INTERPRETING
EARLY AMERICA

*Historiographical
Essays*

INTERPRETING EARLY AMERICA

Historiographical Essays

Jack P. Greene

UNIVERSITY PRESS OF VIRGINIA
Charlottesville and London

THE UNIVERSITY PRESS OF VIRGINIA

Copyright © 1996 by the Rector and Visitors
of the University of Virginia

First published 1996

♾The paper used in this publication meets the minimum requirements of the
American National Standard for Information Sciences—Permanence of Paper
for Printed Library Materials, ANSI z39.48-1984.

Library of Congress Cataloging-in-Publication Data
Greene, Jack P.
  Interpreting early America : historiographical essays / Jack P.
Greene.
    p.   cm.
  Includes index.
    ISBN 0-8139-1622-4 (alk. paper).—ISBN 0-8139-1623-2 (pbk. :
alk. paper)
    1. United States—History—Colonial period, ca. 1600–1775—
Historiography.   2. United States—History—Revolution, 1775–1783—
Historiography.   I. Title.
E188.5.G74   1996
973.3'072—dc20   95-42866
                                                            CIP

Printed in the United States of America

To the Memories of
William Baskerville Hamilton and
John Tate Lanning,
Model Teachers

Contents

Preface   ix

PART ONE: Changing Historical Perspectives   I

ONE   The "New" History   3

TWO   Perspectives on American History   6

THREE   Beyond Power: *Paradigm Subversion and Reformulation and the Re-Creation of the Early Modern Atlantic World*   17

PART TWO: Colonial British America   43

FOUR   The Colonial Era: *An Interview*   45

FIVE   Changing Interpretations of Early American Politics   79

SIX   The American Colonies during the First Half of the Eighteenth Century   113

SEVEN   The Development of Early American Culture   120

EIGHT   Autonomy and Stability: *New England and the British Colonial Experience in Early Modern America*   126

NINE   Society and Economy in the British Caribbean during the Seventeenth and Eighteenth Centuries   156

TEN   Coming to Terms with Diversity: *Pluralism and Conflict in the Formation of Colonial New York*   180

ELEVEN   Chesapeake Transformations: *The Traditionalizing of an English New World Society*   200

TWELVE   The Southern Colonial Mind and American Culture   214

THIRTEEN   Reconstructing British-American Colonial History WITH J. R. POLE   221

FOURTEEN   Colonial New England in Recent Historiography   240

FIFTEEN   Reading *Pursuits of Happiness: A Primer*   281

SIXTEEN   Interpretive Frameworks: *The Quest for Intellectual Order in Early American History*   289

PART THREE: The American Revolution   309

SEVENTEEN   The Flight from Determinism: *A Review of Recent Literature on the Coming of the American Revolution*   311

EIGHTEEN   The Plunge of Lemmings: *A Consideration of Recent Writings on British Politics and the American Revolution*   334

NINETEEN   The Reappraisal of the American Revolution in Recent Historical Literature   367

TWENTY   Beyond the Neo-Whig Paradigm: *Trends in the Historiography of the American Revolution, 1968-76*   441

TWENTY-ONE   Jeffersonian Republicans and the "Modernization" of American Political Consciousness   460

TWENTY-TWO   From the Perspective of Law: *Context and Legitimacy in the Origins of the American Revolution*   467

TWENTY-THREE   The American Revolution Revisited   493

Index   511

Preface

FEW HISTORIANS of my generation became writers of historiographical and critical essays by design. Graduate training in history emphasized subject mastery, and one achieved mastery by learning what
had happened in the times and places studied, not by considering very
deeply, much less lingering over, conflicting interpretations of what had
happened. Lecturers concentrated upon the important historical actors,
events, and developments, not upon the scholars who had written about
them. Of course, graduate teachers instructed their students in the principles of historical criticism and taught them to evaluate works of history
in terms of whether they made sense of known evidence and shed new
light on the field, but they put far more emphasis upon training them to
apply those principles to the documents.

The expansion of historical studies during the 1950s and 1960s significantly changed this orientation. As the number of historians and the
volume of historical work grew, historians became far more attentive to
the methodological and philosophical problems inherent in the act of
writing history, to the operating assumptions that guided their work, to
their varying approaches to the study of the past, and to the differing
interpretations they constructed to explain the same events. In turn,
these developments helped to create within historical studies an enhanced self-consciousness about the craft of history. In the process, they
also made the historian an important part of historical studies. The vast
majority of historians continued to do empirical work on specific times
and places but with a heightened sensitivity to the relationship of their
findings to those of their predecessors and contemporaries. Along with

the need to make sense of a proliferating historical literature, this sensitivity created a demand for critical appraisals of that literature, for the identification of emerging issues, and for the evaluation of conflicting interpretations.

The earliest manifestations of this development in the field of early American history appeared during the mid-1950s. Three of the best minds in the field—Frederick B. Tolles,[1] Richard B. Morris,[2] and Edmund S. Morgan[3]—published masterful articles on the historiography and interpretive issues of the American Revolution. Indeed, Morgan's article, "Revisions in Need of Revising," which I heard him present as a paper at my second meeting of the Mississippi Valley Historical Association in Pittsburgh in the spring of 1956, was primarily responsible for stimulating my interest in historiographical issues in early American history and profoundly influenced the way I would organize my advanced course on the American Revolution when I began teaching at Michigan State University that fall.

Of the thirty courses I taught during my eight quarters at Michigan State University from 1956 to 1959, however, only two were advanced courses, and a more intense involvement in trying to sort out the issues in early American history awaited my move to Western Reserve University in the fall of 1959. All of the courses I designed to fulfill my responsiblity to teach advanced undergraduate and graduate courses and seminars over the entire range of early American history revolved around a critical consideration of controversial or unresolved problems. My intent was not just to familiarize students with existing scholarly debates but to lead them to an appreciation of the problematic character of the colonial and Revolutionary eras and of the vast number of topics that had been either wholly ignored or only casually investigated.

From the time I left graduate school in 1956, William Baskerville Hamilton, my former field superviser in early modern English history at Duke University and editor of the *South Atlantic Quarterly*, had been endeavoring to sharpen my analytical and critical skills and to improve my prose style by annually feeding me several books to review in early American history. In response to his request that I review new books by

---

[1] Frederick B. Tolles, "The American Revolution Considered as a Social Movement," *American Historical Review* 60 (1954): 1–12.

[2] Richard B. Morris, "The Confederation Period and the American Historian," *William and Mary Quarterly*, 3d ser., 13 (1956): 139–56.

[3] Edmund S. Morgan, "The American Revolution: Revisions in Need of Revising," ibid., 14 (1957): 3–15.

Bernhard Knollenberg[4] and Carl Ubbelohde,[5] I proposed a longer essay that would seek to identify and explain recent interpretive directions in studies of the origins of the American Revolution. With Hamilton's encouragement, I labored through much of the late spring and early summer of 1961 to produce this essay, boldly entitled "The Flight from Determinism: A Review of Recent Literature on the Coming of the American Revolution." Taking off from Morgan's 1957 article and a 1958 pamphlet he had produced for the American Historical Association[6] and incorporating much of the analysis of the secondary literature I had undertaken for my advanced course on the American Revolution, it was the first of many similar essays I would write over the following thirty years.

Although I did a long analysis of the literature of early American politics in the mid-1960s, most of my historiographical essays before the mid-1970s focused on some aspect of the American Revolution. As, in the late 1960s and early 1970s, my research interests and those of my doctoral students began to shift away from the Revolution and political history toward the colonial period and social and cultural history, I began to write what I can see in retrospect was a series of closely related review essays and articles trying to sort out the implications of new research on colonial regions and developments. Since the mid-1970s, my historiographical essays have been about equally divided between the Revolution and the colonial period.

Such essays take a lot of time. They require a close reading of the secondary literature and an enormous amount of attention to defining general issues. I have never been entirely persuaded that they are worth the investment of time necessary to produce them, and I am struck by the fact that, except for the very first one, every one of the pieces I have written in this genre has been undertaken in response to an invitation from an editor and not on my own initiative. Nevertheless, as the sheer volume of my historiographical essays powerfully attests, I must like doing them, and I cannot recall ever turning down an opportunity to do one. Closely linked with my graduate teaching obligations at Western Reserve, the University of Michigan, The Johns Hopkins University, and the University of California, Irvine, such essays have been one of

---

[4] Bernhard Knollenberg, *Origin of the American Revolution 1759–1766* (New York, 1960).

[5] Carl Ubbelohde, *The Vice-Admiralty Courts and the American Revolution* (Chapel Hill, N.C., 1960).

[6] Edmund S. Morgan, *The American Revolution: A Review of Changing Interpretations* (Washington, D.C., 1958).

the principal devices by which I have kept abreast of new scholarship and have remained a credible teacher of graduate students in early American history. More important, they test my powers of synthesis, they provide a forum through which I can share with others my thoughts about where my field is going and why, and they help to express my impulse to contribute to the formation of—and to operate within— larger interpretive structures that, while always in flux, help us to locate the significance of specific pieces of research and to give, at least provisionally, some coherence to the field as a whole.

This volume is a collection of twenty-three essays, all but one previously published, which may be roughly classified as historiographical. These pieces are arranged in three parts: "Changing Historical Perspectives," which has three chapters, "Colonial British America," which contains thirteen, and "The American Revolution," which includes seven. In Part One, chapter one, "The 'New' History," is a short general piece that seeks to spell out for a lay audience the underlying assumptions of the more inclusive approach to historical studies that emerged during the 1960s and 1970s. Chapter two, "Perspectives on American History," considers the limitations of the national-state paradigm for the study of colonial history and advocates a less anachronistic approach. Previously unpublished, chapter three, "Beyond Power: Paradigm Subversion and Reformulation and the Re-Creation of the Early Modern Atlantic World," describes the process by which the emerging conception of the Atlantic world over the last forty years has helped to undermine the paradigm of power in early modern studies.

Except for chapter four, "The Colonial Era: An Interview," which John A. Garraty published in 1970 in his book *Interpreting American History: Conversations with Historians* and which provides a long overview of many of the issues involved in the interpretation of the colonial era, the thirteen essays in Part Two and the six essays in Part Three are arranged in the chronological order in which they were written.

Chapters five through twenty-two fall into several different categories. In Part Two, six chapters may be described as review articles that consider several works on a particular problem or area: chapter five, "Changing Interpretations of Early American Politics"; chapter eight, "Autonomy and Stability: New England and the British Colonial Experience in Early Modern America"; chapter nine, "Society and Economy in the British Caribbean during the Seventeenth and Eighteenth Centuries"; chapter ten, "Coming to Terms with Diversity: Pluralism and Conflict in the Formation of Colonial New York"; chapter eleven, "Chesapeake Transformations: The Traditionalizing of an English New World Society"; and chapter fourteen, "Colonial New England in Recent Historiography." Three chapters—chapter six, "The American Colonies during the First Half of the Eighteenth Century"; chapter seven, "The Development of Early American Culture"; and chapter twelve, "The Southern Colonial Mind and American Culture"—are review essays on important single books. Chapter thirteen, "Reconstructing British-American Colonial History," jointly written with J. R. Pole, and chapter sixteen, "Interpretive Frameworks: The Quest for Intellectual Order in Early American History," represent efforts to comment on general trends in the study of colonial America. Chapter fifteen, "Reading *Pursuits of Happiness:* A Primer," is a commentary on Michael Zuckerman's reading of my book.[7]

The chapters in Part Three fall into four categories. Chapter seventeen, "The Flight from Determinism: A Review of Recent Literature on the Coming of the American Revolution"; chapter eighteen, "The Plunge of Lemmings: A Consideration of Recent Writings on British Politics and the American Revolution"; and chapter twenty-two, "From the Perspective of Law: Context and Legitimacy in the Origins of the American Revolution," are review articles. Chapter twenty-one, "Jeffersonian Republicans and the 'Modernization' of American Political Consciousness," and chapter twenty-three, "The American Revolution Revisited," focus on a single book and its historiographical context and implications. Chapters nineteen, "The Reappraisal of the American Revolution in Recent Historical Literature," and twenty, "Beyond the Neo-Whig Paradigm: Trends in the Historiography of the American Revolution, 1968–76," are surveys of the literature.

In preparing this volume for publication, I have been careful to make no substantive changes in the twenty-four republished pieces. I have, however, made many small editorial changes; standardized form, spelling, and citations; eliminated or shortened in later chapters substantial passages that had been repeated from earlier essays included in this volume; and added at the end of each chapter a short paragraph recounting its history and giving its place of publication.

Several people helped in putting this volume together. Robert M. Calhoon and Peter S. Onuf advised me about selection and organization. Amy Turner Bushnell made valuable editorial suggestions. Sarah

---

[7] Jack P. Greene, *Pursuits of Happiness: The Social Development of the Early Modern British Colonies and the Formation of American Culture* (Chapel Hill, N.C., 1988).

Springer retyped older essays that were not already on computer disks. The Johns Hopkins University provided financial assistance. Michelle LeMaster and Nuran Çinlar read proofs, and Michelle did the index.

This volume is dedicated to the memory of two of my former graduate teachers at Duke University, William Baskerville Hamilton, who played such a prominent role in encouraging me to write essays of the kind reprinted in this volume, and John Tate Lanning, who supervised my doctoral field in colonial Hispanic American history. Known among graduate students as "Bulldog" or, playing on his middle name, "The Hound," Hamilton was a gruff iconoclast who, impatient with intellectual timidity and softness, delighted in unsettling students and colleagues alike. He never precipitated an argument he did not enjoy and he most enjoyed those arguments that he goaded students or former students into winning. His intellectual style scared away the faint of heart, but I found it so thoroughly congenial that I have never ceased trying to imitate it.

Equally demanding, Lanning cultivated an aura of inaccessibility that was epitomized by the three long flights of stairs that only a most determined—and dedicated—student would be likely to climb to reach his office at the top of the tower of the Duke University library. Affectionately referred to by his graduate students as "The Don," he had no time for small talk but was invariably forthcoming with advice on professional and intellectual matters for those who he thought took history as seriously as he did. Both much gentler with students and much harder on colleagues and peers than Hamilton, he imparted, by example and by word, three valuable pieces of advice for aspiring historians: be productive, work on large problems, and always address the widest possible professional audience, advice I have always tried to follow and to pass along to later generations of doctoral students.

PART ONE
Changing Historical Perspectives

—One—

The "New" History

ONLY A GENERATION AGO well-socialized historians in the United States had no doubt what the most important—and prestigious—subjects of study were. Here, as in Britain, history was preeminently the study of great public events (national elections, wars, civil strife, revolutions), large-scale transformations (the Renaissance, the Enlightenment, the Industrial Revolution), or great figures in politics, economic life, or the worlds of art and ideas. By definition, powerful social groups and nations were more important than weak ones. "Subordinate" social groups were largely considered only insofar as they interacted with elites, and smaller or non-Western nations were discussed only to the extent that they were involved in "the rise of the West."

So pervasive was this conception of the past that it was virtually unquestioned. The very greatness of the subjects on which it focused seemed to endow them with intrinsic importance: their extraordinary impact and visibility made it unnecessary, almost impossible, to raise the question of why they should be studied to the exclusion of less glamorous aspects of the past, aspects that were either left unexamined or relegated to the periphery of the historical discipline.

Since the mid-1960s, this conception of history has come under sharp attack from the exponents of a radically different view of what should be studied in the past. Inspired by the work of the so-called *Annales* School in France, a growing number of British and American scholars have developed a "new history" that differs from the old in scope, focus, approach, and assumptions. In scope, it is far more comprehensive. All human behavior, the actions and thoughts of peoples from all cultures and all segments of all societies within those cultures, comes within its purview. Its focus is not just upon powerful Western nations but upon peoples in all kinds of political contexts in cultures formerly considered "primitive" or "marginal," not merely upon elites but upon people in all

[3]

social categories, and not only upon prominent events but upon underlying economic, social, and cultural processes.

To date, attention has been concentrated in three areas. One of these has been the basic conditions of life—birth, education, marriage, death, diet, disease, material possessions, housing, work, and man's relationship to nature—and the fundamental units of social organization: household, family, and community. A second has been the structure of economic and social life, including the mode of production and social organization in its broadest sense. And third, the new history has focused upon "collective mentalities," the belief systems and perceptual frameworks that determine the ways people interpret the routine and the extraordinary in their lives.

The new history thus reorders our priorities about the past. It abandons the central assumption of traditional history, what might be called the doctrine of implicit importance. Prominence and visibility no longer constitute a prima facie case for historical significance. On the contrary, the value of every subject depends entirely upon how much it reveals about larger historical processes. From the perspective supplied by the new history, it has become clear that the experiences of women, children, servants, slaves, and other neglected groups are quite as integral to a comprehensive understanding of the past as those of lawyers, lords, and ministers of state; that in terms of explaining social behavior, popular culture is far more revealing than high culture; and that great events are important objects of study only when they open a window upon otherwise obscure aspects of more basic processes of social change.

To recover the history of relatively invisible groups of people, to recreate structures and processes that were usually only dimly perceived in the past, has required unusual resourcefulness and imagination. Scholars have had to seek out and devise ways to manipulate sources—censuses, parish registers, public records, visual materials, oral traditions—that have previously been either ignored or insufficiently utilized. They have also had to move sharply in an interdisciplinary direction, as they have found the methods and concepts developed in fields such as sociology, anthropology, psychology, and linguistics useful in their efforts to reconstruct the societies of the past. From the social sciences, they have also learned to use theory more explicitly and to be more systematic in the formulation of problems, more self-conscious about procedures, and more rigorous about proof. Thus, they have come to insist upon precise quantitative measures whenever possible and have perforce begun to use advanced statistical techniques and the digital computer.

Certainly one of the most significant by-products of the new history has been unprecedented—for historians—intellectual boldness. The demand for rigor has taught historians that all too often the more susceptible a problem is to proof, the more trivial it is. To handle many questions of central concern to the new history, scholars have had to go beyond the historian's traditional question—how do you know that?—to ask the intellectually more demanding question: how much can plausibly be said on the basis of always imperfect sources?

As a cursory examination of publishers' lists or of course offerings at most of the more prestigious American universities will quickly reveal, traditional history is still very much alive. Excessively technical and often seemingly arcane, the new history puts very heavy demands upon practitioners and readers alike and lacks the narrative power that has for so long given the best traditional history some popular appeal. For these reasons alone, the new history may never—and probably should never—entirely supplant the old.

But because it has raised such intriguing and challenging questions about the context and quality of people's lives at all levels of society in past times, it does seem to be waging a winning battle for the possession of the best young minds in the profession. These minds have been inspired by the promise that history may ultimately be able to provide more than the entertainment and moral inspiration that have been its traditional stock in trade, that it may also be able to give us explicit insights into the nature of the human condition through time and space, insights that may finally enable history to come closer to delivering on its seldom-fulfilled promise to provide a rich perspective upon the present and the future, as well as upon the past. To do so, however, young historians must now rise to the additional challenge of devising a literary form that will attract the wider audience that their work deserves.

In response to an invitation from the editorial staff of the op-ed page of the *New York Times*, this chapter was written in the late fall of 1974 in Washington, D.C., while I was a Fellow of the Woodrow Wilson International Center for Scholars. It is reprinted with permission and with minor verbal and paragraphing changes from "The New History: From Top to Bottom," *New York Times*, Wednesday, Jan. 8, 1975, p. 37, copyright © 1975 by the New York Times Company. This chapter also appeared in the *International Herald Tribune*, Jan. 11–12, 1975, 4, and the *Montreal Star*, Jan. 11, 1975.

—Two—

Perspectives on American History

Should the West Indies be included in a course on either early American history or United States history? These are the joined but separate questions posed by Alison Games's plea for a reorientation in the teaching of these two courses.[1] Similar kinds of questions have been paramount in the American historical establishment's intensifying debate over what constitutes or ought to constitute *American,* by which, following our traditional and parochial definition of that term, we mean pre–United States and United States history. This debate flows from two sources. First is the worldwide movement among professional historians over the past generation toward a broader approach to the past, an approach that considers both genders, all ages, all social and ethnic groups, all regions, and all forms of human experience. Second is the related and increasingly powerful emphasis upon the cultural diversity of the populations and regions within the United States. Among historians of the United States, these two developments have together generated the widespread conviction that Americans need a more inclusive national history, one that takes such diversity into account. What is principally at issue at the moment is the form that such a history should take.

The position emerging as dominant holds that American history ought to be the history of all the peoples who have ever occupied the geographical areas that are now part of the United States. No longer limited to the Europeans and their descendants who settled the thirteen English colonies on the eastern seaboard, such peoples include the many native groups of Amerindians on the North American continent and Polynesians in Hawaii, who had occupied their areas long before the Europeans arrived; the large numbers of Africans and their descendants, of

[1] Alison Games, "History without Borders: Teaching American History in an Atlantic Context," *Indiana Magazine of History* 91 (1995): 159–78.

[6]

whom before 1865 the vast majority worked as legally voiceless slaves; the other Europeans and their descendants—the Spanish in Florida, New Mexico, Texas, and California; the French in the St. Lawrence and Mississippi River valleys; the Dutch and Swedes in the Hudson and Delaware River valleys, and the Russians on the west coast—who were the first to settle areas that would eventually be incorporated into the English seaboard colonies or the United States; and the vast numbers of Europeans, Asians, Latin Americans, and West Indians who have emigrated to the United States during the past two centuries.

There is much to be said on behalf of this *national state perspective.* In contrast to older approaches, it focuses attention upon not just the English but the British, European, African, Amerindian, and Asian roots of American culture. This broader perspective requires historians to analyze at last the complex process by which an intricate and continuing process of negotiation among groups from radically different Western and non-Western cultures produced a culture that could be called "American." For those historians who are mainly interested in the question of how we have gotten to where we are and principally concerned with understanding a *national* experience or creating a *national* past, the national state perspective may be adequate. For those historians who regard themselves as students of nonnational entities, however, the national state perspective appears limited, anachronistic, and only slightly less parochial than the perspective it replaces. *Which one? national past?*

Historians of Amerindians provide one important example. The history of Aboriginal America, America before the intensive penetration of Europeans and Africans, simply cannot be contained within contemporary national boundaries. Like medieval and early modern Europe and Africa, Aboriginal America consisted of a large number and an enormously complex array of shifting political and cultural entities that, unlike Europe and Africa, were spread over not one but two huge continents and many islands. Each of these entities occupied a particular area and manifested a cultural orientation and forms of economic, social, and political organization that were, at least to some extent, peculiar to it.

The histories of those groups who have always lived within the boundaries of a single contemporary national state presumably can be told within the parameters of the national history of that state, but the histories of those many groups who were so inconsiderate of later geopolitical developments as to occupy an area transected by a subsequent boundary cannot. To remain true to the logic that underlies it, the national state perspective must exclude any segment of a group that either remained in or fled to an area that was never to be incorporated into the state.

If such artificial and anachronistic divisions of the histories of particular Amerindian groups make no sense from the perspective of Amerindian historians, the focus, characteristic of the national state perspective, on only those Amerindians who lived within the boundaries of those states greatly inhibits understanding of the richness and diversity of Amerindian cultures. To mention only one of the most striking examples, many different types of Amerindian societies existed within the area that became the United States, from relatively sedentary agricultural or marine societies to nomadic hunting and gathering societies with various forms and levels of political organization appropriate to the ways they sustained themselves. But there were no complex and sophisticated imperial states of the sort that existed in central Mexico and the Andes. Obviously, a comprehension of the full variety and range of the history of Aboriginal America requires its practitioners to ignore modern national boundaries and to look comparatively at societies throughout the Americas.

Historians writing from a national perspective may use the work of Amerindian historians to encourage an appreciation of those societies that have resided in the area of the United States and to provide the descendants of those Amerindian groups who survived their encounters with Europeans with a sense of their place in and continuing relevance to the national experience of the country. These are laudable goals in themselves that enable historians to rewrite the history of the country from the point of view of the conquered as well as the conquerors, to conceive of it not only in the traditional sense of how the West was won but also (in the catchy course title used by Amy Turner Bushnell for her course in Amerindian history) of how the East was lost. Quite apart from its relationship to the history of the United States, however, Amerindian history has an integrity—and a perspective—of its own, one that demands consideration of Amerindian groups in relation to each other as well as to the European and African invaders who began to intrude upon their world in the late fifteenth century. Amerindian history can best be written from not a national but a continental or, preferably, a hemispheric perspective.

Similar kinds of observations can be made about the pre–national state histories of the activities of European settlers and their descendants in the Americas. During the three and a half centuries following Columbus's encounter with America in 1492, several emerging European national states, principally Spain, Portugal, the Netherlands, England, and France, managed to establish, initially with little state investment, their political and cultural hegemony over large regions of the Americas. Even in the many places where Europeans and their descendants remained a minority, this hegemony was always manifest in the reconfiguration of American social landscapes along European lines and the emergence of European-style polities replete with European legal systems and institutions.

Both separately and as a whole, the histories of the several European Americas, like the history of Aboriginal America, can be thoroughly understood only comparatively and in terms of contemporary frames of reference. In the case of colonial English or (after the union of Scotland and England in 1707) British America, the contemporary frame of reference included vastly more than the thirteen colonies that the English established along the North American coast and that subsequently formed the United States. By the 1760s, on the eve of the American Revolution, colonial British America stretched from Barbados in the eastern Caribbean to Hudson's Bay in the north, from the Atlantic colony of Bermuda in the east to the Mississippi River in the west. At the time of the Declaration of Independence in 1776, colonial British America consisted of thirty-one colonies: the thirteen revolting colonies, eleven colonies in the West Indies (Barbados, Antigua, St. Christopher, Montserrat, Nevis, Jamaica, the Virgin Islands, Tobago, St. Vincent, Grenada, and Dominica), two Atlantic island colonies (Bermuda and the Bahamas), two colonies on the southeastern coast of North America (East and West Florida), and three colonies to the north of New England (Nova Scotia, Canada, and St. John, now Prince Edward Island). In addition, colonial British America included several long-established social entities in the process of becoming colonies: permanent fishing settlements in Newfoundland, fur-trading posts in Hudson's Bay and in the Great Lakes and Ohio and Mississippi River basins, and log-cutting settlements in Belize on the coast of Central America. In turn, British America was part of an even larger British imperial world that included not just the home kingdoms of England, Scotland, and Wales but the kingdom-colony of Ireland, slave-trading factories on the West African coast, and spice-trading enclaves in India.

Historians have found it convenient to construct the history of colonial British America in terms of several distinctive regions, each composed of two or more colonies and defined by the ecological zones the inhabitants occupied, the socioeconomic activities they developed to sustain themselves, and the sociocultural landscapes and demographic regimes they established. Each of these regions—the Chesapeake, New England, the West Indies, the Middle Colonies, the Lower South, and the Atlantic islands—was peculiar. Although each region drew large numbers of immigrants from Britain, only in New England did English people constitute an overwhelming majority of the population. People of African descent, present in significant numbers throughout colonial British America, were a majority in the Atlantic islands and a vast majority in the West Indies and the coastal areas of the Lower South. Staple agriculture and slave labor were prominent in the economies of most of the colonies from the Chesapeake southward, while mixed farming with family labor predominated in the economies of the Middle Colonies and New England.

Notwithstanding these important differences, all of the regions formed part of the large cultural complex that we now call colonial British America. Each colony in this complex was constitutionally connected to Great Britain. In form and in substance its political institutions were British and its inhabitants were subjects of the British crown. In each colony the vast majority of the free governing population—members of families who were not slaves, who enjoyed the benefit of existing law, and whose male members were entitled to participate in political life— was British, with strong claims to a British identity as people who lived in liberty under a parliamentary government of laws to which the free inhabitants had given their consent. Proud to be the heirs of British political traditions, they debated public issues in terms of British political ideologies, made and enforced laws in a British style, and lived under a legal system that, whatever peculiarities had developed in response to local conditions, was distinctively British. Like Britons in the home islands, they were Protestant in religion. Reinforcing these powerful political and cultural ties were equally strong economic links. Most colonies looked to Britain as a major market—often the only overseas market—for their products and the principal source of the goods and skills they needed to build societies in the New World. Within this expanded British world, trade goods, information, correspondence, and people flowed freely and extensively back and forth across the Atlantic and through the intercolonial trading and communication networks that increasingly bound the colonies to each other as well as to Britain.

Of the many parts of the vast cultural complex of colonial British America, the British political and commercial establishment set most value on the plantation colonies in the Chesapeake, the Lower South, and, most especially, the West Indies. Both because of their proximity to Spain's wealthy American empire and because the Caribbean was the scene of the most intense economic and naval competition among the British, French, and Spanish throughout the colonial era, British officials regarded the West Indian colonies as the most strategically significant of the American colonies. Equally important, in terms of their economic worth to Britain, the West Indian colonies also enjoyed pride of place. Barbados, earliest of the sugar colonies, and Jamaica, largest of the British sugar colonies, were the most valued colonies in the eighteenth century. For the North American colonies, these and other West Indian colonies were the source of sugar and molasses for a growing distilling industry and a substantial market for fish, animal, cereal, lumber, and some manufactured products. A vigorous exchange in such products, in slaves, in people, and in information closely linked the continental colonies and the West Indies.

Colonial Spanish America was even more extensive and culturally far richer and more complex than colonial British America. Its principal centers were in New Spain (now Mexico) and Peru, each of which had long been a viceroyalty with several territorial audiencias under its jurisdiction. Other, less important areas were organized into captaincies general. Within these various political entities, Spaniards and their creole (American-born) descendants used Amerindian or imported African labor in mining, ranching, and agricultural activities that supported elaborate societies and yielded vast riches that were sent to Spain. In one form or another, colonial Spanish America reached from the eastern Caribbean to the Pacific and from the southernmost point of South America north to Florida and New Mexico in the sixteenth century and to Upper California in the late eighteenth century.

Other European powers also presided over similar, if less far-flung, cultural complexes. Colonial French America included the rich sugar colonies of Martinique, Guadeloupe, and St. Dominigue and, before 1763, the continental colonies of Acadia, Canada, Illinois, and Louisiana. Colonial Portuguese America, more concentrated, consisted of several large donatary captaincies or colonies in Brazil. During the seventeenth century, colonial Dutch America was composed of colonies in Brazil,

Surinam, New Netherlands, and several West Indian islands. By the mid-eighteenth century, however, it was confined to a few Caribbean settlements: Surinam on the mainland and Curaçao and other smaller islands.

These several colonial European Americas were in no sense self-contained worlds. Among adjacent island colonies and along international borders between continental colonies, economic interaction was constant and commercial and religious rivalry common. At these points of interaction—between, for instance, Spanish Florida and British Carolina and Georgia, French Canada and British New England and New York, or Spanish New Granada and English Jamaica—neighboring political entities directly interacted with one another. Their exchanges revolved around competition for Amerindian goods, souls, and allegiance; struggles over territory; disputes over runaway slaves; and clandestine trading. In these interactions, the histories of these several colonial European Americas came together to form part of a larger story of conflict and competition over America.

At the same time, however, the histories of such colonies must be understood principally in terms of their relationship not to adjacent colonies belonging to another European America but to the specific European America of which they formed a part and to which they were, in the deepest cultural sense, intimately tied. To be fully comprehended within its contemporary context the history of any segment of these European Americas thus must be placed within a framework provided by the full range of experiences within the national cultural complex to which it belonged.

A history of any one of these European Americas that did not include the histories of each of its many component parts would be incomplete. For that reason, a full appreciation of the history of colonial British America cannot fail to include histories of the West Indian colonies. They represent an important part of that history, not only because London authorities thought them the strategically and economically most significant part of the British colonial world but also, and more importantly, because their experiences were an integral part of the history of that world and represented a major variation within it.

This broad pan-British perspective on colonial British America is scarcely a new one. During the first half of the century, Charles M. Andrews and Leonard W. Labaree emphasized the unities between those British colonies in America that became part of the United States and those that did not. They wrote about colonial political and constitutional developments as if the histories of the West Indian and continental colonies in those areas were interchangeable—as they were.[2] In the early 1940s, Max Savelle published an excellent textbook, *The Foundations of American Civilization: A History of Colonial America* (New York, 1942), that devoted as many chapters—three—to the West Indies as it did to Virginia.[3] During the last decade, general works on the colonial economy by John J. McCusker and Russell Menard[4] and on colonial constitutional and social development by Jack P. Greene[5] have given major attention to the West Indies.

Yet the broader perspective that such works represented and that Professor Games now advocates has never been the predominant one. Parallel to these works has been a vastly larger corpus of literature, the focus of which was evident in the titles. Thus, in 1922 Evarts B. Greene entitled his colonial history text *The Foundations of American Nationality,*[6] and in 1938 Curtis P. Nettels called his *The Roots of American Civilization.*[7] A perusal of these texts quickly told the reader that the term *American* did not include West Indians, Bermudans, or Nova Scotians. Indeed, none of the authors of the many "colonial" history texts published since World War II has followed Savelle's example and given more than passing attention to the West Indies.[8] When in the early 1980s J. R. Pole and I endeavored to persuade the other fourteen contributors to *Colonial British America* to include the West Indies in their discussions of the problems we had assigned them, only two, Richard B. Sheridan and Richard S. Dunn, devoted significant space to the West Indian colonies,

---

[2] See, for instance, Charles M. Andrews, *The Colonial Background of the American Revolution* (New Haven, 1924), and Leonard Woods Labaree, *Royal Government in America* (New Haven, 1930).

[3] Subsequent revisers of Savelle's text, Robert Middlekauf in 1964 and Darold D. Wax in 1973, continued Savelle's emphasis.

[4] John J. McCusker and Russell R. Menard, *The Economy of British America, 1607–1789* (Chapel Hill, N.C., 1985).

[5] Jack P. Greene, *Peripheries and Center: Constitutional Development in the Extended Polities of the British Empire and the United States, 1607–1788* (Athens, Ga., 1986); *Pursuits of Happiness: The Social Development of Early Modern British Colonies and the Formation of American Culture* (Chapel Hill, N.C., 1988).

[6] Evarts B. Greene, *The Foundations of American Nationality* (New York, 1922).

[7] Curtis P. Nettels, *The Roots of American Civilization* (New York, 1938).

[8] To cite only four examples from a whole shelf of such texts in my library, Clarence Ver Steeg, *The Formative Years, 1607–1763* (New York, 1964); David Hawke, *The Colonial Experience* (Indianapolis, 1966); R. C. Simmons, *The American Colonies from Settlement to Independence* (New York, 1976); and Richard Middleton, *Colonial America: A History, 1607–1760* (Cambridge, Mass., 1992).

and only about a third made any mention of them at all.[9] A more recent collection of essays included a piece on the West Indies as part of the "Cultural *Margins* of the First British Empire."[10]

Among most historians of the subject, colonial British America has thus remained largely the history of the minority of British colonies that revolted in 1776. Colonial history is nothing more than the prehistory of the United States. Within this prevailing conception, the history of the West Indies and of other nonrevolting colonies is at best peripheral. By taking such an approach, historians differentiate between separate parts of the same history merely because those parts did not wind up—or so far have not wound up—as part of the same national state. In so doing they condemn themselves to produce a history of colonial British America that is at once partial, parochial, and anachronistic.

Current efforts to make United States history more inclusive and multi-cultural by employing an expanded conception of the colonial past that takes in not only the thirteen British colonies but also the Spanish and French colonies in areas that later became the United States[11] enable historians to bring in Spanish Florida, New Mexico, and California and French Illinois and Louisiana without challenging the principal tradi-tional criteria for inclusion: whether or not an area eventually became part of the United States. The colonial history that this approach prom-ises to produce may be less parochial than one that focuses exclusively on the history of the thirteen revolting British colonies, but it will be no less anachronistic.

For this new colonial history violently wrenches the histories of these non-British colonies out of their contemporary contexts as parts of colo-nial Spanish or French America and shoehorns them into an uneasy asso-ciation with colonies with which during the colonial era they had either (as was the case with Florida, Louisiana, and Illinois) small common

---

[9] Jack P. Greene and J. R. Pole, eds., *Colonial British America: Essays in the New History of the Early Modern Era* (Baltimore, 1984). Of course, Dunn and Sheridan have written large books on aspects of the West Indian colonial history.

[10] Italics added. Michael Craton, "Reluctant Creoles: The Planters' World in the British West Indies," in Bernard Bailyn and Philip D. Morgan, eds., *Strangers within the Realm: Cultural Margins of the First British Empire* (Chapel Hill, N.C., 1991), 314–62.

[11] See James A. Hijiya, "Why the West Is Lost," *William and Mary Quarterly,* 3d ser., 51 (1994): 276–92.

heritage and a mostly antagonistic relationship or (as in the case of New Mexico, Texas, and California) no relationship at all. The cultural, economic, and administrative ties of Spanish New Mexico, Texas, and California ran not east to the British colonies but south to New Spain. Those of Spanish Florida ran not north to the British colonies but east to Spain, south to Cuba, and southwest to New Spain. Those of Illinois ran northeast to French Canada or south to Louisiana, and those of Louisiana ran north to Illinois or east through the French Caribbean colonies to France. A serious history of these outposts of Spanish and French empire cannot stop at the future borders of the United States but must treat them as what they were: extensions or peripheries of the much larger Spanish and French American worlds that constituted their contemporary frame of reference and to which they belonged.

This is a major enterprise that can best be approached as an exercise not in national state history but in comparative colonial history. My own advocacy of such a history goes back a long way: to my study of colonial Latin American and Brazilian history as a graduate student, my teaching of comparative colonial history at Western Reserve University in the early 1960s, and my unsuccessful efforts, in collaboration with my colleague Charles Gibson, to form an institute for the comparative study of the colonial histories of the Americas in association with the William L. Clements Library at the University of Michigan in the mid-1960s. My growing conviction that such a history could only be written from a broad transatlantic perspective that comprehended European and African as well as American developments informed the Atlantic History and Culture Program that my colleagues and I created at The Johns Hopkins University in the early 1970s. For more than a quarter century, this program has encouraged graduate students to take a broadly comparative Atlantic approach to the histories not just of early modern American colonies but of societies and polities throughout the Atlantic world from the fifteenth century forward.

But this approach is not typical of graduate programs in early, much less later, American history, and for that reason alone, I am skeptical that Professor Games will win many converts to her proposal to substitute a course with a broad Atlantic focus for the present United States survey with its national state perspective. Before that proposal could succeed, historians who teach that survey would have to undergo a massive conversion involving a fundamental reconception of the history that American students ought to be taught. Still imprisoned within a national state conception of the past, multiculturalists are unlikely to stimulate such a sweeping change.

With regard to the sort of reorientation of colonial history courses that Professor Games advocates, I am somewhat more sanguine. As more historians of early modern European British, Spanish, French, Portuguese, and Dutch colonies come to understand that the integrity of their subjects requires them to move beyond a conception of colonial history as nothing more than a prelude to national history, more colonial history courses may come to resemble those taught by Professor Games and her mentor, Richard Dunn, and by my students and me. Additionally, the *William and Mary Quarterly*, the principal journal for colonial history in the United States, may rise further above the national state and parochial implications of its subtitle as "A Magazine of Early American History and Culture"; textbooks for colonial history courses may become more inclusive; and more comparative colonial or even early modern Atlantic history courses may appear in college and university catalogs. Only if and when these developments take place will the West Indian colonies once again hold the central place they occupied throughout the long history of colonial British America during the early modern era.

Written in the fall of 1994 in response to an invitation from the editor of the *Indiana Magazine of History* to produce an extended comment on an article by Alison Games, this chapter is reprinted with permission and with extensive verbal changes from "Perspectives on American History," *Indiana Magazine of History* 91 (1995), 179–88.

THREE

Beyond Power:
Paradigm Subversion and Reformulation and the Re-Creation of the Early Modern Atlantic World

D URING THE PAST forty years, within my professional lifetime, historical studies have undergone a radical transformation. When I came into the profession in the early 1950s, historical studies, at least in Western countries, invariably followed power. Studies of antiquity focused on the great civilizations of Greece and Rome, their formation, expansion, decline, and eventual conquest. Analyses of the Middle Ages concentrated on the spread of the Christian faith outward from Rome and the eventual dominion of the Roman Catholic church. Renaissance studies stressed the flowering of learning and the arts and the recovery of the great achievements of antiquity among the Italian city-states and in the Low Countries of the fourteenth, fifteenth, and sixteenth centuries, while Reformation history emphasized the struggle for and against the Roman church's monopoly of religious authority in western Christendom. Evidently the most efficient and effective contrivance for collecting, organizing, and exerting political power, the nation-state, a development of the early modern era, was the principal conceptual device for organizing both early modern and modern history. In this schema, Europe was more important than other continents. Indeed, the Americas, Africa, Asia, and Australia entered history only after they came into contact with Europeans.

[17]

A broad range of governing, if unarticulated, assumptions flowed from this conception of the past. Because they occupied a higher level on the ladder of political evolution of which the nation-state occupied the top rung, nation-states were more important than other kinds of polities —principalities, duchies, city-states, sultanates, confederacies, tribes. Older nation-states were usually more important than newer ones. Nation-states with empires were more important than those without them. Continents that were composed of mostly self-governing states— Europe and North America—were more important than continents that were colonized or dominated—Africa, Asia, South America, and Australia. Within polities, capitals were more important than provinces, centers than peripheries, and of course metropolitan or imperial states than their colonies. Within colonies, areas settled or controlled by Europeans and their descendants were more important than frontiers or the areas beyond them, not yet under European hegemony. Finally, in both imperial states and colonies, urban areas were more important than rural ones.

This nation-centered conception of the past privileged the study of public life. History was past politics, and political history was preeminently the analysis, on the national level, of struggles for power and resources among rival groups of leaders and their followers, organized into formal parties, and the constitutional arrangements, political institutions, and, to a modest extent, legal systems that evolved from those struggles. The focus was upon prominent leaders—monarchs, prime ministers, premiers, cabinet heads, presidents, revolutionary leaders— whose names often tagged the eras with which they were associated. Insofar as there was a history on a level above that of the nation-state— an international history—it was the history not of comparative cultures or development but of diplomacy, war, and the spread of political influence, all of which were stories told primarily in terms of the great events—treaties or battles—and of the great actors—political leaders or generals—who presided over them. Guided by similar assumptions, economic history was the study of the development of major economic institutions such as guilds, trading companies, factories, and corporations, while intellectual history reviewed the appearance and influence of major ideas, the principal figures associated with those ideas, and the intellectual, cultural, or religious movements that marked the transition to the modern age. Like political history, both economic and intellectual history emphasized the role of great actors, economic innovators, and people whose writings or cultural productions marked them as persons of prominence and achievement. History was, in short, the study of winners, not losers, of successes, not failures.

A similar hierarchy determined which levels to study within a political society. The powerful were more important than the powerless, the wealthy than the poor, the propertied than the propertyless, the educated than the uneducated, masters than servants or slaves, employers than employees, adults than children, husbands than wives, sons than daughters. Implicit indices not just of power but also of civility and modernity informed judgments about the relative significance of social groups. Historical significance was also color coded. Lightness of skin correlated almost precisely with historical attention. In this celebration of dominant groups and individual achievements, considerations of power, class, gender, and race determined who acquired a historical presence—and who did not.

From the perspective of our own time, this paradigm of power is as striking for what it left out or relegated to the margins of historical studies as for what it included. Social history was almost entirely an adjunct to political history, cultural history was the study of the production and consumption of high culture, and demographic history scarcely existed. Local history, family history, the history of women or children, the history of less powerful groups—all were distinctly subordinate and less prestigious enterprises, often dismissed by academic establishments throughout the Western world as antiquarian and insignificant.

For a century after the emergence of professional history during the last quarter of the nineteenth century, most historians concerned with exploring the early modern interaction between Europe and the wider world that began in the fifteenth century operated within this conceptual framework. Because the impulse to study this process was much stronger in former colonies, where historians were principally concerned to recover the origins of the societies in which they lived, historians in such entities conceived of this process under the rubric of *colonization.* At bottom, the colonial histories these historians constructed were narratives of exploration and incorporation. They recounted the events and developments by which Europeans brought the native peoples and the spaces they occupied in America first into their consciousness and then under their hegemony. Colonization turned round a series of implicit sequences. Discovery, always the prerogative of Europeans and always referring to the incidents by which peoples and places were brought to European attention, was followed by exploration, trade, conquest, settlement, and mastery—all by Europeans and their creole descendants.

Colonial historians sometimes recognized that the indigenous peoples who occupied the "new" worlds being acted upon by Europeans had histories, especially those who seemed as in Mexico and Peru to have achieved high, that is, Europeanlike, levels of cultural development and those who either, like the Chichimecas in New Spain, the Araucanians in Chile, or the Pueblos in New Mexico, offered sustained and effective resistance or, like the Iroquois in New York or the Calusas in Florida, were numerous enough, strong enough, or isolated enough to preserve their political autonomy for several generations. Historians also recognized that indigenous peoples who occupied territories contested by rival European powers and were able to maintain their independence by shifting support from one side to the other—for instance in North America between the northern British colonies and New France or among the southern British colonies, Spanish Florida, and French Louisiana—had important roles in the European struggle for power. Once an indigenous people had been conquered or brought under settler domination, however, colonial historians mostly brought them into the story only as nameless laborers, objects of European evangelization, producers of skins or furs for European markets, or consumers of European trade goods. The study of both the prehistory—that is, the experience before the availability of the written records on which historians based their accounts—of most Amerindian groups and the impact of Europeans upon the subsequent culture and development of those groups fell to anthropology, the discipline responsible for studying those who, in Eric Wolf's sardonic phrase, were the "people without history."[1]

Nor were very many anthropologists concerned with the history of Amerindians. Archaeologists studied their prehistory, but social and cultural anthropologists focused on contemporary societies, at best including a chapter on the historical background, which was rarely more than a brief and random collection of information on what their informants had told them had "gone before." Except for a few pioneers, historical anthropology or, as it came to be called with specific reference to Amerindian

---

[1] Eric R. Wolf, *Europe and the People without History* (Berkeley, Calif., 1982).

studies, ethnohistory and historical archaeology simply did not exist as fields.[2]

Much the same can be said about the Africans imported as slaves to supply the labor necessary to make the fields, mines, and ranches of the New World productive. No colonial historian put much emphasis upon the fact that far greater numbers of Africans than Europeans came to the New World between 1492 and the 1820s. Because Africa, like Aboriginal America, itself was largely outside history as it was then understood and came into the story only as it came into the consciousness or struggles of Europeans, no colonial historian even appreciated, much less stressed, the extraordinary ethnic complexity among these unwilling immigrants. No colonial historian thought to consider what histories and cultural attributes they might have brought with them from the "old" worlds of Africa. To an even greater extent than Aboriginal America, Africa was a subject left to anthropologists, very few of whom expressed much interest in the experience of Africans and their creole descendants in the Americas.

Within colonial history, these African Americans received little attention. Largely oblivious to the insistent calls of W. E. B. Du Bois for greater attention to African roots of American cultures,[3] colonial historians were slow to acknowledge the vast and essential contribution of slave labor to the building of the new worlds of America. They showed scant interest in the legal and intellectual constructions that sustained American slave regimes, in slave resistance to those regimes, or in the character and variety of slave life. No colonial historian considered whether Africans might have brought any expertise or special skills to European projects of refashioning the Americas or have had anything to do with the success of those projects. Only a few entertained the possibility that African Americans might have made contributions of their own to the content of the many New World cultures that took shape after 1492. The only detailed investigation of African-American life for any area of colonial British America focused not on one of the regions of major concentration of African Americans but on New England.[4]

---

[2]On the first stirrings of the ethnohistory movement, see William N. Fenton, *American Indian and White Relations to 1830: Needs and Opportunities for Study* (Chapel Hill, N.C., 1957).

[3]W. E. B. DuBois, *The Negro* (New York, 1915); *Black Folk: Then and Now* (New York, 1939); and *The World and Africa: An Inquiry into the Part Which Africa Has Played in World History* (1946, rev. ed., New York, 1965).

[4]Lorenzo J. Greene, *The Negro in Colonial New England* (New York, 1942).

Colonial history, in short, focused on the European conquerors and settlers and their creole descendants, and, in those populations, on the adult males. White men founded the colonies. They fought the battles that wrested control of American territories from the indigenous inhabitants. They supplied, organized, or presided over the labor that reconfigured American landscapes along European lines and created the economies needed to sustain new and growing populations of settlers and slaves. They established and then controlled the political, economic, social, and religious institutions. They wrote the laws that defined the rules and the standards under which the inhabitants of the colonies lived, determining what was and was not normative behavior, what was and what was not legitimate. They owned the property and headed the families sustained by that property. They named the places within the new societies they were creating and made the maps that displayed their achievements. Through the laws and the histories and other narratives they wrote, they constructed the identities that distinguished one place or society from another. They supplied the leadership of the settler revolts that, beginning during the last decades of the eighteenth century, resulted in the independence of many American political societies. The strategic, powerful role of white men in every phase of the colonization of America was so clear that few suggested that a colonial history focusing upon them and constructed around their activities and achievements might be in any way deficient.

Insofar as, before the late 1950s or early 1960s, there was a rival to this conception of New World history as the history of colonization, it was the view of New World history as part of a much wider movement encompassed within the idea of the *expansion of Europe.* No less, perhaps even more, celebratory of European achievements and no less sure of the narrative centrality of Europeans, this view took shape in academic circles, in the late nineteenth and early twentieth centuries, not so much in former colonies as near the centers of the great European empires that came to dominate such a large part of the globe after 1850. Its proponents, several of whom filled newly created chairs of imperial history at universities like Oxford, Cambridge, and London, were principally concerned to lay out the history of European expansion in the modern era. In their efforts to link the early modern phase of this expansionary movement with the modern, however, some of them reconceived early modern New World history as *imperial* history.

Written from the point of view of the imperial centers, this history stressed the ways in which the detached parts of the Spanish or British Empire, in America and elsewhere, were themselves Spanish or British.

It emphasized the formal and informal links that bound colonies to the metropolis and to one another in a single political and cultural imperial system and decried the parochialism that had enabled historians of former colonial states, such as the United States, to ignore the strength of metropolitan-colonial ties or the sometimes intimate connections between political societies that had once been but no longer were part of the same extended imperial polity. From this perspective, settler populations in colonies became the agents or conduits through which European power, authority, culture, political and legal institutions and traditions, and forms of economic and social organization flowed into and transformed the New World. Quite as much as in colonial history, however, the focus in imperial history remained fixed upon the activities of white male settlers, albeit they now had to share the stage with and surrender some of their agency to prominent figures in metropolitan centers.

The only important exceptions to these general observations occurred in Latin American countries, several of which experienced the development of a new pride in the plural character of their populations. *Indigenismo*, which emphasized the importance of Amerindians in the Peruvian and Mexican heritage, and *La Raza*, which glorified the racial mixture in Mexico, led, even before World War II,[5] to the emergence among historians such as Silvio Zavala of a new consciousness of the role of nonwhites in the national past.[6] Similarly in Brazil, the historical sociologist Gilberto Freyre's celebration of that country's plural racial past in his 1946 study, *The Masters and the Slaves: A Study in the Development of Brazilian Civilization*,[7] effectively began to bring the large Afro-Brazilian mixed race population into the consciousness of professional historians. But neither of these developments, occurring as they did in countries that according to the paradigm of power were well beyond the boundaries of mainline historical studies, had much immediate effect on the reigning paradigm of historical analysis and the implicit and still deeply embedded hierarchy of priorities associated with it.

Over the last half century, several developments have combined to

---

[5] See Frederick C. Turner, *The Dynamic of Mexican Nationalism* (Chapel Hill, N.C., 1968), 72–76, 170–79; Frederick B. Pike, *The Modern History of Peru* (New York, 1967), 233–36, 306–8.

[6] Silvio Zavala, *New Viewpoints on the Spanish Colonization of America* (Philadelphia, 1943).

[7] Gilberto Freyre, *The Masters and the Slaves: A Study in the Development of Brazilian Civilization*, 2d ed. (New York, 1956), originally published in Portuguese in 1933.

undermine, if by no means yet entirely to eliminate, this pattern of historical consciousness. Perhaps the most important has been the flowering of the social sciences. Already by the early 1940s, geography, economics, political science, and psychology were well ensconced in the curricula of most academic institutions throughout the Western world, but in most universities anthropology and sociology were still marginal subjects and carried less prestige. The drive to solve world problems by reconstructing socioeconomic and political institutions produced an upsurge in government funding for the social sciences after World War II, and all of them except geography quickly underwent a dramatic expansion and especially in the United States acquired a new respectability and sophistication. Displaying a degree of theoretical and conceptual rigor and a range of social and globally inclusive interests that were virtually unknown among contemporary historians, they focused upon not just elites in the West but on all segments of societies all over the globe. In search of additional subjects for analysis, a few social scientists by the 1960s were even turning from the contemporary world to the past, thereby stimulating the development of new subfields such as historical geography, econometric history, historical sociology, historical demography, ethnohistory, historical archaeology, and psychohistory.

As the influence of the social sciences penetrated the undergraduate curricula of United States universities and generated a popular literature, historians themselves began to employ, more and more openly, the language, concepts, methods, and concerns of the social sciences, especially sociology, psychology, economics, and anthropology. In time, this development encouraged a growing interest in the explicit use of theory and methods, including statistics and quantification, drawn very largely from the social sciences. Even more important, by fostering a new and more broadly oriented concern with social, economic, demographic, and cultural history, the new interest in the social sciences among historians helped to provide the foundations for a significant enlargement of the scope of historical inquiry.

In the United States, this movement was powerfully reinforced by the example of new schools of historical methodology and inquiry in France and Britain. By 1945, the French *Annales* school (named for the journal *Annales*) had for a generation been striving for a *histoire totale* that would subordinate the history of public life to a more expanded concern for the recovery of all aspects of a population's experience, from the environmental and material to the social and intellectual, from the macrolevel to the microlevel, and from the most prominent to the most marginal inhabitants. The early *Annalistes* focused almost exclusively upon the history of France and adjacent areas in Europe and the Mediterranean and so were relatively unknown to historians of any areas of the early modern Americas. By the early 1960s, however, students of other parts of early modern Europe, inspired by the French example, were beginning to turn their attention to social, economic, demographic, and cultural subjects. Founded in 1952, the English journal *Past and Present* provided an early showcase for their work. Initially, they studied the social sources of political events, such as the English Revolution or the Revolt of the Netherlands, but they soon began to concern themselves with aspects of the relationships among social structure, culture, and belief systems. Animated in part by Marxist interests in the history of the oppressed, they manifested from the beginning a concern with recovering the history of "peasants," workers, and other social groups long marginalized by a historiography preoccupied with power. At the same time, some of these scholars, including especially the Cambridge Group for the History of Population and Social Structure, studied interactions between population history and economic, social, and political change.

Works produced by these historians provided students of the early modern Atlantic world with attractive new models of how the new interest in the concerns of social science could translate into the illumination of a particular era in the past. Among students of the early modern western Atlantic, those concerned with Hispanic America were the earliest to follow the lead of the *Annalistes*, probably because the societies they studied had the same sorts of serial and notarial records that had provided the documentary base for so much of the early *Annaliste* history. Indeed, François Chevalier, author of the first modern book-length study of a New World social institution, *Land and Society in Colonial Mexico*, published in French in 1952,[8] was himself an *Annaliste* historian. But students of the early modern English, French, and Portuguese colonies soon began to work in this new tradition, and by the late 1960s and early 1970s, studies of family, community, population, and social structure were replacing politics as the main focus of colonial studies throughout the Americas. This new interest can be followed by noting the changing content of well-established journals like the *William and Mary Quarterly* and the *Hispanic American Historical Review* and by the appearance of new journals that catered to the new methodological, theoretical, and comparative interests of historians and historically minded social

---

[8] François Chevalier, *Land and Society in Colonial Mexico* (Berkeley, Calif., 1963).

scientists, including *Comparative Studies in History and Society* (1958), *History and Theory* (1961), the *Latin American Research Review* (1966), the *Journal of Social History* (1967), and the *Journal of Interdisciplinary History* (1970).

This receptivity to British and European models of historical investigation was, at least in part, a function of a general opening to the wider world on the part of Western academic institutions after World War II. Led by the social sciences and stimulated by the rapid decolonization of Asia, the Middle East, and Africa and the global competition between the Western alliance and the Eastern bloc for influence over the many new postcolonial nations, American academic institutions, always less parochial than their European counterparts, moved quickly in the 1950s and 1960s into the study of the non-Western world that they had formerly ignored. To their traditional emphasis upon American, western European, and, to a much lesser extent, Latin American studies, universities in the United States added courses and programs on eastern Europe, Asia, the Middle East, and Africa. By the late 1960s, most major history departments offered courses on Europe and Asia. In historical studies, this influence was reflected in the founding of new journals such as the *Journal of African History* (1960), *Middle Eastern Studies* (1964), or the *International Journal of African Historical Studies* (1968). Although Howard University had been offering courses in African history since 1922[9] and other traditionally black colleges and universities had followed its lead, the study of Africa and the Middle East at the doctoral level was still restricted to a few of the largest departments.

At least implicitly, these three developments—the flowering of the social sciences, the turn away from political to other forms of history inspired by the *Annalistes,* and the growth of non-Western studies—together challenged the predominant paradigm of power with its privileging of the history of the West and its predominant populations. But they by no means overturned it. This point is vividly illustrated by the contents of three highly sophisticated and still useful studies written by three American scholars in the 1950s and early 1960s, one each in the fields of American, European, and world history. Regarded as pathbreaking by contemporaries, these volumes made clear that the old Eurocentric or Western- and elite-centered vision of the past was still alive and well in American historical studies.

---

[9] Primarily through the pioneering efforts of William Leo Hansberry. See Joseph E. Harris, ed., *Pillars in Ethiopian History: The William Leo Hansberry African History Notebook* (Washington, D. C., 1974), 3–30.

Published in 1954, David Potter's *People of Plenty*[10] was informed by the latest social science theory and an ironic awareness of the extent to which, for many, the American dream of economic success had often proven illusory. Yet Potter placed no emphasis upon the facts that the land that had been the basis for American abundance had been wrested from Amerindians or that much of the labor that contributed to that abundance had been supplied by enslaved Africans and their descendants.

Published in 1959 and 1964, R. R. Palmer's two-volume *The Age of the Democratic Revolution*[11] took a broad transatlantic approach virtually without precedent among American historians of Europe. Reflecting an emerging appreciation of the relevance of the history of the United States to the development of the West, this appreciation was, of course, in some major part a function of the power of the United States in the post–World War II world. In this effort at a comprehensive history of late eighteenth-century political revolutions, Palmer both brought the American Revolution into the mainstream of Western history and provided detailed analyses of the many contemporary and subsidiary revolutions associated with the French Revolution in Europe. Yet he failed even to mention the black revolution in St. Domingue, certainly the most "democratic" revolution of the period he covered.

Published in 1963, William H. McNeill's *The Rise of the West*,[12] a response to the new globalism in politics and historical studies, represented an impressive and learned effort to provide a more inclusive and broader alternative to the history of Western civilization. Yet, in this early volume, McNeill, as his title announced, could only conceptualize world history in terms of the centrality of the West. Although his volume contained a large segment on the development of those civilizations that were most directly antecedent to Western civilization and even a chapter on the development of what he referred to as "peripheral civilizations" in India and China, he brought the history of areas outside Europe into his story as they seemed relevant to the history of western Europe. The Americas and Africa received very little attention indeed, the former getting less than fifteen pages and the latter only about five.

---

[10] David E. Potter, *People of Plenty: Economic Abundance and the American Character* (Chicago, 1954).

[11] R. R. Palmer, *The Age of Democratic Revolution: A Political History of Europe and America*, 2 vols. (Princeton, N.J., 1959–64).

[12] William H. McNeill, *The Rise of the West: A History of the Human Community* (Chicago, 1963).

McNeill's work was not unrepresentative of contemporary historical interest in non-European areas. Fundamentally little more than an extension of imperial history, interest in areas that had only recently been under European control was very largely a history of European activities in those former colonies. In its earliest stages of development, the history of India or Africa was the history of Europeans in India and Africa. Moreover, when historians first began to try to move beyond such an emphasis and to write the histories of indigenous populations, they very often tried to make sense of those histories by organizing them under the rubrics, terms, and categories derived from the histories of Western societies, without pausing to ponder the extent to which those rubrics, terms, and categories were themselves culture bound and perhaps inappropriate for the organization of knowledge about radically different cultures.

In other words, the initial broadening of historical studies to include more people than elites, socioeconomic and cultural as well as political and intellectual systems, America as well as Europe, and even areas beyond the West did not radically shake the old correlation between history and power. Thus, colonial historians of both the Americas during the 1960s and 1970s took a far more inclusive approach to their subjects, emphasizing the demography, economic structures, settlement patterns, community, family, and household organizations, wealth structures, social and cultural divisions, and value systems in Europe's new American colonies. Probably because the traditional conception of history as the history of politics was far less strongly entrenched in areas in which so little political history was shared, colonial historians of both the Americas moved earlier and more fully into this new social history than did historians in the national period. But the emphasis in this enterprise was always on the dominant settler populations of Europeans and their creole descendants. Indeed, one of the principal effects of this work was an emerging appreciation of how European these American extensions of Europe actually were. The adjective in the title of James Lockhart's *Spanish Peru, 1532—1560*, a superb study, published in 1968, of the first generation of Spanish settlement in Peru,[13] heralded this development.

These studies had at least three important short-term effects. The first was to stimulate an interest in the comparative history of the colonizing or Europeanizing process, one example of which was Charles Gibson's and my unsuccessful effort to establish a Center for the Compara-

---

[13] James Lockhart, *Spanish Peru, 1532—1560* (Madison, Wis., 1968).

tive Study of American Colonization at the William L. Clements Library in 1965–66 during the brief period when we were both on the faculty of the Department of History at the University of Michigan. The second was to tie the history of the Americas after 1492 even more closely into the reigning paradigm. As the American colonies of Europe more and more came to be seen as extensions of Europe, they acquired greater historical importance. The third was to make even clearer how European penetration into the New World had created a vast, interconnected *Atlantic* world in which people, cultures, institutions, goods, and ideas flowed back and forth between the Old World and the New.

As yet, this emerging Atlantic world had no obvious place for Africans, African Americans, or Amerindians. Dating from the early 1950s, Charles Gibson's pioneering works on the Amerindians of Central Mexico[14] attracted no imitators, and, except for Freyre's impressionistic work, interest in slavery among historians—represented by influential works by Eric Williams,[15] Frank Tannenbaum,[16] Kenneth M. Stampp,[17] and Stanley M. Elkins[18]—concentrated more upon the institution of slavery and the comparative treatment of slaves than upon the slaves themselves, and far more upon the generation that saw the abolition of slavery than upon the many generations that experienced it.[19] Indeed, historians of race, such as Roy Harvey Pearce[20] or Winthrop D. Jordan,[21] concentrated on the attitudes of the master class. Before the early

---

[14] Charles Gibson, *Tlaxcala in the Sixteenth Century* (New Haven, 1952), and *The Aztecs under Spanish Rule: A History of the Indians in the Valley of Mexico, 1519–1810* (Stanford, Calif., 1964).

[15] Eric Williams, *Capitalism and Slavery* (Chapel Hill, N.C., 1944).

[16] Frank Tannenbaum, *Slave and Citizen: The Negro in the Americas* (New York, 1946).

[17] Kenneth M. Stampp, *The Peculiar Institution: Slavery in the Ante-Bellum South* (New York, 1956).

[18] Stanley M. Elkins, *Slavery: A Problem in American Institutional and Intellectual History* (Chicago, 1959).

[19] Peter Kolchin, "American Historians and Antebellum Southern Slavery, 1959–1984," in William J. Cooper, Jr., Michael F. Holt, and John McCardell, eds., *A Master's Due: Essays in Honor of David Herbert Donald* (Baton Rouge, La., 1985), 87–111, provides a comprehensive discussion of this and later literature on slavery in antebellum America.

[20] Roy Harvey Pearce, *The Savages of America: A Study of the Indian and the Idea of Civilization* (Baltimore, 1953).

[21] Winthrop D. Jordan, *White over Black: American Attitudes toward the Negro, 1550–1812* (Chapel Hill, N.C., 1968).

1970s, only the wide-ranging work of the anthropologists Melville J.
Herskovits[22] and Roger Bastide[23] persistently raised and tried to answer
questions about the transmission of African culture to America and its
survival and perpetuation in a variety of settings.

What thrust African Americans into history and inaugurated a profound explanatory revolution in the history of the early modern Atlantic
world were the activities of the descendants of the slaves and their allies
during the 1960s. The civil rights movement that culminated in that
decade demanded not only an end to segregation and racial inequality
in American life but a recognition of the role of African Americans in the
colonial and national history of the United States. More than any other
single development, I would argue, the impulses flowing out of these
demands were responsible for subverting the paradigm of power that had
dominated modern historical studies from the beginning.

Initially, historical studies of African Americans continued to operate
within that paradigm. In the United States, scholars seemed to be principally concerned to identify African Americans who had made important contributions to American life and to incorporate them into
standard accounts of the American past. In so doing, they were endors-
ing the traditional equation of achievement, prominence, and power
with historical significance. But some scholars quickly realized that such
an approach would never reveal the full contribution of African Americans to the shaping of American life and culture and that that contribution could only be recovered through an approach similar to that represented by the new social history, an approach that gave as much
attention to the ordinary and the obscure as to the extraordinary and
the visible.

New work in the emerging field of African history greatly facilitated
the adoption of such an approach. In the decades after World War II,
the founding of universities in tropical Africa, the establishment of African studies centers in European and American universities, the creation
of chairs in African history in Britain and France, the early flow of pro-
fessors from Europe to Africa and of African students to Europe and the
United States, and the demand within African universities for a history

---

[22]Melville J. Herskovits, *The Myth of the Negro Past* (New York, 1941), and *The New World Negro* (Bloomington, Ind., 1966).

[23]Roger Bastide, *African Civilisations in the New World* (New York, 1971), originally published in French in 1967, and *The African Religions of Brazil: Toward a Sociology of the Interpenetration of Civilizations* (Baltimore, 1978), originally published in French in 1960.

of the broader African experience—all led to the rapid development and professionalization of African history.[24] Between 1950 and 1970, a growing number of research students from Europe, the United States, Africa, and the West Indies, drawn to the new graduate training centers such as those at the School of Oriental and African Studies in London, the Program in Tropical History at the University of Wisconsin, or the African Studies Center at the University of Ibadan, dramatically expanded the volume of work in African history. Although non-Africans, including Roland Oliver,[25] David Birmingham,[26] and Jan Vansina,[27] initially dominated the field, already by the mid-1950s African scholars such as K. O. Dike were achieving prominence and distinction.[28]

In stimulating an appreciation of Africa's role in creating the early modern Atlantic world, Philip D. Curtin's *The Atlantic Slave Trade*, published in 1969,[29] was especially significant. An effort to provide a statistical portrait of the transatlantic slave trade from its beginnings early in the sixteenth century until its final abolition in the 1870s, Curtin's book brought a new specificity to the understanding not just of the total volume of the trade, which he estimated at just under ten million, but also of the African sources and the American destinations of slaves as those sources and destinations shifted over time. By relating slave imports to slave population growth, he underlined the appalling mortality and waste of life among slaves all over tropical America. Only in British North America, which absorbed less than 10 percent of the total trade, and possibly in nonplantation areas of Hispanic America did slave populations manage to show a natural increase before the last days of slavery. Nevertheless, Curtin's hard figures about the volume of the trade and the numbers of Africans entering the Americas made it vividly clear that the early modern Atlantic world involved an interaction not just between Europe and the Americas but also among those continents and Africa and that, from the beginning to the end of colonization, interactions with Africa were extensive and continuous. By thus explicitly and force-

---

[24] On these developments, see Roland Oliver, "Western Historiography and Its Relevance to Africa," in T. O. Ranger, ed., *Emerging Themes of African History* (Dar es Salaam, 1968), 53–60.

[25] Roland Oliver and Gervase Mathew, eds., *History of East Africa* (Oxford, 1953), 1.

[26] David Birmingham, *Trade and Conflict in Angola: The Mbundu and Their Neighbors under the Influence of the Portuguese, 1483–1790* (Oxford, 1966).

[27] Jan Vansina, *Kingdoms of the Savanna* (Madison, Wis., 1966).

[28] K. O. Dike, *Trade and Politics in the Niger Delta, 1830–1885* (London, 1956).

[29] Philip D. Curtin, *The Atlantic Slave Trade: A Census* (Madison, Wis., 1969).

fully inserting Africa and Africans into the early modern Atlantic world, Curtin's work implicitly raised the question of whether any comprehensive account of that world could be written without considering not just the *Europeanization* of the Americas emphasized by the new social historians but also their *Africanization.*

But early work in early modern African-American history did not immediately address itself to this grand problem of the Africanization of America. Instead, it concentrated on using serial evidence of the kind employed by social historians (records of slave-trading companies, port books, censuses, taxable lists, individual plantation records—all documents generated by European and creole master classes) both to refine and expand Curtin's figures on the numbers of slaves sent from specific African regions into particular American destinations and to sort out patterns of slave use, work regimes, sources and quantities of food, household organization, material life, mortality, reproduction, and resistance. While few historians attempted to investigate these phenomena comparatively, a series of conferences brought together people studying different branches of the slave trade, different slave regimes, and different aspects of those regimes in all their complexity and variety. These conferences stimulated an interest in comparative slavery and an understanding of the relatedness of African-American experiences in the New World. No other group of studies in the 1960s and 1970s did more to foster an interest in comparative history in early modern America or to expand, deepen, and alter the concept of an interconnected early modern Atlantic world.[30]

---

[30] See David W. Cohen and Jack P. Greene, eds., *Neither Slave nor Free: The Freedmen of African Descent in the Slave Societies of the New World* (Baltimore, 1972); Robert Brent Toplin, *Slavery and Race Relations in Latin America* (Westport, Conn., 1974); Stanley L. Engerman and Eugene D. Genovese, eds., *Race and Slavery in the Western Hemisphere: Quantitative Studies* (Princeton, N.J., 1975); and Vera D. Rubin and Arthur Tuden, eds., *Comparative Perspectives on Slavery in New World Plantations* (New York, 1977). Important early single-author studies that fostered an interest in the comparative study of slavery and African Americans, David B. Davis, *The Problem of Slavery in Western Culture* (Ithaca, N.Y., 1966), and Carl Degler, *Neither Black nor White: Slavery and Race Relations in Brazil and the United States* (New York, 1971), were especially important. More recent collections include Barbara L. Solow, ed., *Slavery and the Rise of the Atlantic System* (Cambridge, 1991); Ira Berlin and Philip D. Morgan, eds., *The Slaves' Economy: Independent Production by Slaves in the New World* (London, 1991); Berlin and Morgan, eds., *Cultivation and Culture: Labor and the Shaping of Slave Life in the Americas* (Charlottesville, Va., 1993); and Joseph E. Inikori and Stanley L. Engerman, eds., *The Atlantic Slave Trade: Effects on Economies, Societies, and Peoples in Africa, the Americas, and Europe* (Durham, N.C., 1992).

Through its deconstruction and reconstruction of the institution of slavery throughout the Western hemisphere, this body of work taught historians to distinguish between newly-imported Africans and creoles, plantation slaves and urban slaves, slaves working in unspecialized agricultural, industrial, or mining production and slaves working as artisans, skilled workers, managers, or domestics closer to the white power structures, slaves in places where they constituted a majority of the population and slaves in places where they were a tiny minority. Through its attention to their resistance and rebellion, to their rejection of European belief systems such as Christianity, to their activities in feeding themselves and marketing, and to their efforts to manumit themselves and their relatives, this work made it clear that, however repressive the regimes under which they toiled, slaves retained some agency. Yet the serial records on which these studies were based had relatively little to say about the question of how the massive presence of Africans and African Americans contributed to the Africanization of the societies and cultures of the Americas.

Borrowing a term from Jewish history, students of African Americans had already begun by the late 1960s to speak broadly of the transportation of Africans to and their dispersal throughout the New World as an African *diaspora*, and the use of the term *diaspora* represented a conceptual breakthrough, an alternative view of early modern Atlantic history.[31] Concepts such as *colonization* or *expansion of Europe* implied a process of social and cultural formation dominated by European organizers and their descendants and operating within national boundaries. The concept of *diaspora*, by contrast, emphasized the flow and mixture of peoples and cultures and implied a process of social and cultural formation that, far from being imposed from the top down, derived from a continuing process of negotiation or exchange among the various peoples and cultures involved. It was as applicable to Europeans as to Africans, and a few scholars actually did begin the refer to the English or the Spanish diaspora in the New World.

Yet it remained unclear precisely how historians might recover the African contribution to this exchange. The first problem involved the very term *African.* Curtin's book on the Atlantic slave trade had already called attention to the extraordinary ethnic and regional diversity of the slaves, a point previously made by Herskovits and Bastide. The growing volume of historical work on Africa during the 1960s and 1970s made it

---

[31] Joseph E. Harris, ed., *Global Dimensions of the African Diaspora* (Washington, D.C., 1982).

clear that, however one looked at it, precolonial Africa was a far more complicated entity than early modern Europe. Stretching over a physical area vastly larger than Europe, Africa included a much wider number of ecological zones, and its inhabitants represented a much greater range of political, economic, and social organizations, cultural traditions, languages, and religions. If the people sent to America as slaves came mostly from the western and central portions of this enormous physical space, they still represented a diversity far greater than could be found among the peoples of western Europe, long bound by a centralized religious culture. The growing awareness of the diversity of Africa's peoples and cultures rendered the term *African* as problematic as the term *European*. Indeed, it powerfully suggested that the diverse peoples brought to the Americas as slaves from the Gold Coast, the Congo, or Angola (themselves rather crude modern analytical constructs) became *African* only *after* they were jumbled together in America and that any understanding of what African Americans brought to the negotiations that produced the various societies and cultures of America would have to be informed by a comprehension of how they had first formed new African-American cultures and what the dimensions and contents of those new cultures were.[32]

The traditional methods and assumptions of Western historiography were ill-suited to this enterprise, and progress in it depended upon another approach developed in the first instance by a second generation of historians of Africa. Endeavoring to move beyond the sorts of questions that could be addressed on the basis of the written serial records kept by Europeans, younger historians of Africa began, already in the late 1960s, to explore other types of sources and other approaches that would enable them to look at African pasts through African lenses. Historical archaeology provided one avenue of approach.[33] A second, pioneered by historians like Jan Vansina, was through the dense and rich oral traditions through which many African societies preserved and passed along to succeeding generations what they deemed to be meaningful about their pasts.[34] A third was to apply the ethnographic methods developed by anthropologists for the analysis of contemporary societies and groups

---

[32] See the insightful analysis of Sidney W. Mintz and Richard Price, *The Birth of African-American Culture: An Anthropological Perspective* (Boston, 1992), written in 1972–73 and first published in 1976.

[33] Merrick Posnansky, "Archaeology: Its Uses and Abuses," in Ranger, *Emerging Themes of African History*, 61–73.

[34] Jan Vansina, *Oral Tradition: A Study in Historical Methodology* (Chicago, 1965).

to the study of earlier times in Africa. This last approach involved the intensive examination of remaining visual evidence and the close questioning of written texts of a kind seldom used by political, economic, or social historians, such as travel reports, chronicles, or observations made by traders, missionaries, and others working among African peoples.[35] Together, these three approaches held out the possibility of reconstructing the histories and past cultures of peoples, including African Americans, for whom written records, the foundation of traditional Western historiography, were nonexistent or sparse.

The new perspective arising out of all these developments informed the Program in Atlantic History and Culture, which my colleagues and I created at The Johns Hopkins University in 1971–72. The *Atlantic* of the program was a quadrangular entity; it included Africa, as well as Europe and the two Americas. Although the program asserted its intention to deal with all the peoples and cultures on all four continents, the focus, as could be seen from the research interests of new faculty appointed to teach in the program—Sidney Mintz and Richard Price in anthropology and Franklin Knight, A. J. R. Russell-Wood, Ray Kea, and, somewhat later, Philip Curtin and Willie Lee Rose in history—was mostly upon Africa, Europe, and areas occupied by Europeans and Africans in the Americas. The heavily slave and African societies of the West Indies, Brazil, and southern North America were to be a special area of concentration. Amerindians got relatively little attention. The inclusion of the term *culture* in the title of the program announced that it was a joint venture between history and anthropology, providing historians with training in the use of anthropological concepts and methods and nontraditional sources and encouraging anthropologists to venture out of the present and into the past. Starting with a recognition of the great disparities in power and resources among cultures, the program also assumed that the purpose of studying cultures comparatively and in interaction with other cultures was not to establish a hierarchy of cultures but, insofar as possible, to understand each culture on its own terms. A final set of assumptions underlying the program was that each of the societies surrounding the Atlantic not only had its own history but also a role in shaping the character of the socioeconomic and cultural region to which it belonged and thus also of the larger Atlantic world.

How the history of an entity in the early modern Americas looked

---

[35] See David William Cohen, "Doing Social History from Pim's Doorway," in Olivier Zunz, ed., *Reliving the Past: The Worlds of Social History* (Chapel Hill, N.C., 1985), 191–235.

when Africans, too, were undersood to be active participants could be
seen in Peter H. Wood's important *Black Majority*, published in 1974.[36]
Offering the best portrait of the character of a slave culture in an English
colony published up to that time, Wood made a powerful case that South
Carolina's majority African-American population contributed not just its
labor but its technical expertise to the rice culture on which South Carolina depended for its economic sustenance throughout the eighteenth
century. Seven years later, in *Rice and Slaves*, Daniel C. Littlefield,[37] one
of the first historians to come out of the Program in Atlantic History
and Culture, reinforced Wood's thesis by linking, in an imaginative and
persuasive exposition, planter preferences for Senegambian slaves with
those slaves' experience with rice culture in Senegambia.

   Still other works explored the ways in which people from various areas
of Africa came together to negotiate a coherent culture. In his pioneering
The Sociology of Slavery, published in 1969, Orlando Patterson imaginatively reconstructed Jamaican slave society before emancipation.[38] Gerald W. Mullin, *Flight and Rebellion*, a study of eighteenth-century Virginia slavery published in 1972,[39] and David Barry Gaspar, *Bondmen and
Rebels*, an analysis of slave resistance in early Antigua published in
1985,[40] explored patterns of interaction between creole and African
slaves in their relations with and resistance to their masters. In the late
1980s, Margaret Creel Washington, *"A Peculiar People,"*[41] and William
D. Pierson, *Black Yankees*,[42] both published in 1988, discussed some of
the ways in which African Americans were able to re-create aspects of
their African heritage in the New World.

   These and many other excellent works written about the Euro-African

---

[36] Peter H. Wood, *Black Majority: Negroes in Colonial South Carolina from 1670 through
the Stono Rebellion* (New York, 1974).

[37] Daniel C. Littlefield, *Rice and Slaves: Ethnicity and the Slave Trade in Colonial South
Carolina* (Baton Rouge, La., 1981).

[38] Orlando Patterson, *The Sociology of Slavery: An Analysis of the Origins, Development,
and Structure of Negro Slave Society in Jamaica* (Rutherford, N.J., 1969).

[39] Gerald W. Mullin, *Flight and Rebellion: Slave Resistance in Eighteenth-Century Virginia*
(New York, 1972).

[40] David Barry Gaspar, *Bondmen and Rebels: A Study of Master-Slave Relations in Antigua
with Implications for Colonial British America* (Baltimore, 1985).

[41] Margaret Creel Washington, *"A Peculiar People": Slave Religion and Community-
Culture among the Gullahs* (New York, 1988).

[42] William D. Pierson, *Black Yankees: The Development of Afro-American Subculture in
Eighteenth-Century New England* (Amherst, Mass., 1988).

societies of early modern plantation America,[43] culminating in John Thornton, *Africa and Africans in the Making of the Atlantic World, 1400—1680*, published in 1992,[44] were paralleled by and, in colonial British-American history, inspired a resurgence and reorientation of Amerindian studies. This development appeared first and has been most extensive in the study of Mexico, Peru, Central America, and other places in Hispanic America where, despite severe demographic loss following the Spanish conquest, Amerindian populations during the colonial era and after were always substantial and often lived intermixed with or in close proximity to Euro-American and African-American populations. But it was also powerful in North American, Brazilian, and Caribbean studies. Principally concerned with explaining how Europeans were affected by their interactions with Amerindians, earlier studies of Amerindians in the colonial world had, with a few notable exceptions such as the works of Charles Gibson, focused on European-Amerindian relations. During the two decades beginning about 1970, however, historians and anthropologists, self-consciously working as "ethnohistorians" and following the example of students of Africa and African America in employing historical archaeology and the sensitive application of ethnographic concepts and methods to traditional written sources, successfully sought to reconstruct the histories of many Amerindian groups before and after contact with Europeans and to look at those contacts through Amerindian eyes. No less than precolonial Africa, pre-contact America increasingly came to be seen as a rich, variegated, and complex panoply of societies and cultures.[45]

By introducing the term *encounter* to refer to the process of mutual discovery that began when Amerindians met Europeans or Africans for

---

[43]Peter H. Wood, "'I Did the Best I Could for My Day': The Study of Early Black History during the Second Reconstruction, 1960–1976," *William and Mary Quarterly*, 3d ser., 35 (1978): 185–225, discusses literature on African Americans in the British colonies published before 1978. On African Americans in the Hispanic world, see Leslie B. Rout, Jr., *The African Experience in Spanish America* (Cambridge, 1976), and the historiographical discussion in John E. Kicza, "The Social and Ethnic History of Colonial Latin America: The Last Twenty Years," *William and Mary Quarterly*, 3d ser., 45 (1988): 480–86.

[44]John Thornton, *Africa and Africans in the Making of the Atlantic World, 1400–1680* (Cambridge, 1992).

[45]For surveys of this literature, see James H. Merrell, "Colonial Historians and American Indians," *William and Mary Quarterly*, 3d ser., 46 (1989): 94–119, for colonial British North America, and Kicza, "Social and Ethnic History of Colonial Latin America," 470–80, for colonial Hispanic and Portuguese America.

the first time, these ethnohistorians achieved a conceptual breakthrough comparable in significance to that made by students of African Americans when they began to use the term *diaspora*. Perhaps even to a greater extent than the concept of *diaspora*, the notion of encounter suggested that none of the parties involved was passive and thereby demonstrably took agency away from Europeans. It implied an interaction not between superiors and inferiors but among groups of strangers, each of which viewed the other as *others*. By reconceiving this interaction as an encounter, ethnohistorians effectively substituted for the traditional notion that Europeans had *discovered* America the idea that Europeans and Amerindians had discovered one another.

In the process, of course, Amerindians acquired a new historical importance. As peoples with histories and cultures with their own integrity, they could no longer be dismissed as inferior, unimportant, and, from a European perspective, culturally backward peoples who were unworthy of historical attention, whose point of view did not need to be taken into account, and whose resistance to Europeans could be regarded primarily as a nuisance on the road to the Europeanization—the civilization—of the Americas. The concept *encounter* implied that there were at least two sides to exchanges, events, and developments and two stories to be told. Moreover, ethnohistorians made clear that encounter did not lead always and immediately to domination by Europeans, whatever the final outcome. Rather, it could be followed by a wide variety of possible outcomes: trade, war, conquest, repulsion, coexistence, absorption, annihilation, expulsion, or reorganization of peoples and cultures.[46]

Parallel to these revolutions in African-American and Amerindian studies was the emergence of two other areas of vigorous historical inquiry. The first was women's history, responsible for the most exciting and significant changes in historical approaches over the last two decades.[47] The second was the study of ethnicity and the history of immigrants from outside the country of the charter culture—in the case of

---

[46] James H. Merrell, "'The Customes of Our Country': Indians and Colonists in Early America," in Bernard Bailyn and Philip D. Morgan, eds., *Strangers within the Realm: Cultural Margins of the First British Empire* (Chapel Hill, N.C., 1991), 117–56, and Philip D. Morgan, "British Encounters with Africans and African-Americans, circa 1600–1780," ibid., 157–219, summarize the findings of the literature on culture encounters between British settlers and, respectively, Amerindians and people of African descent. See also Ida Altman and Reginald D. Butler, "The Contact of Cultures: Perspectives on the Quincentenary," *American Historical Review* 99 (1994): 478–503.

[47] See Mary Beth Norton, "The Evolution of White Women's Experience in Early America," *American Historical Review* 89 (1984): 593–619.

the United States, non-English peoples.[48] For several years now, United States historians have been labeling the larger history that has developed out of these studies *multicultural*. The primary characteristic of multicultural history is its inclusiveness. Not political power or public prominence or socioeconomic clout or high cultural achievement but existence as a coherent cultural entity is the principal criterion for historical significance. Of course, this paradigm of inclusiveness directly challenges many aspects of the traditional historical paradigm of power.

Where the new multicultural history will lead is not at present clear. Notwithstanding its origins in a strong impulse toward inclusiveness, it has shown tendencies toward the production of exclusive histories. As historians have painstakingly reconstructed the history of each group, often in effect studying it as an entity unto itself and thereby providing it with its own history, the general history to which it is presumably attached has tended to become little more than a collection of separate group histories, the larger purpose of which is merely to provide each group with a historical space. If we stop here, however, we will, in my view, be settling for far too little and retreating from the ambitious goal of subverting the paradigm of the powerful.

For the great ambition articulated in the 1960s was to understand how larger historical worlds were created through the interactions of peoples and cultures, a project for which the New World of the early modern Atlantic offered an excellent laboratory. The assumption was that Amerindians, Europeans, and Africans were mutually involved in a competitive and ongoing social interplay. Which aspects of which cultures survived and prospered was a function of what worked best in any given situation and was most socially congenial. Among several excellent examples of this approach are Edward Brathwaite, *The Development of Creole Society in Jamaica, 1770–1832*, published in 1971,[49] and Mechal Sobel, *The World They Made Together: Black and White Values in Eighteenth-Century Virginia*, published in 1987,[50] the title of which effectively captured the largest ambition of the first generation of early mod-

---

[48] See A. G. Roeber, "'The Origin of Whatever Is Not English among Us': The Dutch-speaking and the German-speaking Peoples of Colonial America," in Bailyn and Morgan, *Strangers within the Realm*, 220–83, and Maldwyn Jones, "The Scotch-Irish in British America," ibid., 284–313.

[49] Edward Brathwaite, *The Development of Creole Society in Jamaica, 1770–1820* (Oxford, 1971).

[50] Mechal Sobel, *The World They Made Together: Black and White Values in Eighteenth-Century Virginia* (Princeton, N.J., 1987).

ern Atlantic historians. Brathwaite proposed the concept *creolization* as a device through which historians might study the ways in which Africans and Europeans had adapted to the New World of Jamaica and to one another, while Sobel analyzed the formation of eighteenth-century Virginia culture as a process to which both white and black Virginians made major contributions.

For the grand project of understanding the New Worlds of early modern America as a product of such interactions, the concept of *diaspora*, with its emphasis upon the spread of peoples, and the concept of *encounter*, which, like the related term *contact*, suggests a transitory situation, may not in themselves be sufficient. Although they are improvements on the notions of early modern Atlantic history as either colonization or European expansion, neither concept captures the dynamic and continuous character of the process of social and cultural formation that characterized that history. As an alternative, some scholars have begun to use the related concepts of *mastery, negotiation,* and *exchange. Mastery* calls attention to the great inequalities of power in defining the cultural spaces of the early modern Americas. *Negotiation,* which suggests process, and *exchange,* which stresses outcomes, acknowledge, even emphasize, the agency of those with less formal power in the transactions and interactions that produced those spaces and suggest the ongoing character of the process.

However useful the concepts of *mastery, exchange* and *negotiation* may turn out to be, and preliminary usage suggests that they are highly promising, the idea of *Atlantic* history has always been at odds with the much older and more deeply entrenched conception of the past as, preeminently, the history of nation-states, a mainstay and the last vestige of the paradigm of power. The project to create or to uncover an Atlantic history called not just for considering events and developments in a broad transoceanic framework but, more importantly, for reconceiving the entire historical landscape in which they occurred, a landscape in which contemporary regional or cultural similarities, not ultimate membership in some as yet uncreated national state, would provide the principal criteria of organization.

But the goal of getting beyond the nation-state paradigm has fallen short, and in the effort to achieve that goal the development of multicultural studies has not been very helpful. If it, and all the developments it is built upon, have taken us far away from the idea that history is the study of dominant social groups, it has actually contributed to reinforce the national state paradigm. The surprising liaison between that paradigm and multiculturalism has manifested several parochializing and anachronistic tendencies. It has created artificial distinctions among Amerindians of the same linguistic stock, culture, and political affiliation and among colonies that were once extensions of the same national culture, merely because they did not wind up in the same national state. It has violently wrenched the colonial experiences of some sociocultural entities out of the contemporary national contexts to which they belonged and shoehorned them into an uneasy relationship with the early history of places with which they had little or no contemporary connection. It has focused attention away from the commonalities among the experiences of African Americans in areas that wound up in different countries. Although we have succeeded in getting away from the idea that history is past politics, we have not been able to divest ourselves of the teleological notion that history has to or should be organized along national lines, that colonial diasporas and encounters are prenational history. As long as they remain imprisoned within a national state perspective, multiculturalists are unlikely to complete the project of subverting and reformulating the paradigm of power.

If historical studies are still a long way from where, a quarter of a century ago, I thought they should be by the end of the century, perhaps people of my persuasion expected too much. We should be pleased that they have changed as much as they have. As a result of the careful work of hundreds of historians, anthropologists, and other scholars, the conception of an Atlantic world emerging out of the interchange among peoples, polities, and cultures on the four continents that face the Atlantic has acquired definition and focus, and our understanding of the complex unities, contrasts, and interactions that characterized that world has been enormously enriched. In particular, this conception has helped focus attention upon the ubiquitous presence of people of African descent throughout the early modern New World, upon the significance, even, in many cases, the centrality, of slavery in the construction of those worlds, and upon the agency of African Americans in the formation of the cultures that came to characterize those worlds.

At Johns Hopkins, the Atlantic History and Culture Program turned out to be a vigorous institution that, run at various times by American, African, Latin American, and even European historians, lasted for nearly a quarter century until, two years ago, the anthropologists assumed responsibility for it and, in the manner of anthropologists, globalized and changed it, replacing it with an Institute for the *Global* Study of Culture, Power, and History. But the Atlantic focus retains appeal. In May 1995 the College of Charleston, situated in the place that, as Peter Wood pointed out to us twenty years ago, was the Ellis Island of

Black America, announced the establishment of an Institute for the Study of the Lowcountry and the Atlantic World. The previous January, at a session of the American Historical Association, Bernard Bailyn reported that even Harvard University had decided to take the radical step—radical at least for Harvard—of setting up a center for Atlantic history.

Historians who are committed to a larger Atlantic focus will never be able to rest, however, until the nation-state paradigm, the final trace of the paradigm of power, is finally divested of its hold on the historical mind.

This chapter was written in the spring of 1995 in response to an invitation from Darline Clark Hine and Barry Gaspar to deliver one of several keynote addresses at a symposium on the "Comparative History of Black People in Diaspora" at Michigan State University, East Lansing, April 14, 1995. I wish to thank Adell Patton, Jr., and Peter Kolchin for their suggestions in revising it. It is published here for the first time.

PART TWO
Colonial British America

—FOUR—

The Colonial Era:
An Interview

John A. Garraty Professor Greene, the colonial period of American history is so vast as to defy easy characterization. Can you subdivide it and explain the criteria on which the divisions are made?

Jack P. Greene The range of criteria which might be used to divide the colonial era into periods is infinite, and whatever criteria are chosen by an individual scholar will depend upon his particular sense of what are the most important and enduring themes about the area and the special angle of vision which that sense gives him.

My own feeling is that the most useful (because it is the most basic) breakdown would be in terms of the changing character of colonial society. Such a division is extremely difficult, however, because colonies and regions were settled at different times and developed at widely varying rates, so that they moved through similar stages of development at different times. Nevertheless, colonial social development can be roughly broken down into two phases. The first phase was characterized by relatively inchoate kinds of society. Because they lacked real functional integration, because social and political leadership was not beyond dispute, and because the organization of the economy was still in doubt, societies during this stage were extraordinarily brittle and unstable. During the second phase, by contrast, society was much more coherent and infinitely more stable, as the lines of social and political authority had become clearer, the structure of the economy had been settled, and a considerable degree of social integration had been achieved.

Although most areas had moved from the first to the second of these stages by the early decades of the eighteenth century, and although it does therefore make some sense to say that the first phase corresponds generally with the seventeenth century and the second with the eighteenth century, it is always necessary to keep in mind that some areas—such as tidewater Virginia—had already reached the second stage by the

[45]

last decades of the seventeenth century, while other areas—backcountry Carolina or New Hampshire—did not move into the second phase until after the middle of the eighteenth century.

J. A. G.   Let's start in the beginning. Why did the English become interested in colonies in the first place?

J. P. G.   The initial interest of the English in colonies can be considered under the two general headings: the example of Spain and the peculiar thrust of English domestic development during the sixteenth and early seventeenth centuries. Spain had obviously made such a good thing of colonization, especially with the stunning discoveries of the great caches of gold and silver in Mexico and Peru, that every other western European nation wanted to emulate it.

J. A. G.   If British interest in colonization was partially a response to the success of the Spaniards, can you explain the long delay between the beginning of Spanish colonization in the New World and the first English settlements? The Spanish economy was certainly not more advanced than England's.

J. P. G.   Of course not. The Spanish venture depended initially upon heroic efforts by a relatively small number of people, efforts very similar to those made by earlier Spaniards in driving the Moors out of Spain. Once they had conquered the great native empires in Mexico, Peru, and Central America, once they had obtained access to and control over the rich stores of gold, silver, and jewels in those regions, they had the economic wherewithal to sustain a vast colonial effort, and during the initial decades of settlement the Spanish colonies were self-sustaining to an extent that the English colonies never were. If John Cabot had discovered another Mexico in 1497 instead of Newfoundland or Nova Scotia and had returned to England laden with gold and silver, the English would probably have founded colonies much earlier.

But Spain also had another important advantage. It had been unified in the late fifteenth and early sixteenth centuries, whereas England was distracted by domestic problems throughout most of the sixteenth century. Henry VII was involved in trying to consolidate the authority of the Tudor monarchy, while Henry VIII and his successors were absorbed with the problems of the Reformation and the unstable political and social situation that followed. These domestic problems diverted energy and attention from overseas expansion and colonization until the last half of the reign of Elizabeth I.

J. A. G.   You are implying, then, that the example of Spain was not by itself a sufficient explanation for the development of English interest in colonization?

J. P. G.   Yes. Although it provided a powerful stimulus to ambitious Englishmen interested in glory and gold, the example of Spain was far less important than certain economic and social developments within England, developments which both made possible and encouraged English colonizing activities. For England, the years 1480 to 1660 were years of profound change, in which a fundamental shift took place from the still largely feudal society of the fifteenth century to the fully developed market society of the seventeenth. Increasingly, during the sixteenth century, Englishmen, spurred on by the promise of ever greater profits, began to produce goods for the market or to participate in some phase of the marketing process. The direction of English economic life began to move outward. English traders expanded their activities all over the world—to the Levant, northern Russia, the Baltic, and even down the African coast. This push outward inevitably carried them into the American orbit.

More than that, however, these developments contributed to the colonizing process both by providing incentives, resources, and tools such as the joint-stock trading company which encouraged investors to back colonial enterprises and by contributing to the creation of conditions in England which encouraged Englishmen of all ranks to consider settling, at least temporarily, in the colonies. The shift to a market society created severe social and psychological strains. Traditional social arrangements seemed to be breaking down as a result of new expanded economic opportunities. Rapid horizontal and vertical mobility, the relative decline of older elites whose power rested upon land and their displacement by newer groups whose fortunes depended on business, the rapid rise of lawyers whose services were required to handle a growing volume of land sales and commercial transactions, the volatile character of mercantile life—all of these evidences of rapid and fundamental social change resulted in an unsettledness that almost certainly made it easier for men to overcome their traditional attachments to place and their reluctance to forsake the known for the unknown and perhaps even predisposed them to move.

J. A. G.   That is very interesting. Are you suggesting that these social and economic changes you describe produced more geographic mobility within England, as well as the movement to America?

J. P. G.   Apparently, though we still do not have sufficient evidence to say with much precision just how great an increase in geographical or horizontal mobility there actually was. Certainly, contemporaries thought there was a great increase in both kinds of mobility, however.

J. A. G.   Did not the Reformation also contribute to this unsettledness?

J. P. G. Of course. By breaking up the monasteries, Henry VIII and his advisers stimulated a considerable redistribution of land and much social movement. Even more important, the Reformation caused extraordinary intellectual and religious ferment. Combined with the disorientation induced by the rapid social changes, this ferment predisposed people to look around for certainty and to be preoccupied with the problem of social and religious order. The extreme popularity during the Elizabethan and Jacobean periods of the ancient idea that there was a grand order in the universe established by God and that every individual had a settled place in that order was one form of response to these conditions. Another was the urge, represented by all of the different species of Puritanism, to create a purer church and to use that church as a model for establishing a more orderly, less corrupt, and more coherent social and political order.

Some of the formulae that were proposed to settle social conditions and to purify the church could be undertaken at home. But when men began to dream about the creation of a purer society, they naturally thought about going to virgin America to create it.

J. A. G. Are you implying that English colonization of America was basically utopian in character?

J. P. G. Only partly. Once colonization came to be considered seriously during the last decades of the sixteenth century, the men most interested—people like Richard Hakluyt, Sir Humphrey Gilbert, and Sir Walter Raleigh—articulated a comprehensive rationale for founding colonies. Occasionally utopian in impulse, the writings of such men were largely promotional and tended to put primary emphasis upon more mundane benefits that could be expected to derive from colonies: individual profit, national glory, the advancement of Protestantism, and the rescue of at least part of America from popery.

Yet among many writers and potential settlers there was a pronounced ambivalence about the New World. For every paean to its promises, there was a warning about its dangers. This ambivalence is perhaps best seen in *The Tempest*, where Shakespeare juxtaposes English civilization, represented by Prospero, against the barbarism of remote, uncultivated places, exemplified by Caliban. The tension between these two symbolic figures is revelatory of the contradictory perceptions Englishmen had of the New World. There was great hope that it might be converted into a new Eden, but there was also widespread fear that the wilderness would prove uncongenial to English culture and would so undermine the power of traditional values and institutions as to reduce the English settlers to the savage level of the Indians.

J. A. G.   Was there any strain within this ambivalent perception that was stronger than the others?

J. P. G.   Although there is no way to discover what motives were uppermost in the minds of the vast majority of colonists, there can be little doubt that the central thrust of the English colonizing movement was economic. Even those Puritans who came to New England largely for religious and social reasons also, in many cases, had strong material aspirations. As I indicated earlier, there had been a tremendous release of economic energy and an extraordinary stimulation of economic and social ambition in England on the eve of colonization, and the opportunities presented by the New World—which was so vast that no one group could monopolize all resources or preempt all social status—provided an outlet for this energy and greatly increased its power. The result was that even those colonists who came for other than economic reasons often found it difficult to restrain their material appetites.

However, it would be a mistake to put too much emphasis upon these material aspirations. Religious motives were present everywhere and, among the leaders of the New England colonies, were almost certainly predominant. Besides, in every colony there was a powerful movement to re-create in the New World an idealized version of English society. This movement to anglicize the New World was accentuated by the colonial fear of the barbarizing and corrosive effects of the wilderness. Because it envisioned the imposition of traditional "civilized" restraints upon individuals and groups within colonial society, the movement often ran directly counter to the materialistic impulses of the colonists and took the form of efforts to bridle those impulses through legislation and exhortation.

J. A. G.   Is it useful to distinguish between the motives of the founders of the colonies and the mass of people who came to them and did the fundamental work of colony building?

J. P. G.   In general, the colony planners had much more comprehensive and more fully articulated goals, which they invariably set down at the time of colonization. With the individual settlers, on the other hand, the larger objectives of the planners probably—I say "probably," because most of the settlers obviously did not leave much record behind of why they did what they did—were not of central importance. What concerned such people were the myriad problems presented by their daily lives. Especially in the early years of settlement, simple problems of survival were paramount.

J. A. G.   Did the early colonists anticipate accurately what they were going to find in America?

J. P. G.   Certainly not in the case of Virginia. It took twenty-five years for that colony to get on its feet, for the settlers to accept it for what it was and to learn how to live in and utilize that particular environment. But later colonizers probably expected harsher conditions than they actually found.

The other question, which Sigmund Diamond has addressed in several important articles, is to what extent the aspirations and objectives of the colonizers had to be modified in response to conditions encountered in the colonies. The stated objectives of the colony planners in England invariably gave primary consideration to the corporate interests of the colony and looked forward to the achievement of a tightly integrated society in which each segment—and each individual—contributed to the welfare of the whole. But these objectives, at least in their initial forms, were unattainable and were everywhere quickly abandoned. In Virginia, for instance, the Company early found that it could not recruit settlers to work for the Company in perpetuity as it had originally planned. To make Virginia attractive to prospective colonists, the Company had to relax the harsh discipline and rigid work-camp-style social structure of the early years and to offer incentives in the form of easy access to land and participation in the political process. In the wake of these concessions, the control of the Company over individual settlers became ever more tenuous and its original objectives virtually impossible to maintain. This pattern was repeated again and again during the following century.

J. A. G.   Were new kinds of institutions developed in response to the conditions the colonists discovered in America?

J. P. G.   Except for certain modifications in the labor system which occurred during the last half of the seventeenth century, very few new institutions developed in the colonies. The settlers naturally sought to establish the same institutions with which they had been familiar in England. Inevitably, these failed to function as they had at home, and over a period of time a subtle process of differentiation in both form and content took place. Most important, perhaps, English institutions rarely had the same force and effectiveness in the colonies that they had had in England. Economic opportunity and social mobility tended to erode the authority of these institutions. Their authority was maintained longer in New England, where the inhabitants had a stronger commitment to the values underlying them and where neither economic opportunity nor social mobility was as great. In Virginia and the West Indian colonies, on the other hand, the authority of all institutions was quickly undermined and maintained with extreme difficulty during the early decades of settlement as the settlers, engrossed in the pell-mell rush for profits, dispersed themselves over the landscape, displayed little willingness to let the welfare of the whole society interfere with their own individual ambition, and tried to turn all institutions into vehicles for individual advancement.

J. A. G.   Is it possible that the comparatively strong sense of community which marked New England arose from the difficulty of life there and from the fact that men needed one another? May we, therefore, have overemphasized the role of religious ideas in giving New England such a remarkable amount of social cohesion?

J. P. G.   Although the more difficult conditions of life in New England doubtless were an important factor in the emergence and maintenance of a greater sense of community than existed elsewhere, one should not underestimate the powerful role of religious ideas, especially among colony and community leaders. The Puritan leadership in Massachusetts Bay came to America with hopes of creating a new kind of church and a new kind of society, and they enjoyed considerable authority and confidence among the people, who, in comparison with colonists elsewhere, were a relatively homogeneous group. The result was that they were able to impose their ideas—their religious and social goals—upon the colony to a much greater degree than could other colony leaders, such as Lord Baltimore in Maryland or the early Quakers in Pennsylvania. No matter how much Baltimore might have liked to make Maryland into a Catholic colony or how much the Quakers wanted to build Pennsylvania exclusively upon the principles of the Society of Friends, they were unable to do so because of the diversity of religious and social groups in their colonies.

The fact that economic opportunity was less in New England than elsewhere was also important, however. People stuck together in small communities during the first century of settlement because they rarely made enough from one crop to expand very much for the next. If it were possible to measure it, the pace of economic growth in New England during the seventeenth century would almost certainly turn out to be much slower than it was in Virginia and infinitely less than it was in the sugar islands.

J. A. G.   How have historians' views of New England Puritanism changed over the last generation?

J. P. G.   The change has been extraordinary. In 1927 Vernon L. Parrington published the first volume of his *Main Currents of American Thought.*

This volume was a superb statement of the standard view of the Puritans that had taken shape over the previous century. According to this view, the Puritans were a drab, morbid people, preoccupied with saving their own souls, busily looking into everybody else's affairs, authoritarian in government, and bigoted in religion. Like many others before him, Parrington chastised the Puritans for opposing religious toleration and democracy. In 1932—just five years later—Perry Miller published his *Orthodoxy in Massachusetts,* the first of a brilliant series of studies of American Puritanism in which he presented a much more sympathetic portrait.

The differences between Parrington and Miller primarily arise out of their contrasting perspectives. Parrington viewed the Puritans from the perspective of the 1920s. From that vantage point—which was nearly three hundred years after the initial Puritan settlements—the Puritans looked curiously un-American: they did not permit people free rein over their individual impulses, they tried to stifle individual initiative and deviation, and so on. What Miller tried to do, by contrast, was to get back inside the Puritans and to try to understand them on their own terms and to measure them against the standards not of later generations but of their own.

Consider the matter of religious toleration. Miller and later historians following his example pointed out that in opposing toleration the Puritans were like all other Christian groups in western Europe at that time. The old charge was that they had come to America seeking religious freedom and had then immediately proceeded to deny it to everyone else. But Miller showed that they came to America not to achieve toleration but to construct the "true" church. As John Winthrop said, they intended to found a city upon a hill to which people in England could look for inspiration. That city, they hoped, would provide a model form of church, state, and society which could be transported back to England and used to rebuild English political, social, and religious institutions along lines more acceptable to God. Precisely because they believed that there was only one true way in religion and that any other way was not merely in error but a sinful deviation from God's one way, any idea of toleration was anathema.

J. A. G.   In what other ways has our view of the Puritans changed?

J. P. G.   We have also recognized that Puritanism in general was not all that different from Anglicanism. This is not to say that there were not important differences over theology, church polity, and other matters of religion, but only that in terms of their social views—their conceptions of human nature, the process and character of historical change, and the proper organization of society—the two groups had a considerable amount in common. For instance, the Puritans began with the notion that all men, except for the very few who were numbered among the elect, were innately sinful, and that, therefore, very strong social and political institutions were needed to restrain this darker side of human nature. The Anglicans operated out of a very similar conception, albeit they may have had a more charitable attitude toward those men who could not seem to cope with their own frailties. But what has impressed recent students is not the differences but the similarities between Puritan social, political, and economic assumptions and those of Anglican and other contemporary English and European Protestant groups.

J. A. G. It seems to me you are saying that the change in the view of the Puritans has only been to argue that everyone else was just as bad.

J. P. G. I did not mean to suggest that. No one any longer seems very interested in whether the Puritans were "bad." It is easy enough to judge groups in the past by present-day norms and to find them deficient. But that defeats the larger purpose of history, which is not to evaluate the past in terms of the present but to understand the present from the perspective of the past, to use the past as a kind of cosmic backdrop, which, by furnishing us with a wide range of contrasts with the present, can enable us to understand our own behavior and our own societies more clearly. To do this requires us to comprehend the past as much as is humanly possible in its own terms. Thus, what we want to know about the Puritans is how they stand up against their contemporaries, not against us, and how successful they were in achieving their own goals, not ours. From this point of view, it becomes clear that in one sense the Puritans far exceeded most of their contemporaries. To the extent that, as Edmund S. Morgan has pointed out, the Puritans tried to develop a perfect society while recognizing the imperfections of man, there was a certain nobility to their enterprise and an element of high tragedy in their failure. No other group of colonists and few Englishmen at the time set their sights so high.

J. A. G. Is there any connection between the increasing respect for the Puritans and our own contemporary disillusionment and pessimism about human nature?

J. P. G. I am sure there is. The burning or gassing of thousands of Jews by the Nazis, the dropping of the bomb at Hiroshima, and the many other human cruelties manifest in the twentieth century have contributed to a much less optimistic view of both human nature and the historical process. We have thus come around to a point of view quite similar to that of the Puritans and can thereby appreciate them much more than could earlier generations.

J. A. G.   In looking generally at religious life in the colonies, is it fair to say that there was a greater degree of religious toleration than in England, and if so, why?

J. P. G.   Wherever there were strong competing religious groups—that is, just about everywhere in the colonies except in New England before 1720 and in Virginia before 1750—each was forced to tolerate the others simply because no one group had sufficient power to compel the others to conform. Although it is difficult in this area to speak comparatively, this situation may well have resulted in more practical and legal toleration than existed in England. It should be pointed out, however, that the Toleration Act of 1689 established a high degree of toleration for Christians in Britain. I doubt, in fact, whether during the eighteenth century there was more legal toleration in most colonies than there was in Britain.

J. A. G.   Would you describe the structure of the colonial economy in the seventeenth century?

J. P. G.   The economy rested on an agricultural base. Farming was the principal occupation, and not simply subsistence farming. All over the colonies, farmers were to some extent oriented toward producing a surplus for the market, and this orientation meant the early development of market mechanisms complete with a mercantile community to handle the distribution and exchange of colonial products.

There were, of course, important regional variations. New England agriculture was devoted mostly to the production of foodstuffs, while the Chesapeake colonies organized their agricultural activities around the production of a staple crop, tobacco, for which there was great demand in Europe. The tobacco trade was largely handled by English rather than colonial merchants, who channeled the tobacco to markets both in England and on the Continent. In New England, on the other hand, such entrepreneurial functions were handled by a native group of merchants who developed a brisk trade with the West Indies and the European continent as well as with England and the other continental colonies. This trade involved the export of furs, skins, and fish, as well as agricultural products. Thus, the economic capital of Massachusetts was Boston, but the economic capital of Virginia and Maryland was London.

One result of these dissimilar economic orientations was that the status orders in the two regions were organized rather differently. In Chesapeake society the socioeconomic structure was arranged according to whether one had a lot of land or a little, while in New England the large merchants stood at the apex of economic society.

J. A. G.　What were the major economic problems faced by the colonists?

J. P. G.　There were at least three major problems. The first was finding something that was marketable, that could be exchanged for goods or money in England, on the Continent, or in the West Indies. This problem was solved relatively early just about everywhere. Within a generation, or at most two, the colonists had learned how to utilize the resources in their environment and had worked out an economic structure that would change very little during the following century.

A second problem, in many ways the toughest in the beginning, was labor. The demand for labor was initially met largely through the use of indentured servants, and then after 1660 increasingly by African slaves.

A third problem, which was never adequately solved during the colonial period, was how to get enough capital to finance economic expansion and to keep the economy functioning smoothly. Some mercantile groups in Philadelphia, Charleston, New York, Boston, Newport, and other colonial seaports accumulated considerable amounts of capital, though they often invested it in land or other nonliquid resources. Planters and farmers, however, rarely seem to have had enough specie to meet even the relatively small costs of household purchases. The result in the early days was a heavy reliance upon barter and later upon bills of exchange, promissory notes, and credit. In Virginia and Maryland, the larger planters managed on credit from English merchants, and the smaller producers on credit from the large planters. Older historians used to consider these arrangements a major source of alienation—of the large planters from England and of the smaller producers from the larger—but that is only part of the story. As debtors at all levels were very much aware, the credit represented by their debts was a resource as well as a burden. Without that credit, economic expansion and opportunity would have been greatly restricted.

The need for an internal medium of trade was satisfied largely by the issuance of paper money by the colonial governments. Although there was strong opposition to such issues from British creditors who feared that colonials would try to pay their debts in depreciated paper, and although there was a considerable amount of depreciation in cases where paper issues were not well secured and well managed, many of these issues obtained a considerable amount of stability and functioned to the advantage of all parties.

J. A. G.　Could we go back to the second problem you mention, the need for labor? Why did slavery develop in the American colonies, and can you particularly explain why it expanded so rapidly beginning in the closing decades of the seventeenth century?

J. P. G.   That question, as Winthrop D. Jordan has pointed out in his important book *White over Black,* is an extraordinarily complicated one. The standard argument, which contains a great deal of truth, is that plantation agriculture had certain labor requirements which could best— "best" in an economic sense—be met by a system of bound labor, and that blacks were available and were therefore enslaved. A corollary of this argument is that prejudice against blacks came about as a result of the debasement involved in slavery. But Jordan has argued convincingly that the origins of both slavery and prejudice are considerably more complicated. The Spanish colonies had had slavery for almost a hundred years before it was introduced into the English colonies, and it was a thriving institution in the English West Indian colonies for at least a quarter of a century before it was employed on a large scale by the continental colonies, and these examples clearly predisposed men on the continent to regard and to treat blacks, especially after they began to come in large numbers, as chattel slaves. Prejudice, as Jordan points out, clearly antedated slavery and seems to have depended in major part upon the Englishman's association of blackness with evil. This attitude toward the blacks' color interacted with slavery to degrade blacks and deeply reinforce prejudice against them in the minds of whites.

One can explain the rapid expansion of black slavery on the mainland toward the end of the seventeenth century by the simple fact that it turned out to be an excellent labor system in a staple-crop economy. The initial investment was fairly high, but the slave owner got perpetual work out of slaves, who reproduced themselves and thus continually replenished and added to the owner's labor force.

Essentially, of course, slavery arose as a result of the unwillingness of the white man to content himself with the kind of profits he could make from his own, his family's, or free labor. Slavery was rooted precisely where Black Power advocates suggest that prejudice is rooted today—in the white man's avarice and in his fear of allowing any great measure of freedom to such an exploited and obviously different-looking group. This is not to suggest that only white men were avaricious, but the whites were the dominant group in the colonies, and though other black men may have originally been responsible for selling blacks into slavery in Africa, the whites were responsible for its introduction and perpetuation in the colonies.

J. A. G.   How would you describe the relationship between England and the colonies in the seventeenth century?

J. P. G.   Initially, the relationship was very ambiguous. It was not very clearly defined, because the English had had no experience with such distant possessions. In the beginning, the English looked at the colonies primarily as units for economic production. The relationship was essentially contractual: the crown gave certain things to certain people in return for certain services, although initially not much more than allegiance was required. This essentially commercial relationship was peculiarly appropriate to a market society, and it encouraged the notion among the colonists that a contract had been made with the English government which guaranteed them the right to pursue their own interests in return for their allegiance and a commitment to set up governments closely resembling the government of England.

The English government looked at the colonies from two points of view: what can these colonies contribute to national wealth; and how do they contribute to national prestige?

J. A. G.   When did the English begin to see the colonies as a kind of branch of the English government and begin to think of establishing a general colonial administration?

J. P. G.   When the crown took over the Virginia colony in 1624, it was for the first time thrust into the position of having to administer the day-to-day life of a colony. But there was only one crown colony until 1660. In the early seventeenth century, the term *empire* had quite a different connotation from what it has today. It meant pretty much the same as *dominion:* the colonies were part of the king's domain, under his rule. But exactly what kind of status they occupied within the empire was not very clear before 1660, and became so only gradually thereafter.

J. A. G.   If the English viewed the colonies primarily in economic terms, what kind of control did they place on colonial economic activity?

J. P. G.   They began to place controls on aspects of colonial economic life as soon as any element began to loom importantly in the English economy. The first regulations were in relation to tobacco; in 1621 the metropolitan government required that all tobacco be shipped to England. Later, it encouraged tobacco production in Virginia and Maryland by prohibiting the growing of tobacco in England. But there was no general attempt to set up a system of economic regulation until the value of the colonies had become obvious, in the 1640s and 1650s. When the Dutch began during the English civil war to engross a large part of the colonies' carrying trade, English merchants got upset and demanded some kind of regulation. The early Navigation Acts of 1650 and 1651 were not very effective, but the system was regularized in 1660 and then expanded in 1663 and 1673 in an effort to establish a national monopoly of colonial production. No foreign vessels were allowed to trade at colonial ports, certain categories of goods had to be sent to England before they could be shipped elsewhere, and goods going to the colonies from foreign countries had first to pass through England.

J. A. G.   To what extent did this system of regulation result from practical ideas of what was economically profitable for England, and to what extent was it based on economic theory—that is, the theory of mercantilism?

J. P. G.   The theory, in my view, was a response to the particular need. Insofar as mercantilism implied only that the state had the right to regulate any aspect of economic life, it was a very old idea, deeply ingrained in English habits. But as a set of doctrines about the desirability of national self-sufficiency, of a national monopoly of all trade and resources in the colonies, it grew up in the seventeenth century. It was a theory related to the notion of scarcity, to the idea that resources, capacity for production, and buying power in the world were limited, and that a nation should get as much of them as possible so that other nations should get as little as possible.

Mercantilism, like capitalism, was really a label for describing a whole series of ideas which came into being and continued to operate precisely because they seemed to be accurately descriptive of the conditions out of which they emerged. Once they were conceived of as a system, they acquired a life of their own and controlled the way men looked at economic arrangements.

J. A. G.   It seems to me that the emphasis on mercantilism as a theory tends to distort contemporary realities by suggesting that colonial developments were inspired by the state, whereas colonial developments were primarily inspired by individuals for personal motives. The state simply supervised and responded to their actions. Is that correct?

J. P. G.   I think so.

J. A. G.   Did the economic regulations imposed by the British hamper colonial economic growth in the seventeenth and early eighteenth centuries?

J. P. G.   That is an especially difficult question. No thorough study over time has been made, and there is no clear consensus among historians. My own impression is that they did not, though they might have, had they been strictly enforced. In fact, however, they were never so enforced before the eve of the American Revolution. I should add, of course, that there is no doubt that metropolitan economic regulations did affect the development of the colonial economy by encouraging production of some items and discouraging the production of others, though the acts of encouragement seem to have had a much greater influence than the acts of discouragement.

J. A. G.   Is it possible to be more precise? For example, if you were in the port of Boston or New York or Philadelphia in, say, 1690, would you be likely to see a Dutch or French ship in the harbor?

J. P. G.   In 1690 probably not, but in 1681 or 1682 you might very well have seen a Dutch ship in the harbor, or in a remote cove down the coast. Apparently there was considerable trading with the Dutch and French even as late as that. Smuggling and the evasion of duties, however, were probably more common forms of violation.

J. A. G.   How did the British system of regulating colonial trade affect private British interests?

J. P. G.   The dominant power in this situation was the mercantile groups in Britain. Colonials were forced to accommodate their interests to those of powerful British groups. It is true that in a great many cases their interests were the same, but when they were not, the decision of the British government was always in favor of the British merchants.

J. A. G.   How would you characterize the internal political life of the colonies in the seventeenth century?

J. P. G.   Over the past twenty years, historians have come to describe colonial politics as chaotic, even convulsive. Colonial governments seem to have been often in turmoil: colonists expelled governors, rebelled against properly constituted authority, and engaged in internecine strife as they vied among themselves for power and access to primary sources of wealth and status. Political instability, according to this view, derived out of the release of economic and social ambition in the New World and the collision among rival interests in pursuit of their ambitions.

This conception explains a considerable amount of colonial political life; it may, however, have been somewhat overstressed. Given the character of life in the colonies, given the lack of a settled social structure, the absence of clear lines of political authority, and the diversity of the settlers, what was probably more remarkable than the brittle quality of colonial public life was the extraordinary amount of stability that was actually achieved after the first few generations of settlement. This stability was especially manifest in the localities where the vast bulk of political activity took place—in the towns in New England and in the counties, municipalities, and parishes elsewhere. There were personal feuds, sectarian clashes, and economic rivalries in every locality, but the striking feature of colonial public life on this level, especially by the early decades of the eighteenth century, is the extent to which the agencies of local government were able to maintain order, enforce laws, and solve local problems to the satisfaction of the vast majority of the free inhabitants—to perform, in short, with an effectiveness that very nearly equaled that of their counterparts in Britain.

Similarly, on the provincial level, there was a lot of disorder and upheaval, but nowhere, after the early years, was disorder the normal state of politics for long periods of time. My point is simply that government was not merely a vehicle for the realization of individual or group ambitions but also a way to achieve a much more fundamental psychological need: the need for order, which though common to all peoples may have been even stronger in the unsettled and unsettling environment of the New World than it was in older and more established societies. Governments were not yet conceived primarily as instruments through which people could express themselves but as agencies whose paramount task was to restrain the antisocial passions of imperfect men so that they could live together peacefully if not always harmoniously. This deepseated drive for order acted as a countervailing force against the disintegrative tendencies in colonial politics.

J. A. G.   When and why did the English begin to devise political institutions for controlling the colonies, as distinct from economic regulations?

J. P. G.   They began to see the need for some sort of political control very early. But only in the 1660s, after they had realized that the Navigation Act system was at least partially a failure, did they seriously try to establish political uniformity in the colonies. The later Stuart monarchs, Charles II and James II, had a conception of the colonies very different from earlier monarchs. They saw them not only as units for economic production but also as political entities, part of the king's dominions. The first effective central governing agency was the Lords of Trade, a committee of the Privy Council established in 1675. That committee adopted a series of policies. The first was to try to convert all the private colonies into royal colonies on the grounds that the private colonies had too many privileges, too many exemptions from central control. The second policy was to tighten up administration by making policy much more specific and precise.

The Lords also attempted to restrict the power of the colonial assemblies—those local representative institutions which had emerged in response to a variety of local pressures during the early years of each colony and had become both a critical element in the legislative process and the primary agency through which dominant local interests expressed their economic, social, religious, and political aspirations. The Lords of Trade tried to restrict the power of these bodies by applying the principle of Poyning's Law, an old statute which required the crown's prior assent to any legislation passed by the Irish parliament, to Virginia and Jamaica. Local interests strongly opposed this effort, and the policy was a failure. But the Lords at least articulated a set of beliefs about the way colonies were to be governed and about the nature of the assemblies.

The third policy was centralization. With the Dominion of New England in 1688–89, crown officials sought not only to centralize the northern colonies into one unit but to do away with representative government altogether. This experiment was cut short by the Glorious Revolution, however, and the English never again attempted to govern without assemblies.

J.A.G.   If it was official policy after 1660 to convert private colonies into crown colonies, how do you explain the creation of the Carolinas, New York, and Pennsylvania as private colonies after that date?

J.P.G.   The argument against private colonies achieved wide currency only after the Carolina, New Jersey, and New York grants had been issued. As a matter of fact, the New York grant and the Carolina grant were made at the very time the first royal commission was sent out to investigate conditions in the colonies. Opposition to private colonies developed over the next decade and came to be widely accepted in metropolitan governing circles only after the investigation of the colonies by Edward Randolph, a royal commissioner, in 1675–76.

The Pennsylvania case was special. The elder William Penn had loaned some money to Charles II, and his son used this loan to pry a colony out of the king. There was great opposition to the grant from the Lords of Trade, and, as a result, the Pennsylvania charter was significantly different from earlier private charters. It both required that Penn enforce the Navigation Acts and asserted the jurisdiction of Parliament over the colony, two stipulations not in earlier charters.

J.A.G.   How in general did the Glorious Revolution affect colonial policy?

J.P.G.   Initially, it was not clear how it was going to affect colonial policy. But the issuance of a second charter to Massachusetts Bay in 1691 was an indication that the English were no longer seriously considering doing away with representative institutions. Neither of the other two central goals of the policy of the Lords of Trade was abandoned, however. By the new Navigation Act of 1696, metropolitan authorities sought to tighten up the navigation system by expanding the administrative network in the colonies, establishing vice-admiralty courts to enforce the Navigation Acts, and asserting Parliament's jurisdiction over colonial matters. Although they did not again attempt to consolidate the colonies into larger and more easily administered units, crown officials repeatedly considered such a step during the eighteenth century.

Perhaps the most significant legacy of the Glorious Revolution was a new attitude toward the role of Parliament in the colonies. Increasingly, after 1689, crown officials generally assumed that any time they could not handle colonial affairs Parliament could be called to the rescue. Both Charles II and James II were reluctant to admit Parliament into any share of the internal governance of the colonies, but William III and his successors operated in a different milieu in which the cooperation of Parliament in most major matters of state was assumed. During the early decades of the eighteenth century, crown officials several times threatened parliamentary intervention in attempting to intimidate recalcitrant colonial assemblies into voting a permanent revenue with which to pay the governor and other local royal officials. The threat was that Parliament would vote such a revenue if the assemblies did not. Parliament never actually did that until 1767 with the Townshend Acts, but the threat revealed that the metropolitan government had few doubts about the authority of Parliament to tax the colonies.

J. A. G.   If Parliament had such extensive authority over the colonies, at least in theory, what was the constitutional position of the colonial assemblies, and what was their relationship to Parliament?

J. P. G.   The answer is that neither their constitutional position nor their relationship to Parliament was ever entirely clear. Initially, the assemblies resembled the governing bodies of English corporations: they were gatherings of representatives of the stockholders to make by-laws and regulations for their various enterprises. But they had to deal with so many problems which were so similar in character to problems handled by Parliament in England that they very early came to assume that they were the equivalents on the colonial level of Parliament. Especially after 1680, as the emergent colonial elites who dominated the assemblies became more and more intent upon re-creating English society in America, the members of the assemblies self-consciously sought to mimic the House of Commons in procedures, forms, and behavior. But English authorities never fully accepted the pretensions of the lower houses. The result was a great divergence between colonial and English attitudes on the legal position of the assemblies. One of the undefined questions was whether the assemblies had exclusive authority over the internal affairs of the colonies or cooperative authority with Parliament. As the constitutional debate over the Stamp Act in 1765–66 revealed, colonists had come to assume that the authority of the assemblies was exclusive, whereas the British believed the opposite. But this question had never been fully or explicitly canvassed before the Stamp Act crisis.

J. A. G.   In general terms, how was life in the colonies in the eighteenth century different from life in the seventeenth?

J. P. G.   There were many differences, most of them the result of the extraordinary expansion that took place in the eighteenth century. There was a rapid acceleration of the economy beginning during the second and third decades of the new century and a corresponding growth in settled territory and in population.

With this great expansion came a number of developments. Commercial towns with populations and amenities equal to those of provincial towns in England developed along the seacoast. Elite groups whose economic dominance and social and political leadership were acknowledged by the rest of society emerged in all of the older settled colonies. The institution of slavery expanded rapidly in the plantation colonies and was accompanied by a change in the nature of indentured servitude. Colonial culture and society became more and more anglicized as the century wore on, and the institutional organization of the colonies became clearer and more firmly established. In short, the expansion of the colonies was accompanied by a sophistication and complexity that made life in the eighteenth-century colonies much different from that in the more rudimentary societies of the seventeenth century. This process was beginning to take place in most of the older colonies in the 1680s and 1690s, but the big change came between the end of Queen Anne's War (a phase of the great European War of the Spanish Succession) in 1713 and 1750.

J. A. G.   Did the structure of the economy change markedly in the eighteenth century?

J. P. G.   About the only structural changes occurred with the addition of new staple products. In South Carolina, for example, the introduction of rice in the 1690s changed the organization of society considerably. Similarly, the development of the naval stores industry in the Carolinas, encouraged by the Navigation Act of 1705 which put bounties on naval stores, was another important addition. Besides these and similar additions, however, there were no substantial changes in the economy such as the introduction of a factory system, the growth of urban areas devoted exclusively to manufacturing, or the reorganization of labor. Urban centers still retained their character as commercial towns, the bulk of the economy was organized around the production of staples or other products extracted from the soil or the sea, and market mechanisms did not change.

One might argue that the beginnings of iron manufacturing, which was by no means insignificant in Pennsylvania and Maryland, represented a new development. But the organization of those enterprises was very much like that of older plantation enterprises. No new techniques of labor relations, management, or marketing were involved, and very little technological advance was made.

J. A. G.   Were British regulations of colonial industry very important?

J. P. G.   British regulations applied to three products—woolens, hats, and iron—and I am not sure how they affected the hat industry because there has been no close study of that topic. But the Iron Act restricted only the *export* of finished iron products, and what finished iron the colonists were producing was for local consumption. The act did not prohibit the production of crude iron, to which most of the industry was devoted. As for the woolen industry, the inclusion of the colonies in the Woolen Act of 1699 was an afterthought. The act was really directed against Ireland, and I do not think it had very much effect on the American economy.

J. A. G.   Would you describe the character of business relations that developed between Englishmen and colonists during the eighteenth century?

J. P. G.   Well, they varied considerably from place to place. As Bernard Bailyn has pointed out, much of the trade in the early days developed within kinship networks. New Englanders started to trade with the West Indies, and they found that sometimes this trade carried them to England. So they began to appoint agents, quite often younger sons of the family, or other relatives, in England and the West Indies. This developed by the end of the seventeenth century into a fairly well established system of kinship connections radiating out of the home port in the colonies.

The marketing of tobacco, on the other hand, was quite different; it changed dramatically, beginning in the 1730s. Some British importers maintained close family connections with colonial planters, but by the mid-eighteenth century there were many people in the tobacco trade who had at best only distant family connections with Americans, and there developed among the planters an antagonism to or suspicion of the merchants.

The same was true of the sugar trade. West Indian planters became suspicious of the men who marketed their sugar in England. All kinds of opportunities for fraud existed, and, lacking control over the situation, planters felt at the mercy of these English middlemen. Planter animosity was directed not toward the government or its economic policies but against the British mercantile community. I also suspect that as the colonial economy grew more complex, old family merchant networks tended to break down somewhat and a new, more impersonal kind of business arrangement developed.

J. A. G.   Were there any changes in the navigation system during the eighteenth century?

J. P. G.   Aside from the development of the bounty system and the regulation of colonial manufacturing, which I have already mentioned, the only important change was the passage of the Molasses Act of 1733, which was an attempt to regulate economic relationships within the empire in favor of a particular segment of the empire, the West Indies, by putting a heavy tax on "foreign molasses" imported into the continental colonies. If the British had looked carefully at trade statistics, they would have realized that the continental colonies were far more valuable than the West Indies because they consumed such an extraordinary amount of British goods. But the old idea that the Caribbean sugar colonies were the real jewels of the empire because they produced the most valuable staple was so firmly fixed in English minds that whenever they had to make a choice, they favored the West Indies. The Molasses Act was the one potentially harmful piece of legislation in the whole navigation system during the eighteenth century, but because it was not enforced, it does not seem to have caused widespread or sustained discontent.

All of these new policies—the encouragement of some products by bounties, the prohibition of manufacturing, and the Molasses Act—fit in with the framework of mercantilist assumptions as they had been worked out in the seventeenth century. There was no real change in the rationale of the navigation system in the eighteenth century. New policies were adopted, but for old ends.

J. A. G.   What changes occurred in the character of the labor force in the eighteenth century?

J. P. G.   The most important was the extraordinary expansion of slavery. This development had begun in the seventeenth century but was greatly accelerated in the eighteenth century. The demand for slaves was continual, especially in new areas, in the western part of Virginia and Maryland, and then in the Carolinas. Slavery even expanded in the northern colonies, especially in the cities.

In areas where there were not large numbers of slaves—in rural Pennsylvania, for instance—indentured servitude maintained the same character it had had all along: servants were primarily undifferentiated workers in agricultural pursuits. But in the cities, where slaves were doing much of the heavy work that servants had formerly done, and on the plantations in the southern colonies, servants tended to be used for more specialized kinds of skilled labor. Many more of the indentured servants in the eighteenth century were of non-English origin, a large proportion of them Germans. But I do not think that these changes in national origins affected the organization of the labor force very much.

J. A. G. Was there any significant opposition to slavery among the colonists in the eighteenth century?

J. P. G. As Winthrop Jordan has made clear, what is so extraordinary about the institution of slavery in the eighteenth century is the ease with which people accepted and used it. That seems to me the most remarkable fact about slavery. Instances of articulate, well-reasoned criticism of slavery are relatively rare before the 1740s. The primary group which opposed slavery, beginning in the 1740s and increasingly thereafter, were the Quakers, who did so largely on religious grounds. But opposition to slavery before the Revolution was limited.

J. A. G. What was the effect of slavery on slaves? Was slavery in the colonial period any different than in the period just before the Civil War?

J. P. G. We do not know very much about the effect of slavery upon the slaves. What we do know is that it was never the happy system apologists in the middle of the nineteenth century claimed. On the other hand, the system seems to have been less harsh in the eighteenth century than it later became. Conditions varied from the north to the south; the fewer the slaves in an area, the freer the system seems to have been. In the West Indies slavery was terribly harsh. The ultimate threat for a slave who would not behave himself in Virginia was that he would be shipped out to Jamaica or Barbados. In Carolina and Georgia, where the ratio of slaves to whites was much higher, slavery was far harsher.

One example of the more lenient treatment in the eighteenth century, at least in Virginia, is revealed by the diary of Landon Carter, a wealthy planter. Carter's diary reveals that the slaves on his plantation lived within a fairly fixed family structure. Carter was always very careful to spell out the relationships of one slave to another: this person is so-and-so's mother, or so-and-so's father, or so-and-so's husband. This provides a different picture from that of slavery in the new sections of the South during the 1840s and 1850s. Apparently, at that time in such areas family relationships were neither clearly established nor respected by the slave owner.

J. A. G. What effect did slavery appear to have on the slaveholder? Does the Landon Carter diary, for instance, throw light on how slavery affected Carter?

J. P. G. Slave owners were not very explicit about this matter, but by reading between the lines in the Carter diary and in a great many other documents, one can discern several effects of slavery upon slaveholders. Jefferson wrote in his *Notes on Virginia* that the real problem with slavery was not so much what it did to slaves (although he was concerned about that) but what it did to owners. He argued that it made them imperious, even barbarous, because it gave them such unlimited power over other men. A great many others disliked slavery for this reason. Even in South Carolina, where there was very little opposition to slavery, a man like the merchant Henry Laurens, who was active in the slave trade, attacked slavery precisely on these grounds.

Another, more subtle effect, frequently noted by travelers in the eighteenth century, was that in the southern colonies both slaveholders and nonslaveholders displayed an extraordinary reverence for their own independence. Being a slaveholder made Landon Carter much more sensitive to the value of his own freedom. His slaves were perpetual reminders of how terrible the condition of slavery was. When the possibility of "enslavement" by the British government arose before the Revolution, the mere use of the term *slavery* in that connection carried an emotive force that was very strong in the southern colonies.

J. A. G. Could we return to the money problem in colonial history and its relationship to the problem of accumulating capital in a growing economy? Did the colonists ever find a satisfactory solution to this problem before the Revolution?

J. P. G. Not any long-term solution. From time to time various colonies did in fact have favorable balances of trade; this was the case in South Carolina in the 1750s. Considerable specie came into the New England colonies as a result of their trade with the West Indies, as well as into New York and Philadelphia. But ultimately the colonies relied on credit, most of it from English sources, and on the paper money issues referred to earlier.

J. A. G. Is it fair to say that British restrictions on colonial paper money were not really the fundamental cause of the shortage of capital, but rather that a growing yet primitive economy with enormous needs for capital could not supply its own needs by any means?

J. P. G. I think that is a fair interpretation. But I would point out that of all the potential economic grievances against the mother country, the policy of prohibiting paper currency, which eventually led to parliamentary prohibition of legal tender issues in New England by an act of 1751, caused most discontent.

J. A. G.　Could one then also say that the British prejudice against legal tender was probably dysfunctional from the British point of view?

J. P. G.　Yes and no. The fears of British merchants were not groundless. In New England during the 1730s and 1740s and in North Carolina during the French and Indian War, depreciation of colonial paper money was very rapid, and there were some attempts to make sterling debts payable in depreciated currency. On the other hand, there are a number of examples of self-regulated currency systems in the colonies which attained remarkable stability over long periods. What the merchants should have done was to have encouraged Parliament to authorize the issue of a currency for the colonies.

J. A. G.　What were the major changes in the composition and structure of colonial society during the eighteenth century?

J. P. G.　Most obviously, as I suggested earlier, there was a remarkable increase in size, diversity, and complexity in just about every aspect of life: population, settled territory, towns, religion, social organization. The diversity was most apparent in the non-English groups who migrated to the colonies—Germans, Scotch-Irish, Highland Scots, and other groups—and in the proliferation of religious sects. But the diversity was also directly related to the complexity that came with the increase in size, for the complexity produced a whole new range of economic opportunities in commerce, the professions, and the trades. In commerce, merchants began to specialize, becoming either exporters or importers, concerning themselves with either internal trade or overseas commerce. Among the professions, the law became of great importance. In earlier days men could go to court and argue their own cases, but as society became more complex, so did social and economic relationships, with the results that the legal system grew more and more sophisticated and lawyers had to handle an increasing number of specialized tasks. Although we know much less than we need to know about the development of the law and the legal profession—there are no good, comprehensive studies—it is clear that by the middle decades of the eighteenth century the law was the best route for rapid upward mobility. In the trades, especially in the cities, there was a growing multiplication and specialization, which created new sources of employment for men and women as free laborers, apprentices, or indentured servants. Whether these new opportunities created sufficient room for upward social mobility to offset the closing up of agricultural opportunity that was obviously occurring in older settled areas by the mid-eighteenth century, and whether there was in such areas an overall increase or decrease in vertical mobility, is a matter of great debate at the moment. But there was clearly still considerable opportunity for the ambitious in newly settled areas, and there seems to have been a major rise in horizontal mobility—migration from one place to another—during the middle decades of the eighteenth century, as colonials began to demonstrate a penchant for that restless movement and rootlessness which have subsequently come to be thought of as two of the most important elements in the American character.

Of course, the class structure varied considerably in its specific form from one place to another. More fluid in new areas and in expanding towns, it was less open in older inhabited areas not undergoing any marked economic expansion. The social order continued to be based primarily upon material success, though merchants and planters (the groups who had earlier stood at the top of the prestige order) had to make room for lawyers.

J. A. G.   The emphasis that you place on specialization and complexity seems not to have applied to ministers, or to religion. Would you comment more specifically on how social change affected religion in America?

J. P. G.   We have traditionally looked at the eighteenth century as a period of considerable secularization. In a general sense that image is accurate, but most people were still by modern standards extraordinarily pious. Interest in theology may have waned, and the Deity may have occupied a less prominent place in the everyday lives of men, but belief remained strong. More significantly, in a heterogeneous society, experiencing great social and economic change and constantly expanding, the old religious uniformity could not be maintained. New people with new faiths were coming to America, and along with the extensive religious divisions produced by the Great Awakening in the 1730s and 1740s, this fragmentation greatly altered religious life in the colonies and further stimulated the pressures toward religious toleration that had been present in a number of colonies since the beginnings of settlement. Another change was the continuing decline of the social standing of the clergy. Even in New England, where the clergy was still remarkably influential, young men—John Adams is a good example—who would formerly have gone into the ministry were increasingly turning to the law or to commerce.

J. A. G.   What effect did these social changes you have been describing have on politics?

J. P. G.   That depended on the degree of integration in the society of each colony. In societies lacking functional integration, political life tended to be quite fragile already, and rapid changes in the eighteenth century only exacerbated this condition. Because most of the societies of the colonies were not yet well integrated, the politics of most colonies was, as Bernard Bailyn has pointed out, unstable, organized around continually shifting factions representing opposing interests, and fiercely competitive. But no single formula will accurately characterize all colonial political systems. A few colonies—Virginia after 1720 and South Carolina after 1745—managed to avoid this kind of intensive factional turmoil altogether. Specifically, in the case of Virginia, society was sufficiently well integrated—the social and political leadership of the large planters being so widely acknowledged and the dominant planter group so homogeneous in interest—that the social changes that took place in the colony in the mid-eighteenth century did not lead to factional politics.

J. A. G.   How did the changes of the eighteenth century affect the colonists psychologically? How did change affect their hopes, and also their behavior, in all the areas you have been talking about: religion, politics, and cultural life generally?

J. P. G.   From a psychological point of view, the most difficult problem faced by Euro-Americans, even after several generations, was learning how to live with prosperity. Coming out of a society of scarcity, where people actually died of hunger, where whole populations had lived in perpetual poverty not just for one generation but for hundreds of years, they had a hard time learning how to be comfortable with prosperity and the more relaxed form of life it permitted, how not to feel guilty or anxious because they had things so good.

They were able to adjust to prosperity in varying degrees according to the extent of the prosperity. They adjusted most quickly in the West Indies, where a set of values quickly emerged that emphasized acquisitiveness for its own sake. By the end of the seventeenth century, a supremely materialistic society had developed in the West Indies. On the continent, during the eighteenth century, the colony which best adjusted to prosperity was South Carolina. After 1745 the expansion there had been dizzying. Rice and indigo production and distribution, the slave trade, and the law were so profitable that men starting with very little made enormous fortunes in only one generation. In the 1730s South Carolinians were just as uncomfortable with prosperity and the extravagance, idleness, and frivolity that seemed to accompany it as people in other colonies. Even as late as the 1760s, people still thought in these terms in Virginia, New England, Pennsylvania, and New York, but not in lowcountry South Carolina, which by the 1760s was perhaps the place where people were most completely adjusted to what would become during the next century probably the most conspicuous feature of American behavior: unrestrained acquisitiveness and pursuit of individual ambition.

Until quite recently, historians assumed that the Revolutionary generation was committed to social and economic equality, by which they meant social and economic leveling. But no idea was further from their minds. When they talked about equality in a social or economic sense, they meant no more than that each man should have an equal right to achieve the best material life he could within the limits imposed upon him by his ability, means, and circumstances. Because it was obvious that men were unequal in their abilities, would start on unequal bases, and would achieve varying degrees of success, and because it was also assumed that one of the primary functions of laws, constitutions, and governments was to guarantee that men's property (their material acquisitions) as well as their liberty would be eternally secure, any idea of equality in the sense of social leveling was perforce totally foreign.

From the beginnings of settlement, the day-to-day life of most colonists had been oriented in this way, toward the fulfillment of the economic and social aspirations of individuals. Except for the West Indies and lowcountry South Carolina after the 1740s, however, there was a marked reluctance to accord full intellectual legitimation to the highly individualistic modes of action that this orientation seemed to imply, to develop new values which would correspond to and accurately describe prevailing forms of behavior. Instead, the leaders clung desperately to an older conception that emphasized the organic character of society, the obligation of all individuals to sacrifice their own private interest to those of the public in general, and the antisocial nature of much individualistic behavior.

This conception was an integral part of the intellectual baggage of the earliest settlers, but throughout much of the seventeenth century colonial leaders had watched helplessly as it had been eroded and social order had seemed to give way to social chaos. Toward the end of the century and throughout the rest of the colonial period, emergent elites all over the colonies responded to this condition by trying to superimpose upon colonial society an order very similar to that originally attempted by the founders and still thought to be characteristic of the more settled society of the parent state. Guilt-ridden about the unstable, antisocial, and uncultivated character of colonial society, these groups reacted in one or both of two ways. They either looked back to the glorious day of the early founders when men allegedly had been more religious, more industrious, more frugal, and more public-spirited, or they looked across the Atlantic to an idealized conception of England for standards to which the colonists should aspire.

One of the main themes of eighteenth-century social development was, in fact, the attempt by elites to re-create in America societies more closely resembling that of an ideal England. They tried to impose traditional English values upon society, to make colonial political systems conform more closely to that of England, to copy English institutions, and to imitate English patterns in virtually every aspect of cultural life. An obvious manifestation of the frequently observed tendency of provincial societies to seek to model themselves after the metropolis, these mimetic impulses ran very deep. What is so significant about them is that they represented to a very large degree a rejection of many aspects of colonial life and an attempt to substitute for them an idealized Old World, specifically English, conception of the way New World societies should function. And they were not very successful, despite the fact that, as colonial societies became more complex and more settled during the eighteenth century, they came increasingly to resemble England. But appearances, as elites in the colonies fully understood, were deceiving, and the central question facing them on the eve of the pre-Revolutionary disturbances was whether America's material success might not be a direct measure of its moral and cultural failure.

How far these worries reached down into colonial society is revealed by the Great Awakening, which to a significant degree constituted a rejection of the materialistic and secular character of American life. Although some groups among the evangelical clergy began during the Awakening to develop a millennial view of America's future, a view that stood in sharp contrast to the pessimistic forebodings of many of the elite, it is significant that their vision of a future in which men with God's help would lead selfless lives and live together in an affectionate union displayed a profound discontent with the present.

J. A. G. But did not the colonists come to see themselves as Americans rather than as transplanted Europeans before the Revolution?

J. P. G. I think they came to see themselves as *British* Americans, not as a separate people with separate values and a different kind of psychology. They were Britons who lived in America, different from the people in Britain, but nonetheless British, and they were very concerned to make that point. The degree to which they had not yet become fully and obviously British was the distance they still had to cover before they could realize the full potential of the colonies and make colonial societies complete.

J. A. G.   By the middle of the eighteenth century, the word *American* begins to be used. Does not that suggest a sense of similarity among the residents of different colonies which had not existed in earlier periods of time? Where does the word come from, and what does it signify?

J. P. G.   It comes from the fact that they all lived in America; it may have been no more than a geographical designation. I do not think that when it was first used it involved an increasing awareness of the cohesiveness or the similarities of the various colonies. What tied Massachusetts and South Carolina and Virginia most closely together before 1763 was their common connection with England.

J. A. G.   How did these social aspirations, these desires to make the colonies more British, affect colonial attitudes toward Britain in the middle of the eighteenth century?

J. P. G.   In general, the colonists were very happy to be British and proud of their connection with Britain. Because it forced them to be concerned with a national (British) problem, the French and Indian War between 1754 and 1763 actually strengthened British patriotism in the colonies. In none of the earlier wars had the colonists contributed so much to an imperial cause nor had the theater of action been so much in the colonies. The result was an ever closer identification of colonial interests with those of Britain. The great British victories, beginning in 1759, in Canada, the West Indies, and India added enormously to the extent of British territory, and for the colonists it was exhilarating to be a part of what everybody in Britain and the colonies was saying was the greatest empire in history since Rome. From New England to Georgia, colonists took pride in this common achievement, and the significant part they thought they had played in the war both indicated to them that they had finally achieved a position of importance within the British Empire and created expectations that they would play a still greater role in the future. Benjamin Franklin's suggestion at this time that the rapid increase in the population of the colonies might eventually require that the capital be moved from London to Philadelphia revealed the full extent of these expectations.

On the other hand, the war also brought the colonists themselves closer together by forcing them to realize that they had many interests in common. As is well known, a delegation of colonial representatives at the Albany Congress of 1754 proposed a defensive union of the colonies, which was subsequently rejected by local leaders back in the colonial capitals. Traditionally, historians have interpreted this incident as an indication of how disunited the colonies were. But the proper point to make about this episode is not that union was rejected but that it was proposed, that some colonial leaders had so far escaped from limitations of vision imposed upon them by the habitual particularism of the colonies as to be able to see that the colonists had certain common problems that might best be solved by common action.

J. A. G.   Were there any indications before 1763 that the colonies might be about to break free from their English ties? Was the Revolution inevitable, or was it a response to the particular changes in British policy that occurred after the French and Indian War?

J. P. G.   There were no manifest indications that a revolution was going to occur fifteen years later. All signs, as a matter of fact, point in just the opposite direction. There was no major discontent with the Navigation Acts. There was considerable tension between royal officials in London and the colonies and local legislatures, especially during the war, but, because the colonists had been able to exercise a considerable amount of local autonomy through their legislatures, there was little basic dissatisfaction with existing political relations between Britain and the colonies. The colonists were full of British patriotism. There seemed to be no reason, in short, why the colonists might not have stayed in the empire indefinitely, or have evolved in the way Canada, Australia, and New Zealand later did.

But when one looks beneath the surface, one sees that the colonists were happy with the navigation system only because the parts of it that they would have found particularly onerous were not rigidly enforced, that the political relationship was satisfactory only because the English were not making a sustained attempt to enforce certain traditional policies that the colonists regarded as highly objectionable. And one recognizes that the extreme British patriotism of the colonists was dependent upon a conception of their own future role in the empire that was at marked variance with expectations in Britain. It is also very clear that, since at least 1748, powerful British colonial officials had been intent upon moving in directions that would alter existing economic and political relationships in such a way as to raise colonial resentment and to disappoint colonial expectations.

Through much of the period from 1721 to 1748, relationships between Britain and the colonies were dominated by what Edmund Burke called a policy of "salutary neglect." What Burke meant was that the colonists were permitted an enormous amount of freedom and by and large were allowed to go their own way, except in a few areas in which their behavior impinged adversely upon powerful British interests. None of the old ideals of British colonial policy was actually abandoned during these years, but there had been no systematic attempt to enforce them.

Some of the adverse fruits—adverse from the vantage point of White-hall—of this policy began to become apparent in the late 1740s. The governors of New York and South Carolina were writing to England constantly, complaining that they had no authority, that they commanded no respect in their colonies, that the assemblies had all the power. A civil war raged in New Jersey. Royal government had broken down almost entirely in New Hampshire and North Carolina. In Bermuda royal authority had sunk so low that the speaker of the legislature reportedly put a price on the governor's head. Understandably, there was a sense in London that a real crisis had developed in the empire. Something had to be done. So the earl of Halifax, an energetic and ambitious man, was made head of the Board of Trade, the chief agency concerned with governing the colonies. He proceeded to try to enforce regulations that had been ignored for twenty or thirty years. Although he encountered a great amount of difficulty in getting official support for many of the more drastic changes he wanted, he used all the powers at his command to try to enforce royal authority in every specific situation that he could, until the outbreak of the French and Indian War forced him to abandon his efforts because of the need for colonial cooperation against the French.

Because almost all of his efforts were directed against particular colonies, the colonists as a whole had little sense of the general meaning of his actions. An objectionable instruction to a single governor or disallowance of one or more laws of an individual colony did not seem to portend a general assault upon colonial liberties. In fact, the full meaning of these actions did not become clear for a decade or more. Christopher Gadsden of South Carolina correctly analyzed the situation when he reported that it was not until after delegates from various colonies had gotten together at the Stamp Act Congress that it became clear that all of these seemingly isolated acts were part of a large movement to strengthen royal authority in the colonies, a movement that could only be interpreted by men like Gadsden as a general conspiracy by some figures in the British government to undermine existing colonial constitutions and perhaps eventually to "enslave" the colonies. Only from the perspective of a common grievance such as the Stamp Act, however, could the supposed existence of this conspiracy become clear. Only then, only with the open and explicit reexamination stimulated by the Stamp Act crisis and the events that followed it did men in the colonies begin to realize that there were certain things about the metropolitan-colonial relationship that were injurious, or potentially so, for the colonies. Even then, they tended to focus their discontent upon events that occurred after, rather than before, 1763 and to idealize the earlier relationship. My answer to your question is, therefore, that although the essential preconditions for revolt can be found before 1763, the revolt was a specific response to British policies undertaken after that date.

J. A. G. What is your opinion of the so-called New Left interpretation of colonial history?

J. P. G. So far as I know, the New Left has no interpretation of *colonial* history. Staughton Lynd and Jesse Lemisch have written about the Revolution, but no one has really worked on the colonial period.

To the extent that New Left historians are insisting that American historians (like a great many historians of the French Revolution, such as George Rudé and Richard Cobb) should look at the Revolution or society "from below," I think that they are on a profitable track. We have spent so much time in the last twenty years looking at early American history from the point of view of the elite, the dominant groups, that we have tended to ignore other elements in society. It is obviously very important to understand what their attitudes and aspirations were.

J. A. G. What are the half-dozen or so books that you would recommend to persons interested in the subject we have been discussing? In each case, could you indicate the chief contribution of the volume?

J. P. G. I would prefer, I think, to talk about historians rather than about books. The only towering figure, the only historian of the very first importance who has thus far produced work of the highest distinction specifically on the colonial period, is Perry Miller. Taken together, his many works on American Puritanism have both stimulated a major revolution in the way historians have understood that subject and, vastly more important, demonstrated the potentiality for the understanding of colonial life through intensive investigations of colonial ideas as they were manifested at a variety of levels. It is extremely difficult to make a choice among his several important works, but my own preference is *The New England Mind: From Colony to Province* (1953), which describes the Puritan response to basic social and economic changes in New England society between the mid-seventeenth century and 1730.

Once you move beyond Miller, there are a number of very good historians. The most important figure in the generation that preceded Miller is of course Charles M. Andrews. Among a massive corpus of excellent work, *The Colonial Period of American History* (1934–37), in four volumes, and *The Colonial Background of the American Revolution* (1924) are of continuing importance. The first three volumes of the former work provide the most comprehensive narrative of the public history of the colonies in the seventeenth century yet available, while volume 4 and

The Colonial Background together constitute the most complete and well-balanced analysis of British commercial and colonial policy.

Among Miller's contemporaries, Louis B. Wright and Carl Bridenbaugh have contributed an amazing number of important pioneer studies in colonial cultural and social history, but in quality the work of Wesley Frank Craven is second only to that of Miller. Craven's *The Southern Colonies in the Seventeenth Century* (1949), which traces the political and socioeconomic history of the colonies from Maryland to South Carolina down to 1689, and his recent *The Colonies in Transition, 1660—1713* (1968), which presents the closest thing we have to a composite political history of any segment of colonial history, are filled with penetrating insights and wise judgments and will be of lasting significance.

Five men stand out in the generation that followed Miller: Frederick B. Tolles, Edmund S. Morgan, Bernard Bailyn, Daniel J. Boorstin, and Alan Heimert. Tolles has carried the study of cultural history to a new level of sophistication, especially in *Meeting House and Counting House: The Quaker Merchants of Colonial Philadelphia* (1948), a work that employs the intensive study of a single group to illuminate the broader social tensions and cultural trends present in colonial society. The most artful and probably also the most prolific writer of his generation, Morgan has produced several works of major importance on seventeenth-century New England which both amplify and qualify the earlier work of Perry Miller in a number of respects. His *The Puritan Dilemma: The Story of John Winthrop* (1958) is the best introduction to Puritanism during the first generation. Bernard Bailyn's most significant work on the colonial period is *The New England Merchants in the Seventeenth Century* (1955), a work that employed the functional approach of the sociologists to raise our understanding of the socioeconomic and political history of early New England to a new level. In *The Americans: The Colonial Experience* (1958), Daniel J. Boorstin both contributed a provocative general account of colonial development and threw out a multitude of suggestive hypotheses that invite consideration and testing, while Alan Heimert's massive *Religion and the American Mind from the Great Awakening to the Revolution* (1966), despite a number of obvious flaws, is a book of enormous learning that towers over the landscape of eighteenth-century colonial religious history. There are a number of others in this generation whom one would have to mention were he concerned with Revolutionary as well as colonial history, and, indeed, the most important books of both Morgan and Bailyn—respectively, *The Stamp Act Crisis: Prologue to Revolution* (1953) and *The Ideological Origins of the*

American Revolution (1967)—properly fall within the period of the Revolution.

From a still younger generation, there have been several highly competent works, and it is impossible to mention them all here. I would single out Winthrop D. Jordan's *White over Black: American Attitudes toward the Negro, 1550—1812* (1968), the title of which is accurately descriptive, as the most impressive contribution to colonial history yet published by anyone from this age group.

Originally entitled "Colonial Institutions," this interview, done at my home in Baltimore in the summer of 1969, is reprinted with permission and with minor verbal changes from John A. Garraty, ed., *Interpreting American History: Conversations with Historians* (New York: Macmillan, 1970), 29–62.

—FIVE—

Changing Interpretations
of Early American Politics

IN MANY RESPECTS the extraordinary ferment in the study of early
American politics over the past two decades seems to have produced
at least as much confusion as understanding. Subjecting various portions
of the early American political fabric to a thorough and rigorous scrutiny,
a variety of scholars have demonstrated that long-accepted interpretations and categories simply do not fit their particular objects of study.
Unfortunately, the negative thrust of their work, though enormously
valuable, has not been matched by an equally vigorous attempt at reconstruction. We now have a rather clear idea of what the nature of early
American politics was not, but we are still not very sure about what
exactly it was. Moreover, the bewildering mass of data produced by the
new studies seems, on the surface, to defy any effort at rational classification and refinement, any attempt to make explicit and conscious the
network of unrecognized, inarticulated, and, in many cases, seemingly
contradictory assumptions that lie behind their conclusions. The immediate impression is that the politics of every colony was completely idiosyncratic, that there were as many species of political life as there were
political environments. Yet one can discern in the literature as a whole a
slow and tentative groping toward some common, if still largely implicit,
conclusions. To sort out, identify, and classify those conclusions and to
put them in the perspective of the historiography of early American politics is the purpose of this essay.

The nineteenth-century approach was predominantly Whig. That is, it
rested upon the standard Whig assumptions about the nature of man
and the historical process: that man is animated largely by the desire
for freedom, that self-government is, therefore, necessarily the central

concern of political life, and that history itself, at least in the western
European world, is the story of man's inexorable progress toward liberty
and democracy. Colonial politics was, then, simply another chapter in
the age-old struggle of liberty against tyranny in which liberty-loving
colonials from their first landing at Jamestown in 1607 until the successful conclusion of the War for Independence in 1783 had steadily opposed
the arbitrary and tyrannical attempts of the English government to interfere in their affairs, to restrict that freedom and self-government to
which all men naturally aspired and for which the American environment was itself peculiarly well suited. Writers like George Bancroft, the
most prolific and most admired nineteenth-century historian of early
America, whose massive *History of the United States* traced the narrative
of American development through the adoption of the Constitution and
was the standard account of early American political development for
over half a century, fitted all political happenings into this mold. The
various colonial rebellions, the many manifestations of opposition to the
Navigation Acts, the friction between assemblies and royal and proprietary governors, the resistance to parliamentary taxation after 1763, the
War for Independence itself—all were part of the colonists' relentless
striving for self-government and freedom from British control.[1]

Long before Herbert Butterfield wrote his devastating exposé of this
approach in 1931,[2] early American historians had sensed its many inade-
quacies. Fiercely partisan to those men and groups who seemed to be
aligned on the side of liberty, it was, because it insisted upon reading the
past in terms of the present, shot through with anachronisms. Worst of
all, it was starkly simplistic. Rarely more than a narrative of consecu-
tive, if often otherwise unrelated, public events, it ignored political divisions within the colonies, made no effort to identify, much less to explain,
the intricate and complex interplay of forces that normally determine
political events, and failed completely to fit politics into its broad social
context, to look at it, in the words of one recent critic, "in conjunction
with other elements of social activity."[3]

The Whig interpretation of early American politics first came under serious attack during the closing years of the nineteenth century when a

---

[1] George Bancroft, *History of the United States*, 10 vols. (Boston, 1834–74).

[2] Herbert Butterfield, *The Whig Interpretation of History* (London, 1931).

[3] Bernard Bailyn, "A Whig Interpretation," *Yale Review*, n. s., 50 (1961): 438–41.

number of scholarly studies appeared stressing the importance of internal divisions within the colonies in shaping early American political life;[4] but an alternative framework of interpretation, one which attempted to relate politics to social and economic life, emerged only gradually during the first three decades of the twentieth century. The basic structure of the new interpretation was first worked out in detail in two studies of politics in the Middle Colonies in the years immediately preceding the Declaration of Independence: C. H. Lincoln, *The Revolutionary Movement in Pennsylvania* (1901), and Carl Becker, *History of Political Parties in the Province of New York, 1760–1776* (1909). Lincoln and Becker found that politics in both Pennsylvania and New York was conditioned by deep-seated internal conflicts between rival social groups. In Pennsylvania there were "two opposing forces, one of them radical," composed of Scotch-Irish Presbyterians and Germans in the west and non-Quaker lower- and middle-class Philadelphians in the east, and the other "conservative," consisting of the Quaker mercantile oligarchy in the east. In New York it was the radical unprivileged and unfranchised common freeholders, tenants, mechanics, and artisans against a tightly knit landowning and commercial aristocracy. Unleashed by the contest with Britain between 1763 and 1776, this "latent opposition of motives and interests between the priviliged and unprivileged"—the struggle of the radicals to push their way into the political arena and to achieve a wider area of economic and social freedom, the fight over "who should rule at home," and the radical demands for the "democratization of . . . politics and society"—this internal contest, and not the debate over Parliament's colonial authority, was the central issue in the politics of both colonies in the years immediately before the War for Independence.[5]

The striking similarity between developments in Pennsylvania and in New York strongly suggested that what was true for those two colonies was also true for the others, that the debate with Britain had everywhere been accompanied by an internal struggle for democracy between groups representing mutually antagonistic sectional and class interests, and that such a struggle was the distinguishing feature of early American politics. Over the next three decades, a number of scholars pushed this suggestion back into the colonial period and ahead into the years after

---

[4]See, e.g., Brooks Adams, *The Emancipation of Massachusetts: The Dream and the Reality* (Boston, 1887).

[5]C. H. Lincoln, *The Revolutionary Movement in Pennsylvania* (Philadelphia, 1901), 3–4, 7, 14, 39, 53–54, 77, 96–98, 150, 189–90; Carl L. Becker, *History of Political Parties in the Province of New York, 1760–1776* (Madison, Wis., 1909), 5–24, 27–28, 51–52, 275–76.

1776,[6] and it became the central theme of two powerful and vividly written general interpretations of the early American past: Charles and
Mary Beard, *The Rise of American Civilization*,[7] and Vernon Louis Parrington, *Main Currents in American Thought: The Colonial Mind*.[8]

By 1940 the study of early American politics had undergone a profound and seemingly permanent transformation. Applied generally to
many areas of early American political life, the suggestions of Lincoln
and Becker had been converted into dogma. New categories had replaced the old ones completely. Not American patriots and British tyrants but radicals and conservatives, lower classes and upper classes,
democrats and aristocrats, debtors and creditors, westerners and easterners, tenants and landlords, laborers and capitalists had become the

---

[6] Among the more important studies that applied some variant of this interpretation to
early American politics are James Truslow Adams, *The Founding of New England* (Boston, 1921), and *Revolutionary New England in the Republic, 1776—1850* (Boston, 1926);
Charles A. Beard, *An Economic Interpretation of the Constitution* (New York, 1913); Robert L. Brunhouse, *The Counter-Revolution in Pennsylvania, 1776—1790* (Harrisburg, Pa.,
1942); H. J. Eckenrode, *The Revolution in Virginia* (Boston, 1916); J. Franklin Jameson,
The American Revolution Considered as a Social Movement (Princeton, N.J., 1926); Merrill Jensen, *The Articles of Confederation: An Interpretation of the Socio-Constitutional
History of the American Revolution, 1774—1781* (Madison, Wis., 1940); Irving Mark,
Agrarian Conflicts in Colonial New York, 1711—1775 (New York, 1940); John C. Miller,
"Religion, Finance, and Democracy in Massachusetts," *New England Quarterly* 6 (1933):
29–58; Allan Nevins, *The American States during and after the Revolution* (New York,
1924); Arthur M. Schlesinger, *The Colonial Merchants and the American Revolution* (New
York, 1917); J. Paul Selsam, *The Pennsylvania Constitution of 1776: A Study in Revolution-
ary Democracy* (Philadelphia, 1936); Ernest W. Spaulding, *New York in the Critical Period, 1783—1789* (New York, 1932); Richard Upton, *Revolutionary New Hampshire: An
Account of the Social and Political Forces Underlying the Transition from Royal Province
to American Commonwealth* (Hanover, N.H., 1936); and Thomas Jefferson Wertenbaker,
Patrician and Plebeian in Virginia (Charlottesville, Va., 1922), and *Torchbearer of the
Revolution: The Story of Bacon's Rebellion and Its Leader* (Princeton, N.J., 1940). About
the only works published during these years on any aspect of early American politics
which did not emphasize the importance of internal class and sectional divisions were
those which treated constitutional relations between Great Britain and the colonies and
took for their main theme the opposition of colonial lower houses of assembly to royal
governors. The most important studies in this category are Charles M. Andrews, *Colonial Background of the American Revolution* (New Haven, 1924), and Leonard W. Labaree, *Royal Government in America* (New Haven, 1930).

[7] Charles Beard and Mary Beard, *The Rise of American Civilization* (New York, 1927).

[8] Vernon Louis Parrington, *Main Currents in American Thought: The Colonial Mind*
(New York, 1927). A decade later Curtis P. Nettels systematically developed the same
theme at greater length in a general textbook on colonial history, *The Roots of American
Civilization: A History of American Colonial Life* (New York, 1938).

principal actors upon the political stage. Politics was no longer an autonomous and disembodied sphere of activity but a reflection of economic and social cleavages within the colonies, and the essence of political activity was economic and social conflict between "natural" rivals: the little men—the yeomen farmers, agricultural tenants, artisans, and town laborers—against aristocratic merchants, landowners, and professional men, with the former contending for human rights and democracy—the demand for greater popular participation in politics and a general equality of social and economic condition—and the latter for property rights and the maintenance of special privileges in all areas of early American life for the upper classes. If the categories had changed, however, and if the contours of political life seemed to have been thoroughly altered, the ultimate end of the political process, the standard against which every particular event and development were to be judged, remained essentially the same as it had been in the Whig version. For the new historians, as for their nineteenth-century predecessors, the essential meaning of early American politics was to be found in the slow and at times halting advancement toward freedom and democracy that reached its culmination in the halcyon days of Andrew Jackson and the political triumph of the common man. The past continued to be read in terms of the present.

Although there were endless local variations, the broad outlines of early American political development according to the new interpretation seemed reasonably clear. After some early contests between the privileged and unprivileged that culminated in a series of rebellions at the end of the seventeenth century and resulted in some temporary victories for the unprivileged, the privileged, composed of relatively small groups of wealthy men connected by kinship and interest, gained control of the political life of every colony. Although they were everywhere a small minority of the population, they managed to maintain their hold on government by restricting the suffrage to property holders, refusing to extend equitable representation to egalitarian frontier areas, dominating the elective lower houses of assembly, and securing a monopoly on all appointive offices from seats on the royal and proprietary councils down to the lowest administrative posts in towns and counties.[9] Between 1765 and 1776 radical leaders, devoted to the achievement of social democracy if also at times to their own advancement, "seized on British acts as heaven-sent opportunities to attack the local aristocracy . . . under the

---

[9] For a capsule statement of this view, see Merrill Jensen, "Democracy and the American Revolution," *Huntington Library Quarterly* 20 (1957): 321–41.

guise of a patriotic defense of American liberties" and united the unprivileged "in what became as much a war against the colonial aristocracy as a war for independence."[10] The chief significance of the American Revolution was, in fact, not that it brought the colonies their independence but that it provided the opportunity for the unprivileged to score the first great victory for American democracy by driving some of the privileged to become loyalists and compelling others to give the forces of democracy a larger share in the direction of public affairs. Enabled by the pressures of 1774–76 to wrest the lion's share of political power from the conservatives, the radicals over the next decade pushed through the Declaration of Independence, the embodiment of their ideals, and inaugurated a program of democratic reform that succeeded in the various states according to the strength and determination of the radicals but was checked, if only temporarily, in 1787–88 by the Constitution and the conservative resurgence it represented.

This version of early American political development— frequently designated as Progressive because it was obviously shaped by the rhetoric and assumptions of Progressive politics[11]—was so widely accepted and so integral a part of American historical consciousness that it seemed, even as late as 1950, eternally viable. In a real sense, however, the Progressive interpretation of early American politics was the victim of its own success. Its very symmetry and neatness, its apparent comprehensiveness, and its seemingly easy adaptability to almost every situation combined to render it as lifeless and abstract, as little descriptive of the complex and continually changing realities of colonial society and politics, as the old Whig interpretation. Although some scholars continued to produce works set within the Progressive mold,[12] in the years since

---

[10] Jensen, *Articles of Confederation,* 11.

[11] See Charles Crowe, "The Emergence of Progressive History," *Journal of the History of Ideas* 27 (1966): 109–24; Richard Hofstadter, "Beard and the Constitution, History of an Idea," *American Quarterly* 2 (1950): 195–213; Douglass Adair, "The Tenth Federalist Revisited," *William and Mary Quarterly,* 3d ser., 8 (1951): 48–67; and Cecelia M. Kenyon, "'An Economic Interpretation of the Constitution' after Fifty Years," *Centennial Review* 7 (1963): 327–52.

[12] The most important are Merrill Jensen, *The New Nation* (New York, 1950); Jerome R. Reich, *Leisler's Rebellion: A Study of Democracy in New York, 1664–1720* (Chicago, 1953); Elisha P. Douglass, *Rebels and Democrats: The Struggle for Equal Political Rights and Majority Rule during the American Revolution* (Chapel Hill, N.C., 1955); Richard Walsh, *Charleston's Sons of Liberty: A Study of the Artisans, 1763–1789* (Columbia, S.C., 1959); Jackson Turner Main, *The Anti-Federalists: Critics of the Constitution, 1781–1788* (Chapel Hill, N.C., 1961); Staughton Lynd, *Anti-Federalism in Dutchess County, New*

World War II study after study investigating a wide range of phenomena has shown that it is inapplicable to many political situations in early America, that it cannot be superimposed upon existing evidence without serious distortion. The resulting erosion, gradual, piecemeal, and still incomplete though it is, now seems to have left the Progressive interpretation as little more than a series of clichés, of continuing importance only for what they reveal about the intellectual fashions of the first half of the twentieth century.

The most direct assault upon the Progressive interpretation of early American politics has come from Robert E. Brown. In *Middle-Class Democracy and the Revolution in Massachusetts, 1691—1780* (1955), he presented a massively documented case for the propositions that Massachusetts throughout the eighteenth century was a "middle-class society in which property was easily acquired and in which a large portion of the people were property-owning farmers," that 95 percent of the adult males were qualified to vote, that there was virtually no inequality of representation, that the farmers—not the merchant aristocracy—had by virtue of their superior numbers "complete control of the legislature," and that there was no "sharp internal class conflict." Far from being an aristocracy, Massachusetts, Brown concluded, was a middle-class democracy, and the Revolution, instead of being "an internal class conflict designed to achieve political, economic, and social democracy," was in fact a movement "to preserve a social order rather than to change it," to protect the democratic practices which the British government was trying "to curtail . . . as a necessary step toward the recovery of British authority and the prevention of colonial independence."[13]

What "was true in Massachusetts," Brown suggested in a general projection of his findings, was probably also "true in the other colonies,"[14] and he immediately set to work to substantiate this suggestion with a

York: *A Study of Democracy and Class Conflict in the Revolutionary Era* (Chicago, 1962); Staughton Lynd and Alfred Young, "After Carl Becker: The Mechanics and New York City Politics, 1774–1801," *Labor History* 5 (1964): 215–76; and Bernard Friedman, "The New York Assembly Elections of 1768 and 1769: The Disruption of Family Politics," *New York History* 46 (1965): 3–24.

[13] Robert E. Brown, *Middle-Class Democracy and the Revolution in Massachusetts, 1691–1780* (Ithaca, N.Y., 1955), 401–8.

[14] Robert E. Brown, "Reinterpretation of the Revolution and Constitution," *Social Education* 21 (1957): 103.

similar investigation of Virginia. Undertaken in collaboration with his wife, B. Katherine Brown, this study was published in 1964 under the title *Virginia, 1705–1786: Democracy or Aristocracy?* Based upon an even greater amount of research and more systematic analysis, it demonstrated, at least, that what was true for Massachusetts was almost true for Virginia. The percentage of adult white males who could meet the property requirement for voting was only 85 percent instead of 95 percent, but the electorate was still wide, economic opportunity and social mobility were great, class antagonism was slight, representation was fairly equitable throughout the colony, and the only instance of internal social conflict before or during the Revolution occurred after 1740 between a growing group of dissenters and the Anglican establishment over the privileged position of the Anglican church. These findings led the authors to conclude that Virginia society, like Massachusetts society, was "fundamentally middle-class," with a political system that was "a middle class, representative democracy," and that the Revolution in Virginia, as in Massachusetts, was not an internal social upheaval but a conservative protest movement against the attacks of the British government upon Virginia democracy.[15]

A torrent of criticism followed the publication of both of these volumes. Several critics objected that the Browns' definition of democracy as any system in which social and economic opportunity was open to all and a majority of free adult males could vote was both anachronistic and inaccurate. It was anachronistic because it was derived from twentieth-century rather than eighteenth-century conceptions of democracy and inaccurate because almost all public offices—whether appointive or elective—were held by men from upper-class groups.[16] In the most elaborate critique of the Massachusetts volume, John Cary showed that Brown's

---

[15] Robert E. Brown and B. Katherine Brown, *Virginia, 1705–1786: Democracy or Aristocracy?* (East Lansing, Mich., 1964).

[16] Among the most searching reviews of the Massachusetts volume were those by Robert J. Taylor, *Mississippi Valley Historical Review* 43 (1956): 111–13, and Clifford K. Shipton, *Political Science Quarterly* 71 (1956): 306–8, while David Alan Williams, *William and Mary Quarterly*, 3d ser., 22 (1965): 149–52, is perhaps the best review of the Virginia volume. Other, more extended criticisms of the Browns' assumptions, use of terms, and conclusions may be found in Jensen, "Democracy and the American Revolution"; Roy N. Lokken, "The Concept of Democracy in Colonial Political Thought," *William and Mary Quarterly*, 3d ser., 26 (1959): 568–80; J. R. Pole, "Historians and the Problem of Early American Democracy," *American Historical Review* 67 (1962): 626–46; and John M. Murrin, "The Myths of Colonial Democracy and Royal Decline in Eighteenth-Century America: A Review Essay," *Cithara* 5 (1965): 53–69.

sampling techniques were faulty, that his statistics were unreliable, and that, at least for certain selected towns, the percentage of qualified voters, though still quite high, was 20 to 30 percent lower than Brown had originally indicated.[17]

When the smoke cleared, however, two points became clear. The first was that the Browns had not departed very far from the Progressive historians they had set out to criticize. So preoccupied were they with demonstrating the factual and interpretive mistakes of the Progressive account that they permitted that account to dictate the questions they asked of their materials. Borrowing wholesale their assumptions, categories, and terminology from the earlier interpretation, the Browns, like the Progressive historians, were completely committed to a democratic point of view which assumed, among other things, that in any given political situation it is the people in general and what they want that are of primary importance; that the middle and lower classes have strong political interests and aspirations; and that the struggle for democracy—even though it was a struggle to preserve rather than to obtain democracy—was the central issue in early American politics. As the title of the Virginia book indicated, the Browns assumed, as had their Progressive progenitors, that colonial society had to be either aristocratic or democratic, that it had to fit into one or the other of two rigid, abstract, largely self-contained, and mutually exclusive political categories. By insisting upon working entirely within two such broad and abstract polar classifications, the Browns did great violence to the diverse tendencies in early American political life and precluded the possibility of developing new and more meaningful categories for describing those tendencies.

The second point that can be made about the Browns' work is more positive. However unscientific their sampling techniques and however inexact their statistics, they established beyond serious doubt two basic facts about the societies of Massachusetts and Virginia that necessitated serious modifications in the Progressive conception of early American politics. First, by showing that the economic structure was highly fluid, property widely distributed, and lower-class economic and social discontent minimal, they made it clear that neither colony was so rigidly stratified as to produce the kind of social conflicts which Progressive historians thought were the stuff of colonial politics. Second, by showing that

---

[17] John Cary, "Statistical Method and the Brown Thesis on Colonial Democracy," *William and Mary Quarterly*, 3d ser., 20 (1963): 251–64. See also the rebuttal by Brown, ibid., 265–76.

the franchise was considerably wider than had previously been supposed, they demonstrated that the predominance of the upper classes in politics did not depend upon a restricted franchise, that they had to have the support of men from all classes to gain elective office. That both of these conclusions are equally applicable to the rest of the colonies is indicated by the findings of a number of recent independent studies.

Investigations of voting requirements and voter eligibility in Plymouth, Connecticut, Rhode Island, Virginia, New York, New Jersey, and Pennsylvania have revealed that the franchise in those colonies was also very wide and that the vast majority of free adult males could expect to acquire enough property during their lifetimes to meet the suffrage requirements.[18] Similarly, Jackson Turner Main, in a general examination of *The Social Structure of Revolutionary America,* has argued that American society in the late eighteenth century was everywhere relatively free from poverty and had, especially by European standards, a high rate of vertical mobility, great social and economic opportunity, and a remarkably supple class structure. This combination of economic abundance and social fluidity, Main has concluded, tended "to minimize those conflicts which might have grown out of the class structure and the concentration of wealth" that was occurring in older settled areas.[19]

Even before the Browns mounted their vigorous assault, a number of other scholars had been busy turning out a series of detailed studies of the political life of individual colonies that had been quietly effecting a major revolution in the interpretation of early American politics. This movement, which is still in progress, was inspired in part by the early

[18] See George D. Langdon, Jr., "The Franchise and Political Democracy in Plymouth Colony," ibid., 513–26; David S. Lovejoy, *Rhode Island Politics and the American Revolution, 1760–1776* (Providence, R.I., 1958), 5–31; Charles S. Grant, *Democracy in the Connecticut Frontier Town of Kent* (New York, 1961); Milton M. Klein, "Democracy and Politics in Colonial New York," *New York History* 40 (1959): 221–46; Nicholas Varga, "Election Procedures and Practices in Colonial New York," ibid., 41 (1960): 249–77; Richard P. McCormick, *The History of Voting in New Jersey: A Study of the Development of Election Machinery, 1664–1911* (New Brunswick, N.J., 1953); Theodore Thayer, *Pennsylvania Politics and the Growth of Democracy, 1740–1776* (Harrisburg, Pa., 1953), 6; and Lucille Griffith, *Virginia House of Burgesses, 1750–1774* (Northport, Ala., 1963), 53–79.

[19] Jackson Turner Main, *The Social Structure of Revolutionary America* (Princeton, N.J., 1965), esp. 270–87, quotation from 163.

works of Lincoln and Becker and in part by the prosopographical studies of eighteenth-century British politics by Sir Lewis Namier and his followers.[20] Like Lincoln and Becker, the authors of these studies have been primarily interested in penetrating behind the formal institutional arrangements, ostensible issues, and dominant rhetoric of political life to the hard, concrete, and underlying realities. In marked contrast to the Progressives, however, they have in general found broad economic and social divisions within the colonies to have been less important in determining the nature and form of political activity than the conflicting interests and ambitions of rival groups within the upper strata of society. In imitation of Namier, they have tried to sort out and describe the networks of interest, kinship, religious affiliation, and regional ties that presumably formed the basis for the major political groupings and to show how those networks related to the social and economic structure of the colonies in which they existed. In the process they have shown how inadequate the old polar categories employed by the Progressive historians actually were, how profoundly those categories obscured and distorted the complex and variegated nature of early American politics.

The first of these studies, John Bartlett Brebner's *The Neutral Yankees of Nova Scotia,* appeared as early as 1937. An exhaustive survey of the development of Nova Scotia from 1749, the year the British government inaugurated its program to turn what had previously been no more than a military garrison presiding over an unassimilated French population into a full-fledged British colony, until the conclusion of the War for Independence, this volume showed that the political life of the colony quickly came under the dominance of a powerful "little commercial group" centered in Halifax and headed by Joshua Mauger, the "economic overlord" of the colony who presided over its fortunes from a London base. By virtue of Mauger's influence among metropolitan officials at Whitehall, members of this group by the 1760s filled most of the public offices in the colony, including the lieutenant governorship and a healthy majority of seats on the royal council. With such extensive political power they were able to secure a virtual monopoly over both the distilling industry—the chief pillar in Nova Scotia's rudimentary economy—and the colony's London trade and to reap handsome profits from the sale of lands granted to themselves and from manipulating both the public and private debts of the colony.

---

[20] Especially Sir Lewis Namier, *The Structure of Politics at the Accession of George III* (London, 1929), and *England in the Age of the American Revolution* (London, 1930).

Because of its economic stranglehold over Halifax and because the bulk of the population, widely scattered over the rest of the province and preoccupied with eking out an existence in a new and not always hospitable environment, was politically inarticulate, disorganized, and acquiescent, this "office-holding clique" usually managed even to get its friends elected to a majority of the seats in the lower house of assembly. On the rare occasions when men from outside the clique were able to obtain a majority in the house, they only infrequently acted in concert against the merchant-official oligarchy, and when they did, the members of the oligarchy in the council could always block their efforts. Thus, except for an occasional and usually ineffective challenge from a royal governor or a newly arrived merchant who resented its monopolization of power, office, and economic opportunity, the oligarchy was free to govern Nova Scotia as its private interests demanded. Its tight political control, Brebner concluded, was one of the main factors in Nova Scotia's failure to join the other colonies in the American Revolution.[21]

Brebner's work on Nova Scotia, by the author's own admission a "marginal" and relatively new colony, did not in itself demand a reexamination of the Progressive conception of early American politics, but two volumes on Maryland politics published in the 1940s indicated that that conception clearly did not apply uniformly to the older colonies. After a close look at Maryland society and politics through the middle decades of the eighteenth century, Charles Albro Barker found in *The Background of the Revolution in Maryland* that political divisions in that colony contained no elements of "western populism, or evangelical democracy," or "'class struggle.'" The conflict was not between classes, not between "plebeian and patrician," but "within the upper class," a classic struggle between "country" and "court" in which the "local squirearchy," which dominated "every phase of the growing life of the province" and expressed itself politically through the elective House of Delegates, was aligned against the absentee proprietor and his representatives who monopolized the seats on the proprietary council and all major public offices.[22] Although individuals sometimes changed sides as the proprietor sought to lure influential members of the gentry into the proprietary

---

[21] John Bartlett Brebner, *The Neutral Yankees of Nova Scotia* (New York, 1937), 149–57, 207–42, 291–353.

[22] The extensive patronage of the Maryland proprietor is analyzed in detail by Donnell MacClure Owings, *His Lordship's Patronage: Offices of Profit in Colonial Maryland* (Baltimore, 1953).

camp by appointment to lucrative offices,[23] the issues which divided these two groups—the special privileges, powers, and revenues of the proprietors—remained constant, subtly shaping every political battle in pre-Revolutionary Maryland. The "country party" took the lead in the protest against British policy between 1763 and 1776, and, although the increasing incidence of "election pledges, instructions to delegates, mass meetings, committees and associations" during those years tended to give "increasing force, from outside legislative doors, to the politics of protest," it resulted, Barker argued, not in the diminution but the enlargement of the influence of the gentry by bringing its members into "closer connection with the people" and giving "practical . . . meaning to the phrases about popular rights" employed in the Revolutionary debate.[24]

That the same group—"a relatively small class of planters, lawyers, and merchants"—continued to dominate Maryland politics after 1776 without serious challenge from below was the argument of Philip A. Crowl in *Maryland during and after the Revolution: A Political and Economic Study*, published in 1942 just two years after Barker's volume. Crowl found plenty of political conflict in Maryland, but it was neither class nor sectional in nature. Rather, it took the form of a series of struggles over opposing interests, ideas, and personalities between ad hoc coalitions of rival groups of leading men.[25]

In the years after World War II, investigations of segments of the political history of Connecticut, New Jersey, and Rhode Island revealed both their distinctive features and how far the politics of each colony-state departed from the Progressive model. In *Connecticut's Years of Controversy, 1750—1776*, published in 1949, Oscar Zeichner showed that the tradition of political tranquillity that had earned for Connecticut its reputation as the "land of steady habits" had been shattered by the Great

---

[23] The classic case is that of Daniel Dulaney, Sr. For the details of his switch as well as additional confirmation of the general conclusions reached by Barker, see Aubrey C. Land, *The Dulanys of Maryland: A Biographical Study of Daniel Dulany, the Elder (1685—1753), and Daniel Dulany, the Younger (1722—1797)* (Baltimore, 1955).

[24] Charles Albro Barker, *The Background of the Revolution in Maryland* (New Haven, 1940), esp. 24, 182–83, 372–77. Additional insight into the nature of "out-of-doors politics" in Maryland is provided by Neil Strawser, "Samuel Chase and the Annapolis Paper War," *Maryland Historical Magazine* 57 (1962): 177–94.

[25] Philip A. Crowl, *Maryland during and after the Revolution: A Political and Economic Study* (Baltimore, 1942), esp. 11–15. See also Crowl's "Anti-Federalism in Maryland, 1787-1788," *William and Mary Quarterly*, 3d ser., 4 (1947): 446–69.

Awakening, which by fragmenting the colony into a variety of religious groups—Separates and New Lights on the one hand and Old Lights, Arminians, and Anglicans on the other—paved the way for a succession of "long and bitterly fought factional and party conflicts." Because the eastern half of Connecticut was the main center of New Light strength while the western half was the primary stronghold of the Old Lights and Anglicans, these conflicts were to some extent sectional. But they also came to represent rival economic interests as eastern merchants and lawyers who formed the core of the Susquehannah Company, a speculative enterprise intent upon securing the support of the Connecticut government for its land schemes in Pennsylvania's Wyoming Valley, came into conflict with western leaders who opposed their project. Because the previously dominant western, Old Light, anti–Susquehannah Company group was too moderate in its resistance to the Stamp Act, the eastern, New Light, Susquehannah Company faction was able to gain the ascendancy in 1766 as the imperial question became an important issue in local politics. The New Light faction retained power until 1776, and the Old Light group gradually disintegrated as first the Old Lights and then the Arminians came to support the New Light opposition to British policy, leaving only the Anglicans, many of whom subsequently became loyalists, in opposition. As in Maryland, these conflicts were not along class lines. The leaders of both groups were drawn from Connecticut's "ruling aristocracy of magistrates and ministers."[26]

Similarly, Richard P. McCormick in *Experiment in Independence: New Jersey in the Critical Period, 1781–1789*, published in 1950, found that "'men of interest'" with powerful family connections played the preponderant role in New Jersey politics. On the statewide level they were loosely organized into two broad sectional factions, the East Jersey and the West Jersey. But this split did not represent the "sectionalism of tidewater against backcountry, of plantation owners against yeomen, of a metropolis against the hinterlands, of a trading region against an agricultural region, or of an over-represented minority against an under-represented majority." Rather it was a sectionalism that was peculiar to New Jersey, one that followed a familiar historical and cultural cleavage that dated from the earliest settlement of the colony and had been inten-

---

[26]Oscar Zeichner, *Connecticut's Years of Controversy, 1750–1776* (Chapel Hill, N.C., 1949), 3–43, 219–35. Zeichner's account of the religious origins of Connecticut's political divisions has been amplified in several important respects by Robert Sklar, "The Great Awakening and Colonial Politics: Connecticut's Revolution in the Minds of Men," *Connecticut Historical Society Bulletin* 28 (1963): 81–95.

sified during the War for Independence as East Jersey leaders took the lead in prosecuting the war while West Jersey leaders, many of whom were Quakers, adopted "a negative or neutral attitude."[27]

David S. Lovejoy showed in *Rhode Island Politics and the American Revolution, 1760—1776* (1958), that in the decades just before the American Revolution, Rhode Island politics also revolved around sectional and factional disputes. Like the disputes in Connecticut and New Jersey, these were not the result of "the attempt of one class of people to tear down another and broaden the basis of government" but of a "struggle between equals, between people who already enjoyed the right to vote and who fought to control the government for their own ends." In contrast to the New Jersey factions, those in Rhode Island were sharply defined and well organized around two rival leaders—Samuel Ward from Newport and Stephen Hopkins from Providence—and reflected an overt and explicit contest between Newport and Providence for economic and political supremacy within the colony. That personality was of critical importance in the Ward-Hopkins controversy was indicated by the virtual dissolution of the Ward faction after Hopkins's alliance with the Wantons of Newport resulted in a humiliating defeat for Ward in the election of 1770 and his retirement from politics.[28]

Other studies have shown similarly unique political patterns in still other colonies. Between 1741 and 1767 New Hampshire politics closely resembled those of Nova Scotia. A remarkably close-knit oligarchy—centered around Governor Benning Wentworth, bound together by close family, social, and economic ties and well connected in official circles in London—occupied most of the important appointive offices and dominated the mast and naval stores industries, the disposition of public

---

[27] Richard P. McCormick, *Experiment in Independence: New Jersey in the Critical Period, 1781—1789* (New Brunswick, N.J., 1950), 69–102. The origins of this split and some of its manifestations in the period before the American Revolution can be traced in John E. Pomfret, *The Province of West New Jersey, 1609—1702: A History of the Origins of an American Colony* (Princeton, N.J., 1956), and *The Province of East New Jersey, 1609—1702: The Rebellious Proprietary* (Princeton, N.J., 1962); Donald L. Kemmerer, *Path to Freedom: The Struggle for Self-Government in Colonial New Jersey, 1703—1776* (Princeton, N.J., 1940); and Richard P. McCormick, *New Jersey from Colony to State, 1609—1789* (Princeton, N.J., 1964).

[28] Lovejoy, *Rhode Island Politics*, 1–30, 193–94. A briefer and more pointed analysis of Rhode Island's factional dispute is Mack E. Thompson, "The Ward-Hopkins Controversy and the American Revolution in Rhode Island: An Interpretation," *William and Mary Quarterly*, 3d ser., 16 (1959): 363–75. Both Lovejoy and Thompson make the point that before 1755 Rhode Island politics was dominated by representatives of the agrarian towns against the opposition of commercial interests in Newport.

lands, and the overseas trade, the most lucrative segments of the New Hampshire economy. By an effective use of patronage and other varieties of political influence, this group even managed to control the elected lower house. The failure of an early challenge from a rival group of leading men in the 1740s and early 1750s resulted in the disappearance of faction and the total and unchallenged political ascendancy of the Wentworth family, which governed with the support of the "vast majority of provincial inhabitants."[29] In Georgia, which, like Nova Scotia, was comparatively new and underdeveloped throughout the colonial period, there were no significant internal sectional or class conflicts before the Revolution, and only on the question of opposition to British policy after 1763 was there any clear political division, as Governor James Wright and a small coterie of crown officers lined up in support of British authority against the vast bulk of the colony's leading men, some of whom occupied seats on the royal council but most of whom expressed themselves through the elected Commons House of Assembly.[30] A mild form of sectionalism appeared in the 1780s as leaders from the rapidly expanding upcountry began to compete for political prominence with traditional lowcountry leaders, but this split neither resulted in the development of coherent and permanent factions nor determined voting behavior on the major public issues.[31]

Politics in Delaware after the Declaration of Independence continued to manifest a long-standing sectional rivalry between the leaders of the two dominant agricultural southern counties and the dynamic Scotch-Irish minority representing the commercial interests of New Castle in the north.[32]

Factional disputes over proprietary powers, religion, and economic interests characterized the politics of both Carolinas during the proprietary period. Under the crown, however, the old factional disputes subsided in South Carolina after a chaotic battle over paper currency, which in general pitted the Charleston mercantile community against the

---

[29] Jere R. Daniell, "Politics in New Hampshire under Governor Benning Wentworth, 1741–1767," *William and Mary Quarterly*, 3d ser., 23 (1966): 76–105.

[30] W. W. Abbot, *The Royal Governors of Georgia, 1754–1775* (Chapel Hill, N.C., 1959). For somewhat different conclusions and an analysis of the snarled political life of Georgia during the War for Independence, see Kenneth Coleman, *The American Revolution in Georgia, 1763–1789* (Athens, Ga., 1958).

[31] W. W. Abbot, "The Structure of Politics in Georgia, 1782–1789," *William and Mary Quarterly*, 3d ser., 14 (1957): 47–65.

[32] John A. Munroe, *Federalist Delaware, 1775–1815* (New Brunswick, N.J., 1954).

planters, ended in the early 1730s with the stabilization of the colony's
paper money system. Thereafter there were no significant political divisions.[33] Even the Regulator movement of the late 1760s, a recent writer
has found in sharp contrast to the old interpretation, did not reveal or
produce any deep-seated class or sectional antagonism, because the Regulators—a combination of small planters and leading men in the backcountry—were primarily concerned with the establishment of law enforcement agencies adequate to deal with the lawless conditions that
prevailed in the backcountry and laid aside other subsidiary grievances
against the eastern government once effective courts had been secured.[34]
The foundations for these grievances—a discriminatory tax system and
insufficient representation for the backcountry in the legislature—were
presumably to a large extent remedied by the new constitution in 1776.[35]

By contrast, North Carolina during the royal period continued to be
torn by factional strife over the disposition of lands, payment of quitrents, and the unequal representation of the rapidly expanding southern
section of the colony in the legislature. After a dramatic attempt by leaders of the southern counties to change the representation system had
been squelched by London authorities in the early 1750s, the north-south
quarrel gradually subsided, but in the late 1760s and early 1770s the colony was again plagued by sectional antagonisms as western Regulators
rose in protest against corrupt local administration by "eastern" ap-
pointees intent on enriching themselves at the expense of the western
inhabitants. This protest, which was eventually put down with force,
apparently produced a deep sectional rift that continued to affect North
Carolina politics even after the conditions that produced it had disappeared.[36]

---

[33] These generalizations are drawn largely from M. Eugene Sirmans, *Colonial South Carolina: A Political History, 1663–1763* (Chapel Hill, N.C., 1966). See also Sirmans's "Politics in Colonial South Carolina: The Failure of Proprietary Reform, 1682–1694," *William
and Mary Quarterly*, 3d ser., 23 (1966): 33–55, and "The South Carolina Royal Council,
1720–1763," ibid., 18 (1961): 373–92.

[34] Richard Maxwell Brown, *The South Carolina Regulators: The Story of the First American Vigilante Movement* (Cambridge, Mass., 1963).

[35] There is no adequate study of South Carolina politics immediately after 1776, but see
the introduction to William E. Hemphill and Wylma Anne Wates, eds., *Extracts from
the Journals of the Provincial Congresses of South Carolina, 1775–1776* (Columbia, S.C.,
1960), i–xxxiv.

[36] The fabric of North Carolina politics has not been completely unraveled, but some of
the more important developments are dealt with in Charles G. Sellers, Jr., "Private
Profits and British Colonial Policy: The Speculations of Henry McCulloh," *William and*

That the Progressive model is also inapplicable to the politics of the two oldest colonies, Massachusetts and Virginia, can be inferred from a spate of specialized investigations of each. In Massachusetts after the Restoration, the old Puritan leadership, which had previously been able to maintain its political predominance despite occasional challenges from a variety of discontented groups in the colony,[37] began to crack under pressures from both without and within. The external pressures, described by Michael Garibaldi Hall in *Edward Randolph and the American Colonies, 1676—1703*,[38] derived from the attempts of the crown to assert its authority over the colony, and the internal pressures, discussed by Bernard Bailyn in *The New England Merchants in the Seventeenth Century*,[39] largely from a rising group of interrelated merchants, who, though in many cases Puritans themselves, were discontented with orthodox Puritan leadership. Together with other dissatisfied groups, the merchants at first cooperated with the crown in the hope of breaking the power of the Puritans and formed the bulk of the provisional council which in 1685 and 1686 governed Massachusetts during the interim period between the recall of the charter and the arrival of royal governor Edmund Andros. But this group, too "multifarious" to constitute a party, as Richard S. Dunn has emphasized in an excellent study of the changing political orientation of New England at the end of the seventeenth century and the beginning of the eighteenth century,[40] made com-

---

Mary Quarterly, 3d ser., 8 (1951): 535–51; Lawrence F. London, "The Representation Controversy in Colonial North Carolina," *North Carolina Historical Review* 11 (1934): 255–70; and Desmond Clarke, *Arthur Dobbs, Esquire, 1689—1765: Surveyor-General of Ireland, Prospector and Governor of North Carolina* (Chapel Hill, N.C., 1957). Hugh T. Lefler and Paul Wager, eds., *Orange County—1752—1952* (Chapel Hill, N.C., 1953), contains the best discussion of the North Carolina Regulator movement.

[37] Together, George Lee Haskins, *Law and Authority in Early Massachusetts: A Study in Tradition and Design* (New York, 1960), and Edmund S. Morgan, *The Puritan Dilemma: The Story of John Winthrop* (Boston, 1958), provide a satisfactory account of the political life of Massachusetts Bay before the Restoration. The social and political divergencies from the ideas of the dominant group are emphasized by Darrett B. Rutman, *Winthrop's Boston: Portrait of a Puritan Town, 1630—1649* (Chapel Hill, N.C., 1965), and "The Mirror of Puritan Authority," in *Law and Authority in Colonial America: Selected Essays,* ed. George A. Billias (Barre, Mass., 1965), 149–67.

[38] Michael Garibaldi Hall, *Edward Randolph and the American Colonies 1676—1703* (Chapel Hill, N.C., 1960), esp. 21–128.

[39] Bernard Bailyn, *The New England Merchants in the Seventeenth Century* (Cambridge, Mass., 1955).

[40] Richard S. Dunn, *Puritans and Yankees: The Winthrop Dynasty of New England, 1630—1717* (Princeton, N.J., 1962), 212–57.

mon cause with the old Puritan leadership against Andros as soon as it became clear that it could not control the dominion government. Under the new government established under the Charter of 1691, the council, Bailyn has argued, became the "political voice of the merchants," who over the next forty years used their connections in Great Britain and cooperated with the country party representing lesser property owners in the House of Representatives to make and break a succession of governors in an attempt to secure their "permanent interests."[41]

This process can be seen in John A. Schutz's account of the intrigues and maneuvers that preceded the removal of Jonathan Belcher and the appointment of William Shirley as governor of Massachusetts in 1741.[42] Though heated political controversies—which, as George Athan Billias has recently shown in connection with the land bank struggle,[43] were usually between rival groups of leading men representing opposing economic interests—occasionally arose thereafter,[44] Shirley's appointment ushered in a period of political stability that lasted until his removal from the governorship in 1756 and was based upon his deft manipulation of the House of Representatives and a clever distribution of patronage that enabled him to draw many of the colony's leading men into his political orbit and to build a powerful political machine around "a solid core of supporters and a shifting number of auxiliaries."[45] By the 1760s resentment against the engrossment of power and office by this "oligarchy" had become widespread among the wealthy and ambitious who were not a part of it, and, when the oligarchy was cautious in opposing British measures after 1763, its opponents seized the opportunity to discredit it and to reduce its power by excluding its members from the royal council.[46]

---

[41] Ibid.; Bailyn, *New England Merchants*, 143–97.

[42] John A. Schutz, "Succession Politics in Massachusetts, 1730–1741," *William and Mary Quarterly*, 3d ser., 15 (1958): 508–20.

[43] George A. Billias, *The Massachusetts Land Bankers of 1740* (Orono, Maine, 1959), 17–53.

[44] See Paul S. Boyer, "Borrowed Rhetoric: The Massachusetts Excise Controversy of 1754," *William and Mary Quarterly*, 3d ser., 21 (1964): 328–51.

[45] John A. Schutz, *William Shirley, King's Governor of Massachusetts* (Chapel Hill, N.C., 1961), quotation from p. 269.

[46] Ellen E. Brennan, *Plural Office-Holding in Massachusetts 1760–1780: Its Relation to the "Separation" of Departments of Government* (Chapel Hill, N.C., 1945), 3–106; Edmund S. and Helen M. Morgan, *The Stamp Act Crisis: Prologue to Revolution* (Chapel Hill, N.C., 1953), 7–20, 207–19; John Cary, *Joseph Warren: Physician, Politician, Patriot* (Urbana, Ill., 1961); Francis G. Walett, "The Massachusetts Council, 1766–1774," *William and Mary Quarterly*, 3d ser., 6 (1949): 605–27.

This internal political battle, sharpened by the Revolutionary controversy and ending in 1775 with the outbreak of war and the dissolution of
the oligarchy, was played out against a backdrop of western agrarian
distrust of the commercial East, which though temporarily submerged
during the war, openly manifested itself again in the disturbances of the
1780s.[47] Although westerners seem to have taken the revolutionary ideal
of popular sovereignty more seriously than easterners, they revealed,
just like Massachusetts citizens in the eastern portion of the colony, a
pronounced tendency to trust political affairs at every level of government to leading men except in times of extreme economic distress such
as those which accompanied Shays' Rebellion.[48]

Virginia politics, like those of Massachusetts, proceeded through several distinct phases. The chaotic factionalism and chronic disarray of the
colony's first few decades gave way under the careful efforts of Governor
Sir William Berkeley to a more stable political environment after the
Restoration. Berkeley, as Bernard Bailyn has shown, gathered around
him many of the most successful among a new wave of immigrants who
began coming to Virginia in the 1640s. Bound to Berkeley by "ties of
kinship and patronage," this group, called the Green Spring faction after
Berkeley's plantation, formed "an inner circle of privilege" with a virtual
monopoly over the important public offices and the seats on the governor's council, easy access to the public lands which constituted the chief
form of wealth in the colony, and sufficient political influence to dominate the proceedings of the elective House of Burgesses. Bacon's Rebellion, which, as Wilcomb E. Washburn has emphasized, began over a
disagreement on Indian policy and had few of the populist-democratic
overtones traditionally associated with it,[49] became an occasion for the
venting of pent-up resentment among county leaders outside the official group.

No sooner was the rebellion over and Berkeley removed from the
scene, however, than this bitter rivalry between court and country and

---

[47] The basic study of western attitudes is Robert J. Taylor, *Western Massachusetts in the
Revolution* (Providence, 1954).

[48] Ibid.; Lee Nathaniel Newcomer, *The Embattled Farmers: A Massachusetts Countryside
in the American Revolution* (New York, 1953), 79–87; Benjamin W. Labaree, *Patriots and
Partisans: The Merchants of Newburyport, 1764–1815* (Cambridge, Mass., 1962), 1–15;
and David Syrett, "Town-Meeting Politics in Massachusetts, 1776–1786," *William and
Mary Quarterly,* 3d ser., 21 (1964): 352–66.

[49] Wilcomb E. Washburn, *The Governor and the Rebel: A History of Bacon's Rebellion in
Virginia* (Chapel Hill, N.C., 1957).

the incipient factionalism it represented began to subside as the leading men in both groups united against a series of royal governors who, unlike Berkeley, were not intimately connected through kinship, patronage, or economic interest with the emergent planter group. For thirty-five years after the rebellion, the leading planter families—a "league of local oligarchs" who were becoming increasingly self-conscious and expressing themselves largely through the council—drove one governor after another out of office.[50]

Not until the end of the second decade of the eighteenth century, when Lieutenant Governor Alexander Spotswood gave up the fight and allied himself with the local leaders, was this pattern broken and the political infighting it had produced stopped. For the most part Spotswood's successors followed the same course, and Virginia politics through the middle decades of the eighteenth century acquired a degree of stability that was rare in colonial America.[51] Personal rivalries among leading politicians never hardened into factions, and the local oligarchy, dominating the council, the House of Burgesses, and the county courts, governed, as Charles S. Sydnor has demonstrated, with rare skill and responsibility, to the general satisfaction of the entire Virginia political community.[52] Even the apparent challenge by Patrick Henry and the heated political discussions that followed the disclosure in 1766 that a longtime speaker of the House of Burgesses and colony treasurer had loaned large sums of public money to his friends among the gentry did not produce any permanent or significant divisions within the Virginia polity.[53] Not until the war and Confederation periods did a serious split, apparently

---

[50] Bernard Bailyn, "Politics and Social Structure in Virginia," in *Seventeenth-Century America: Essays on Colonial History*, ed. James Morton Smith (Chapel Hill, N.C., 1959), 90–115. On the self-consciousness of the Virginia gentry, see Louis B. Wright, *The First Gentlemen of Virginia: Intellectual Qualities of the Early Colonial Ruling Class* (San Marino, Calif., 1940).

[51] See Jack P. Greene, *The Quest for Power: The Lower Houses of Assembly in the Southern Royal Colonies, 1689–1776* (Chapel Hill, N.C., 1963), 22–31.

[52] Charles S. Sydnor, *Gentleman Freeholders: Political Practices in Washington's Virginia* (Chapel Hill, N.C., 1952). See also Griffith, *Virginia House of Burgesses;* Jack P. Greene, "Foundations of Political Power in the Virginia House of Burgesses, 1720–1776," *William and Mary Quarterly*, 3d ser., 16 (1959): 485–506; and Carl Bridenbaugh, *Seat of Empire: The Political Role of Eighteenth-Century Williamsburg* (Williamsburg, Va., 1950), 1–43.

[53] Thad W. Tate, "The Coming of the Revolution in Virginia: Britain's Challenge to Virginia's Ruling Class, 1763–1776," *William and Mary Quarterly*, 3d ser., 19 (1962): 323–43; David John Mays, *Edmund Pendleton, 1721–1803: A Biography*, 2 vols. (Cambridge, Mass., 1952).

based upon both opposing sectional and economic interests and personal political rivalries, appear.[54]

A number of recent studies suggest that not even in Pennsylvania and New York, the prototypes for the Progressive model, did the politics fit that model well. Until the mid-1770s Pennsylvania politics seems to have resembled the Maryland pattern more closely. From the first decades of the colony's history there was a more or less continuous struggle between court and country over the distribution of power between the proprietor and the assembly. During the first quarter of the eighteenth century both the country party and the court party were Quaker, but the country party, led by lawyer David Lloyd and operating primarily through the assembly, drew its strength mostly from the country, while the court party, "dominated by city merchants under the leadership of the Proprietor's secretary, James Logan," and in complete control of the council, was most powerful in Philadelphia, the seat of the proprietor's government.[55] Fanned by personal rivalries and ambitions, this bitter party strife temporarily subsided after 1725 as unparalleled commercial prosperity, the tactful administration of Governor Patrick Gordon, and the disappearance of old political issues ushered in an era of good feeling and resulted in the virtual extinction of the old parties.

Political peace proved to be short-lived, however, and with the end of Gordon's administration in 1736 the old wrangling began anew, this time between a united "Quaker party"—composed of remnants from both of the older factions and supported by many non-Quakers—and the "Proprietary party"—consisting of a growing body of Anglicans, proprietary officeholders, and some Presbyterian and German back settlers—over "the authority of the Proprietors and the best means of achieving a *modus vivendi* with the Indians."[56] These two parties continued to be the principal rivals in Pennsylvania politics up through the middle 1770s, although after the exclusion crisis of 1756—after many Quakers with-

---

[54] The exact nature and precise importance of this split is unclear, but see Jackson Turner Main, "Sections and Politics in Virginia, 1781–1787," *William and Mary Quarterly*, 3d ser., 12 (1955): 96–112.

[55] Roy N. Lokken, *David Lloyd, Colonial Lawmaker* (Seattle, 1959), and Frederick B. Tolles, *James Logan and the Culture of Provincial America* (Boston, 1957), discuss the role and behavior of the central protagonists.

[56] Frederick B. Tolles, *Meeting House and Counting House: The Quaker Merchants of Colonial Philadelphia* (Chapel Hill, N.C., 1948), 11–28; Thayer, *Pennsylvania Politics*. On the composition of the proprietary group, see G. B. Warden, "The Proprietary Group in Pennsylvania, 1754–1764," *William and Mary Quarterly*, 3d ser., 21 (1964): 367–89.

drew from the assembly rather than betray their pacifist principles in what, as Ralph Ketcham has recently emphasized, was a move to preserve, not relinquish, Quaker political power—many of the leaders of the Quaker party were no longer Quakers.[57] The annual election battles between these two parties were occasionally extremely hard fought, especially from 1764 through 1766, when the proprietary party managed to exploit western discontent over the Paxton affair and resentment over the Quaker party's moderate response to the Stamp Act to secure its only clear victories, and both parties appealed broadly to the electorate.[58] But this conflict, as William S. Hanna has underlined, was largely a mere "jousting at the top among the gentlemen rulers and their factions" with no basic social issues at stake.[59]

For reasons not entirely clear, this contest subsided after 1766, and over the next decade the internal politics of Pennsylvania were remarkably smooth. Only in 1776, when traditional leaders were slow in deciding for independence, did a rival group of radical "independents," composed primarily of men not previously prominent politically, arise to seize control of Pennsylvania government. But this new group, David Hawke has argued in a recent assault upon the earlier interpretation of Lincoln, was not the mouthpiece of the unprivileged West (which, indeed, does not appear to have been the source of any mass discontent), nor even of the urban masses of Philadelphia, but was rather the political arm of a relatively small group of middle-class ideologues intent upon gaining independence and reconstructing the government of Pennsylvania to give the people a greater share in it. The trouble was that when they "gave the people democracy" in the constitution of 1776, "the people spurned the gift," still preferring "the elite to run their affairs."[60] Although the nature of the political struggles of the fifteen years after

---

[57] Ralph Ketcham, "Conscience, War, and Politics in Pennsylvania, 1755–1757," *William and Mary Quarterly*, 3d ser., 20 (1963): 416–39; John J. Zimmerman, "Benjamin Franklin and the Quaker Party, 1755–1756," ibid., 17 (1960): 291–313.

[58] See Sister Joan de Lourdes Leonard, "Elections in Colonial Pennsylvania," ibid., 11 (1954): 385–401; J. Philip Gleason, "A Scurrilous Colonial Election and Franklin's Reputation," ibid., 18 (1961): 68–84; and David L. Jacobson, "John Dickinson's Fight against Royal Government, 1764," ibid., 19 (1962): 64–85.

[59] William S. Hanna, *Benjamin Franklin and Pennsylvania Politics* (Stanford, Calif., 1964), quotation from 201.

[60] David Freeman Hawke, *In the Midst of a Revolution* (Philadelphia, 1963), quotation from 198.

1776 remains to be reexamined, Hawke's conclusions suggest that they may have been largely between rival political groups with opposing conceptions of the way the polity ought to be organized and may not, therefore, have represented any fundamental divisions within society.[61]

A still different variety of factionalism characterized the politics of New York. Leisler's Rebellion—in part a protest against the monopolization of office and economic resources by a small group surrounding the royal governor—and its ruthless suppression inaugurated a thirty-year-long feud between Leislerians and Anti-Leislerians in which the objective was not just political control of the New York government with the economic advantages that such control represented, but, as Lawrence H. Leder has stressed, the complete extinction of the opposition party. Although Robert Livingston and others helped arrange a political truce during the administration of Governor Robert Hunter between 1710 and 1719, which eventually resulted in the disappearance of the old parties,[62] new factions appeared in the 1720s and remained a constant on the political scene. For the most part loose and temporary alliances, these factions were based upon family rivalries, conflicting economic interests, ethnic and national differences, religious tensions, sectional antagonisms, personal ambition, and political alliances with the royal governors. The principals shifted sides with astonishing ease as their interests or inclinations decreed until the 1750s, when factions solidified "around the Livingston and De Lancey families, and it was their political rivalry which underlined the history of New York until the Revolution" and shaped New York's response to British measures between 1763 and 1776.[63]

The debate between the Livingston and De Lancey parties, like the debates between the amorphous factions that preceded them, usually centered upon bona fide issues, and the parties vied with each other for

---

[61] The analysis of these struggles in Charles Page Smith, *James Wilson, Founding Father, 1742–1798* (Chapel Hill, N.C., 1956), would seem to support this view.

[62] Lawrence H. Leder, *Robert Livingston, 1654–1728, and the Politics of Colonial New York* (Chapel Hill, N.C., 1961) and "Robert Livingston: A New View of New York Politics," *New York History* 40 (1959): 358–67.

[63] The best short descriptions of these shifting factions as well as the most thoughtful analyses of the nature of New York politics are two articles by Milton M. Klein, "Democracy and Politics," and "Politics and Personalities in Colonial New York," *New York History* 47 (1966): 3–16. Stanley Nider Katz also discusses the factionalism of the early 1730s in his edition of James Alexander, *A Brief Narrative of the Case and Trial of John Peter Zenger, Printer of the* New York Weekly Journal (Cambridge, Mass., 1963), esp. 2–7.

support from a wide electorate;[64] but at bottom this contest was primarily an "intra-class wrangle" between rival upper-class groups and never the struggle between aristocracy and democracy on which Becker had insisted. Far from being democratic upheavals, the small farmer and tenant uprisings that culminated in the "Great Rebellion of 1766," Milton M. Klein has argued, were essentially apolitical in character and concerned largely with such basic economic questions as "land-titles, rents, security of tenure, and . . . personal obligations to the manor lord."[65] Even the radical Sons of Liberty, who played so conspicuous a part in New York politics between 1768 and 1776, Roger Champagne has demonstrated, were largely under the control of the Livingston party and, although they held ideas with more radical implications than party leaders, had no democratic program of their own, being so loosely bound together as to be unable to play a significant role in the Livingston party's shaping of the new independent state government in 1776.[66]

Although the picture is far from complete, it can be safely inferred from this survey that every colony-state displayed a unique combination of characteristics that produced its own peculiar configuration of politics and that the old Progressive conception is either totally inapplicable or seriously distorting at every point for which there has been a detailed study. But the more important question is whether these seemingly disparate, contradictory, perpetually changing, and highly volatile political systems had enough in common to make it possible to construct an alternative framework of interpretation. Although there has been no systematic attempt to deal with this question, certain preliminary conclusions can be drawn on the basis of the findings of the specialized studies published thus far.

Politics everywhere was primarily elitist in nature. Public office—both appointive and elective—and political leadership were securely in the

---

[64] Klein, "Politics and Personalities," 9–10; William Livingston et al., *The Independent Reflector or Weekly Essays on Sundry Important Subjects More Particularly Adapted to the Province of New York*, ed. Milton M. Klein (Cambridge, Mass., 1963), 20–48; Lawrence H. Leder, "The New York Elections of 1769: An Assault on Privilege," *Mississippi Valley Historical Review* 49 (1963): 675–82; Varga, "Election Procedures and Practices."

[65] Klein, "Democracy and Politics," 231, 238–40; Roger Champagne, "Family Politics versus Constitutional Principles: The New York Assembly Elections of 1768 and 1769," *William and Mary Quarterly*, 3d ser., 20 (1963), 57–79; Don R. Gerlach, *Philip Schuyler and the American Revolution in New York 1733–1777* (Lincoln, Nebr., 1964), quotation from xvii.

[66] Champagne, "Family Politics versus Constitutional Principles," and "New York's Radicals and the Coming of Independence," *Journal of American History* 51 (1964): 21–40.

hands of upper-class groups, and, although there were occasional manifestations of social and economic discontent among the lower classes,
that discontent never resulted in widespread demands for basic changes
in the customary patterns of upper-class leadership. Political divisions
were not along class lines. Rather, they revolved around the ambitions
of rival factions, each faction drawing support from all segments of a
broad electorate. The chaotic and explosive nature of these divisions in
many places—the ease with which groups formed, dissolved, and reformed, leaders appeared "first on one side and then on another," and
issues precipitated "formations without apparent relationship to previous or succeeding groupings"[67]—has led Bernard Bailyn to conclude that
colonial politics was "a constant broil of petty factions struggling almost
formlessly, with little discipline or control, for the benefits of public authority." According to this characterization, the object of these "shifting,
transitory, competitive groupings"—the primary and impelling force behind colonial politics—was "the search for wealth, power, and prestige"
by the individuals who composed them.[68] "Uncommitted to any broad
principle or program," these factions were "preoccupied with immediate
concerns," "local questions and selfish interests." Ideas, theories, principles thus become "mere rhetoric," weapons in the factional armory employed to rationalize the conduct of the protagonists and to distract the
unwary among the electorate or the unaligned politicians from the "real"
objectives in dispute.[69]

   That "chaotic factionalism" is an appropriate rubric for large segments
of early American politics, that the competition for wealth, power, and
prestige was involved to some extent in almost every factional contest,
and that ideas were always closely related to the interests of the people
who used them seems beyond dispute, but this formulation, recently applied by Forrest MacDonald to the period between 1776 and 1789,[70] is

---

[67] Bernard Bailyn, "The Beekmans of New York: Trade, Politics, and Families," *William and Mary Quarterly*, 3d ser., 14 (1957): 601–2.

[68] Bernard Bailyn, ed., *Pamphlets of the American Revolution, 1750–1776*, vol. 1 (Cambridge, Mass., 1965), 1:91, 188–89, 191.

[69] See Lovejoy, *Rhode Island Politics*, 2–3; Hanna, *Benjamin Franklin*, ix; Gerlach, *Philip Schuyler*, xiv–xvii; and Klein, "Democracy and Politics," 238–40. The Introduction to his edition of the *Pamphlets of the American Revolution* indicates that Bailyn does not now hold this view of the role of ideas in early American politics, though it was implicit in much of his earlier work.

[70] Forrest MacDonald, *E Pluribus Unum: The Formation of the American Republic, 1776–1790* (Boston, 1965), and previously *We the People: The Economic Origins of the Constitution* (Chicago, 1958).

not free from objection. For one thing, it assumes, like the Progressive conception, an "extraordinary rationality in the political behavior of men," the ability of politicians not only to see "their interests clearly" but also "precisely how to go about securing them."[71] Second, it rests upon a blanket assumption—which is clearly not universally valid—that in politics, ideas are always subordinate to concrete and tangible factors. Third, it does not accurately describe all portions of early American political life. Some factional divisions were extraordinarily stable, and some political environments were free from factionalism altogether. Finally, unless it falls back upon the old Progressive formula of repression, manipulation, propaganda, and control, which posits a degree of efficiency and sophistication not easily associated with colonial and Revolutionary America, it does not by itself explain why the electorate tolerated such a patently irresponsible brand of politics. To remedy these objections it is necessary to turn to recent writings on the "political culture" of the colonies.

As here used, the term *political culture* applies to that intellectual and institutional inheritance which inevitably conditions, however slightly in many instances, *all*, even the most revolutionary and impulsive, political behavior. For early America the most visible elements of that culture— the formal concepts of political thought and the external forms of institutional development—have received a considerable amount of attention from historians during the past seventy-five years.[72] What until recently has been almost completely ignored, and what it now appears is vastly more important, is that elusive and shadowy cluster of assumptions, traditions, conventions, values, modes of expression, and habits of thought and belief that underlay those visible elements. Although the inquiry into this area has not yet proceeded very far, work already published has yielded some extremely important results.

The findings of one group of independent studies help to resolve a

---

[71] This comment was made recently by Cecelia M. Kenyon in "'An Economic Interpretation of the Constitution' after Fifty Years," 338.

[72] Among the most important recent studies in this category are Leonard W. Labaree, *Conservatism in Early American History* (New York, 1948); Max Savelle, *Seeds of Liberty: The Genesis of the American Mind* (New York, 1948); Clinton Rossiter, *Seedtime of the Republic: The Origin of the American Tradition of Political Liberty* (New York, 1953); Morgan and Morgan, *Stamp Act Crisis;* and Greene, *Quest for Power.*

problem that to the Progressive historians and the Browns was an in-comprehensible paradox: why, in the words of J. R. Pole, "the great mass of the common people might actually have given their consent to con-cepts of government" that by "systematically" excluding them "from the more responsible positions of political power" restricted "their own par-ticipation in ways completely at variance with the principles of modern democracy."[73] What these studies have found, through an intensive ex-amination and "imaginative reconstruction of the values and assump-tions" of early American political thought, is that colonial *and* Revolu-tionary society was essentially what Walter Bagehot called "a deferential society" that operated within an integrated structure of ideas that was fundamentally elitist in nature. That structure of ideas assumed, among other things, that government should be entrusted to men of merit; that merit was very often, though by no means always, associated with wealth and social position; that men of merit were obliged to use their talents for the benefit of the public; and that deference to them was the implicit duty of the rest of society. All society was therefore divided among the rulers and the ruled, and the rulers, including the representa-tives of the people, were not the tools of the people but their political superiors. "The mass of the people," Richard Buel, Jr., has argued in the most thorough exposition of these ideas, thus "elected representatives not to order them around like lackeys to do the people's bidding, but to reap benefit from the distinguished abilities of the few upon which the safety of society might in large measure depend" and to utilize the "polit-ical expertise of the realm in the people's behalf."[74]

Another group of studies has suggested that more than the simple pursuit of wealth, power, and prestige may have been involved in the factional struggles of colonial politics. Works by Perry Miller, Edmund S. Morgan, George Lee Haskins, and others on the Puritans[75] and by

---

[73] Pole, "Historians and Early American Democracy," 626–46, quotations from 628, 641.

[74] Richard Buel, Jr., "Democracy and the American Revolution: A Frame of Reference," *William and Mary Quarterly,* 3d ser., 21 (1964): 165–90, quotations from 178, 188. See also Pole, "Historians and Early American Democracy," 629, for the phrase from Bage-hot. The importance of these ideas in determining political behavior is indicated by McCormick, *Experiment in Independence,* 102; Labaree, *Partisans and Patriots,* 14–15; and my own investigation of Virginia politics immediately before the Declaration of In-dependence.

[75] Especially Perry Miller, *The New England Mind: The Seventeenth Century* (Cambridge, Mass., 1939); Morgan, *Puritan Dilemma;* and Haskins, *Law and Authority in Early Mas-sachusetts.*

Frederick B. Tolles on the Quakers[76] have indicated how important the special religious, social, and political ideas of each were in shaping the political behavior of the leaders of early Massachusetts Bay and Pennsylvania. Of vastly more general influence appears to have been the group of ideas analyzed by Z. S. Fink and Caroline Robbins[77] and called by J. G. A. Pocock the "Country ideology."

This ideology, which appeared with minor variations and modifications in all parts of the British political world during the seventeenth and eighteenth centuries, shared certain dominant assumptions about human nature and the function and process of government: that men were imperfect creatures, perpetually self-deluded, enslaved by their passions, vanities, and interests, confined in their vision and understanding, and incapable of exercising power over one another without abusing it; that government and constitutions existed to restrain the vicious tendencies of man by checking them against one another; that to fulfill that function, each of the elements in the polity had to be balanced against the others in such a way as to prevent any one of them from gaining ascendancy over the rest; and that history was the record of a continual struggle between liberty and power, purity and corruption.

A mixed constitution was the device by which this delicate balance was to be achieved, but the tendency of men in power, especially men connected with the administration (the court), to seek to increase that power by corrupting Parliament—the voice of the men of independent property (the country)—was so great that the country members in Parliament had to keep a wary eye on the court to see that it did not succeed in throwing the constitution out of balance or overturning it altogether and establishing an unrestrained executive tyranny that would make free with the liberties and property of the citizenry. It was essential, therefore, both that every seeming abuse of ministerial power be immediately detected and rooted out of the polity and that every representative of the country be constantly on guard lest he somehow be seduced into the conspiracy of power and thereby betray his country and lose his own

---

[76] Tolles, *Meeting House and Counting House* and *James Logan.*

[77] Z. S. Fink, *The Classical Republicans: An Essay in the Recovery of a Pattern of Thought in Seventeenth-Century England* (Evanston, Ill., 1945); Caroline Robbins, *The Eighteenth-Century Commonwealthman: Studies in the Transmission, Development, and Circumstances of English Liberal Thought from the Restoration of Charles II until the War with the Thirteen Colonies* (Cambridge, Mass., 1959).

personal independence, which was regarded as the basis of "all human excellence."[78] This fetish of independence led to the condemnation of *parties*, which perforce were the instruments of *partial* men, and to the idealization of the virtuous patriot, the man of preeminent virtue whose behavior was determined not by self-interest, not by the narrow interests of some group or region with which he was associated, but by nothing less than the welfare of the entire country.[79]

The state of knowledge is still too imperfect for historians to be able to assess with any certainty the importance of the country ideology in giving shape and coherence to the configuration of early American politics. That all of its components including its several stock personae—the court villain, dependent court lackey, independent country patriot—as well as its conventions of behavior, its rhetoric, and its patterns and categories of thought were transferred in toto to the colonies is clear enough from the frequent application of the terms *court* and *country* to colonial politics, the oft-expressed dread of arbitrary power and aversion to parties, the extent to which those components infused the thought and informed the behavior of individuals,[80] the conscious cultivation of

---

[78] J. G. A. Pocock, "Machiavelli, Harrington, and English Political Ideologies in the Eighteenth Century," *William and Mary Quarterly*, 3d ser., 22 (1965): 547–83, esp. 563–72. The court-country dichotomy as it was expressed in British politics after 1714 is discussed by Archibald S. Foord, *His Majesty's Opposition, 1714–1830* (Oxford, 1964). The essential components of the mid-eighteenth-century version of the country ideology as it had developed in the colonies are discussed by Buel, "Democracy and the American Revolution"; Bailyn, *Pamphlets of the American Revolution*, 38–59; and H. Trevor Colbourn, *The Lamp of Experience: Whig History and the Intellectual Origins of the American Revolution* (Chapel Hill, N.C., 1965).

[79] There is no adequate modern investigation of this particular political motif. The classic expression of it in eighteenth-century Britain was Henry St. John, Viscount Bolingbroke, *A Dissertation upon Parties* (The Hague, 1734), and *Letters on the Spirit of Patriotism: On the Idea of a Patriot King; and On the State of Parties, at the Accession of King George the First* (London, 1749), both written during the author's "country" period.

[80] In this connection, see Gerald Stourzh, "Reason and Power in Benjamin Franklin's Political Thought," *American Political Science Review* 47 (1953): 1092–1115, and *Benjamin Franklin and American Foreign Policy* (Chicago, 1954); Paul W. Connor, *Poor Richard's Politicks: Benjamin Franklin and His New American Order* (New York, 1965); Jack P. Greene, ed., *The Diary of Colonel Landon Carter of Sabine Hall, 1752–1778*, 2 vols. (Charlottesville, Va., 1965), 1:28–48; Zolta'n Haraszti, *John Adams and the Prophets of Progress* (Cambridge, Mass., 1952); John R. Howe, Jr., *The Changing Political Thought of John Adams* (Princeton, N.J., 1966); Edward Handler, *America and Europe in the Political Thought of John Adams* (Cambridge, Mass., 1964); Douglass, *Rebels and Democrats*; Arthur O. Lovejoy, *Reflections of Human Nature* (Baltimore, 1961), 37–65; Cecelia

those components by colonial leaders through the middle decades of the eighteenth century, and the more or less continuous efforts of the lower houses of assembly to check the prerogative and undermine executive authority—attempts which persisted both because and in spite of the factional disputes and internal divisions in colonial politics and resulted in a roughly uniform pattern of constitutional development in all of the colonies.[81]

But it is not enough to know that the country ideology was an integral part of early American politics. We need to know as well the precise nature of its role and its relationship to other elements of political life. That role and that relationship will, of course, be different for every situation, and any generalization will therefore have to await a series of detailed investigations similar to the one conducted by Bernard Bailyn for the pre-Revolutionary debate. But Bailyn's study suggests what those answers may be. He finds that ideas expressed by Americans in the debate, many of which were descended directly and in a fairly undiluted form from the country ideology, had a dual role.

First of all they were *explanatory*, both in the sense that they enabled the principals to explain to themselves and the world what they were about and to see themselves in some kind of cosmic, or at least historical, perspective, and in the sense that they revealed "not merely positions taken but the reasons why positions were taken." Only through these ideas, only through the beliefs, attitudes, assumptions, motivations, and professed goals that "lay behind the manifest events of the time," he insists, can the "contemporary meaning" of the Revolution be understood. However much those ideas may have distorted underlying realities, they were always thought by the participants to be true and were, therefore, as Gordon S. Wood has phrased it, "psychologically true." Because these ideas—these inherited values and habits of thought—also exerted a powerful influence upon the way Americans perceived reality, shaping into predictable and familiar patterns their interpretations of

---

M. Kenyon, "Men of Little Faith: The Anti-Federalists on the Nature of Representative Government," *William and Mary Quarterly*, 3d ser., 12 (1955): 3–43; and Adrienne Koch, *Power, Morals, and the Founding Fathers: Essays in the Interpretation of the American Enlightenment* (Ithaca, N.Y., 1961).

[81] See my *Quest for Power*, and my review of F. G. Spurdle, *Early West Indian Government: Showing the Progress of Government in Barbados, Jamaica, and the Leeward Islands, 1660–1683* (Palmerston North, N.Z., 1963), in *William and Mary Quarterly*, 3d ser., 22 (1965): 146–49; and Murrin, "Myths of Colonial Democracy and Royal Decline," 61–66.

and response to metropolitan actions, they were also in an important and fundamental sense *determinative.*[82]

Ideas, then, in all of their several forms, operate to impede men's perception of reality at the same time that they give it shape and meaning, and in some situations they may even become as real as the more tangible elements of political life and exercise greater causative power than the manifest events or the underlying interests or ambitions they were first called into the political arena to serve.

Despite the impressive accomplishments of the past three decades, our knowledge is still too fragmentary and the character of the subject too complex to permit any firm or easy generalizations about the nature of early American politics. Out of the overwhelming tangle of interests, ideas, and ambitions that seem, at least on the surface, to make colonial politics incomprehensible, however, emerge certain basic regularities that make it possible to establish at least a rough typology of political forms into which, after the elimination of certain individual variants, most pre-1776 colonial political activity can be fitted.[83] On the basis of present knowledge, this typology would seem to require at least four distinct, if also overlapping, and not necessarily sequential classifications.

For the first, which is probably also the most common, we can use Bailyn's term, *chaotic factionalism.* It involved a ruthless competition for dominance, power, and economic advantage among rival groups of leading men, groups which were largely ad hoc and impermanent, formed as temporary alliances on specific occasions, then dissolving as quickly as they appeared only to have the individuals who had composed them regroup in different combinations in response to later events. This form seems to have been typical of Virginia before 1660, Massachusetts from 1684 to 1741, New York from 1720 to 1755, Pennsylvania from 1680 to 1720, Maryland before 1689, South Carolina and New Hampshire before 1730, and North Carolina until 1745. To some extent, it was present

---

[82] Bailyn, *Pamphlets of the American Revolution*, 1–202, esp. 8, 20, 60; Wood, "Rhetoric and Reality in the American Revolution," *William and Mary Quarterly,* 3d ser., 23 (1966): 31.

[83] This is not to suggest that those variants are not of enormous importance but only that their significance will appear more clearly when they are seen in relationship to the more generalized features of colonial political development.

in every classification, but it was the dominant characteristic only in the first.

The second type may be called *stable factionalism.* It was distinguished by the emergence of two semipermanent opposing interest groups with relatively stable memberships and representing explicit regional—perhaps a more precise and appropriate term than sectional—economic, religious, or kinship rivalries (occasionally in combination) and, in some cases, standing for rather well-defined sets of principles and beliefs. This type appears to have predominated in Massachusetts from 1760 to 1776, Rhode Island and Connecticut after 1750, New Hampshire in the 1730s and 1740s, New York from 1690 to 1720 and again from 1755 to 1776, in New Jersey, Maryland, and perhaps Delaware through most of the eighteenth century, in Pennsylvania from 1735 to 1776, in North Carolina in the 1740s and 1750s, and in South Carolina from 1720 to 1740.

The third classification may perhaps best be described as *domination by a single, unified group.* In this type of politics all of the avenues to political power and most of the primary sources of wealth were monopolized by a dominant elite bound together by common economic interests, religious beliefs, patronage and kinship ties, or some combination of these factors. In this system faction was submerged by some form of repression, manipulation, or corruption—in the "country" sense of the term—of potential leaders of opposition elements. Massachusetts Bay before 1684 and again from 1741 to 1760, New York before Leisler's Rebellion, Virginia between 1660 and 1720, and New Hampshire and Nova Scotia after 1750 are examples of this type.

The fourth and rarest form was almost wholly *faction free with a maximum dispersal of political opportunity within the dominant group* composed of the elite and potential members of the elite. This type, which appears to have existed over a long period only in Virginia after 1720 and South Carolina after 1740, depended upon a homogeneity of economic interests among all regions and all social groups, a high degree of social integration, and a community of political leaders so large as to make it impossible for any single group to monopolize political power. It was, in a real sense, the epitome of the country ideal of a government composed of independent men and, at least in Virginia, was in part the result of the conscious cultivation of that ideal by the leaders of the polity.

Whatever its defects, however much it stands in need of refinement, clarification, modification, and elaboration, this typology may by providing a general frame of reference at least make it easier to discuss early American politics. Hopefully, it may also be a first step toward the development of new, less abstract categories which will more accurately reflect the political life they seek to describe. Perhaps even, it will serve as a foundation for achieving some understanding of the relationship between these early political forms and the more sophisticated party structure that emerged in the United States after 1790.

In response to an invitation from Ray A. Billington to contribute an essay on the historiography of early American politics to the festschrift of John Edwin Pomfret, who, as director of the Henry E. Huntington Library, had befriended me while I was a fellow at that institution in the summer of 1962, I wrote this chapter in the fall of 1965 during my first and, as it turned out, my only semester of active teaching at the University of Michigan. It is reprinted with permission and with minor verbal changes from Ray A. Billington, ed., *The Reinterpretation of Early American History* (San Marino, Calif.: The Henry E. Huntington Library, 1966), 151–84.

—Six—

The American Colonies during the First Half of the Eighteenth Century

RICHARD HOFSTADTER'S *America at 1750: A Social Portrait* is a badly needed book. Traditionally, American historians have concerned themselves largely with the description and exploration of great public events. The implications of this orientation for our understanding of early American history have been profound. For one thing, it has meant that a disproportionate amount of scholarly attention has been focused upon the two great events at either end of the colonial period: the settlement of the colonies during the seventeenth century and the origins and development of the American Revolution after 1760. It has also been in large part responsibile for the corresponding neglect of the long and relatively uneventful, if scarcely unimportant, years between the Glorious Revolution of 1689 and the end of the Seven Years' War in 1763, years during which each of the colonies seemed to settle down into a period of relatively self-contained development and during which, for the colonies as a whole, there was little common public history with the exception of the four intercolonial wars and the momentous spiritual explosion known as the Great Awakening.

In the past, concern with these years has usually centered upon either the description of these important events or the exploration of some prominent general themes—the development of representative political institutions or of a common political culture—that seemed to have a direct bearing upon the coming of the American Revolution. As American historians have to some extent moved away from event-oriented history over the past generation and especially since 1960, an increasing number of scholars have produced a growing collection of monographs on many specific aspects of colonial life during these neglected years. But their studies have contributed almost as much to confuse us about the general picture as to enlighten us about detail. For what they have re-

vealed is a tangle of seemingly discrete and idiosyncratic local developments and characteristics that have thus far largely defied systematic
classification and comparison. The result is that we still do not have any
firm grasp upon the period, we still do not have any clear sense of what
either the general outline or the underlying themes that presumably gave
it some unity and coherence may be or whether it constituted a single,
relatively undifferentiated, unit of development or was rent by fundamental discontinuities.

This gracefully written and penetrating volume goes further toward
remedying this deficiency than any previous book. Not intended as a
separate study, it was to be only the first section of an ambitious "three-
volume history of American political culture from 1750 to the recent
past," a *"general interpretive synthesis"* that would *"cull out . . . from the
extraordinary mass of significant historical research . . . produced in our
time"* that which was *"sound and translatable into broad public terms."* At
the author's tragic and untimely death in October 1970, however, not
even this first section had been completed. A chapter on colonial elites
was only partially written and "too fragmentary for publication," his
widow tells us, and two important sections which the author "had
planned, one on colonial politics, the other on imperial wars, had not
even been started."[1]

But the eight chapters that were completed along with a partially finished introduction constitute an important work in their own right. Like
all of Hofstadter's earlier books and essays, they combine a superb mastery of secondary materials and an extraordinary talent for characterization, distillation, and synthesis with a remarkable capacity to ferret out
and give clear verbal expression to what is most meaningful and general
in the subject. As the subtitle suggests, the volume purports to be no
more than a "portrait" of the society of the continental colonies in 1750.
But it is not simply a still life. Indeed, it is a bold and analytic exploration of the underlying conditions and guiding themes of American life
during the important formative years of the early eighteenth century.

Some of the most prominent themes developed by Hofstadter are, un-
surprisingly, neither unfamiliar nor peculiar to the period of colonial history he is considering. Thus, like many earlier scholars, he is especially
impressed with "the inability of the English political [and social] order
to reproduce itself effectively in the New World." Colonial society, he
argues, was essentially "a kind of distillation of certain aspects of the
new European world" that had taken shape since the end of the Middle

---

[1] Richard Hofstadter, *America at 1750: A Social Portrait* (New York, 1971), vii–x.

Ages, "a scene in which the basic institutions of Old World society were represented by shadowy substitutes." With no court, no nobility, an extremely weak and in some colonies nonexistent religious establishment without "a deeply rooted place in the texture of society," no ancient universities, and no "magnificent estates manned by scores of servants and capable of feeding scores of brilliant and fashionable guests," colonial society was "a preponderantly middle-class world" with "the simpler agencies of the middle class . . . in strong evidence: the little churches of the dissenting sects, the taverns . . . , the societies for self-improvement and 'philosophical' inquiry, the increasingly eclectic little colleges; the contumacious newspapers, the county court houses and town halls, the how-to-do books, the *Poor Richard's Almanack*." Even the aristocracy, which "*constituted* itself out of the business class," was a pale imitation of the English model. It had "only a slender sense of the personal prerogative, the code of honor, or the grand extravagance in life-style that goes with hereditary aristocracy." Instead, it manifested "the disciplined ethic of work, the individual assertiveness, the progressive outlook, the preference for dissenting religions, and the calculating and materialistic way of life associated with the middle class."[2]

Two related and equally familiar themes developed by Hofstadter are the erosion of traditional European attitudes toward authority in the colonies and the emergence of a psychology of accommodation out of the pressures created by the increasingly pluralistic character of the population, especially after 1700. Speculating that migration itself may have been a selective process in which only "the most venturesome or visionary, the most impatient and restive under authority, the most easily alienated, the most desperate and cranky" participated, Hofstadter suggests that the initial population of the colonies brought with it "a strong bias toward dislike of authority" that was subsequently nurtured by the circumstances of life in America. Most free men and even some former servants quickly became independent proprietors who were beholden to no one except themselves and their families for their survival, while the labor of those free men who were not was in so much demand that they were at once free from both "dire need" and any "spirit of subservience."[3]

By "presenting a choice between religious styles, church affiliations, and pastors," the Great Awakening further contributed to undermine traditional authority even in the religious world by heightening "the sense that people, as individuals, had the power to act and decide." Simi-

---

[2] Ibid., xii, 133–34, 138, 204.

[3] Ibid., 32, 141.

larly, the intermingling of peoples of divergent cultural and national backgrounds and competing religious persuasions slowly edged people toward a habit of accommodation and compromise. Colonial society remained basically English even after the great immigration of non-English groups after 1713 and became even more thoroughly Protestant as a result of the Great Awakening. But the result of both experiences, Hofstadter argues, was an increasing capacity for the toleration and acceptance of ethnic, cultural, and religious diversity.[4]

If ethnic and religious diversification was a distinguishing and extremely important theme of the period after 1700, it was probably not the most significant or pervasive one. As Hofstadter emphasizes, "growth—growth consistently sustained and eagerly welcomed, growth as a source of grand imperial hopes and calculating private speculation . . . was the outstandingly visible fact of mid-eighteenth century life in the American colonies"—and, one might add, had been so since the negotiation of peace at Utrecht in 1713.[5] Hofstadter bases this observation exclusively upon the broad geographical dispersion and the rapid and previously unparalleled increase in the colonial population, which multiplied six times between 1700 and 1760.

The case could have been made much stronger—and the character of this period of colonial development brought more clearly into focus—had Hofstadter used economic indices as well. For, although he has provided excellent characterizations of the economic life of six major economic areas—the five substantial seaboard cities and the varied rural societies of the New England villages, Hudson River estates, Chesapeake society, South Carolina planting society, and the backcountry—he has not made any attempt to describe the phenomenal economic, as distinct from demographic, growth of the colonies between 1700 and 1760, perhaps a more serious omission than politics in a social portrait of this particular period. Extant data are not nearly so complete as we would like, and they are only just now being systematically compiled and analyzed. What is already available makes it fairly clear, however, that the economy, like the population, was growing at an extraordinary rate. During the six decades after 1700, the volume of agricultural production increased at least six times, the amount of overseas exports about four times, and the value of imports from Britain alone (which is also a rough indicator of the rise in colonial buying power) nearly seven times.

Together with the population figures cited by Hofstadter, these data

---

[4] Ibid., 291.

[5] Ibid., 3.

vividly indicate the degree to which growth, extraordinary rapid and extensive economic as well as demographic growth, was a fundamental—and probably the most decisive single—characteristic of the colonial experience during the first half of the eighteenth century. By transforming the colonies from relatively slowly growing entities with, at best, a mildly promising social and economic future in 1700, into dynamic units, it put the colonies, for the first time, upon a solid social and economic base, opened up previously unimagined possibilities for still greater expansion and development, and significantly enlarged the range and level of colonial aspirations.

One of the most widespread, if subtle, side effects of this growth was to push the colonists toward an even greater degree of secularism. Both because the New England Puritans left behind such a wealth of data and because their experiment was so bold in its design and remains so fascinating in detail, they have received a disproportionate amount of emphasis from colonial historians. Perhaps because he was not a specialist on the colonial period, Hofstadter has managed to transcend the limitations of the Puritan perspective. More clearly than most colonialists, he has perceived that "the center of gravity of the colonial population" lay not in New England but in the Chesapeake, "the mainland provinces most prized in the mother country," and "that the majority of white colonials may have come for very mundane reasons—not to reach the glories of the other world but to relieve the hardships of this." "With our eyes too firmly fixed on the Puritans," he writes, we have failed "to see that hundreds of thousands of immigrants were rounded up and persuaded to come to America by men moved by secular motives of empire and profit; and that so many of them came without firm religious attachments (or at least without seeking to reproduce them here) that the American colonies at the end of the eighteenth century were perhaps the most unchurched regions in all Christendom. Religious tolerance, and after it religious liberty, were the creations of a jumble of faiths too complex to force into any mold, and of a rising secularism too urbane to care to try."[6]

In three excellent chapters, which together constitute what is perhaps the best available short description of mid-eighteenth-century colonial religious life, Hofstadter makes clear the extent to which "the profit motive undermined the desire to impose a creed," while "prosperity and materialism" slowly but inexorably weakened the foundations even of Puritanism. Given the power of the psychological forces unleashed by

---

[6] Ibid., xv–xvi, 157, 180–81.

the great economic growth, he suggests, "what is impressive is not that the pristine Puritan way finally faded, but that it survived so long and left so lasting an imprint upon the New England mind and character." This is not to say that the colonists ever completely adjusted to their growing prosperity. As Hofstadter implies, the Great Awakening, which he accurately sees as part of a wider transatlantic "Second Reformation," was at least in part a response to the "greater secularism" and, as I have suggested elsewhere, to the rising levels of guilt that prosperity helped to produce.[7]

If the remarkable economic growth of the colonies had serious psychological costs, it also to a very great extent was built upon enormous human misery. In three chapters Hofstadter offers brilliant summaries of our present and, in several respects, extremely inadequate knowledge of the institutions of servitude and slavery. His sensitivity to "the anguish of the early American experience" as represented in the lives of the servants and slaves could scarcely be more acute. He points out how few servants (one out of ten) achieved even a "tolerable comfort" and "the measure to which the sadness that is natural to life was overwhelmed in the condition of servitude by the stark miseries that seemed all too natural to the history of the poor."[8]

For the thousands of Africans who had been forcibly torn from their homelands, the experience was far more shattering. It tended both "to reduce their African identity to the withered husks of dead memories" and, Hofstadter believes, to deprive them of virtually every vestige of their African heritage. And it was not only the slaves who lost in this repressive "system of power." Slavery dehumanized white society just as the slave trade brutalized white captains and crews, and whites had to learn to live with the anxieties and fears that derived from the usually remote but always present possibility of servile insurrection.[9]

A growing tendency toward *intensive* social and economic development in older settled areas, especially after the 1730s, provides a final and, with the exception of the great *extensive* growth of the colonies, perhaps the most basic theme of the eighteenth-century colonial experience. Perhaps because he was unable to complete his chapter on colonial elites, Hofstadter touched upon but did not explicitly formulate or ade-

---

[7] Ibid., 188, 209–10, 218. See Jack P. Greene, "Search for Identity: A Consideration of Selected Patterns of Social Response in Eighteenth-Century America," *Journal of Social History* 3 (1969–70): 183–200.

[8] Hofstadter, *America at 1750*, 64–65.

[9] Ibid., 90, 119.

quately develop this theme. It was manifest in several tendencies he describes: the growing diversity in population and religion, the emergence of some degree of exclusiveness among the urban elite, and the expansion of higher education. But it was even more powerfully evident in the increasing social differentiation that had accompanied the growing social stratification and the rising specialization in overall occupational structure as well as in business, the trades, the professions, and perhaps even commercial farming. And it was also apparent in a strong movement toward social consolidation spearheaded by the emergent economic elites. At midcentury those elites everywhere were seeking, with considerable success, to establish their political, social, and cultural predominance over the societies of the colonies. As improving communications, more extensive economic ties, and, especially during the last two intercolonial wars, greater military and political cooperation drew them ever more closely into the ambit of British culture, they were also endeavoring, with equally positive results, to reproduce the society and culture of Britain in—that is, to anglicize—the colonies.

Although it is regrettable that Hofstader's inability to complete his chapter on colonial elites prevented him from dealing fully with this important theme, the absence of the sections on politics and the imperial wars may be less disadvantageous. Because he was such an astute student of political history, one of course regrets that he was unable to finish these sections. By omitting any consideration of politics, however, this volume manages perhaps to achieve a much sharper and probably only a somewhat exaggerated sense of the profound importance of demographic, economic, social, and religious developments and the relative unimportance of politics in shaping the lives of the colonists. This achievement makes the volume the most penetrating and plausible characterization of the early eighteenth-century colonial experience we have had to date.

Written in the winter of 1972–73 in response to an invitation from Stanley Kutler to contribute a review essay to the first number of his new journal, *Reviews in American History*, this chapter is reprinted with permission and with minor verbal changes and the addition of footnotes to quotations from *Reviews in American History* 1 (1973): 69–75.

Seven

The Development of Early American Culture

BEFORE 1960, when Bernard Bailyn published his pathbreaking essay *Education in the Forming of American Society,* historians of education concerned themselves almost exclusively with the history of formal pedagogy, institutions of learning, and concepts of education. Bailyn's compelling plea for a new approach to the subject based upon a broad definition of education as nothing less than "the entire process by which a culture transmits itself across the generations" has, however, stimulated a major reconception of the field.[1] Historians of education have subsequently pressed their inquiries well beyond the traditional confines of their discipline and have concerned themselves with the whole range of formal and informal institutions that perform educative functions in society, the relationship between those institutions and the society in which they exist, and the content and nature of the intellectual traditions and value systems transmitted through them.

Lawrence A. Cremin's rich and wide-ranging *American Education: The Colonial Experience, 1607–1783* is an admirable example of the work now being done within this expanded conception. Cremin does not employ quite so inclusive a definition of the subject as Bailyn recommended. But his conception of education "as the deliberate, systematic, and sustained effort to transmit or evoke knowledge, attitudes, values, skills, and sensibilities" is broad enough to have enabled him to produce the most comprehensive study ever published of seventeenth- and eighteenth-century Anglo-American culture.[2] Indeed, although the volume contains a number of specific new conclusions, it is most remarkable

---

[1] Bernard Bailyn, *Education in the Forming of American Society: Needs and Opportunities for Study* (Chapel Hill, N.C., 1960), 14.

[2] Lawrence A. Cremin, *American Education: The Colonial Experience, 1607–1783* (New York, 1970), xiii.

for its scope and for the author's impressive mastery of a vast and intricate subject.

Sponsored by the American Historical Association and the United States Office of Education and supported by the Carnegie Corporation of New York, this volume is the first of a projected three-volume history of American education. It is divided into two parts. The first part provides a full and succinct treatment of the intellectual heritage and educational institutions the colonists brought with them from England and describes the colonists' selective utilization of that inheritance in the period down to 1689. The second discusses the continuing flow of ideas and institutions from England and increasingly also from Scotland; the impact of growing religious diversity, material and demographic expansion, and the dispersion of political authority upon the traditional concepts and agencies of education; and the resulting "emergence of characteristically American modes of education in the provincial era" from 1689 to 1783.[3]

Cremin finds that the nature of education in these two periods differed markedly. During the seventeenth century colonial concepts of education were largely traditional and almost wholly derivative from England. Cremin's description of the rich intellectual heritage upon which the colonists drew, which is easily the most systematic and concise treatment of that subject presently in print, is organized around a consideration of the major books available to the colonists and, especially, of the popular handbooks of piety and civility and the extensive literature on the character of the learned man and of learning itself. Cremin is particularly careful to point out the extraordinary diversity and richness of this inheritance. But, he argues in an important insight, its many strands were sufficiently similar in content and orientation to comprise a kind of "Anglo-American *paidea*," a vision, common to Englishmen and colonists in both Virginia and New England, of what constituted the good life and of the modes through which that vision was to be transmitted to the young.[4]

In their advocacy of a kind of easy pragmatism in which the chief life goal was "to get ahead in a troubled world," some writers, like Francis Osborne, spoke with particular force to individuals "seeking to rise in the relatively fluid social structure of the New World."[5] But the primary

---

[3] Ibid., 266.

[4] Ibid., 42.

[5] Ibid., 75–76.

emphasis that ran through all of this literature and was shared by Anglican and Puritan alike was upon the role of education in contributing to
the preservation of order, to "the maintenance of personal, doctrinal,
and social stability" and the "network of mutual obligations and responsibilities that holds a Christian society together."[6] Education was the
central means through which man might someday establish his mastery
over both his environment and himself and the chief agency for the individual attainment of wisdom and virtue, the only true measures of
personal achievement; and it was the duty of every individual to use
his learning not merely for personal advancement but for social service.
Increasingly, also, there emerged the convictions that education should
be more widely available and that it should function as an agency for
personal advancement and a confirmation of personal merit rather than
a mere recognition of social status—convictions that spoke with special
relevance to upwardly mobile people in the New World.

In England a complex of institutions—churches, schools, colleges, and
communities—shared responsibility for education with the family, and
the author describes in detail the internal structure, character, and educational role of the many varieties of each of those institutions. Though
this entire complex of institutions was brought over to the colonies,
it was transferred in a vastly simplified form. Such new and relatively
simple societies could not support such an elaborate institutional structure. A general blurring of distinctions and overlapping of functions was
accompanied by an erosion of the traditional authority of many institutions and a corresponding decline in standards, especially in professional training.

An even more important result of this process of social simplification,
the author argues in challenging earlier interpretations, was the shift of
the balance of educational responsibility to the family. The church and,
in New England, the community continued to play a large part; there
were more schools outside New England than it has usually been supposed; and Harvard College was an institution of surprisingly high quality. But the relative weakness of these supportive institutions, especially
outside New England, meant that the family had to assume a greatly
expanded role, and it rapidly became "the critical agency for institution-
alizing change—for nurturing the versatility, the flexibility, and the
pragmatism so vital to the successful planting and modification of
metropolitan institutions."[7]

---

[6] Ibid., 46–47.

[7] Ibid., 137.

Symbolized by the writings of Newton and Locke, the intellectual up-heavals surrounding the Glorious Revolution of 1689, the author argues, marked a "watershed between an overwhelmingly derivative colonial culture of the seventeenth century and an increasingly creative provincial culture of the eighteenth."[8] Over the following century the relative harmony of ideas that had characterized the earlier period gave way to an ever-increasing diversity that was manifest in every area of colonial life. Educational goals became less traditional and more utilitarian; the content and orientation of education became less religious and more secular. As the colonies grew in size and material resources, moreover, a process of social "redifferentiation" took place; the colonies began to replicate the more complicated educational structure of England; and the colonial educational system became more and more complex. The "stabilization of community life in the older settlements, coupled with the growing prevalence of churches, schools, and colleges, led to a gradual easing of the formal burdens" that had earlier devolved upon the family, and the colonies developed a variety of "autochthonous" (indigenous) concepts, practices, and institutions that were more appropriate than their English equivalents to conditions of life in America.[9]

As the colonists were drawn ever closer to one another and to the metropolis through an expanding commerce and improved communications during the eighteenth century, the localism of the seventeenth century gave way to a new cosmopolitanism, and the intellectual interaction between metropolis and colonies became less of a one-way process and more of a mutual exchange. An increasing emphasis upon the practical application of learning and upon learning as a vehicle for self-improvement made the utilitarian writings of men such as Daniel Defoe, Richard Steele, and, later, the thinkers of the Scottish Enlightenment especially congenial to the colonists. This emphasis, along with the growth of denominationalism in religion and growing interest in public affairs, fostered a "general expansion of schooling," while high levels of literacy, running, the author argues, from 70 to 100 percent of adult males all over the colonies—in Virginia, Pennsylvania, and New York, as well as in New England—were reflected in rising productivity, increasing technical skills, and a growing political sophistication among the citizenry at large. Stimulated by a rapid increase in the amount of accessible reading matter, this new sophistication encouraged broad participation in politics and constituted an important precondition for the American Rev-

[8] Ibid., 253.
[9] Ibid., 226, 485, 519.

olution. By the end of the "provincial era" in 1783, Americans had thus experienced a rapid development of "human capital," and certain fundamental characteristics of American education were already well developed: the prevalence and accessibility of schooling, the diversity of substance and modes of available education, and the popularization of control of educational institutions at all levels.[10]

Precisely because the author has given us so much, it is disappointing that he did not use his rich materials as the basis for working out a new framework for the interpretation of colonial culture and a less conventional and more refined scheme of periodization. Instead, he has relied upon the traditional framework according to which the transplantation of metropolitan culture was quickly followed by its transformation and eventual Americanization, and the proper focus of attention is upon the emergence of autochthonous (that is, American) values and institutions.

Such a framework is probably suitable for treating seventeenth- and perhaps even very early eighteenth-century developments in most of the colonies. But a considerable amount of evidence presented in the second part of Cremin's work strongly suggests that it may distort in serious and fundamental ways our understanding of colonial development through the middle decades of the eighteenth century. The increasing differentiation of colonial society may have resulted during the half century before the Revolution in a growing, rather than a lessening, correspondence between colonial and metropolitan culture, while the increasing economic, intellectual, social, political, and religious ties between Britain and the colonies over the same period may have accelerated an already strong movement toward anglicization in the colonies to such a degree as to cause many colonials to regard autochthonous developments as evidence of colonial cultural inferiority and to prevent the full legitimation of those developments until after the Revolution had produced a revulsion against all things British.

The important points are, of course, that before the Revolution the pressures toward anglicization in some segments of colonial culture may have been quite as important as those toward Americanization, and that by focusing on the latter, one will almost certainly tend to underestimate the strength of the former. If these suggestions turn out to be plausible, it is clear that we will need a more refined conceptual framework that, proceeding from a recognition that colonial cultural development was not entirely a linear process, will take as its central focus the tension between the pull of metropolitan culture and the transforming power of

---

[10] Ibid., 545, 551, 553.

the American environment; that will not treat the whole period from 1689 to 1783 as a single, undifferentiated unit; and that will take special care to distinguish between developments that occurred before and during the Revolution.

The above reservation notwithstanding, this tightly integrated and lucidly written volume is a major work of synthesis and analysis and a reliable guide to the main lines of colonial cultural development. It will also be a necessary starting point for all subsequent studies of the first two centuries of American education.

Perhaps because it was late, the *New York Times Book Review,* for which this chapter was originally written, did not print it, which left it free to be published in *Reviews in American History* after Stanley Kutler had gotten an unsatisfactory essay on Cremin's book from another reviewer. It is reprinted with permission and with minor verbal changes and the addition of citations to quotations from *Reviews in American History* 1 (1973): 183–87.

—EIGHT—

Autonomy and Stability:
New England and the British Colonial Experience in Early Modern America

EXCEPT FOR Renaissance Florence, pre–Civil War England, and Revolutionary France, colonial New England has perhaps received more historical attention than any other segment of the early modern world. In a continuing quest for understanding the nature and meaning of the New England experience and its relationship to the larger themes of American development, scholars in previous generations have focused upon three main problems: the character and evolution of New England Puritanism, the nature of the New England town, and the contribution of the region to the American Revolution. Perry Miller's great works on Puritan thought[1] certainly deserve to be ranked among the first and very best examples of one important branch of social history: the study of collective mentalities.

Until quite recently, however, there has been relatively little interest in other aspects of New England social history. The result has been that our knowledge of colonial New England, though far more extensive than that for any other portion of colonial British America, has lagged far behind that of equally heavily studied areas in early modern Europe. The publication within a period of a few months of the four books here reviewed suggests that we are finally upon the threshold of an explosion of interest in the history of early New England society. By shifting the focus of inquiry from the intellectual and the political to the social realm,

---

[1] Especially Perry Miller, *Orthodoxy in Massachusetts, 1630–1650* (Cambridge, Mass., 1933); *The New England Mind: The Seventeenth Century* (Cambridge, Mass., 1939); and *The New England Mind: From Colony to Province* (Cambridge, Mass., 1953).

these volumes, along with a few earlier works,[2] bring the search for the nature of colonial New England to a new and deeper level of analysis.

At first glance it is obvious that each of the four volumes has its own peculiar shape, the nature of which has been determined by a combination of the character of existing data and the questions brought by the author to the material. Yet despite many important dissimilarities in form and content, they share a common orientation, approach, and set of concerns. Each focuses upon rural New England, upon one or more of the farming communities where the vast majority of the inhabitants lived until well after the colonial period, and upon the "ordinary people" and the "basic circumstances" of their lives. Each is concerned to some degree with the structure, character, and dynamics of rural life as revealed in the workings of local institutions, including the town, church, household, and family; with conditions of life and health and standards and styles of living; and with the quality and mechanisms of interpersonal and intracommunity relations. Each is based almost entirely upon the spare official records of local institutions: the papers of town, church, and court, including especially probate, land, and vital records. In manipulating this intractable data, each of the authors has displayed remarkable resourcefulness and imagination, quantifying data wherever possible and making explicit and responsible use of theories, concepts, and methods drawn from the related social sciences of anthropology, psychology, and demography.

The nature of the records has made it inevitable that each of these studies should be primarily and most satisfactorily a study of "what men did." Despite the many obvious and well-known difficulties of establishing concrete linkages between data on behavior and statements about beliefs and motivations, each of the authors has, however, made a laudable and intelligent effort to discern and to describe not merely the general and recurrent patterns of behavior in the discrete actions recorded in the data, but also the underlying and ordering values and assump-

---

[2] Kenneth A. Lockridge, *A New England Town: The First Hundred Years* (New York, 1970); Michael Zuckerman, *Peaceable Kingdoms: New England Towns in the Eighteenth Century* (New York, 1970); Philip J. Greven, Jr., *Four Generations: Population, Land, and Family in Colonial Andover, Massachusetts* (Ithaca, N.Y., 1970); and John Demos, *A Little Commonwealth: Family Life in Plymouth Colony* (New York, 1970). Among earlier works, see especially Charles S. Grant, *Democracy in the Connecticut Frontier Town of Kent* (New York, 1961); Sumner Chilton Powell, *Puritan Village: The Formation of a New England Town* (Middletown, Conn., 1963); and Darrett B. Rutman, *Winthrop's Boston: A Portrait of a Puritan Town, 1630–1649* (Chapel Hill, N.C., 1965).

tions—what Michael Zuckerman has called "the operative arguments and axioms"—implied by those patterns.[3] Finally, each of the authors has also taken pains to specify the general implications of his work for our understanding of broader trends within colonial New England as well as within comtemporary social history.

This essay will consider these four volumes largely in terms of two general questions. The first, explicitly raised by the authors themselves, is what these microstudies reveal about the macroworld of colonial New England. The second, not directly confronted by any of the authors, is forced upon the reader by the heavy concentration of energy and intelligence upon the analysis of colonial New England within these works. It is the larger question of perspective and meaning, of what we know when we know about colonial New England, of where New England fitted into and what it can tell us about the wider British-American colonial experience of which it was a part.

Outside New England, at least, Anglo-Americans of both the seventeenth and the eighteenth century would no doubt have been surprised by the amount of historical attention that has subsequently been devoted to the New England colonies. They would have had no doubts that the most dynamic—and, hence, most important—centers of colonial activity were to be found in the Caribbean sugar colonies, the Chesapeake tobacco colonies, and, beginning in the eighteenth century, the rich farming regions running south from New York to the Carolinas and the rice-growing areas of South Carolina and Georgia. Far from being in any sense prototypical of British colonial development, the New England colonies, by comparison with many of the colonies to their south, always seemed to be outside the mainstream of colonial life—their societies cast into a different form, their inhabitants animated by different impulses, their economies growing at a slower tempo, and their involvement in the larger world of Anglo-American society less direct, intensive, and vital.

The extent of the subsequent interest in New England coupled with the relative neglect of the other colonies, from New York south to Barbados, makes it clear that there has somehow been a reversal of priorities or a major reordering of the criteria by which priorities are determined, between eighteenth-century Anglo-Americans and twentieth-century historians. The complex reasons for this shift are important subjects in themselves and deserve careful study and analysis. But when they are

---

[3] Zuckerman, *Peaceable Kingdoms*, vii.

untangled they will doubtless tell us more about later American cultural development than about the misperceptions of eighteenth-century Anglo-Americans.

The important point, in any case, is that interest in New England has run so deep that the importance of its study has come to be taken for granted. The result has been that no one any longer bothers to ask the question of why New England should be studied, why its investigation should be given priority over that of other areas of the British-American colonial world, or what it might tell us about that world that the experience of other colonies would not.

The question of what these local studies reveal about larger trends in New England is confronted most explicitly by Kenneth A. Lockridge and Michael Zuckerman, who both present the thesis that the characteristics and developments they describe were central to the New England, even the American, experience. Each addresses himself to the traditional problems of whether and in what senses the towns were hierarchical or egalitarian, democratic or oligarchical, open or constricted, static or dynamic, conflicted or consensual; and each organizes his study around two of the classic questions of New England historiography: the nature of town life and the character and direction of change during the colonial era.

Lockridge's study of the first hundred years of Dedham, Massachusetts, is a work of elegant simplicity. Cleanly structured, clearly argued, and lucidly written, it is the classic story of New England declension, much refined and retold at the community level in terms of not merely the religious but also the broad social, political, and economic experiences of the residents of the town. Moved by a vision, both Puritan and "peasant" in origins, of "a unified social organism" knit together by Christian love and composed only of like-minded people, the founders of Dedham, Lockridge argues, succeeded to an amazing degree in implementing their original ideal, to achieve what he calls a "Christian Utopian Closed Corporate Community." For its first fifty years, from 1636 to 1686, Dedham was "a remarkably stable agricultural community" in which the inhabitants, clustered together in a nuclear village around the church and living in daily interaction with one another, subordinated self-interest to the public good, shunned all public disputes, and systematically excluded the contentious and the deviant from the town. Dedicated to the achievement of perfection in the church, they routinely denied membership to those who could not "prove they had received saving grace," without a murmur of complaint from those excluded. Believing in the natural inequality of men, they allocated land on the basis of differences in rank as well as size of family and accepted the implications (in terms of the absence of possibilities for upward social mobility) of an ideal of a static community presided over by the town's most distinguished (restrained and industrious) men. A yearning for order was obviously the central underlying tendency shaping their behavior in all areas of their lives.[4]

The achievement and perpetuation of this ideal for so long was fostered by the simplicity of the economy and the abundance of land, both of which ensured that the vast majority (over 85 percent) would be farmers, that social differentiation would be slow to develop, and that men's economic expectations would remain modest. The result was "an isolated, small, stable, homogeneous agricultural community which resembled the rural society of seventeenth-century Europe as much as it resembled the 'land of opportunity' dear to the hearts of generations of American students and scholars." Indeed, Dedham's population was considerably less mobile than comparably sized English villages: "less than one percent of the adult males . . . in a given year would be newcomers, while less than one percent of the adult males would emigrate." Its steady, if undramatic, rise in population was primarily attributable to natural increase, in all probability the result not of a higher birthrate or earlier ages at marriage, neither of which differed significantly from those in Europe, but of a lower death rate, which Lockridge ascribes to either "better diet or better housing."[5]

The tenor of life within Dedham changed markedly during its second half century, from 1686 to 1736. The gradual diminution of the spiritual energies and utopian impulses of the founders, already evident during the 1670s and 1680s, was an important ingredient of change. Even more significant in destroying the "original integrity" of the village community was the steady growth and dispersion of population. The rapid spread of people across the landscape led to the physical and social disintegration of Dedham village. What had formerly been one community now split into a series of semi-independent and sometimes antagonistic townships, and instead of settling together in clusters, men established their

---

[4] Lockridge, *New England Town*, 16, 18, 24.

[5] Ibid., 63–64, 67.

families on individual farmsteads. Population growth resulted in more social diversity and more intense pressures upon available land.[6]

Together, dispersion and growth greatly weakened the consensual impulses within the community and profoundly altered the character of politics. Public life became overtly contentious, the town increasingly politicized. Whether because of a growing lack of trust in the customary leaders of the town, as Lockridge implies, or rising confidence on the part of rank-and-file townsmen, the power of traditional leaders gradually declined, the townsmen moved from a passive to an active political role, and the social locus of authority shifted downward. But, Lockridge emphasizes, these themes of change ran in counterpoint to the theme of inertia. Therefore growth, dispersion, diversity, and disharmony had little effect upon many of the town's basic patterns of existence. After a hundred years Dedham remained predominantly rural, agricultural, simple, and isolated. Its population continued to be largely immobile and deeply rooted in the town, and a heavy concentration of resources had not yet destroyed the rough equality of wealth or removed the opportunities for modest upward social mobility that had characterized earlier generations.

Looking ahead to Dedham's next half century, Lockridge suggests— and here his evidence is sufficiently thin and scattered as to require him to be highly speculative—that much more important and fundamental changes occurred. On the one hand, he sees an irreversible movement away from the "powerful corporate impulse" of the seventeenth century toward a more open society of "pluralism, individualism, and liberty," as continued growth created new economic opportunities in nonfarming occupations and a rising spirit of enterprise turned Dedham away from its traditional isolation and more and more toward the outside world. On the other hand, he sees an ominous tendency toward scarcity and stratification, as the continuing decline in the amount of available land, failure to develop new agricultural techniques, and reluctance of most inhabitants to emigrate seemed to point toward growing inequalities of wealth, increasing numbers living in poor circumstances, and, ultimately, a genuine "crisis of overcrowding." By the 1760s, Lockridge posits, the tension "between this rapidly developing individualism and the social Europeanization" of the town, "between individual expectations" for a continued opening of society and the persistence in fact of the "old immobility and the actual deterioration of economic opportunity," had

---

[6] Ibid., 90.

become sufficiently great as to predispose the inhabitants toward—and to be directly related to—the American Revolution.[7]

Lockridge uses the Dedham experience to construct a general three-stage model of New England social development. According to this model, the social and religious harmony and coherence of the first generations gave way under the pressures of growth and dispersion to a more diverse, contentious, and open society during the early eighteenth century before finally turning into an increasingly divided, differentiated, closed, and "Europeanized" society in the decades just before the American Revolution.[8] A useful corrective to earlier studies which have tended to see the development of New England as a relatively uncomplicated linear process moving from social corporatism to social atomism, Lockridge's model may well be a fairly accurate representation of the experience of the more developed towns in New England, those that Edward M. Cook, Jr., has classified as cities and county towns.[9] Whether it applies so clearly to Dedham itself is, from Lockridge's own study, less apparent.

However extensive the changes that occurred in the town during its second fifty years, Dedham does not (before 1736) appear to have experienced the rapid acceleration of the economy and increase in opportunity that elsewhere—in the more dynamic regions of New England—significantly whetted economic appetites, raised material aspirations, and generated a torrent of individual opportunism.[10] Perhaps a more thorough analysis of the experience of the town after 1736 will show that the pace of economic activity increased sufficiently to produce a major rise in individual expectations through the middle decades of the eighteenth century. But unless the opening of Dedham society was considerably greater after 1736 than Lockridge seems to show that it was before that date, it is doubtful that the trend toward scarcity and stratification was so sharply felt as he suggests. That the trend had actually reached "crisis" proportions by the 1760s is especially questionable.

If such a crisis actually existed, one would expect to find some concrete evidence that Dedhamites either perceived or were behaving in ways that suggested that they felt or sensed that existing degrees of

---

[7] Ibid., 160–61, 165.

[8] Ibid., 177.

[9] Edward Marks Cook, Jr., "Local Leadership and the Typology of New England Towns, 1700–1785," *Political Science Quarterly* 86 (1971): 595–96.

[10] See, especially, Richard L. Bushman, *Puritan to Yankee: Character and the Social Order in Connecticut, 1690–1765* (Cambridge, Mass., 1967).

"crowding" and stratification were becoming intolerable. But Lockridge adduces no such evidence. Indeed, what his account seems to suggest is that the extent of social opening had been so modest and the subsequent process of social closing so gradual as, in all probability, to make its consequences less apparent (and less unacceptable) to contemporaries than to later historians.

Before we will know whether this projected "crisis of overcrowding" is anything more than simple hyperbole, we will need to know much more about whether and in what ways the changes Dedhamites experienced during their first century affected their capacity to adjust to shifting social circumstances, whether and to what extent those changes may have prepared them for the acceptance of adversity as well as opportunity.[11] And we will also need to know more precisely how they responded to the growing complexity of the town and the decreasing availability of land after 1736 and whether there were compensating developments that created opportunities aside from tilling the soil.[12]

If Dedham had not advanced as far as some other towns on the road from social corporatism to social atomism, and if, as Lockridge argues, the degree of political contention was an important measure of how far along that road any given community had traveled, then, as Zuckerman's volume makes clear, there were still many other towns in Massachusetts which had not gone nearly as far as Dedham by the middle decades of the eighteenth century. The product of an extremely agile and inventive mind, Zuckerman's ambitious attempt "to comprehend the culture of provincial Massachusetts whole" is a lucidly written, brilliantly argued, and relentless assault upon the convention which "posits the diminution or disappearance of the original settlers' sharp sense of community as the forces of the frontier or the winds of destiny imposed more individualistic modes." Zuckerman's central thesis is "that the consciousness of community, in Massachusetts, continued at least three quarters of the way through the eighteenth century as a prime value in public life." "Themes of concord and consensus," he argues, were "as strong in 1770, or 1750, as in 1700, in values and in behavior."[13]

The explanation for the continuing vitality of the communal impulse, Zuckerman contends, is to be found in the pressures of life in the towns.

---

[11] Lockridge, *New England Town*, 161.

[12] In the meantime, see Edward Marks Cook, Jr., "Social Behavior and Changing Values in Dedham, Massachusetts, 1700–1775," *William and Mary Quarterly*, 3d ser., 27 (1970): 546–80.

[13] Zuckerman, *Peaceable Kingdoms*, vii.

Following the transfer of central authority to London by the charter of 1691, the initial concentration of authority among the magistrates (and clergy) on the provincial level in Massachusetts gave way to a broad diffusion of power among the towns. As a result of this localization of authority, called by Zuckerman "the essential institutional development of the era between settlement and the American Revolution," the towns acquired a degree of power and autonomy previously unknown. Thenceforth, "the locus of power and influence over the lives of the people lay primarily in the towns, not in the province"; the provincial House of Representatives was, as Robert Zemsky has also recently emphasized, reduced "to a virtual congress of communities"; and the provincial government "became, in practice, the creature of its constituents," the towns.[14]

This shift in power also meant that the towns were almost exclusively responsible for maintaining order and enforcing values. If the inherited ideological attachment to peace as a prime value was to be maintained, two conditions had to be met. First, the denseness of the communal experience, the very physical and social contiguity that inevitably brought the inhabitants of these simple rural villages into daily contact with one another, required, Zuckerman argues, that "accommodation to others" would be expected and contention discountenanced. Second, the absence of adequate agencies of enforcement, of any satisfactory means of institutional coercion, meant the towns would have to rely largely on internal compliance and the moral suasion of the community rather than on external compulsion, for the achievement of the ideal of the town as a "homogeneous communal unit."[15]

Hence, according to Zuckerman, every aspect of the social organization of the town was oriented toward the promotion of concord and consensus. The preeminent goal of child rearing and education was the inculcation of restraint, as the perils of the three Ds—Death, Depravity, and Damnation—received every bit as much emphasis as the three Rs, and self-assertion was discouraged in favor of self-abasement. The town meeting, the "institutional site of the translation of larger values into local behavior," insisted upon being inclusive, upon not excluding any independent men from participation, and upon resolving all disagreements and thereby preventing disharmony. Even the social structure itself encouraged these tendencies. With very little social distance between

---

[14] Ibid., 16, 18, 20, 35; Robert Zemsky, *Merchants, Farmers, and River Gods: An Essay on Eighteenth-Century American Politics* (Boston, 1971).

[15] Zuckerman, *Peaceable Kingdoms*, 49, 118.

the poorest and the richest inhabitants and no substantial economic specialization, there was no basis for an entrenched oligarchy or a system of deferential politics. The result was a kind of rough political and economic equality that militated against the development of the sharp social divisions that sometimes rend more complex societies.[16]

Under these conditions, Zuckerman contends, men shunned litigation and dispute, a "striking . . . domestic tranquility" prevailed, and dissent "was generally surreptitious, rarely long-sustained, and usually smoothed over immediately." If accommodation was impossible, separation was the only alternative, because conflict was an intolerable state. But separation, as Lockridge has also suggested in the case of Dedham, was itself merely a tactic for "turning contention into consensus." Obviously, the restraints on individual expression and initiative in such communities were enormously powerful.[17]

Somewhat ironically, the Revolution, which for the towns had initially represented an assertion of local independence, eventually undermined their autonomy by setting up a new and more formidable central authority, yet it did little to alter the character of community life. Until well after the Revolution, the towns of Massachusetts were still "governed by the canons of community rather than the individualistic canons of contract." "Self-suppression for the sake of social harmony" continued to be the basic organizing principle of town life. But the situation had scarcely been a static one. Over the course of the eighteenth century, the "iron inflexibility" of the first generations "had edged steadily into the accommodative character" of the mid-eighteenth century, and this shift "from coercive to accommodative consensus" to some extent rendered the "perils of pluralism" less frightening by providing a glimpse of the possibility for "an accommodation that could secure concord even out of genuine conflict in the community." By the end of the Revolution, however, few inhabitants, according to Zuckerman, had yet had anything more than a glimpse of this future order.[18]

A strikingly original and compellingly argued statement, the Zuckerman book thus challenges the conventional view of eighteenth-century New England society at virtually every important point. But the extraordinary incongruity between it and the findings of other scholars raises the serious questions of whether, to what extent, and in what sense

---

[16] Ibid., 154.

[17] Ibid., 104, 124, 139.

[18] Ibid., 8, 237, 253, 255–56.

Zuckerman has offered us an accurate characterization of the realities of life in the colonial New England town. The enduring consensus and aversion to litigation he describes stand in sharp contrast to the increasing economic and religious conflict and the rise in litigation found by Richard L. Bushman, John M. Murrin, C. C. Goen, and Lockridge, among others.[19] Zuckerman's emphasis upon the relative social, economic, and political equality within the towns is difficult to reconcile with the tendencies toward increasing stratification and differentiation found by Charles S. Grant, Lockridge, and especially, Edward M. Cook, Jr., for some towns.[20] His emphasis upon the denseness of the communal experience does not fit easily with David H. Flaherty's characterization of the amount of individual space available in rural settings in colonial New England.[21] Moreover, whereas Zuckerman argues that crowding discouraged contention, Lockridge and John Demos suggest that it encouraged it.[22] Finally, the limited scope of individual behavior stressed by Zuckerman simply does not seem to fit the vigorously competitive and individualistic activities described by many scholars, especially Bushman. Is it possible that all of these scholars have been wrong?

A more plausible answer, and one that, not surprisingly, seems to be achieving some sort of rough consensus among historians of colonial New England, is that Zuckerman is the one in error; that he has been, at best, playfully perverse and, at worst, irresponsible in his choice and use of data. Primary grounds for these suspicions are to be found in some obvious problems with regard to his sample. He bases his conclusions on the analysis of sixteen Massachusetts towns, certainly a number large enough to constitute a valid sample, at least for Massachusetts, if they were chosen with a view to achieving some representative distribution of towns according to size, location, age, type, and other variables.

But Zuckerman's main criteria of selection seems to have been the availability of published records. Whether he has analyzed these records accurately can only be determined by careful study of the records them-

[19] Bushman, *Puritan to Yankee;* John M. Murrin, "The Legal Transformation: The Bench and Bar of Eighteenth-Century Massachusetts," in Stanley N. Katz, ed., *Colonial America: Essays in Politics and Social Development* (Boston, 1971), 415–49; C. C. Goen, *Revivalism and Separatism in New England, 1740–1800: Strict Congregationalists and Separate Baptists in the Great Awakening* (New Haven, 1962).

[20] Grant, *Democracy in the Connecticut Frontier Town of Kent,* 29–104, 143–68; Cook, "Local Leadership and the Typology of New England Towns," 586–608.

[21] David M. Flaherty, *Privacy in Colonial New England* (Charlottesville, Va., 1972).

[22] Demos, *Little Commonwealth,* 50.

selves. What is obvious from a quick rundown of the list of towns is that only two of the sixteen—Worcester and possibly Braintree—could possibly be considered active centers of economic activity during the early eighteenth century. The rest were rural farming or fishing villages which were relatively isolated from the main currents of economic development and relatively unaffected by the pressures of growth and increasing diversity that Bushman analyzed so superbly for Connecticut and that swept through other parts of New England as well.

In these eddies and backwaters of Massachusetts society, it is unsurprising that the social structure remained only slightly differentiated and political life highly egalitarian, that the towns themselves should display an "adamant insularity" and a broad indifference in relation to most provincewide affairs, or that the inhabitants should have adhered to their commitment to harmony and consensus in behavior, as well as in values, more tenaciously and for a longer time than people living in towns undergoing more rapid and far-reaching change. What Zuckerman seems to have described, then—and what certainly is an important contribution to our understanding of eighteenth-century New England society—is not *the* New England town but a particular and perhaps numerically dominant type of Massachusetts town at a rather early and static stage of economic and social development.[23]

Although Zuckerman may thus be guilty of trying to stretch his evidence too far, it is also highly probable that by doing so he has made an additional—and no less important—contribution. By showing how deep consensual impulses ran in more static areas of eighteenth-century rural New England, he raises the strong possibility that important residues of those impulses may to one degree or another have continued to have a significant bearing upon behavior even in the more dynamic centers of growth. Certainly, he casts serious doubt, as does surviving literary evidence, upon Lockridge's assertion that eighteenth-century New England thinkers deemphasized "the notion of an organic society held together by voluntary restraint."[24]

Yet, it is obviously undesirable to overemphasize the power of "other-oriented communalism" in New England society. Even in towns where the communal impulse was strongest, the limits of acceptable behavior for individuals was probably expanding during the eighteenth century. The insistent localism of the towns, and their selective compliance with the regulations and directives of the provincial government, represented

---

[23] Zuckerman, *Peaceable Kingdoms*, 35.

[24] Lockridge, *New England Town*, 55.

a new attitude toward authority that, by encouraging the townsmen to put the interests of a part of society above that of the whole, may well have subtly undermined the strength and logic of the consensual mode while at the same time loosening the restraints upon the individual in terms of his relationship to the community. Moreover, the movement from coercive to accommodative consensus described by Zuckerman may have produced a similar result, for accommodation and compromise are concepts that contain an implicit recognition of the divergency and legitimacy of individual interests.[25]

As pure or self-contained categories, community-mindedness and individualism have no approximations in social reality in colonial New England or anywhere else. To assess where any given community might fall on a continuum between these two ideal extremes, one needs to know what the specific mixture was in that particular place. Zuckerman's towns probably belong well along toward the pole designated community-minded. But they were not without some scope for individualism. The question is whether that scope was increasing during the eighteenth century even as a result of, and within, the very tendencies to which he attributes the continuing strength of the drive toward consensus.

Philip Greven and John Demos have taken a somewhat different approach in the attempt to define the character of the colonial New England experience. Unlike Lockridge and Zuckerman, they have focused not upon such classic New England public institutions as the town meeting and the church but upon the family, one of the most basic and pervasive of all human institutions and, presumably, one of the most resistant to change. They have chosen to look at the traditional problem of the nature of communal life in New England in terms not of the dynamics of public life but of the social history of the family as revealed through such hitherto largely neglected subjects as the structures of families and households, relations between parents and children, marriage and inheritance practices, the nature and operation of broader kinship ties, standards of life and health, patterns of settlement and migration, and, in the case of Demos, the physical context of family life.

The Greven volume, certainly one of the best first books published in any area of early American history over the past decade and, in many ways, the most impressive of the four works considered here, is an extraordinary, if quiet, display of the systematic and inventive application of intellect to the difficult problem of explicating the relationship between family development and social change in Andover, Massachusetts, from its founding in 1646 through the third quarter of the eighteenth century. Using some of the techniques of historical demography, especially family reconstitution, Greven has built his study around a probing analysis of the genealogical histories of the 28 first-generation families who settled in Andover during the 1640s and 1650s and their progeny through the next three generations. He has not collected the histories of the many families who came to the town after the 1650s. He suggests that they probably were "not very different from the histories of the settler families," and his analysis of the settler families alone required him to handle data for more than 247 families and 2,000 individuals! But he has supplemented his study of this core group with demographic analyses of the aggregate population of the town. Greven uses this data to consider five basic phenomena as they changed over time: the effect of the "fundamental events of birth, marriage and death" upon both particular families and the larger community of the town, the relationship of families to the land, relations between fathers and sons, family structure, and family mobility.[26]

Just twenty miles from Boston, Andover (like Dedham) was never anything more than a simple rural village during the seventeenth century. The dependence of its inhabitants upon the land was fundamental. The only alternative to husbandry was physical labor, which in an underdeveloped agricultural economy was relatively unremunerative. Largely "men of limited means and humble social background," the first settlers were tied to the scale and traditions of agricultural life as they had known them in England. They employed the open-field system, settled in close proximity to one another in a nuclear village, and were sparing in their distribution of land, the range of landholding being remarkably narrow. But the shift to a dispersed pattern of settlement, accompanied by a heightened concern over legal titles to private property, began in the late 1650s, somewhat earlier than in Dedham. By 1680 nearly half of the inhabitants had moved to the southern portion of the town, "remote from the original village center." This early and widespread dispersion, Greven theorizes, "diminished the cohesive force of the community and

---

[26]Greven, *Four Generations*, 1, 5.

augmented the significance of the individual family, settled on its own lands at an appreciable distance from other neighbors."[27]

Although the process of migration from England evidently limited the degree to which families were likely to be extended in structure among the first settlers, a combination of abundant land, large families, a proclivity to remain in Andover, and long delays in the transmission of land to the second generation "fostered the development of families which were extended in their structures, patriarchal in character, and rooted" in Andover. A majority of households remained nuclear into the second generation in the sense that sons usually lived apart from their parents after they were married. But the proximity of residences, Greven finds, laid the basis "for elaborate kinship networks" which continued to expand for generations. The most salient characteristic of the Andover family was the strength of parental authority, as fathers retained control of land to ensure that sons would continue dutiful and dependent.[28]

This picture began to change between 1680 and 1720 largely as a result of rapid demographic growth. From the beginning Andover had been a remarkably healthy place to live. Infant mortality was low—of an average of 8.3 children born to a group of sample families, 7.2 survived to age 21—and those who lived to 21 could anticipate long and healthy lives: 71.8 years for men and 70.8 for women among the first generation and 64.2 for men and 61.6 for women among the second. Combined with relatively young ages for first marriages for women (19.0 for the first generation and 22.3 for the second) and a correspondingly high and increasing number of births per marriage, this low rate of mortality sent the population surging upward.

Such explosive demographic growth began to alter the character of family life in subtle but profound ways by inaugurating a long-term tendency toward the diminution of paternal authority. Many fathers of the second generation simply did not have enough land to provide adequately for all of their sons, many of whom now received money, training in a trade, or a liberal education for their inheritance. Almost a quarter of second-generation sons followed a trade, and whereas little more than a fifth of first-generation sons moved away from Andover, nearly two-fifths of second-generation sons migrated from the town, many to new towns in Connecticut or New Hampshire where land was cheaper. Sons going into trades or moving away acquired their independence earlier than those (the majority) who stayed behind. But those who remained

[27] Ibid., 49, 56–57.

[28] Ibid., 73, 98.

also began to demand—whether because of the example of their more mobile and autonomous siblings or for some other reasons, Greven does not say—and in many cases to receive, through deeds of gift and deeds of sale, their economic and personal independence much earlier than had their fathers.

These tendencies toward more complex patterns of family life, earlier independence for children, attenuation of available economic resources within Andover, and high out-migration accelerated during the half century from 1720 to 1770, a period that corresponded roughly with the emergence of the fourth generation. Rates of population growth slowed perceptibly for two sets of reasons. First, Andover suddenly became less healthy, as the mortality of both children and young adults increased markedly, the former largely because of successive epidemics of the throat distemper and the latter left unexplained by Greven. The longevity of women actually increased somewhat, but that of men declined steadily from 64.2 in the second generation to 62.4 in the third and 59.8 in the fourth. At the same time, the birthrate slowed. Although the average age at marriage for men decreased a little, women married later (24.5 for the third generation), and intervals between births increased.

Despite this slowing rate of demographic growth (which was almost stagnant during the second and fourth quarters of the eighteenth century) and a heavy out-migration, which included between one-half and three-fifths of third-generation sons, pressure on family land mounted steadily, with the result that those who stayed in Andover (like those who remained in Dedham, if Lockridge is correct) actually suffered a declining standard of living during the fourth generation. The degree of economic accumulation and the disparity of wealth had never been very great in Andover, but among the fourth generation there was a decided "trend toward smaller estates" at all economic levels.[29]

Although the persistence of strong extended family networks "provided a basic source of stability and continuity" in this increasingly uncertain situation, these many changes contributed to a further loosening of family ties. The continuing decline in patriarchal authority and increasing independence of sons was manifest, Greven posits, in a sharp drop in the average age of marriage (among women as well as men in the fourth generation), a rising proportion of impartible inheritances, a tendency to convey lands to sons at earlier ages, and the increasing willingness of sons to leave the family and community. Assuming that many other communities and regions had also experienced these

---

[29] Ibid., 224.

"changes in the relationships between fathers and sons," Greven also suggests that they may "have been connected closely with the movement for independence [from Britain] itself during the third quarter of the eighteenth century—that period in which the fourth generation in Andover was coming to maturity and establishing its own independence from fathers and families." Increasingly accustomed to independence from family control, he surmises, these independent sons turned more easily toward political independence in 1776.[30]

Greven's findings, like those of Lockridge, may be used as the basis for a model of social and, specifically, generational change for colonial New England as a whole. In such a model, the first generation—the settlers— founded an extraordinarily stable and closely integrated community based primarily upon the successful establishment of strong patriarchal families, with the strength of the fathers deriving largely from their iron-clad control of the land. The second generation put their roots down even more deeply into the town, developed a series of complex and overlapping extended family networks within the community, and responded to the generally benign conditions of life and the seeming plentifulness of land by producing large numbers of offspring. By the third generation, which came to maturity during the early eighteenth century, Andover had come to resemble many Old World communities, as kinship ties became ever more intricate; the occupational structure became more highly specialized, land became less and less plentiful, mortality rates rose, and there appeared an "increased disparity of wealth" and, for the first time, some noticeable concentration of property among the wealthier individuals in the town. At the same time the pressure of population growth and the decreasing availability of land encouraged men to "move away in appreciable numbers in search of more abundant land and opportunity elsewhere" and thereby contributed to a significant loosening of family ties. Confronted by the same problems and a declining standard of living as well, members of the fourth generation moved in even greater numbers, produced children at a sharply decelerated rate, and were considerably less tied to their families. Throughout this long process, however, the family—and patriarchalism—remained strong and functioned as a prime agency of stability within the community even as late as the 1770s.[31]

Clearly, this model of generational change seems in many respects to be congruent with the model of social change advanced by Lockridge.

[30] Ibid., 221, 280.

[31] Ibid., 224, 275.

Both emphasize the extraordinary stability achieved by the first generation and its perpetuation through later generations, even in the face of a wide assortment of important changes in the social context of the community. Greven does not consider the extent of public contention in Andover, but, like Lockridge, he describes the growing "Europeanization" of the community, the glacially slow but inexorable movement toward land scarcity and social complexity as represented by increasing occupational specialization and social differentiation. Like Dedham, Andover does not seem to have experienced major economic growth or the social dislocations and tensions such growth could produce. Andoverites seem to have been less rooted to their community, but had Lockridge carried his study forward into the mid-eighteenth century, he might well have discovered that Dedhamites responded to the decline in the amount of available land in much the same way as did Andoverites, by moving away in growing numbers and becoming "a seedbed for the new communities being established elsewhere."[32]

Also a "case study in early American family life," the Demos volume differs from Greven's in several important respects. Demos's major objective is to present a synchronic portrait of "the fundamental sources of strength and strain" among families in Plymouth colony during the seventeenth century. Thus, he is only incidentally concerned with the problem of how families changed over time, and he treats a number of towns instead of only one. He also uses a wider range of sources. Moving beyond official records and literary sources, Demos relies heavily upon such surviving physical artifacts as houses, furniture, tools, utensils, and clothing in an intuitive and suggestive attempt to recreate the physical context of family life. Finally, although he is thoroughly aware that the theory is too sophisticated for the crude data with which he has to work, he makes responsible and profitable use of Erik Erikson's model of individual development in an imaginative effort to reconstruct the life cycle of the individual.[33]

Despite these many differences in scope and orientation, Demos's concern with describing the fundamental circumstances of life and the structure of households and families in Plymouth makes it possible to compare many of his findings with those of Greven. The economy of Plymouth, like that of most of the rest of rural New England, remained simple, underdeveloped, and agricultural throughout the seventeenth century. Almost every man—even those who, like tradesmen, artisans,

---

[32] Ibid., 258.

[33] Demos, *Little Commonwealth*, ix, xiv.

and ministers, worked at some other calling—was a farmer. Standards of life and health were somewhat lower than those in Andover but still remarkably high by contrast with the societies of contemporary Europe. At the outside no more than one in four children died before reaching 21 and, among those who survived to that age, men could expect to live until 70 and women to 63.

Patterns of marriages and births were also roughly comparable. Women married relatively young—at 20 during the early years of the colony, rising to 22 at the end of the century—while men, as in Europe, continued to marry later—at 27, declining to 25. In part because of earlier marriages, wives were extraordinarily fecund: between eight and nine children per couple "was pretty standard." As with Andover, most households were nuclear in structure, consisting of a father, mother, and children, with an occasional apprentice or servant. The town of Bristol, for example, averaged six persons per household in 1689. By the end of the century, in old towns, there were also a number of trigenerational households which included an aged parent or relative. But these nuclear units, again as in Andover, were knit together into physically contiguous extended kinship groupings and family networks.[34]

Demos devotes considerably more attention than Greven to describing the multiple functions of the family and to speculating about the nature of relationships within it. The primary agencies for owning, using, and distributing property, "families served as the central units of production and exchange," and as schools, vocational institutions, churches, houses of correction, and welfare institutions, taking the place of hospitals, orphanages, old peoples' homes, and poorhouses. In the absence of a complex institutional framework for handling the problems of the society, the family, Demos makes clear, occupied much more social space and carried broader social obligations than the modern family.[35]

Within Plymouth families, wives may have gradually achieved a somewhat better position than their counterparts in the same social strata enjoyed in England: husbands clearly occupied a superior status, but there "does *not* seem to have been a . . . really pervasive, and operational norm of male dominance." Control over children was extremely strict, however, with parents being generally indulgent until a child reached the age of 2, when it was subjected to a crushing discipline. As in Andover, "questions of inheritance were . . . closely intertwined with discipline," and parents routinely concerned themselves directly in the

---

[34] Ibid., 68.

[35] Ibid., 183.

lives of their children even after they had acquired families of their own. Plymouth was not a society "which conferred an unusual degree of power and privilege upon youth." Admission to freemanship often came as early as 25 and usually by 40, but office rarely came before 40. Yet, parents do not seem to have aspired to achieve control over their adult children's lives to the degree that they did in Andover; certainly, fathers never succeeded in establishing such a strong patriarchal system. Demos suggests several reasons why it was difficult for Plymouth residents "to maintain the traditional subjection of youth to age." But the most convincing one—and clearly a major distinguishing variable between Plymouth and Andover—was the failure of Plymouth "to sustain a tight pattern of community organization."[36]

The relative weakness of the ties of community in Plymouth probably also was a central ingredient in and was simultaneously exacerbated by still another important difference between it and Andover: a marked degree of geographical mobility. Whereas the settlers of Andover put down deep roots within the town, those of Plymouth found the "magnetic influence of empty land . . . too powerful" and early broke through the fragile bonds of community, as William Bradford complained, because they would not "be content with their condition" and were more concerned "for the enriching of themselves." These expansive pressures and the resulting dispersion quickly eroded whatever ideals of community the settlers had brought with them and may ultimately have somewhat weakened traditional lines of authority within the family itself. But its short-run effect was actually to strengthen the nuclear family unit by forcing it to assume many obligations that would have been born by the community in a more settled society.[37]

Employing some contemporary insights of modern psychiatry, Demos offers two intriguing, but probably highly anachronistic, explanations for the erosion of community in colonial Plymouth, both of them based upon the modish but still questionable assertion that the colonies were marked by an *unusual* degree "of contention, of chronic and sometimes bitter enmity." First, he argues that the heavy obligations of the family made the maintainence of family harmony imperative and that, in combination with the lack of privacy and the cramped living conditions within the household, this imperative placed strong unconscious restraints "on the expression of hostile impulses against the members of one's own household," which were turned outside the family upon the

[36] Ibid., 95, 103, 174, 189.

[37] Ibid., 11.

neighbors. Second, he argues that the extreme severity of child discipline after the initial period of indulgence created both "a tight cluster of anxieties about aggression" that was an element of "special potency in the culture at large" and "a preoccupation with shame" that was manifest, for example, in the "legion of court cases that had to do with personal disputes and rivalries."[38]

But neither of these suggestions, both of which might presumably hold for all New England communities, explains why, from the beginning, Plymouth's sense of community should have been sufficiently weaker than that of Andover, Dedham, or the many towns considered by Zuckerman to have produced such a much more open and fluid pattern of social and family development. Certainly, this is one of the most important questions raised by Demos and is one he nowhere explicitly confronts. Which of a number of possibilities—theological differences, varying social origins, differential identity models, or whatever—will turn out to be the crucial variables is a problem that deserves extensive consideration.

At the same time that the strength of attachment to community was thus waning, Plymouth was growing steadily more diverse. By the end of the seventeenth century, this trend was readily apparent in housing which was of "greater size and greater differentiation," in physical possessions which were "more ample and more diversified," and in patterns of personal relations within and the organization of affluent households which were much more complex. A tendency in such households to keep an increasing number of servants more and more apart from the family proper implied the existence of a "significant principle of differentiation" and a "variety of status definitions" much in the style of "the medieval manor house." The addition of more rooms—separate kitchens and parlors reserved for special occasions—both inaugurated "some tendency toward the separation of various domestic functions" and "foreshadowed major realignments in the whole network of human relations" that would come, well beyond the seventeenth century, with the gradual provision of more space—hence more privacy—for individual members of the household.[39] Flaherty recently explored this development in greater detail and showed it to have been characteristic of the whole of colonial New England.[40] But this trend toward greater accumulation and greater

---

[38] Ibid., 50, 136–38.

[39] Ibid., 34, 37, 47–48, 111.

[40] Flaherty, *Privacy in Colonial New England*, 26–27, 34–35, 38.

diversity was, of course, infinitely more evident among the wealthy. Although "the whole community moved slowly toward greater material prosperity," the wealthy moved at a vastly more accelerated pace than the rest of society, with the result "that the *distance* between the richest and the poorest citizens widened steadily as the years passed."[41]

Although there are major differences in scope and focus among these four volumes, each of the authors has thus analyzed the rural community or communities he has investigated in terms of several of the following overlapping criteria: the degree of (1) community or family cohesion; (2) continuing strength of the ideals and institutions of the founders; (3) geographical mobility and dispersion of the inhabitants; (4) social, political, and religious conflict; and (5) social differentiation and economic opportunity. The extent of overlap is sufficient to make it possible to use the findings of these volumes to suggest some tentative answers to the two questions raised at the beginning of this essay: first, what was the direction and nature of social change within colonial New England, and, second, what is the place, meaning, and explanatory utility of New England within the larger British-American colonial experience?

With regard to the first question, the initial and in many ways most vivid impression to emerge from these works is that there were wide variations in the nature of the New England experience not only from one category of communities to another but from one community to another within the same category. Plymouth towns seem to have been far less cohesive than the others, and change came much more rapidly to Plymouth than to Andover and Dedham, and considerably faster to Andover and Dedham than to Zuckerman's towns. Moreover, as between Andover and Dedham, which seem to have been roughly similar sorts of communities, there appear to have been significant differences in the degree and kind of changes that took place—a clear reminder of the old truism that each town had its own peculiar history.

Yet, and even more interestingly, these works also reveal certain common patterns of development, especially in Plymouth, Andover, and Dedham. For one thing, despite the authors' concern with change, there was, as each of them takes pains to emphasize, an extraordinary degree of continuity and stability within all of these communities. They were in no sense inert, and change was not so glacial as it seems to have been in

[41] Demos, *Little Commonwealth*, 37.

Zuckerman's villages. But old values and old patterns of behavior exhibited a remarkable resiliency, especially in Andover and Dedham, and change was nowhere very sweeping in character. However undramatic, the changes that did occur, though they of course varied in pace and depth according to local circumstances, followed a similar general and clearly discernible pattern, one that corresponds quite closely to the models of social and generational change suggested by Lockridge and Greven. They included impressive population growth, a response to highly favorable conditions of life, and a reflection of a correspondingly high birthrate and low mortality; the dispersion of the population out from the original village centers to individual farms; an increasing differentiation of society and complexity of kinship networks; and a growing diversity in many aspects of town life. These changes were in turn accompanied by a moderate acceleration of the economy during the late seventeenth and early eighteenth centuries; the eventual attenuation of the social and religious synthesis of the founders, the bonds of community, and the cohesiveness of families; a growing demand for and exhibition of autonomy among the sons of each successive generation; more individualism and more conflict within the public life of the towns; a decline in older forms of opportunity through the exhaustion of original supplies of land; and a marked rise in geographical mobility, as children moved away from their birthplaces in search of greater opportunity.

As a device for conveying the thrust of these changes to the reader, Lockridge has employed the familiar dichotomy between *American* and *European*, with the former standing for an unusually open society with great room for individual maneuver (such as presumably characterized Jacksonian America) and the latter for a more settled society with a definite social hierarchy and a relative lack of opportunity. Thus, insofar as colonial New England displayed a tendency toward greater individualism, personal autonomy, and social fluidity, it may be said to have been becoming more American; while to the very important extent that it was moving in the direction of a more pluralistic, complex, fixed, differentiated, and constricted society, it may also be described as becoming more European. This is an extremely useful device that provides us with two different standards of comparison—Jacksonian America and early modern Europe—through which we can obtain a clearer idea of what colonial New England was and was not. The explicit comparisons made by Greven and Demos between the demographic history and family and household structures of New England and those of old England and other continental European communities, as well as the implicit contrasts drawn by Zuckerman between the values and behavior in his eighteenth-century towns and those of early nineteenth-century America, are especially illuminating.

But are these the most fruitful standards for comparison? It is hardly surprising that colonial New England came more and more to resemble the societies of Europe as, with age, its communities achieved a more fixed and differentiated social structure. Nor is it surprising that it did not yet appear much like the bustling urban centers and frontier settlements of the 1830s and 1840s. New England in 1740 or 1770 was neither an elaborate Old World society nor a part of that post-Revolutionary, aggressively egalitarian world of Jacksonian America. Rather, it was a new *colonial* society bounded in time, space, culture, and circumstance.

A potentially far more illuminating basis for comparison would, therefore, seem to be other contemporary colonial societies, specifically, because of their rich variety and similarity of national origins, other contemporary British colonial societies on the continent and in the Caribbean. Only when such comparisons have been made will we be able to see clearly the peculiar features of colonial New England and to put its experience in its proper perspective vis-à-vis that of the several other constituent components of the colonial world of early modern Anglo-America.

Even from the perspective provided by these four volumes, it is unclear what many of the broad outlines of such a comparison might be. We simply do not have enough precise information on family and household structure, marriage and inheritance patterns, or birth and mortality rates for the other mainland and Caribbean colonies. The chronic shortage of women, extending even into the middle of the eighteenth century, and high rates of mortality in the Caribbean colonies may have resulted in considerable deviation from the patterns observed in New England. Given the broad similarity in household and family structure over much of western Europe and New England and the comparable rates of population growth in New England and the rest of the continental colonies, however, it is doubtful that there was so much variation among the colonies on the continent. But firm conclusions obviously await much further study.

With regard to the strength of the corporate impulse, however, the results of such a comparison are, on the basis of what we already know, much more predictable. For when one looks at the New England experience as described by these four and earlier volumes from the perspective of that of the colonies to the south—both continental and Caribbean—the single most vivid impression with which one comes away is of the marked extent to which the New England experience deviated from the normal pattern. The slow movement "away from a powerful corporate impulse" toward "pluralism, individualism and liberty" described by Lockridge, Greven, and Demos, the transition from a peasant or pre-modern to a modern mentality,[42] is remarkable primarily because it occurred so late in the development of the region. No other colony—not even the utopian ventures in Carolina, Pennsylvania, and Georgia—managed to resist the winds of change for so long. An explanation for this phenomenon may be approached through the consideration of two sets of conditions: those that inhibited and those that eventually facilitated the processes of change that took place with such amazing rapidity everywhere else.

Any evaluation of the conditions inhibiting change in New England must begin with a recognition of the most obvious difference in methods of colonization between it and the rest of the colonies, what Richard Hofstadter has referred to as its "measured approach" to settlement.[43] As the important variations in the persistence and degree of social cohesion exhibited by Plymouth on the one hand and Dedham and Andover on the other strongly suggest, however, far more important would seem to be the depth and strength of the corporate impulse. As the last and most protective bastions of the corporate impulse within the colonies, Zuckerman's communities—by the very aberrance of their behavior—probably illuminate far better than any other places the conditions under which that impulse could survive, even flourish. For that reason, one can perhaps best turn to them in the search for those conditions.

Three circumstances stand out as distinguishing most of Zuckerman's communities from Andover and Dedham by the middle of the eighteenth century. In contemporary theories of value change, as Fred Weinstein and Gerald M. Platt have reminded us in their recent analysis of the psychosocial ingredients of the modernization process, it is virtually a commonplace that the "internalization of values occurs most intensively and extensively in relatively undifferentiated groups and communities."[44] It is hardly surprising, therefore, that one distinguishing circumstance was the relative lack of social differentiation, or that a second was the comparatively undeveloped and static character of the economy and the corresponding absence of economic opportunities and structures that might have encouraged more autonomous and less community-oriented

---

[42] Lockridge, *New England Town,* 165.

[43] Richard Hofstadter, *America at 1750: A Social Portrait* (New York, 1971), 144–45.

[44] Gerald M. Platt and Fred Weinstein, *The Wish to Be Free: Society, Psyche, and Value Change* (Berkeley and Los Angeles, 1969), 32.

behavior. A third was what Zuckerman calls the "adamant insularity" and relative isolation of the towns, a condition which to a great extent may have insulated them from many of the larger currents of development in the more dynamic centers of New England life. To a considerable degree, Andover and Dedham seem to have shared each of these three characteristics during their first fifty years in the period before the serious diminution of the original corporate impulse in those communities.[45]

What these three conditions all strongly suggest, then, is that in marked contrast to the situation in the Caribbean and southern mainland colonies, environmental pressures all over *rural* New England initially were extremely weak. The physical setting simply did not generate a material abundance, an intensity of economic activity, or a complexity of social patterns sufficient to limit the capacity of the Puritan synthesis to analyze and explain the environment. Only in Boston—which, as Darrett B. Rutman has shown in his excellent study of the first two decades of that town,[46] early became a prosperous mercantile center with a relatively large, concentrated, heterogeneous population, differentiated society, and considerable contact with the outside world—does any extensive erosion in this synthesis seem to have occurred during the initial years of settlement. In the absence of intensive economic and social change, however, rural New England, existing largely on the margins of the bustling economic and social activity of the larger Atlantic world and representing the most tranquil pole of life within the old British Empire, continued to provide a fertile setting for the sustenance of the original corporate impulse of the Puritans.

If powerful cultural restraints, a stingy physical environment, and relative isolation combined to keep much of New England from going the way of the other colonies by sliding into any easy acceptance of social atomism and the behavioral mandates of initiative and autonomy, still other conditions gradually emerged to push it inexorably in that direction. As Lockridge, Greven, and Demos have shown, the search for better agricultural lands early pulled families away from village centers to individual farmsteads widely dispersed over the countryside. In this setting, somewhat removed from the powerful institutional matrix present in many village centers, the problems of maintaining family cohesion, providing an adequate inheritance for one's children from a niggling na-

---

[45] Zuckerman, *Peaceable Kingdoms*, 35. On the relative isolation, see Greven, *Four Generations*, 120; Lockridge, *New England Town*, 63–64, 139–41.

[46] Rutman, *Winthrop's Boston*.

ture, and otherwise achieving an active mastery over a harsh environment required resourcefulness and initiative on the part of heads of households.

To the extent that fathers responded to this situation by showing an impatience with any external restraints that interfered with their ability to cope with it and, in the process, necessarily assumed a somewhat autonomous stance in relationship to the rest of the community, they were, by their own example, providing a model for their children that, inadvertently and ironically, operated to undermine the communal impulse to which they were themselves so strongly devoted as well as to loosen their own control over their adult offspring. But, as the findings of Greven and Lockridge would seem to suggest, well into the early eighteenth century in many rural areas—and even longer in communities of the kind described by Zuckerman—the imperatives of independence and competitive mastery over the environment were never sufficiently powerful to gain ascendancy over the traditional mandates of dependence and obedience to authority. The wish for autonomy, as yet culturally illegitimate, existed in a state of tension with a much stronger need to remain dependent upon the traditional cultural agencies of community, church, and family, the first two of which at least continued to display a vitality that was considerably less evident elsewhere in the British-American colonies.

Only with the acceleration of the economy as a result of rapid internal population growth and the increasing integration of the New England economy into the larger Atlantic economy during the early eighteenth century, did the mandates of initiative and autonomy begin to gain ascendance over the older corporate impulse.[47] This development not only stimulated greater social differentiation and geographical and economic mobility but drew many communities out of a relatively isolated existence. By opening up many new opportunities for profit and wealth, it also, as Bushman has suggested,[48] whetted men's material appetites and thereby paved the way for nothing less than a behavioral revolution in the more dynamic areas of rural New England—a revolution that scarcely touched still isolated communities like Zuckerman's, had a strong impact upon central places and suburban towns such as Andover and Dedham, and had a transforming effect upon cities and new towns.[49]

---

[47] The analysis here relies heavily upon the explanatory model developed by Weinstein and Platt in *The Wish to Be Free.*

[48] Bushman, *Puritan to Yankee.*

[49] These classifications are derived from Cook, "Local Leadership and the Typology of New England Towns."

Far from playing a merely passive role, as Lockridge implies,[50] men became active agents in this process, as they increasingly ignored traditional restraints and turned energies formerly devoted to religious and community endeavors to the pursuit of personal gain.[51]

By encouraging a high degree of autonomous and aggressively competitive behavior, this revolution also provided new identity models and new standards of personal conduct for the society at large. No longer was the moral and psychological necessity of obedience to the authority of the community and its traditional leaders—magistrates, pastors, and fathers—automatically assumed. Rather, the new models of behavior emphasized the authority of self rather than the authority of community; individual economic achievement and success rather than ascriptive criteria for political leadership and social status; the fulfillment, privacy, and comfort of the individual rather than self-denial in favor of the common good;[52] and the "capacity of the individual to direct his own existence rather than . . . an unquestioning response to public morality."[53]

With this behavioral revolution the accumulation of wealth became both an assertion of the new mandate of personal autonomy and a necessary denial of passive dependence. Failure to acquire wealth and thereby to demonstrate one's autonomy "led to a sense of moral unworthiness and fear of the loss of self-esteem in one's own eyes and the eyes of the community." The autonomous pursuit and accumulation of wealth thus represented the only available escape from failure, from potential "regression to the abiding wish for love and protection" that lay at the heart of and continued to sustain the communal impulse. If, however, through this revolution, the wish for autonomy became "conscious and generalized" in the more dynamic areas of New England society, "the morality necessary to sanction it was not yet available": the revolution in behavior had not yet been accompanied by a revolution in values.[54] As was indicated by persistent demands for return to the traditional imperatives of community and obedience to authority, the fear that an excess of atomistic behavior would lead to social chaos and loss of control—that man

---

[50] Lockridge, *New England Town,* 134.

[51] On this point, see, especially, Miller, *New England Mind: From Colony to Province,* and Bernard Bailyn, *The New England Merchants in the Seventeenth Century* (Boston, 1955).

[52] See Flaherty, *Privacy in Colonial New England,* 242–44.

[53] Weinstein and Platt, *Wish to Be Free,* 31.

[54] Ibid., 36, 200–203.

could not tolerate freedom without strong societal restraints—was still too close to the surface and too easily activated to permit the development of an alternative morality that would be a more accurate reflection of prevailing modes of behavior.[55]

But the protests against the new patterns of behavior were clearly a retrograde action with little chance of success. Belatedly and with great screaming and kicking from some of its inhabitants, much of rural New England—following the earlier example of Boston and presumably of the other seaport towns—had finally been drawn out of the eddies and backwaters and into the mainstream of Anglo-American economic life. Although, as Zuckerman shows, pockets of the old premodern mentality continued to exist in many static, undifferentiated, and isolated communities throughout the colonial period, the resulting transition from a premodern to a modern mentality was irreversible. That the spread of autonomous behavior did not immediately lead to social chaos enabled New Englanders to live with the behavioral revolution even when they could not bring themselves to endorse it and eventually would help to persuade them that in a society with so much space and so many resources individual autonomy was not necessarily incompatible with—and could even be an essential precondition for—social stability.

The behavioral revolution that occurred in many areas of rural New England during the eighteenth century and the accompanying transition from a premodern to a modern mentality had, of course, taken place far earlier in the histories of the Caribbean, Chesapeake, and other British-American colonies. From the perspective supplied by their development, it is possible to see how atypical, peculiar, even anachronistic the New England experience was in Anglo-American history during the seventeenth and early eighteenth centuries, how weak were the pressures exerted by the New England environment, how powerful the restraints imposed by Puritan culture upon all aspects of rural New England life, and how long it took for New England to assimilate to a pattern of behavior that, to one degree or another, had long since come to dominate the societies of the rest of the colonies. Only from the peculiar vantage point supplied by the New England colonies, however, can one see vividly just how weak the corporate impulse was in other British colonies, how unimposing were their figures of traditional authority, how great were the possibilities for material gain, and how rapid and pervasive was the de-

---

[55] See Jack P. Greene, "Search for Identity: An Interpretation of the Meaning of Selected Patterns of Social Response in Eighteenth-Century America," *Journal of Social History* 3 (1969–70): 189–224.

velopment of highly autonomous behavior. Therein, in this special perspective upon the other, more vital colonies, lies the particular significance of and the primary justification for the study of New England in the consideration of the British colonial experience in early modern America.

Throughout the early 1970s my administrative duties at The Johns Hopkins University were considerable. As chairman and ex-chairman of the Department of History, I was deeply involved in expanding, rebuilding, and reorienting that department. I also had principal responsibility for establishing a new interdisciplinary Program in Atlantic History and Culture, for overseeing the recruitment of the first faculty members for a new Department of Anthropology, and for securing the external funding and negotiating the internal politics required for these initiatives to succeed. These local administrative responsibilities quickly enhanced my reputation as a person who never agreed to a deadline he did not miss. When in early 1971 I accepted an invitation to write this chapter as a review essay for the *Journal of Social History*, I had no idea that I would not find time to finish it until January 1973, while I was in Jamaica for a month helping to oversee an interdisciplinary exercise on Jamaican slave society jointly sponsored by Johns Hopkins and the University of the West Indies, Mona, for history and anthropology students. The chapter is reprinted with permission and with minor verbal changes and citations to quotations from the *Journal of Social History* 7 (1974): 171–94.

—Nine—

Society and Economy in the British Caribbean during the Seventeenth and Eighteenth Centuries

"THE SUGAR COLONIES," the agricultural writer Arthur Young estimated in 1770, "add three millions a year to the wealth of Britain; the rice colonies near a million, and the tobacco ones almost as much."[1] Young's estimation doubtless was imprecise, but his remarks vividly underline a conviction widely shared by his contemporaries: the Caribbean sugar islands were both the most valuable of the British colonies in America and a major source of wealth for the mother country. Whatever the view of eighteenth-century Britons, modern historians have not previously given these colonies an amount of attention anywhere nearly commensurate with their early importance. In this century there has been a trickle of monographs on the internal constitutional development of the islands and their external relations with the mother country.[2] Ex-

---

[1] Arthur Young, *Annals of Agriculture*, 2 vols. (London, 1784), 1:13, as cited by Richard B. Sheridan, *Sugar and Slavery: An Economic History of the British West Indies, 1623–1775* (Baltimore, 1974), 471.

[2] Especially C. S. S. Higman, *The Development of the Leeward Islands under the Restoration, 1660–1688* (Cambridge, 1921); Lillian M. Penson, *The Colonial Agents of the British West Indies: A Study in Colonial Administration, Mainly in the Eighteenth Century* (London, 1924); Vincent T. Harlow, *A History of Barbados* (Oxford, 1926), and *Christopher Codrington, 1668–1710* (Oxford, 1926); Agnes M. Whitson, *The Constitutional Development of Jamaica, 1660–1729* (Manchester, Eng., 1929); Richard Pares, *War and Trade in the West Indies, 1739–1763* (Oxford, 1936); A. P. Thornton, *West-India Policy under the Restoration* (Oxford, 1956); F. G. Spurdle, *Early West Indian Government: Showing the Progress of Government in Barbados, Jamaica, and the Leeward Islands, 1660–1783* (Palmerston North, N.Z., 1964); and George Metcalf, *Royal Government and Political Conflict in Jamaica, 1729–1783* (London, 1965).

cept for the valuable studies of Eric Williams, J. Harry Bennett, and, especially, Richard Pares, there has been remarkably little serious study of the economic development of the Caribbean colonies, while in the area of social history the impressive early works of Frank Wesley Pitman and Lowell J. Ragatz have been followed by almost forty years of nearly total neglect, perhaps in part because of the judgment of both of these scholars that, to the extent the West Indian colonists had succeeded in establishing a society at all, it was a "wilderness of materialism," a "degraded" and monstrous creation that bore little resemblance to the "healthy and progressive" social organisms found on the mainland, and, more particularly, in New England.[3]

As a result of the sudden efflorescence of scholarship represented by the works considered here and a few other recently published studies, however, we are now on the verge of achieving a more systematic and thorough understanding of the economic and social development of the Caribbean colonies than we have for any other segment of the early modern British overseas empire, including perhaps New England. By making it clearer than ever before exactly what the new settlers—Africans as well as Europeans—created in the West Indies during the seventeenth and eighteenth centuries, as well as how and why they created it, this understanding provides for the first time a reasonably adequate basis for evaluating the judgments of Pitman and Ragatz.[4]

Intended as comprehensive social histories of the six major British West Indian islands—Barbados, Jamaica, and the four Leeward islands of

---

[3] Eric Williams, *Capitalism and Slavery* (Chapel Hill, N.C., 1944); J. Harry Bennett, *Bondsmen and Bishops: Slavery and Apprenticeship on the Codrington Plantations of Barbados, 1710—1838* (Los Angeles and Berkeley, 1958); Richard Pares, *A West India Fortune* (London, 1950), *Yankees and Creoles: The Trade between North America and the West Indies before the American Revolution* (Cambridge, Mass., 1956), and *Merchants and Planters* (Cambridge, 1960); Frank Wesley Pitman, *The Development of the British West Indies, 1700—1763* (New Haven, 1917), quotations from 2, 39, 41; Lowell J. Ragatz, *The Fall of the Planter Class in the British Caribbean, 1763—1833* (New York, 1928).

[4] Carl and Roberta Bridenbaugh, *No Peace beyond the Line: The English in the Caribbean, 1624—1690* (New York, 1972); Richard S. Dunn, *Sugar and Slaves: The Rise of the Planter Class in the English West Indies, 1624—1713* (Chapel Hill, N.C., 1972); Orlando Patterson, *The Sociology of Slavery: An Analysis of the Origins, Development, and Structure of Negro Slave Society in Jamaica* (Cranbury, N.J., 1969); Richard Sheridan, *The Development of the Plantations to 1750* and *An Era of West Indian Prosperity, 1750—1775,* Chapters in Caribbean History, no. 1 (Barbados, 1970), and *Sugar and Slavery;* Michael Craton

Antigua, Montserrat, Nevis, and St. Kitts—during the seventeenth century, the volumes by Carl and Roberta Bridenbaugh and by Richard S. Dunn cover much of the same ground. Each volume recounts the familiar story of the original English settlement in the Lesser Antilles in the 1620s, the heavy English migration and search for a staple during the 1630s, the sugar revolution and the massive importation of African slaves (beginning in Barbados during the 1640s and extending to the Leeward Islands and Jamaica after the Restoration), the subsequent drift toward monoculture and a declining ratio of Europeans to Africans, and the vigorous competition for possession of the islands by rival European powers over much of the seventeenth century.

But they are very different books and represent two distinct, if also complementary, approaches to the study of past societies. One approach, of which Carl Bridenbaugh is one of the most skilled practitioners among American historians, may be referred to as *social history by example.* For its effectiveness it relies chiefly upon an intelligent blending of illustrations from the surviving literary, pictorial, and material record. A second and new approach, of which the Dunn book is a superb example, depends much more heavily upon the systematic presentation and analysis of existing quantitative data. Its success derives largely from the firmness of the data and the author's sensitivity in interpreting them. These divergent paths do, however, lead the authors to the same general conclusion. Echoing Pitman and Ragatz, as well as many contemporary commentators, they agree that, at least for the seventeenth century, the West Indian colonies were social failures.

Indeed, this is the central theme of the Bridenbaughs' study, *No Peace Beyond the Line: The English in the Caribbean, 1624–1690.* Written from "the insular rather than the imperial point of view," this vigorously argued volume provides a comprehensive narrative of the economic and social development of the British Caribbean colonies from 1624 to 1692, with special focus upon the lives of the people—white and black—and "their outlook." At least in part the book is a success story. The authors admire the "astounding English vitality" displayed by the settlers and their extraordinary economic achievement. With the help of the Dutch, who provided expertise and capital, Barbadian planters in just twenty years, from 1640 to 1660, effected an agricultural and social revolution that was little short of spectacular. In doing so, they not only generated

---

and James Walvin, *A Jamaican Plantation: The History of Worthy Park, 1670–1970* (Toronto, 1970); Edward Brathwaite, *The Development of Creole Society in Jamaica, 1770–1820* (Oxford, 1971).

enormous wealth for many of themselves and their backers but established an economic model that could be—and was—transferred to the
rest of the English islands. But the price of this "impressive material
accomplishment," the Bridenbaughs argue, was nothing less than "social
failure and human tragedy." The human tragedy can be measured in part
by the enormous toll in human life, especially among the unwilling immigrant African slaves, who died in droves on slave ships and were worked
so hard and mercilessly on the plantations that the mortality rate had
reached at least as high as 6 percent per annum by 1690.[5]

For the Bridenbaughs, however, the even greater tragedy was the failure of the English settlers to establish "a sound white society." They went
out to the islands determined "to improve their fortunes . . . and . . . to
transplant as much of Old England as possible." But two related factors
combined to prevent them from forming a "society resembling any in the
Old World." First, the Bridenbaughs argue, although the "seventeenth
century was not fundamentally a materialistic age" for the English, for
the West Indian settlers "it was little else"; and the "overweening greed
for profit and a persisting overemphasis on things material" simply "prevented any successful rooting and growth of English civilization." Living
in "a continual state of transition" and never committed to permanent
residence, the white settlers, mostly young, male, and drawn from "a low
grade set of people," with only a smattering of gentlemen leaders and no
"substantial number of those middling Englishmen who figured at the
same time in the building of the New England and Chesapeake societies,"
constructed only "inadequate institutions" and a "way of life" that was
religiously and morally deficient and culturally and intellectually
barren.[6]

Second, insular life was "blighted" by the massive importation of alien
and unwilling African slaves. The "all-embracing difficulty" arising from
this excessive materialism and the overwhelming numbers of alien Africans, according to the Bridenbaughs, was the "incomplete adjustment"
of Englishmen "to the New World." The "family, the church, and the
community"—the "prime institutions that had made English civilization
what it was" and "provided the safeguards against barbarism"—"never
grew to form a healthy, rounded, friendly society of white people." Coming from the more similar climate of West Africa and with no hope of
escape, the blacks were better "able to live as families and to develop a
genuine sense of community life which they expressed so fascinatingly in

---

[5] Bridenbaugh, *No Peace beyond the Line*, 3, 407, 412.

[6] Ibid., 3, 35, 102, 150, 165, 263, 377, 411.

music and the dance." But the arrested social development of the whites, the Bridenbaughs insist, left the Caribbean islands in a condition that closely resembled Thomas Hobbes's state of nature, with "no commodious Building[,] . . . no Arts, no Letters, no Society, and, which is worst of all, continued feare and danger of violent death; And the life of man was solitary, poore, nasty, brutish, and short."[7]

That the British West Indies were "disastrous social failures" during the seventeenth century is also the judgment of Richard S. Dunn in *Sugar and Slaves: The Rise of the Planter Class in the English West Indies, 1624–1713.* Like the Bridenbaughs, Dunn has sought to produce "a composite portrait of English life in the Caribbean." As his subtitle implies, however, his primary concern is not with the failure to reproduce English institutions but with the "rapid rise of a cohesive and potent master class," in Dunn's view, the "chief distinguishing feature of island society in the seventeenth century." Making ingenious use of maps, census materials, and a wide variety of other data, Dunn describes the emergence, "practically overnight" in Barbados, of "the most perfectly articulated colonial aristocracy in English America" and of the formative stages in the slower development of similar groups in the Leeward Islands and Jamaica before 1713. The result is a study of major importance: the first systematic and extended account of the emergence and character of an elite group for any of the English colonies during the seventeenth and eighteenth centuries.[8]

These scrabbling West Indian elites, Dunn argues, quickly created a "very durable social pattern" that, with its highly stratified social structure and great disparities in wealth and styles of life, bore a superficial resemblance to English rural society, but it was one that "had no counterpart . . . elsewhere in the English experience" within England. "The one outstanding attraction to life" in the islands, according to Dunn, "was the opportunity for making a quick fortune," and in the race for profits members of the rising elite rejected "most of the social values associated with the gentry in seventeenth-century England" at the same time as they tried to cultivate many gentry habits that were entirely inappropriate to a tropical environment. By surrounding themselves with "hordes of restive black captives" whom they simultaneously "hated and feared," they created a situation for themselves that was so insecure as to make the islands "almost uninhabitable." Moreover, an alien climate and an unfamiliar and virulent disease environment turned

---

[7] Ibid., 102, 264, 411, 413.

[8] Dunn, *Sugar and Slaves*, xvii, 46, 48, 340.

the islands into "a demographic disaster area," where life expectancy was low, families were characteristically broken, deaths were usually in excess of births, and the number of young adults was extremely high.[9]

In these circumstances the plantation became a ruthlessly capitalistic institution. With little of the paternalism that helped to soften relations between landlords and tenants on English estates, the sugar plantations mercilessly exploited the slaves in the conviction that "it was more efficient to import new slaves of prime working age from Africa than to breed up a creole generation of Negroes in the Caribbean." For those whites who survived, Dunn argues, there could be no permanent attachment to such a society. The only viable goal was escape, as the failures drifted off to other colonies and the successes either sold out and migrated or retired to England, leaving their estates in the hands of managers. The result was a society that was "radically different" from that of England: family structure never followed a normal pattern, traditional supportive social institutions were virtually nonexistent, there was a rapid circulation among the elite, and the entire white population was highly transient and unstable. With "a small cadre of white masters driving an army of black slaves," the British West Indies in 1713 more closely resembled a nineteenth-century industrial factory than a traditional European society.[10]

In constructing this portrait of these "fast-living, fast-dying tropical" communities, Dunn not only provides the most solid and precise account ever written of the social development of the British West Indies down to 1713, he also challenges some traditional historical clichés. Specifically, he argues plausibly that the extent of British migration to the Caribbean has been seriously exaggerated and "that the stream of migration to the mainland colonies was always larger, even before the English Civil War." More conclusively, he also shows that historians have similarly exaggerated the white depopulation of Barbados during the seventeenth century and the degree of concentration of landholding. With 20,000 whites in 1680, Barbados was exceeded in numbers only by Massachusetts and Virginia among all the English colonies in America, and the great majority of Barbados property holders at that date were still small farmers.[11]

Nor do Dunn's conclusions agree with those of the Bridenbaughs in all

---

[9] Ibid., 45, 47, 116, 188, 334.

[10] Ibid., 47, 320, 335.

[11] Ibid., 16, 77.

respects. In particular he denies that "slaves adjusted better than their masters to life in the tropics," that Negro family life was any less stunted than that of whites, or that slave acclimation to the tropics was a critical consideration in the shift from indentured to slave labor. Rather, Dunn attributes this shift largely to the slaves' availability, cheapness, and dependability as a labor force. More important perhaps is a subtle distinction in emphasis in explaining the social failure of the West Indian colonies. Whereas the Bridenbaughs attribute that failure to the "incomplete adjustment" of the English colonists to the New World, Dunn seems to trace it to the totality of that adjustment, to their almost complete capitulation to conditions of life they found in the islands and their successful manipulation of those conditions for a single purpose: material gain.[12]

In *The Sociology of Slavery: An Analysis of the Origins, Development, and Structure of Negro Slave Society in Jamaica,* an inventive and perceptive book that, concentrating on Jamaica and covering the whole period from the beginning of British occupation to the emancipation of the slaves in 1838, goes well beyond the works of either the Bridenbaughs or Dunn in the depth and scope of its treatment of slave culture, Orlando Patterson reiterates even more forcefully the Bridenbaughs' and Dunn's harsh judgment. According to Patterson, Jamaica not only failed to replicate its parent culture but was "a monstrous distortion of human society" chiefly characterized by "the astonishing neglect" and perversion "of almost every one of the basic prerequisites for normal living." The early attempts to establish "a *colonie de peuplement*" failed as Jamaica settlers abandoned all other considerations in the race for sugar profits. The result was cultural disintegration—the "almost complete disorganization" of the "values of both masters and slaves" and a society that "existed for the pursuit of one goal—that of making vast fortunes as quickly as possible from growing sugar."[13]

After 1730 "both a slave and a white creole society emerged," but by that time the society was so deeply materialistic and so malintegrated that whites were unable to perpetuate what little sense of "local patriotism" they had developed during the first half century of settlement and fled the colony for Britain as fast as they could afford to, thus depriving the colony of "the wealthiest and most talented sector of the white creole group." The consequences of this deprivation of leadership for white society were profound: an utter lack of the educational and other social and

---

[12] Ibid., 313; Bridenbaugh, *No Peace beyond the Line,* 102.

[13] Patterson, *Sociology of Slavery,* 9, 284.

cultural institutions of British society, "a complete breakdown of religion and morality," "the almost complete breakdown . . . of marriage and the family," "the gross mismanagement of the economic affairs of the island," and a repressive slave system that placed "total power" in the hands of the masters, with almost none of the mitigating agencies provided for dependents in other societies by state, community, and bureaucracy.[14]

But Patterson's most important contribution is in describing the lives and culture of the slaves under this repressive regime. Making imaginative and resourceful use of a wide variety of sources, Patterson provides much hard information and a series of intriguing hypotheses about such topics as the structure and disposition of the workforce, conditions of life and work, the tribal origins and social institutions of the slaves, the "slave personality," and patterns and meanings of slave resistance.

Patterson challenges the conventional belief that "Gold Coast Negroes dominated the rest of the Africans," arguing instead that the survival of so many Gold Coast cultural elements in modern Jamaica is attributable to their insistence upon keeping to themselves and that, in any case, "the Akan and Ga-Adangme peoples of the coastal strip of Ghana" were able, as the largest component of the slave population for the first fifty years, "to impose their own patterns of behavior and speech on the creole slave society which was then in its nuclear stage." Virtually every ethnic group from West Africa was represented among Jamaican slaves, and this complex ethnic diversity continued to be a divisive social force among slaves throughout the slave period. Eventually, ethnic diversity became less important than the larger distinction between Africans and creoles (American born). Although the slaves were not yet able to reproduce themselves, and large numbers of Africans had to be imported to maintain a stationary level among the slave population, by 1760 the mortality rate had decreased and the birthrate had increased enough for creoles to outnumber—and dominate—the African-born. On plantations, slaves were further divided according to place and character of work, with domestics, skilled workers, and drivers having a higher status than field hands.[15]

An important result of the creolization of this fragmented population between 1730 and 1780 was its successful adjustment to the harsh conditions of slave life. The creoles had learned English, mastered their roles in the system, and developed patterns of behavior through which they

---

[14] Ibid., 34, 40–41, 43, 92, 285.

[15] Ibid., 142, 153.

could "best adjust" to their thralldom.[16] The predominance of the Quashee personality syndrome, which in its manifestations of a persona of childlike inefficiency, frivolity, and ignorance bears a marked similarity to the American Sambo as described by Stanley Elkins,[17] is a case in point. But Patterson, in contrast to Elkins, stresses the extent to which the slaves in assuming the Quashee mask were simply catering to white stereotypes for their own ends—according to the Jamaican proverb, playing the "fool to catch wise"—rather than actually internalizing them. In any case adjustment did not mean acceptance. Servile revolt was both "continuous and intense": among American slave societies, only Brazil may have experienced more frequent or larger-scale revolts. Moreover, as Patterson skillfully shows, slave songs and folktales reveal a sharply developed and persistent "sense of injustice and persecution."[18]

Despite the repressiveness of the system, all slaves had some space of their own. Most slaves had a half acre of ground assigned to them on which they grew their own provisions, and the custom of the country permitted them to sell any surplus at regional Sunday markets, which brought the slaves from neighboring plantations together. Because they were farthest removed from their white masters, field slaves, Patterson seems to be implying, may have had more privacy, more latitude, and less pressure to socialize to white norms. This space and scope permitted the slaves, as individuals, to preserve some sense of individuality and integrity and, collectively, to maintain some elements of their African religions and to develop seasonal recreations to a high level.

Yet, Patterson stresses, the most vivid effect of the slave society of Jamaica upon both slaves and masters was its overall destructiveness. Legally the slaves had "no civil character, no personality," and the whole system constituted an overwhelming and "constant onslaught on the self-dignity and pride of slaves" and led, Patterson argues, not entirely persuasively, to the "complete breakdown of all major institutions—the family, marriage, religion, organized morality"—the slaves had brought with them from Africa. Only after emancipation was there any significant reversal in these destructive tendencies, the result of two autonomous developments: the consolidation and amplification of the Afro-Jamaican cultural system that had begun to develop under slavery and

---

[16] Ibid., 285.

[17] Stanley Elkins, *Slavery: A Problem in American Institutional and Intellectual Life* (Chicago, 1959).

[18] Patterson, *Sociology of Slavery,* 180, 257, 273.

"the revival of British civilization in the island after its disintegration under slavery."[19]

❀ ❀ ❀

By placing the British Caribbean colonies in their general economic context and a longer time perspective, Richard B. Sheridan in his two volumes both amplifies and modifies the findings of Patterson, Dunn, and the Bridenbaughs. The product of over twenty years of research and an unparalleled mastery of existing sources, *Sugar and Slavery: An Economic History of the British West Indies, 1623–1775* is the most comprehensive and authoritative study yet published on the socioeconomic development of the early British Caribbean. Like the Bridenbaughs and Dunn, Sheridan is concerned with Barbados, Jamaica, and the four Leeward Islands. Unlike them, he carries his story down to 1775, devoting more space to the eighteenth century. Admirably succinct, Sheridan's two essays for the new series Chapters in Caribbean History (which will eventually constitute a cooperative history of the Caribbean in fifty chapters)[20] summarize most of the main findings of the larger work and place them in a comparative framework that includes consideration of the French islands of Martinique and St. Domingue as well as the Spanish island and mainland colonies.

Sheridan focuses upon the organization and operation of the sugar plantation and the role of the sugar colonies in the emerging Atlantic economy; his primary thesis is "that, however inhumane, the sugar industry made a notable contribution to the wealth and maritime supremacy of Great Britain." The "economic growth of Great Britain," he argues, "was chiefly from without inwards," "the Atlantic was the most dynamic trading area," and, next to the metropolis, "the most important element" in the growth of the Atlantic before 1776 "was the slave-plantation, chiefly of the cane-sugar variety in the islands of the Caribbean." By generating new trades and shipping, shifting "millions of hoe cultivators from one side of the Atlantic to the other," redirecting the movement of capital, stimulating the production of intermediate products in the temperate-zone colonies, and creating a wealthy class of

---

[19] Ibid., 85, 178, 247, 287.

[20] Previously published in the same series are Elsa V. Goveia, *The West Indian Slave Laws of the 18th Century* (Barbados, 1970), and C. J. Bartlett, *A New Balance of Power: The 19th Century* (Barbados, 1970).

planters and merchants, the plantation, Sheridan contends, "was truly an innovation in the Schumpeterian sense."[21]

Thus the sugar industry not only became the "chief source of new wealth" (much of it channeled into Britain) during the seventeenth and eighteenth centuries, it also helped, as the most important sector of the new colonial export economies, to give rise to a variety of economic linkages that in turn induced changes in productive techniques and organization within the home islands. More than "elements . . . indigenous to the domestic economy," Sheridan believes, these changes were critical to the emergence of the Industrial Revolution.[22]

Sheridan is especially effective in tracing long-term fluctuations in the economic and political context of the sugar boom. Prices fluctuated, showing a consistently higher trend only during the periods 1680–1713 and 1734–58, but both the volume and market value of sugar products moved inexorably upward over the whole period 1643–1775. This movement reflected a continuous expansion of the sugar industry, the result of (1) a steady increase in per capita sugar and tea consumption throughout the Anglo-American world so that supply never quite caught up with demand, (2) the almost total exclusion of foreign sugar from the British market, and (3) the rising political influence of the West Indian "interest" in British politics. Early opposition to the Navigation Acts gave way to demands for strict enforcement as the West Indians won one concession after another from the metropolitan government, concessions, one contemporary estimated, that brought them £8 million in profits during the thirty years from 1730 to 1760!

Fixed capital costs in labor, buildings, and machinery, as well as depreciation costs (mainly the result of high replacement rates for slaves), were much higher than for any other colonial agricultural industry; and there were no important changes in the technology and methods of cultivation, processing, or transportation. Nevertheless, expansionary tendencies were so strong that profits were extremely high, during the mideighteenth century up to 8.5 percent in newer areas in good years and no lower than 4 percent in older colonies like Barbados.

The longer time perspective permits Sheridan to chart important temporal and spatial variations in the developmental sequence described by the Bridenbaughs and Dunn. During the eighteenth century Barbados continued its inexorable movement toward "a capital-intensive, power-intensive system of agriculture conducted on a sustained-yield ba-

---

[21] Sheridan, *Sugar and Slavery,* xii, 306–7, 475.

[22] Ibid., 11, 16.

sis," as declining soil fertility and higher processing costs required more and more capital and labor to yield ever-diminishing rates of return. But the drive toward intensive monoculture and many of the tendencies associated with that drive either lost vigor or changed in character between 1700 and 1775. An actual turning away from sugar to livestock was manifest as early as the 1730s, and the movement toward property consolidation had leveled off by 1750, with roughly a third of the proprietors owning somewhat more than half of the estates and windmills.[23]

Although white migration continued through the 1740s, there was a reversal in the formerly steady decline in white settlers after 1710. Over the next sixty-five years the number of whites grew by about 50 percent, to 18,500 in 1773. The slave population continued to rise, doubling over the same period, but imports, which remained fairly high, accounted for a declining proportion of the slave population. Annual mortality rates among slaves declined from 6 percent in 1700–1725 to 3.8 percent in 1750–75, the result, Sheridan surmises, of a growing ratio of creoles to the total number of slaves and better diet and health care, as, with declining profits, it became more profitable to breed slaves locally than to import new ones.

For reasons also described by Dunn, the heavy influx of African slaves, large-scale property consolidation, loss of white settlers, and intensive concentration on sugar experienced by Barbados during the half century after 1640 took place in the Leeward Islands mainly after 1713, with Nevis, which had already experienced substantial development in that direction, leading the way, followed by Montserrat, St. Kitts, and Antigua. But these islands differed from the Barbados model at least before 1775 in that there was no turning away from monoculture and no reversal in the decline of white settlers. In Nevis and Montserrat there was a steady loss from the 1670s to a low point in 1745, followed by a slight rise over the next decade and a continuation of the downward trend thereafter. In the later developing islands of St. Kitts and Antigua, white population continued to climb in the 1720s and then dropped slowly but steadily thereafter. Because the black population tripled in all four islands between the second and seventh decades of the eighteenth century, the ratio of blacks to whites was much higher than in Barbados—15 to 1 in Antigua, 12 to 1 in St. Kitts, 11 to 1 in Nevis, and 7.5 to 1 in Montserrat—with the result that the Leeward Islands were little more than sugar factories with a few white managers and a large gang of black workers. Far more than Barbados they had been transformed by 1770

---

[23] Ibid., 147.

from colonies of settlement into colonies of exploitation with an impoverished cultural and political life of the kind attributed by the Bridenbaughs and Dunn to all of the islands by the end of the seventeenth
century.

Despite many similarities, Jamaica diverged considerably from the
patterns exhibited by the smaller islands. Although much larger, it did
not export as much sugar as Barbados until early in the eighteenth century, and it continued to grow slowly from 1713 to 1740 because of the
decline of the sugar market, the engrossment of lands by large holders,
an inadequate slave supply, and the fierce opposition of the Maroons,
bands of runaway slaves who terrorized outlying areas of the colony, especially between 1725 and 1739. After the cessation of hostilities with the
Maroons and in response to a rising sugar market, Jamaica experienced a
spectacular growth from 1740 to 1775 as the number of slaves and sugar
plantations doubled. By 1775 Jamaica was exporting ten times as many
sugar products as Barbados and had three times as many slaves. Over
the same period the aggregate value of the colony's economy increased
from just over £3.5 to over £15.1 million.

But this rapid expansion produced significantly different results from
those arising from the similar development of Barbados a century earlier
or of the Leeward Islands a half century before. Jamaica never became
a sugar monoculture. Four out of ten slaves were in nonsugar production, and more than half of the plantations were devoted to livestock,
provisions, and minor staples. Similarly, there was still much uncultivated land and considerable land wastage in Jamaica, where the plantation economy was more land-intensive and less labor- and capital-
intensive. Moreover, Jamaica experienced no loss of white population,
which increased slowly but steadily from 7,000 in 1703 to over 18,000 in
1774. Also, slave mortality was somewhat lower, ranging from 4 percent
down to 2 percent annually, the probable result, Sheridan thinks, of better dietary standards deriving from the allowance to each slave of a small
plot of provision ground and one and one-half days per week for his or
her own activities. Finally, Jamaica slaves developed a vigorous internal
marketing system, and the free colored population of Jamaica exceeded
that of Barbados by 10 to 1.

In several important respects Sheridan's findings strongly suggest that
the picture of emerging Caribbean society as drawn by the Bridenbaughs
and Dunn for the end of the seventeenth century requires some modification. On the question of absenteeism, Sheridan argues that, although
it was present from the beginning of sugar culture, it did not become "a
movement of consequence until the eighteenth century." In the Leeward

Islands a substantial number of proprietors may have been absentees, in
St. Kitts perhaps as many as half by the early 1730s. Barbados and Jamaica never had such large proportions, although during the silver age
of sugar, which began around 1740, up to 30 percent of sugar plantations
in Jamaica belonged to absentees. But before 1775, Sheridan emphasizes,
absentees were only a fraction of the British proprietors in the tropics,
albeit a highly visible fraction because of their disproportionate wealth
and influence in the British government. Absenteeism, Sheridan agrees,
"drained away wealth and income that might otherwise have gone into
public and private improvements" and "contributed to the impover-
ishment of political and social life" in the islands, but along with continuing, if probably somewhat declining, high mortality rates, it also functioned to keep avenues of social mobility open.[24]

Indeed, throughout the eighteenth century white society was more
open and more attractive to white immigrants than might have been
expected from the extent of property consolidation and tendencies toward monoculture and white population loss that were so strongly manifest by 1713. Even in the older and smaller islands, Sheridan shows, "each
generation witnessed the rise of new men and at times the establishment
of new family dynasties alongside the stagnation and decline of planters
whose indebtedness and absenteeism [or death] made their estates ripe
for the plucking." Some enterprising immigrants acquired instant wealth
through marriage, while others first accumulated the capital necessary
to purchase a plantation through trade, office, or the law. In Jamaica,
where there was uncultivated land as late as the 1760s, it was still possible for those with sufficient capital to establish a sugar plantation from
scratch or for those with fewer resources to begin with minor staples and
build up a sugar estate gradually from reinvested profits, apparently the
most common pattern of estate building in the Caribbean throughout
the period from 1640 to 1775. In any case, opportunities were sufficient
so that many planters rose up from the lower and middle ranks of society,
with "one stream of recruits" coming from "the professional, administrative, and especially the mercantile groups in the colonies" and a second
"from subordinate managerial personnel on plantations." Many of these
recruits seem to have come not from the creoles but from the newcomers
and especially from the Scots, who came in large numbers after 1710.[25]

Finally, Sheridan adduces considerable evidence that, even in terms
of the Eurocentric standards imposed by the Bridenbaughs, Dunn, and

---

24 Ibid., 13, 385–86.

25 Ibid., 177, 387–88.

Patterson, Britain's Caribbean colonies were not the total social failures those writers suggest. Sheridan does not deny that the social costs of the "sugar lottery" were burdensome or that "by European standards of the time" the sugar colonies "were notoriously deficient in education, social services, and public improvements," but he does suggest that the stereotyped images of the West Indies as a social wasteland and the planter "as an improvident, indolent, and sensuous gentleman" are both one-dimensional and "in need of revision." He shows that the quality of plantation management was improving after 1750; many planters were obviously hardworking and thrifty; religious and cultural factors influenced white behavior; the professions, especially the law, were well developed, and "middle-class mercantile and professional men exerted an influence that was disproportionate to their numbers"; "family life coexisted with bachelorhood"; and "it was not unusual for families to remain in possession of plantations for many generations."[26]

One family of large planters who did not flee the Caribbean before the 1780s was the Price family of Jamaica, owners of Worthy Park, one of three Jamaica sugar estates with a continuous history of three hundred years and the subject of Michael Craton and James Walvin's useful microstudy *A Jamaican Plantation: The History of Worthy Park, 1670–1970*. Commissioned by the present owners to commemorate the tricentennial of the plantation, the volume follows the history of the estate beyond emancipation in 1834 through a long period of decline and three changes in family ownership to its revival and expansion under the Clarkes between 1918 and 1970. But more than two-thirds of the volume is devoted to the history of the estate during the first half of its existence. In the experience of Worthy Park and the Price family one can see how the general developments described by Dunn, Patterson, and Sheridan were refracted through the experience of one estate and one family. Most specifically, the history of the Prices illustrates the life cycle of a great Jamaica sugar family.

Establishment of the family fortune, as Sheridan suggests was generally the case, was a slow process. Francis Price, founder of the fortune and veteran of Cromwell's army, had had a small estate on which he raised indigo, cocoa, and a little sugar for seven years before he acquired by patent in 1670 the original 840 acres of Worthy Park in a lush but remote inland valley. Over the next nineteen years Price prospered. He rose from lieutenant to major of militia, twice served as member of the assembly for St. John's Parish, established a fruitful business connection

---

[26] Ibid., 364; Sheridan, *Era of West Indian Prosperity,* 105–7.

with Peter Beckford, "co-founder of the largest of all Jamaica fortunes," and made an important dynastic connection through the marriage of his daughter to Francis Rose, scion of another emerging planter family. He also cleared fields, built roads and a great house, and acquired another 900 acres at Worthy Park with the intention of turning it into a sugar plantation. At his death in 1689 it was still devoted to provisions and livestock and was "an extremely modest pioneer farm, such as might have been found in the backwoods of Virginia or the Carolinas at much the same time."[27]

The spectacular growth in the fortunes of the Price family came over the next two generations. Charles Price, Sr., who died in 1730, turned Worthy Park into a sugar estate and became one of Jamaica's "more substantial planters." Aided by the favorable economic climate after 1713 and his own great energy and enterprise, he accumulated an estate worth over £100,000, including a house in Spanish Town, the seat of fashion and power, and, though he lived all his life in Jamaica, he sent his children to England for their education. Whereas Charles Price, Sr., "was chiefly notable as an estate builder" and only dabbled in public life, his son Charles Price, Jr., became the most prominent political figure in the colony at the same time he was expanding family holdings in land and wealth. Indeed, he combined "territorial megalomania with an exaggerated sense of duty." Known to his contemporaries as "The Patriot," he was a member of the assembly for thirty-one years and speaker for eighteen years (beginning in 1745), the leading spokesman for the Spanish Town or sugar planter interest in the island, and for four years before his death in 1772 a member of the council.[28]

Political influence brought access to land and public works projects that raised the value of his holdings, and his activities as a speculator and developer were on a scale unequaled in the Anglophone Caribbean. At his death he owned 26,000 acres, "perhaps the largest portion of Jamaica ever owned by a single individual," and 1,800 slaves, 1 percent of the entire slave population of the island. During the silver age of Jamaica sugar beginning around 1745, returns were so large that he was relatively free from the scarcities of capital and labor that had limited his father and grandfather. He built a costly aqueduct at Worthy Park, an expensive town house in Spanish Town, and an elaborate country house. Yet he did not avoid the Jamaica malady of expanding his holdings far beyond his capacity to finance them. At his death his real estate empire

---

[27] Craton and Walvin, *Jamaican Plantation*, 38, 41.

[28] Ibid., 46, 58, 72.

was "staggering under the weight of mortgages." Charles Price III was unable to save much of his father's estate in the unhappy economic climate after 1775 and finally deserted Jamaica for England in 1787, the first Price in the main line of the family to become an absentee. Although the Price family fortunes revived briefly in the 1790s under the vigorous stewardship of Charles's heir and cousin, Rose Price, and the family managed to retain control of Worthy Park down to 1863, the fortunes of the family in Jamaica subsequently ebbed and flowed according to general economic conditions and quality of management.[29]

To the extent that the experience of the Price family is revelatory of broader trends, it may be used to evaluate the conclusions of the more general works considered here. In at least two senses the harsher assessments of the Bridenbaughs, Dunn, and Patterson would seem to be confirmed. First, Jamaica, if not quite a demographic disaster area, was clearly unhealthy for whites as well as for blacks. Among the first three generations of Prices, life expectancy was only twenty-four (though for those who reached adulthood it was dramatically higher), while the slaves at Worthy Park continued to suffer a natural decrease through the 1780s and 1790s long after the balance among them had shifted from Africans to creoles. Second, beginning with the third and fourth generations, the Prices were to some degree guilty of the extravagance usually attributed to Caribbean planters, devoting some share of the family's resources to conspicuous consumption, including the assignment of an excessive number of slaves to domestic statuses.

But in many other respects the experience of the Prices deviates sharply from the projections of Dunn and the characterizations of Patterson. The first four generations revealed none of the sloth of the planter stereotype; no serious improvidence appeared until the third generation, and even then in an attenuated form. Indeed, the energy and industry of the first three generations were as impressive as those of any Boston or Philadelphia merchant family. Similarly, the Prices did not become absentees until the late 1780s, and even then they were not the stereotyped absentees who fled Jamaica as soon as they had acquired "sufficient wealth to live in ostentatious luxury abroad" but rather, in the authors' words, the "battered" victims "of an implacable system, seeking relief from the daily mounting weight and tension of plantation debt, in abdication."[30]

The behavior of the Prices in this respect raises questions not only

---

[29] Ibid., 73, 79.

[30] Ibid., 164.

about the authors' judgment that sugar wealth for the first Charles Price was primarily "a means of escape" from the island but also about the conventional wisdom concerning the extent, timing, and causes of the major flow of absentees from Jamaica. Clearly, the deliberate choice of Charles Price, Jr., to remain in Jamaica was not dictated by the lack of means to leave. On the contrary, along with other aspects of his behavior, including his building of elaborate houses in Spanish Town and at his country estate, his massive reinvestment of profits in capital improvements and labor for his estates, and his devotion to public life, it shows a degree both of commitment to the island and of local patriotism that do not easily fit the clichés about planter behavior.[31]

Far more closely than these clichés, the history of the Price family would seem, before its eventual, and perhaps reluctant, abandonment of Jamaica in the 1780s, to have resembled the experiences of the great planting families on the continent—the Carters, Robinsons, Randolphs, and Lees in Virginia and the Pinckneys, Bulls, and Smiths in South Carolina—with the early generations laboring to build a large estate, later ones playing an increasingly prominent role in politics, and still later ones failing, in either the economic or political realm, to match the achievements of their progenitors.

In his *Development of Creole Society in Jamaica, 1770—1820,* Edward Brathwaite has issued an even more direct challenge to the view of the British West Indian colonies as social failures. Far from being merely "a loose 'collection of autonomous plantations,'" he argues, Jamaica "had developed, from the beginning of its history, an establishment of governmental and social institutions capable not only of organizing and controlling life within its territory, but comparable in many ways (at least up to the American Revolution) to similar institutions on the mainland of British North America." Although he does not explore the composition of white society for late eighteenth-century Jamaica so thoroughly as Dunn does for late seventeenth-century Barbados, Brathwaite shows that it was not limited to a handful of resident managers of large sugar estates. As many as a fifth of island whites were from large landholding or wealthy and substantial mercantile or professional families. In addition, there were many small planters and urban artisans, clerks, or shopkeepers, as well as estate managers.[32]

Unlike the Leeward Islands, Jamaica thus managed to sustain a "self- conscious, articulate, cohesive social class of proprietor-administrators"

---

[31] Ibid., 67.

[32] Brathwaite, *Development of Creole Society,* 307.

well into the later eighteenth century. Like most colonial ruling groups, its orientation was much more practical than aesthetic, and its primary capital—and social—investment in the island was in the form of material improvements such as roads, bridges, public buildings, and forts. But the members of this class were not as yet "passengers only." They were "creoles" in the fullest sense of that term: that is, they were "committed settlers" who supported an active press; built churches, schools, and hospitals; and exerted political and social control through dynamic and self-conscious political institutions, especially the assembly, the "most perfect expression of (white) creole society." The grand houses they built in growing numbers after 1750 mark the emergence "of a creole style, a Jamaican 'vernacular,'" that makes it apparent, Brathwaite argues, "that considerable effort was [still] being made . . . to 'civilize the wilderness,'" much like that of wealthy North Americans in their own rural settings of the same time.[33]

The political attitudes of Jamaicans and continentals were strikingly similar in the years before the American Revolution, and what primarily distinguished Jamaica from the mainland plantation colonies was not, as Brathwaite supposes, less "significant cultural development" or the absence of a desire to reorder society but its relatively greater vulnerability to metropolitan military might and economic sanctions. Only after 1776 was the vigor of white society weakened, Brathwaite suggests, as the American Revolution in many ways isolated Jamaica "from the wider English-speaking New World area of which it was a part" and the humanitarian revolution challenged the foundations and sapped the self-confidence of Jamaican society. Together these revolutions pushed the island into an ever greater dependence upon "the essentially 'absentee' cultural and material influence of the Mother Country" and a revulsion against creole forms and institutions.[34]

But the most important contribution of Brathwaite's book is not in showing that even within the Eurocentric perspective assumed by the Bridenbaughs, Dunn, and Patterson, Jamaica's "social failure"[35] came a full century later than those writers have suggested but in proposing a new frame of reference for approaching the analysis of colonial societies. Like Patterson and Elsa Goveia, whose earlier study of the slave society

---

[33] Ibid., xiv, 39, 67, 124; Sheridan, *Sugar and Slavery*, 232.

[34] Brathwaite, *Development of Creole Society*, xiii–xiv, 71.

[35] Bridenbaugh, *No Peace beyond the Line*, 412.

of the Leeward Islands[36] served as an admirable model for Brathwaite's study, Brathwaite analyzes in detail and with sensitivity the culture of Jamaica's African population. In a brilliant chapter on the folk culture of the slaves, he argues that Jamaica blacks developed and maintained a powerful "'little' tradition" in a rich variety of contexts. Afro-creole life, he maintains in a significant elaboration of Patterson, was not confined to the regimes of the sugar plantation and the routines of domestic service. The number of freedmen was not inconsequential, and, although many of them lived in isolation near the borderline of poverty, others were small planters, fishermen, pilots, overseers, clerks, artisans, shopkeepers, schoolmasters, and builders. Among the slaves there were mechanics, tradesmen, preachers, seamen, woodsmen, and higglers who worked independently and whose activities provided them with considerable scope for privacy and individual autonomy.[37]

But Brathwaite's main point is not simply that, despite the internalization of a belief in Negro inferiority among slaves and freedmen, an Afro-creole tradition was able to survive and even flourish in a complex structural context. Rather, it is that that tradition constantly interacted with the dominant, if weak, Euro-creole tradition to produce a culture or way of life that was distinctively Jamaican, albeit it was also "part of a wider New World or American Culture complex" and "essentially different from the metropolitan model." To understand this process, Brathwaite emphasizes, we must view "white and black, master and slave," not as "separate nuclear units, but as contributory parts of a whole," as "two cultures of people, having to adapt themselves to a new environment and to each other." We have to think in terms not of acculturation of black people, a one-way process, but of transculturation between blacks and whites, a process of exchange.[38]

Enormously intricate, this process was most intense at points of most direct and continuous contact—at markets and army camps and in the great houses—and among groups on the boundaries between black and white society—among mulattoes and domestics in the Afro-creole group and among whites "at the book-keeper or 'walking buckra' level." But it was pervasive. Among blacks it was most clearly manifest in their learning of the master's language and work routines, their identification with

---

[36] Elsa V. Goveia, *Slave Society in the British Leeward Islands at the End of the Eighteenth Century* (New Haven, 1965).

[37] Brathwaite, *Development of Creole Society,* 309.

[38] Ibid., xiii, 101, 307.

local symbols of authority and places of work, and, ultimately, among elite blacks and free coloreds, their imitation of the whites and rejection of many aspects of their African heritage. For whites it was apparent in language, food, dress, amusements, and sexual relationships, although the pull of the metropolis and the need to justify slavery were sufficiently powerful to prevent them from explicitly embracing or coming to terms with Jamaica's Afro-creole tradition and to force them to cling desperately to a "bastard metropolitanism." Nonetheless, Brathwaite stresses, despite white and black resistance, the debasements caused by slavery, and the excessive imitativeness of Jamaican life, an entirely "'new' construct" emerged in colonial Jamaica that was viable and creative even while no group within it managed to appreciate its creativity.[39]

Failure to appreciate this creativity has persisted in modern scholarly judgments that the Anglo-Caribbean colonies were "social failures" or "monstrous distortions of human society."[40] Such assertions, first advanced among modern scholars by Pitman and Ragatz and now echoed by the Bridenbaughs, Dunn, and Patterson, are patently ethnocentric, specifically Eurocentric. The question is not *whether* European immigrants to those colonies established societies, but *what kind* of societies they—along with the much larger stream of immigrants from Africa—established.

Some colonial societies approximate to the metropolitan model of their dominant members more closely than others, and various groups within colonial societies actively cultivate many features of that model. By definition, however, colonial societies are not metropolitan ones: at most, they are no more than moderately strong reflections of the metropolis. As Dunn's work in particular illustrates, it is illuminating to contrast colonial societies to the society of their metropolis. But we may never fully understand the nature and range of colonial societies in the early modern or any other period until we stop evaluating them in terms of the standards of the metropolis and recognize that they constitute a related but significantly different category of societies. To one degree or another each colonial society was a new society that existed within a symbiotic relationship with one or more metropolitan societies.

---

[39] Ibid., 296, 304, 307.

[40] Dunn, *Sugar and Slaves,* 340; Patterson, *Sociology of Slavery,* 9.

But it also existed within a distinctive and confined ecosystem and was profoundly influenced by a number of factors, including especially the organization of its economy, the virulence of its disease environment, and the ethnic composition of its population; and the necessity of adapting to a new environment and, in many cases, to a polyethnic milieu required a process of cultural reformulation and adaptation—to use Brathwaite's phrase, of creolization—that produced perceptions, institutions, social forms, and modes of behavior that invariably deviated from those of its metropolis at the same time that many of its members were striving to keep such deviations to a minimum.[41]

For this reason it is misleading—and pointless—to condemn a colonial society for not reproducing the society of its metropolis. A more promising approach would seem to be to look at the often subtle and, as Brathwaite so strongly underlines, inevitably creative process of reformulation and adaptation against the comparative background supplied by not only the metropolis but also other colonial societies across space and time.

From such a perspective, it will become clear that, as the Bridenbaughs, Dunn, and Patterson have emphasized, the Anglo-Caribbean colonies did have social configurations that differed in many important respects from traditional England. But it will also become apparent that, as Sheridan reminds us, those configurations were always changing in response to a variety of exogenous and endogenous factors and were by no means unique. Rather, they were simply an Anglophone variation of a more general south Atlantic pattern that stretched from southeast Brazil north to the Narragansett Bay, a pattern chiefly characterized by the systematic exploitation of some people—mostly Africans—for the economic benefit of others—almost entirely Europeans. What articles were produced at what profit, how readily immigrant populations could become self-sustaining, and how fully the social features and processes of the metropolis could be replicated varied from one ecological zone to another. But every society within this system was, to a considerable degree, exploitative and materialistic, while most were also markedly polyethnic.

Within the early modern colonial Anglophone world, the Caribbean colonies were doubtless the most fully exploitative and the most thor-

---

[41] See Jack P. Greene, "Search for Identity: An Interpretation of the Meaning of Selected Patterns of Social Response in Eighteenth-Century America," *Journal of Social History* 4 (1970): 189–220.

oughly materialistic at every stage of their development. But from the beginning the dominant impulse was material in all of the colonies from New York south; even in New England the quest for profit was never weak and became increasingly vigorous during the eighteenth century. Except perhaps in the Leeward Islands, where by the mid-eighteenth century the white society was little more than a handful of loosely orga- nized plantation managers, the material impulse, as Brathwaite shows for Jamaica, was never so strong as to crush the complementary desire, to use the Bridenbaughs' phrase, "to transplant as much of Old England as possible."[42]

For a number of reasons that desire was doubtless more difficult to realize in the Caribbean and the coastal areas of the Carolinas and the Chesapeake: a more virulent disease environment meant that immigrant populations, both European and African, took longer to become self- sustaining; higher returns per unit of labor meant that the proportion of Africans (the most available source of durable labor for tropical and semitropical zones) to Europeans was greater than in more northerly areas; and larger profits meant that more European settlers could reemi- grate to Britain. But neither in their materialistic orientation, their dis- ease environments, their number of African inhabitants, their concern to cultivate British values and institutions, nor perhaps even their commit- ment to the colony was there a sharp break between island and mainland societies. Rather, there was a social continuum that ran from the Carib- bean through Georgia and South Carolina to the Chesapeake through Pennsylvania and New York to urban and then rural New England. The social contrast between a sugar plantation in Barbados and a small ho- mogeneous farming community in New England was considerable. But it would no doubt have been less apparent to a contemporary traveler had he proceeded not directly from the one to the other but through a series of intermediate stops along the coast.

Thanks to the works here considered, and especially to the careful quantitative analyses of economic and social data by Sheridan and Dunn, the imaginative reconstructions of Afro-creole life by Patterson and Brathwaite, and the detailed analysis of the experience of the Price family by Craton and Walvin, we now have a fuller picture than ever before of the Caribbean end of this social continuum and a solid basis for constructing a clear typology of the societies of the Anglophone Ameri- can world of the seventeenth and eighteenth centuries, a typology built

---

[42] Bridenbaugh, *No Peace beyond the Line,* 3.

on the recognition that colonial societies must be described and assessed in terms of the constrictions and possibilities inherent in the specific type of society they represent.

This chapter developed out of an invitation from the *American Historical Review* to review three books published in 1972 and 1973 on the English colonies in the early modern West Indies. It is reprinted with permission and with minor verbal changes and citations to quotations from the *American Historical Review* 79 (1974): 1499–1517.

—TEN—

Coming to Terms
with Diversity:
Pluralism and Conflict
in the Formation of
Colonial New York

S INCE THE EARLY 1960s a growing interest in the sociology of early
modern Anglo-American colonization has been manifest in the proliferation of studies of many aspects of the organization and character
of the "new" societies founded by the English in America beginning with
Virginia in 1607. Recently, considerable attention has been focused on
New York, other than Jamaica, the only English colony established during the seventeenth century that was conquered from a rival European
power. In Jamaica the Spanish settlers fled into the Blue Mountains with
their slaves when the English invaded in 1655 and eventually drifted off
to other Spanish settlements around the Caribbean. But in New York
the vast majority of the roughly 9,000 Dutch inhabitants of old New
Netherlands remained following the English conquest in 1664.

From the beginning the presence of this large, firmly established alien
Dutch population gave New York a pluralistic character that was largely
missing in the relatively ethnically homogeneous colonies established
earlier in the Chesapeake, New England, and the West Indies. Social
heterogeneity subsequently came to characterize most of the English-
American colonies, especially those founded after 1660. But New York
continued, as Michael Kammen puts it in his general history of the colony, to be "the most polyglot and socially mixed of them all."[1] Perhaps
because it seems to prefigure in many ways the subsequent history of the

---

[1] Michael Kammen, *Colonial New York: A History* (New York, 1976), xvi.

United States, New York's pluralism has long fascinated colonial historians. How that pluralism affected the political and social dynamics of the colony provides the common theme that links the five volumes considered in this essay.[2]

One of a series of recent case studies of the political development of an English colony during a carefully defined period, Robert C. Ritchie's admirably concise, clearheaded, and unpretentious *The Duke's Province* considers New York during the first generation following its conquest from the Dutch in 1664. Like previous studies in this genre, it analyzes the social context of politics and describes the major social changes in this important "era of transition between rough-hewn settlements and established provincial life," including the emergence of a powerful Anglo-Dutch mercantile elite and the rapid concentration of wealth in New York City, the shifting economic balance within this elite in favor of the English, and the increasing regional variations in social structure. But the volume is essentially a political, and not a social, history.[3]

The proprietary fief of Charles II's brother, the duke of York, New York was the only English colony of the period that did not have an elected assembly, and the struggle of the English settlers to secure such an institution against the determined resistance of proprietary governors has been the classic theme for this period of New York history, the duke's persistant reluctance to grant such an institution being seen as a precursor of his more general effort to dispense with representative government in the colonies through the Dominion of New England after he became king in 1685. Earlier scholars, especially Wesley Frank Craven and David S. Lovejoy, have pointed out the simplistic character of this formulation,[4] but no one has previously shown so clearly the extent to which the colonists' demand for representative government was less the "fulfill-

---

[2] Robert C. Ritchie, *The Duke's Province: A Study of New York Politics and Society, 1664–1691* (Chapel Hill, N.C., 1977); Thomas J. Archdeacon, *New York City, 1664–1710: Conquest and Change* (Ithaca, N.Y., 1976); Sung Bok Kim, *Landlord and Tenant in Colonial New York: Manorial Society, 1664–1775* (Chapel Hill, N.C., 1978); Douglas Greenberg, *Crime and Law Enforcement in the Colony of New York, 1691–1776* (Ithaca, N.Y., 1975); and Kammen, *Colonial New York.*

[3] Ritchie, *Duke's Province,* 3.

[4] Wesley Frank Craven, *The Colonies in Transition, 1660–1713* (New York, 1968), 208–10; David S. Lovejoy, *The Glorious Revolution in America* (New York, 1970), 98–121.

ment of a belief in a liberal ideology" than "an attempt to protect and extend . . . gains made by individuals and local communities."[5]

Ritchie does not deny that New Yorkers, particularly the New Englanders on Long Island, strongly objected to paying taxes levied without their consent. But he argues that the demand for local autonomy and control over the economic resources of their own areas against the aggrandizement of a "powerful political interest group" composed of New York City merchants and fashioned by Sir Edmund Andros in an attempt to consolidate proprietary political power during his governorship (1673–80) was what primarily animated the demand—temporarily realized in the mid-1680s during a brief period of proprietary weakness—for a representative assembly. Throughout this long struggle the colonists' behavior, Ritchie insists, "was characterized by particularism and selfishness rather than lofty ideals."[6]

Whether or not ideals are not often, perhaps invariably, the products of such impulses, Ritchie probably attaches insufficient importance to the New Yorkers' resentment at being—alone among English colonists in America—deprived of the central attribute of civic competence as defined by early modern Englishmen. To have "an arbitrary and absolute power . . . exercised over us[,] . . . and the inhabitants wholly shut out . . . of any share, vote, or interest in the government," meant, as the New York grand jury poignantly phrased it in 1681 in an address quoted by Ritchie, that "we are esteemed as nothing," excluded, like other presumably unworthy groups, from a civic space and thereby deprived of the most vital ingredient in their identity as free Englishmen.[7]

Yet, if Ritchie may underestimate the force of the colonists' indignation at being thus, in effect, civilly emasculated, he is entirely persuasive in arguing that Andros's successful creation of a court clique of "merchant-landowners" was the "most important long-term result" of the period. Also nourished by the patronage of his successor, Thomas Dongan, who lavished profitable offices, trading concessions, and huge land grants upon his favorites, this privileged coterie, an amalgam of English and assimilating Dutch merchants, formed the nucleus of "an elite group that was to dominate life in New York for over a century." By engrossing an ever more disproportionate share of the colony's economic resources, they also elicited the hatred of rural settlers in the Hudson

[5] Ritchie, *Duke's Province*, 4.

[6] Ibid., 4, 100.

[7] Ibid., 159.

River valley and on Long Island and stimulated the growth of a "strong sense of regionalism" that made itself manifest in a fierce antagonism to privilege and a distrust of the city that, as Patricia Bonomi and other scholars have shown, was an enduring feature of colonial New York politics.[8]

Together with mounting ethnic tensions between the English and the Dutch, who, resentful of growing English economic competition and domination of political office at all levels, longed for a return to the days when they had had the colony entirely to themselves, these strains contributed to an explosive situation. That it did not earlier erupt in a massive rebellion is a testimony, Ritchie suggests in an important original point, to the extreme reluctance of colonists "to overthrow a properly constituted government." Only when authority faltered in the wake of the Glorious Revolution did these combustible materials finally produce the "explosions of frustration" that came to be known as Leisler's Rebellion. Primarily the work of men like its leader, the wealthy Dutch merchant Jacob Leisler, who had never been a part of the group of families that had dominated New York for the previous three decades, this uprising represented a last hurrah for those Dutch who had resisted anglicization. Far from allaying existing tensions, it created new and equally complex divisions that persisted through the following generation without destroying the privileges of the old elite, which came out of the rebellion with its political and economic power stronger than ever.[9]

Thomas J. Archdeacon's *New York City, 1664—1710*, examines the ways in which, during the first half century of English occupation, ethnic rivalries affected life in the town of New York, the colony's largest population center. The first detailed and systematic quantitative study of any segment of the history of any major urban center in early modern Anglo-America, it is an especially important addition to the emerging picture of early American society that significantly expands and deepens our knowledge of political and social currents in early New York. Building on a thorough analysis of two surviving tax lists for 1677 and 1703, Archdeacon makes imaginative use of church records, freemanship lists, customhouse records, and other government documents to examine changes

---

[8] Ibid., 4, 82, 107. See also Patricia U. Bonomi, *A Factious People: Politics and Society in Colonial New York* (New York, 1971).

[9] Ritchie, *Duke's Province*, 211, 235.

in social stratification, ethnic makeup, occupational structure, patterns of residence, elite composition, and distribution of political power.

In many respects, his findings reveal that the town conformed rather closely to patterns of development previously observed in other primarily materially oriented colonial areas settled for a comparable length of time. Thus, by 1703 New York exhibited a high degree of social stratification, a marked concentration of political power, and a strong impulse to resort to the use of African slaves. The richest 10 percent of the inhabitants owned just under half of the taxable resources, less than 3 percent of adult males exercised over "half of the official civic power" (as determined by a weighted ranking of offices), and 43 percent of the whites owned slaves, who, together with a small number of free people of African descent, constituted as much as a fifth of the population. Despite increasing stratification, however, society was still open: the vast majority of newlyweds either "began married life in, or quickly obtained, their own homes." If, moreover, the political life of the town, like that of the rest of colonial Anglo-America, was highly deferential, the franchise was broad, and the political domination of the wealthy depended, as elsewhere, upon a largely passive electorate.[10]

Like those in other colonial urban centers, few New York slaveholders had more than two or three slaves, a fact the author interprets as meaning that most slaves were domestics. But the heavy concentration of slaves among the wealthy merchants suggests that many of them may have been used as dockworkers and in other similar capacities.

What distinguished New York from comparable colonial towns was the growing socioeconomic competition between the old Dutch and the new English and French Huguenot immigrants, a competition in which the Dutch came out second best. The period from 1677 to 1703 witnessed the gradual erosion of the Dutch position in the town. In the former year almost four-fifths of identifiable assessed inhabitants were Dutch, while Dutch merchants dominated the town's economic life, despite a significant rise in the number of English among the wealthier merchants over the previous decade. By the latter date this situation had changed dramatically. Together with a small group of apparently highly assimilable French Huguenots, the English constituted over two-fifths of the population. Even more impressive, members of these two new ethnic groups were disproportionately represented among the wealthiest fifth of the population.

A significant number of Dutch merchants managed to accommodate

---

[10] Archdeacon, *New York City,* 94.

themselves to the new regime, including Rip Van Dam, Abraham De Peyster, and Jacobus Van Cortlandt, who were among the wealthiest and most prominent residents of the town. But the English and French together outnumbered the Dutch among the richest group of merchants by almost two to one and dominated every phase of commercial activity. More than any other single indicator, Archdeacon concludes, the "rise to prominence of the English and French merchants exemplifies the way in which New York became an English city during the last quarter of the seventeenth century."[11]

Further evidence of this shift in ethnic predominance can be seen in changing occupational and residential patterns. By 1703 the English and French outnumbered the Dutch in the five leading occupational categories, as the Dutch increasingly "gravitated towards the central ranges" of the economic spectrum, where they had "twice the representation of the English and the French" in such "middle-ranking" employments as blacksmithing, carpentry, and cooperage. Similarly, by ranking streets according to the economic standing of the people who lived on them, Archdeacon is able to show, in a highly original chapter on the social geography of the town, that the English and French minority formed a heavy majority of the inhabitants of the wealthiest and most prestigious districts in 1703, while the Dutch had been largely "relegated to more marginal areas" and accounted for "four of every five families in the poorest areas."[12]

For most of the Dutch inhabitants, then, Archdeacon shows conclusively, the English conquest meant a relative decline in power and status. Whether, given their comparative lack of autonomy under the Dutch regime and the marginal role of New Netherlands in the Dutch overseas empire, it also meant an absolute decline is much less clear. But Archdeacon argues that the accumulated frustration arising from the deteriorating position of the Dutch primarily accounts for the "tumultuous events" that shook the town during the closing decades of the seventeenth century. This frustration "drew many Dutch residents in 1689 to Jacob Leisler's Rebellion." "Unmistakably Dutch," Leisler and his lieutenants represented "an earlier elite which latecomers had bypassed" and attracted support from "the many Dutch citizens who had not been able to succeed within the new English order" and longed "for older, better days." Unlike the uprisings in other English colonies during the last quarter of the seventeenth century, then, Leisler's Rebellion, Archdea-

---

[11] Ibid., 76.

[12] Ibid., 51–52, 95.

con contends, represented "not the final drive for power by an aspiring elite, but rather a futile last grasp by a declining one."[13]

The suppression of the Leislerians in 1690 paved the way for a temporary rapprochement, most vividly manifested in rising numbers of interethnic marriages among the Dutch and the English. But this rapprochement turned out to be extremely fragile and premature. When in 1698 a new governor sided with the old Leislerians against the narrow English clique that had seized power in the wake of the rebellion, the town split—largely along ethnic lines—into two feuding parties. The ensuing struggle lasted for almost fifteen years, until the slave uprising of 1712 "reemphasized a fundamental similarity of interests among European colonists of all national backgrounds" and, symbolically, marked the "beginning of a new period of politics" and social development.[14]

While Archdeacon's book helps to reshape our understanding of the role of ethnicity in the social and political dynamics of the town of New York, Sung Bok Kim's *Landlord and Tenant in Colonial New York* focuses upon rural New York. Far and away the most ambitious and important of these five books, Kim's volume brings an impressive amount of evidence and analysis to bear upon one of the classic problems in the historiography of colonial New York: relations between landlords and tenants.

This problem was not peculiar to New York. Tenantry existed in all of the colonies, even in yeoman New England. But New York was the only colony with a large tenant population, six to seven thousand by 1776. In a setting in which so much land was seemingly so easily available, New York's peculiar land system has struck most analysts as anomalous, even un-American. Motivated by what Kim refers to as an "ingrained animus against landlordism" and a correlative "worship of the yeomanry," most earlier historians have painted landlord-tenant relations in New York in bleak colors, employing all the familiar elements—oppressive landlords, exploited and degraded tenants, tenant revolt, and landlord repression—that have been used to depict similar systems in early modern Europe. They have also emphasized its "feudal" character and focused primarily upon the series of violent confrontations that oc-

[13] Ibid., 8, 109, 115, 155.

[14] Ibid., 144–45.

curred on some New York estates after 1750 and culminated, on the eve of the American Revolution, in the "Great Rebellion of 1766."[15]

Going much more deeply into the sources than any previous scholar, Kim has undermined the old view at almost every significant point. About thirty in number, the "great baronial estates" of colonial New York occupied more than two million acres and were about equally divided between manorial and nonmanorial patents. Kim's book is a detailed "study of the rise, structure and functioning of the four largest manors": Rensselaerswyck (1,000,000 acres) and Livingston (160,000 acres) in the northern frontier county of Albany, and Cortlandt (86,000 acres) and Philipsburgh (92,000 acres) in Westchester County just to the north of New York City. All four estates concentrated on wheat throughout the colonial period, though the Westchester manors also produced significant quantities of meat and dairy products for the urban market after 1730. Together, the four estates accounted for more than half of the total acreage of the colony's developed estates; for this reason, as well as because of their representative geographic distribution and the absence of any important distinction between manorial and nonmanorial estates after 1720, Kim claims that his book may be taken as a study of New York tenant society "as a whole."[16]

Created in the 1680s for a complex of reasons, the most important of which, in Kim's judgment, was the proprietary desire to create "an aristocratic bastion" to counter the Whiggish proclivities of the advocates of representative government, the manors all carried privileges of feudal lordship, including the right to hold civil and criminal courts and to extract fowl and labor rents from tenants. Without investigating how the manors actually worked, earlier historians seized upon these grants of privilege as evidence that New York's manors were feudal in character. But Kim shows clearly that neighboring local jurisdictions, abetted by the assembly that was established following the Glorious Revolution, early swallowed up most of these privileges, until by 1720 only the erratically collected fowl and labor rents remained. Similarly, the further privilege enjoyed by three manors of sending a representative to the assembly also worked to undermine landlord power by requiring them to put many leases on a lifetime basis so that a sufficient number of tenants could meet franchise requirements. Although landlords continued to exercise great influence on the provincial level, they thus wielded considerably

[15] Kim, *Landlord and Tenant*, x, 17, 347.

[16] Ibid., vii, x.

less authority in their localities than would appear from the terms of their grants, and the influence they did have, Kim concludes, derived "from their wealth, prestige, and . . . positions as landlords" and "not from the feudal privileges of lordship, which suffered a quick death in New York."[17]

The difficulty of obtaining tenants, Kim shows, eroded even the landlords' economic power. The opening up of American lands for agriculture set in motion a vast rustication process that significantly extended—to broad segments of European populations—the "aspiration to farm a piece of land absolutely one's own." The hold of this "yeoman psychology" upon potential settlers constituted a "formidable deterrent to the settlement of the great manors," and there was a "persistent demographic disparity" between them and neighboring areas throughout the early eighteenth century. Nevertheless, Kim finds in opposition to earlier scholars, during the fifty years before the American Revolution, "mounting pressures on land resources in the old settlements" and, before 1763, warfare on the frontiers enabled the manors to achieve even more success in recruiting settlers than the rest of the colony.[18]

But it was not only these external conditions that made the manors more attractive. "Not a closed community," the manors, Kim reminds us, were "an integral part of American colonial society," and landlords, utterly unable to develop their estates without tenants, had to offer favorable terms to overcome the "avowed reluctance of farmers to accept leasehold tenure in the midst of abundant economic opportunity." These terms included material help, such as a year's provisions, farming equipment, seeds, livestock, and sometimes a house; secure (on all but Philipsburgh, usually life-term) leases with an initial rent-free period and low annual rents thereafter; local services such as gristmills, sawmills, and stores; and, most important, equity in whatever improvements tenants made to their holdings in the form of buildings, orchards, fences, cleared fields, and gardens. Such enticements were especially appealing for people who lacked the resources necessary to purchase a freehold and make the large capital outlay required to start an independent farm.[19]

Although the fortunes of individual tenants varied, most tenants under these favorable conditions managed to achieve a good standard of living, especially—and surprisingly—when compared to freeholders in

[17] Ibid., 32, 127.

[18] Ibid., 130, 236–39.

[19] Ibid., 129, 142.

adjacent areas; many acquired the financial capability to move on to their own freeholds (leases turning over on an average of every ninth year); and some even obtained an equity in their leaseholds equal to that of the landlord. Thus functioning as "an asylum for the impoverished" and, in many cases, as a step to an independent freehold, tenancy in colonial New York was neither oppressive nor degrading. A significant measure of tenant independence was the total failure of landlord efforts to preempt their tenants' produce. Far "more capitalistic . . . in character than feudal," Kim concludes, leaseholding as it evolved on the manors was thus essentially no more than "a rental agreement in money terms" in which the tenant, immediately upon entering into it, effectively "transformed himself into a propertied man and a co-partner in the land with his landlord."[20]

Far from producing "a seething kettle of discontents," then, this system, before 1750, Kim argues powerfully, had yielded "a stable and peaceful manorial society" that permitted economic advancement. As evidence of the system's success, Kim points both to the low level of overt tenant opposition to landlords before 1750 and to the growing reliance of manorial families upon rents. Whereas the founding and second generations of landlords were, except for the Van Rensselaers, principally merchants whose interests in their lands were clearly ancillary to commercial enterprise, the third generation, which came into control during the middle of the eighteenth century, began to deemphasize their commercial activities and "settle down as rentiers and sedentary country gentlemen."[21]

Their repose was, however, interrupted in the 1750s when violence flared along the disputed border area between Massachusetts and the two estates of Rensselaerswyck and Livingston Manor. Though it quickly subsided following the settlement of the boundary in 1757, violence erupted again over a much broader area with the "Great Rebellion of 1766."[22] Earlier historians, notably Oscar Handlin and Patricia Bonomi,[23] have suggested that these uprisings were more the result of conflicting land claims than of endemic tenant unrest. But no one has previously shown so fully the extent to which this suggestion is true. The earlier riots, Kim demonstrates, were provoked by Massachusetts land

---

[20] Ibid., 234, 244, 251.

[21] Ibid., viii, 161, 280.

[22] Ibid., 347.

[23] Oscar Handlin, "The Eastern Frontier of New York," *New York History* 18 (1937): 50–75; Bonomi, *A Factious People*, 218–28.

speculators who were trying, with the support of an expansionist-minded legislature in Boston, to secure control over eastern portions of the two northern manors and who encouraged tenants to follow them with the prospect of freehold titles from Massachusetts. Though Kim admits that leaseholding was an exploitable issue among some tenants, he denies that it had widespread appeal, pointing out that only twenty-seven tenant families—less than 5 percent of the total tenant population of the two manors, and all from a limited area along the disputed border—took part in the uprisings.

Though more complex in its origins and more general, the rebellion of 1766 was also "primarily an extension of the controversy over land titles." With the Stamp Act riots of 1765 fresh in their minds, squatters on disputed portions of Philipsburgh Manor initiated the rebellion after they had exhausted all legitimate channels through which they might have secured legal title and after expected support from royal officials who wanted to break up New York's large estates had failed to materialize. Only when the riots spread to the holdings of Stephen Van Cortlandt, an "autocratic landlord" whose "harsh and arbitrary practices" had long been a source of discontent among the tenants on his portion of Cortlandt Manor, did the rebellion take on the character of a classic tenant rising for better lease terms, the only such uprising in the whole history of the manors in colonial New York.[24]

As in the 1750s, the participation of some regular tenants indicated some dissatisfaction with landlords, but the tenants of all the proprietors of Cortlandt Manor other than Stephen Van Cortlandt remained quiet. The landlords came under attack in 1766, Kim contends, "not because of their landlordism but because of their claims to certain disputed lands," and the overwhelming majority of their tenants conspicuously failed to join the rebellion. Kim interprets the failure of the rebellion to generate "a tidal wave of antirent agitation" as certain proof that colonial tenants did not, for the most part, live under conditions they regarded as hard and oppressive and considers the preoccupation of rebel leaders with obtaining "freehold property for themselves" a clear indication that they were "neither social revolutionaries nor a jacquerie but simply petty landed bourgeois" whose "concern for property was as great as that of the landlords."[25]

Such a hasty summary can scarcely convey an adequate appreciation of the richness and subtlety of Kim's analysis. He takes pains to point

---

[24] Kim, *Landlord and Tenant,* 347, 384.

[25] Ibid., 347, 414–15.

out exceptions to his argument. Thus, he notes that many tenants disliked paying rents and shows that where, as on Philipsburgh Manor, they had tenure only at the will of the landlord, they were considerably more exploitable than was generally the case. Nevertheless, it is probable that Kim overemphasizes the virtues of the New York manor system. If favorable lease terms and other conditions combined to keep the vast majority of tenants quiet throughout the colonial period, the strong fear of tenant rebellion among the elite that was so widely manifest during and following the rebellion of 1766 strongly suggests that landlords themselves thought there was sufficient unhappiness among tenants to make them potential participants in a general uprising of the canaille, a fear that would seem to have been given at least some substance by the tendency, noted by several scholars of the American Revolution, of tenants to choose sides in that conflict in opposition to their landlords.

Yet even if Kim has painted somewhat too roseate a picture of the New York manors, he has written an unusually valuable book that persuasively and thoughtfully revises our understanding of landlord-tenant relations in colonial New York. It provides a striking example of how our comprehension of early America is being expanded and refined through the painstaking investigation of the conditions, institutions, and processes of colonial life. At the same time, it further underlines the extent to which the old liberal conception of the colonial experience as defined by a polar conflict among classes has severely obscured its richness and complexity.

Douglas Greenberg explores other sources of disharmony in his pioneer study of New York's criminal justice system. Based upon a careful examination of all 5,297 criminal cases for which records survive during the years from the crown's assumption of the colony in 1691 to the Declaration of Independence, *Crime and Law Enforcement in the Colony of New York, 1691–1776*, focuses upon two specific questions: who were the criminal defendants and what happened to them. Greenberg's primary concern, however, is "not so much to draw a composite picture of criminal behavior in colonial New York as . . . to demonstrate that the fragmented and heterogeneous nature of New York society was reflected in the records of the criminal courts."[26]

In many respects the patterns of accusations and judgment discovered

---

[26] Greenberg, *Crime and Law Enforcement*, 35.

by Greenberg are remarkably similar to those found in other contemporary societies for which there are comparable studies. Most criminals were male, young, and rootless. Single women, "natural" pariahs in societies that put a high premium upon family life, were more likely to be prosecuted than married women. Theft and convictions were most common among the poorest and most marginal social group, in New York's case, enslaved Africans. Women were more often acquitted than men and very rarely accused of violent crimes. The crime rate was especially high among British soldiers and sailors—a fact, Greenberg suggests persuasively, that may have contributed significantly to the peculiar intensity of New York's resistance to quartering British troops in private houses or even in town during the decades just before the American Revolution.[27]

Even more interesting, perhaps, are the regional variations in patterns of prosecutions and convictions. There were significant differences between the town of New York and the countryside. In the former, convictions were more difficult to obtain, acquittals were more frequent, and crimes of personal violence, theft, and keeping disorderly houses— all of which increased with intensity of settlement—were more numerous; in the latter, convictions were more frequent, acquittals were fewer, and crimes involving the abuse of public office—which seem to have risen with distance from the capital—and violations of public order were higher.

Much less prevalent in urban New York than in contemporary London, rioting and other forms of collective resistance to constituted authority were thus "largely a rural phenomenon." Within the country, moreover, there were important divergencies. Settled mostly by Puritan New Englanders, Suffolk County on Long Island had a conviction rate of 75 percent and just over 6 percent acquittals, a higher conviction rate and fewer acquittals than any other area; the counties surrounding Manhattan and stretching north up the Hudson River had just over 50 percent convictions and just under 15 percent acquittals; while the more extensive northern counties along the Canadian frontier (Albany and Charlotte) had only 35 percent convictions and 7 percent acquittals, leaving nearly 60 percent of all cases unresolved. Law enforcement was thus most efficient on Puritan Long Island and least so in those rural areas farthest removed from central authority in the town of New York. To the extent that the treatment of crime is an important indicator of

---

[27] Ibid., 80.

the character and cohesion of a society, New York, Greenberg concludes, was not a single social unit but "a congeries of societies under the aegis of a single political system with each society functioning with relative autonomy" and, one might add, responding to a different set of social priorities.[28]

Two categories of crime—contempt of authority and personal violence—were, however, common to every area. The former was disproportionately high among the Dutch, who seem to have had continuing difficulties in accepting the legitimacy of British authority. Thus, Myndert Courten, apparently expressing a widespread attitude among the Dutch inhabitants, told the court of King's County in 1706 that "he did not value the Courts order a fart . . . and would obey none of their orders." But it was not only the Dutch who were contemptuous of established authority. Governor Hardy reported in 1756 that it was a common belief "among the Lower Class of Mankind in this part of the world that after warning" a law "Officer to desist [from making an arrest] and bidding him stand off at his Peril, it was lawful to oppose him by any means to prevent the arrest." Greenberg attributes this "deep strain of anti-authoritarianism in the people of New York" partly, especially among the Dutch, to the individualistic character of settlement and the corresponding absence of much sense of community, but "primarily" to the colony's "social and ethnic heterogeneity" and unstable political life, which "engendered doubts about the legitimacy of government which, in turn, encouraged challenges to that legitimacy."[29]

From the author's own analysis, however, it would seem that the anti-authoritarianism of New Yorkers was attributable less to social heterogeneity per se than to the weakness of the system of law enforcement. For that system, as Greenberg shows conclusively, was "not nearly so complex as the society it protected." With "no professional police establishment," a "severe shortage" of competent officials from constables up to judges, inadequate jails, and widespread public aversion to jury service, the system never had strong enforcement capabilities, and it became even less effective after 1750 because it did not expand as rapidly as did the population. Crime rates remained steady or even decreased slightly over the period studied, but increases in the amount of violent crime, the number of unresolved cases (nearly 40 percent), the average duration of prosecutions, and the rate of recidivism, along with the frequency

[28] Ibid., 56, 218.

[29] Ibid., 160, 181–83.

of resort to brutal punishments after midcentury—all suggest that the colony's institutions of law enforcement were under considerable strain and becoming less and less adequate to fulfill their critical function as instruments of social control. The situation was most acute in rural areas, where cases involving violations of public order and rioting—some of them arising from tenant uprisings against landlords—rose by 20 percent after 1750 and, with the exception of Suffolk County, the average duration of cases increased to between five and six months, twice the average for the town of New York.[30]

To determine whether the experience of New York was typical of other "new" Anglo-American societies of the period will require the assemblage of comparable data for other colonies. So far, such data are available only for Massachusetts. They show that New York had a dramatically higher crime rate. Whereas Massachusetts in 1723 had only 12.5 prosecutions and 4.7 convictions per 100,000 residents, New York never had fewer than 150 prosecutions and 80 convictions in any given year. From these figures we can safely conclude, with Greenberg, that New York was not the sort of "peaceable kingdom" some scholars have found in many Massachusetts towns during the eighteenth century. Greenberg also suggests on the basis of this comparison that New York had an abnormally high crime rate that helped to make its society peculiarly unstable and was itself "directly attributable to the [heterogeneous] composition of the population." But we know from many earlier studies that Puritan Massachusetts displayed a degree of social discipline, respect for authority, and strength of social institutions (community, church, and family) that made it totally unlike any other contemporary Anglo-American colony with the single exception of Connecticut, and it is, therefore, highly probable that its crime rates were abnormally low and the efficiency of its legal institutions abnormally high.[31]

The rate of indictments in New York also seems to have been somewhat higher than that for the county of Surrey in England.[32] But Surrey, a well-established society with well-developed institutions of justice, scarcely provides a satisfactory basis for comparison with a new and relatively primitive colonial society. Before we can know whether New York's crime rate and judicial efficiency deviated sharply from the colo-

---

[30] Ibid., 35, 156.

[31] Ibid., 69, 114.

[32] J. M. Beattie, "The Pattern of Crime in England, 1660–1800," *Past and Present*, no. 62 (1974): 47–95.

nial norm and, if so, precisely why, we will have to have studies of crime and law enforcement in colonies that, on the face of it, were not so dissimilar from New York.

In the meantime Michael Kammen points to several additional conditions that affected the social development of colonial New York. Certainly the best available one-volume history of the colony and as good a one-volume account as exists for any of Britain's American colonies, *Colonial New York* traces the history of the colony from its initial settlement by the Dutch to the Declaration of Independence. It describes the marginal character and slow development of the colony under the Dutch, the destabilizing tensions between the conquered Dutch and conquering English for a generation after the English conquest, the growing anglicization of all aspects of New York life after 1691, the acceleration of economic growth and the increasing political, social, and economic stability after 1710, the relatively slow demographic growth, and the colony's involvement in the Seven Years' War and the preliminaries of the American Revolution.

Like Ritchie, Archdeacon, and Greenberg, Kammen stresses the importance of ethnic, linguistic, and regional heterogeneity in shaping the colony's social development. An "excess of pluralism" and its "attendant instabilities and lack of cohesion" worried early Dutch administrators, helped to make New York "one of the less attractive Edens in eighteenth-century America," and meant that the quarrel with Britain after 1764 would be peculiarly divisive. But Kammen puts equal stress upon two additional characteristics of New York society not emphasized by either Archdeacon or Greenberg: its materialism and its secularism. "No other group of colonists," Kammen speculates, "may have been quite so pervasively materialistic and intent upon the exclusive quest for creature comforts. Unlike New England, where getting and spending were partially restrained by Puritan inhibitions, and unlike the South, where proto-English elegance became a mitigating ethic of sorts, the New Yorkers' materialism was undiluted by divinity, gentility, or propriety."[33]

Whether New Yorkers actually were more materialistic than the vast majority of English colonists in the early modern era is open to serious doubt; that they were deeply materialistic, however, no one can deny.

---

[33] Kammen, *Colonial New York,* xvi, 63, 127, 179.

From its very beginning as a European settlement, the quest for gain had been the animating impulse among the inhabitants: the first seal of New Netherlands had appropriately featured the beaver, whose pelt was the primary reason for Dutch interest in North America.

With such a strong material orientation, social institutions, religion, and community-mindedness tended to be weak, while self-interest—what Kammen euphemistically calls "privatism"—and secularism were strong. Augmented by the rapid commercial growth of the colony after 1710, this "exploitive opportunism and a bourgeois ethos," Kammen argues, "ran roughshod over concern for human rights and civic consciousness." With the exception of the Puritan towns on Long Island, material wealth was the measure of all things, and spiritual life remained stunted. "As to religion," observed a visitor in 1744, "they have little of it . . . and of enthusiasm not a grain." The Great Awakening which swept through the continental colonies during the 1740s, Kammen conjectures, "may have had less impact in New York than in any colony north of the Carolinas."[34]

Nowhere was this excessive materialism and undeveloped sense of community more apparent than in the extraordinary engrossment of most of the best lands by a few large proprietors. No wonder that New York attracted relatively fewer immigrants than its neighbors or that it experienced such severe and widespread land riots in the 1750s and 1760s! Having been "chiefly" induced to come to America by "the hopes of having land of their own & becoming independent of Landlords," as one New Yorker put it, few people were willing to settle quietly for tenant status. As Kammen correctly points out in seconding Kim, the land rioters of the mid-eighteenth century "were not 'levelers' eager to alter an unjust system of social class and vicious economic exploitation," but "landowners *manqués* . . . who wanted a piece of the system."[35]

Excessive "pluralism and materialism combined with a lack of coherent community"—these, according to Kammen, were "the major trends and themes in New York's colonial history." Ethnic and regional diversity, uneven land distribution, intense localism, rapid demographic and economic growth, increasing urbanization, and, after 1750, the nascent development of urban and rural proletariats, Kammen argues, continued to prevent New York from resolving its "most critical social prob-

[34] Ibid., 189–90, 230.

[35] Ibid., 299, 302.

lem": how to achieve "community in a heterogeneous and burgeoning society." Throughout the colonial period New York continued to be "more of an artificial designation than a conscious cohesive entity."[36]

But this reading of the New York experience, on the surface so strongly supported by the more detailed studies of Archdeacon and Greenberg, may very well overstress the adverse social effects of pluralism, materialism, and growth. Certainly, it makes it extremely difficult to understand how New York ever managed successfully and without far more social and political upheaval than it actually experienced to pass from colonial to independent status in 1775–77.

Many indications, all of them discussed by Kammen, suggest that New York was not falling apart but coming together during the mid-eighteenth century. The development of "protoparties out of the older system of chaotic, impermanent factions," the achievement of an underlying consensus "on the basic nature of the political system," the increasing acceptance of the existence of an organized political opposition, the emergence of religious toleration and a kind of "ecumenical 'civil religion,'" the growing perception of society as a series of competing "economic interest blocs," the establishment of a variety of cultural institutions—clubs, societies, libraries, schools, professional organizations—in the town of New York, the rise in social spending and civic consciousness represented by improvements in private and public buildings and public services, the decline in the strength of the manorial system, and an evident growth, apparent in the newspapers, "in provincial consciousness and native chauvinism"—all suggest that New Yorkers were rapidly coming to terms with their extraordinarily "heterogeneous society."[37]

New Yorkers may indeed have started out with the conventional western European belief that, as Greenberg puts it, "held heterogeneity to be politically disruptive, socially untenable, and potentially revolutionary."[38] But their common devotion to the pursuit of material gain, a powerful social cement in a society with so many unexploited resources, seems early to have forced them to begin to come to terms with their diversity and to develop attitudes and forms of behavior appropriate to it. In the process they also seem to have acquired a psychology of accommodation, a receptivity to change, and a tolerance for diversity

---

[36] Ibid., 215, 278, 348.

[37] Ibid., 192, 231, 250, 276, 279.

[38] Greenberg, *Crime and Law Enforcement*, 38.

that provided the basis for an emerging cohesiveness and a sense of identity that, while quite unlike those in many more homogeneous societies
and still fragile in situations where material interests or competing ambitions were in sharp conflict, enabled New York to make the transition
to independence without falling apart. Contrary to Kammen's view, the
success of that transition may have been achieved because of, not "despite[,] . . . its historical tradition of diversity"—and materialism.[39]

Historians have learned from modern social science that diversity,
growth, change, and undiluted individualism are disorienting and corrosive of social cohesion and stability, and over the past decade, early
American social and political historians, in particular, have been guilty
of an almost uncritical and mechanical application to the early American
past of the general "social model" represented by such notions. But the
degree of applicability of such generalized models necessarily varies from
one context to another, and in a situation such as that in early America,
where social space and economic opportunity were (relatively) widely
available and the unrestrained quest for individual gain was not necessarily (or perhaps not even very often) socially disruptive, diversity and
growth could not only be tolerated to a high degree but could also contribute powerfully to the achievement of political and social coherence
and stability. William Penn, the progenitor of another heterogeneous colony in America, appreciated as much in 1675, when he wrote that "Many
Inquisitive Men into Humane Affairs have thought that the *Concord
of Discords* hath not been the infirmest basis Government can rise or
stand upon."[40]

To call attention to Penn's insight is not necessarily to argue that we
should turn from modern social science to early modern political apho-
risms for explanatory models of social systems but only to point out that
there is a competing theory of the social effects of heterogeneity and to
suggest that it may provide a more appropriate framework for the analysis of the pluralistic societies of early America than the more modern
models implicitly applied to colonial New York by Greenberg and Kammen. In the meantime, all five of the books considered in this essay con-

---

[39] Kammen, *Colonial New York*, 375.

[40] William Penn, *England's Present Interest* (London, 1698), 100–101, as cited by Caroline
Robbins, "The Efforts of William Penn to Lay a Foundation for Future Ages," in *Aspects
of American Liberty: Philosophical, Historical, and Political* (Philadelphia, 1977), 80.

tribute significantly to illuminate the question of how New Yorkers came to terms with their particular forms of pluralism during the colonial era.

This chapter combines material from two reviews essays, "The Making of New York," *Times Literary Supplement,* no. 3938 (Sept. 2, 1977), 1053–54, and "The Pursuit of Property," *Times Literary Supplement,* no. 3988 (Sept. 8, 1978), 982–83. They are reprinted with permission and citations for the quotations.

—Eleven—

Chesapeake Transformations:
The Traditionalizing of an English New World Society

D URING THE FIRST three quarters of the eighteenth century, the in-habitants of Virginia took enormous pride in its status as Britain's "most ancient American possession"[1] and "most extensive, richest and most commanding colony in America."[2] During the American Revolution it seemed only natural, as contemporaries from Georgia to New Hampshire acknowledged, that Virginians should assume the leadership of both the opposition to Britain and the creation of the new American nation. Virginia, reported the noted French visitor La Rochefoucauld-Liancourt in the mid-1790s in repeating a common observation, "was one of the first colonies to take part in the revolution: and no one of the states made more vigorous efforts, expended greater sums, or displayed more signal energy, to accomplish that happy object."[3] Similarly, follow-ing the achievement of independence, when the American Union seemed on the verge of collapse, Virginians again took "a leading, active, and influential part in bringing about" a stronger national government.[4] Such "generous attention . . . to the general interest," exclaimed John Daly Burk, author of Virginia's most extensive post-Independence his-

---

[1] John Daly Burk, *History of Virginia*, 4 vols. (Richmond, 1904–16), 3:373.

[2] Edmund Randolph, *History of Virginia*, ed. Arthur H. Schaffer (Charlottesville, Va., 1970), 251.

[3] Duc de La Rochefoucauld-Liancourt, *Travels through the United States of North America*, 2 vols. (London, 1799), 1:387.

[4] Marquis de Chastellux, *Travels in North America in the Years 1780, 1781, and 1782*, trans. Harold C. Rice, Jr. (Chapel Hill, N. C., 1963), 2:435.

tory, at the beginning of the nineteenth century, "produced everywhere a sentiment of tender respect and just admiration."[5] How deep and widespread that sentiment ran was richly manifest in the election of Virginians in eight of the first nine presidential terms under the new Federal Constitution.

This astonishing contemporary appreciation of Virginia's preeminent role in colonial and Revolutionary America did not, however, persist much beyond the Revolutionary generation. For a variety of complex reasons, the colonial history of Virginia, its near neighbor Maryland, and the other southern colonies received relatively little attention in the initial construction of an American national past during the nineteenth century. The prolonged commitment of the southern states, until 1865, to the blatant and embarrassing anomaly of chattel slavery marked them as deviant from, not central to, the emergence of republican America, while, after 1865, the subsequent cultural hegemony of the northeastern states, which contained almost all of the major graduate training institutions in history, virtually guaranteed that American history would continue to be written with scant emphasis on the role of the southern colonies.

As Thad W. Tate explains in a masterful survey of the historiography of the seventeenth-century Chesapeake, which constitutes an introduction to the first of the two volumes considered in this chapter,[6] the establishment of a new school of historical studies at Johns Hopkins University in Maryland in the mid-1870s yielded, over the next forty years, several monographs on various aspects of the history of colonial Virginia and Maryland. Quantitatively, however, these in no way equaled the output of studies of the northern colonies then coming out of the many new graduate departments of history in the area from Philadelphia north to Boston. Nor, despite publication of a few outstanding works by scholars such as Louis B. Wright and Wesley Frank Craven, did this situation change much over the following half century.[7]

Indeed, as Tate suggests, only in the mid-1960s did the analysis of the

---

[5] Burk, *History of Virginia* 3:373.

[6] Thad W. Tate, "The Seventeenth-Century Chesapeake and Its Modern Historians," in Thad W. Tate and David L. Ammerman, eds., *The Chesapeake in the Seventeenth Century: Essays on Anglo-American Society* (Chapel Hill, N.C., 1979), 3–50.

[7] Louis B. Wright, *The First Gentlemen of Virginia: Intellectual Qualities of the Early Colonial Ruling Class* (San Marino, Calif., 1940); Wesley Frank Craven, *The Southern Colonies in the Seventeenth Century, 1607–1689* (Baton Rouge, La., 1949).

southern colonies in general and the Chesapeake colonies in particular begin to proceed at a pace that was anywhere nearly as intensive as that devoted to the Puritan colonies of New England since the mid-1920s. This new interest in the southern colonies is in part a logical extension of a powerful resurgence of interest in America's colonial past in the years since the Second World War. Intimately linked to the establishment in Williamsburg, Virginia, in the mid-1940s of the Institute of Early American History and Culture, the institution responsible for publication of the two works here considered and many other important studies of British colonial America, this resurgence has pulled literally hundreds of young scholars from all over the world into the field and, increasingly, sent them scurrying into relatively neglected areas, including the seventeenth-century Chesapeake, in quest of significant research subjects. Probably more important, the new concern with the southern colonies has also been inspired by the shifting focus toward social history in early modern British and European historical studies over the past twenty-five years. Such a focus, as Tate points out, is far more congenial to the exploitation of surviving records for the southern colonies than was the preoccupation with intellectual history which dominated colonial American historiography for much of the period from the mid-1920s to the mid-1960s.

Whatever its sources, this new interest has resulted in, among other things, what Thad Tate and David Ammerman appropriately describe as a "remarkable renascence of interest in the seventeenth-century Chesapeake,"[8] a renascence which has already produced several notable books[9] and is now superbly represented by this volume. Composed of selected papers from a 1974 conference and a few commissioned pieces, the eight substantive contributions it contains exemplify the kinds of sophisticated social history now being done on early modern Anglophone America and collectively provide a lucid portrait of the first century of social development in Britain's "most ancient" area of overseas settlement in the New World. Intended to "illuminate the most significant aspects of the development of Anglo-American society in the Chesapeake," the essays concentrate on four major subjects: immigration patterns, mortality and its social effects, socioeconomic opportunity, and

---

[8] Tate and Ammerman, *Chesapeake in the Seventeenth Century,* vii.

[9] In particular, Wesley Frank Craven, *White, Red, and Black: The Seventeenth-Century Virginian* (Charlottesville, Va., 1971), and Edmund S. Morgan, *American Slavery, American Freedom: The Ordeal of Colonial Virginia* (New York, 1975).

the political and cultural implications of the emergence of a predominantly native or creole population around the end of the seventeenth century.[10]

In sharp contrast to New England, which was settled mostly by a massive influx of religious dissidents during the single decade of the 1630s, the Chesapeake colonies continued to attract large numbers of immigrants throughout the seventeenth century. An estimated 70 to 85 percent were servants imported to meet an expanding demand for labor to produce tobacco, the region's principal staple. James Horn has used several of the surviving lists of servants who left London, Bristol, and Liverpool at various periods during the seventeenth century to contribute an intelligent and highly useful analysis of the character of this emigration. What he finds, briefly, is that the servants were young (fifteen to twenty-four, a majority being between twenty and twenty-one) and predominantly male (ranging from six to two and a half males for every female). Drawn from a broad cross section of English society, about half of them were minors or unskilled workers, "while the rest came from agricultural occupations that defy any simple classification." Almost wholly people who had not yet acquired much stake in society, they came from a multitude of different places, mostly within a forty-mile radius of the port of embarkation. Perhaps because of the nature of his data, Horn puts heavy emphasis on push factors, including contraction of the agrarian labor market, decline of the cloth industry, personal tragedy (particularly the loss of parents), and harvest failure, at the expense of pull factors, in the decision to emigrate.[11]

He argues persuasively that emigration to America was simply an extension of internal English migratory patterns from villages and countryside into large urban centers and suggests that the decision to leave the British Isles usually occurred, not when a person left home, but after he or she had arrived in London or elsewhere and found little opportunity. Along with his finding that Chesapeake emigrants differed in no important respect from those who went as servants to other colonies, this suggestion places the migration to the Chesapeake squarely within the mainstream of population movements within England.

Horn's stress upon push factors may derive at least in part from his

---

[10] Burk, *History of Virginia* 3:373; Tate and Ammerman, *Chesapeake in the Seventeenth Century*, 45.

[11] James Horn, "Servant Emigration to the Chesapeake in the Seventeenth Century," in Tate and Ammerman, *Chesapeake in the Seventeenth Century*, 65.

knowledge of the high mortality which awaited emigrants to the Chesa-peake, the causes and effects of which are the subject of three pieces in this collection. In an ingenious contribution Carville Earle, a historical geographer, offers the most compelling explanation yet advanced for the high death rate in Virginia during its first two decades of settlement. Finding that annual mortality fluctuated between 4 and 30 percent, ac-cording to whether the population was dispersed or concentrated in the vicinity of Virginia's principal settlement at Jamestown, Earle argues that it was not, as most earlier historians have contended, either starva-tion or an unfamiliar disease environment that primarily accounted for the heavy toll but Jamestown's situation in a "deadly estuarine zone" in which an annual summer invasion of saltwater contaminated the water supply with salt, sediment, and fecal material containing pathogens of typhoid and dysentery that floated back and forth past Jamestown with the summer tide. Typhoid, dysentery, and salt poisoning, he estimates, probably accounted for two-thirds of all deaths, and the subsequent re-distribution of population to higher land and freshwater zones between 1624 and 1634 brought about a sharp improvement in mortality rates.[12]

That this improvement was insufficient to bring mortality down even to metropolitan, much less to New England, levels is amply revealed by two suggestive case studies on the impact of high mortality upon pat-terns of family life, one by Lorena S. Walsh on Maryland and the other by Darrett B. and Anita H. Rutman on Middlesex County, Virginia. Already drastically limited by the disproportionate number of men to women among immigrants, families were deeply affected by the frequent death of parents. In Maryland, half of all marriages had been broken by death within seven years, while in Middlesex a quarter of all children had lost one or both parents by the age of five, one-half of them by thir-teen, and three-quarters by twenty-one. Parental death was such an in-tegral part of the fabric of life that it was the norm for most children. Because men died younger than women, Walsh suggests, women "were accorded an unusually influential role in managing the estate and bring-ing up the children," while, as the Rutmans astutely observe, the omni-presence of death both accentuated the importance of extended kinship and quasi-kinship connections as refuges for orphaned children and im-pelled fathers to set their sons up independently as soon as they reached their maturity. Indeed, with so many young children without natural parents in both colonies, parental control and sexual mores were weak, and autonomy and adaptability, not dependence and inflexibility, were

---

[12]Carville Earle, "Environment, Disease, and Mortality in Early Virginia," ibid., 107.

the qualities prudent parents must have sought to encourage in their offspring.[13]

The material prospects that awaited those who could survive in the Chesapeake are the subject of two further essays, one on Maryland by Lois Green Carr and Russell R. Menard and another on Surry County, Virginia, by Kevin P. Kelly. The more or less continuous expansion of the tobacco industry from 1617 to 1680 meant that not only free immigrants with capital but servants could do well in the rich soils surrounding the Chesapeake. Before 1660, indeed, surviving servants, especially those fortunate enough to acquire wives and families, often achieved substantial property, with a few even acquiring fortunes sufficient to attain membership in a nascent Chesapeake gentry. Opportunity declined somewhat over the next two decades and became ever slimmer after 1680 as a result of a long-term depression in tobacco prices that persisted for three decades. Whereas servants arriving between 1660 and 1680 could still expect to become small, independent landholders and minor local officeholders, those who came after 1680 found themselves under the necessity of moving, either to less productive areas, such as Surry County, where they lived on small plots in typically single-person households with little hope of acquiring families or substantial wealth, or out of the Chesapeake altogether, to the newer colonies of the Carolinas, New Jersey, or Pennsylvania. The older Chesapeake settlements now became a funnel for immigrants into an expanding area of the North American coast.

Drawing upon his own research for Maryland and that of Martin H. Quitt for Virginia, David W. Jordan describes patterns of political life generally comparable to family patterns. Given the low life expectancy and the dearth of immigrants with much political experience, officeholding at all levels was distinguished by considerable discontinuity, lack of sustained and qualified leadership, and the absence of a governing elite capable of perpetuating itself from one generation to another. Almost to the end of the century, a "continuing progression of relatively young men, almost exclusively first-generation settlers," presided over the politics of the Chesapeake, with the "prolonged ascendancy of immigrants" constituting "the most striking feature" of its political life.[14]

---

[13] Lorena S. Walsh, "'Till Death Us Do Part': Marriage and Family in Seventeenth-Century Maryland," ibid., 137.

[14] David W. Jordan, "Political Stability and the Emergence of a Native Elite in Maryland," ibid., 246.

The picture that emerges of Britain's oldest region of American settlement during most of its first century is thus one of a largely immigrant society populated mostly by people who, having been in uneasy or tenuous circumstances at home, had joined the vast internal migration to English cities and had then moved on to the Chesapeake, where the survivors among them often managed to improve their material and social status substantially. The names they gave to the places in which they lived betrayed their desire to re-create in America something resembling the society they had left behind.

But the excess of men over women, late age of marriage, high death rates, heavy concentration upon producing tobacco on dispersed plantations, and rough equality among free people made it extremely difficult for them to replicate traditional patterns of English social, family, and political life. The editors and several of the contributors emphasize the "fragile character" of this society. But from the contents of this volume, a more descriptive term would seem to be "improvisational" or "contingent," for the single most powerful impression one takes away from these essays is of the resourcefulness and resilience of the Chesapeake's new inhabitants in adapting old habits and institutions to such radically different circumstances.[15]

As many of the essays emphasize, the Chesapeake colonies lost much of their contingent character after 1675 when they gradually began to undergo a profound social transformation. As black slavery slowly began to displace servitude as the predominant form of labor between 1680 and 1720 and opportunity for new settlers to acquire land in older settled areas declined, immigration slowed. Simultaneously, improved life expectancy, a more equal sex ratio, and earlier marriages raised the birthrate. Together, these developments contributed to the emergence of a native-born majority at the end of the century, at the core of which was an increasingly wealthy slave- and plantation-owning creole elite that was becoming ever more sharply differentiated from people of less wealth. Between 1690 and 1710 this elite both took control of politics and began to provide more continuous, sustained, and experienced leadership.

In a perceptive closing essay, Carole Shammas explores the cultural effects of the emergence of a creole majority among the Virginia elite after 1690. The earlier, discontinuous immigrant elite had been primarily interested in making fortunes and returning to England as quickly as material circumstances would permit. Stung by metropolitan condescen-

---

[15] Tate and Ammerman, *Chesapeake in the Seventeenth Century,* vii.

sion and anxious about Virginia's almost wholly unsavory reputation in England, the new creole elite self-consciously set about trying to make Virginia more recognizably English and threw themselves into its "improvement" through the creation of towns, a college, a richer public life, more responsive and active political institutions, and even a history, which provided Virginia with "a sense of permanence and legitimacy . . . it had never before possessed." By these and other actions, Shammas suggests, Virginia creoles manifested their commitment to the place of their nativity and finally provided some of the most essential foundations for the achievement of that proud sense of place and preeminence which, despite the Chesapeake's tenuous early history, Virginians displayed so fully to the admiration of their contemporaries during the late colonial and Revolutionary years.[16]

Especially since World War II, historians have emphasized the remarkable stability of Virginia's public life during the Revolutionary era. The political system that produced George Washington and Thomas Jefferson, George Mason and James Madison, Patrick Henry and Richard Henry Lee, John Marshall and James Monroe, to name only the more prominent members of the Virginia political galaxy, was, historians have mostly agreed, both responsive to the needs of its constituents and, particularly in comparison with most other colonies at the time, extraordinarily free from serious internal conflict. Depicting a society that was crude, unhealthy, permissive, and marked by conflict, historians like those represented in the Tate and Ammerman volume have pointedly raised the questions of when and how the profoundly improvisational and contingent world of seventeenth-century Virginia was transformed into the vastly more settled world of Washington's generation.

This major transformation is not, however, the one Rhys Isaac alludes to in the title of his ambitions study, *The Transformation of Virginia, 1740–1790*. He focuses instead upon the alleged breakup of the ordered society of the mid-eighteenth century as a result of what Isaac refers to as a "double revolution in religious and political thought and feeling." Concentrating on religious, social, and cultural life rather than on politics and considering all segments of society and not just the elite, Isaac

---

[16]Carole Shammas, "English-Born and Creole Elites in Turn-of-the-Century Virginia," ibid., 294.

offers a formidable challenge to the standard view of Revolutionary Virginia as a society at peace with itself.[17]

To provide the necessary background for this transformation, Isaac begins his book with a long synchronic portrait of "traditional" ways of life in Virginia during the second quarter of the eighteenth century. His approach is largely derived from symbolic anthropology and will be of interest not just to students of colonial Anglo-America but also to those historians who are concerned with trying to recover the mentalities of societies in which the volume of literary production was low and there was comparatively little systematic record keeping. His characterization is both insightful and compelling. Analyzing Virginia society in terms of its arrangement of social space, its principal actors, its primary sites and occasions for social action, and its "textures of community," he describes an extensive, personal, and rank-ordered society arranged in a series of scattered and loose-knit communities. Although it was based upon the impersonal "principle of money," this society, Isaac argues, was organized largely around "the great cultural metaphor of patriarchy" and was dominated by hegemonic local elites, whose eminence depended not merely upon the great wealth and offices their members enjoyed but upon the number of their dependents—slaves, servants, family members, and people of lesser wealth and status who accorded the gentry deference and services in return for patronage and credit.[18]

Isaac considers how members of the gentry expressed their status and authority through their demeanor, mode of discourse, classical learning, refined style of living, personal independence, and new "great houses," the last functioning as centers for the display of the liberal hospitality only they could afford. They revealed their social authority through their dominance of the two most prominent public institutions, the county courts and parish churches, both of which served as inclusive ceremonial "centers for community assembly" and were contrived "to offer a powerful representation of a structured, hierarchical community."[19]

Based on economic competition and requiring substantial physical severity to police its expanding slave labor force, Virginian society contained considerable latent potential for violence. By the mid-eighteenth century, however, these underlying propensities had been largely chan-

---

[17] Rhys Isaac, *The Transformation of Virginia, 1740–1790* (Chapel Hill, N. C., 1982), 5.

[18] Ibid., 9, 20, 115.

[19] Ibid., 35, 58, 64.

neled into a series of "contest pastimes" that consumed much of the colony's social energy. In an intense jockeying for personal advantage and social recognition, free men of all classes danced, courted, drank, gambled, fought, and otherwise asserted their manly prowess, while the wealthy vied with one another in extravagant displays of magnificence and liberality. The outward self-abasement and exaggerated shows of submissiveness demanded from black slaves by whites and a growing communalism within the slave quarters contrasted sharply with the blatant assertions of self so prevalent among the free population.[20]

The heart of the volume consists of six lively vignettes, each of which is intended to illustrate through a careful explication of a specific episode how developments in religion and politics brought conflict and change to the colony's "traditional" order after 1760. Nominally inclusive, Virginia's Anglican establishment had already been weakened by serious internal squabbling between the laity and the clergy before the appearance of widespread organized dissent in the mid-1760s. Two decades earlier Presbyterians, largely confined to a few localities, had assumed a posture of quiet accommodation toward the Anglican establishment. But the Separate Baptists, whose numbers increased rapidly after 1765, presented a much more militant challenge.[21]

Standing for a pious, austere, and deeply emotional way of life that emphasized a "search for deep fellow feeling" within a "close, supportive, and orderly community," they represented an aggressive "counter culture" that defined itself by its opposition to the formal distance and the worldly, extravagant, convivial, competitive, and egocentric orientation of the existing order. They sought neither control of the political system nor a "redistribution of worldly wealth." But, appealing primarily to less affluent segments of the population, they nonetheless managed, according to Isaac, to create "a cultural disjunction between the gentry and sections of the lower orders where hitherto there had been a continuum." At the same time their "open rejection of deference" seemed to the gentry to be "highly subversive of established authority."[22]

What made the Baptist challenge even more serious, Isaac contends, was its coincidence with the decade of bitter controversy between Britain and the colonies preceding the American Revolution, and Isaac explores this controversy, in which Virginia took a prominent part, through an

---

[20] Ibid., 136.

[21] Ibid., 9.

[22] Ibid., 164–65, 173, 265.

analysis not of familiar political events but of two separate conflicts within the religious sphere. Specifically, he uses these incidents to illustrate the gentry's growing ambivalence toward the colony's previously almost sacrosanct connection with metropolitan Britain, an ambivalence in which the gentry were at once eager cultural provincials and increasingly wary of what they took to be the growing corruption of metropolitan society. More and more, according to Isaac, the gentry felt trapped between the evident degeneracy of Britain and the ignorant enthusiasm of the evangelicals.

Isaac shows how Virginia's traditional leaders deftly used the controversy with Britain to resolve this dilemma. Taking the lead in the resistance to Britain, they equated the self-denial and communal solidarity it required with opposition to corruption in general. They thus placed themselves at the forefront of those who, like the evangelicals, advocated "a world reshaped in truly moral order" and thereby managed to revive "the spirit of the traditional deferential social order."[23]

But this revival, Isaac maintains in a brief conclusion, was only momentary. The old order had already been too thoroughly undermined by what he refers to as a "radical individualization," epitomized by the evangelical stress upon personal conversion. According to Isaac, this development was also apparent during the last decades of the eighteenth century in a growing "privatization" of household living arrangements, a palpable separation of family from community, and a manifest decline in the social idealization of the metaphor of patriarchy in favor of the metaphor of money, now in association with a "greatly enhanced metaphor of the self-sustaining individual." It was further evident in the only "great institutional transformation" that accompanied Virginia's transition to independence: the total separation of church and state provided by the 1784 "Act for Establishing Freedom of Religion" was "utterly without precedent in the Atlantic world."[24]

Notwithstanding its power and subtlety, this imaginative reading of Virginia's Revolutionary experience has many problems. Perhaps most serious, the characterization of Virginia's "traditional" order seems to have been constructed largely for the purpose of providing the author with a stable backdrop against which to assess the impact of the religious and social developments in which he is primarily interested. As a result, it tends both to overestimate the coherence and rigidity of that order and to underestimate its fluidity and receptivity to change. Thus, al-

---

[23] Ibid., 255, 269.

[24] Ibid., 273, 284, 312.

though Isaac points out that the old order was still relatively new and "gentry dominance . . . hardly consolidated" by 1750, he nevertheless presents that order as far more coercive and deeply entrenched and its gentry leaders as far more thoroughly committed to the status quo and more monolithic in outlook than they probably were.[25]

The gentry's social authority was almost certainly stronger in Virginia than in any of the other new English societies in America. Even in Virginia, however, aspirations for the patriarchy, authority, patronage, and deference enjoyed by the English gentry seem to have remained, to an important degree, unfulfilled, and the predominance of the elite probably rested far less upon the sort of coercive hegemony depicted by Isaac than upon their own acute awareness that to retain power they could not violate the interests of the lower orders of free people, whose tacit consent had always been essential to gentry authority everywhere in early modern Anglo-America.

Certainly, it seems unlikely that gentry aspirations for patriarchy ever predominated over the concern for money that had been so conspicuously evident in Virginia from its first founding. As Virginia's leaders had increasingly endeavored to reshape the colony into something resembling English rural society after 1690, such aspirations were indeed widely evident. No less than their contemporary British counterparts, however, the Virginia gentry were always alive to new economic opportunities— whether in land development, new crops, or iron production—with the result that Virginia, rapidly expanding in settled territory, population, and economic production throughout most of the eighteenth century, never seems to have settled into the kind of "traditional" socioeconomic stasis in which their aspirations for patriarchy could flourish. Nor was the Anglican gentry by any means so united in defense of an extravagant style of living against its evangelical critics as Isaac suggests. Indeed, more and more after 1740, a concern with proliferating luxury and immorality extended far beyond dissenters to include what appears to have been a large majority of the most visible and politically powerful members of the gentry. Even without the evangelical challenge, these men would have welcomed the opportunity presented by the imperial controversy to try to recover Virginia's lost virtue.[26]

Similarly, Isaac appears to overstate the strength of the Anglican religious establishment, whose influence, never very deep in this highly secular society, seems to have depended heavily upon its toleration of a wide

[25] Ibid., 9, 141.

[26] Ibid., 9.

diversity of religious orientations and its compatibility with the loose and permissive character of Virginian life. The Baptists appealed strongly to those many people who did not find this establishment spiritually satisfying. But they never constituted more than a small fraction—Isaac says 10 percent—of the population during the colonial period. Reaffirming the society's long-standing cultural preference for a more relaxed mode of religious life, the vast majority of Virginians remained, at least in the short run, either nominally Anglican or blissfully unattached to any denomination.

If, in these ways, Isaac has exaggerated the coherence of the old order, he has probably also given insufficient attention to the continuities between the old order and the new. From a perspective stressing the underlying fluidity and dynamism of the old order, the decision to separate church and state does not seem all that revolutionary: it looks, rather, like yet another display of the gentry's awareness of the extent to which its authority depended upon a broad social consensus and of its capacity to adapt to new social conditions. As earlier historians have argued, this remarkable flexibility was an important reason why the Revolution did not produce more radical social results in Virginia and why, arguably, the elite emerged from the Revolution stronger than it had ever been before.

It can also be contended that in the wake of the Revolution the new emphasis upon the metaphor of the self-sustaining individual was less an expression of declining interest in community than a rationalization which extended social approbation to modes of individualistic behavior prevalent in Virginia from its first establishment. Similarly, at the same time that it undermined the older—and probably never very strong—forms of communal unity, the new religious order, with the evangelicals' stress upon the fraternity of true believers, may even have enhanced community in Virginia by reorganizing it along denominational lines. Along with the slowing pace of territorial, demographic, and economic growth, these developments actually appear to have left the gentry in a position from which, during the first half of the nineteenth century, they could preside over not the *modernization* of Virginia but a greater *traditionalization* than their ancestors had managed to achieve during the colonial period.

Although Virginia's late eighteenth-century history is susceptible to alternative readings, Isaac's engaging and intelligent account is certainly the most powerful and sophisticated interpretation now available. One of the best—and most provocative—books written on colonial Anglo-America during the 1980s, it must be the starting point for all further work on the subject. Equally important, his efforts to demonstrate how historians can profitably employ some of the tools of symbolic anthropologists, a process he discusses at length in a concluding section, deserve close inspection. *The Transformation of Virginia* is one of those rare works of history that is as significant for its methodology as for its substantive findings. By both broadening and deepening the range of inquiry, Isaac's approach promises considerable enrichment to the rapidly developing field of social history.

This chapter combines two essays, "Adapting to the New World," *Times Literary Supplement*, no. 4048 (Oct. 31, 1980), 1237, and "Challenges to the Gentry," *Times Literary Supplement*, no. 4169 (Feb. 24, 1983), 177. It is reprinted with permission and with the addition of citations to quotations.

Twelve

The Southern Colonial Mind
and American Culture

T HE LONG-TERM neglect of the history of those British colonies that
subsequently became part of the American South has severely
hampered efforts to understand the origins of southern distinctiveness.
Traditionally, students of early America have devoted far more attention
to the northern colonies, specifically to New England, where the dominant and historically conscious Puritan settlers left behind a rich and
easily accessible cache of literary sources. Historians of the South have
rarely interested themselves in the history of the region before it began
to become self-consciously "southern" in the decades after 1815. Over
the past quarter century, the resurgence of scholarly interest in early
America has yielded several impressive studies of many aspects of the
demographic, economic, social, and political history of the southern colonies; we now, finally, seem to be well on the way toward a more detailed
and comprehensive understanding of them.

The new concern with the southern colonies among scholars of early
America has, however, hitherto produced surprisingly little solid work
on their intellectual life. Whereas interest in New England Puritanism
as an intellectual and cultural system has been proliferating wildly, older
works by Louis B. Wright and Carl Bridenbaugh[1] have continued to be
the standard sources of information about thought and culture in the
southern colonies. As a result, the intellectual and cultural history of
Britain's North American empire in the seventeenth and eighteenth centuries has been written almost as if the southern colonies had never existed, and the emergence of an American culture during the colonial and
Revolutionary eras has been depicted as having been to an astonishing

---

[1] In particular Louis B. Wright, *The First Gentlemen of Virginia: Intellectual Qualities of
the Early Colonial Ruling Class* (San Marino, Calif., 1940); Carl Bridenbaugh, *Myths and
Realities: Societies of the Colonial South* (Baton Rouge, La., 1952).

degree simply an extension of New England culture, the American self deriving directly and almost exclusively out of the Puritan self and American moral sensibilities out of the Puritan ethic. The fact is, however, that we have not had the detailed work necessary either for assessing the role of the southern colonies in the emergence of American culture or for analyzing the extent to which, as the work of most early American cultural historians implicitly assumes, those colonies may or may not have already comprised a distinctive cultural unit that stood outside the mainstream of American development.

Richard Beale Davis's massive *Intellectual Life in the Colonial South, 1565–1783*, represents a heroic effort to remedy this problem. The product of a quarter century of enterprising labor, it is impressive for its broad scope, the extensiveness and ingenuity of the research on which it is based, and its disarming lack of pretension. Despite the title, it is actually a wide-ranging cultural history. Focusing on the five southern mainland colonies of Maryland, Virginia, North Carolina, South Carolina, and Georgia during the first century and a half of British occupation, it is the single most comprehensive description ever undertaken of the cultural life of any segment of Britain's early modern American empire. Together comprising over three hundred pages, the bibliographies and notes leave no doubt that the effort expended in the search for relevant materials has been proportionate to the grandness of the subject. Yet the author modestly eschews any claims to completeness and insists that his volumes are no more than a "starting point," an introduction to "relatively unfamiliar materials vital to a comprehensive understanding of the American mind."[2]

But such modesty, however engaging, is all too frequently a mask for timidity, and the author's excessive timidity in the conception and execution of his book renders it as exasperating as it is admirable. Conceiving of it as essentially "an assemblage, a reportage, when possible an interpretation of documented fact," he is throughout far more interested in presenting than in analyzing his materials. This preference determines both how he arranges his evidence and what he says about it. He organizes his data not around the several potentially unifying interpretive themes that suggest themselves from his evidence, but according to "aim, subject matter, and form." In ten book-length chapters, ranging from 74 to 200 pages in length, he treats successively the literature of description and history, Indians, formal education, books, religion, sci-

---

[2] Richard Beale Davis, *Intellectual Life in the Colonial South, 1585–1763*, 3 vols. (Knoxville, Tenn., 1978), xxxi.

ence and technology, the fine arts, belles lettres, and political and economic life. He then breaks each chapter down into shorter—and more
digestible—units, mostly according to spatial or broad temporal categories, the discussion of each topic proceeding colony by colony, first in the
seventeenth and then in the eighteenth century.[3]

"THE MIND"

Similarly, he does not in his analysis reach for a high level of generalization. Except for a few paragraphs in the introduction and a cursory
effort to set forth a few general characterizations in a brief eighteen-page
epilogue, he shows little interest in developing the sort of sustained and
comprehensive interpretation of the southern colonial "mind" that
Miller and his successors have wrought for the Puritan mind of New
England during the same period.[4] Rather, Davis's leading concerns are
simply, as he puts it in the introduction, "to demonstrate that the colonial southerner had a mind" and that that mind was both creative and
productive.[5] Although he is careful to consider the several influences that
seem to have shaped the many and varied products of that mind, he is
usually content simply to bring each of those products before the reader
for review, making no systematic effort to come to grips with the difficult
but ultimately more significant question of whether those products
reveal important commonalities that, by providing an underlying coherence and unity, may have formed the basic components of an emergent southern culture. The result resembles nothing so much as a
crowded museum, arranged according to topic, in which the curators
have made only minimal effort either to relate objects from one room to
those in others or to stress any unities among various exhibits other than
their common temporal and spatial origins.

THE MOVES

Predictably, in a work of this character, the intermediate-level generalizations around which the author organizes each chapter constitute the
most vivid and compelling impressions produced by the book and are
probably its most important contribution. In particular, Davis shows in
abundant detail that southern colonists (1) produced "the most discern-
ing and complete discussions in existence of the American red man as the
white Englishmen found him," discussions that, in sharp contrast to
New England captivity narratives, revealed a remarkably modern so-

---

[3] Ibid., xxvi, 1310.

[4] See, especially, Perry Miller, *The New England Mind: The Seventeenth Century* (Cambridge, Mass., 1939), and *The New England Mind: From Colony to Province* (Cambridge,
Mass., 1953); Sacvan Bercovitch, *The Puritan Origins of the American Self* (New Haven, 1975).

[5] Davis, *Intellectual Life in the Colonial South*, xxvi.

phistication in their ethnographic emphasis; (2) displayed "from the beginning a *persistent* desire for schools and colleges," albeit that desire was rarely translated into the creation of permanent institutions; (3) included many people who by the early eighteenth century "owned and read books" in impressive quantities; (4) had a strong interest in religion even if it was infinitely less "all-absorbing" than that of Puritan New Englanders; (5) showed an acute interest in their physical environment, which yielded a respectable body of scientific literature and advances in agricultural technology that were "probably equal" to those of their contemporaries in rural Britain; (6) exhibited increasingly good taste in the fine arts, especially in architecture and landscape gardening, even though they made few "distinctive contributions" in the area; (7) produced a "great deal" of belletristic writing, much of it good and some of it fine; and, what has always been more widely appreciated, (8) excelled in politics and the law.[6]

On the level of detail, the yield is even richer—so rich, in fact, that it is possible to list here only a few of the more important and interesting findings. For instance, the author shows that the southern colonies had far more private schools than any one had previously suspected, that the plain style characterized southern Anglican quite as much as northern Puritan colonial sermons; that there was virtually no cultural lag between the southern colonies and the metropolis in terms of literary and artistic tastes; that in belles lettres southerners followed contemporary British models more closely than did New Englanders; and, somewhat surprisingly, that slavery, despite its ubiquity throughout the southern colonies after 1710, was "curiously inconspicuous" on the "cultural surface" of southern colonial life, at least before 1763. Similarly, he provides valuable correctives to fashionable clichés among early American literary historians (and by example shames them for their lack of industry and ingenuity in research) by showing that, contrary to prevailing opinion, the southern colonists had a strong elegiac tradition and nature poets who showed a deep appreciation for the world around them.[7]

The author's failure to offer a coherent and sustained analysis of the emergence and character of southern colonial culture does not mean that he eschews higher-level generalizations altogether. Indeed, underlying his discussion are two general propositions that deserve serious consideration. First, he suggests that there were important continuities "in certain features of southern intellectual character from the colonial era to

---

[6] Ibid., 106, 261–62, 626, 631, 987, 1121, 1313.

[7] Ibid., 987.

at least the mid-twentieth century." Second, he argues that the southern "mind did at least as much toward the shaping of the later national mind as did that of New England."[8]

Whether the cluster of characteristics that later defined the South as a distinctive—and deviant—section of American culture was already manifest during the colonial period is not a question that has much interested earlier historians. Yet it is one of evident significance. If the South was a deviant section, we need to know if it was always that way and, if not, what made it that way and when—questions that can scarcely be satisfactorily answered without going back to the beginnings of the South in the southern colonies. The author's case for southern distinctiveness from the earliest days of settlement rests upon two related premises: first, that the cultural similarities among the five southern colonies were far more impressive than the differences, and second, that what made those colonies alike also made them different from other British-American colonies. The first, for which the author piles up an enormous amount of evidence from one chapter to the next, can be accepted without major reservations; the second is far more problematic.

What makes it problematic is the author's use of the Puritan colonies as a basis for comparison. Quite properly, he decries the excessive influence ascribed by historians to the Puritans in the formation of the later American mind. Yet he inadvertently adds weight to such ascriptions by himself using the Puritans as a standard against which to assess the achievements and contributions of southern colonials. Throughout, he emphasizes the important and undeniable differences between the southern and Puritan colonies: in motives for and patterns of early settlement, in attitudes toward nature and Indians, in the mix of emphases accorded to religious and secular concerns, and in the degree of receptivity to metropolitan cultural influences.

However, recent scholarship has strongly suggested that those aspects of early New England culture that seem to have been most distinctly Puritan—the strong religious orientation, the communal impulse, the perfectionist aspirations, the sense of "chosenness," and the belief in social and religious exclusivity—were not even typical of New England as a whole but were largely confined to the two colonies of Massachusetts and Connecticut, and that even there they seem to have become weaker over time. Thus, it can be argued that what in contrast to the Puritan colonies appears to Davis to be peculiarly southern—the counterpointing of hedonism and spirituality, acquisitiveness and social responsibility,

---

[8] Ibid., xxvi, 1636.

and activity and indolence—were not only, as his evidence seems to confirm, more typically English than the cultural patterns exhibited by Puritan Massachusetts and Connecticut but also almost certainly characteristic of most other early modern British colonies from Barbados north to Rhode Island and New Hampshire.

Within the larger framework of Anglo-American colonial life, then, not the southern but the Puritan colonies appear to have been distinctive, and even they seem to have been rapidly assimilating to the dominant cultural patterns by the late colonial period. Indeed, as all of the colonies were drawn more and more tightly into the ambit of metropolitan life, especially after 1710, convergence, not divergence, seems to have characterized the cultural development of mainland colonial Anglo-America.

To advance this line of argument is not to deny that the seeds of southern distinctiveness were present during the colonial period. In particular, the relatively greater affluence derived by southern colonists from staple-crop agriculture enabled them to purchase more black slaves, to devote more time both to the pursuit of the good life and to politics and law, to cultivate metropolitan cultural models more assiduously, to rely more heavily upon metropolitan cultural institutions rather than to develop their own, and to be more self-indulgent and less industrious. Before the American Revolution, however, these differences were largely ones of degree, and, given the strong convergence of cultural development in colonial Anglo-America by the 1740s and 1750s, it is by no means preposterous to suggest that all of the colonies, including Massachusetts and Connecticut, would have gone as far as the southern colonies in the same cultural direction had they had the resources to do so. Only later, after the northern states had both abandoned slavery and defined it as morally reprehensible, were the cultural divergencies that had arisen out of the relatively more profuse material abundance of the southern colonies defined as distinctive and labeled, by critics, as deviant.

From the perspective supplied by this line of argument, the author's second major proposition would seem to have been badly formulated. For if the southern colonies were both typically English and typically colonial Anglo-American, the question is not whether the southern colonies made a substantial contribution to the shaping of the American mind but precisely what that contribution was. To take one example, suggested by the author, the pursuit of the good life has been perhaps the most important ingredient in what he refers to as the "American Dream"; as such, it has also been a major determinant of American national culture. The Puritans' ambition of erecting a city upon a hill and

their conception of themselves as God's chosen people did indeed become
visible and at times powerful components of that culture. But it is doubtful that they have ever been so pervasively and persistently influential
as the quest for the good life. Nowhere during the colonial period in
British America was the commitment to that quest more evident than
in the southern colonies.[9]

Comprehension of the great extent to which the southern colonies
were at the center rather than on the peripheries of Anglo-American cultural development during the seventeenth and eighteenth centuries
makes it clear that the important questions about southern distinctiveness are when and how this region—during the first 150 years of its
existence the very embodiment of what is arguably the single most important element in the shaping of the American mind—came to be perceived not as the highest expression but as the very denial of some of the
central tenets of American life.

For indirectly bringing us to these questions as well as for providing
such an ample display of so many of the cultural artifacts of the colonial
southern mind, the author of these sprawling volumes has, despite his
maddening analytical caution, made a useful contribution to the ongoing
effort to describe the topography of early American culture and to reconstruct the processes through which it was formed.

I wrote this chapter in the summer of 1979 while I was in Florence for a month exploring
suggestions that The Johns Hopkins University use its Villa Spelman as a site for a
program for European students in American studies. A long strike prevented the *Times
Literary Supplement*, the journal that commissioned it, from publishing it, and it subsequently appeared in the *Journal of Interdisciplinary History* 12 (1982): 515–21, © 1982
by the Massachusetts Institute of Technology and the editors of the *Journal of Interdisciplinary History*, from which it is reprinted with the permission of the editors of the
journal and the MIT Press, Cambridge, Massachusetts, and the addition of citations to
quotations.

[9] Ibid., 273.

—THIRTEEN—

Reconstructing British-American Colonial History

With J. R. Pole

I F HISTORY is impossible to predict, so are the changing interests of historians. In March 1947 ten prominent early American historians assembled at Princeton to consider the state of their field. The following December in Cleveland, Carl Bridenbaugh, director of the recently created Institute of Early American History and Culture in Williamsburg, reported on their deliberations to the annual meeting of the American Historical Association. If Bridenbaugh's report accurately reflected their mood, they must have felt like an endangered species. By every measure Bridenbaugh could devise—the amount of time devoted to the period in survey courses, the numbers of specialized courses on the period offered in colleges and universities, the quantity of publications and new dissertations in the field, the numbers of scholars and graduate students engaged in active research—interest in colonial and Revolutionary America, eras that had absorbed a large proportion of the attention of the first two generations of professional historians between 1875 and 1925, seemed to have declined dramatically during the previous quarter century. Indeed, several leading graduate training centers—Princeton, Pennsylvania, Johns Hopkins, Chicago, and Berkeley—no longer had any historian actively working in the field; at still others, including Columbia, Northwestern, and Duke, teaching responsibilities for early American history fell entirely upon people whose primary field of interest was the early national period. Probably correctly, Bridenbaugh attributed this decline largely to the widespread impression within the profession that "colonial history" had "all been written." Decrying the notion that America's colonial and Revolutionary pasts had been "mined out," Bridenbaugh called attention to how little was known about the social and cultural history of colonial America, especially during the years from about 1680 to 1750, and exhorted his listeners to join in "a concerted effort to re-establish the field as a prominent [area of] study."[1]

But Bridenbaugh's jeremiad did not immediately lead to a palpable revival of interest in American colonial history. Notwithstanding the gradual emergence of the *William and Mary Quarterly* as the liveliest and most interesting medium of historical discourse in the United States and the appearance of important and sophisticated new works—by, among others, Wesley Frank Craven on the early southern colonies; Perry Miller on the New England mind; Louis B. Wright, Bridenbaugh, Max Savelle, and Frederick B. Tolles on aspects of the sociocultural life of the colonies; and Merrill Jensen, John R. Alden, John C. Miller, and Edmund S. Morgan on the American Revolution—it would have been impossible as late as the mid-1950s to predict the remarkable renaissance in early American studies that would occur over the following quarter century, much less to anticipate the course that renaissance would take.

Indeed, the landscape of colonial American history had changed very little over the previous generation. The major problems had been identified mainly during the three decades between 1890 and 1920, and the main interest had long been, and continued to be, in making slight additions to existing information or modest shifts in points of view. In both a formal and a substantive sense, colonial history before 1763 was dominated by its characterization as "the colonial period." Despite the insistence of Charles M. Andrews, Lawrence Henry Gipson, and other historians of the imperial school that the proper frame of reference for British-American colonial history included all the British colonies in America and not just the thirteen that revolted in 1776, the prevailing conception of colonial history, even for Andrews and Gipson, was strongly conditioned by the knowledge that the colonial period had been followed by the American Revolution and the foundation of the American nation. Such questions as arose from the operation of the navigation laws, the character of British imperial policy, the quality of British colonial administration, and the development of provincial and local political institutions in the colonies all tended to be colored by an implicit consensus that the underlying questions to be addressed were how such matters affected the movement for independence, how far and in what ways they were "responsible" for the Revolution, and how far back such responsibility might be traced. Even a local uprising in Virginia in 1676,

---

[1] Carl Bridenbaugh, "The Neglected First Half of American History," *American Historical Review* 53 (1948): 506–17.

a full hundred years before the Declaration of Independence, could be interpreted and was thought to be best understood as a "forerunner" of the eventual revolt against Britain. These observations do not hold for the careful contextual work of Wesley Frank Craven or the profound scholarship of Perry Miller, who analyzed the New England mind in terms that took their bearings from the contemporary interplay between theological aspirations and secular conditions. But the power and implications of Miller's work were slow to intrude upon the existing conception of the subject, a testimony to the force that conception continued to exert over the contracting world of early American studies.

Nor was that force much shaken by contemporary trends in the interpretation of later periods of American history. For at least fifteen years after World War II the prevailing conception of the American past continued to be that formulated during the first three decades of the twentieth century by Charles Beard, Vernon L. Parrington, and others and now known as the "Progressive" point of view. As John Murrin has pointed out, these "Progressive historians" were not much interested in, wrote very little about, and hence had relatively little impact upon the ways historians looked at the colonial period per se.[2] Equally important, the Progressive interest in history primarily as the analysis of *political* conflict meant that their salutary concern with getting at underlying social and economic development was limited largely to an interest in how those developments affected political life. Thus, to the small degree that the Progressive point of view influenced the ways colonial historians thought about their area of study, it tended to encourage a search for the socioeconomic roots of political behavior, especially as they were manifested during the Revolutionary era. It thereby served to strengthen the traditional view of the colonial period as interesting chiefly as a prelude to the Revolution. Moreover, because it held the focus of attention so directly upon politics, the Progressive point of view failed to engender a new comprehension of the significance of socioeconomic history as a subject worthy of study in its own right and probably even helped to inhibit the immediate development of a full appreciation of the important implications of the new work in sociocultural history for understanding the colonial past.

Much the same can be said about the initial effects of the growing interest in American studies between 1945 and 1960. Throughout these

---

[2] John M. Murrin, "Political Development," in Jack P. Greene and J. R. Pole, eds., *Colonial British America: Essays in the New History of the Early Modern Era* (Baltimore, 1984), 409.

years the American studies movement was guided by two basic assumptions. First was the definition of American studies as the analysis of only those areas that were or would become part of the United States. Thus, no less than the Progressive conception, the American studies approach was at bottom a variation on the Whig interpretation of history. Important in the colonial period were those aspects that seemed to explain the Revolution and the subsequent development of United States history. As a consequence, at the same time that it stimulated a renewed interest in many aspects of colonial culture, the American studies movement tended to channel that interest into an anachronistic search for the colonial roots of later American culture and to analyze colonial developments largely in terms of the extent to which they exhibited a process of Americanization.

A second pervasive assumption underlying the American studies approach was that America, at least in its continental British-American variant, was and had always been fundamentally different from Europe and that any variations among localities and regions within America were far less important than the similarities that made American culture, defined as the culture of the United States, different from that of Europe. This emphasis upon *American exceptionalism,* reinforced by the new postwar notion of *consensus,* tended to homogenize differences in time as well as in space in the American past and thereby further helped to blur the boundaries between the colonial and national periods and to inhibit the emergence of a conception of the colonial period as having an integrity of its own.

Precisely why and how the colonial period came during the next quarter century to acquire such an integrity and to become one of the most exciting and attractive areas of American historical study is complex and probably not yet very well understood. A subject of such considerable significance for an appreciation of the transformation of historical knowledge during the last half of the twentieth century demands far more serious and extended analysis than can be attempted here.

But any such analysis will have to give primary attention to three interrelated developments *within* the field of early American history itself. First, during the 1950s the works of Perry Miller finally began to exert an influence commensurate with their subtlety and brilliance. A growing recognition that Miller was not only the most original and profound historian in the entire history of American history but perhaps the only American historian whose work was qualitatively comparable to that of the great European historians of his and the previous generation inevitably stimulated interest in early America and set a high standard of historical discourse that in itself attracted prospective young historians into the field. Second, primarily through the *William and Mary Quarterly* and an increasingly distinguished book publication program, the Institute of Early American History and Culture was both providing an outlet for a steadily expanding volume of high-quality research in the field and serving as a forum for the exchange of new ideas and points of view. Third, a well-situated group of unusually effective graduate teachers in several of the major graduate training centers—Edmund S. Morgan at Brown and Yale, Oscar Handlin and Bernard Bailyn at Harvard, Richard B. Morris at Columbia, Wesley Frank Craven at Princeton, and Merrill Jensen at Wisconsin, to name only the most productive teachers—attracted into early American history a growing proportion of the enlarging pool of graduate students who began, especially after 1955, to seek a career in professional historical studies. Within a decade students of these and other teachers were assuming posts at major universities and beginning to train students of their own. To cater to the new interest, universities and colleges that before World War II had abandoned work in early American history revived the subject, and some universities doubled—a few eventually tripled—the number of historians teaching in the field.

Whatever the explanations for the proliferation of interest in early American history during these years, by the late 1950s, a mere decade after Bridenbaugh's 1947 lament, it was no longer possible to speak of early American history as "a neglected subject."[3] While the number of people teaching in the "first half" of American history was still equal to only a fraction of those covering the nineteenth and twentieth centuries, the proportions had shifted dramatically within a relatively short period. By the last half of the 1960s the number of Ph.D.'s in early American history produced in any given year considerably exceeded those for entire decades between 1920 and 1950, and the same could be said for the quantity of publications. Nor was interest in early America confined to historians and students of early American literature and art. Young scholars in the social sciences—sociology, historical geography, econometric history, anthropology, even psychology, psychiatry, and political science—began to find attractive research opportunities in the early American period.

Of course, by no means all of this new interest was directed at the

---

[3] Lester J. Cappon, "'The Historian's Day': From Archives to History," in Ray Allen Billington, ed., *The Reinterpretation of Early American History: Essays in Honor of John Edwin Pomfret* (San Marino, Calif., 1966), 234–38.

colonial era. Indeed, until the late 1960s a large proportion centered on the Revolution and the deepening of the analysis of such traditional questions as why the Revolution occurred, what kind of phenomenon it was, and how it related to the new Constitution of 1787–88, itself a focus of major investigation. Even among those scholars who did choose to concentrate upon the earlier period, attention was initially rather strongly directed toward conventional institutional and political subjects within established frameworks of interpretation. With the dramatic proliferation of scholars working in early American history through the 1960s, however, more and more of them began to investigate an ever-widening range of topics relating to the 150 years before the Revolutionary disturbances. Increasingly, they directed their questioning less toward existing answers than toward the questions themselves. Inspired by Miller's work on Puritanism as a moral and explanatory system that changed with social and economic circumstances, they turned first to intellectual history, working out and modifying Miller's own portrait of Puritan religious and intellectual development, analyzing the history of political and social thought, showing how inherited notions about themselves and other peoples conditioned European attitudes toward the non-Europeans they encountered in America.

This revived respect for ideas and values as important components of historical situations, a respect that was very greatly enhanced by intensive studies by Bailyn, Gordon S. Wood, and others on the political ideology of the late colonial and Revolutionary years, was soon accompanied by a new interest in the economic, demographic, and social history of the colonies, areas that had previously been only vaguely charted. To some small extent this development seems to have been a function of ever larger numbers looking for new research topics in unexplored areas and of an internal, almost self-generating logic that operated to push the boundaries of inquiry from one new area outward into another. For example, when publications on suffrage and representation revealed that ownership of property had been more widespread and the suffrage itself more widely distributed than earlier historians had supposed, others were led to look more closely at probate records as sources of information about social structure, standards of living, and economic expectations.

Probably much more important, however, were powerful stimuli deriving from two external sources. Perhaps the most significant of these came from related social science disciplines, which in the decades immediately after World War II acquired, especially in the United States, a new respectability and a new sophistication. Social science influences intruded upon colonial history in two ways. First, a few social scien-

tists—primarily econometric historians, historical geographers, historical sociologists, and cultural anthropologists—made important contributions to the field. But the impact of the social sciences upon British-
American colonial historical studies was far too pervasive to be explained
solely by the examples of so few people. As the influence of the social
sciences penetrated into the undergraduate curricula of most universities
and colleges, at least in the United States, and reached even into popular
social literature, historians themselves increasingly began to take over
and to employ, if usually only implicitly, the language, concepts, methods, and concerns of the social sciences, especially sociology, psychology,
economics, and anthropology. In time, this development encouraged a
demonstrable interest, unusual in historians for earlier generations, in
the explicit use of theory and methods, including statistics and quantification, drawn very largely from the social sciences. To the extent that
the impact of the social sciences was both earlier and greater among colonial historians than among students of later periods of American history,
it was probably because the traditional conception of history as the history of politics was far less strongly entrenched in an area in which so
little political history was shared.

But the new interest among colonial historians in social, economic,
demographic, and other areas of history was also powerfully reinforced
by the example of new schools of methodology and historical inquiry
on the other side of the Atlantic. The French *Annales* school had for a
generation been striving for an *histoire totale* that would subordinate the
history of public life to a more expanded concern for the recovery of all
aspects of a population's experience, from the environmental and material to the social and intellectual, from the macrolevel to the microlevel,
and from the most prominent inhabitants to the most marginal.

By the early 1960s the orientation of this group had been taken up by
those involved in the study of early modern England, where a powerful
intensification of interest in Tudor and Stuart history was already in
progress. Scholars concerned with the social sources of the English Revolution of the mid-seventeenth century; with the relationship between
social structure, culture, and belief systems; and, especially as it was
manifested by the recently formed Cambridge Group for the History of
Population and Social Structure, with the interaction between population history and economic, social, and political change, provided students of colonial British America with attractive new models of how the
new interest in the concerns of social science could translate into an illumination of a particular era of the past.

At the same time, the findings of these historians provided colonial historians with an expanded context for their work and served to draw them more fully than ever before into the historian's world of the past, a world in which subjects were judged to be significant less for what they might reveal about subsequent events than for what they told about the specific world of which they were a part. If the social sciences turned the attention of colonial historians in the direction of socioeconomic and cultural history, the work of early modern historians in France and Britain taught them the virtues of endeavoring to re-create past societies in their own integrity, within their own terms of reference, and, insofar as possible, without the distortions of teleology. An important concomitant of this development was a renewed respect for and interest in various levels of local history.[4]

Whatever the influences that aroused so much new interest in British-American colonial history and turned that interest so strongly in the direction of an expanded conception of the subject in the 1960s and 1970s, the result was a veritable explosion of monographs and articles and a profusion of information about many aspects of the field. Not all of the results of this new prosperity have been entirely salutary. For some time now, it has been clear that the wealth of new information generated annually by students of colonial history has given rise to a severe case of intellectual indigestion. As knowledge has become more abundant and detailed, scholars have become more and more specialized, and the field of colonial British America has fragmented into a series of subspecialties, regional, temporal, thematic, and methodological. To a deplorable extent specialists in one area of colonial British America claim no more expertise about the other areas than about, for instance, nineteenth- or twentieth-century history in general.

At the same time, while many of the old general contours and themes around which the field had traditionally been organized have been destroyed or rendered obsolete, there has been a notable lack of systematic attention to the problem of replacing them with new ones. As scholars have concentrated more and more upon smaller and smaller units in their laudable efforts to recover the context and texture of colonial life in as much detail as the sources and scholarly ingenuity will permit,

---

[4] In stressing these particular influences from within the disciplines of historical studies, we do not wish to minimize general social developments, such as the disillusionment with the American dream which, beginning in the mid-1960s, sent many people off on what now appears in retrospect to have been a nostalgic search for a more attractive, communal past, one that some of them found in the relatively egalitarian and communally oriented family farming communities of preindustrial New England.

there has been surprisingly little effort to relate their findings to the larger picture of British-American development over the whole period from the beginning of the seventeenth century through the middle decades of the eighteenth. One paradoxical result of the reinvigoration of British-American colonial history has thus been a signal loss of overall coherence, to the point that we are now less clear than ever before about precisely what the central themes and the larger questions are in the field as a whole.

A second problem is that the profusion of scholarship about colonial America inevitably has been uneven. We know vastly more, for instance, about New England and the Chesapeake than we do about other areas, about rural life than about urban, about religion than about secular culture, about external trade than about internal, about political ideology than about political process, about static wealth structures than about the dynamics of social developement, about adult, white, independent males than about other elements in the population. Yet, although everyone is aware that we know more about some areas and questions than about others, no one has sought in a systematic and comprehensive way to assess what we do know and what we do not or to identify those areas and problems—and they are many—to which scholars in the field might now profitably turn their attention.

In a conscious effort to address these problems, the authors of this chapter organized a conference to consider a series of papers by mature scholars who had both lived through and themselves made significant contributions to the first impressive stages of the current transformation of colonial British-American history. The goal was to recruit scholars primarily from among members of the generation who, having received their doctorates in the 1950s or early 1960s and having now held professional posts for between one and two decades, were already in mid-career and who, because of their past, present, or prospective roles in training doctoral students, seemed to be strategically well placed to be able both to define developments to date and to suggest guidelines for the future.

Our intention was for the conference to be as intellectually comprehensive as possible. This objective might have been achieved through either a spatial or a temporal approach. But considerations of economy, as well as our feeling that the current preoccupation with distinctions observable over space and time had been a powerful contributing force in undermining a holistic conception of the subject, decided us to adopt a structural approach, and we divided the subject into fourteen topics, each of which was to be covered by a scholar with a demonstrated interest in it: Jacob M. Price and Richard B. Sheridan on economic development; James T. Lemon on spatial organization and settlement patterns; Jim Potter on population trends; Richard S. Dunn on labor systems; Timothy H. Breen and Gary B. Nash on cultural interaction and social relations; James A. Henretta on social structure; Joyce Appleby, David D. Hall, and Richard L. Bushman on value systems and aspects of religious and social behavior; and William A. Speck, John M. Murrin, and Stanley N. Katz on political, constitutional, and legal developments. The particular subject division we adopted reflects contemporary notions about the sociology of knowledge as it has been defined over the past generation by the social sciences and, more specifically in historical studies, by the *Annales* school. Its heavy emphasis upon the economic, demographic, spatial, social, and cultural dimensions of the colonial past also mirrors the contemporary distribution of interest and activity within the field itself.

In setting out guidelines for the authors, we asked each of them to treat his or her topic in its broadest possible dimensions, to cover both the seventeenth and the eighteenth centuries, both the island colonies and those on the continent, and all segments of society. Insofar as relevant, they were to consider regional variations, changes over time, external and internal (metropolitan and colonial) dimensions, and the role of women and minorities as well as of the dominant male members of society. Specifically, we asked them to focus upon (1) where we are now and how we got here; (2) what problems require more attention; (3) what, in view of existing sources and ways of manipulating them, the best strategies for attacking these problems are; (4) how problems and findings in the topic area relate to those in the other areas; and (5) what *general* themes that seem to be emerging from research already published or under way might help to structure studies not just of the subject area of the paper itself but in the field of British-American colonial history as a whole. Finally, we requested the authors to try to detach themselves from the teleology imposed by the American Revolution and the establishment of a separate American nation and to consider colonial British America between 1607 and 1763 as a broad socioeconomic, cultural, and political unit only some portions of which seceded between 1776 and 1783.

Predictably and probably desirably, the final essays as published in *Colonial British America: Essays in the New History of the Early Modern Era*,[5] all of which were revised in the light of the discussions at the conference at which they were initially presented in August 1981, do not

---

[5] Greene and Pole, *Colonial British America.*

conform in all cases to these prescriptions. Some authors, specifically Henretta and Katz, felt that they could best elucidate their topics by looking at them from the vantage point of later, specifically American developments, while a majority, including Appleby, Lemon, Potter, Nash, Henretta, Hall, Bushman, and Katz, either ignored the Caribbean colonies completely or gave them only cursory mention. No one treated in a systematic or sustained way the less populous island colonies of Bermuda, the Bahamas, and Newfoundland or the northern most continental colony, Nova Scotia. Similarly, although they were by no means ignored, the roles of women and children certainly, and those of Amerindians and lower-class whites probably, were not accorded the prominence that their numbers, contemporary socioeconomic and cultural importance, and recent scholarly attention demand and that they will, we hope, receive over the next few decades. To a considerable degree, these underemphases, like the relative inattention to the colonies of the Lower South, arise out of the absence of extensive research on which the contributors might have drawn. To that extent, they provide powerful testimony to the continuing failure of a significant proportion of the colonial American historical community to adopt a larger conception of their subject or, perhaps, fully to accept the desirability of a nonteleological *histoire totale.*

To the degree that our original objective of comprehensiveness was not completely fulfilled, it cannot be attributed only to the orientations of individual authors. Several important topics, including the development of language, communications networks, occupational structures, the professions, and secular social institutions above the level of the family simply fell through the interstices of our topical division of the subject, and we must take full responsibility for these and similar omissions. Yet, even by virtue of its failure to achieve a comprehensive treatment of the subject, *Colonial British America* implicitly fulfilled one of its major objectives: the denotation of important areas demanding additional research.

Nor do these omissions represent the only failure of objectives that can be attributed to the organization of the volume. As critics of the *Annales* school have frequently pointed out, one of the most obvious weaknesses of a sectoral approach to historical and social analysis is the difficulty of tying various sectors together and showing how through a series of complex interactions they operate to shape the historical or social process, and this weakness is doubtless enhanced when each sector is treated by a different author. Thus, it is scarcely surprising that few of the authors displayed much concern with trying to articulate systematically "*general* themes that . . . might help to structure studies . . . in the field of British-American colonial history as a whole."

This is not to suggest, however, that they have been inattentive to the utility of explanatory frameworks and models in the organization of historical analysis. Indeed, several authors affirmed the continuing usefulness of existing models for explaining developments within the particular sectors for which they had responsibility, albeit they often recommended changes in those models to make them fit the complex situations they purport to help analyze. Thus, Price and Sheridan both seemed to agree that a combination of the staple and population-market models still provides the most productive approach to colonial economic development. Lemon found no better substitute for a modified central-place theory for explaining colonial settlement patterns; Breen advocated the use of a revised interactionist model in looking at relations among cultures; Bushman proposed what was essentially a diffusion framework for the interpretation of colonial cultural development; and Appleby pointed out many positive benefits to be derived from a critical employment of the value-and-society approach to the study of colonial belief systems.

On a more general level, however, the authors seemed to be almost unanimous in their conviction that no existing model was very satisfactory, and this negative judgment seems to apply equally to older and more recent frameworks of explanation. The early twentieth-century interpretive systems associated with Frederick Jackson Turner, the imperial historians, or the Progressives all now seem to be far too one-dimensional to be of more than limited use, and none of the authors showed any disposition to try to revive them. Similarly, except for Hall, none of them had a good word to say for the concept of American exceptionalism, which provided the intellectual underpinning for both Turnerian analysis and much of the work deriving out of the post–World War II American studies movement and the so-called consensus school of American history.

Nor are they any happier with the gemeinschaft-gesellschaft model, with its view of Western historical development as a process of "declension" from an organic, communal subsistence, religious, and personal society to a more individualistic, market-oriented, secular, and impersonal one. Perhaps because it seemed to fit rather well the New England experience as it was limned by Miller and several younger historians of the New England community, over the past quarter century this model has been used more widely by colonial historians than any other. During the 1970s and early 1980s, however, it became powerfully obvious that it fundamentally distorted the experiences of all of the colonies outside New England and, perhaps more serious, that it gave excessive emphasis to the power of tradition and the resistance to change at the same time that it underestimated the adaptive capacities of societies and the individuals who composed them.

Much the same can be said about the more recent variant of this conception that looks at change in the early modern era in terms of a movement from traditional to modern. Both the gemeinschaft-gesellschaft and the traditional-modern frameworks are teleological and almost invariably laden with distorting value judgments. While the former proceeds from a lament for the passage of older, presumably warmer forms of social interaction, the latter is rooted in a celebration of the rush into an enlightened present. Finally, insofar as the authors show any explicit concern for the problem, none of them demonstrates much optimism that the social sciences may yield new general models that either will prove more suitable for analyzing colonial development as a whole or will not be freighted with theory that, in Appleby's words, overdetermines the interpretive outcomes.

If, however, existing general frameworks are all unsatisfactory and none of the authors of the chapters in the *Colonial British America* volume has proposed an alternative, those chapters do, we would suggest, provide a foundation for the development of a new, more inclusive framework for the reconstruction of colonial history. Although this is not the place to attempt to elaborate it in detail, we can suggest, in a preliminary way at least, what its most essential features may be.

What seems to be indisputably clear from this collection of essays is that any workable general framework will have to be based upon recognition that colonial British America comprised several distinctive socioeconomic regions that transcended political boundaries. Colonial historians have of course traditionally distinguished between the island and the continental colonies and between the southern and the northern colonies on the continent. More recently, a few scholars have also divided the colonies into two broad categories: *colonies of exploitation* and *colonies of settlement,* the former term referring to those colonies that employed large numbers of slaves to produce staples on plantations in the Caribbean and southern North America and the latter to those colonies that did not.[6]

---

[6] See, for instance, Franklin W. Knight, *The Caribbean: The Genesis of a Fragmented Nationalism* (New York, 1978), 50–60. A highly sophisticated elaboration of a similar typology can be found in Philip Mason, *Patterns of Dominance* (London, 1971), 66–136.

Originally developed by students of nineteenth-century imperialism to distinguish between colonies in which a small population of Europeans conquered and exploited the labor and resources of a large indigenous population and colonies in which large numbers of European immigrants and their increase occupied previously only thinly settled lands as permanent settlers, this particular typology is fundamentally misleading when applied to the early modern British-American colonies. Every one of these was a colony of settlement in the sense that it involved the expropriation and settlement of land with new immigrants—whether voluntary, as in the case of most Europeans, or forced, as in the case of virtually all Africans—and the subsequent organization of settler societies. Strictly speaking, not even the small British trading factories on the African coast or in India during this period were colonies of exploitation in the original sense of the term.[7]

An earlier typology developed before the advent of the new imperialism and the establishment of large numbers of colonies of exploitation of the classic type during the later nineteenth century would seem to be more useful. In his *Lectures on Colonization and Colonies*, a collection of lectures delivered at Oxford between 1839 and 1841, Herman Merivale also separated colonies into two types. But his distinction was between those that had *"no peculiar advantages for the production, by agricultural or mining labour, of articles of value in the foreign market"* and those that did, the former being characterized by mixed farming, free labor, less involvement in international markets, and a less stratified social structure and the latter by staple agriculture, bound labor, deep involvement in international markets, and greater extremes of wealth.[8] Of course, this distinction between *farm colonies* and *plantation colonies* cannot be too rigidly applied. No early modern British-American colony was entirely without large landholdings worked by bound labor, and none, not even in the Leeward Islands, was a purely plantation colony without

---

[7] To argue that all British-American colonies were settler societies does not imply either that some of them (notably those in the Caribbean) did not subsequently become colonies of exploitation (in the Leeward Islands this may have already happened by the middle of the eighteenth century) or that they were not basically exploitative in character. Indeed, in addition to being settler societies, all of the colonies were fundamentally exploitative of both the environments in which they lived and of any subordinate groups of people within them whose labor and persons could be exploited by those with greater power and resources. For an illuminating discussion of the problem of developing a workable typology of colonies, see M. I. Finley, "Colonies: An Attempt at a Typology," Royal Historical Society, *Transactions*, 5th ser., 26 (1976): 167–88.

[8] Herman Merivale, *Lectures on Colonization and Colonies* (New York, 1967), 260–61.

small agricultural landholders. But it nevertheless can serve as a useful classificatory device for distinguishing between the two broad categories of colonies of settlement within the early modern British-American world.

As scholars have moved strongly away from political history to social and economic history during the 1960s and 1970s, however, they have recognized the crudeness of these older categorizations and have gradually developed a more refined system of *regional* classification based largely upon differences in methods of land use, settlement patterns, socioeconomic organization, and cultural orientation. As will be apparent from the chapters published in *Colonial British America,* there is by no means yet complete agreement as to precisely how many regions there were or how and where the boundaries among them should be drawn. But a strong preference seems to be emerging for a five-part division. By order of settlement, these parts are the *Chesapeake,* comprising Virginia, Maryland, northern North Carolina, and perhaps southern Delaware; *New England,* composed of Massachusetts and its offshoot colonies Connecticut, Rhode Island, New Hampshire, and Nova Scotia; the *Caribbean,* including until 1763 Barbados, the Leeward Island colonies of Antigua, Montserrat, Nevis, and St. Christopher, and Jamaica; the *Middle Colonies,* comprising New York, New Jersey, Pennsylvania, and northern Delaware; and the *Lower South,* containing South Carolina, southern North Carolina, and Georgia. To these five groups some scholars would add two others, neither of which received much mention in *Colonial British America:* first, a group of non-staple-producing small Atlantic island colonies made up of Bermuda and the Bahamas, and second, the New West, which beginning in the 1730s formed in the backcountries of Pennsylvania, Maryland, Virginia, and the Carolinas.[9]

It is interesting that in this more refined system of regional classification, before 1763 only three regions—New England, the Atlantic island colonies, and the New West—can be defined as almost wholly farm colonies, and only two—the Caribbean and the Lower South—as predominantly plantation colonies. Both the Chesapeake and the Middle Colonies fall somewhere in between these two types. No doubt, this seven-part division will be refined still further as scholars develop an even more acute appreciation of important differences between areas within these larger regional categories. Already, in fact, it is obvious that

---

[9] In this connection, see the suggestive essay by Robert D. Mitchell, "The Formation of Early American Cultural Regions: An Interpretation," in James R. Gibson, ed., *European Settlement and Development in North America: Essays on Geographical Change in Honour and Memory of Andrew Hill Clark* (Toronto, 1978), 66–90.

before 1763 there were at least three important subregions within both New England and the Caribbean and two within the Chesapeake and the Middle Colonies.

If, however, we are ever going to develop a satisfactory comprehensive general framework for interpreting the whole of the early modern British-American experience, we will have to move beyond an appreciation of regional differences to an emphasis upon important similarities— underlying unities that make it possible, indeed necessary, to conceive of these separate regions as parts of a larger British-American world.

Five major similarities now appear to have been of special importance. First, each region was initially a *new* society whose members were faced with the problems of organizing an unfamiliar landscape, finding ways to exploit that landscape so as to satisfy their basic material needs, and creating a social and political system that would enable them to live together in an orderly manner. Second, each region was tied into the emerging transatlantic trading network, itself, like the colonies, a result of the vigorous commercial (and military) expansion of Europe outward during the early modern period. Third, unlike people in the European societies from which the dominant white settlers emanated, the settlers all lived, as both Breen and Nash emphasized in their chapters in *Colonial British America,* in multiracial and, within each racial category, multiethnic societies whose plural character was sooner or later reflected in considerable heterogeneity in both religious and secular life. Fourth, no less than the societies from which they came, these new societies were all fundamentally exploitative in character, not just of their new environments but of any of the people living in those environments who were susceptible to exploitation. Indeed, in colonies as well as in the metropolitan societies of Europe, people's status was in great measure determined by the extent to which they could or could not exploit other people.

Fifth and finally, it cannot be emphasized too strongly that all these new American societies were also *colonial* societies. Most obviously, their status as colonies meant that they were subjected to a common imperial policy and operated within a roughly similar political framework. It also meant that they not only were frequently engaged in hostilities with neighboring Indians and colonists of rival European nations but were also drawn into imperial wars between Britain and its French, Spanish, and Dutch enemies for at least half of the long period between 1607 and 1763. Finally, their status as colonies also meant that they were economic and social extensions of Britain and that their existence, material well-being, and, until very late in the colonial period, actual safety were in important degrees intimately dependent upon Britain. Even more important, however, their colonial status meant that no matter how distant they might be from Britain or how much latitude they may have had in their internal development (and notwithstanding the ethnic diversity of their populations), they were all cultural provinces of Britain whose legal and social systems, perceptual frameworks, and social and cultural imperatives were inevitably in large measure British in origin and whose inhabitants thereby shared a common identity as British peoples living in America.

Arguably the most important similarity among the several regions of colonial British America, this common identity imposed upon British Americans in all regions a common set of expectations for their new societies, which they looked upon not merely as vehicles for their own sustenance and enrichment but also as places that would eventually be recognizable approximations of Albion itself. They thus came to the New World expecting not to create something wholly new but, insofar as possible, to re-create what they had left behind, albeit without some of its less desirable aspects. Their expectation, their hope, was that the simple societies with which they began in time would develop into complex, improved, and civilized societies as those terms were defined by their metropolitan inheritance.

These contemporary expectations provide a basis for the further elaboration of a general *developmental framework* of the colonial process that can encompass the experiences of all regions of colonial British America before 1763. Like the emerging system of regional classification, this conception is doubtless in need of much further refinement, but it encourages and permits us to conceive of the development of the several colonial regions as part of a long-range social process that can be divided into three sequential phases.

The first phase involved the *social simplification* of inherited forms that so many scholars have noted for the first generations in every new colony. With very few exceptions, this early phase was characterized by much unsettlement and disorientation, as people sought to find ways to manipulate their new environments for their own sustenance and advantage while endeavoring, with limited success, to impose upon that environment social arrangements that, except possibly in the orthodox colonies of Puritan New England, bore little more than a crude resemblance to those they had left behind.

As social arrangements gradually became more settled, population grew more dense (and usually more heavily creole), and the inhabitants acquired greater economic wherewithal, the simple social conditions that had characterized the first phase of settlement gave way to more elaborate ones. This second phase, one of *social elaboration,* thus involved the articulation of socioeconomic, political, and cultural institutions, structures, and values that, although they were usually highly creolized variants of those found in the more developed areas of Britain, were sufficiently functional to enable local populations to assimilate to them with relatively little difficulty.

If this second phase was marked by a growing acculturation of the inhabitants to their social environment, that acculturation was not so complete as to inhibit demands, emanating largely from emerging elites, for a restructuring of their societies along lines that would make them more demonstrably British. Through the last decades of the period, colonial societies became more populous, offered prospects for greater comfort and affluence, grew more settled (if not in all cases much more orderly), and became internally more complex. In the common language of the times, these developments were subsumed under the term *improvement.* With these and other "improvements," colonial societies approximated more closely to the established societies of the Old World and entered into still a third phase of development, a phase of *social replication.*

In this phase members of strategically placed elites, who by the late colonial period almost everywhere dominated and gave tone and definition to their societies, displayed a keen desire to re-create British society in America and took pride in the extent to which their societies were becoming increasingly anglicized. By no means all members of the less affluent ranks of society shared this desire so fully, however, and some of the signs of sharp conflict in the colonies over religion, economics, and politics during the three or four decades before the Revolution can be attributed to opposing notions about precisely what directions the process of social development should take. For this reason, this third phase cannot by any means be seen as one of harmonious solidification under an image of anglicized replication.

The timing of this process and the duration of each phase varied from region to region, and these differences led to widely varying results. The rate and character of population growth (including the changing ratios among the sexes, racial groups, and immigrants and creoles), economic growth, territorial expansion, and date of settlement would seem to have been the central variables in determining differences in timing. Variations in results, on the other hand, were obviously a function of a much more numerous group of variables, including the nature of economic organization and the labor system, levels of socioeconomic differentiation, the depth and character of the religious orientation and goals of the populace, the healthfulness of the situation, the authority and responsiveness of colonial political leaders and institutions, and the degree of direct involvement with metropolitan Britain.

At every stage in this process of social development, it is important to keep in mind, these variables operated within a general framework of persisting tension between what we might, for convenience, refer to as experience and inheritance. By *experience* we mean to connote the complex of demands made upon the inhabitants by the necessity for their societies to function effectively within their several specific physical and social environments. By *inheritance* we mean to signify those traditions, cultural imperatives, and conceptions of the proper social order that the colonists derived initially from the metropolis—traditions, imperatives, and conceptions that they or their ancestors had brought with them from the Old World and that subsequently had been reinforced or modified through a process of continuous interaction with that world. The balance of force between experience and inheritance shifted from one phase of social development to the next according to local circumstances and the imperial and international context. But the general direction of movement before 1763 seems to have been toward the growing importance, though not necessarily in all cases the predominance, of inheritance.

If our aims in putting forth this conception seem ambitious, the spirit in which we do so is both tentative and inquiring. We offer it as no more than a preliminary effort to call attention to the need for and to articulate a general framework that will help historians of colonial British America to process the enormous amount of data they are assembling without losing sight of the underlying coherence of the field as a whole or doing violence to the period, places, and structures they study. As R. G. Collingwood observed, all history is an interim report on work in progress. The fourteen substantive essays in *Colonial British America*, like the general model they helped to inspire, are tendered to the reader as precisely that, a series of provisional reflections upon what has been achieved and what areas require additional research. In this spirit, we commend the essays to our own and succeeding generations of historians of colonial British America.

Jointly authored with J. R. Pole in the late summer of 1982, this chapter is reprinted with permission and minor revisions from Jack P. Greene and J. R. Pole, eds., *Colonial British America: Essays in the New History of the Early Modern Era* (Baltimore: The Johns Hopkins University Press, 1984), 1–17.

—Fourteen—

Colonial New England in Recent Historiography

T<small>HE HISTORIOGRAPHY</small> of colonial New England, like that of colonial British America in general, underwent a profound reorientation during the 1970s and 1980s. The classic theme of the nature, implementation, and subsequent metamorphosis of Puritanism in Massachusetts Bay and Connecticut has continued to receive major attention from historians. Indeed, no other subject in the vast and variegated history of colonial British America has yet attracted more scholarly attention. Increasingly, however, religious history has had to share the stage with social history. How this development has changed our conceptions of colonial New England is the subject of this paper. For convenience, the subject has been broken down into three rough periods, the first stretching from the founding to 1660, the second from 1660 to about 1720, and the third from 1720 to about 1770. To the rather considerable extent that Nova Scotia was a socioeconomic and cultural extension of New England during the third quarter of the eighteenth century, this analysis may help to illuminate important aspects of the immediate background of its early development.

Much of the work done on the first generation of English settlement in New England before 1660 speaks most directly to the question of the typicality of the New England experience in the process of establishing English colonies in the Americas. Early American historians have widely, if usually only implicitly, assumed that the New England experience can serve as a model for the English-American colonial experience in this regard. But recent research on New England and other areas of settlement has seriously undermined this assumption. With regard to almost every area of life, the New England experience, at least insofar as it was manifest in the histories of the two major colonies of Massachusetts Bay and Connecticut, deviated sharply from that of every other region of English colonial settlement—in Ireland, in North America, and in the Atlantic and Caribbean island colonies.

Demographically, for instance, the experience of New England was quite peculiar. Although a few hundred people had migrated to Plymouth and other small coastal settlements in the 1620s, New England, in contrast to most other areas, was initially peopled largely by a short, sudden, and carefully organized burst of immigration. Between 20,000 and 25,000 English people poured into the colony and adjacent areas in just twelve short years between 1630 and 1642. As many as 70 percent of these immigrants, moreover, came not, as was the case elsewhere, as unmarried, young, and unfree servants but as members of established families, independent farmers and artisans with some accumulated resources. Virtually from the beginning, therefore, the age structure and sex ratio in New England resembled those of established societies all over western Europe far more closely than was the case with any other new society established by the English in America during the early modern era. Unlike the Chesapeake colonies, which could never have sustained themselves without a constant flow of new arrivals from England, New England was the destination of relatively few new immigrants following the outbreak of the English Civil War in 1642. Nor does it appear that immigration from England to New England ever again became substantial at any later time during the colonial period.[1]

Nevertheless, New England population grew rapidly from the large base of initial immigrants. Largely free of serious epidemics, New England experienced much lower rates of mortality than either England or any of its other colonies. Studies in the early 1970s by Philip Greven and Kenneth Lockridge suggested that infant mortality was low—of an average of 8.3 children born to a group of sample families in Andover, 7.2 survived to age 21—and those who lived to 21 could anticipate long and healthy lives: 71.8 for men and 70.8 for women among the first gen-

[1] Terry L. Anderson and Robert Paul Thomas, "White Population, Labor Force, and Extensive Growth of the New England Economy in the Seventeenth Century," *Journal of Economic History* 23 (1973): 639–41; T. H. Breen and Stephen Foster, "Moving to the New World: The Character of Early Massachusetts Immigration," *William and Mary Quarterly*, 3d ser., 30 (1973): 189–222; Virginia Dejohn Anderson, "Migrants and Motives: Religion and the Settlement of New England, 1630–1640," *New England Quarterly* 68 (1985): 340, 346–67; N. C. P. Tyack, "The Humble Puritans of East Anglia and the New England Movement: Evidence from the Court Records of the 1630s," *New England Historical and Genealogical Register* 138 (1984): 79–106.

eration of settlers and 64.2 for men and 61.6 for women among the second. Combined with relatively young ages for first marriages for women (19.0 for the first generation and 22.3 for the second) and a correspondingly high number of births per marriage, this low rate of mortality sent population surging upward. Within a generation population had doubled. By 1660 New England as a whole contained between 55,000 and 60,000 inhabitants of European descent, more than twice the number in the Chesapeake colonies, which had been in existence for a full generation longer. In vivid contrast to the Chesapeake, moreover, most of these people were native-born, New England becoming the first region of Anglo-American settlement to develop a predominantly creole population.[2]

We have long known of course that the New England colonies had a much more deeply religious orientation than other English colonies; perhaps the most important finding of new scholarship in this area is the considerable religious diversity among the early settlers. As William Stoever and Philip Gura have both emphasized, participants in the great migration were far from being all of one mind with regard to theology, church government, and other religious questions, and the congregational church polity preferred by most of them was conducive to the accommodation of a wide range of religious opinion. At the same time, however, this scholarship has continued to emphasize, with Perry Miller, the extent to which leaders of these colonies were moved by the vision of establishing a redemptive community of God's chosen people in the New World. They saw themselves as a special group joined in a binding covenant with God and sent by him into the wilderness to establish the true Christian commonwealth that would thenceforth serve as a model for the rest of the Christian world. In the societies they created, the church and the clergy thus necessarily had unusually powerful roles, the relationship between clerical and secular leaders was both intimate and mutually supportive, and full civil rights, including the franchise, were in many communities limited to church members.[3]

---

[2] Anderson and Thomas, "White Population," 639–42; Philip J. Greven, Jr., *Four Generations: Population, Land, and Family in Colonial Andover, Massachusetts* (Ithaca, N.Y., 1970), 21–40; Kenneth Lockridge, "The Population of Dedham, Massachusetts, 1636–1736," *Economic History Review*, 2d ser., 19 (1966): 318–44.

[3] David D. Hall, "Understanding the Puritans," in Herbert Bass, ed., *The State of American History* (Chicago, 1970), 330–49; Michael McGiffert, "American Puritan Studies in the 1960's," *William and Mary Quarterly*, 3d ser., 27 (1970): 36–67; and Anderson, "Migrants and Motives," 367–83. David D. Hall, "A World of Wonders: The Mentality of the Supernatural in Seventeenth-Century New England," in Hall and David Grayson

If most of these conclusions are generally compatible with the work of an earlier generation of historians, recent historians, especially Stephen Foster, have perhaps put more emphasis upon the social dimensions of the initial Puritan vision. Puritan colonists came to America not only because they were unable to realize their religious aspirations in old England; they were also driven by a profound disquiet over the state of contemporary English society. In towns and rural areas alike, new social and economic forces seemed to be producing a disturbing and ever-widening gap between inherited prescriptions of social order and actual circumstances of life, while the crown and its agents were more and more intruding into many aspects of local affairs, civil as well as religious. To an important degree, the great migration to New England was an "essentially defensive, conservative, even reactionary" response to these developments. Hence, its members were determined not only to achieve perfection in the church but also to create a society that, in contrast

---

Allen, eds., *Seventeenth-Century New England* (Boston, 1984), 239–74; William K.B. Stoever, *"A Faire and Easie Way to Heaven": Covenant Theology and Antinomianism in Early Massachusetts* (Middletown, Conn., 1978); and Philip F. Gura, *A Glimpse of Scion's Glory: Puritan Radicalism in Seventeenth-Century New England, 1620–1660* (Middletown, Conn., 1984), stress the religious diversity among Puritan settlers. See also Stephen Foster, "New England and the Challenge of Heresy, 1630 to 1660: The Puritan Crisis in Transatlantic Perspective," *William and Mary Quarterly,* 3d ser., 28 (1981): 624–60, "The Godly in Transit: English Popular Protestantism and the Creation of a Puritan Establishment in America," in Hall and Allen, *Seventeenth-Century New England,* 185–238, and "English Puritanism and the Progress of New England Institutions, 1630–1660," in David D. Hall, John M. Murrin, and Thad W. Tate, eds., *Saints and Revolutionaries: Essays on Early American History* (New York, 1984), 3–37; J. F. Maclear, "New England and the Fifth Monarchy: The Quest for the Millennium in Early American Puritanism," *William and Mary Quarterly,* 3d ser., 32 (1975): 223–60; and Sacvan Bercovitch, *The American Jeremiad* (Madison, Wis., 1978), 3–61. Relations between church and state, ministry and magistracy in early New England are treated in David D. Hall, *The Faithful Shepherd: A History of the New England Ministry in the Seventeenth Century* (Chapel Hill, N.C., 1972); George Selement, *Keepers of the Vineyard: The Puritan Ministry and Collective Culture in Colonial New England* (Lanham, Md., 1984); and B. Katherine Brown, "The Controversy over the Franchise in Puritan Massachusetts, 1654 to 1674," *William and Mary Quarterly,* 3d ser., 33 (1976): 228. Other works on the complex issue of the franchise are T. H. Breen, "Who Governs: The Town Franchise in Seventeenth-Century Massachusetts," ibid., 27 (1970): 460–74; Stephen Foster, "The Massachusetts Franchise in the Seventeenth Century," ibid., 24 (1967): 613–23; Arlin I. Ginsberg, "The Franchise in Seventeenth-Century Massachusetts: Ipswich," ibid., 34 (1977): 444–52; Robert E. Wall, "The Franchise in Seventeenth-Century Massachusetts: Dedham and Cambridge," ibid., 453–58, and "The Decline of the Massachusetts Franchise, 1647–1666," *Journal of American History* 59 (1972): 303–10; and James A. Thorpe, "Colonial Suffrage in Massachusetts," *Essex Institute Historical Collections* 106 (1970): 169–81.

to the seemingly increasingly anarchic and beleaguered world they were leaving behind, would conform as closely as possible to traditional English conceptions of the ideal, well-ordered commonwealth.[4]

This determination accounted for the peculiar social organization of New England. In their grand design of building the ideal traditional ordered English world in the untamed American wilderness, Puritan settlers tried to organize their new societies around a series of tightly constructed and relatively independent settled permanent communities in which the inhabitants formally covenanted with each other to comprise unified social organisms. As David Grayson Allen and others have shown, there was considerable diversity in the form of these communities. Joseph Wood's recent research shows that only a few, like Andover, were the classical kind of nucleated villages in which the inhabitants lived around the meetinghouse and went forth each working morning to fields arranged according to the traditional open-field system that still prevailed in some areas of England. Most, like Sudbury, quickly broke up into dispersed rural settlements with the inhabitants living on individual farms. How any group of settlers organized themselves upon the land seems to have been determined to some significant degree by their own prior experience in England.[5]

But everywhere, at least in the three "orthodox colonies" of Massachu-

---

[4]T. H. Breen, "Transfer of Culture: Chance and Design in Shaping Massachusetts Bay, 1630–1660," *New England Historical and Genealogical Register* 132 (1978): 3–17, and "Persistent Localism: English Social Change and the Shaping of New England Institutions," *William and Mary Quarterly*, 3d ser., 32 (1975): 3–28; Andrew Delbanco, "The Puritan Errand Re-Viewed," *Journal of American Studies* 18 (1984): 342–60; Allen Cardin, "The Communal Ideal in Puritan New England, 1630–1700," *Fides et Historia* 17 (1984): 25–38. The clearest and most perceptive discussion of Puritan social goals in New England is Stephen Foster, *Their Solitary Way: The Puritan Social Ethic in the First Century of Settlement in New England* (New Haven, 1971).

[5]Diversity among New England towns is admirably treated in David Grayson Allen, *In English Ways: The Movement of Societies and the Transferal of English Local Law and Custom to Massachusetts Bay in the Seventeenth Century* (Chapel Hill, N.C., 1981). See also Joseph S. Wood, "Village and Community in Early Colonial New England," *Journal of Historical Geography* 8 (1982): 333–46; Sumner Chilton Powell, *Puritan Village: The Formation of a New England Town* (Middletown, Conn., 1964); Kenneth A. Lockridge, *A New England Town, the First Hundred Years: Dedham, Massachusetts, 1636–1736* (New York, 1970); Greven, *Four Generations;* John J. Waters, "Hingham, Massachusetts, 1631–1661: An East Anglian Oligarchy in the New World," *Journal of Social History* 1 (1968): 351–70, and "The Traditional World of the New England Peasants: A View from Seventeenth-Century Barnstable," *New England Historical and Genealogical Register* 130 (1976): 3–21.

setts Bay, Connecticut, and New Haven, the objective of their settlement was the same. Although they were by no means disinterested in achieving sustenance and prosperity, they put enormous emphasis upon establishing well-ordered communities knit together by Christian love and composed of like-minded people with a common religious ideology and a strong sense of communal responsibility. These tightly constructed and communally oriented villages were only one means of achieving order and harmony. Strong extended and highly patriarchal families, Greven's work on Andover suggests, also helped to preserve social control and guarantee a relatively high degree of peace throughout the first generation of settlement. So also did the quick establishment of an educational system that was designed to promote religious and social cohesion and was extraordinarily elaborate for a new colonial society.[6]

The Puritan colonial experiments in Massachusetts, Connecticut, and New Haven were also unusual in the extent to which they were presided over by a numerous and highly visible group of established secular and clerical leaders. To a far greater extent than any other English colonists in America, the Puritans brought their leaders with them to New England. Political and religious authority and social status survived the Atlantic crossing and the process of reimplantation in the New World without serious disruption. Unlike the hothouse elites that sprang up among the winners in the race for profits in other early colonies, New England leaders at both the local and the provincial levels were to a significant degree during the first decades people who had brought all the traditional attributes of sociopolitical authority with them to the New World.

As Stephen Foster has pointed out, the political societies of the New England colonies were based not upon the "customary engines of social coercion of early modern Europe," not upon "a hereditary monarch, a titled nobility, a church hierarchy, and a landlord class," but upon "a radical voluntarism" deriving out of the logic of the social covenants that served as the foundations for colonies and communities alike. Because all freemen, initially defined as church members who had assumed full civil rights, were theoretically parties to those covenants, and because the proportion of freemen usually ran as high as 60 to 70 percent of the adult male population in most towns, the potential for political participation was—by English standards—extraordinarily high. Most of the time, however, they willingly deferred to the magistrates, who assumed

---

[6] Foster, *Solitary Way,* 11–64, 99–152; Timothy H. Breen and Stephen Foster, "The Puritans' Greatest Achievement: A Study of Social Cohesion in Seventeenth-Century Massachusetts," *Journal of American History* 60 (1973): 5–22.

the dominant role in establishing political institutions, allocating land, making laws, dispensing justice, and reinforcing the position of the clergy and churches.[7]

A comparatively slow pace of economic development was also an important element in enabling the Puritans to succeed in their socioreligious goals in New England. Many immigrants, including even some of the clergy, certainly had economic as well as religious and social reasons for coming to New England, and, although the economy of the region seems to have been reasonably prosperous and even to have enjoyed a considerable rate of growth over much of the seventeenth century, neither the soil nor the climate was conducive to the development of staple agriculture. Very early, fish, timber, furs, and shipping brought some people more than ordinary returns, and in seaboard towns the proportion of the population engaged in fishing was substantial. But most settlers had no alternative source of income than cereal agriculture and animal husbandry, which yielded only modest profits. Hence, except in the emergent port centers of Boston and Salem, the wealth structure of the New England colonies, at least down to 1660, remained far more equitable than in other colonies. Nor, except perhaps in the fishing industry, did New Englanders have the need, the incentive, or the resources to recruit a large force of unfree laborers. The labor of family members and perhaps a few servants who resided in the nuclear family household was all that was either necessary or profitable for most economic enterprises in the region.[8]

---

[7]Greven, *Four Generations*, 41–99; James Axtell, *The School upon a Hill: Education and Society in Colonial New England* (New Haven, 1974), 166–244; Robert Emmet Wall, Jr., *Massachusetts Bay: The Crucial Decade, 1640–1650* (New Haven, 1972), esp. 21–40; Foster, *Solitary Way*, 67–98, 155–72; T. H. Breen, *The Character of the Good Ruler: A Study of Puritan Political Ideas in New England, 1630–1730* (New York, 1970), 1–86.

[8]Terry Lee Anderson, *The Economic Growth of Seventeenth-Century New England: A Measurement of Regional Income* (New York, 1975); Anderson and Thomas, "White Population," 661; Bernard Bailyn, *The New England Merchants in the Seventeenth-Century* (Cambridge, Mass., 1955), 1–111; Daniel Vickers, "Work and Life on the Fishing Periphery of Essex County, Massachusetts, 1630–1675," in Hall and Allen, *Seventeenth-Century New England*, 83–117; William Cronon, *Changes in the Land: Indians, Colonists, and the Ecology of New England* (New York, 1983), 127–56; Charles F. Carroll, *The Timber Economy of Puritan New England* (Providence, 1973); Darrett B. Rutman, *Winthrop's Boston: A Portrait of a Puritan Town, 1630–1649* (Chapel Hill, N.C., 1965), 164–201; William I. Davisson and Dennis J. Dugan, "Commerce in Seventeenth-Century Essex County, Massachusetts," *Essex Institute Historical Collections* 107 (1971): 113–18; Davisson, "Essex County Wealth Trends: Wealth and Economic Growth in 17th Century Massachusetts," ibid., 103 (1967): 291–342; Donald W. Koch, "Income Distribution and Polit-

Along with the strong cohesive force that the church, village, family, schools, and visible and authoritative leaders exerted in New England villages, the absence of exceptional economic opportunities inhibited the urge to scatter that was so powerfully manifest among the settlers in the Chesapeake. The initial colonists moved about quite a bit during the first two decades of settlement, and people who either had tenuous ties to the community or lived in the economically most active areas tended to be highly mobile. But those with close economic, family, political, and religious involvement seem to have developed a deep emotional attachment to their communities, an attachment that in turn seems to have fostered a degree of persistence and spatial immobility that may have been lower even than in most established village populations in England.[9]

These same conditions also helped to produce several decades of "relative social peace." Notwithstanding the well-known theological controversies between Bay Colony magistrates and religious rebels such as Roger Williams and Anne Hutchinson, the challenges presented by the arrival of the Quakers in the mid-1650s, and the presence of considerable controversy in the churches and contention in the courts, major social discord was rare and conflict restrained throughout most of the seventeenth century. As Timothy Breen and Stephen Foster have aptly observed in regard to Massachusetts, this characteristic of New England society placed it in contrast not only to the Chesapeake but to virtually the whole of the contemporary civilized world and constituted perhaps the single "most startling accomplishment" of the orthodox Puritan colonies of Massachusetts, Connecticut, and New Haven.[10]

---

ical Structure in Seventeenth-Century Salem, Massachusetts," ibid., 105 (1969): 50–71; Terry L. Anderson, "Wealth Estimates for the New England Colonies, 1650–1709," *Explorations in Economic History* 12 (1975): 151–76; Richard Waterhouse, "Reluctant Emigrants: The English Background of the First Generation of the New England Clergy," *Historical Magazine of the Protestant Episcopal Church* 44 (1975): 473–88; Breen, "Transfer of Culture," 3–17; Stephen Innes, "Land Tenancy and Social Order in Springfield, Massachusetts, 1652 to 1702," *William and Mary Quarterly*, 3d ser., 35 (1978): 33–56.

[9] Breen and Foster, "Moving to the New World," 209–13; David Grayson Allen, "Both Englands," in Hall and Allen, *Seventeenth-Century New England*, 77–80; Linda Auwers Bissell, "From One Generation to Another: Mobility in Seventeenth-Century Windsor, Connecticut," *William and Mary Quarterly*, 3d ser., 31 (1974): 79–110; W. R. Prest, "Stability and Change in Old and New England: Clayworth and Dedham," *Journal of Interdisciplinary History* 6 (1976): 359–74; John M. Murrin, "Review Essay," *History and Theory* 11 (1972): 231.

[10] See David Thomas Konig, *Law and Society in Puritan Massachusetts, 1629–1692* (Chapel Hill, N.C., 1972); Paul R. Lucas, *Valley of Discord: Church and Society along the Connecticut River, 1636–1725* (Hanover, N.H., 1976), 1–57; Carla Pestana, "The City

The picture that emerges of the Puritan colonies during the first generation of settlement is thus of a self-conscious and successful effort to re-create a traditional society in the New World. With low mortality, rapid population growth, a benign disease environment, and a far more fully and rapidly articulated Old World–style society, the intensely religious colonies of Massachusetts, Connecticut, and New Haven, moved by powerful millennial and communal impulses, exhibited rapid community and family development. With strong patriarchal families, elaborate kinship networks, and visible and authoritative leaders, localities quickly developed vigorous social institutions, including many schools, and deeply rooted populations. Mostly involved in cereal agriculture and with no generalized source of great economic profit, the Puritan colonies displayed a relatively egalitarian wealth structure and an extraordinarily low incidence of social discord and contention.

Increasingly after 1660 and in a few places even before, this carefully constructed and coherent social and cultural order began to change. To many contemporary Puritan settlers, in fact, these changes seemed to portend failure, and they interpreted them as evidence of social and moral declension, a pervasive and steady turning away from the original goals of the founders by their descendants. The explanatory structure they articulated to make this development comprehensible to themselves still provides the basic framework for the declension model that modern historians have conventionally employed to characterize the process of historical change in colonial New England. Positing a largely linear process of change from gemeinschaft to gesellschaft, from community to individualism, from traditional to modern, this model has come under sharp attack in recent years.

Among the most important of the conditions pushing the orthodox New England colonies into social patterns that suggested declension to contemporary inhabitants was their rapid demographic growth. Immigration continued low, in all probability amounting to no more than 10,000 to 12,000 for the last half of the seventeenth century and never averaging more than a few hundred per year before the American Revolution. Yet the population grew rapidly in response to highly favorable

---

upon a Hill under Seige: The Puritan Perception of the Quaker Threat to Massachusetts Bay, 1656–1661," *New England Quarterly* 56 (1983): 323–53; Breen and Foster, "Puritans' Greatest Achievement," esp. 5–6.

conditions of life. With an abundant food supply, a relatively equal sex ratio, a low population density, and a low incidence of epidemic diseases, New England settlers, especially in the rural areas that were the homes of all but 5 percent to 10 percent of them, enjoyed low mortality and exhibited a high percentage of married women and a vigorous birthrate that, for most of the seventeenth century, produced completed families averaging in excess of seven children. Notwithstanding considerably less favorable conditions in seaport towns such as Boston and Salem, the number of people of European descent in Massachusetts, Connecticut, Plymouth, Rhode Island, and New Hampshire soared from just over 30,000 in 1660 to over 90,000 by 1700.

During the eighteenth century the rate of population growth slowed significantly in New England. For the quarter of a century beginning in 1690, one case study has shown, the age of marriage rose, while the number of children per completed family fell by nearly 40 percent to 4.6 before rising again to around seven in subsequent decades. At the same time, mortality increased, partly as a result of periodic epidemics that were in turn, to an important degree, probably a function of higher population density and closer ties with the outside world. Declining life expectancy seems by midcentury to have brought mortality figures closer to those long characteristic of Britain and recently achieved in the Chesapeake. Despite these developments, natural population growth remained vigorous, averaging between 26 and 28 percent per decade through the first seven decades of the eighteenth century. Total numbers, surpassing 115,000 by 1710 and 215,000 by 1730, had reached nearly 450,000 by 1760.[11]

---

[11] Henry A. Gemery, "Emigration from the British Isles to the New World, 1630–1700: Inferences from Colonial Populations," *Research in Economic History* 5 (1980): 193, 195; James H. Cassedy, *Demography in Early America* (Cambridge, Mass., 1969), 40, 175; Clifford K. Shipton, "Immigration to New England, 1680–1740," *Journal of Political Economy* 44 (1936): 225–39; Philip J. Greven, Jr., "The Average Size of Families and Households in the Province of Massachusetts in 1764 and the United States in 1790: An Overview," in Peter Laslett and Richard Wall, eds., *Household and Family in Past Time* (Cambridge, 1972), 545–60, and *Four Generations*, 185–97; Anderson and Thomas, "White Population," 639, 647–48; Daniel Scott Smith, "The Demographic History of Colonial New England," *Journal of Economic History* 32 (1972): 165–83; Maris A. Vinovskis, "Mortality Rates and Trends in Massachusetts before 1860," ibid., 195–202; Lockridge, "Population of Dedham," 324–26, 332–39; Susan L. Norton, "Population Growth in Colonial America: A Study of Ipswich, Massachusetts," *Population Studies* 25 (1971): 433–52; Douglas R. McManis, *Colonial New England: A Historical Geography* (New York, 1975), 66–72; Robert Higgs and H. Louis Stettler III, "Colonial New England Demography: A Sampling Approach," *William and Mary Quarterly*, 3d ser., 27 (1970):

The effects of this burgeoning population were profound. Intensifying an already powerful demand for land, it supplied the energy for the rapid expansion of settlement. Although King Philip's War in the mid-1670s and the first set of intercolonial wars between 1689 and 1713 operated as a temporary brake on expansion, by the early eighteenth century New Englanders had occupied a broad band extending fifty to seventy miles inland and from New York north to southern Maine. Driving out the Indians or shunting them off to marginal areas, settlers were rapidly replacing the forests with a European-style landscape of farm buildings, fields, orchards, pastures, and fences. By 1700 the four remaining New England colonies of Massachusetts, Connecticut, Rhode Island, and New Hampshire contained about 120 towns. This expansive process accelerated after 1713. Over a hundred new towns were founded during the next fifty years, and the area of settlement both became far more compact in areas of older occupation and spread over all of southern New England and north and east into New Hampshire, Maine, and Nova Scotia.[12]

Already by the 1660s within the oldest settlements, population growth had led to the dispersal of people out from the early clusters of settlement. In the few places that had been initially settled as nucleated villages, this process sometimes resulted in the physical and social disintegration of the original village centers. Instead of settling together in close proximity, people tended more and more to establish their families on individual farmsteads, while some people moved so far away from the original meetinghouses that they found it desirable to form new semi-

282–94; Stettler, "The New England Throat Distemper and Family Size," in H. E. Klarman, ed., *Empirical Studies in Health Economics* (Baltimore, 1970), 17–27; Rose Lockwood, "Birth, Illness, and Death in 18th Century New England," *Journal of Social History* 12 (1978): 111–28.

[12] McManis, *Colonial New England*, 46–66; Douglas E. Leach, *Flintlock and Tomahawk: New England in King Philip's War* (New York, 1966); Charles E. Clark, *The Eastern Frontier: The Settlement of Northern New England, 1610–1763* (New York, 1970); Bruce C. Daniels, *The Connecticut Town: Growth and Development, 1635–1790* (Middletown, Conn. 1979), 8–44, and *Dissent and Conformity on Narragansett Bay: The Colonial Rhode Island Town* (Middletown, Conn., 1983), 23–47; Eric H. Christiansen, "The Emergence of Medical Communities in Massachusetts, 1700–1794: The Demographic Factors," *Bulletin of the History of Medicine* 54 (1980): 66; Jere R. Daniell, *Colonial New Hampshire: A History* (Millwood, N.Y., 1981), 133–64; David E. Van Deventer, *The Emergence of Provincial New Hampshire, 1623–1741* (Baltimore, 1976), 62–82; Andrew Hill Clark, *Acadia: The Geography of Early Nova Scotia to 1760* (Madison, Wis., 1968), 330–69. Cronon, *Changes in the Land*, 54–81, 127–70, suggestively discusses the changing social landscape of New England during the colonial era.

independent and sometimes antagonistic settlements. Contrary to the designs of the original Puritan leaders, they thereby contributed to destroy the prescriptive unity of the towns and perhaps to weaken the bonds of neighborhood and the authority of political and social institutions.

Despite this dispersion, second- and even third-generation settlers may have been more rooted and less mobile than those of the first generation. When they moved, they did not usually leave the political jurisdictions in which they had been born, and even then often stayed within fifteen to thirty miles of the places of their birth. With growing population, however, land in the older agricultural communities was by the third and fourth generations usually all taken up, and young people coming into their maturity found that they either had to go into nonfarming occupations or move to new towns to the north, west, or east. Out-migration from old communities and the founding of new towns proliferated after 1715, as New Englanders became increasingly mobile. Although a significant proportion of long-distance migrants consisted of middle-aged people who moved with their children only after the death of their parents to what they hoped would be better lands, many others were young, unmarried adults who by the 1730s and 1740s displayed little resistance to moving away from their homes and families. This willingness to migrate by young adults in turn seems to have weakened parental authority and pushed children more and more toward the imperatives of autonomy and independence that had been so powerfully manifest everywhere else in the English-American world throughout the seventeenth century.[13]

---

[13] Wood, "Village and Community in Early New England," 333–46; Greven, *Four Generations*, 41–71, 175–221; Lockridge, *New England Town*, 79–118, and "Land, Population, and the Evolution of New England Society, 1630–1790," *Past and Present*, no. 39 (1968): 62–80; Bissell, "From One Generation to Another," 79–110; Thomas R. Cole, "Family, Settlement, and Migration in Southeastern Massachusetts, 1650–1805: The Case for Regional Analysis," *New England Historical and Genealogical Register* 132 (1978): 171–81; John W. Adams and Alice Bee Kasakoff, "Migration and the Family in Colonial New England: The View from Genealogies," *Journal of Family History* 9 (1984): 24–44, and "Migration at Marriage in Colonial New England: A Comparison of Rates Derived from Genealogies with Rates from Vital Records," in Bennett Dyke and Warren T. Morrill, eds., *Genealogical Demography* (New York, 1980), 115–38; Darrett B. Rutman, "People in Process: The New Hampshire Towns of the Eighteenth Century," *Journal of Urban History* 1 (1975): 268–92; Douglas Lamar Jones, *Village and Seaport: Migration and Society in Eighteenth-Century Massachusetts* (Hanover, N. H., 1981); John J. Waters, "Patrimony, Succession, and Social Stability: Guilford, Connecticut, in the Eighteenth Century," *Perspectives in American History* 10 (1976): 131–60; Charles S. Grant, "Land

Even before population growth had helped to accelerate the general processes of dispersion and mobility, the intense spiritual energies and utopian impulses that had been so central to the founding generation of Puritan colonists began to attenuate. Relative to population growth, church membership seems to have declined from about 1650 until 1675. Although absolute numbers remained fairly steady and there was even a revival of spiritual interest and church membership during the last quarter of the seventeenth century among the third generation, the clergy throughout these years decried the decay in godliness and the growth in worldliness among the laity. In response to this situation, many ministers sought to broaden the base of church members beyond the visible saints. Though it was never adopted by all congregations, the Halfway Covenant of 1662 permitted baptized but unconverted children of church members to be "half-way" members and to have their children baptized. By the 1680s and 1690s a few clergymen like Solomon Stoddard of Northampton advocated even further liberalization of membership requirements. Discovering "that a pure membership was a flimsy foundation on which to construct an ecclesiastical system, and that the restraining influence of the church on the entire community was more important than the preservation of a [pure] congregation of saints," the churches opted to sacrifice purity to community.[14]

Problems involving church membership were compounded by dissension within and among churches. By the 1660s the search for a single orthodox way in theology and church government to which the emigrants had been committed had been revealed to be a chimera. While the autonomy of individual congregations rendered any attempt to achieve

---

Speculation and the Settlement of Kent, 1738–1760," *New England Quarterly* 27 (1955): 51–71.

[14] Robert G. Pope, *The Half-Way Covenant: Church Membership in Puritan New England* (Princeton, N. J., 1969), 128–36, 210–11, 233–35, 276; Gerald F. Moran, "Religious Renewal, Puritan Tribalism, and the Family in Seventeenth-Century Milford, Connecticut," *William and Mary Quarterly*, 3d ser., 36 (1979): 236–54; Moran and Maris A. Vinovskis, "The Puritan Family and Religion: A Critical Reappraisal," ibid., 39 (1982): 32–42; David M. Scobey, "Revising the Errand: New England's Ways and the Puritan Sense of the Past," ibid., 41 (1984): 3–31; Charles E. Hambrick-Stowe, *The Practice of Piety: Puritan Devotional Disciplines in Seventeenth-Century New England* (Chapel Hill, N.C., 1982), 242; Selement, *Keepers of the Vineyard*, 43–59; Perry Miller, "Declension in a Bible Commonwealth," in *Nature's Nation* (Cambridge, Mass., 1967), 25–30, and *The New England Mind: From Colony to Province* (Cambridge, Mass., 1953); Joseph J. Ellis, *The New England Mind in Transition: Samuel Johnson of Connecticut, 1696–1772* (New Haven, 1973), 11.

regional religious uniformity impossible, disagreements among the godly over baptism and other sacraments, predestination, and the proper form of church government revealed deep fissures and contradictions within the Puritan movement. Whether or not, as Paul Lucas has argued, these disputes "made dissension a way of life" in New England during the last half of the seventeenth century, they certainly unleashed "a continuing struggle for control of church government." By seriously eroding "the community's power to suppress dissent," they also eventually forced colony and community leaders into a grudging acceptance of it.[15]

Nor did ministers of the second and third generations enjoy the stature and immediate influence of those of the first. Although it is certainly an exaggeration to speak of the "collapse of clerical authority," strife among the clergy, disputes between the clergy and the laity, and what David Hall has called the "diminished charisma" of the ministers who replaced the first occupants of the pulpits of New England combined to undermine clerical authority. While it may be true that "the clergy's involvement with the mental images of the laity was as intense as ever after 1660" and that "the ministry remained the most important calling in New England," the clergy no longer exerted such a profound influence in defining life in the Puritan colonies, and many congregations revealed a growing reluctance to support their ministers in the style to which their predecessors had been accustomed. By the early decades of the eighteenth century, it was a general lament among ministers that they "did not enjoy the prestige, influence, and social status" of their seventeenth-century predecessors.[16]

All of these developments stimulated the clergy to articulate a broadly diffused sense of religious decline. Increasingly after 1660 declension became the omnipresent theme in sermons, and the jeremiad, which publicly reviewed the "shortcomings of society" and called on the people to renounce their sins and return to the primitive religious and social purity of the emigrants, became the standard form of sermon on all "the great

---

[15] E. Brooks Holifield, *The Covenant Sealed: The Development of Puritan Sacramental Theology in Old and New England, 1570—1720* (New Haven, 1974), 169–230; Scobey, "Revising the Errand," 19, 30; Lucas, *Valley of Discord,* 205; Lillian Handlin, "Dissent in a Small Community," *New England Quarterly* 58 (1985): 193–220; Sydney V. James, "Ecclesiastical Authority in the Land of Roger Williams," ibid., 57 (1984): 323–46; Pope, *Half-Way Covenant,* 260.

[16] Foster, "Godly in Transit," in Hall and Allen, *Seventeenth-Century New England,* 237; Lucas, *Valley of Discord,* xiii; James W. Schmotter, "Ministerial Careers in Eighteenth-Century New England: The Social Context, 1700–1760," *Journal of Social History* 9 (1975): 249–67; Hall, *Faithful Shepherd,* 181.

occasions of communal life, when the body politic met in solemn conclave to consider the state of society." Few modern historians accept these contemporary laments at face value. They recognize that New England was not declining but merely undergoing a series of intellectual and institutional adaptations to reflect the changing needs of the churches and society. As, more and more through the middle decades of the century, hope fell victim to experience and the "ideal of community" dimmed before "the shortcomings of community life," the original New England way, in Stephen Foster's words, simply dissolved "into unrelated, often irreconcilable parts." In the process, as Perry Miller noted nearly a half century ago, it became "something other than it had started out to be, in spite of the fact that many . . . still desired with all their hearts that it remain unchanged."[17]

If the jeremiads of the late seventeenth century cannot be read as literal indications of New England's declension, they certainly revealed a widespread discontent with contemporary religious and social behavior that gripped the laity as well as the clergy. By the 1660s, in fact, few colonists any longer had any very vivid sense of the urgency of the original mission that had brought their parents and grandparents to New England. As the "formulations of the first two decades" lost "their near monopoly position as the fulcrum for their members' imaginative lives," New Englanders seemed—to themselves—to be irresistibly carried "away from the original dedication to holiness and the will of God." The crown's assumption of control over New England in 1684 effectively shattered "any lingering sense among the colonists that they formed a special, divinely chosen community."

By that action the crown at once destroyed the old government that had theoretically "bound the whole community in Covenant with God," rendered impossible any further efforts to enforce a religious orthodoxy by requiring toleration of all Protestant religions, and "left the third generation of settlers with no clear definition of the status" to which their grandparents and even parents had aspired "as the chosen children of God." Subsequently, the founders' prophetic vision of establishing God's city upon a hill became little more than "a pious memory, faithfully recorded by Cotton Mather [and other clergymen] but [largely] exotic to the religious life of the province" as a whole. During the first six decades

---

[17] Miller, "Declension in a Bible Commonwealth," 23, 43; Sacvan Bercovitch, *The American Jeremiad* (Madison, Wis., 1978), 16; Foster, *Their Solitary Way*, xiv–xv; Pope, *Half-Way Covenant*, 261, 275–76, and "New England versus the New England Mind: The Myth of Declension," *Journal of Social History* 3 (1970): 301–18.

of the eighteenth century, the idea of New England's special place in God's plan for humankind increasingly lost force and was gradually merged with the more general conception of the whole Anglo-American Protestant world as the bulwark against popery.[18]

Especially during the late seventeenth century, this declining sense of mission, this pervasive feeling of having fallen away from the faith of the fathers, may have helped to alter still other aspects of the religious landscape of New England. By stirring "severe feelings of inadequacy and insecurity," it may have been largely responsible for driving people more and more "into the terrible wilderness of their own inner selves" and into an excessive preoccupation with the internal strife of the local communities in which they lived. Certainly, the ancient corporate religious impulse was no longer sufficiently strong to provide a vehicle through which communities could join together to contain the astonishing degree of contention and aggression that was so vividly manifest in the rise in criminal prosecutions for deviance and in the various witchcraft episodes, especially the one that occurred at Salem in 1692–93.[19]

Although, as Perry Miller has emphasized, New England religious culture remained vital and adaptable throughout the years from 1670 to 1730, it no longer held its former preeminence in New England life. Despite some occasional local revivals, the spiritual life of New England seemed to the clergy throughout the first three or four decades of the eighteenth century to have become ever more "shamelessly secular." The continuing diminution of religious concern seemed to be indicated at once by further declines in the proportion of the population who were full and active church members and in the authority and status of the

---

[18] Foster, "Godly in Transit," in Hall and Allen, *Seventeenth-Century New England*, 214; Miller, "Declension in a Bible Commonwealth," 25; Breen and Foster, "Puritans' Greatest Achievement," 20; Pope, "New England Versus the New England Mind," 105; Kai T. Erikson, *Wayward Puritans: A Study in the Sociology of Deviance* (New York, 1966), 157; Maclear, "New England and the Fifth Monarchy," 258; Bruce Tucker, "The Reinterpretation of Puritan History in Provincial New England," *New England Quarterly* 54 (1981): 481–98, and "The Reinvention of New England, 1691- 1770," ibid., 59 (1986): 315–40.

[19] Emory Elliott, *Power and the Pulpit in Puritan New England* (Princeton, N.J., 1975), 8; Erikson, *Wayward Puritans*, 157–59, 163–81; John Demos, "Underlying Themes in the Witchcraft of Seventeenth-Century New England," *American Historical Review* 75 (1970): 1319–22, "John Godfrey and His Neighbors: Witchcraft and the Social Web in Colonial Massachusetts," *William and Mary Quarterly*, 3d ser., 33 (1973): 242–65, and *Entertaining Satan: Witchcraft and the Culture of Early New England* (New York, 1982). See also David D. Hall, "Witchcraft and the Limits of Interpretation," *New England Quarterly* 58 (1985): 253–81.

clergy and by the persistence of religious discord in many communities. For the first time, moreover, the Anglican church began to make significant inroads among the formerly almost wholly Congregational population. Already by the 1720s some prominent ministers had defected to the Anglicans, who by 1770 had seventy-four congregations in New England and numbered as many as 25,000 adherents who were drawn from all segments of the population.[20]

Even more subversive of the old New England way was the moderate acceleration and changing character of the economy during the last half of the seventeenth century. Economic goals had never been absent from the Puritan settlements. Despite some religious scruples against excessive profiteering, the colonists had been responsive to economic opportunities from the beginning. If throughout the seventeenth century most of them were involved in agriculture, they successfully sought not simply to produce enough food to feed their families but a surplus to exchange for tools and other finished goods that they were unable to produce efficiently themselves and that had to be imported from England or some other major processing center. This surplus, at first consisting primarily of grains but increasingly composed of meat, dairy, and orchard products, served to sustain a growing non- or semi-agricultural population in the coastal seaports that developed to handle the exchange but also acted as "a primer for overseas trade."

Nor, in contrast to most other early British colonies, was agricultural produce the principal item of trade. Already by the late 1630s and the early 1640s, Boston, Salem, and Charlestown were also developing a vigorous trade in furs, fish, and timber products, including planks, barrel staves, shingles, oars, naval stores, and masts. With the rapid dwindling of the fur supply at midcentury, the fur trade had declined to insignificance by the mid-1670s. But the fish and lumber industries expanded to meet the demands of new markets in the West Indies, the Wine Islands, and the Iberian peninsula. Far and away the most important export venture, fishing employed large numbers of people throughout the colonial period, perhaps never less than 10 percent of the population; and by the early eighteenth century, in Salem, fishing exceeded the value

---

[20] J. William T. Youngs, Jr., *God's Messengers: Religious Leadership in Colonial New England, 1700–1750* (Baltimore, 1976); Laura L. Becker, "Ministers vs. Laymen: The Singing Controversy in Puritan New England, 1720–1740," *New England Quarterly* 55 (1982): 77–96; Ellis, *New England Mind in Transition*, 55–122, and "Anglicans in Connecticut, 1725–1750: The Conversion of the Missionaries," *New England Quarterly* 44 (1971): 66–81; Bruce E. Steiner, "New England Anglicanism: A Genteel Faith?" *William and Mary Quarterly*, 3d ser., 37 (1970): 122–35.

of timber exports, "the second most valuable export," by 12 to 1. Because most exports in all these areas had to be processed and packed in barrels, they all generated significant local processing industries that provided a livelihood for substantial numbers either in the localities where they were produced or in the points of export, while a growing shipbuilding industry emerged along the coast to produce the vessels that carried these products across the seas.[21]

Never a purely subsistence society, the New England colonies were thus from early in their histories and increasingly during the seventeenth century heavily involved in trade. By 1660 it was already clear that, to an important extent, the emerging economy of New England, as Terry Anderson has observed, would "be centered around" its "shipping sector and that many institutions" would have "to be developed or changed to meet the needs of a commercial society." The merchants who presided over this process of commercialization became leading agents of change. Aggressively seeking out new markets in North America, the West Indies, England, and Europe, they first acquired and then supplied the capital and managerial expertise needed to link the "producers and consumers of [the] interior towns" of New England to "the larger world economy," and, when the resource base of the region proved insufficient to support continuous long-term economic growth, they increasingly began to supply "shipping services to major parts of the Atlantic world." By the second and third decades of the eighteenth century, they had thereby "created a well-integrated commercial economy based on the carrying trade."[22]

Nor were the economic activities of this rising commercial elite limited to trade. Especially after King Philip's War in the mid-1670s, they were among the heaviest land speculators and developers, many of them acquiring several thousands of acres which they hoped eventually to sell for a profit to those segments of a burgeoning population eager to move to new lands. In the rich Connecticut River valley, the Pynchon family,

---

[21] McManis, *Colonial New England*, 86–122; John J. McCusker and Russell R. Menard, *The Economy of British America, 1607–1789* (Chapel Hill, N.C., 1985), 91–110; Davisson and Dugan, "Commerce in Seventeenth-Century Essex County," 113–42; Allen, *In English Ways*, 228; Bruce C. Daniels, "Economic Development in Colonial and Revolutionary Connecticut: An Overview," *William and Mary Quarterly*, 3d ser., 37 (1980): 429–34; Carroll, *Timber Economy of Puritan New England*, 57–128; Van Deventer, *Provincial New Hampshire*, 93–106.

[22] Anderson, *Economic Growth of Seventeenth-Century New England*, 21, 23; McCusker and Menard, *Economy of British America*, 107. Bailyn, *New England Merchants*, is the classic study of the role of the merchants in the developing New England economy.

as Stephen Innes has recently shown, turned Springfield into a company town by engrossing a large proportion of the land and exerting a near monopoly of the region's trade. Owning the only store and all the town's grist and saw mills and employing a significant proportion of the adult male population as workmen in their various agricultural, processing, and trading enterprises, the Pynchons presided over a process of progressive social and economic stratification in which by 1680 at least one-half of the adult males in Springfield lived as tenants, renters, and dependents in a socioeconomic system that contrasted sharply with the egalitarian villages envisioned by the first settlers.[23]

As an ever-enlarging circle of towns became involved in producing foodstuffs and other items for export during the last half of the seventeenth century, the hinterlands of both the larger ports and commercialized towns such as Springfield seem to have enjoyed substantial economic growth, to have become far more diversified in terms of occupational structure, and to have experienced substantial economic stratification. Some experts have suggested that economic growth may have averaged as high as 6 percent per annum in some of the more dynamic areas. At least in Connecticut, Jackson Turner Main has recently shown, opportunity to acquire wealth actually seems to have declined for several decades after 1660 before it began to rise again in 1690. But for New England as a whole during the second half of the century, this commercially and demographically driven economic growth, it has been estimated, contributed between 1650 and 1710 to a substantial rise in per capita real income at an annual rate of about 1.6 percent and to a 295 percent increase in real aggregate economic output. Over the same period these same areas supported a growing number of artisans and craftsmen, many of whom continued to engage in farming, and exhibited growing concentrations of wealth in the hands of its richest inhabitants. In Salem, for instance, the amount of inventoried wealth owned by the most affluent 10 percent of the population rose from 21 percent before 1661 to 62 percent thereafter.[24]

---

[23] Theodore B. Lewis, "Land Speculation and the Dudley Council of 1686," *William and Mary Quarterly*, 3d ser., 31 (1974): 255–72; Stephen Innes, *Labor in a New Land: Economy and Society in Seventeenth-Century Springfield* (Princeton, N.J., 1983), and "Land Tenancy and Social Order," 33–56.

[24] Innes, *Labor in a New Land*, 72–122; Jackson Turner Main, *Society and Economy in Colonial Connecticut* (Princeton, N.J., 1985), 68–69; Anderson, *Economic Growth of Seventeenth-Century New England*, 114–19, "Economic Growth in Colonial New England: 'Statistical Renaissance,'" *Journal of Economic History* 39 (1979): 243–47, and "Wealth Estimates for the New England Colonies," 151–76; Davisson, "Essex County Wealth

A far cry from the closed, cohesive, and contained villages originally envisioned by Puritan leaders, Boston, Salem, and other ports and commercial towns thus became prosperous mercantile centers with relatively large, concentrated, heterogeneous populations, many new economic opportunities in nonfarm occupations, significant concentrations of wealth in the hands of leading merchants, marked social and economic distinctions, considerable contact with the outside world, and a rising spirit of enterprise that gradually spread outward to the surrounding countryside. The growing intensity of economic activity and the emerging complexity of social patterns in these more dynamic areas of New England operated to undermine the communal unity, corporate and religious orientation, and social goals of the first settlers. In these dynamic areas the old religious-based corporatism began to give way to the atomistic pursuit of wealth and self-interest.[25]

As Bernard Bailyn has written, the ethos of the mercantile groups which dominated these commercial centers "represented the spirit of a new age. Its guiding principles were not social stability, order, and the discipline of the senses, but mobility, growth, and the enjoyment of life." Among this strategic segment of the population, the desires to "succeed in trade" and emulate the lives of their London trading associates was far "stronger than any counterforce the clergy could exert." Increasingly after 1670, successful merchants and farmers comprised a new *economically* based elite which exerted an influence greatly disproportionate to their numbers in the public life of Massachusetts and to a lesser extent in Connecticut, New Hampshire, and Rhode Island. Certainly at the provincial and, in many areas, also at the local level of government, wealth and property, rather than piety, became the basis for political leadership and participation. Moreover, as rival groups among the elite vigorously competed with one another within the political arena for profits, land, and influence, the old consensual politics gave way to division, conflict, and discord.[26]

Trends," 291–342; Koch, "Income Distribution and Political Structure," 50–71; Richard P. Gildrie, *Salem, Massachusetts, 1626–1683: A Covenanted Community* (Charlottesville, Va., 1975), 155–69; James M. Henretta, "Economic Development and Social Structure in Colonial Boston," *William and Mary Quarterly*, 3d ser., 22 (1965): 75–92.

[25] See, in this connection, Paul Boyer and Stephen Nissenbaum, *Salem Possessed: The Social Origins of Witchcraft* (Cambridge, Mass., 1974), 60–109; Gildrie, *Salem, Massachusetts*, 145–69; Innes, *Labor in a New Land*, 123–50.

[26] Bailyn, *New England Merchants*, 139–42; Innes, *Labor in a New Land*, 151–70; Breen, *Character of the Good Ruler*, 87–202, "Who Governs," 473, and "War, Taxes, and Political Brokers: The Ordeal of Massachusetts Bay, 1675–1692," in Breen, *Puritans and Adven-*

Accompanying this contention and discord in public life was a rising volume of litigation, most of it concerning economic issues involving property and debt. Denounced by many contemporaries in the orthodox Puritan colonies of Massachusetts and Connecticut as an indication of creeping "*Rhode Islandism*," the acrimony and divisiveness produced by these developments certainly revealed the long-term ineffectiveness of religious and social communalism as devices to preserve social harmony in communities undergoing substantial demographic and economic growth and social diversification. "The force of ideological commitment alone," Stephen Foster has noted, "could [not] maintain a system of political and social subordination for which the traditional material and institutional bases were lacking."

As David T. Konig has recently emphasized, however, the founders of New England had never expected to achieve their social vision without viable legal institutions, which they carefully incorporated into the governmental structure during the 1630s. As the force of that original vision continued to attenuate in the face of continued economic growth and the "intensified resentments of compact town life," Konig shows in his analysis of patterns of litigation in Essex County, Massachusetts, individuals increasingly found it useful "to turn to the outside authority of extra-town institutions like the courts" to resolve their differences, and such legal institutions, he persuasively insists, "were to large degree responsible" for the fact that Essex County continued throughout the seventeenth century to be a "remarkably stable society." If, in their passage from "communalism to litigation," the residents of Essex County had become a contentious and disunited people, they were still fundamentally a "well-ordered people," and, so far from being an indication of social disruption, increasing litigation, Konig contends, was "an agent of orderly social change and economic growth."[27]

---

turers: Change and Persistence in Early America (New York, 1980), 81–105; Richard P. Gildrie, "Salem Society and Politics in the 1680s," *Essex Institute Historical Collections* 114 (1978): 185–206; Robert de V. Brunkow, "Officeholding in Providence, Rhode Island, 1646–1686: A Quantitative Analysis," *William and Mary Quarterly*, 3d ser., 37 (1980): 242–60. Richard R. Johnson, *Adjustment to Empire: The New England Colonies, 1675–1715* (New Brunswick, N.J., 1981), provides an excellent account of the imperial context of these developments.

[27] Daniels, *Dissent and Conformity on Narragansett Bay*, 22; Foster, *Solitary Way*, 7; Konig, *Law and Society*, xii–xiii, 89–116, 188–89. That the enforcement of law itself became less exacting during the seventeenth century is suggested by R.W. Roetger, "The Transformation of Sexual Morality in 'Puritan' New England: Evidence from New Haven Court Records, 1639–1698," *Canadian Review of American Studies* 15 (1984): 243–57.

Existing largely on the margins of—if by no means entirely cut off from—this increasingly bustling economic and social world, much of rural New England was relatively untouched by these social and economic developments during the seventeenth and early eighteenth centuries. Many inland towns, places described by Edward M. Cook as "small, self-contained farming villages," remained comparatively isolated, economically underdeveloped, socially egalitarian, and religiously homogeneous. Certainly during the seventeenth century, all but a few Connecticut towns seem to have belonged to this category: in Jackson Turner Main's words, they were "not very flourishing, predominantly agricultural and middle class, with few large property holders." In these "peaceable kingdoms," traditional institutions of community, family, and church continued to display a vitality that was considerably less evident either in the bustling market centers and seaport towns of New England or in the other Anglo-American colonies, and the corporate impulse probably remained strong.[28]

With the further acceleration of the economy as a result of rapid internal population growth and the increasing integration of the New England economy into the larger Atlantic economy during the early decades of the eighteenth century and especially after 1720, however, more and more of New England was drawn out of a relatively isolated existence and pushed in the direction of greater social differentiation, geographical and economic mobility, and individualism. The vast majority of New Englanders continued to live on farms. Recent scholarship has, however, effectively challenged the ancient myth that these farms were self-sufficient and independent units of production on which yeomen families, concerned with little more than their own security, produced all that was required to meet their needs without the help of additional labor.

As Bettye Hobbs Pruitt has recently shown in the case of the agricultural society of mid-eighteenth-century Massachusetts, "interdependence rather than self-sufficiency" is the concept that best describes that

---

[28] Edward M. Cook, Jr., *Fathers of the Towns: Leadership and Community Structure in Eighteenth-Century New England* (Baltimore, 1976), 179; Main, *Society and Economy in Colonial Connecticut*, 87–88; Michael Zuckerman, *Peaceable Kingdoms: New England Towns in the Eighteenth Century* (New York, 1970); Christopher M. Jedrey, *The World of John Cleaveland: Family and Community in Eighteenth-Century New England* (New York, 1979).

society. Although local communities were often self-sufficient, at least in foodstuffs and other primary services, most individual units were not. Only those few farms with relatively large amounts of both labor and land under cultivation did not have to involve themselves in local networks of exchange in which they traded products, labor, and skills simply to meet the subsistence requirements of their families. In this situation, Pruitt emphasizes, "production for home consumption and production for sale or exchange were complementary . . . objectives."[29]

If virtually all New England agricultural communities were thus "not atomistic but integrated" into a series of "local networks of exchange involving all sorts of goods and services," they were also increasingly "linked either directly or through . . . dealings with others" to the larger provincial and Atlantic worlds. New England's rapid demographic growth not only generated dozens of additional rural settlements but also produced significant urbanization. New England had only two major cities: Boston, which, despite a decline in its population and relative importance as a commercial entrepôt after 1740, continued to be the region's primary urban center, and Newport, which developed impressively after 1710. As the second largest city in New England, Newport had more than two-thirds as many people as Boston by 1775.

After 1715 and increasingly during the boom years of the 1740s and 1750s, however, a large number of towns, many of which had been little more than hamlets through most of the seventeenth century, developed into important secondary commercial centers. These included seaports— Portsmouth in New Hampshire; Salem, Marblehead, and Gloucester in Massachusetts; Providence in Rhode Island; and New Haven, New London, and Norwich in Connecticut—and inland commercial and administrative centers—Worcester and Springfield in Massachusetts and Hartford and Middletown in Connecticut. Perhaps as many as another two to three dozen places were distinctly urbanized by 1770.[30]

---

[29] Carole Shammas, "How Self-Sufficient Was Early America?" *Journal of Interdisciplinary History* 13 (1982): 247–72; Bettye Hobbs Pruitt, "Self-Sufficiency and the Agricultural Economy of Eighteenth-Century Massachusetts," *William and Mary Quarterly,* 3d ser., 41 (1984): 333–64; Winifred B. Rothenberg, "The Market and Massachusetts Farmers, 1750–1855," *Journal of Economic History* 41 (1981): 283–314.

[30] Pruitt, "Self-Sufficiency and the Agricultural Economy," 349; Gary M. Nash, *The Urban Crucible: Social Change, Political Consciousness, and the Origins of the American Revolution* (Cambridge, Mass., 1979), 111–18, 172–76, 180–97, 244–47; G. B. Warden, "Inequality and Instability in Eighteenth-Century Boston: A Reappraisal," *Journal of Interdisciplinary History* 6 (1976): 585–620; Lynne Withey, *Urban Growth in Colonial*

To a significant extent, this urbanization was a function not merely of growing population but also of a steady expansion of external trade. Although New England's exports were relatively unimpressive compared to those of all of the other regions of colonial British America, they were nonetheless substantial and underwent "an enormous expansion" during the century from 1660 to 1760. Not including the coastal trade, which may have accounted for as much as 40 percent of the value of its total trade, New England annually exported products worth almost £440,000 by 1770. Fish accounted for around 35 percent of this total; livestock, beef, and pork for 20 percent; wood products for 15 percent; whale products for 14 percent; potash and grain products each for 5 percent; rum for 4 percent; and a variety of other items for the remaining 2 percent. Far and away the largest proportion of this trade—63 percent—went to the West Indies. Britain and Ireland with 19 percent and southern Europe with 15 percent were, respectively, second and third, while Africa with only 3 percent to 4 percent was a distant fourth.[31]

Though the growing populations that inhabited New England's increasing number of urban places produced some of their own food and necessities, they all required significant supplements of both food and timber products, and, together with the additional demand for those products for export to the West Indies and elsewhere, these requirements inevitably acted to produce a lively commercial exchange between town and country, which were more and more linked by a proliferating network of roads, bridges, and ferries. This exchange in turn helped to raise levels of agricultural production and to stimulate timber industries in the countryside, first in the immediate vicinities of the towns and then in areas farther away. By the mid-eighteenth century, as Pruitt has remarked, few New England "communities existed wholly beyond the reach of [these] market forces," while most were inextricably tied into,

---

Rhode Island: Newport and Providence in the Eighteenth Century (Albany, N.Y., 1984); Daniels, *Connecticut Town*, 140–80, and "Emerging Urbanism and Increasing Social Stratification in the Era of the American Revolution," in John Ferling, ed., *The American Revolution: The Home Front* (Carrolton, Ga., 1976), 15–30; Cook, *Fathers of the Towns*, 172–79; Jones, *Village and Seaport;* Christine Leigh Heyrman, *Commerce and Culture: The Maritime Communities of Colonial Massachusetts, 1690—1750* (New York, 1984).

[31] McCusker and Menard, *Economy of British America*, 107–10; James G. Lydon, "Fish for Gold: The Massachusetts Fish Trade with Iberia, 1700–1773," *New England Quarterly* 54 (1981): 539–82; David C. Klingaman, "The Coastwise Trade of Colonial Massachusetts," *Essex Institute Historical Collections* 108 (1972): 217–33.

and deeply affected by, not just the local regional markets with which they had long been associated but also "the larger provincial and Atlantic economies of which they were a part."[32]

Compared with their counterparts elsewhere in colonial British America, eighteenth-century New England farmers were, perhaps, "not highly commercialized." Yet the commercialization of agriculture and the expansion of the fishing, timber, and whaling industries in response to growing internal and external demand had a significant impact upon the social landscape of the region. That impact can be seen clearly in the development of regional specialization. Of course, fishing and whaling had always been confined to the coast, the former concentrated in the area north of Boston and the latter in the coastal and island area along the southeastern coast of Massachusetts.

During the seventeenth century most other products had been diffused throughout the region. As time went on, however, the timber industry came to center in New Hampshire and Maine, grain production tended to concentrate in the breadbasket areas of the Connecticut River valley and in Middlesex and eastern Worcester County in Massachusetts, grazing and livestock production in hilly and rocky regions and along the southern coast of New England, and dairying in areas near to urban centers. The Narragansett region of Rhode Island was particularly noted for its large estates, which concentrated upon stock, especially horses, and dairy farming.[33]

Although a few farmers in eighteenth-century New England—the Narragansett planters and the owners of the larger farms in the rich Connecticut River valley and along the southern coast of New England—seem to have "crossed a line where commercial production brought sufficient returns to warrant a preponderant investment" in large landed estates and market crops, the principal beneficiary of the growing commercialization of New England seems to have been the expanding service

---

[32] Pruitt, "Self-Sufficiency and the Agricultural Economy," 362, 364; Rothenberg, "Market and Massachusetts Farmers."

[33] Pruitt, "Self-Sufficiency and the Agricultural Economy," 359–61, 364; Van Deventer, *Provincial New Hampshire,* 93–106, 159–78; Daniels, "Economic Development in Colonial and Revolutionary Connecticut," 429–50; Elinor F. Oakes, "A Ticklish Business: Dairying in New England and Pennsylvania, 1750–1812," *Pennsylvania History* 47 (1980): 195–212; Karen J. Friedmann, "Victualling Colonial Boston," *Agricultural History* 47 (1973): 189–205; William D. Miller, "The Narragansett Planters," American Antiquarian Society, *Proceedings* 43 (1934): 49–115; Christian McBurney, "The South Kingstown Planters: Country Gentry in Colonial Rhode Island," *Rhode Island History* 45 (1986): 81–93.

sector of society. To an important extent the result of the population's strenuous and purposeful efforts to wrest economic returns from disadvantageous circumstances, as well as an indication of the growing economic and social diversity of the region, this development led to an increasingly complex occupational structure that provided new opportunities for young men who did not inherit land or did not want to stay on the farm. Most numerous of these service occupations were the artisans and craftsmen, ranging in status and wealth from shoemakers, tailors, and weavers at the bottom through coopers, carpenters, and joiners in the middle up to millers and tanners at the top. The last two often operated comparatively large-scale enterprises. Representatives of all these occupations could be found in rural as well as urban areas. But some more specialized artisans—shipwrights, distillers, silversmiths, printers, and rope and iron manufacturers—rarely resided outside the larger towns. Out of this proliferating body of skilled artisans derived the well-known New England penchant for mechanical ingenuity that during the closing decades of the eighteenth century would make such a powerful contribution to the beginnings of industrial change in the new American republic.[34]

Two other groups, merchants and professionals, also expanded in numbers, wealth, and influence in the increasingly diverse society of eighteenth-century New England. The mercantile group, consisting of large overseas traders, shipowners, ship captains, shopkeepers, and pedlars, was increasingly complex and prosperous. The large overseas merchants who organized and presided over the region's commerce with the outside world and, as in the case of Rhode Island slave traders, provided freight and shipping services for other areas of the Atlantic commercial world were usually the richest people in the region. Professionals—ministers, doctors, and lawyers—were far fewer in number. But the last two became far more numerous during the eighteenth century, while lawyers were more and more often also among the wealthiest and most influential inhabitants. Together with some prominent officeholders, the wealthier lawyers, overseas merchants, and inland traders played an entrepreneurial role in New England's economic development and profited disproportionately from it. Often among the investors in industrial enterprises such as shipbuilding, distilling, and iron production, they were

---

[34] Richard L. Bushman, "Family Security in the Transition from Farm to City, 1750–1850," *Journal of Family History* 6 (1981): 240; Main, *Society and Economy in Colonial Connecticut*, 151, 241–56, 381; Daniels, "Economic Development in Colonial and Revolutionary Connecticut," 438–43.

also frequently involved as land speculators in the development of new towns on the eastern, northern, and western frontiers.[35]

The acceleration and growing complexity of the economy during the eighteenth century also helped to produce and to reinforce a more typically British social structure. The comparative economic equality that had characterized much of early New England had never obtained in Boston, where from the late seventeenth century onward the concentration of wealth remained relatively high and relatively stable over time, with the wealthiest 30 percent of property holders possessing around 85 percent of the town's private wealth. By contrast, during the eighteenth century, rural areas experienced a slow but steady growth in the concentration of property until by the 1760s and 1770s the richest 30 percent owned between 65 percent and 75 percent of total wealth. In urban areas this trend toward wealth consolidation was even more pronounced, with towns like Portsmouth, Salem, Newport, Providence, New Haven, and Hartford already moving powerfully toward Boston levels by the early decades of the century.

While it is undoubtedly true that, in comparison with most of the rest of the British-American world, the wealthiest men in late colonial New England enjoyed only "moderate rather than large fortunes," had fewer servants and slaves, lived less genteelly, and had to share political office with men "entirely lacking in family connections and large estates," some

---

[35] Main, *Society and Economy in Colonial Connecticut,* 262–65, 278–313, 370, and "The Distribution of Property in Colonial Connecticut," in James Kirby Martin, ed., *The Human Dimensions of Nation Making: Essays on Colonial and Revolutionary America* (Madison, Wis., 1976), 64–70; Withey, *Urban Growth in Colonial Rhode Island,* 123–32; Elaine F. Crane, *A Dependent People: Newport, Rhode Island, in the Revolutionary Era* (New York, 1985), 16–46; Jay Coughtry, *The Notorious Triangle: Rhode Island and the African Slave Trade, 1700–1807* (Philadelphia, 1981); Alison Jones, "The Rhode Island Slave Trade: A Trading Advantage in Africa," *Slavery and Abolition* 3 (1981): 226–44; Van Deventer, *Provincial New Hampshire,* 78–82, 174–78, 215; Christiansen, "Medical Communities in Massachusetts," 64–77; John M. Murrin, "The Legal Transformation: The Bench and Bar of Eighteenth-Century Massachusetts," in Stanley N. Katz, ed., *Colonial America: Essays in Politics and Social Development* (Boston, 1971), 415–49; David H. Flaherty, "Criminal Practice in Provincial Massachusetts," Colonial Society of Massachusetts, *Publications* 42 (1984): 191–242; McManus, *Colonial New England,* 132–39; Grant, "Land Speculation and the Settlement of Kent," 51–71, and *Democracy in the Connecticut Frontier Town of Kent* (New York, 1972), 55–65; Richard L. Bushman, *From Puritan to Yankee: Character and the Social Order in Connecticut, 1690–1765* (Cambridge, Mass., 1967), 73–82; Julian Gwyn, "Money Lending in New England: The Case of Admiral Sir Peter Warren and His Heirs, 1739–1805," *New England Quarterly* 44 (1971): 117–34.

individuals, especially in the towns, managed to accumulate impressive wealth. In New Hampshire, for instance, David E. Van Deventer has found that only two people whose estates were probated before 1740 had estates valued at more than £3,000 in New Hampshire old tenor currency, whereas twenty-one people who went through probate between 1741 and 1760 and twenty-seven between 1761 and 1770 had estates that exceeded that amount. Indeed, the wealthiest decedents after 1740 greatly exceeded that amount. The estate of Ebenezer Smith who died in 1764 was valued at just over £90,000, that of John Gilman in 1751 at nearly £48,000, and that of Nicholas Gilman in 1749 at just under £34,000. Three other decedents had estates valued at over £20,000, and twelve others at over £10,000.[36]

If few New Englanders enjoyed such impressive wealth, those who did aspired, as did rising elites elsewhere in colonial British America, to recreate the genteel culture of contemporary Britain. To that end, they built larger and more commodious houses and filled them with English and Continental furnishings and other fashionable consumer items, made charitable bequests, filled their towns with impressive public buildings, created a host of urban voluntary associations, and otherwise sought to reproduce the urban amenities of British provincial cities. The elite of Newport, where the old Puritan sanctions against conspicuous consumption were less powerful, could carry this process further than its counterparts in either Boston or smaller cities in the orthodox Puritan colonies of Massachusetts and Connecticut. Everywhere, however, elite behavior in New England was calculated to reinforce the traditional

[36] Main, *Society and Economy in Colonial Connecticut*, 122, 132–33, 278–366, 368, 381, and "Distribution of Property in Colonial Connecticut," in Martin, *Human Dimensions of Nation Making*, 77–90; Bruce C. Daniels, "Long Range Trends of Wealth Distribution in Eighteenth-Century New England," *Explorations in Economic History* 11 (1973): 123–35, "Defining Economic Classes in Colonial New Hampshire, 1700–1770," *Historic New Hampshire* 28 (1973): 53–62, "Money-Value Definitions of Economic Classes in Colonial Connecticut, 1700–1776," *Histoire Sociale* 7 (1974): 346–52, and "Defining Economic Classes in Colonial Massachusetts, 1700–1776," American Antiquarian Society, *Proceedings* 83 (1973): 251–59; Alice Hanson Jones, "Wealth Estimates for the New England Colonies about 1770," *Journal of Economic History* 32 (1972): 98–127, and *The Wealth of a Nation to Be: The American Colonies on the Eve of the Revolution* (New York, 1980), 50–194; G. B. Warden, "The Distribution of Property in Boston, 1692–1775," *Perspectives in American History* 10 (1976): 81–128, and "Inequality and Instability in Eighteenth-Century Boston: A Reappraisal," 585–620; Withey, *Urban Growth in Colonial Rhode Island*, 123–32; Crane, *Dependent People*, 25–29; Van Deventer, *Provincial New Hampshire*, 173–78.

prescriptive association among wealth, social status, and political authority.[37]

To an increasing extent during the eighteenth century, New England's wealthy inhabitants, as Edward Marks Cook has shown in his study of political leadership in a large sample of towns, also monopolized public office. To be sure, patterns of officeholding in many small agricultural towns remained relatively egalitarian throughout the century. But towns with more developed economic structures all showed a powerful tendency toward oligarchy, with a handful of wealthy and prominent families, often as few as one to three, dominating both appointed and elective offices. In most towns these family political dynasties were based, to an important degree, upon long association with the town's history. But in a few towns, those in which a coherent and continuous elite had been slow to develop—Marblehead provides one example and, perhaps, Portsmouth, New Hampshire, another—a significant number of relative newcomers could be found among the eighteenth-century elite. In large towns like Boston and Newport, the structure of local elites was too complex, too open, and too broadly based and economic power too often independent of political power to permit such heavy concentrations of political power in a few families. Whatever the local variations, however, most commercially oriented towns displayed a strong correlation between wealth and officeholding. The growing number of Anglicans who held political office in communities where they were numerous testifed to the diminishing importance of Congregational church membership in New England public life.[38]

---

[37] See Robert J. Dinkin, "Seating in the Meeting House in Early Massachusetts," *New England Quarterly* 43 (1970): 450–64; Anthony G. Roeber, "'Her Merchandize . . . Shall Be Holiness to the Lord': The Progress and Decline of Puritan Gentility at the Brattle Street Church, Boston, 1715–1745," *New England Historical and Genealogical Register* 131 (1977): 175–91; Christine Leigh Heyrman, "The Fashion among More Superior People: Charity and Social Change in Provincial New England, 1700–1740," *American Quarterly* 34 (1982): 107–24, and *Commerce and Culture*, 143–81, 330–65; Withey, *Urban Growth in Colonial Rhode Island*, 13–50; Crane, *Dependent People*, 47–62; Van Deventer, *Provincial New Hampshire*, 217–25; Main, *Society and Economy in Colonial Connecticut*, 278–366.

[38] Cook, *Fathers of the Towns*; Michael Zuckerman, "The Social Context of Democracy in Massachusetts," *William and Mary Quarterly*, 3d ser., 25 (1968): 523–44; Van Deventer, *Provincial New Hampshire*, 218–23; Main, *Society and Economy in Colonial Connecticut*, 317–66; Bruce C. Daniels, "Family Dynasties in Connecticut's Largest Towns, 1700–1760," *Canadian Journal of History* 8 (1973): 99–110, "Large Town Officeholding in Eighteenth-Century Connecticut: The Growth of Oligarchy," *Journal of American Studies* 9 (1975): 1–12, and "Democracy and Oligarchy in Connecticut Towns: General Assembly Officeholding, 1701–1790," *Social Science Quarterly* 56 (1975): 460–75; Withey, *Urban*

Increasing concentrations of wealth and the solidification of an economic and familial elite were also accompanied by the spread of both slavery and poverty. Slavery was a direct function of growing wealth. From early on in the settlement of New England, there had been a few Indian and black slaves. As late as 1690, however, there were fewer than 1,000 blacks—about 1 percent of the total population—in the entire region. Over the next three decades they increased slowly if steadily to over 6,000, or about 3 percent of the total population. Though their numbers continued to increase to over 15,000 by the early 1770s, and though slavery was still an expanding institution in all the New England colonies on the eve of the American Revolution, the proportion of blacks in the population remained steady at around 3 percent for the rest of the colonial period.

But these aggregate figures mask much greater concentrations of slaves in the more commercialized areas, particularly in the port towns, where they served as domestics, artisans, watermen, dockworkers, and emblems of conspicuous consumption for urban elites. Although Jackson Turner Main is certainly right to point out that there were few incentives to develop a plantation-style agriculture with a large servile labor force in most parts of New England and although most rural slaves were distributed in small numbers of one or two among farm families, for whom they performed agricultural or household labor, they were present in more substantial numbers on many of the commercial plantations in the Narragansett country of Rhode Island, where some estates employed as many as twenty slaves as stockmen and in the dairy industry. Indeed, as Louis Masur has recently emphasized, "slavery flourished in eighteenth-century Rhode Island." Slaves comprised as high as 18 percent of the population of Newport in 1755, and in 1774 as many as 30 percent of white households in several Rhode Island towns "contained slaves or blacks bonded in some manner." For the colony as a whole, 14 percent of households owned slaves. Without dispute, these figures represent "a substantial commitment to the institution." If New England as a whole was not, like colonies farther south, heavily dependent on slave labor, it

Growth in Colonial Rhode Island, 9–11, 130–31; G. B. Warden, "Officeholding and Officials in Boston, 1692–1775," *New England Historical and Genealogical Register* 131 (1977): 267–90; Robert M. Zemsky, "Power, Influence, and Status: Leadership Patterns in the Massachusetts Assembly, 1740–1755," *William and Mary Quarterly*, 3d ser., 26 (1969): 502–20, and *Merchants, Farmers, and River Gods* (Boston, 1971); Heyrman, *Commerce and Culture*, 143–81, 330–65; Bruce E. Steiner, "Anglican Officeholding in Pre-Revolutionary Connecticut: The Parameters of New England Community," *William and Mary Quarterly*, 3d ser., 31 (1974): 369–406.

was certainly a society that condoned slavery, and it contained a few areas that had concentrations of slaves roughly comparable to those in the Chesapeake during the early period of its transition to a slave plantation system after 1680.[39]

If the increasing social stratification of New England during the eighteenth century provided some families with the wherewithal to live a genteel life and own slaves, it does not seem to have resulted in a manifest proletarianization of the population. To be sure, as Charles Grant, Kenneth Lockridge, and several other historians have observed, by the third and fourth generations in most towns vigorous demographic growth rendered existing land resources inadequate to enable many families to provide a viable farm for each of their male offspring. As a result, there was a sharp increase in the number of young adult males with minimal levels of property. By the mid-eighteenth century as many as a third of the adult males in most communities were landless laborers. As Jackson Turner Main has shown in the case of Connecticut, however, this development was very largely a function of age. Typically, laborers were young men who were either waiting a few extra years until they inherited land from their fathers or preparing themselves to enter a craft, a profession, or trade, while those who found inadequate opportunity within their own communities simply joined the stream of immigrants to new settlements or to urban areas.

Whichever of these choices they made, Main has found, laboring was, for the vast majority of whites, only "a temporary line of work." If more and more young men began adult life with few assets, almost all of them could expect to obtain property "as they passed through the life cycle,"

---

[39] Robert C. Twombly and Robert H. Moore, "Black Puritan: The Negro in Seventeenth-Century Massachusetts," *William and Mary Quarterly*, 3d ser., 24 (1967): 224–41; "Estimated Population of the American Colonies: 1610–1780," in Jack P. Greene, ed., *Settlements to Society, 1584–1763: A Documentary History of the American Colonies* (New York, 1966), 238–39; Daniels, *Dissent and Conformity on Narragansett Bay*, 57–59; Withey, *Urban Growth in Colonial Rhode Island*, 71–73; Crane, *Dependent People*, 76–83; Miller, "Narragansett Planters," 67–71; McBurney, "South Kingstown Planters," 81–93; Main, *Society and Economy in Colonial Connecticut*, 129–30, 176–82, 309, 378; Louis P. Masur, "Slavery in Eighteenth-Century Rhode Island: Evidence from the Census of 1774," *Slavery and Abolition* 6 (1985): 140–50; Van Deventer, *Provincial New Hampshire*, 113–14. On conditions of slavery in New England and the Black response to it, see Robert C. Twombly, "Black Resistance to Slavery in Massachusetts," in O'Neill, *Insights and Parallels*, 11–32, and Lorenzo J. Greene, *The Negro in Colonial New England* (New York, 1942). On the decline of slavery in Massachusetts after 1770, see Elaine MacEacheren, "Emancipation of Slavery in Massachusetts: A Reexamination 1770–1790," *Journal of Negro History* 55 (1970): 289–306.

and the "great majority of Connecticut's people fared as well in 1774 as in 1700 or 1670." "By contrast with most pre-industrial societies," Main concludes, "virtually all of the married men and their families . . . did not simply escape poverty but enjoyed real plenty." Main's findings have been reinforced by recent work on the changing diet of colonial New England by Sarah F. McMahon, who has found that changes in land use and improvements in food production and preservation over the course of the colonial period meant that the region produced enough food so that few families could fail to enjoy a "comfortable subsistence."[40]

Yet this is not to suggest that eighteenth-century New England was without poverty. Poor relief had been a feature of New England life from the beginning, and it increased visibly during the eighteenth century as population growth, personal misfortune, the typically high loss of males in a seafaring economy, and other factors arising out of the increasingly complex character of New England society produced, in both city and country, an expanding class of both transient poor in search of employment and impoverished people unable to care for themselves. The towns dealt with this problem either by "warning out" nonresidents or providing public relief for residents. But the costs of placing poor people in families or caring for them in almshouses became so high in major urban centers that several of them—Newport in the 1720s, Boston in the late 1730s, Providence and other towns in the 1750s and 1760s—built workhouses in an effort to make the able-bodied poor pay for themselves.

But the extent of this problem is easy to exaggerate. A close examination of people in the ranks of the poor reveals that they contained few adult male heads of households. Rather, the vast majority seem to have fallen into one or the other of two principal categories: first, young unemployed single men and women who, if Main's findings for Connecticut can be extended to the rest of New England, presumably eventually found employment and rose out of the ranks of the poor, and, second, members of traditionally dependent groups—widows, the aged, the sick, the disabled, and orphans, only the last of which could be expected ever

---

[40]Grant, *Democracy in the Connecticut Frontier Town*, 83–103; Lockridge, "Land, Population, and the Evolution of New England Society," 62–80; Main, *Society and Economy in Colonial Connecticut*, 149–51, 377–78, and "Standards of Living and the Life Cycle in Colonial Connecticut," *Journal of Economic History* 43 (1983): 159–65; Gloria L. Main, "The Standard of Living in Colonial Massachusetts," ibid., 101–8; Jones, *Village and Seaport*, 103–21; Nancy R. Folbre, "The Wealth of Patriarchs: Deerfield, Massachusetts, 1760–1840," *Journal of Interdisciplinary History* 16 (1985): 208; Sarah F. McMahon, "A Comfortable Subsistence: The Changing Diet in Rural New England, 1620–1840," *William and Mary Quarterly*, 3d ser., 42 (1985): 26–65.

to escape their dependence upon the community for their support. Yet, while transiency and poverty were increasing throughout New England in the eighteenth century, they were still far below levels exhibited by contemporary British or European cities. With never more than 5 to 7 percent of a given locality's population receiving poor relief—and in most rural areas the percentage was much lower—New Englanders, as David Flaherty has observed, "had only limited experience with poverty in comparison with their fellow country men in Great Britain," where as "much as one-third of the . . . population may not have been able to feed and clothe themselves adequately."[41]

Along with the continuing internalization of Puritan religious constraints and a "high standard of law enforcement," students of legal records have cited this relative lack of poverty as at least part of the explanation for a low incidence of serious crime in New England. Throughout the last half of the seventeenth century, Roger Thompson has found in his study of sexual misbehavior in Middlesex County, Massachusetts, "New Englanders in general . . . were markedly more law-abiding" than English people in the home islands. Although infractions involving fornication, "by far the largest part of the criminal business" of local sessions courts, were being progressively and "effectively decriminalized" during the eighteenth century, the "rate of prosecution for crimes of violence, sexual offenses, and miscellaneous crimes," David Flaherty has found in the case of Massachusetts, was far higher than in England. But a much lower incidence of crimes against property, traditionally associated with poverty, meant that the per capita crime rate in Massachusetts was 43 percent less than that in Essex County, England, and far below that in London.[42]

---

[41] Charles R. Lee, "Public Poor Relief and the Massachusetts Community, 1620–1715," *New England Quarterly* 55 (1982), 564–85; Douglas Lamar Jones, "The Strolling Poor: Transiency in Eighteenth-Century Massachusetts," *Journal of Social History* 8 (1975): 28–54, and "Poverty and Vagabondage: The Process of Survival in Eighteenth-Century Massachusetts," *New England Historical and Genealogical Register* 133 (1979): 243–54; Daniels, *Dissent and Conformity on Narragansett Bay,* 57–59; Withey, *Urban Development in Colonial Rhode Island,* 51–71, 133–36; Nash, *Urban Crucible,* 71–74, 88, 125–27, 185–89, 217, 245–46, 253–55, 263, 310, 326–28, 337; Allan Kulikoff, "The Progress of Inequality in Revolutionary Boston," *William and Mary Quarterly,* 3d ser., 28 (1971): 375–412; David H. Flaherty, "Crime and Social Control in Provincial Massachusetts," *Historical Journal* 24 (1981): 352–53.

[42] Roger Thompson, *Sex in Middlesex: Popular Mores in a Massachusetts County, 1649–1699* (Amherst, Mass., 1986), 194, 198; Flaherty, "Crime and Social Control," 339–60; Hendrik Hartog, "The Public Law of a County Court: Judicial Government in Eighteenth-Century Massachusetts," *American Journal of Legal History* 20 (1976): 282–329.

A low crime rate did not, however, betoken inactivity on the part of the courts. At least in Massachusetts, civil litigation increased dramatically throughout the eighteenth century. Though inhabitants of some more isolated communities continued to eschew the courts and to try to resolve differences through the church or the town government, litigation rose steadily, at a much faster rate in rural areas than in towns, and there was a marked increase in the number of cases involving disputes across town boundaries. An indication of the penetration of the commercial economy into the countryside, the growing interdependence between urban and rural areas, and the further attenuation of the consensual communalism of the founders, these developments, together with low crime rates and high prosecution rates for criminal offenses, provide powerful testimony to both the public acceptance and efficacy of the courts as "instruments of social control."[43]

Increasing civil litigation may have been linked to a general "withering of traditional parental and community control." The first generation of rural New Englanders founded remarkably stable and closely integrated communities around a base of strong patriarchal families, while the second generation put down even deeper roots and developed a series of complex and overlapping extended kinship networks within the community. However, already by the third generation, which came to maturity in the early eighteenth century, and certainly by the fourth generation, which reached adulthood beginning in the 1730s and 1740s, the pressure of population growth, the decreasing availability of land, the opening up of new towns, and the emergence of many new opportunities for young men outside agriculture in an increasingly varied occupational structure all contributed to a significant diminution of patriarchal authority and loosening of family ties.

As evidence of these changes, historians have noted a rising proportion of impartible inheritances, a tendency to convey land to sons at earlier ages, a steady increase in the outmigration of sons, a sharp drop

---

[43] William E. Nelson, *Dispute and Conflict Resolution in Plymouth County, Massachusetts, 1725–1825* (Chapel Hill, N.C., 1981), 13–75, and *Americanization of the Common Law: The Impact of Legal Change on Massachusetts Society, 1760–1830* (Cambridge, Mass., 1975), 13–63; Murrin, "Review Essay," *History and Theory* 11 (1972): 250–51; David Grayson Allen, "The Zuckerman Thesis and the Process of Legal Rationalization in Provincial Massachusetts," *William and Mary Quarterly*, 3d ser., 29 (1972): 456–59; L. Kinvin Wroth, "Possible Kingdoms: The New England Town from the Perspective of Legal History," *American Journal of Legal History* 15 (1971): 318–27; Flaherty, "Crime and Social Control," 355; Bruce H. Mann, "Rationality, Legal Change, and Community in Connecticut, 1690–1760," *Law and Society Review* 14 (1980): 187–221.

in the age of marriage among both men and women, a major rise in daughters marrying out of the birth order, a diminution of parental control in marriage and a corresponding rise in the importance of romantic love in mate selection, a surge in premarital pregnancy, a shift away from parent-naming and Bible-naming, the provision of more space—and, hence, more privacy—for individual members of households, and, perhaps even, a rise in female offenders in the courts. Along with an apparent improvement in the status of women as suggested by "their more frequent petitions for divorce and their greater success in obtaining it," all of these developments have been interpeted as indications that the circumstances of eighteenth-century New England life were forcing fathers and husbands to redefine their roles, changing the character of the family, and helping to accelerate a powerful process of individuation among children and young adults.

The effects of these changes upon the basic character of New England life were profound. No longer "patriarchs grandly presiding over an ancestral estate and minutely controlling the lives of their sons and heirs," fathers now tended to act as "benefactors responsible for the future well-being and prosperity of their offspring." At the same time the tendency for parents to find fulfillment "in the success of their children" has been alleged to have produced a "new and different type of family life . . . characterized by solicitude and sentimentality towards children and by more intimate, personal, and equal relationships" among members. Finally, this new "organization of family life contributed to the emergence of a liberated individual, a person who was exempt from all except voluntary ties to the family of his birth and free to achieve his own goals."[44]

---

[44]Greven, *Four Generations*, 125–258; John J. Waters, "Family, Inheritance, and Migration in Colonial New England: The Evidence from Guilford, Connecticut," *William and Mary Quarterly*, 3d ser., 39 (1982): 64–86; Jedrey, *World of John Cleaveland*, 58–94; Daniel Scott Smith, "Parental Power and Marriage Patterns: An Analysis of Historical Trends in Hingham, Massachusetts," *Journal of Marriage and the Family* 35 (1973): 419–39, and "Child-Naming Practices, Kinship Ties, and Change in Family Attitudes in Hingham, Massachusetts, 1641 to 1880," *Journal of Social History* 18 (1985): 541–66; Smith and Michael Hindus, "Premarital Pregnancy in America, 1640–1966," *Journal of Interdisciplinary History* 6 (1975): 537–70; David H. Flaherty, *Privacy in Colonial New England* (Charlottesville, Va., 1972), 26–27, 34–35, 38; Nancy F. Cott, "Divorce and the Changing Status of Women in Eighteenth-Century Massachusetts," *William and Mary Quarterly*, 3d ser., 33 (1976): 586–614, and "Eighteenth-Century Family and Social Life Revealed in Massachusetts Divorce Records," *Journal of Social History* 10 (1976): 20–43; Folbre, "Wealth of the Patriarchs," 199–220; C. Dallett Hemphill, "Women in Court: Sex-Role Differentiation in Salem, Massachusetts, 1636 to 1683," *William and Mary Quarterly*, 3d ser., 39 (1982): 164–75; Lyle Koehler, *A Search for Power: The "Weaker Sex"*

By further undermining the coercive power of the old socioreligious regime that the founders of the orthodox Puritan colonies had set out to implement and thereby opening up New England society, increasing population growth and the changing character of religious, economic, social, and familial life provided, as Richard L. Bushman has argued, the necessary preconditions for nothing less than a behavioral revolution that stretched over and had a transforming effect upon all but the least dynamic areas of New England. Far from playing merely a passive role, people became active agents in this process. Increasingly ignoring traditional ideological and social restraints, they turned energies formerly devoted to religious and community endeavors to their own private pursuits of personal and individual happiness.

By encouraging a considerable amount of autonomous and aggressively competitive behavior, this behavioral revolution also provided identity models and standards of personal conduct for the society at large that stood at marked variance with the original values of the leaders of the founding generation. No longer was the moral and psychological necessity of obedience to the authority of the community and its traditional leaders—magistrates, pastors, and fathers—automatically assumed. Rather, contemporary models of behavior emphasized the authority of self rather than the authority of community; individual economic achievement and success rather than ascriptive criteria for political leadership and social status; the fulfillment, privacy, and comfort of the individual rather than self-denial in favor of the common good; and the "capacity of the individual to direct his own existence rather than . . . an unquestioning response to public morality." With this behavioral revolution the pursuit of wealth and gentility became as important as the pursuit of salvation and even more important than the pursuit of consensus and community.[45]

If all of these developments combined to push New England in the direction of greater individualism, personal autonomy, and social fluid-

---

in Seventeenth-Century New England (Urbana, Ill., 1980), 345–46, 361, 366; James A. Henretta, *The Evolution of American Society, 1700–1815: An Interdisciplinary Analysis* (Lexington, Mass., 1973), 30–31; Winifred B. Rothenberg, "Markets, Values, and Capitalism: A Discourse on Method," *Journal of Economic History* 44 (1984): 175–76. Thompson, *Sex in Middlesex,* 190–200, has recently persuasively questioned the coerciveness of patriarchal authority in late seventeenth-century Middlesex County, Massachusetts.

[45] Bushman, *From Puritan to Yankee.* See also Richard S. Dunn, *Puritans and Yankees: The Winthrop Dynasty of New England, 1630–1717* (Princeton, N.J., 1962). The quotation is from Fred Weinstein and Gerald M. Platt, *The Wish to Be Free: Society, Psyche, and Value Change* (Los Angeles and Berkeley, 1969), 31.

ity, the revolution in behavior exemplified by these developments was by
no means universal. Nor did it produce a social environment that could
be exclusively characterized in terms of "fluid, unstable social relations
[that were] conducive [only] to individual mobility and a competitive
ethos." Not just rural areas like those described by Michael Zuckerman
and Christopher Jedrey but also urban communities continued, throughout the colonial period, to show remarkable stability in family life and
to exhibit many other powerful residues of their Puritan cultural inheritance. "Rather than being at odds with the ideals of Puritanism or the
ends of communitarianism," Christine Heyrman argues in her recent
study of eighteenth-century Gloucester and Marblehead, "commercial
capitalism coexisted with and was molded by the cultural patterns of the
past." As Heyrman shows, New England communities could become
more populous, stratified, complex, diverse, and mobile without lapsing
into social disorder. In Gloucester and Marblehead, at least, civic consciousness, deference to leaders and institutions, church membership,
"traditional patterns of association," and, perhaps, family authority remained strong. The abiding power of these traditional elements of the
old Puritan social order, Heyrman plausibly contends, testifies to both
the resilience of that order and the enduring authority of inherited beliefs
and values.[46]

Certainly, the revolution in behavior suggested by the growing evidence of increasing individuation had not yet been accompanied by a
revolution in values. In their quest for land and wealth, men might challenge traditional leaders and established institutions. What they could
not challenge so easily, however, was the old system of values which de-
plored both self-oriented behavior and resistance to authority. Notwithstanding the continuing strength of so many aspects of the old social
order, the increasingly palpable divergence between the values attached
to that order and individual behavior produced a gnawing guilt that was
evident in persistent demands, especially from the clergy, for a return to
the traditional imperatives of community and obedience to authority.
The fear that excessively atomistic behavior would lead to social chaos
and loss of control and the belief that man could not tolerate freedom

---

[46]Toby L. Ditz, *Property and Kinship: Inheritance in Early Connecticut, 1750—1820*
(Princeton, N.J., 1986), 159; Zuckerman, *Peaceable Kingdoms*; Jedrey, *World of John
Cleaveland*, 58–94; Heyrman, *Commerce and Culture*, 15–19, 407–14. Laurel Ulrich, *Good
Wives: Image and Reality in the Lives of Women in Northern New England, 1650—1750*
(New York, 1982), emphasizes the role of women in sustaining the communal impulse in
New England communities.

without strong societal restraints were still too deeply embedded in cultural consciousness and too easily activated to permit the development of an alternative morality that would more accurately reflect the new modes of behavior.

Although the old millennial impulses of the founders had been severely attenuated by the latter decades of the seventeenth century, they had been "replaced by a conservative determination to perpetuate the symbols and institutions of the colonial founders." Cotton Mather and others engaged in what Robert Pope has referred to as "an oppressive filiopietism that transformed the founding generations into paragons of social virtue, wisdom, and saintliness," constantly holding them up as a model for later generations and as a contrast that provided a framework for the interpretation of American Puritan history as a process of steady declension. The guilt felt by later generations over this declension and the disjuncture between the values of the founders and their own behavior made people, as several scholars have suggested, peculiarly susceptible to the atavistic appeals of the mid-century Great Awakening, the first large-scale religious revival in American history.[47]

Though it helped those people most deeply affected by it to cleanse themselves of guilt by throwing off their worldly ambitions, the Great Awakening did not result in a return to the old communal mode and the old values. Instead, as Bushman and other scholars have shown, it intensified religious divisions. Although some communities managed to contain those divisions within the existing church, many others split into rival congregations, thereby shattering all hope of religious unity. Such developments and the bitter enmity they engendered further undermined the authority of the church and the clergy and made it clear that "revivalism, the ministry's favorite panacea [for the restoration of the old Puritan social order], could no longer be counted on to preserve [communal] order and harmony." Because they inevitably spilled over into politics and brought into the open personal and factional animosities which had previously operated beneath the surface of public life, the religious disputes generated by the Awakening also helped to transform politics by legitimizing factionalism and contention in the public realm

---

[47] Maclear, "New England and the Fifth Monarchy," 259; Pope, "New England versus the New England Mind," 107; Bushman, *From Puritan to Yankee.* See also Axtell, *School upon a Hill,* on the role of schools in perpetuating Puritan social ideology, and Kenneth A. Lockridge, *Literacy in Colonial New England: An Enquiry into the Social Context of Literacy in the Early Modern West* (New York, 1974), on one of the unintended modernizing effects of the widespread schooling.

and thereby weakening the traditional deference accorded magistrates.

The egoistical impulses and frank pursuit of self-interest set free by the Awakening seemed to New England leaders of all persuasions to portend only social and political chaos. Many of them demanded a return to the old social order and decried attempts by a few "worldly individuals" to develop a new conception of the social order that, by giving "self-interest . . . a free rein" and making "the satisfaction of human desires the main end of government," would once again bring values and behavior into harmony. At best, however, such people were only fighting a delaying action. Already by the mid-eighteenth century, the expansive impulses in New England economic and religious life had sufficiently "relaxed the restraints of men's feelings and actions" and sufficiently sapped the authority of traditional social institutions that they had significantly altered both the character of life and the character of the inhabitants. That the spread of autonomous behavior did not immediately lead to social chaos did, however, enable New Englanders to live with the behavioral revolution even when they could not bring themselves to endorse it.[48]

Despite the enduring vitality of so many aspects of the original Puritan social order, New England, recent historiography thus reveals, had changed dramatically between 1660 and 1760. Far more populous and more densely settled and stretching over a far larger area, it had a much more complex economy. Less reliant on family agriculture and more

[48] Bushman, *From Puritan to Yankee*, ix, 276, 279; Harry S. Stout and Peter Onuf, "James Davenport and the Great Awakening in New London," *Journal of American History* 71 (1983): 577; Onuf, "New Lights in New London: A Group Portrait of the Separatists," *William and Mary Quarterly*, 3d ser., 37 (1980): 627–43; Stout, "The Great Awakening in New England Reconsidered: The New England Clergy," *Journal of Social History* 8 (1974): 21–47; James Walsh, "The Great Awakening in the First Congregational Church of Woodbury, Connecticut," *William and Mary Quarterly*, 3d ser., 28 (1971): 543–62; James W. Schmotter, "The Irony of Clerical Professionalism: New England's Congregational Ministers and the Great Awakening," *American Quarterly* 31 (1979): 148–68; Robert D. Rossel, "The Great Awakening: An Historical Analysis," *American Journal of Sociology* 75 (1970): 907–25; James W. Jones, *The Shattered Synthesis: New England Puritanism before the Great Awakening* (New Haven, 1973); Patricia J. Tracy, *Jonathan Edwards, Pastor: Religion and Society in Eighteenth-Century Northampton* (New York, 1979); Gregory H. Nobles, *Divisions throughout the Whole: Politics and Society in Hampshire County, Massachusetts, 1740–1775* (Cambridge, Mass., 1983), 36–106.

heavily involved in trade, it had developed a number of important urban areas that were closely linked by an already well-articulated transportation and marketing network with the countryside, many parts of which were engaged in more specialized and market-oriented agriculture and small-scale processing and natural resource manufacturing. Except perhaps in some isolated rural areas, its society was considerably more differentiated, with greater extremes between the richest and poorest inhabitants and a more complex occupational structure. That society was also far less cohesive as the social agencies of church, community, and family had all become much less coercive while the individuation process had become considerably more powerful.

In the words of Perry Miller, this "progression of the communities from primitive simplicity to complexity and diversity . . . irresistibly" carried New England "away from the original dedication to holiness and the will of God." In the process it not only, as Miller suggested, made religion less central to the lives of its people but also sapped the strength of the corporate impulse that had been so powerfully manifest during the first and even second generations of settlement and greatly loosened the old Puritan social order. As New England society became both more complex and looser, it also lost many of the distinctive features it had exhibited during the seventeenth century. While it may be an exaggeration to say, as have John J. McCusker and Russell R. Menard, that by the late colonial period the region's well-integrated agricultural and commercial society "resembled nothing so much as old England itself," through the long process of social change over the previous hundred years it had certainly become by the middle decades of the eighteenth century far more demonstrably English than it had been during the decades immediately after its establishment.[49]

To the extent that these changes can be seen, as so many clerical leaders at the time saw them, as an attenuation of the original Puritan social order and can be represented as a decline from the radically traditional world envisioned, and, to a remarkable degree, actually achieved, by the founding generations of orthodox Puritans, the declension model can still plausibly be used as a framework for describing the social history of colonial New England. As has been suggested above, however, the process of social change in New England during the century after 1660 also involved considerable demographic and economic growth as well as social

---

[49] Miller, "Declension in a Bible Commonwealth," 25; McCusker and Menard, *Economy of British America*, 92.

elaboration, stratification, and consolidation, and such trends can be at best only partially and inaccurately comprehended within a declension model.

Written in the early fall of 1987 while I was a fellow at the National Humanities Center, Research Triangle Park, North Carolina, for presentation as a paper at a session on the "Historiography of Eighteenth-Century Colonial America," at a conference on "New England Planters in Maritime Canada" sponsored by the Planter Studies Committee of Acadia University, at Wolfville, Nova Scotia, October 23, 1987, this chapter was initially published as "Recent Developments in the Historiography of Colonial New England," *Acadiensis* 18 (1988): 143–77. It is here reprinted with permission and minor verbal changes. It was previously reprinted in Margaret Conrad, ed., *They Planted Well: New England Planters in Maritime Canada* (Fredericton, N.B., 1988), 61–96.

FIFTEEN

Reading *Pursuits of Happiness:*
A Primer

WHETHER AUTHORS should endeavor to correct misreadings of their work is a question I have always answered in the negative. By writing their own reviews in their prefaces, taking pains to make their intentions and interpretations as explicit as possible, and similar devices, authors can endeavor to shape the ways readers encounter their work. Because each reader brings a peculiar set of concerns to a text, however, authors have little control over how their published works are interpreted. Always the product of a dialectic between authorial intentions and the multiple perspectives brought to a work by its readers, the meanings books acquire depend very heavily on how they are read and may or may not have much to do with the author's original goals. Indeed, precisely because every work—and whatever body of literature may grow up around it—is engaged anew by each reader, it is subject to a continuous process of elaboration and interpretation that makes it difficult even to think in terms of "correct" or "incorrect" readings. To the extent that, even as they move on to new concerns, authors retain a proprietary interest in an earlier work, they probably ought to be content simply to sit back and observe, with as much detachment as possible, the process by which it is reshaped as a result of its encounters with other minds. By thus distancing themselves from their offspring, they can at once acknowledge that it now has a life of its own, gracefully permit it to enjoy its own history, and get on with other work.

If my conviction that authors should let their works stand or fall on their own merits makes me reluctant to try to rescue *Pursuits of Happiness* from some of the more imaginative features of Michael Zuckerman's creative reading of it, so also does the appreciative nature of that reading.[1]

---

[1] Michael Zuckerman, "Farewell to the 'New England Paradigm' of Colonial Development," *Pennsylvania History* 57 (1990): 66–73.

Zuckerman's mastery of hyperbole, unsurpassed among early American historians, is surely one of his most engaging qualities, especially when it is turned in one's favor. To make any objections to so positive an assessment can only appear ungrateful. Yet two considerations prompt me to overcome my reluctance and to offer the following primer for reading *Pursuits of Happiness*. First, both implicitly and explicitly, Zuckerman's objections to my use of the explanatory model proposed in *Pursuits of Happiness* raises issues that are of considerable importance to the ongoing effort to reconstruct the colonial British-American past. Second, his analysis provides a pointed example of the way a given reader's special intellectual concerns can shape his reading of a work.

As Zuckerman points out, *Pursuits of Happiness* proposes what I have called a *developmental model* as an alternative to the declension or gemeinschaft-gesellschaft or modernization model employed by so many students of early America since World War II. Derived out of my reading of the monographic literature on English, Irish, and colonial British-American social history and implicit in much seventeenth- and eighteenth-century literature, the proposed framework posits that the colonial experience in the early modern British Atlantic world can best be understood as an ongoing process of adaptation, institution building, and expansion of human, economic, social, and cultural resources in association with a transformation of the simple and inchoate social entities of the earliest years of settlement into the ever more complex, differentiated, and well-articulated societies of the late colonial era.

Among other objections Zuckerman contends that my use of this model in *Pursuits of Happiness* subordinates crucial regional differences to an abstract general theme. To whatever slight extent this objection may be valid, the model worked against the book's purpose, which was diametrically the opposite. To quote the preface, the book was intended not to minimize but "to call attention to the considerable diversity within the British-American social world."[2] As we all know, uncritical applications of explanatory models, both implicit and explicit, can produce exactly the sorts of distortions and inattention to context and variety that Zuckerman claims to have found in *Pursuits of Happiness*. As I believe to be the case with the developmental model, however, they can also serve to focus attention upon variations in context, process, and development. Indeed, my concern to point up such differences and to emphasize regional (and subregional) distinctions was one of the princi-

---

[2] Jack P. Greene, *Pursuits of Happiness: The Social Development of the Early Modern British Colonies and the Formation of American Culture* (Chapel Hill, N.C., 1988), xii.

pal reasons why the volume included detailed reconstructions of the social histories of every one of the major regions of the early modern British colonial world and why that concern was highlighted by the incorporation of the word *variations* in the titles of each of the chapters in which those reconstructions were adumbrated.

Whether or not the developmental model actually functioned as intended in *Pursuits of Happiness* to produce an understanding of the distinctiveness of these several regional cultures the readers of the book must judge, but the very abstractness and open-endedness of the model should have facilitated that goal. By not proposing a set of highly specific outcomes that each region had to achieve, the model should have—and I think does—promote an understanding of spatial and temporal variations at the same time that it provides "an analytical framework within which these distinctive regional experiences can be both related to one another and comprehended as part of a generalized process of social formation that may help to provide some larger coherence to colonial studies."[3]

Citing the treatment of the Middle Colonies to illustrate how he believes my use of the developmental model inhibited appreciation of regional peculiarities, Zuckerman contends that those colonies did not fit the developmental model "because they did not become more solidified or settled with time."[4] But that model does not posit the attainment of any particular degree of solidity or settledness. Rather, it suggests only that as the new societies of early modern America moved through time toward greater complexity, they found ways to balance whatever elements composed them. Contrary to structural-functionalist theory, which has been much too casually employed by early American historians and seems still to inform some of Zuckerman's commentary, pluralism of the sorts found most extensively (among the free segments of society) in the Middle Colonies did not automatically produce chronic instability and incoherence. It simply required that whatever coherence they achieved should be built on a more variegated base. Far from representing "increasing incoherence,"[5] then, religious toleration and acceptance of party politics in the Middle Colonies seem rather to have been implements for the development of a coherence compatible with the plural foundations of Middle Colony societies. Whether that coherence was

---

[3] Ibid.

[4] Zuckerman, "Farewell to the 'New England Paradigm,'" 71.

[5] Ibid., 72.

substantially more fragile than or only different from the coherence attained by less plural societies is a question that can only be determined by empirical research and comparative analysis.

Zuckerman's suggestion that the developmental model is also excessively reductive also strikes me as wrong. In the sense that they seek to identify particular variables that account for continuities, changes, and variations, all explanatory models are reductive. But it is simply inaccurate to say that in the final analysis the developmental model "reduces to the solitary aspect of private acquisitiveness."[6] To be sure, that model places heavy emphasis upon the material aspirations that were brought to the colonies by free (and prospectively free) immigrants and that were there nourished by the opportunities that they and their descendants found and created. As the book takes pains to emphasize, however, the pursuit of happiness involved far more than the simple quest for individual gain. Everywhere, even in the West Indies, possessive individualism was accompanied by a collective desire to transform the new colonial societies into "improved" societies on the model of metropolitan England, a social expectation that settlers actively cultivated as part of their several pursuits of happiness.

As many students of early modern colonization have recognized, the successful adaptation and reformulation of metropolitan cultures in the New World neither automatically produced a demand for a new "American" identity nor reduced the authority and pull of the metropolitan cultures from which the settlers emanated and to which they remained politically, economically, and culturally attached. On the contrary, as their own societies became more complex and sophisticated and the prospects for attaining the improved state to which they aspired came more within their grasp, the attractive power of the metropolis appears to have intensified, even among many of those segments of the population who could not trace their ancestry directly to it. As much as the demographic, economic, and social results of the expansive and, for free people, empowering conditions shared by every region between 1720 and 1770, this quest for anglicized improvement was a primary component of the social convergence that by the third quarter of the eighteenth century had made the North American colonies more alike than they had ever been before or, perhaps, would be again before the present century.

Pursuits of Happiness nowhere suggests, that that convergence produced identical societies. Rather, the developmental model postulates that, through the conjoint processes of creolization (adaptation to local

---

[6] Ibid.

conditions) and metropolitanization (successful cultivation of the principal values and forms of the parent culture), it did provide the foundations for both the loose political confederation that came into being during the century after 1775 and the emergence of a rudimentary national culture, a process that remained incomplete until the last half of the twentieth century.

To understand colonial development in terms of a series of creative interactions between these two processes as they functioned differentially from region to region strikes me as potentially more promising than a reversion to the presumed, and almost certainly greatly exaggerated, tension between individualism and collectivism that has always been the central analytic device in the declension model and that yet informs Zuckerman's characterization of the Middle Colonies. In any case, a comprehension of how that tension was played out in the several regions of the early modern British-American world, as well as an appreciation of the differential operation of the many centrifugal and centripetal impulses in that world, can be accommodated within the developmental model. In this effort attention to British social developments is useful not because much light can be gained through a comparison of the still (even in the 1770s) relatively new and simple colonial societies with a much older, larger, more dense, and infinitely more complex Old World society but because it shows how the metropolitan inheritance itself was changing and how, as the parent society underwent alterations, those changes were replicated in the colonies to the extent permitted by regional conditions. For as long as they remained colonies and even for a long time thereafter, the metropolis continued to be an authoritative exemplar.

If Zuckerman's remarks about the obscuring and reductive character of my use of the developmental model are misleading, his assertion that that model cannot explain "the momentous transformations of our national life" is irrelevant.[7] Specifically set forth as a model to explain the development of early modern *colonial* societies, that model may very well be applicable to the experiences of most of the new colonies established by other European powers during that era. As Peter S. Onuf's recent book *Statehood and Union*[8] would seem to suggest, it may also facilitate understanding of the process of regional social formation in the West during the century and a half after the Revolution. Less possibly,

---

[7] Ibid.

[8] Peter S. Onuf, *Statehood and Union: A History of the Northwest Ordinance* (Bloomington, Ind., 1987).

it might even, with modifications and refinements, be useful in analyzing some types of regional *social* and *economic* change involved in the shift from the rural and commercial societies of the colonial and Revolutionary eras to the urban and industrial societies of the mid- and late nineteenth century. But it was never presented as a paradigm for the development of a national society or a national culture, a task for which the declension model would seem to be even less well-suited and for which there are already several other explanatory models, the utility of which must be evaluated by historians of later periods and of national entities.

Zuckerman's principal contention, that *Pursuits of Happiness* fails to identify the Middle Colonies as the primary crucible for the generation of American culture, has no necessary connection to his observations on the utility of the developmental model. Indeed, that contention can perhaps best be understood as a reiteration of a position to which Zuckerman has been committed since at least the beginning of the 1980s. The introduction to a collection of essays entitled *Friends and Neighbors: Group Life in America's First Plural Society* (Philadelphia, 1982), his provocative essay "Puritans, Cavaliers, and the Motley Middle" not only, like *Pursuits of Happiness,* attacked the uncritical reliance of so many early American historians on the New England paradigm but also vigorously and effectively championed the contention "that the configuration of American civilization first found its essential contours in the mid- and south Atlantic regions, and especially in the province of Pennsylvania." Emphasizing the extent to which "the pluralistic modes of the middle colonies" both prefigured the subsequent development of American culture and "spread irresistibly in national affairs," Zuckerman argued in that essay that "in political, economic, social, and even religious life, Pennsylvania provided the pattern for the nation more than Massachusetts [or Virginia] ever did."[9]

If one accepts the premise, employed by both the advocates of the New England paradigm and Zuckerman, that it is important to show which region of colonial America more nearly typified the culture of later America, Zuckerman, in my view, has by far the stronger case, albeit I also think that he exaggerates the social uniqueness of the Middle Colonies and the extent of their similarity to later American "civilization." Had he done no more than merely take the opportunity provided by *Pursuits of Happiness* to restate this position, I could scarcely object. In

---

[9] Michael Zuckerman, "Puritans, Cavaliers, and the Motley Middle," in Zuckerman, ed., *Friends and Neighbors: Group Life in America's First Plural Society* (Philadelphia, 1982).

fact, however, his concern to reiterate that position has shaped his reading of my book in ways that can only mislead his readers as to its purpose and argument. In particular, his commentary implicitly functions to involve my volume in a debate to which it was not intended to contribute on a question that its author thinks both impossible to resolve and unpromising to pursue.

Rather than entering the debate over which region merits priority as the seedbed of American culture, as Zuckerman implies, *Pursuits of Happiness*, in fact, attacks the impulse behind that debate as "reductionist."[10] The book does not argue that American culture derived exclusively or even principally out of the Chesapeake. Rather, it contends only that a pervasive pattern of behavior that was powerfully evident in early modern England and Ireland and that quickly became a dominant feature in all of the new English societies in America found its *earliest* expression in English America in the first permanent settlements in the Chesapeake, that the orthodox Puritan New England colonies in many respects during their earliest generations represented a deliberate if ultimately largely unsuccessful rejection of that pattern of behavior, but that it was nevertheless central to the cultures that developed everywhere in English America, including eventually even in New England. This contention does not in any way suggest, as Zuckerman implies, that the culture of the Middle Colonies or any other colonial region derived from that of the Chesapeake. Rather, it posits a series of independent beginnings from a common cultural base that resulted in similar but quite distinctive regional cultures, with the distinctions being a function of several significant variables relating to situation and time.

As the preface declared, *Pursuits of Happiness* sought "to depict the emergence of American cultural patterns during the century beginning around 1660 as the product not of the influence of one predominant region but of a powerful social convergence among all four of the broad cultural regions . . . that beginning in 1776 would constitute the United States."[11] As a corollary, it also argued that, far from being deviant or distinctive areas, both the Chesapeake and the Lower South "were before 1800 in the mainstream of British-American development" and "perhaps as much as any of the several distinctive regional cultures in colonial British America during the early modern era . . . epitomized what was arguably the most important element in the emerging British-American

---

[10] Greene, *Pursuits of Happiness*, xii.

[11] Ibid.

culture: the conception of America as a place in which free people could pursue their own individual happinesses in safety and with a fair prospect that they might be successful in their several quests."[12]

In the summer of 1989, the editors of *Pennsylvania History* invited me to comment on Michael Zuckerman's extended commentary on my book *Pursuits of Happiness*. In my response, I sought, by clarifying my intentions in that book, both to discourage the sort of reading that Zuckerman had given it and to readdress the larger question of regional influences in the creation of early American culture. Published under the title "Michael Zuckerman's *Pursuits of Happiness:* A Comment," it is reprinted with permission from *Pennsylvania History* 57 (1990): 73–78.

---

[12] Ibid., 5.

SIXTEEN

Interpretive Frameworks:
The Quest for Intellectual Order in Early American History

FOR AT LEAST three decades, growing numbers of historians have been churning out an increasingly specialized and fragmented literature on many aspects of the new societies created in America under the aegis of the English state during the early modern era. The extraordinary volume, range, and inventiveness of this scholarship have generated enormous intellectual excitement. Initially, the excitement was channeled into empirical research; the contributors to this literature were mostly content to set their findings within established intellectual frameworks, often the gemeinschaft-gesellschaft model or some related variant of modernization theory. Two volumes published in the mid-1970s—James A. Henretta, *The Evolution of American Society, 1700—1815* (1973),[1] and Richard D. Brown, *Modernization: The Transformation of American Life, 1600—1865* (1976)[2]—represented succinct and useful early efforts to synthesize some of the new scholarship within this older tradition.

As the literature on the colonial era continued to expand, two points became clear: first, the findings of much of the new empirical research did not fit easily into existing interpretive frameworks; second, these findings actually called into question many of the general themes and underlying assumptions associated with those frameworks. As J.R. Pole and I pointed out in 1984 in the introduction to *Colonial British America: Essays in the New History of the Early Modern Era,* a collection of pieces

---

[1] James A. Henretta, *The Evolution of American Society, 1700—1815* (Lexington, Mass., 1973). In collaboration with Gregory H. Nobles, Henretta has revised this volume as *Evolution and Revolution: American Society, 1600—1820* (Lexington, Mass., 1987).

[2] Richard D. Brown, *Modernization: The Transformation of American Life, 1600—1865* (New York, 1976).

by sixteen authors designed to identify and articulate "the central themes and the larger questions" that had emerged from the new scholarship, this development destroyed any sense of coherence for the field as a whole and demanded an effort to formulate new explanatory frameworks that would be compatible with the growing body of empirical data and would enable historians to make some general sense out of those data.[3]

Bernard Bailyn reiterated this point two years later. "The sheer amount of accumulated information," he remarked, "has overwhelmed the effective organizing principles, the major themes or interpretive structures that have heretofore contained it." "What is most urgently needed," he wrote in the early pages of *The Peopling of British North America: An Introduction*, is "a fresh look at the whole story, and a general interpretation or set of related interpretations that draws together the great mass of available material . . . and that provides a framework for a comprehensive, developmental narrative of early American history."[4]

During the 1980s historians responded to this need in two complementary ways. Several produced syntheses covering specific sectors of colonial development. These include John J. McCusker and Russell R. Menard's bold explication of the main findings of the expanding literature on the economic development of the colonies,[5] Ian K. Steele's investigation of the development of communications within the Anglophone world during the six or seven decades after 1675,[6] my own analysis of the emer-

---

[3] Jack P. Greene and J. R. Pole, "Reconstructing British-American Colonial History: An Introduction," in Greene and Pole, eds., *Colonial British America: Essays in the New History of the Early Modern Era* (Baltimore, 1984), 7 [chap. 13 above].

[4] Bernard Bailyn, *The Peopling of British North America: An Introduction* (New York, 1986), 6–7.

[5] John J. McCusker and Russell R. Menard, *The Economy of British America, 1607–1789* (Chapel Hill, N.C., 1985). Using a regional framework that combines the staples approach, which stresses the importance of external markets, with the so-called Malthusian tradition, which emphasizes the significance of internal population growth, McCusker and Menard provide for the economic realm a model that depicts colonial economic history as a story of growth, development, and prosperity for the free segments of the population and frightful exploitation for black slaves and Indians. This model is compatible with the more general ones proposed by Bailyn and myself and discussed below.

[6] Ian K. Steele, *The English Atlantic, 1675–1740: An Exploration of Communications and Community* (New York, 1986). Steele examines the ways in which improved communica-

gence of a viable distribution of authority within the extended polity of the early modern British empire,[7] and Patricia U. Bonomi's exploration of religious life in colonial British North America.[8]

Still other scholars have endeavored to work at an even more general level. The first half of the 1980s yielded two such efforts, both published in 1981. Kenneth A. Lockridge, in *Settlement and Unsettlement in Early America: The Crisis of Political Legitimacy before the Revolution,* offered a brief, suggestive "personal synthesis" around the general theme implicit in the subtitle.[9] Much more ambitious, Angus Calder, in *Revolutionary Empire: The Rise of the English-Speaking Empires from the Fifteenth Century to the 1780s,* provided an informed "large-scale historical narrative" of economic, social, cultural, political, and military development for England and all "the areas overrun and governed by English-speakers," including Wales, Scotland, Ireland, the North American and West Indian colonies, and the trading factories and marcher societies in Africa and India.[10] But neither of these works aspired to produce a comprehensive synthesis with an explicit new framework of interpretation of the kind called for by Pole and me and by Bailyn.

Four ambitious efforts to articulate such a framework appeared during the second half of the decade. Each written from a different perspective, these include the concise interpretive essay by Bailyn quoted above and

---

tions resulting from increasing trade, travel, and contact, the improvement of the postal system, and the proliferation of newspapers and printing contributed to the emergence of a more integrated transatlantic world during the six or seven decades after 1675, a development that presumably added to the pull of metropolitan culture during the late colonial period.

[7] Jack P. Greene, *Peripheries and Center: Constitutional Development in the Extended Polities of the British Empire and the United States, 1607–1788* (Athens, Ga., 1986). This work uses a core-periphery framework to illuminate the ambiguous nature of constitutional relationships within the early modern British Empire and the emergence and persistence of incompatible interpretations of that relationship at the empire's center and in its peripheries.

[8] Patricia U. Bonomi, *Under the Cope of Heaven: Religion, Society, and Politics in Colonial America* (New York, 1986). Exploring the process of institution building in the religious realm, Bonomi shows how the proliferation of churches and rising church attendance helped give colonial regions, many of them for the first time, a more deeply and self-consciously religious culture.

[9] Kenneth A. Lockridge, *Settlement and Unsettlement in Early America: The Crisis of Political Legitimacy before the Revolution* (New York, 1981), 3.

[10] Angus Calder, *Revolutionary Empire: The Rise of the English-Speaking Empires from the Fifteenth Century to the 1780s* (New York, 1981), xviii–xix.

a substantial synthesis, *Atlantic America, 1492–1800,* from the point of view of historical geography by D. W. Meinig,[11] both published in 1986; my own book-length effort to interpret the recent findings of social and cultural historians, *Pursuits of Happiness: The Social Development of Early Modern British Colonies and the Formation of American Culture,* issued in 1988;[12] and David Hackett Fischer's attempt to delineate the origins of early American cultural development in *Albion's Seed: Four British Folkways in America,* which appeared in 1989.[13] These four works offer colonial British Americanists an abundance of possibilities for bringing some intellectual order to their field. The essay that follows offers a preliminary evaluation of the interpretive models suggested by these four books.

Fischer's volume makes no claim to being a comprehensive synthesis. It provides massive amounts of information on selected aspects of early modern colonial life but reveals little concern for coming to terms with either the data or the implications of much of the new literature on colonial British America. At least implicitly, however, *Albion's Seed* does offer a general framework for the analysis of the colonial era and thereby represents a potential contribution to the emerging search for an explanatory order for early America.[14]

The principal emphasis in the framework suggested by Fischer is the many transatlantic cultural continuities in the formation of the new British societies in North America during the early modern era. Such an emphasis is by no means new. The "germ theory" historians during the

---

[11] D. W. Meinig, *Atlantic America, 1492–1800* (New Haven, 1986). *Atlantic America* is the first in a proposed three-volume work, *The Shaping of America: A Geographical Perspective on 500 Years of History.*

[12] Jack P. Greene, *Pursuits of Happiness: The Social Development of Early Modern British Colonies and the Formation of American Culture* (Chapel Hill, N.C., 1988).

[13] David Hackett Fischer, *Albion's Seed: Four British Folkways in America* (New York, 1989).

[14] For a more extensive commentary on the explanatory framework suggested by *Albion's Seed,* see my "Transplanting Moments: Inheritance in the Formation of Early American Culture," *William and Mary Quarterly,* 3d ser., 48 (1991): 224–30, my contribution to "Forum: *Albion's Seed: Four British Folkways in America*—A Symposium," ibid., 223–308. That contribution is an expanded version of a section initially written as part of this essay that, at the request of the organizers of the forum, I adapted for use as the introductory piece in that enterprise.

1880s and 1890s and Edward Eggleston's pioneering 1901 study of *The Transit of Civilization from England to America in the Seventeenth Century*[15] focused upon such continuities. Throughout the twentieth century many early Americanists, including, among the most powerful advocates of such a perspective, Charles M. Andrews in the 1920s and 1930s, Louis B. Wright in the 1940s and 1950s, and J. G. A. Pocock in the 1970s and 1980s,[16] have emphasized the metropolitan sources of emerging colonial American cultures and the broader English or British context to which those cultures were attached. Indeed, few contemporary students of colonial America would deny the crucial significance of the colonists' ties to metropolitan culture.

Fischer goes well beyond any of these scholars in stressing the centrality of the British inheritance in the formation of the four regional cultures that, in his view, developed into major cultural hearths during the colonial era. Also to a far greater extent than any previous historian, Fischer seeks to depict each of these American regional cultures as an extension of a specific British regional culture: Massachusetts of East Anglia, Virginia of southern and western England, the Delaware Valley of the north Midlands, and the backcountry of the borderlands of England, Scotland, and Ulster.

As a framework for explaining this process of colonial regional cultural formation, Fischer employs a cultural diffusion model in which a large-scale, regionally specific migration dominated by an influential immigrant elite operated as the principal agency of cultural transfer. Functioning as the "governors" of the new cultures being created in America, these elites presided over a short three-stage process in which the period of initial transit of people and culture was followed by "a cultural crisis of great intensity" and then by a third period of cultural consolidation during which they succeeded in reproducing much of the culture of their British regions of origin. Within a generation, Fischer argues, each

---

[15] Edward Eggleston, *The Transit of Civilization from England to America in the Seventeenth Century* (New York, 1901).

[16] See Charles M. Andrews, *The Colonial Period of American History*, 4 vols. (New Haven, 1934–38); Louis B. Wright, *The First Gentlemen of Virginia: Intellectual Qualities of the Early Colonial Ruling Class* (San Marino, Calif., 1940); and J. G. A. Pocock, "British History: A Plea for a New Subject," *New Zealand Journal of History* 8 (1974): 3–21, and "The Limits and Divisions of British History: In Search of the Unknown Subject," *American Historical Review* 87 (1982): 311–36. Pocock appeals for the incorporation of the histories of all the cultures of the Atlantic archipelago of Britain and Ireland and of the new settler societies in America and elsewhere into a new history of "Greater Britain" of the kind written by Calder.

new American regional culture had acquired a distinctive character that proved extraordinarily durable and remarkably resistant to change.[17] Though less explicitly formulated and supported with infinitely more detail, this view of the rapid articulation and subsequent persistence of cultural forms is powerfully reminiscent of Louis Hartz's fragment thesis with its emphasis upon "the traditionalizing impact of fragmentation."[18]

Fischer uses *folkways*, which he defines as "the normative structure of values, customs, and meanings that exist in any culture," as his principal analytical device. For each region he illustrates the processes of cultural formation and persistence through extended synchronic descriptions of twenty-four separate categories of folkways ranging from speech and building to order, power, and freedom.[19] This approach is similar to the one anthropologists developed early in this century and employed to characterize and compare cultures.[20] Like many earlier analysts, Fischer nowhere explicitly confronts the questions of whether cultures are no more than the sum of their folkways and whether the process of cultural transfer might be more fully illuminated by an effort to arrange the several categories of folkways into some sort of hierarchy of significance.

Fischer's use of this framework in *Albion's Seed* presents serious problems. First, his evident exaggeration of the role of the metropolitan inheritance leads him to neglect many other elements that were inherent in the complex process of cultural reformulation that occurred in the new settler societies of early modern America. As identified by many other students of this subject, these include material considerations, environmental limits and potentials, the resistance and receptivity of existing native cultures, and the diverse regional origins of the settler populations. Similarly, Fischer's preoccupation with showing the fullness of cultural transfer prevents him from considering the extent to which the imported culture was subjected to what anthropologist George M. Foster calls a "local screening process" characterized "by a 'stripping down' or 'reduction'" in which many components of the imported culture are

---

[17] Fischer, *Albion's Seed*, 896, 819–820.

[18] Louis Hartz, *The Founding of New Societies: Studies in the History of the United States, Latin America, South Africa, Canada, and Australia* (New York, 1964), 4.

[19] Fischer, *Albion's Seed*, 7.

[20] As, for instance, George P. Murdock et al., *Outline of Cultural Materials* (1938; 4th ed., New Haven, 1961).

"eliminated and the complexity and variety of many configurations . . . simplified."[21]

Equally problematic, Fischer's emphasis on the role of elites in the creation of new culture hearths seems to be unnecessarily one-dimensional. However decisive the influence of those who were most strategically situated among the first arrivals in every region, those elites neither, as Fischer's analysis seems to suggest, acted as independent agents of cultural transfer nor were immune to forces arising out of local American conditions. Along with his virtually exclusive focus on the British settler population, Fischer's formulation of the role of elites precludes him from considering how necessary interactions with Amerindians, Africans, and even other Europeans may have affected the shape and content of the cultural constructs those populations were together creating or from appreciating the degree to which elite goals had to be purchased at the price of significant concessions to other social groups. Finally, Fischer's framework provides no way for taking into account, explaining, and characterizing any temporal changes that may have occurred during the long era between the achievement of cultural consolidation and the end of the colonial period.

Whereas the model Fischer proposes for understanding colonial British America thus highlights the moment (often stretching over one or more generations) of transplantation in each of several distinctive regions and upon the character of the cultures (as manifest in their folkways) created under the disproportionate influence of elites during those moments, Bernard Bailyn builds his "preliminary effort to . . . identify major themes" around "the early history of the American population," especially the history of the large-scale migrations of peoples that produced that population.[22] Like Fischer, Bailyn uses a regional framework, takes

---

[21] George M. Foster, *Culture and Conquest: America's Spanish Heritage* (Chicago, 1960), 12–13, 227, 232–33. For an application of a similar view to the whole of the early modern European expansion process, see R. Cole Harris, "The Simplification of Europe Overseas," *Annals of the Association of American Geographers* 67 (1977): 469–83, and the symposium it generated: Robert D. Mitchell, "The Simplification of Europe Overseas," ibid., 59 (1979): 474–76; Adrian Pollock, "Commentary: Europe Simplified," ibid., 476–77; Harris, "Comment in Reply," ibid., 478–80.

[22] Bailyn, *Peopling*, ix–x.

a broad transatlantic perspective, emphasizes the significance of the British connection, and focuses strictly upon the North American settlements.

The similarities between these two models are, however, superficial in comparison to the many dissimilarities. Primarily designed to explain, through a description of their folkways, what kinds of cultures settlers created in America and why, Fischer's model stresses the initial immigration into each region, the British regional specificity of those migrations, the extent to which colonial regional cultures were replicas of deep-rooted and stable British regional cultures, and the relatively unchanging character of the cultural constructs implanted in America.

Using the more dynamic concept of peopling, Bailyn focuses on the continuing movement of people into America, not just from Britain but also from the European continent; classifies those people not according to their regional origins but according to whether they came from metropolitan or provincial areas; suggests that early modern Britain was less a coalition of discrete regional cultures than a fluid, mobile, rapidly changing, and increasingly integrated society; stresses the continuing importance of the British connection in the development of American cultures; takes special note of the reverse flow of influence from America to Britain; and places far more emphasis on the role of the recipient environment in shaping societies established in America.

Indeed, the world Bailyn seeks to explain was a world in extraordinary flux, a world in which "all was movement, change, growth, dispersal." Principally interested in why and in what patterns immigrants came to the colonies and in the long-term impact of that migration on the Old World, Bailyn depicts the migration to America as "an extension outward and an expansion in scale of domestic mobility in the lands of the immigrants' origins," in which the continuing need for labor and the feverish activities of land speculators became the "major stimuli to population recruitment and settlement." Through "the sheer magnetism of economic betterment and religious toleration," the "pull of the American colonies" eventually created such "a mighty flow" that it reshaped traditional "patterns of European domestic mobility" and became "one of the greatest events in recorded history," transforming "at first half the globe, ultimately the whole of it, more fundamentally than any development except the Industrial Revolution."[23]

As he formulates the concept of peopling, Bailyn proposes to move beyond the process of migration to include settlement patterns, land use,

---

[23] Ibid., 60, 20, 60, 37, 36, 4, 5, 4.

mobility, the "mingling and clashing of diverse groups and races, the evolution of social patterns, of community and family organization, population characteristics—the whole world of cultural-anthropological, social-structural, and demographic history."[24] The model Bailyn offers to describe this complex array of topics relies primarily upon two explanatory devices.

The first is a concept of the cultural region similar to that employed by Fischer. Through a summary of a hypothetical "domesday book for the periphery" in 1700, Bailyn identifies four "distinct zones" of British North America: New England, a "middle circuit" consisting of the settlements around the Hudson and Delaware rivers, the Chesapeake colonies, and two less densely settled areas in the Carolinas. Far from having achieved a state of cultural coherence, as Fischer suggests, these zones, according to Bailyn, at the beginning of the eighteenth century were still in a state of "soft" plasticity in which "what would become familiar and obvious to later generations was just emerging, unsurely, from a strange and unfamiliar past." But Bailyn agrees with Fischer in emphasizing the distinctiveness of these cultures one from another.[25]

The second explanatory device is the distinction between core and periphery. Indeed, the one "inner quality" that supplied some commonality to these dissimilar regions, Bailyn contends—the "single, complex characteristic" that "was just then emerging and which would continue to characterize American society throughout the pre-industrial era and perhaps afterward as well"—was their peripheral relationship to British culture. "American culture in this early period," he posits, "becomes most fully comprehensible when seen as the exotic far western periphery, a marchland, of the metropolitan European culture system."[26]

Following a tradition epitomized by Frederick Jackson Turner, Bailyn emphasizes the magnetism of a "maturing American economy" and the extent to which social behavior revealed "not the gradual re-creation of traditional forms but a new and dynamic process that was a central force in the peopling of America." But he challenges Turner's view of "the colonial world as a *frontier*—that is, as an advance, as a forward- and outward-looking, future-anticipating progress toward what we know eventuated." Rather, he insists that it should be seen as a marchland—"a typically disordered border country," "a ragged outer margin of a central

[24] Ibid., 7–8.

[25] Ibid., 50, 87, 91.

[26] Ibid., 112.

world, a regressive, backward-looking diminishment of metropolitan ac-complishment," where life was marked by "primitiveness and violence" and a "bizarre, quite literally outlandish quality" and in which law and religion, "those fragile integuments" of civilization, were too weak to contain the "savagery of life."[27]

This perspective enables Bailyn to appreciate that the savagery repre-sented by the Amerindian wars, slavery, and transportation of criminals to America at once constituted an abandonment of "the ordinary re-straints of civility" and a distention "of elements that existed in the par-ent cultures, but that existed there within constraints that limited, shaped, and in a sense civilized their growth." It also enables him to perceive the extent to which the regional cultures of British North America were cultures at odds with themselves. For already in 1700 the "disorder of life in a marchland" existed in tension with the "self-conscious gentility" of an emerging creole population, and this "inter-mingling of savagery and developing civilization," in Bailyn's view, was "the central characteristic of" the emerging colonial world, the one that primarily gave rise to its "distinctive way of life."[28]

Far more than Fischer's cultural diffusion model, Bailyn's peopling ap-proach seems to have the potential to yield an inclusive understanding of the process of regional cultural formation in colonial British America. Though he could scarcely have developed it fully in a volume as brief as *The Peopling of British North America*, it might serve as the basis for assessing the role not just of cultural inheritance but of physical and material conditions and interactions with Amerindians in the crystalli-zation of early settlement cultures as well as the contributions of later arrivals, both voluntary and involuntary, to subsequent changes in those cultures. Though it is ostensibly only a synchronic portrait, Bailyn's analysis of these cultures in 1700 reveals a strong awareness of how they had already changed in significant ways from their early years, and his use of the core-periphery framework implicitly suggests the extent to which the pull of the metropolitan core would serve as a powerful agency of change in the peripheries of the expanding transatlantic British cul-tural system.

In its present general form, however, Bailyn's model is more useful for explaining why and how people moved into the several regions of colo-nial British America than in organizing our understanding of what they did when they got there. His emphasis upon the emerging gentility of a

---

[27] Ibid., 37, 85, 112–13.

[28] Ibid., 113, 122, 114.

segment of the creole populations contains at least a latent conception of comparative social zones and thus implies the existence of some sort of social process by which those zones moved from relative savagery to relative civility. As Bailyn employs it in this volume, however, the core-periphery framework is too broad and too static to make sense out of the manifold changes he sees as endemic to the life of every region. Indeed, Bailyn's emphasis upon the ubiquity of change only directs attention to his failure, in this volume, to explore and explicate the general underlying patterns inherent in those changes. What is crucially lacking in Bailyn's model, as in Fischer's, is an explicit theory of sequential development, a coherent framework for charting in a systematic way the process by which disordered marchlands became more recognizably British cultural provinces, to the extent that they did.

In *Atlantic America, 1492–1800,* D. W. Meinig reveals considerably more sensitivity to the sequential order of change. Conceived as "a geographic complement to the work of historians," his "synthesis of important themes" takes a much more expansive temporal and spatial approach than either Fischer's or Bailyn's, albeit the focus quickly narrows to North America and the West Indies after the English and other northwest Europeans began to take an active interest in America during the second half of the sixteenth century. Setting for his central theme "the creation of a vast Atlantic circuit, a new human network of points and passages binding together four continents, three races, and a great diversity of regional parts," Meinig devotes considerable space to the period of initial outreach by European powers into Africa and the Americas during the late fifteenth and the sixteenth centuries.[29]

Emphasizing that this outreach led to "a sudden and harsh encounter" among "three Old Worlds," Meinig, alone among the authors of the principal works considered here, gives sustained analytical attention to the tragic impact of this encounter upon Amerindians, especially through the catastrophic dispeopling that, in its North American manifestation, contributed essentially to prepare the way for the subsequent peopling that interests Bailyn. To clarify the nature of this encounter, of this "progressive integration" of Europeans and Amerindians "into a single New World," Meinig distinguishes among three possible modes of interaction: "stratification within a single complex society," as in Mexico and Peru;

---

[29] Meinig, *Atlantic America,* xv, 3.

"benign articulation of two peoples at a point of exchange," as in French Canada; and "expulsion of the native population from the colonized area and the creation of a firm frontier of separation between the two peoples," as throughout the English settlements. This last mode ultimately led to the appearance of three broad zones of Amerindian-white relations: "a coastal zone of conquest and encapsulation," an intermediate zone "of articulation and interdependence," and a more distant interior zone "beyond sustained massive" contact "but markedly affected by it."[30]

As his definition of these zones strongly suggests, Meinig is primarily interested in developing a sequential framework to explain how Europeans established their dominance in America and thereby unleashed a process that reshaped the American world. To this end, he depicts European encroachments upon the American seaboard as proceeding in three phases, from *seafaring*, including exploration, gathering, barter, and plunder; to *conquering*, consisting of the establishment of commercial outposts and the imposition of some degree of political, military, and religious control over strategic sites; to *planting*, including the permanent settlement of Europeans, the transfer of European institutions and other aspects of culture, and the organization of settlements into colonies. Meinig divides the planting phase into two subphases, a long period of *implantation*, during which "major production districts" and culture hearths were articulated, and a period of *reorganization*, during which metropolitan authorities tried to bring these many implantations under tighter central control.[31]

Like Fischer and Bailyn, Meinig employs the concept of the cultural region as a central explanatory device for the implantation process. Casting a broad net to include all those regions that either remained British or subsequently became part of the United States, he traces the

---

[30] Meinig, "The Continuous Shaping of America: A Prospectus for Geographers and Historians," *American Historical Review* 83 (1978): 1190; *Atlantic America*, 70, 72, 208. To explain the effects of this process upon Amerindians, Meinig uses the framework proposed by Francis Jennings in which contact, producing depopulation and social and cultural disturbance, is followed by a reordering of dominance-dependence relationships between whites and Amerindians, gradual Amerindian demographic revival, establishment of new large-scale institutions through acculturational processes, and the eventual stabilization of a cultural mode in which all participating groups have undergone substantial change. Jennings, *The Invasion of America: Indians, Colonialism, and the Cant of Conquest* (Chapel Hill, N.C., 1975), 329; Meinig, *Atlantic America*, 207.

[31] Ibid., 7, 65–66, 80; "Continuous Shaping of America," 1195.

emergence of eleven separate regional cultures in North America and the West Indies: Greater New England, the St. Lawrence River valley, Hudson's Bay, the Hudson River valley, Pennsylvania, Greater Virginia, the Tropical Islands, the Carolinas, Florida, Louisiana, and Texas and the Lower Rio Grande River valley.

Defining these cultures in terms of their "functional coherence, cultural similarity, and regional consciousness," Meinig describes their development within a framework that gives "special attention to localities and regions, networks and circulations, national and intercontinental systems." The key analytic concepts are *spatial system,* which refers to "a network of nodes and links that channeled the movements of people, goods, and messages within the bounds of a defined territory"; *cultural landscape,* which connotes "the result of the domestication of a particular kind of country by a particular group of immigrants that imprinted an area with a geometry, morphology, and architecture of settlement; introduced a selection of crops, animals, technology, and economic activities; and created particular patterns of ecological alteration"; and *social geography,* which means "the distribution and demographic character of its population, the locations of important social groups (however identified), and the basic social institutions and contexts (such as the village, market town, county, plantation, tenanted estate, freehold farm, and so forth) that served as matrices for the emergence of distinctive local societies."[32]

Perhaps because of his enlarged focus, Meinig never develops or applies these concepts or the broader framework in a sustained and systematic way, but two general themes do emerge from his discussion of regional formation. First is the idea, previously used by George Foster and R. Cole Harris, of the simplification of European social and cultural forms as a result of the settlers' inability to "recreate on American shores a fully European society." Second is the theme of growing diversity among and within regions. The product of differences in resource exploitation, climate, and the peoples and cultures they contained—peoples and cultures drawn from at least forty distinct Indian groups, a great number of African peoples, and nearly three dozen regional and religious cultures from Europe—this diversity, in Meinig's view, led to ever greater divergence among regions and between those regions and the metropolitan society. As a way to depict this process, Meinig, in a notable refinement of the core-periphery dichotomy, develops a "distance

---

[32] Meinig, *Atlantic America,* xv, 85; "Continuous Shaping of America," 1190–91.

decay" *spectrum* to illustrate graphically the decreasing Europeanness of segments of the colonial populations according to their cultural proximity to the metropolis.[33]

Notwithstanding his appreciation of the importance of environmental constraints and opportunities and climate in the "shaping of America," Meinig thus joins Fischer and Bailyn in putting considerable emphasis upon the role of cultural inheritance in the formation of the regional cultures of colonial British America. He also agrees with Fischer that, through "precedence, prestige, or power," a strategic segment of the founding population exerted a disproportionately influential role in this process. In contrast to Fischer, however, Meinig does not portray any of those cultures as pure and direct transplants from the Old World. Rather, he argues that they emerged out of the settlers' "experience over many years" through an elaborate process of cultural selection, adaptation to American conditions, and interactions with peoples of other races and ethnic groups, who brought their own cultural inheritances into the equation.[34]

Probably because of his preoccupation with its different results in the cultural regions he describes, Meinig's depiction of this experiential process is the least satisfactory component of his explanatory framework. His models for dealing with some aspects of that process—the presettlement phases of European contact with America, modes of interactions among Europeans and native peoples, zones of encounter between Amerindians and whites, and the spatial distribution of metropolitan cultural influences—all provide excellent devices for bringing some intellectual order to early modern British-American history. But his framework for portraying the sequential order of regional cultural formation seems too general to be very useful. Employed to cover several generations of developments, the concept of *implantations* is insufficiently refined. As Meinig uses it, the concept of *reorganization* describes a situation shaped primarily by external political demands and takes little account of internal regional cultural or socioeconomic forces. What seems needed is a more elaborate model of the temporal process of regional formation implied by the concept of implantations.

T. H. Breen proposed such a model in a 1984 essay in which he distinguished between charter societies and creole societies. The former con-

---

[33] Meinig, *Atlantic America*, 215, 265. On pp. 222–25 Meinig does make a cursory attempt to classify North American cultural regions according to the homogeneity of their populations.

[34] Ibid., 221, 85.

cept applies to the founding generations, during which societies were dominated by a "charter group," a term Breen borrowed from John A. Porter to refer to "the first ethnic group" to come into a new area and to establish effective possession. By "making decisions about institutional forms, about the treatment of other races, about the allocation of natural resources," such groups during this charter phase, like the strategic elites emphasized by Fischer and Meinig, "exercised considerable influence over subsequent generations." Breen applies the concept of *creole societies* to later generations, in which a majority of colonial populations were native born, social and cultural practices were more rigidly defined and less open to change and local variation, and demographic and economic growth and increasing social density provided the conditions for the emergence of a greater self-consciousness of membership in an expanding British cultural core. Though developed as a framework for discussing racial and ethnic relations, this formulation, with its distinction between differing phases of development, has potential for more general application to the larger social processes at work in colonial British America.[35]

Both Breen's and Meinig's sequential categories are compatible with those proposed in my *Pursuits of Happiness,* an explicit effort to provide a "framework for a comprehensive, developmental narrative of early American history."[36] In scope, this volume is much less expansive than Meinig's; it considers only those places effectively occupied by the British before 1770 and does not carry the analysis into the era of the American Revolution. Within these limits, however, it takes a wide perspective. Treating the entire British Atlantic world, including Britain and Ireland, it is similar to the volumes of Fischer, Bailyn, and Meinig in that it considers the American colonies as extensions of the metropolitan

---

[35] T. H. Breen, "Creative Adaptations: Peoples and Cultures," in Greene and Pole, *Colonial British America,* 195–232, quotations from 205. Breen cites John A. Porter, *The Vertical Mosaic: An Analysis of Social Class and Power in Canada* (Toronto, 1965), 60. Breen's temporal typology bears some resemblance to the implicit framework developed by James Lockhart and Stuart B. Schwartz to organize their discussion of the social development of Spanish and Portuguese settlements in early modern America. In *Early Latin America: A History of Colonial Spanish America and Brazil* (Cambridge, 1983), chaps. 4, 5, they distinguish between conquest societies and mature colonial societies, with a third category, fringe areas, retaining many features of conquest societies during much later times.

[36] The quotation is from Bailyn, *Peopling,* 7.

British world and employs a broad regional framework. It concentrates on six distinctive colonial American regions—the Chesapeake, New England, Bermuda and the Bahamas, the West Indies, the Middle Colonies, and the Lower South—and it attempts to delineate important variations within each of these regions.

Taking a social perspective that is intended to be inclusive of the folkways stressed by Fischer, the peopling employed by Bailyn, and the spatial systems, cultural landscapes, and social geography utilized by Meinig, *Pursuits of Happiness* uses *social development* as its principal analytic concept. The focus is upon the creation and subsequent histories of colonial regions as defined by the socioeconomic structures and cultural constructs devised and amended by settlers and their descendants to enable them to exploit the economic potentials of their new environments and to express the larger purposes of the societies they were creating. Like the analyses of Fischer, Meinig, and Breen, *Pursuits of Happiness* emphasizes the role of elites in giving shape and coherence to these regions. But the concern is less with identifying the contributions of key actors than with delineating the nature, function, and changing character of defining social processes as they were manifest in population distribution, economic organization, land use, labor systems, social institutions, and social structures, including distributions of occupations and wealth.

These processes, *Pursuits of Happiness* posits, cannot be traced exclusively to either the transit of civilization from Britain or the Americanizing effects of New World conditions. Rather, they were the products of a complex, regionally differentiated interaction between the metropolitan *inheritance*—"those traditions, cultural imperatives, and conceptions of the proper social order that settlers" initially brought with them from the Old World and that were subsequently reinforced through a process of continuous interaction with that world—and *experience*—"the slowly accumulating expertise arising out of the inhabitants' learning through a process of trial and error how best to meet the complex demands made upon them by the need for their societies to function effectively within their specific physical and social environments."[37]

Throughout the course of this interaction, *Pursuits of Happiness* suggests, two general variables were always at work. First were the material aspirations brought to the colonies by free (or prospectively free) immigrants and there nourished by the opportunities that, through the creative exploitation of natural resources and whatever labor they could

---

[37]Greene, *Pursuits of Happiness*, 169.

acquire and capital they could command, they and their descendants found and devised. These opportunities, as Bailyn also emphasizes, expanded throughout the long period of territorial, demographic, and economic growth between 1720 and 1770. The second variable was a broadly shared desire on the part of settlers to transform their colonial societies into "improved" societies on the model of metropolitan England. This social expectation, *Pursuits of Happiness* argues, grew in power as the achievement of more complex and sophisticated societies seemed to make it more attainable.

As a framework for understanding how these processes and variables worked, *Pursuits of Happiness* proposes a developmental model. The explicit underlying assumption is that the colonial experience in the early modern British Atlantic world can best be understood as a process of adaptation, institution building, and expansion of human, economic, social, and cultural resources in association with the transformations of the simple and inchoate social entities of the earliest years of settlement into the ever more complex, differentiated, and articulated societies of the late colonial era. Like those offered by Meinig and Breen, the developmental model depicts this process as a series of overlapping phases. But it includes not two but three sequential stages: an early phase characterized by "the *social simplification* of inherited forms" of the kind emphasized by Foster, Harris, and Meinig; a second stage of *social elaboration* "marked by the continuing articulation of socioeconomic, political, and cultural institutions, structures, and values that were usually at once highly creolized variants of those found in the more settled areas of Britain and sufficiently functional to enable local populations to assimilate to them with relatively little difficulty"; and a third stage of *social replication* characterized by the achievement of sufficient demographic and social density, economic and political capacity, and internal cultural complexity to suggest a closer approximation to established societies in the Old World. Defined in terms of their comparative relationship to the metropolitan society to which the colonial regions were attached at any given point, these stages, like the models proposed by Bailyn and Meinig, stress the peripheral character of those regions within the broad British cultural system but also accent the slow emergence of increasingly refined and more metropolitanized social zones within the peripheries.[38]

The developmental model is centrally concerned to show the common social processes at work in the regions of colonial British America as well

---

[38] Ibid., 167–68.

as important underlying unities they shared, including their newness, membership in the emerging transatlantic trading networks, ethnic and racial diversity, exploitative character, colonial condition, and cultural, political, and strategic dependence upon the parent state. But it is also designed to direct attention to regional and subregional variations in context, process, and development. It is thus put forth as a vehicle both for facilitating an explicit understanding of spatial and temporal variations and for providing "an analytical . . . framework within which . . . distinctive regional experiences can be both related to one another and comprehended as part of a generalized process of social formation that may help to provide some larger coherence to colonial studies." As each region moved from a contingent to a complex society and from lesser to greater social coherence, the coherence it achieved invariably differed according to—and had to be compatible with—the local conditions that sustained it and of which it was an expression.[39]

In contrast to the works of Fischer and Meinig, *Pursuits of Happiness* does not argue that these powerful regional diversities led ineluctably in the direction of cultural divergence, and it certainly does not imply, with Meinig, that the American Revolution was the result of such divergence. Rather, it posits a gradual social convergence during the middle decades of the eighteenth century throughout the anglicized parts of the British Atlantic world. The product, in the colonies, of the conjoint processes of *creolization*—adaptation to local conditions—and *metropolitanization*—successful cultivation of the principal values and forms of the parent culture—that convergence, *Pursuits of Happiness* suggests, provided the foundations for both the loose political confederation that came into being after 1775 and the rudimentary national culture that emerged thereafter. By intensifying demands among colonists for metropolitan recognition of their growing metropolitanness, it also served as a critical precondition for the rupture of the early modern British Empire.

The appearance of so many works of synthesis within such a short period reveals the depth and breadth of the perceived need among historians of colonial British America for restoring general intellectual order to their field. The authors' efforts to articulate explanatory frameworks and models also suggest a widespread recognition of the utility of such devices and the desirability of making them explicit and employing them

[39] Ibid., xii.

self-consciously. The use of regional analysis by all four of the principal works considered here, as well as that by McCusker and Menard, testifies to the extent to which the concept of the cultural region has already been accepted as an appropriate tool for organizing our understanding of early modern American history. The failure of all the frameworks considered here to give much explicit attention to important processes of racial and ethnic interaction is lamentable, and they are in many ways quite different in emphases. Yet, the cultural diffusion model employed by Fischer, the broad parameters of colonial development and especially the process of immigration set out by Bailyn, the concepts and devices for depicting the colonizing process and analyzing its spatial and social dimensions proposed by Meinig, and the sequential model suggested by me are potentially complementary and helpful in the effort to make some sense of the welter of information still being churned out in this vigorous field of historical inquiry.

Written in the spring of 1990, this chapter is reprinted with permission from the *William and Mary Quarterly*, 3d ser., 48 (1991): 515–30. Earlier versions were presented at the National History Day Summer Institute, "Global and Multi-Cultural Historical Perspectives on the Columbian Voyage and Its Legacy," Library of Congress, Washington, D.C., July 25, 1990, and at a seminar of the Program in Atlantic History, Culture, and Society, The Johns Hopkins University, Baltimore, Maryland, October 2, 1991. The chapter provided the starting point for a session on "Frameworks for Synthesizing Colonial History" at the annual meeting of the Organization of American Historians in Chicago, April 3, 1992.

PART THREE
The American Revolution

—Seventeen—

The Flight from Determinism:
A Review of Recent Literature on the Coming of the American Revolution

T HE CAUSES of the American Revolution have been a subject of continuing fascination for American historians, who in the nearly two
centuries since the event have produced a myriad of different interpretations. George Bancroft and his contemporaries in the nineteenth century
found the origins of the Revolution in man's inevitable march toward
progress, God's plan for his chosen people, and the predisposition of
people in the American environment toward freedom. Clearly, against
these powerful forces George III's tyrannical designs were foredoomed to
failure.[1] The reaction to Bancroft's nationalistic treatment set in toward
the end of the century. The years after 1890 saw the rise of two new
schools of interpretation that exerted a powerful influence upon Revolutionary scholarship. The imperial school, led by Charles M. Andrews,
George L. Beer, and Lawrence H. Gipson, insisted that the Revolution
could be understood only when considered in terms of the empire as a
whole and sought to explain why British politicians adopted the measures they did after 1763.[2] At the same time, the socioeconomic or Progressive school, represented by Carl Becker, Arthur Schlesinger, Sr.,

---

[1] See vols. 5–6 of Bancroft's *History of the United States* (Boston, 1858–60). An excellent
analysis of Bancroft as a historian is in Harvey Wish, *The American Historian* (New
York, 1960), 70–87.

[2] Representative of the imperial school are Charles M. Andrews, *The Colonial Background of the American Revolution* (New Haven, 1924); George L. Beer, *British Colonial
Policy, 1754–1765* (New York, 1907); Lawrence H. Gipson, *The British Empire before
the American Revolution*, 10 vols. (Caldwell, Idaho, and New York, 1936–61), and, most
recently, his *The Coming of the Revolution, 1763–1775* (New York, 1954).

J. Franklin Jameson, and Merrill Jensen, investigated social and economic divisions within the colonies in an effort to discover what was revolutionary about the Revolution.[3]

Both schools provided useful correctives to earlier Whig interpretations. The imperialists achieved a deeper understanding of the British side of the conflict, and the Progressives added a new dimension by focusing attention upon the importance of local considerations. Like Bancroft, however, both schools tended to view the Revolution as the product of impersonal and inexorable forces deeply rooted in the colonial past. The imperialists emphasized the growing divergence between Britain and the colonies, the maturing of colonial institutions and attitudes that made it virtually impossible for Americans to continue in a subordinate colonial status.[4] On the assumption that men are moved primarily by economic forces, the Progressives stressed the growing competition between rival capitalist systems and the intracolonial conflict generated by lower-class demands for greater economic and political privileges.[5] Both interpretations played down the importance of traditional American grievances against Britain, and both saw the Revolution as a liberal movement, the imperialists as an attempt to overturn a long-established colonial relationship, and the Progressives as an effort to achieve a wider area of economic and social freedom.[6] Recent scholarship has exhibited a strong tendency to reverse these trends.

---

[3] Among the more important works of this school are Carl L. Becker, *The History of Political Parties in the Province of New York, 1760—1776* (Madison, Wis., 1909); Arthur M. Schlesinger, Sr., *The Colonial Merchants and the American Revolution, 1763—1776* (New York, 1918); J. Franklin Jameson, *The American Revolution Considered as a Social Movement* (Princeton, N.J., 1926); and Merrill Jensen, *The Articles of Confederation* (Madison, Wis., 1948). Among the most recent contributions of this school are Carl Bridenbaugh, *Cities in Revolt: Urban Life in America, 1743—1776* (New York, 1955); Elisha P. Douglass, *Rebels and Democrats: The Struggle for Equal Political Rights and Majority Rule during the American Revolution* (Chapel Hill, N.C., 1955); and Schlesinger's *Prelude to Independence: The Newspaper War on Britain, 1764—1776* (New York, 1958).

[4] See Andrews, "The American Revolution: An Interpretation," *American Historical Review* 31 (1926): 219–32.

[5] The best summaries of this argument are Schlesinger, "The American Revolution Reconsidered," *Political Science Quarterly* 34 (1919): 61–78, and Louis M. Hacker, "The First American Revolution," *Columbia University Quarterly* 37 (1935): 259–95.

[6] An excellent analysis of both the imperial and socioeconomic schools is Edmund S. Morgan, "The American Revolution: Revisions in Need of Revising," *William and Mary Quarterly*, 3d ser., 14 (1957): 3–15. A good brief summary of the major schools of interpretation and survey of recent trends is the same author's *The American Revolution: A Review of Changing Interpretations* (Washington, D.C., 1958). Page Smith, "David Ramsay

Since World War II a new wave of scholars has produced another interpretation that may appropriately be styled neo-Whig. The nature and direction of their inquiries differ markedly from those of earlier writers. Their emphasis has been upon immediate issues and individual actions rather than upon long-range determinants or underlying conditions. Although they have been cautious in using formal psychology, they have been interested mainly in psychological questions involving constitutional principles, political power, liberty, security of property, and legal rights. Moreover, they have taken a broader approach to the problem of human motivation, proceeding upon the assumption that man is not moved by economic considerations alone. Their primary focus has been upon American grievances against Britain, the central question in their studies being why Americans were angry in the fateful years after 1763. To answer this question they have explored the sources intensively and rigorously, concerning themselves with problems at once more limited and more ambitious. The scope of their works has been narrow. They have sought not to write an epic of the American Revolution but to define issues, fix responsibilities, and measure the impact of events and policies. The result has been a remarkable reinterpretation of the Revolution and the virtual elimination of hitherto widely accepted views. It is their contention that the Revolution was essentially a conservative movement, a defense of American rights and liberties against provocations by the mother country.

At the forefront of the new school is Edmund S. Morgan, who recently investigated in detail the crisis provoked by the Sugar and Stamp acts, perhaps the most thoroughly studied of the events that preceded the Revolution. His findings, set forth in two articles and in *The Stamp Act Crisis: Prologue to Revolution*, written in collaboration with his wife, Helen M. Morgan,[7] fundamentally alter older interpretations and demonstrate the value of subjecting familiar materials to a rigorous reexamination. The Morgans found that the offer by George Grenville to entertain suggestions from the colonies for taxing themselves was less than sincere, that he had, in fact, already decided upon a stamp tax by the time he suggested it to Parliament in 1764. Both the Massachusetts as-

---

and the Causes of the American Revolution," *William and Mary Quarterly*, 3d ser., 17 (1960): 51–77, is a recent and suggestive analysis of trends in interpretation since the Revolution.

[7] Edmund S. Morgan, "The Postponement of the Stamp Act," *William and Mary Quarterly*, 3d ser., 5 (1948): 311–41, and "Colonial Ideas of Parliamentary Power," ibid., 7 (1950): 353–92; Edmund S. and Helen M. Morgan, *The Stamp Act Crisis: Prologue to Revolution* (Chapel Hill, N.C., 1953).

sembly and colonial agents in London tried unsuccessfully to act on the offer, but the fact is that Grenville neither communicated it to the colonies through official channels nor formulated it in terms precise enough to permit definite action. The year's delay, the Morgans conclude, was merely to permit the ministry to work out details of the Stamp Act.

This discovery fixes responsibility for the crisis squarely upon Grenville and seriously undermines one of the central arguments of both the imperial and Progressive schools: that the colonists' failure to suggest alternatives to the Stamp Act indicated that they were opposed not to taxation without representation but to taxation in general. That argument is still further weakened by the Morgans' findings that Americans objected to all forms of parliamentary taxation for revenue in 1764–65 and not simply to internal taxes, as writers of both earlier schools had argued. That the colonists had distinguished between internal and external taxes was widely believed in England, but the Morgans found no such distinction in contemporary American statements. Both American legislators and pamphleteers categorically denied Parliament's authority to levy any taxes for revenue purposes, the principle to which they consistently adhered for the next decade.[8]

In the light of this evidence it becomes clear that the traditional charge that Americans were inconsistent and continually enlarged their claims as the situation changed is invalid. Moreover, by demonstrating that the emerging Sons of Liberty organizations were dominated by men from the "better and wiser part" of colonial society, the Morgans have further weakened the Progressive interpretation, which has held that those bodies were an expression of lower-class discontent with existing social and political conditions in the colonies.

The Morgans' study strongly suggests that American devotion to principle was considerably greater than most scholars during the previous half century had assumed and demonstrates the primacy of political and constitutional considerations in the American case against the Sugar and Stamp acts. As the subtitle indicates, the work argues for the decisiveness of the Stamp Act crisis in the unfolding Revolutionary drama. Not only did it raise the issue of the extent of Parliament's jurisdiction in the colonies by forcing American leaders and Parliament into a precise formulation of directly opposing views, but it also created an atmosphere of mutual suspicion that pervaded all subsequent developments and

---

[8]Curtis P. Nettels's defense of the older interpretation was on the whole unconvincing. See his letter, Morgan's reply, and Oliver M. Dickerson's defense of Morgan, *William and Mary Quarterly*, 3d ser., 6 (1949): 162–70, 351–55.

quite possibly precluded any peaceful settlement of the issue. Thereafter, Americans scrutinized every parliamentary action for possible threats to their constitutional rights, while English authorities became increasingly convinced that American opposition was simply a prelude to an eventual attempt to shake off the restraints of the Navigation Acts and perhaps even political dependence.

Two years before the appearance of the Morgan book, Oliver M. Dickerson considered the justice of English suspicions in *The Navigation Acts and the American Revolution.*[9] In this work Dickerson examined the navigation system as it operated in the eighteenth century and found that it worked no serious hardships upon the colonies, a view essentially similar to those of earlier historians of the imperialist school, especially George L. Beer. But Beer and other imperialist writers assumed that the supposed widespread smuggling was symptomatic of American discontent with the Navigation Acts, and it is upon this point that Dickerson disagrees sharply. He denies that the colonists in the period before 1763 either regarded the system as a grievance or made any serious attempt to evade it, except in the case of tea and sugar after passage of the Molasses Act in 1733. In general, he found that the system was well enforced, without major objection from the colonists, for whom its benefits far outweighed its objectionable features. These findings, Dickerson argues, indicate that the Navigation Acts were the "cement of empire," a positive force in binding the colonies to the mother country.

This happy arrangement was upset in 1764 when the British undertook to substitute a policy of trade taxation for the older system of trade protection and encouragement. With the Sugar Act of that year, British officials introduced stricter customs and commercial regulations designed to produce more revenue. This new policy, Dickerson argues, destroyed the empire in little more than a decade. Taxes and incidental charges arising from measures adopted over the next twelve years drained over £600,000 from the colonies, about half of which came from the sugar tax and went not for American uses but directly into the British treasury. The effect of these regulations was compounded because the bulk of the taxes fell most heavily upon the more important commercial towns, which were at the forefront of the Revolutionary movement.[10]

But "England's most fateful decision," Dickerson declares in his most

---

[9] Oliver M. Dickerson, *The Navigation Acts and the American Revolution* (Philadelphia, 1951).

[10] Unlike the sugar tax, the Townshend tax on tea did go for colonial purposes. In "Use Made of the Revenue from the Tax on Tea," *New England Quarterly* 31 (1958): 232–

important new conclusion, was the establishment of a separate Board of Customs for the continental colonies at Boston in 1767 as part of the Townshend revenue program. Previously, American customs collection had been supervised from London, and administration, tempered by the desire of British merchants to keep American trade running smoothly, had been relatively lax. The commissioners of the new board, receiving their salaries out of collections, literally began to wage war on American commerce. Between 1768 and 1772 they engaged in what Dickerson judges was little less than "customs racketeering," employing legal technicalities and unscrupulous methods to plunder large amounts from colonial merchants, including such future Revolutionary leaders as John Hancock and Henry Laurens. The commissioners were also largely responsible for still other measures Americans found distasteful, including extended use of troops in Boston. Moreover, there was a direct connection between their activities and such important manifestations of colonial discontent as the Boston Massacre and the *Gaspee* affair.[11] The more blatant abuses came to an end after 1770 as the commissioners and their supporters lost influence at home as well as in the colonies, but the damage had been done, and it was their wholesale attack on American liberty and property, not American opposition to the navigation system or addiction to smuggling, that caused the intense colonial hostility to the new board.

At no time after 1763, Dickerson concludes, did Americans express dissatisfaction with either the philosophy or the operation of the Navigation Acts. In fact, they opposed the new measures because they were not primarily trade regulations of the older type. Nevertheless, colonial resistance convinced British officials that Americans were trying to throw off the navigation system, leading them to take an increasingly stricter tone and providing the only real foundation for the subsequent charge by some nineteenth- and twentieth-century writers that Ameri-

---

43, Dickerson shows that the tea revenue went to pay salaries of British officials in the colonies.

[11] Dickerson treats several of these subjects in greater detail in "John Hancock, Notorious Smuggler or Near Victim of British Revenue Racketeers?" *Mississippi Valley Historical Review* 32 (1946): 517–40; "England's Most Fateful Decision," *New England Quarterly* 22 (1949): 388–94; "British Control of American Newspapers on the Eve of the American Revolution," ibid., 24 (1951): 453–68; and "The Commissioners of Customs and the Boston Massacre," ibid., 27 (1954): 307–25. For the commissioners' use of writs of assistance and the American reaction, see the same author's "Writs of Assistance as a Cause of the Revolution" in Richard B. Morris, ed., *The Era of the American Revolution* (New York, 1939), 40–75.

cans were unhappy with the Navigation Acts. Only insofar as British efforts to employ new methods to enforce a system they thought was under attack produced American discontent, Dickerson declares, were the Navigation Acts in any sense a cause of the Revolution.[12]

Interestingly, both the Morgan and Dickerson books show that important accepted interpretations that Americans were inconsistent in their objections to parliamentary taxation and that they objected to the restraints of the navigation system were based on contemporary British charges rather than on American statements. Both works attempt to illuminate the extent and nature of American discontent and emphasize that it was the product of measures adopted beginning in 1763. Thus, they tend to shift attention away from long-range forces and earlier colonial developments to events in the period immediately preceding the Revolution and to emphasize the importance of individual actions by the ministry and officials in the colonies in contributing to the rise of the Revolutionary movement.

Bernhard Knollenberg's recent study, *Origin of the American Revolution, 1759—1766*,[13] the first of a projected two-volume account, continues these trends. Knollenberg has chosen to rely primarily upon original sources in attempting to discover the origins of American discontent in the 1760s and to explain why the colonies reacted so violently to the Stamp Act. He finds that, contrary to contemporary British suspicions, there was little sentiment for independence among the colonists during the Seven Years' War and agrees with Morgan and Dickerson that Americans were in general happy with existing political and economic relationships with Britain. Knollenberg's contention is that trouble began not in 1763 but in 1759, when British military successes made it unnecessary to placate the colonies further and permitted metropolitan authorities to inaugurate a stricter policy. Under the leadership of the earls of Granville and Halifax, presidents respectively of the Privy Coun-

---

[12] This view is essentially similar to that of Curtis P. Nettels, "British Mercantilism and the Economic Development of the Thirteen Colonies," *Journal of Economic History* 12 (1952): 105–14, and Lawrence A. Harper, "The Effects of the Navigation Acts on the Thirteen Colonies," in Morris, *Era of American Revolution*, 1–39, and "Mercantilism and the American Revolution," *Canadian Historical Review* 23 (1942): 1–15, the latter to be considered with Dickerson's comment, ibid., 29–34. Harper argues that the burdens placed on the colonies by the Navigation Acts were greater than the benefits but admits that there was little overt dissatisfaction with pre-1763 exploitative features and that Americans objected seriously only to post-1763 regulatory measures.

[13] Bernhard Knollenberg, *Origin of the American Revolution, 1759—1766* (New York, 1960), ix, 486.

cil and Board of Trade and longtime advocates of closer control over the colonies, crown officials undertook a series of new and provocative measures intended to weaken colonial self-government and, Knollenberg implies, to check tendencies which colonial officials feared might be leading toward independence.

Over the next four years a wider and more intensive use of such traditional checks as the royal instructions and legislative review produced serious discontent in Virginia with the disallowance of the Two-Penny Act in 1759, in New York and New Jersey with the issuance of the general instruction of 1761 stipulating that judicial tenure should be at the crown's pleasure rather than during good behavior, and in South Carolina with the disallowance of an election law in 1761 which was in part responsible for the bitter Gadsden election controversy. This reform impulse also led in 1761 to the issuance of writs of assistance in Massachusetts to help restrain smuggling and the support by some crown officials of Archbishop Thomas Secker's efforts to establish an Anglican bishopric in the colonies, both of which aroused strong antagonism in the Bay Colony. Separately, none of these measures was very important, but their concentration within a short period caused serious alarm among colonial leaders.

That the alarm was justified became increasingly clear after the fall of the Newcastle ministry in April 1762. The removal of the moderating influence of Newcastle and Pitt gave a freer hand to the proponents of the new spirit of administration. This spirit, in combination with general inexperience in colonial affairs, the conclusion of the war, and preoccupation with the domestic distraction caused by Wilkes, led the Bute and Grenville ministries to undertake a variety of measures to tighten up the colonial system. In 1763 came a series of steps that were particularly unpopular in New England, including the decision to use the Royal Navy to curb colonial smuggling and to enforce the previously laxly administered Molasses Act of 1733 and various white pines acts. Also in 1763 metropolitan officials decided to station a large standing army in the colonies and to limit westward expansion into the region beyond the Alleghenies. Security was the primary consideration behind both measures, but it was easy for Americans to interpret the former as an attempt to coerce them and the latter as a stratagem to confine them to the seacoast—motives, Knollenberg finds, which actually did play some part in the decisions. The necessity of paying for the army led to the decision to tax the colonies and to Parliament's passage in 1764 of the Sugar Act (called by Knollenberg the American Act) providing for extensive reforms in customs administration and in 1765 of the Stamp Act, which touched off the colonial uprising of 1765–66.

The long list of grievances Knollenberg describes will be familiar to specialists, and most of them have been the subjects of monographs or articles.[14] But no prior student of the American Revolution has emphasized them so heavily or explained so clearly how they contributed to the complex web of discontent in the colonies. From this perspective the Stamp Act, though still the focal point of rebellion, is less decisive than most previous historians have held. Knollenberg's most important contribution is in demonstrating that it was not the Stamp Act alone but the cumulative effect of British policy that drove the colonists to resistance during the Stamp Act crisis. Nor has anyone previously explored the issue of the army so thoroughly. Knollenberg rejects Beer's thesis that troops were stationed in America to provide for colonial defense and to suppress Pontiac's rebellion. He points out that the rebellion began after the decision about the army had been made and that troops organized during the war for frontier fighting were disbanded. Thus, although metropolitan authorities gave some weight to using the army as a coercive force against the Americans and to augmenting the crown's patronage by increasing the number of army officers, the prime consideration, Knollenberg argues, was the general defense of the empire as a whole. Troops for that purpose could be stationed as well in America as elsewhere and with less opposition from Parliament, which still opposed a large standing army in the home islands during peacetime. Furthermore, by stationing troops in America, metropolitan officials could tax the colonies to provide for their support. Thus, Americans found themselves saddled with a standing army and threatened with parliamentary taxa-

---

[14] See Richard L. Morton, *Colonial Virginia*, 2 vols. (Chapel Hill, N.C., 1960), 2:751–819, on the dispute over the Two-Penny Act; Milton M. Klein, "Prelude to Revolution in New York: Jury Trials and Judicial Tenure," *William and Mary Quarterly*, 3d ser., 17 (1960): 439–62, and Donald L. Kemmerer, "Judges' Good Behavior Tenure in Colonial New Jersey," New Jersey Historical Society *Proceedings* 56 (1938), on judicial tenure; Jack P. Greene, "The Gadsden Election Controversy and the Revolutionary Movement in South Carolina," *Mississippi Valley Historical Review* 46 (1959): 469–92, on the Gadsden election dispute; Arthur L. Cross, *The Anglican Episcopate and the American Colonies* (New York, 1902), on attempts to establish Anglican bishops; Howard H. Peckham, *Pontiac and the Indian Uprising* (Princeton, N.J., 1947), on the responsibility for Pontiac's rebellion and the army's failure to quell it; Robert G. Albion, *Forests and Sea Power* (Cambridge, Mass., 1926), on the reaction to the white pines acts; and Clarence W. Alvord, *The Mississippi Valley in British Politics*, 2 vols. (Cleveland, 1916), on British western policy.

tion to support it. To make matters worse, Americans were neither consulted about the disposition of the troops nor given any of the plums of office; and finally, when put to the test against Pontiac, the army proved unequal to the task, and colonial troops had to be called upon for aid.

On the question of parliamentary taxation, Knollenberg takes a position essentially similar to that of McIlwain,[15] arguing convincingly that usage, always "a powerful force in establishing legal rights and constitutional principles under English law," had determined that Parliament should have the right to regulate the trade of the colonies but not to tax them.[16] Moreover, the author contends, to tax the colonies to pay for their own defense upset a long-standing mercantilist tradition by which the colonies traded their allegiance for protection by the mother country. In demonstrating how local conditions influenced and determined the nature of each colony's reaction in 1764 to the proposed taxes, Knollenberg adds substantially to the Morgans' treatment of the Stamp Act crisis. He also shows that two of the early protests, that from Massachusetts in November 1764 implicitly and that from Connecticut of the previous June explicitly, actually distinguished between internal and external taxes. This evidence does not appear to be sufficient to modify the Morgans' view that Americans in general objected to all forms of taxation by Parliament, but it may help to explain why Englishmen thought that Americans had made such a distinction. Similarly, Knollenberg does not present sufficient evidence for his assumption, in contradiction of Dickerson, that there was widespread smuggling in the colonies before 1763, although he is probably right in asserting that the navigation system worked greater hardships on the tobacco colonies of Virginia and Maryland than Dickerson had suggested.

Although the merits of this work far outweigh its limitations, it can be objected that Knollenberg fails to assess the relative importance of the issues he presents and that his arguments sometimes rely more upon deductive reasoning than upon inductive examinations of evidence. It might also be argued that he has presented an ex parte case for the Americans. But that, after all, was what he set out to do. Who was right or wrong makes little difference. The questions are why were Americans

---

[15] Charles H. McIlwain, *The American Revolution: A Constitutional Interpretation* (New York, 1923).

[16] For the most recent statement on the opposite point of view by the leading imperial historian, see Gipson, *The British Empire before the American Revolution* 3 (rev. ed.):273–80.

driven to the brink of rebellion and why did they think they were right? And certainly, the background of American discontent, the complexity of the issues, and the case for American resistance in 1765–66 have never been so well presented in one volume.

Another recent monograph, Carl Ubbelohde's *The Vice-Admiralty Courts and the American Revolution*,[17] attempts to discover why Americans objected to the courts after 1763. The courts, juryless bodies completely dominated by judges, had operated in the colonies since the late seventeenth century, handling problems of seamen and merchants, condemning and disposing of prizes in wartime, and, after 1696, sharing equal jurisdiction with common-law courts in the enforcement of the Navigation Acts. The common-law courts had repeatedly challenged their power, but there had been relatively little other objection to them before 1763, when metropolitan authorities sought to make them "a cornerstone in the new imperial rule."

The demand for stronger courts, Ubbelohde finds, arose during the war as a result of persistent reports of collusion between provincial vice-admiralty judges and American smugglers. At war's end metropolitan officials moved quickly, obtaining in 1763 Parliament's sanction to use the navy as an enforcement agency and in 1764, in the Sugar Act, a number of specific reforms to bolster the vice-admiralty system, including the establishment of a new court with authority over the whole area from Newfoundland to Florida. Metropolitan officials decided to locate the new court at Halifax and to appoint a learned lawyer, Dr. William Spry, as judge, with a handsome annual salary of £800 to be paid from English funds should money obtained from seizures be insufficient. Though it had no appellate power, the Halifax court was to have equal and concurrent jurisdiction with the provincial vice-admiralty courts, which meant that customs officials could choose between the local or Halifax tribunals, the latter presumably being more impartial and less amenable to merchant influence. To strengthen the system further, the Sugar Act provided that the burden of proof should rest on the accused in all cases arising under the Navigation Acts and that, in cases where the defendant was acquitted, a ruling by an admiralty judge that there had been probable cause for seizure would exempt the prosecutor from action in common-law courts.

Americans found much to complain about in the new admiralty regulations. They objected to the inconvenience of the Halifax court, pay-

---

[17] Carl Ubbelohde, *The Vice-Admiralty Courts and the American Revolution* (Chapel Hill, N.C., 1960), xii, 242.

ment of Spry out of seizures, and the probable-cause arrangement. But the bulk of their objections involved the constitutional question. There was, they argued, a fundamental difference between trade regulations and revenue measures such as the Sugar Act; and to try cases arising under revenue laws in the vice-admiralty courts deprived them of their ancient right of trial by jury, especially because such cases in England were tried before juries in the common-law Court of Exchequer. This question became even more important after Parliament had also made the Stamp Act enforceable in the vice-admiralty courts. Here, Ubbelohde argues in one of his most important conclusions, was the root of American complaints against the courts. It was not so much the courts themselves as their association with the new revenue laws that made them onerous. Still, the whole issue was only a minor gust in the tempest over the Stamp Act, and the courts did not come under major attack until after passage of the Townshend Acts in 1767.

Townshend's program called for the execution of an earlier proposal to substitute four new superior courts of vice-admiralty with specific jurisdictions for the general court at Halifax, which had been little used during its brief existence. Located in Charleston, Philadelphia, Boston, and Halifax, the new courts, like the general court, were to supplement, not replace, the provincial courts, and crown officials guaranteed their judges fixed annual stipends from metropolitan sources. There was only one important change in function: the new courts were empowered to hear appeals from the provincial courts.

Originally thought of as a concession to the Americans, who had repeatedly objected to the inconvenience of the Halifax court, the new courts did not meet with a kindly reception in the colonies. Appointment to the benches of the new courts were not calculated to please patriot leaders. Two, Augustus Johnson for Charleston and Jared Ingersoll for Philadelphia, had been former stamp distributors, and the other two, Robert Auchmuty, Jr., for Boston and Jonathan Sewall for Halifax, strong supporters of the crown in Massachusetts. Moreover, the new courts along with the provincial courts again suffered from their associations, first with the enforcement of the Townshend taxes and then with the activities of the new American Board of Customs, particularly in the notorious Laurens-Leigh controversy in South Carolina and the seizure of the *Liberty* in Massachusetts. Resentment continued strong, particularly in New England, where the courts played a conspicuous role in enforcing the white pines acts, but agitation subsided in 1770 after the partial repeal of the Townshend duties and did not erupt again until the onset of a new crisis in 1773.

The courts, then, Ubbelohde concludes, were a minor but persistent "cause" of the American Revolution. American objections to paying judges out of seizures and appointing loyal crown supporters to the judgeships were unjustifiable, he thinks, because the judges received their salaries whether or not they condemned a single vessel and they were fair and impartial in their rulings. Although he argues that the metropolitan policy of enforcing the new revenue acts in the vice-admiralty courts was a natural and defensible continuation of earlier practice, he also thinks that Americans, given their distinction between trade and revenue measures, were also justified in arguing that the policy extended admiralty jurisdiction beyond limits normally exercised in England, thus creating a basic inequality between Englishmen and Americans. This argument became more compelling in the 1770s as Americans began to think increasingly in terms of equal rights.[18]

For the same reason the Americans' most effective and most persistent charge, that empowering the courts to try revenue cases deprived them of their rights to trial by jury, would also seem to be valid, though Ubbelohde suggests, this reviewer thinks mistakenly, that there was actually no break with eighteenth-century custom, and though the Americans themselves adopted a similar system in the 1780s after the failure of experiments using juries in admiralty cases. Still, the fact remains that Americans' hostility to the courts ebbed and flowed with their dissatisfaction over questions of greater moment, and Ubbelohde's conclusion that it was really the courts' link with broader objectives of British policy that brought them into disfavor is inescapable. What matters most, of course, is the simple fact that Americans did consider the courts a grievance. As Ubbelohde perceptively points out, men fight "as much for images as realities."

Another work has thrown new light on still another issue, the British army in America. As Knollenberg has shown, the army played an important part in events from 1763 to 1766. Subsequent disputes over quartering, particularly in New York in 1767, are well known.[19] But the army's role in developments after 1767 has never been thoroughly studied. John R. Alden, though only incidentally concerned with the army as an

---

[18] This aspect of the issue is treated more fully in David S. Lovejoy's excellent article, "Rights Imply Equality: The Case against Admiralty Jurisdiction in America, 1764–1776," *William and Mary Quarterly*, 3d ser., 16 (1959): 459–84.

[19] Perhaps the best and most recent summary is Nicholas Varga, "The New York Restraining Act: Its Passage and Some Effects, 1766–1768," *New York History* 37 (1956): 233–58.

issue, shows what the results of such a study might be in his *General Gage in America* (Baton Rouge, La., 1948). As commander-in-chief of the army in North America from 1763 to 1775, Gage had to deal with all the problems raised by the presence of the army in the colonies. Colonial fears that the army might be used as a coercive force became a reality in September 1768, when British troops, upon order from the ministry, began arriving in Boston to quell the disturbances over the Townshend Acts. As Alden shows, this action raised a storm of protest from Bay Colony leaders, some of whom circulated through the press a weekly report, *A Journal of the Times*,[20] enumerating the evils of the army and bringing the issues to the attention of other colonies. They objected to a standing army in time of peace as unconstitutional and charged both that the removal of troops to Boston left the frontiers exposed to Indian attacks and that the soldiers were a corrupt and lawless influence in the city. Continuous friction between the troops and the townsmen culminated on March 5, 1770, in the Boston Massacre. As most of the troops were removed in the early 1770s, agitation over the army quieted, but the same problems flared up again after the crisis of 1773–75 had led to the recall of the troops and to Gage's appointment as governor of the colony. Perhaps the most important new information presented by Alden is the discovery that Gage's order to march on Lexington and Concord was the result of a ministerial directive to make some show of force in Massachusetts. Thus, it was the ministry, more than Gage, who was responsible for the provocative use of the army on April 19, 1775, just as it was the ministry which was responsible for the earlier provocation of sending troops to Boston in 1768.

Other scholars in the postwar years have approached the Revolution from the perspective of a particular colony. In one sense this development is a continuation of a pattern established early in the century by Charles H. Lincoln and Carl Becker,[21] but the emphasis in the newer studies is different. Whereas Lincoln and Becker were interested primarily in the effect of the Revolution on local developments, in particular the demand of lower-class groups for a greater share of the political pie and increased economic and social privileges, recent writers have been more concerned with the effect of local conditions and developments

---

[20] A modern edition with a valuable introduction is Oliver M. Dickerson, ed., *Boston under Military Rule* (Boston, 1936).

[21] Charles H. Lincoln, *The Revolutionary Movement in Pennsylvania, 1760–1776* (Philadelphia, 1901), and Becker, *History of Political Parties in New York*.

upon the controversy with Britain. Like the writers previously considered, they have sought to explain why the colonists revolted. The tone was set by two excellent pre–World War II studies of Maryland and New Jersey: Charles A. Barker, *The Background of the Revolution in Maryland* (New Haven, 1940), and Donald L. Kemmerer, *Path to Freedom: The Struggle for Self-Government in Colonial New Jersey, 1703–1776* (Princeton, N.J., 1940). Unlike these studies, which sought the origins of the Revolution in earlier colonial developments, most postwar accounts have concentrated on the last quarter century of the colonial period.

Two of the best of these studies are David S. Lovejoy's *Rhode Island Politics and the American Revolution, 1760–1776* (Providence, 1958), and W. W. Abbot's *The Royal Governors of Georgia, 1754–1775* (Chapel Hill, N.C., 1959). Lovejoy finds no class conflict or issues that were peculiar to Rhode Island, though resentment against the strict enforcement of the Navigation Acts was probably stronger than in most other colonies. But he does find two rival factions of equals, one led by Samuel Ward and the other by Stephen Hopkins, competing for election by a broad electorate in a society that had reached a surprising level of political maturity. In the last analysis, Lovejoy concludes, Rhode Islanders revolted to protect the wide area of freedom to which they were accustomed. Similarly, Abbot found that the Revolution in Georgia was singularly lacking in internal economic and social conflict. The difference was that Georgia, newest of the thirteen colonies, lacked political maturity; and, although the debate with Britain greatly accelerated the colony's development, it was, in the end, pulled into the revolt by outside forces and the fear of not having a part in great events.[22]

Other studies of Connecticut and Pennsylvania also show unique patterns of development. In *Connecticut's Years of Controversy, 1750–1776* (Chapel Hill, 1949), Oscar Zeichner shows that a long-standing sectional split profoundly influenced the course of Revolutionary development in Connecticut. But the split was not along class lines. Rather, the east was Congregational, New Light, oriented toward Boston, and interested in western land speculation, while the west was largely Anglican, oriented toward New York, and opposed to the land schemes of the east. Both sides ultimately supported the Revolution, but the intensity with which

---

[22] Kenneth Coleman, *The American Revolution in Georgia, 1763–1789* (Athens, Ga., 1958), supplies some detail that is missing in Abbot's study but agrees with Abbot's general interpretation.

they resisted metropolitan measures differed, with the east taking the more radical position. Similarly, Theodore Thayer in *Pennsylvania Politics and the Growth of Democracy, 1740–1776* (Harrisburg, Pa., 1953), finds that the old split between proprietary and Quaker-led antiproprietary factions conditioned Pennsylvania's reaction to the imperial conflict. Against British policy after 1763 the Quakers, who were trying to persuade the crown to make Pennsylvania a royal colony, took a moderate position which did not satisfy more radical elements in the colony. The resulting rivalry, which to a limited extent was along class lines, saw the eventual triumph of the radicals in 1776.

Like the other neo-Whig studies, these works shift attention away from broad determinants to immediate contingencies in the period after 1760. They also emphasize the absence of serious social or class conflict, the relative harmony with Britain before 1763, and, with the exception of Abbot's study, which did not deal with the voting problem, the existence of a wide franchise. They all agree that the Revolution was a political and defensive movement to preserve rights and liberties under attack from Britain's new colonial policy. Implicitly, then, these works seriously undermine both the imperial and Progressive interpretations.

Robert E. Brown is in essential agreement with these works in his provocative *Middle-Class Democracy and the Revolution in Massachusetts, 1691–1780* (Ithaca, N.Y., 1955), but he seeks the origins of the Revolution much earlier in the colonial period, and his assault upon older interpretations is much more direct and sweeping. His meticulous investigations show that almost all adult males in Massachusetts could meet the property qualifications for voting and that representation was reasonably equitable. There was, therefore, no sizable class or section of underprivileged for which the Revolution provided an opportunity to achieve more political democracy. Massachusetts was already a middle-class democracy. The crown's attempt to restrain this democracy had produced three-quarters of a century of "perpetual discordance" before 1763, and the increase in the tempo of these attempts after that date drove the colony to revolt. Thus, Brown argues, the Revolution, in Massachusetts at least, was a war to preserve democracy and the existing social order, not a movement to gain democracy, as the socioeconomic historians have contended, or an unjustified reaction to measures conceived for the good of the empire, as the imperialists have argued.

Critics have objected that Brown's definition of democracy is too narrow, but it seems to this writer that the difference between his and other recent interpretations is largely semantic. Substitute home rule or colonial rights and privileges for democracy, and the difference disappears. A more important difference arises over the seriousness of pre-1763 discord. Brown, unlike other recent writers, implies—and on this point he is unconvincing—that Massachusetts was unhappy with the imperial system as it existed before 1763 and that there was more continuity than change in post-1763 British policy as it affected that colony.

These neo-Whig works constitute a serious indictment of British policymakers in the years after the Seven Years' War. If their measures were wise and just in terms of the whole empire, they certainly failed to persuade the American colonists of that fact. How this breakdown in understanding could have occurred in a nation celebrated for its political genius has been explained in part by another school of writers who since World War II have been working out the implications of Sir Lewis Namier's earlier studies of British politics during the opening years of the reign of George III.[23] The late Richard Pares in *King George III and the Politicians* (Oxford, 1953) offered a brilliant general discussion of politics during the reign in the light of Namier's work; John Brooke in *The Chatham Administration, 1766–1768* (London, 1956), presented a detailed narrative of the ill-fated Chatham government, the first volume in a projected series under the general heading *England in the Age of the American Revolution*; and the late Eric Robson, in *The American Revolution* (London, 1955), a collection of interpretive essays, considered the Revolution in Namierist terms.[24]

A long line of earlier historians from Horace Walpole to Sir George Trevelyan had charged George III with attempting to destroy the influence of the Whig oligarchy and reestablish the supremacy of the crown over Parliament. The king's American program was part of the same pattern: the Whigs and Americans were aligned against a common en-

---

[23] Sir Lewis B. Namier, *Structure of Politics at the Accession of George III*, 2 vols. (London, 1929), and *England in the Age of the American Revolution* (London, 1930).

[24] In addition to these works, an American disciple of Namier, Charles R. Ritcheson, has published *British Politics and the American Revolution* (Norman, Okla., 1954), an interesting narrative of the course of British politics from 1763 to 1783. Ritcheson is primarily interested in measuring the impact of the Revolution on British politics. His view of the Revolution adheres closely to that of the imperialist school. A recent work, J. Steven Watson, *The Reign of George III, 1760–1815* (Oxford, 1960), incorporates most of the findings of the Namier school but adds little to what earlier writers have said about the coming of the Revolution. A new synthetic study of the Revolution, Esmond Wright, *Fabric of Freedom, 1763–1800* (New York, 1961), 22–34, 259–63, contains an excellent summary of the conclusions of this school.

emy in a struggle against tyranny. Had the Whig party been in power, the argument ran, it would have pursued a more conciliatory policy and prevented the Revolution.[25]

Namier and his followers have overturned this interpretation. They have demonstrated that there were no parties in the modern sense, only loosely organized factions and family groups; that what mattered in politics was not attachment to principle but the struggle for office; that political issues revolved about local rather than national or imperial considerations; that all groups, as well as the king, accepted the traditional Whig principles that had evolved out of the Revolutionary Settlement; and that George III did not have to subvert the constitution to gain control over Parliament because, as in the case of his grandfather, George II, his power to choose his own ministers and his control over patronage assured him of considerable influence in determining Parliament's decisions.

What these discoveries mean in terms of the Revolution, though no one has worked them out in detail, is fairly clear. They reinforce the views of the neo-Whigs on the shortsightedness and ineptness of British policy. If British political leaders were so deeply involved in local matters, it is not difficult to see why they were unable to take a broader view in dealing with the colonies. As Robson has pointed out, it was not tyranny but weakness that caused metropolitan authorities to act as they did. Moreover, though the Namierists absolve George III of tyrannical designs, they do not lessen his responsibility. On the contrary, if the choice of ministers rested with the king, he must bear the ultimate responsibility for their decisions. Finally, if George III was a good Whig committed to the supreme authority of Parliament, then it becomes clear why he was willing to go to such lengths to defend Parliament's authority in the colonies and why he was unable to stand apart from Parliament as a royal symbol of imperial union as the colonies desired.[26]

But neither the Namierists nor the neo-Whigs have explained satisfactorily how Britain and America arrived at the position they did after 1763. Granted that the colonies were reasonably content with the old colonial system until the last years of the Seven Years' War and that only

---

[25] An excellent study of the changing interpretations of the opening years of the reign of George III that is critical of Namierist techniques is Herbert Butterfield, *George III and the Historians* (London, 1957).

[26] A suggestive discussion of the implications of the discoveries of the Namier school for the Revolution is Edmund S. Morgan, "The American Revolution: Revisions in Need of Revising," *William and Mary Quarterly*, 3d ser., 14 (1957): 3–15.

subsequent policies drove them to rebellion, it is still necessary to have some knowledge of earlier developments to understand fully why British politicians adopted the measures they did between 1763 and 1776 and why the colonists resisted.

The imperial historians have been particularly interested in these problems,[27] and a few recent scholars have followed their lead. Two works, Max Savelle's *Seeds of Liberty* (New York, 1948) and Clinton Rossiter's *Seedtime of the Republic* (New York, 1953), have sought to trace the rise of American attitudes and traditions to discover the "origin of the American way of life," the "first pattern of American culture." Both books reflect the current preoccupation with the history of ideas, and both lend support to the neo-Whig view. Savelle explores developments in most aspects of colonial culture. The eighteenth century saw the gradual emergence of common attitudes, ideals, and traditions, the most important of which was freedom. By 1750, Savelle argues, the Americans were, culturally, one people with a latent American loyalty and American nationalism waiting to be nourished by the British challenge after 1763. These findings make it easier to answer one of the most puzzling questions growing out the Revolution: how thirteen diverse and quarreling colonies could offer united resistance to the mother country. Rossiter is concerned largely with the rise of liberty in the colonies and the rationale or political ideas developed to support it. He finds that the arguments put forth by Americans during the Revolutionary crisis were part of a philosophy of "ethical, ordered liberty" that had grown out of a century and a half of colonial experience. Thus, British measures after 1763 struck at the heart of a mature and well-developed political faith, a fact that helps explain the intensity of American resistance.

More recently, another American scholar, Dora Mae Clark, has thrown new light upon changing responsibilities within the metropolitan administration in the eighteenth century and their effect upon British policy after 1763. In *The Rise of the British Treasury: Colonial Administration in the Eighteenth Century* (New Haven, 1960), she argues that the increasing importance of finance had by the 1760s given the dominant voice in colonial affairs to the Treasury, which was responsible for devising most of the policies that precipitated the Revolution. By showing the increasing influence of the Treasury, with its preoccupation with fiscal affairs, she puts the Grenville program in clearer perspective than

---

[27] Particularly valuable are Charles M. Andrews, *Colonial Background of the American Revolution*, and Leonard W. Labaree, *Royal Government in America: A Study of the British Colonial System before 1783* (New Haven, 1930).

ever before and reinforces the neo-Whig interpretation. It was simply a logical continuation of earlier trends, although Americans, accustomed to the lenient policies of Walpole and the Pelhams and unaware of the Treasury's rising power, looked upon it as a radical departure from precedent. The net effect of her work is to lessen the responsibility of the first minister, secretary of state, and Board of Trade in making policy and to focus attention upon less prominent officials in the Treasury, such as Charles Jenkinson, Thomas Whateley, and John Robinson. Moreover, her findings make it easier to understand why metropolitan authorities were willing to go to such lengths in their quest for revenue.

The postwar studies have added greatly to our knowledge of the causes of the American Revolution; equally important, they have suggested still other areas of fruitful research. The Morgans' study of the Stamp Act crisis indicates that it might be worthwhile to take a new look at the American position during the second great crisis, from 1773 to 1776. The works of Dickerson, Knollenberg, Ubbelohde, and Alden demonstrate the need for fresh and intensive studies of still other issues: the army, paper currency, assembly rights, and perhaps even western lands.[28] The accounts of developments in specific colonies have borne sufficient fruit to justify similar studies for Virginia, New York, South Carolina, North Carolina, and New Hampshire. Moreover, the works of the Namier school have called attention to the desirability of examining anew the processes by which policy was formed in England with specific reference to measures Americans found grievous. If the great politicians were too submerged in parochial affairs to deal effectively with colonial

---

[28] Although the subject requires fuller treatment, Richard M. Jellison and I have treated the currency issue in "The Currency Act of 1764 in Imperial-Colonial Relations, 1764–1776," *William and Mary Quarterly*, 3d ser., 18 (1961): 485–518. We found that the Currency Act, which applied to all colonies from New York south to Georgia, was an important grievance in each of those colonies except Delaware. The failure of colonial efforts to obtain repeal and the rigid interpretation by crown authorities of what constituted legal tender currency through the 1760s and early 1770s helped to persuade Americans that British officials did not understand American problems, although Parliament's belated amendment of the act to permit emissions that were legal tender in payment of colonial taxes for New York only in 1770 and then for the other colonies in 1773 helped to mitigate colonial discontent and might have resulted in a satisfactory solution to the currency problem had not the war intervened. Jack M. Sosin, *Whitehall and the Wilderness: The Middle West in British Colonial Policy, 1760–1775* (Lincoln, Nebr., 1961), re-examines the western lands question from the imperial point of view. Although Sosin presents a strong case for British western policy, he is only incidentally concerned with the extent and nature of colonial discontent with that policy. Another study will be necessary before we fully understand the American position.

problems, who did deal with them? Whence the movement for imperial reform derived and whence it drew its strength are intriguing questions that have never been satisfactorily answered. Clark's findings suggest that the bureaucracy had a greater hand in shaping policy than we have previously suspected, and this suggestion would seem to be worth pursuing. Finally, the works of Rossiter and Savelle describe the nature and substance of American political and cultural attitudes on the eve of the Revolution; but, despite several excellent studies of the development of the lower house in the colonies, we still do not know exactly what their constitutional position was in 1763. Some answer to this question is essential to any clear understanding of what it was that Americans were defending over the next two decades.

Though they may disagree on specific questions, there is a remarkable consensus among the new school about the nature and process of the American Revolution. The colonists were generally happy with things as they were in 1760, before metropolitan authorities through short-sighted and mistaken calculations adopted stricter policies that fundamentally challenged American rights and property. The intensity of American protests varied with the seriousness of the threat, but the American position on most questions, including taxation, was consistent throughout the debate, an indication of American devotion to principle. Thus, the Revolution was not the inevitable or necessarily logical result of long-range forces at work since the founding of the colonies but a conservative and defensive movement against recent provocations by the mother country. Moreover, the absence of serious dissatisfaction over the old mercantile system or any sizable amount of lower-class discontent with the existing political system in the colonies means that the Revolution was more political, legalistic, and constitutional than social or economic. The issue then, according to the neo-Whigs, was no more and no less than separation from Britain and the preservation of American liberty.

This view is reflected in most of the newer synthetic and interpretive works on the American Revolution. John R. Alden in *The American Revolution, 1775—1783* (New York, 1954), writes that the Revolution is "to be explained by the mistakes of the British government in dealing with the American colonies after 1763,"[29] and Richard Morris in *The American Revolution: A Short History* (Princeton, N. J., 1955) asserts that it "was a political revolution rather than an overturn of the social order." In

---

[29] The same view is implicit in Alden's *The South in the Revolution, 1763—1789* (Baton Rouge, La., 1957).

The Genius of American Politics (Chicago, 1953), Daniel Boorstin sees the Revolution as "a victory of constitutionalism" and "an affirmation of the tradition of British institutions," a view shared by Louis Hartz when he emphasizes the Revolution's "quality of traditionalism" in *The Liberal Tradition in America* (New York, 1955). The best single comprehensive account, Edmund S. Morgan, *The Birth of the Republic, 1763–1789* (Chicago, 1956), though brief, incorporates most of the new findings and adds still another dimension, arguing that the essence of the Revolutionary experience was the search for the principles first to defend American constitutional rights and then to build a new nation.[30]

Defenders of older interpretations and other commentators have been reluctant to accept the neo-Whig view. They have charged that it has contemporary political overtones, reflecting the conservative mood of the 1950s. The assumption is that one's findings are strongly influenced by environmental factors and that the newer interpretation is no better or worse than older ones. There is no question that social determinants do affect the works of historians, but not necessarily in a way to make them all equally distorted reflections of that elusive, though theoretically attainable goal, objective, historical truth.

It can be argued, in fact, that environmental conditions in the post–World War II years have made possible an increasing detachment among historians of the Revolution. The absence of serious internal economic problems and the general leveling of society has enabled them to avoid that central preoccupation with economic questions that led many scholars of the Progressive school to wrench Revolutionary events out of context by superimposing some of the a priori assumptions and tenets of economic determinism. Similarly, the basic fact and acceptance of Anglo-American cooperation has made it unnecessary for them to fall into the temptation—to which so many of the imperialist historians succumbed—of interpreting the Revolution in such a way as to promote Anglo-American accord.

Moreover, it seems to this reviewer that the quality of any study rises with the amount of evidence it subsumes and the validity of the assumptions on which it is based. Certainly, few previous studies have been the products of such intensive research as have the basic monographs of the

---

[30] The one exception to this trend is Esmond Wright's *Fabric of Freedom.* Wright strikes a middle road between various schools of interpretation, although he relies heavily on the works of the neo-Whigs and would seem to agree with them on the basic nature of the Revolution, suggesting that it was at least in part the result of "a mounting series of irritations."

neo-Whigs, and their assumptions—that individual actions and immediate issues are more important than underlying determinants in explaining particular events, and that in any case single factors rarely suffice to explain problems of causation and motivation—would seem to be sound and to reflect a growing sophistication in historical studies.

Nor would the identification of the neo-Whig school with current political trends seem to be justified. Some commentators have associated a few of the writers, in particular Boorstin, Hartz, and Rossiter, with the new conservatives,[31] who may well find the neo-Whig interpretation of the Revolution congenial. But the principal neo-Whig writings by the Morgans, Dickerson, Knollenberg, Ubbelohde, and others are all decidedly apolitical.

The charge has also been made that the neo-Whigs represent a return to Bancroft. To be sure, their interpretation is essentially a moderate version of the nineteenth-century Whig view as propounded by Bancroft and others. But the differences are more important than the similarities. The neo-Whigs do not have the fiery nationalism, ardent patriotism, moral fervor, or belief in the divine guidance of American development that characterized the old Whigs. They have not been satisfied with the simplistic explanation that the Revolution was the product of British tyranny. On the contrary, their accomplishment has been to produce a greater awareness of complexities, a more precise formulation of issues, and a deeper understanding of the pattern, process, and causes of the American Revolution.

Written in the summer of 1961 in Cleveland, Ohio, while I was at Western Reserve University, this chapter, my first venture in extended historical criticism and synthesis, developed out of an invitation from William Baskerville Hamilton, editor of the *South Atlantic Quarterly*, to review two of the principal books it considers, one by Bernhard Knollenberg and the other by Carl Ubbelohde. Previously reprinted in The Bobbs-Merrell Reprint Series in American History, no. H-348 (Indianapolis, 1967), it is here reprinted with permission and minor verbal changes and corrections from the *South Atlantic Quarterly* 61 (1962): 235–59, Copyright Duke University Press, 1962.

[31] See William J. Newman, *The Futilitarian Society* (New York, 1961), 300–333, and M. Morton Auerbach, *The Conservative Illusion* (New York, 1959), 128, 140, 159–60, 198–99, 245–46, 279.

—Eighteen—

The Plunge of Lemmings:
A Consideration of Recent Writings on British Politics and the American Revolution

T HE STORY of how Sir Lewis Namier as a young man just graduated from Balliol College, Oxford, started to work on the imperial problem during the American Revolution and wound up studying the "British 'political nation' during the American Revolution" is familiar to all students of Anglo-American history in the eighteenth century. So great was the magnitude of his contribution to the latter subject that one can scarcely regret his abandonment of the former. Because Namier's conclusions about the British political nation do have such important implications for any understanding of the imperial problem, however, it is regrettable that neither Namier nor any of his many students and intellectual heirs have ever made any comprehensive or systematic attempt to tell us what these implications are. They have been at some pains to describe the impact of the American Revolution upon British politics, but, except for Namier's own brief preliminary observations in *England in the Age of the American Revolution*,[1] they have not been explicitly concerned with analyzing the influence of British politics upon the American Revolution. The appearance over the last five years of a number of new studies of British politics during the 1760s and 1770s serves both to remind us of the need for and to make possible the formulation of some tentative suggestions about where such an analysis may lead.

---

[1] Lewis Namier, *England in the Age of the American Revolution* (London, 1930).

[334]

Originally set forth in his two major books[2] and a number of related essays and lectures[3] and recently recapitulated, extended, and refined by John Brooke in the introductory survey to his and Namier's collaborative *History of Parliament: The House of Commons, 1754–1790*,[4] Namier's central conclusions about the nature of British politics during the early years of the reign of George III are so well known that they may be briefly summarized here. They are (1) that the "political nation"—the people who took some active role in politics—was largely restricted to a narrow elite consisting mainly of the landed nobility, the rural gentry, and the wealthier bourgeoisie; (2) that the House of Commons, which by twentieth-century criteria appears grossly unrepresentative, was, in fact, remarkably representative—a "marvellous microcosmos"—of the political nation that because of its commitment to trade and promoting the national wealth usually acted in the interests of the nation as a whole; (3) that there were no parties in the modern sense, only loosely organized factions and family groups; (4) that these factions together constituted only one of three broad divisions in the House and no one faction was large enough to govern without major support from both of the other two broad categories, the "permanent *ins*," the placemen and other followers of the court and administration, and the "permanent *outs*," the independent country gentlemen; (5) that all of the groups as well as the king accepted the traditional Whig principles that had evolved out of the Revolutionary Settlement; (6) that at least in part because of this consensus, what mattered most in politics was not ideology or attachment to principle but the struggle for office, power, and advantage among the leading factions; (7) that because of the tremendous expense of elections, few were contested and the participation and influence of the electorate were extraordinarily limited; (8) that political issues both in and out of Parliament usually revolved around local rather than national or imperial considerations; and (9) that the king was still an extremely important factor in politics and that George III did not

---

[2] Lewis Namier, *The Structure of Politics at the Accession of George III*, 2 vols. (London, 1929), and *England in the Age of the American Revolution*.

[3] Conveniently collected together in Lewis Namier, *Crossroads of Power: Essays on Eighteenth-Century England* (London, 1962).

[4] Lewis Namier and John Brooke, *The History of Parliament: The House of Commons, 1754–1790*, 3 vols. (New York, 1964). The Introduction fills about 40 percent of the first volume.

have to subvert the constitution in order to free the crown from the fetters of a ministry imposed upon him by a majority in Parliament or to gain more influence for the crown in legislation; his power to choose his own ministers was secure and his prestige and control of patronage assured him a major voice in all executive decisions as well as in the deliberations of Parliament.[5]

Initially, Namier's reading of British politics had little impact upon the interpretation of the American Revolution, and it was not until the 1950s that scholars gradually became aware of the importance of his contribution to the understanding of the Revolution. By shattering the traditional nineteenth-century Whig portrait of the opening years of the reign of George III as a bitter constitutional struggle between a malevolent king bent upon increasing the influence of the crown and a party of patriotic Whigs determined to preserve the free constitution they had carefully developed since the Glorious Revolution, Namier helped to demolish the legend—already largely discredited by the imperial historians in the United States—of George III as a tyrant king intent upon enslaving the colonies. Second, by showing the parochial nature of British politics and the preoccupation of the key British politicians with the struggle for office, Namier also helped to make clear why they did not take a broader view in dealing with the imperial problem between 1763 and 1783. Finally, by demonstrating that George III was a good Whig committed to the supremacy of Parliament in both the realm and the empire, Namier helped to explain why he was willing to go to such lengths to defend Parliament's authority over the colonies and why he was unable to stand apart from Parliament as a royal symbol of imperial union as the colonies desired.[6]

Yet the recognition of these specific contributions and their incorpora-

---

[5] Recent summaries and analyses of Namier's conclusions may be found in John Owen, "The Namier Way," *New Statesman and Nation,* Jan. 26, 1962, 130–31; J. L. Talmon, "The Ordeal of Sir Lewis Namier: The Man, the Historian, the Jew," *Commentary* 33 (1962): 237–46; Henry R. Winkler, "Sir Lewis Namier," *Journal of Modern History* 35 (1963): 1–19; and John Brooke, "Namier and Namierism," *History and Theory* 3 (1964): 331–47. Richard Pares, *King George III and the Politicians* (Oxford, 1953), considers Namier's conclusions as they apply to the whole reign and suggests some important qualifications.

[6] Eric Robson, *The American Revolution, 1763–1783* (London, 1955); Edmund S. Morgan, "The American Revolution: Revisions in Need of Revising," *William and Mary Quarterly,* 3d ser., 14 (1957): 3–15; Esmond Wright, *Fabric of Freedom, 1763–1800* (New York, 1961); and Jack P. Greene, "The Flight from Determinism: A Review of Recent Literature on the Coming of the American Revolution," *South Atlantic Quarterly* 61

tion into the corpus of literature on the Revolution have been accompanied by a marked failure to perceive clearly the full implications of Namier's findings for the study of the Revolution, with the result that the most crucial question raised by Namier relative to the Revolution has been largely ignored. That question is whether, given the structure of British politics as described by Namier, there were any courses of action open to the British government alternative to those it actually pursued between 1763 and 1783, or, to put the question in another way, whether it was possible for the British to have adopted a posture and measures that would have been sufficiently palatable to the Americans to have prevented the Revolution. Namier himself clearly thought not. "In 1760," he wrote in his brief section on "The Imperial Problem" in *England in the Age of the American Revolution,* "Great Britain had not reached a stage at which it would have been possible to remodel the Empire as a federation of self-governing States under a Crown detached from the actual government of any of its component parts." Such an arrangement, which was actually proposed by the Americans in several forms at various points between 1765 and 1775 and has subsequently been considered a viable alternative by scholars, was impossible, Namier observed, because "royalty . . . was still an active factor in British politics, and to eighteenth-century Englishmen any exercise of its attributes apart from the British Parliament would have seemed a dangerous and unconstitutional reversion to 'prerogative.'" "This junction between King and Parliament," Namier declared, "was by itself bound to carry the supremacy of the British Parliament into the Colonies; and the very fact that George III so thoroughly and loyally stood by the constitutional principles of the time rendered a conflict inevitable."[7]

For purposes of the discussion that follows, it is important to note that Namier's statement contains three interdependent hypotheses. The first is that the devotion of both the king and Parliament to the principle of parliamentary supremacy was *bound* to lead to parliamentary intervention in American affairs in the 1760s. This hypothesis seems to depend in part upon a prior one set forth in an earlier paragraph: that there was widespread sentiment in Britain after the Seven Years' War that "the time had come for settling [the British Empire in America] . . .

(1962): 235–59 [chap. 17 above] have been most implicitly concerned with spelling out the implications of Namier's work for the understanding of the Revolution.

[7] The quotations are from Namier, *England in the Age of the American Revolution,* 2d ed. (London, 1961), 37. All subsequent quotations from this work are from this edition.

on a more regular basis." It does not, of course, imply that Parliament's passage of the Stamp Act or Townshend Acts or any other specific measure Americans found objectionable was inevitable, but only that parliamentary intervention in some form was inevitable. The second hypothesis is that once the Americans had challenged any aspect of Parliament's authority over the colonies, the king and Parliament were *bound* to defend that authority and to regard American opposition as "dangerous and unconstitutional." The third hypothesis, which he reiterated again in his Academy of Arts lecture in 1953, is that the "terms in which the overwhelming majority of the politically minded public . . . considered" the imperial problem at the time made a "true settlement" of it, that is, a solution along the lines advocated by the Americans, absolutely impossible.[8] If each of these hypotheses is true, only one conclusion can follow: the structure of British politics during the earlier years of the reign of George III made the American Revolution inevitable. The demise of the First British Empire was the necessary result of its own structural failure.

Why this proposition has never been seriously entertained, much less directly engaged, can be surmised.[9] For one thing, it was made in brief and general terms without any effort to explain just what it was about the imperial structure that made it susceptible to failure. For another, neither Namier nor any subsequent scholar ever attempted any sustained or systematic demonstration of its plausibility. For still another, the growing realization of the impossibility of establishing the inevitability of any historical event has made historians understandably wary of explanations that seemed to place major limitations upon man's freedom of action, and this view has been strongly reinforced since 1945 by the Bomb and the recognition that the very existence of man may depend upon his ability to manipulate his environment and events. Finally, Namier's argument seems on the face of it to run counter to one of the strongest tendencies in modern Revolutionary scholarship.

Reacting strongly against the more mechanistic explanations of the nineteenth-century nationalists who saw the Revolution as decreed by God and the imperial historians who viewed it as the necessary result of social divergence, most recent scholars have emphasized the alternatives

---

[8] The quotations are from ibid., 36–37, and Namier, *Crossroads of Power*, 124–25.

[9] Robson, *American Revolution*, 16–20; Charles R. Ritcheson, *British Politics and the American Revolution* (Norman, Okla., 1954); and J. Steven Watson, *The Reign of George III, 1760–1815* (Oxford, 1960), 173–206, all employ portions of Namier's argument without following it to its logical conclusion.

available to metropolitan officials at each stage of the Revolutionary conflict. The predominant view has been, as Edmund S. Morgan insisted in 1957, that the "loss [of the colonies] was not inevitable" and that "all the objectives of the Americans before 1776 could have been attained within the empire, and would have cost the mother country little or nothing."[10] The implication is that the Revolution was caused not by *structural* but by *human* failure, not by the absence of viable alternatives (i.e., alternatives that might have been acceptable in terms of the structure of the situation) but by the failure of the men in charge in Britain to recognize the desirability of these alternatives and to attempt to implement them.

For whatever reasons, Namier's argument has never been properly evaluated, and we still do not know after almost forty years to what extent it may or may not be true, to what degree the human failure emphasized by Morgan and other recent scholars may have been the result of the structural failure referred to by Namier. Because all of the new works under consideration confront this question at least indirectly, such an evaluation may now be attempted here.

As a result of the detailed study of *The Chatham Administration, 1766–1768*, by John Brooke,[11] as well as the more general treatments by Charles Ritcheson,[12] Richard Pares,[13] and J. Steven Watson,[14] it has been firmly established for well over a decade that the British political nation was not deeply divided over the American question at any point before the outbreak of war in 1775. The crisis of 1765–66 over the Stamp Act did indeed produce a division of opinion among leading political groups. As Richard Pares has phrased it, the followers of George Grenville—and, one might add, those of the duke of Bedford and Lord Bute—"thought it lawful and expedient to tax the colonies," the old Whigs around Lord Rockingham "thought it lawful but not expedient," and the small knot of supporters of William Pitt, soon to be made Lord Chatham, "thought

---

[10] Morgan, "The American Revolution: Revisions in Need of Revising," 12–13. These comments were made in direct reference to Namier's work.

[11] John Brooke, *The Chatham Administration, 1766–1768* (London, 1956).

[12] Ritcheson, *British Politics and the American Revolution.*

[13] Pares, *King George III and the Politicians.*

[14] Watson, *Reign of George III*, 173–206.

it neither lawful nor expedient," though they did not, of course, question Parliament's general legislative power over the colonies.

However, the consensus seems to be that the respective position of each group, with the possible exception of the Chathamites, was determined not by considerations of policy or sincere convictions about the best way to handle the American question but by the exigencies of politics and the necessity of defending one's behavior in and out of office against the attacks of one's rivals. As Richard Pares has written, men took positions without usually thinking them "out for the future" and then "defended very tenaciously the commitments, even the mistakes, of the past." Thus, Grenville "blundered into the Stamp Act, just as the Rockinghams . . . stumbled upon its repeal. But once the colours were nailed to the mast, there was no taking them down."[15] For the next decade each group adhered rigidly to the position it had taken in 1765–66. Clearly, as John Brooke remarked, the American question, like all other major issues before Parliament in the 1760s and 1770s, seemed to be "subordinate to party conflict."[16]

What may be even more significant than the extent to which these disagreements over a question of such extraordinary import were determined by the struggle for office is that the range of disagreement was so narrow. Except for the Chathamites, the disagreement was not substantive but tactical. The issue was not whether Parliament had the right to tax the colonies but whether it was expedient for Parliament to exercise that right, and even the Chathamites, while denying Parliament's authority to tax the colonies, agreed with every other group "that Great Britain held full sovereignty in America" and that the rightful exercise of that sovereignty resided in Parliament. Of course, in 1765–66 it was not even clear to the Americans that the ultimate issue in dispute was "not taxation, but sovereignty," but, given the consensus among leading politicians of all denominations that Parliament had authority to legislate for the colonies, any subsequent attempt by the Americans to place limitations upon or in any way to deny that authority was bound to be met by almost universal resistance from British politicians and to persuade them that British sovereignty over the colonies could not be maintained without the acknowledgment of Parliament's legislative authority by the colonists.

The existence of so wide a consensus upon such a fundamental point—

---

[15] Pares, *King George III and the Politicians*, 90–91.

[16] Brooke, *Chatham Administration*, xiv.

the omnipresent conviction following the Stamp Act crisis that, in case of any further opposition to parliamentary authority in the colonies, "the sovereignty of this country," as Bedford declared in the summer of 1767, "shou'd be asserted and established with firmness and temper"—meant that the series of individual blunders by leading political figures over the next decade was both less culpable and more disastrous than historians have usually recognized.[17] They were less culpable both because they proceeded from assumptions that were shared by virtually every man within the political community who had access to power and, to the limited extent that the American question impinged upon public consciousness, by the overwhelming majority of the electorate,[18] and because they were, in almost every instance, responses to American challenges to the validity of those assumptions and to widespread demands within the British political community that those challenges be met.

Thus, the Townshend Acts of 1767 were not simply the irresponsible brainchild of Charles Townshend but a direct response to parliamentary resentment of a number of instances of what appeared to be American ingratitude following the repeal of the Stamp Act. Other men might have adopted other measures, measures even that would have been ostensibly less objectionable to the Americans. Given the mood of the political community in Britain, however, any measures adopted at that moment would have had to carry within them at least an implicit assertion of parliamentary supremacy over the colonies—an assertion that Americans would ultimately decide had to be denied at all costs. Individuals such as Townshend or Hillsborough or North blundered in their colonial measures and were, therefore, responsible as individuals for helping to alienate the colonies, but because their behavior proceeded upon assumptions held by the entire community, their failures were in a larger and more important sense also the failures of the community at large.

At the same time, however, it is clear in retrospect that the very universality of those assumptions made the mistakes of individual ministers all the more disastrous. The structure within which they had to operate was clearly so rigid as to preclude any possibility of major political innovation, and each mistake, each new affront to the Americans, only resulted in a further escalation of the controversy and the development of a situation in which such innovation would be required to achieve a

---

[17] Ibid., quotations from 95, 99, 208.

[18] Namier and Brooke, *House of Commons* 1:67–80, discuss the relationship of the American question to the only two elections during this period, those of 1768 and 1774.

satisfactory resolution of the dispute, a situation that was not, as John Brooke has remarked, *"almost"* but *entirely* "beyond the powers of statesmanship to handle."[19]

The crucially limiting effects of this structural rigidity upon the British response to events in the colonies from the Boston Tea Party in December 1773 to the outbreak of the War for Independence in April 1775, may be surmised from Bernard Donoughue's important recent book on that subject.[20] The strength and stability of the North ministry, the weakness of the opposition, the disenchantment of many of the traditional friends of the colonies with the American cause, and the anger of many segments of the political community over other recent events in Massachusetts Bay—especially the publication of the Hutchinson letters—combined to determine the nature of that response. But the most important factor in persuading British politicians that the Boston Tea Party required strong punitive measures was, Donoughue finds, the almost universal conviction among them that the empire could be preserved only if Americans accepted the principle of complete subordination to Parliament and that such subordination could be achieved only by dealing harshly with the Bay Colony. The result was the adoption of the Coercive Acts in the winter and spring of 1774.

Once a policy of coercion had been adopted, Donoughue emphasizes, nothing short of a major reversal in the trend of thought and events could have altered the "inevitable slide into war." Despite the obvious failure of the coercive program in America, however, no such reversal occurred. The opposition made almost no attempt to capitalize on the failure of the government's program in the elections held in the fall of 1774. Over the next few months, Dartmouth in the cabinet, Chatham in the Lords, and Burke in the Commons made proposals for conciliation, but those proposals never received any serious consideration, despite the fact that they all insisted upon maintaining Parliament's general sovereignty over the colonies, at least in principle. Increasingly, the prevailing sentiment was to meet colonial resistance with military force. During the autumn of 1774 George III—to whom Donoughue assigns a major role in pushing for ever stronger measures—and every minister except Dartmouth advocated such a step. In early 1775 the ministry adopted a policy of military reinforcement and blockade in combination with North's extremely limited proposals for conciliation and advised General

---

[19] Brooke, *Chatham Administration*, 26–27.

[20] Bernard Donoughue, *British Politics and the American Revolution: The Path to War, 1773–75* (New York, 1964).

Thomas Gage in Boston to be ready to use force. By mid-April, when war actually broke out at Lexington and Concord, the "changing emphasis in British policy, away from expressing Parliamentary sovereignty through legislation, towards enforcing colonial subordination by military repression, was . . . almost complete."

This change in emphasis, Donoughue points out, was the natural result of the "very logic and consistency with which the British government applied its premises about the colonial situation." The implication here is that it was not the absence of other alternatives—both the First and Second Continental Congresses had proposed one—and not just the events themselves that made the situation irretrievable and limited the range of choices so disastrously, but traditional preoccupations about what colonies were and what their relationship to Britain and Parliament ought to be. That no one either in office or in opposition—not Dartmouth, not Chatham, not Burke—was able to break out of these preconceptions, to escape from the oppressive weight of dominant ideas and habits of thinking and to grapple with the possibility that, as Americans were insisting, the empire might be preserved without totally subordinating the colonies to Parliament is extremely significant. It is significant because it indicates not, as Donoughue suggests, that the men in power lacked vision, magnanimity, and statesmanship but that the political system itself lacked the capacity for adjustment that would have permitted these men to make the kinds of constitutional innovations the Americans were calling for.

Two recent studies of the nature of political opposition during the era of the American Revolution give added weight to this conclusion. The first, *His Majesty's Opposition, 1714–1830*, by Archibald S. Foord,[21] traces the growth of the concept and institution of constitutional opposition under the first four Georges. Until well after the Revolution, prevailing attitudes toward opposition tended strongly to reinforce the existing system. Although the settlement of the great religious controversies of the seventeenth century, the rejection of divine right theory after 1688, and the solution of the dynastic problem after 1714 provided conditions under which an institutionalized opposition did in fact gradually begin to develop, not until the end of the century and later did opposition cease to be "abhorred . . . in theory" by all politicians, even those actually in

---

[21] Archibald S. Foord, *His Majesty's Opposition, 1714–1830* (New York, 1964), xi, 494.

opposition. "The prevalent ideal," Foord points out, "called for national unanimity beneath the sovereign, not party rivalry among his subjects," and opposition was "justified only by maladministration which could not otherwise be corrected."

By definition, therefore, there could be no opposition to the system per se but only to degenerative and corrupt tendencies within it. Thus, the aim of all opposition from Bolingbroke and Carteret in the 1730s and 1740s to Chatham, Rockingham, and Burke in the 1760s and 1770s was never to change the constitution but merely to preserve it from the misguided attempts of wicked ministers to use the resources of the court to overturn it by corrupting Parliament.

In this situation the differences separating political groups did not run very deep, and where any individual stood on a given question "depended much more upon whether he was in or out of office than upon what label was attached to him." Old labels—Whig and Tory, court and country—were still used, and, though they did not designate cohesive party groupings, they did stand for certain well-understood principles. Thus, the Tories continued up through the 1770s to retain a special reverence for monarchy, to regard themselves as the prime "defenders of the Church and the landed interest," and, probably because they were rarely in office, to vote for place bills, reduction of the army, shorter Parliaments, and other measures intended to lessen the power of the ministry and thereby minimize the possibilities of evil ministers' sapping the foundations of the constitution. Similarly, Whigs never lost a chance to claim full credit for the Revolutionary Settlement of 1688–89 and to picture themselves as its rightful guardians. But by the early 1740s, Foord concludes, politicians of all persuasions had come to realize that no great or basic issues were at stake and that "the contest for power was taking place amid agreement on fundamentals." In the 1760s and 1770s this "agreement on fundamentals" necessarily meant that once the Americans had challenged the most important of these fundamentals—the supremacy of the king-in-Parliament over the whole realm—no opposition group would or could fully champion their cause.

A second recent study of the opposition, Harvey C. Mansfield, Jr., *Statesmanship and Party Government,*[22] underlines this point. A brilliant inquiry into the theoretical origins of party government, Mansfield's book analyzes with great thoroughness the writings of the two leading opposition theorists of the eighteenth century, Bolingbroke, whose con-

---

[22] Harvey C. Mansfield, Jr., *Statesmanship and Party Government: A Study of Burke and Bolingbroke* (Chicago, 1965), xii, 281.

demnations of party and exaltation of independent, disinterested, and virtuous patriotism, the author convincingly argues, exercised a powerful and widespread appeal among British political leaders during the 1760s, and Burke, whose *Thoughts on the Causes of the Present Discontents* represents the first important theoretical defense of party. Mansfield's purpose is to illuminate "the arguments for and against party government as they were presented at its origin" and to explain why Burke sought to make party respectable and to substitute party government for the statesmanship recommended by Bolingbroke.

What Mansfield finds, briefly, is that Bolingbroke and his followers opposed party primarily because they were convinced "great" parties would inflame the body politic by disputing over "great" questions involving the very essentials of the existing social and political order, while small parties would pursue the selfish ends of their members to the detriment of the common good. Burke, on the other hand, defended party not just because he wanted to justify the opposition activities of the Rockingham Whigs but because he was genuinely fearful that Bolingbroke's doctrines might, by assigning such a large role to the king in the choice of patriot ministers, lead in time to a major increase in crown power. To preclude a development so dangerous to the "balance of the constitution," Burke advocated the establishment of party government in which parties with well-defined principles and a public record would operate in such a way as to ensure the preservation of the constitution. Parties, according to Burke, would both give party members a mutual interest independent of the court and, because they could function effectively with only honest men of ordinary capacity, lessen the polity's dependence upon statesmen of extraordinary ability who might not always be identifiable or available.

In terms of the present discussion, however, Mansfield's central conclusions are of less interest than his demonstration of the limited objectives of both thinkers. However much Bolingbroke and Burke may have differed in their prescriptions for what they took to be the political ills of Britain, they were in agreement on two basic points: first, that the constitution itself was not defective in any of its essentials, and second, that there had to be in every civil society an absolute and uncontrollable power which in Britain was properly lodged in the king-in-Parliament. Bolingbroke thought it sufficient simply to throw the rascals out and replace them with men of virtue, while Burke, though he suggested limitations on the power of the crown that went "far beyond practice contemporary to him and beyond other constitutional ideas of his time that were not frankly republican," advocated nothing more than the restoration of popular control of the House of Commons and party government, neither of which required "any major change in the constitution."

What these two thinkers had in common, therefore, and what they shared with the very political leaders they were attacking was a reverential regard for the existing constitution as it had evolved out of the Revolutionary Settlement, which by the time Burke wrote was, as Mansfield remarks, so completely successful that it "could be taken for granted" and "no longer had to be defended." The recognition that even the leading opposition theorists were so thoroughly devoted to the existing constitutional structure makes even more clear just what "the true limits of [political] action in the eighteenth century" were, how slight the possibilities were that Americans would receive from any segment of the political establishment anything but resistance to their proposals for constitutional innovations, and how unfruitful it is to condemn British political leaders of that generation "for not doing the impossible."

Just how this widespread devotion to the existing constitutional structure limited the behavior of the British political community during the American crisis is revealed even more strikingly by two other groups of recent books. The first consists of separate studies of four of the principals in that crisis, each representing a somewhat different political and psychological type. The second includes several new investigations of the process of policymaking for the colonies in the 1760s and 1770s.

Easily the most fascinating of the studies of individuals is *Charles Townshend,* begun by Namier and finished by John Brooke after Namier's death.[23] A frankly psychological biography, the volume's underlying argument is that Townshend's erratic behavior in politics was in considerable measure the result of a "mental attitude toward authority" that derived from his "conflicts with his father" during his early life. Along with other early associations, those conflicts, Lady Namier argues in a brief epilogue, damaged Townshend's character "beyond repair" and deprived him of a successful political career by turning him into a restless, irresolute, mercurial, self-destructive, and antisocial being, driven to feeding an insatiable vanity by making one dramatic public show after another and incapable of any genuine friendship or loyalty in public life. Even the one consistent element in his political career—his American program—was, the authors argue, the product of his unhappy relation-

---

[23] Sir Lewis Namier and John Brooke, *Charles Townshend* (New York, 1964).

ship with his father, as Townshend, "the oppressed son, now became the heavy father." His "fatal American measures of 1767" are thus presented as a product of his personal "fantasies," which he was able "to force . . . on to reality" because of the "confusion of the times." Because, in the opinion of the authors, these measures "led inescapably to one of two alternatives—either to the extinction of representative institutions in the colonies, or independence from the mother country," the clear implication is that to a remarkable degree the American Revolution was the result of Charles Townshend's unhappy early years.

The effectiveness of the presentation, due especially to the skillful use of quotation and the responsible character of the authors' judgments, makes this argument plausible. The interpretation is not, however, entirely free from objection. For one thing, the authors' estimate of the importance of the Townshend Acts and consequently of Townshend himself in bringing on the Revolution is greatly exaggerated, as is indicated by the relative harmony that prevailed between most colonies and Britain after Parliament had repealed the bulk of the Townshend duties in 1770. The Townshend Acts certainly helped to poison further the metropolitan-colonial relationship, but they were not *in themselves* fatal to that relationship. More important, however, the authors have not avoided the primary hazard of the psychological biographer, that is, they have not sufficiently taken into account the interpenetration of individual psychology and general culture or, more specifically, the extent to which Townshend's political behavior was conditioned not simply by his personal difficulties but by the interaction between these difficulties and the political culture in which he operated.

On the basis of the evidence presented, for instance, one could argue that Townshend's "weather-cock" behavior was as much the result of his *consistent* devotion to Bolingbrokean ideals of patriotism as of his personal instability. Without in any way suggesting that there may not have been "a vast amount of unconscious self-deception, both in his view of himself and of events in his past," one could make a plausible case for the proposition that each volte-face in his mercurial political career was, at least in his eyes, required by his determination to be, as he declared in November 1762, a "man of business and a man of honour; to be decided by things not men; to have no party; to *follow* no leader, . . . to be governed absolutely by my own judgment[, and] . . . to preserve that independence which I sincerely value above the lustre of popularity or the reward of subservience." These "patriotic" imperatives may have been especially congenial to Townshend because of his own individual psychological makeup. They may have been in large part simply convenient rationalizations for his "self-damaging" movements. Because they were so important in giving coherence to his view of himself, however, no account of his life that does not explicitly take them into consideration will ever be completely satisfactory.

More important, neither the imperatives he professed to follow nor the general pattern of behavior they inspired were peculiar to Townshend. As Mansfield has argued, those imperatives were part of the warp and woof of British political culture in the middle of the eighteenth century, and they were manifest, though in each case in a somewhat different and highly personalized form, in the behavior of individuals as seemingly diverse as George III and Chatham. It is possible, of course, that they and the other men who embraced those imperatives did so because their early lives were similar to that of Townshend, but one cannot dismiss the possibility that the imperatives themselves—for whatever underlying social, historical, or cultural reasons—exercised a powerful determinative influence upon the lives of various public figures of widely varying psychological types.

The dangers of interpreting any individual response that was so similar in character to the reactions of many other contemporaries purely, or even largely, in terms of that individual's psychological makeup may be seen in the authors' explanations for Townshend's American policy. However colored by his early conflict with his father, none of his ideas about the colonies were in any way peculiar to him. The general assumption behind them—that Parliament was supreme throughout the empire—was, as has been so frequently iterated throughout this essay, almost universally held among the dominant elements within the British political nation. What differentiated Townshend from many, but not all, of his contemporaries was his early and repeated insistence upon parliamentary intervention in American affairs. But that insistence can be explained largely by the fact that his long-standing interest in American affairs, an interest which dated back to his five years at the Board of Trade in the early 1750s, made him more aware of and more concerned with colonial problems than most other political leaders. Of his two major proposals, parliamentary taxation was advocated by a great many individuals in the 1760s, and making colonial executives independent of the legislatures was an ancient ideal of colonial officials that was shared by virtually everybody with any experience in colonial administration.

As the most aggressive and publicly confident member of the ministry, Townshend was, of course, primarily responsible for proposing and formulating the revenue act that put those ideals into effect in 1767, but it is especially significant that, as the authors point out, the climate of opinion in Parliament ran strongly in favor of Townshend's program. The refusal of the New York lower house to comply with the Quartering Act, along with the attempt of the Massachusetts house to pardon the Stamp Act rioters of that colony, had convinced even Chatham that "sufficient lenity had been shown to the colonies" and most other M.P.'s that concrete measures had to be undertaken to establish, once and for all, the authority of Parliament over the colonies. That the Townshend Acts were undertaken by a ministry that with the exception of Townshend was notoriously sympathetic to the colonies is only evidence of how widespread that conviction was. The Townshend Acts were thus probably less a case of Townshend's forcing his personal fantasies upon Parliament than of his supplying Parliament with an explicit program through which it could give expression to that conviction, a program tailored to suit the sentiments of the majority of M.P.'s who eagerly accepted it and passed it into law. What is most significant about Townshend's program, therefore, is not that he was able to push it through Parliament but that it encountered no significant opposition within Parliament.

One of the most emphatic exponents of parliamentary intervention in the colonies in 1767 was Lord George Germain, the subject of Gerald Saxon Brown's *The American Secretary*.[24] Not a full biography, this volume focuses primarily upon Germain's tenure as colonial secretary from the time he entered that office in 1775 until the War of Independence broadened out into an international conflict of major proportions in 1778. Presenting a surprisingly strong case for Germain's conduct of the war during that period, the author argues in challenging the traditional view that Germain did a creditable job under the circumstances, though, like just about everyone else in British politics, he failed to appreciate "the force of the Revolution as an idea" and the extent to which it had the support of the people at large.

What is more interesting for the purposes of this essay, however, is the discussion of Germain's attitudes toward the colonies before his appointment as colonial secretary. Like Townshend, Germain was a man of brilliant parts whose political career had been stunted, not, as in Townshend's case, by a long series of peccadilloes but by a major disgrace following his court-martial and conviction in 1760 for disobedience of orders at the Battle of Minden the previous year. Insofar as the author

---

[24]Gerald Saxon Brown, *The American Secretary: The Colonial Policy of Lord George Germain, 1775–1778* (Ann Arbor, Mich., 1963). Another recent, more comprehensive, and less flattering study of Germain is Alan Valentine, *Lord George Germain* (New York, 1962).

could discover, Germain, in contrast to Townshend, had never thought seriously about the colonies or their relationship to Britain before the Stamp Act crisis. In the early 1760s when the various measures of the Grenville program were under discussion, he was still laboring under the political cloud that had enveloped him following his court-martial. In the summer of 1765 he achieved a major goal in his campaign to rehabilitate himself politically with his appointment to office under Rockingham, and he took part in the debate over the repeal of the Stamp Act the following winter.

After listening to arguments from all sides, Germain decided that Grenville was correct in insisting upon enforcement of the act and, deserting the Rockingham government, spoke and voted against repeal. Perhaps in part because he felt it necessary to demonstrate publicly the resolution that had been called into question at Minden, he was little disposed by nature to "compromise and adjustment" and in his subsequent alliance with Grenville thoroughly established his reputation as a "steady advocate of a resolute policy toward America." Following Grenville in calling for measures that would effectively establish parliamentary sovereignty over the colonies at the time of the Townshend Acts and declaring himself strongly in favor of coercion during the crisis that followed the Boston Tea Party, he never doubted that Parliament's authority over the colonies "was complete and absolute" and that any effort to conciliate the colonists would only invite greater resistance to parliamentary authority in America.

To an even greater degree than Townshend, then, Germain seems to have been motivated in his American policy—in "his consistent and uncompromising adherence to a 'plan of coercion'" from the Stamp Act crisis until he resigned as American secretary in 1782—by his devotion to the ideal of parliamentary supremacy over the entire British Empire; and, it is important to add, George III, most of the members of the North administration, and the vast majority in Parliament shared that devotion. Indeed, from 1774 on, they also shared Germain's frequently repeated conviction that only force would produce American acquiescence in parliamentary supremacy. Precisely because he was thus so representative of opinion among the key elements in the political nation, Germain, as Brown suggests, was an especially appropriate choice to take over administration of American affairs once the government had committed itself to the use of force in the fall of 1775.

The American policy of Germain's predecessor as American secretary has been analyzed in detail by B. D. Bargar in *Lord Dartmouth and the*

American Revolution.[25] In terms of personality and approach to politics, no man offered a sharper contrast to Germain. Cautious and conciliatory, Dartmouth had little political ambition and even less taste for public life and took office only because of a deep sense of noblesse oblige and the insistence of family and friends. His position on the American question reflected his personality. Like Germain, he held office under the Rockingham ministry as president of the Board of Trade; unlike Germain, he supported the repeal of the Stamp Act and left office in 1766 with a "reputation as a friend of the colonists."

In his behavior as American secretary during the year and a half after he took office in August 1772, Dartmouth did nothing to alter that image. His handling of a number of problems with individual colonies inherited from his predecessor, Lord Hillsborough, his attempt to reverse the antiexpansionist western policy of Hillsborough, and his "cautious and moderate" response to the *Gaspee* affair all demonstrated an unusual amount of sympathy for the American position coupled with a willingness to make concessions.

Underlying Dartmouth's conciliatory disposition, however, was a firm and abiding commitment to the principles laid down in the Declaratory Act. Neither Townshend nor Germain was any more thoroughly convinced than Dartmouth of Parliament's right to legislate for the colonies "in all cases whatsoever." "If the people of Britain and the colonies were one and the same people," he believed, "they must naturally have but a single head—the King-in-Parliament." The American conception of a divided sovereignty was "illogical and unreasonable." To limit the power of Parliament "by reserving certain essential functions, such as taxation, to the individual colonial assemblies" would "be tantamount to dissolving the empire." Moreover, the suggestion that the colonies were connected to Britain through the king was, Dartmouth believed in common with a wide spectrum of his fellow politicians, "dangerously Tory in its implications" because the colonists might have supplied the crown with a revenue "beyond the control of Parliament" and thereby have destroyed the settlement of 1688–89 by leading "to a revival of the independence of the royal prerogative" and the return of a Stuart-like despotism. What distinguished Dartmouth from Germain, then, was not the content of his "unalterable principles" but his willingness "to interpret those principles in the broadest and most favorable manner."

---

[25] B. D. Bargar, *Lord Dartmouth and the American Revolution* (Columbia, S.C., 1965), ix, 219.

But the Dartmouth approach of expedient conciliation was viable only so long as Americans refrained from once again challenging the fundamental principles of the British constitution, and it could not possibly have survived a constitutional crisis of the scale that followed the Boston Tea Party. Even Dartmouth believed that such an "unwarrantable insult" to parliamentary authority could not go unpunished, and he supported the Coercive Acts in the hope that "a limited amount of punishment would lay the basis for a complete conciliation of differences." Because the necessary precondition for that conciliation was colonial submission to Parliament, because even a man as sympathetic to the Americans as Dartmouth found himself unable to conceive of the possibility that there might be any middle ground between complete submission and total independence, Dartmouth's hopes were in vain. Limited punishment encountered massive resistance, and, although Dartmouth personally opposed extreme measures and continued to clutch at any straw that seemed likely to lead to a resolution of the conflict, the almost universal resentment of American behavior among most political leaders pushed him into harsher and harsher measures until Lexington and Concord shattered all possibility of a peaceful settlement and created a situation with which Germain was logically and temperamentally more suited to cope than he.

A much bolder and potentially more innovative advocate of conciliation was William Petty, second earl of Shelburne, who was in charge of American affairs from 1766 to 1768 under Chatham and who has been freshly evaluated by John Norris in *Shelburne and Reform.*[26] An unusually intelligent and penetrating attempt to assess Shelburne's responsibility "for the liberal reforms that emerged in England at the end of the American war" and to explain why he was "the patron of almost all the precursors of nineteenth-century radicalism," this book concentrates upon describing Shelburne's growing intellectual affinity with many of the chief spokesmen of that radical fringe group, the "Dissenting Interest"; his behavior in opposition and his advocacy of political and economic reform between the Middlesex election of 1769 and the fall of the North ministry in 1782; and his remarkably systematic but only partially successful efforts while in office under the second Rockingham and his own short ministries in 1782–83 to correct the "anomalies and inefficiencies" of administration.

The book also contains a reevaluation of Shelburne's policies and attitudes toward the American question. The preference for *"utilitarian"* as

---

[26] John Norris, *Shelburne and Reform* (New York, 1963).

opposed to "*customary* justifications for political conduct" and the rejection of traditional modes of political behavior, specifically the use of party, that lay behind his association with radical thinkers and contributed to his reputation as the treacherous "Jesuit in Berkeley Square" and were important in his ultimate failure as both politician and reformer made Shelburne considerably more open and flexible on American affairs than almost any of his contemporaries within the political establishment. Like Dartmouth, he advocated conciliation instead of coercion and, although he voted against the Declaratory Act, "supported the authority of Parliament over the colonies." Like his political leader Chatham, however, he also believed that that authority did not include power to levy "internal" taxes and should be used only in cases where "there were clear precedents." In office his goal was to avoid raising such fundamental issues altogether.

In his pragmatic view of the matter, "Anglo-American harmony was essential if the country was to be prosperous, and so long as it was prosperous, . . . claims of sovereignty and taxing rights were dangerous irrelevancies." Thus, he intended his much-derided scheme for raising a revenue in the colonies through improved collection of quitrents in 1767 not to yield all the money thought necessary, as some hostile historians have implied, but to satisfy the widespread demand for a colonial revenue among members of Parliament by supplying "enough of an appearance of one to satisfy them and at the same time not reawaken the outcry from the Americans." As Norris points out, however, the "determination to secure a revenue for America" inevitably doomed any such strategy to failure. So great was that determination that as soon as it became clear that the quitrent scheme would not provide an adequate revenue, Shelburne could do nothing to keep Townshend from pushing his program of taxation and coercion through the cabinet and Parliament. Similarly, in opposition in 1774–76 Shelburne was a vocal opponent of the punitive measures against Boston and subsequent measures of coercion. But just as the clamors for a colonial revenue rendered his American strategy unacceptable in 1767, so the deep consensus that Parliament's authority over the colonies had to be effectively established made his "hope that sovereignty might be secured by mutual agreement" totally chimerical in 1774–76.

The plain fact was, of course, that even Shelburne's chimera fell far short of American visions. Although he denounced coercion and the war as tyrannical measures that would ultimately lead to the destruction of the liberty of all Britons, he never stopped believing, with Chatham, in the "authority of Parliament over all matters of imperial concern, including 'external' taxation." The broad assertion of parliamentary authority implied in that belief was, of course, completely unacceptable to the Americans, and it represented the outermost limits to which anyone within the British political establishment was willing to go to meet American demands. Shelburne's attitudes and behavior in 1774–76 thus boldly underscore the overwhelming power of the prevailing ideology of parliamentary supremacy among the British political community and the improbability of anyone from or acceptable to the establishment being able even to suggest, much less to secure support for, any arrangement by which that ideology could have been modified to satisfy the constitutional claims of the colonists.

In opposition to this line of argument, it might be contended that the real experts on colonial affairs—the bureaucrats behind Shelburne, Dartmouth, and Germain who continued in office through all changes in administration—had a more profound understanding of the nature of the dispute and might, if the Americans had not been quite so forward in pushing their claims, have achieved some mutually satisfactory resolution of the difficulties, but several books that touch on the role of these figures indicate that they operated within the same ideological prison that bound their superiors. John Shy's *Toward Lexington*[27] is one of the best of these books.[28] An unusually thorough and penetrating examination of the changing mission of the army in the colonies from 1763 to 1775, its organization and disposition, and its part in contributing to the outbreak of the Revolution, the Shy book also analyzes how decisions concerning the use of the army were made. In the process it also indicates both the degree of importance of bureaucrats in the several offices involved as well as of a number of "experts" without portfolio in shaping decisions about the army and how similar their basic assumptions about the nature of the relationship between Britain and the colonies were to those of their superiors.

Franklin B. Wickwire makes the same points more explicitly in *British Subministers and Colonial America*,[29] a study of the role of the secretaries

---

[27] John Shy, *Toward Lexington: The Role of the British Army in the Coming of the American Revolution* (Princeton, N.J., 1965), x, 463.

[28] Earlier works that touch on this subject are Dora Mae Clark, *The Rise of the British Treasury: Colonial Administration in the Eighteenth Century* (New Haven, 1960), and Jack M. Sosin, *Whitehall and the Wilderness: The Middle West in British Colonial Policy, 1760–1775* (Lincoln, Nebr., 1961).

[29] Franklin B. Wickwire, *British Subministers and Colonial America, 1763–1783* (Princeton, N.J., 1966), xii, 228.

and undersecretaries of the Treasury, Admiralty, Southern (and later American) Department, Board of Trade, and Customs in shaping "major policy" toward the colonies. The men in Britain who knew most about colonial affairs, the individuals who occupied these offices, Wickwire makes clear, exercised a significant influence upon every important measure to which the colonists took exception between 1763 and 1776 and, although he does not deal with the question directly, it is clear from the nature of their influence that they were at least as conservative in their views on the imperial constitution as the successive administrations they served.

That the wall of assumptions that enclosed the dominant elements of the British political nation was so impenetrable that there was absolutely no way by which the Americans could either scale or breach it is further indicated by the findings of Jack M. Sosin in *Agents and Merchants.*[30] Intended to discover the extent to which British ministers considered the "interests of the North American colonists" in the several measures that applied to them between 1763 and 1775, this work shows that colonial agents and British merchants involved in the American trade constituted "a rudimentary lobby" through which the colonies could make their views known to London authorities and influence colonial policy in their favor. During the 1760s and early 1770s, the author finds, this group was reasonably effective. By concerning itself primarily "with the realities of governmental administration" and playing down whatever "ideological abstractions" were involved, it managed to secure repeal of the Stamp Act, modification of the Townshend program, and a number of other concessions.

As Sosin makes clear, however, the success of the American lobby depended to a great extent both upon the sympathy of the administration in power and, more important, its ability to avoid raising "the explosive question of sovereignty." When, after 1773, the escalation of the dispute made that question the central focus of debate and the agents were *bound* by instructions from the colonies to present arguments explicitly denying the authority of Parliament over the colonies, the effectiveness of the lobby was completely destroyed. Thus, for all its institutional crudity and ad hoc character, it was not the deficiencies of the lobby itself that were primarily responsible for the failure of Americans to persuade British leaders of the virtues of their constitutional arguments—a much more sophisticated and better organized institution with a recognized

---

[30] Jack M. Sosin, *Agents and Merchants: British Colonial Policy and the Origins of the American Revolution, 1763–1775* (Lincoln, Nebr., 1965), xvi, 267.

position in the constitutional structure could, under the circumstances, scarcely have done any better—but the movement of the conflict into a realm that was well beyond the ambit of permissible discussion in the British political culture of the 1770s. So strong and so extensive was the commitment to the ideal of Parliament's omnipotence over the empire that no proposition that seemed in any way to call that idea into question could possibly be taken into consideration.

How far this commitment reached down into the political nation is suggested by still another group of recent books dealing with the campaign for political reform within Britain during the first decades of the reign of George III. Three of them—George Rudé, *Wilkes and Liberty;*[31] Ian R. Christie, *Wilkes, Wyvill, and Reform;*[32] and Eugene Charlton Black, *The Association*[33]—are concerned directly with the reformers themselves. A meticulous attempt to delineate the "social ingredients" of the Wilkite movement, the Rudé book shows that, although Wilkes had some support among the clergy, gentry, and even aristocracy, most of his backers were drawn from three other groups: merchants of the middling and lesser sort in London and other commercial cities, lesser freeholders of both urban and rural districts, and the London mob composed principally of "wage-earners" and other unpropertied elements among the "lower orders of the people." The larger merchants supplied most of the leadership, but the small property owners far outnumbered all other groups. Christie's book, concerned primarily with explaining the content and extent of both the "Wilkite and Wyvillite agitation," concludes that both movements, though supported by men with varying individual goals, were directed toward purifying the existing constitutional system and that most of the energy and support for reform at both periods derived from country gentlemen and substantial yeomen in the counties and commercial groups in the cities. The Black study traces the gradual enlargement of the political nation and explains the role in this process of extraparliamentary assocations as developed from the early Wilkites

---

[31] George Rudé, *Wilkes and Liberty: A Social Study of 1763 to 1774* (New York, 1962), xvi, 240.

[32] Ian R. Christie, *Wilkes, Wyvill and Reform: The Parliamentary Reform Movement in British Politics, 1760—1785* (New York, 1962).

[33] Eugene Charlton Black, *The Association: British Extraparliamentary Political Organization, 1769—1783* (Cambridge, Mass., 1963), xiv, 344.

through the Association movement of 1779–85, the Protestant Association, and the Society for Constitutional Information, to John Reeves's Association for the Preservation of Liberty and Property founded in response to the French Revolution.

In relevance to the present discussion, what is most interesting about these studies of what Black appropriately refers to as "the periphery of political life" is what they reveal about the limited goals of the Wilkite movement. The most radical of any group actually engaged in day-to-day politics between 1760 and 1776, the Wilkites did not call for any fundamental changes in the constitutional structure of Britain, not even for "the extension of the parliamentary franchise," but only for the purification of the existing constitution. Growing out of the "traditional deep-rooted, critical preoccupation with the problem of power" in the British political community, "the general discontent of many of the 'middling sort' in the metropolis against those in power," the almost instinctual distrust of the court by independent country gentlemen, and the ambitions—and fears—of opposition politicians, the Wilkite movement proceeded upon the conviction that the constitution was being thrown out of balance either by the dominant aristocracy—which, the Wilkites believed, had long had far too much weight in government for the good of the nation as a whole—or, more probably, by the misuse of the influence of the crown by "a secret Closet party, beyond the control of Parliament and guided behind the scenes by the sinister combination of the Earl of Bute . . . and the Princess Dowager of Wales," who were intent upon destroying English liberty and the constitution by corrupting Parliament. The "massacre" of St. George's Fields, the persecution of Wilkes, especially Parliament's blatant disregard of the wishes of the Middlesex electors by refusing to seat him in Parliament, and the mistreatment of the colonies all served to confirm the Wilkites in their belief; and their specific reform proposals for a place bill, shorter parliaments, an oath against bribery at elections, the secret ballot, the abolition of rotten boroughs, and more equal representation were all intended, like the later program of the Wyvillites, to purge the constitution of its defects by reducing the "excessive influence" of the aristocracy and crown in Parliament.

The limited nature of the proposals of the Wilkite movement did not mean, of course, that the movement did not have some highly radical implications. The use of oaths and instructions to bind representatives to adhere to the wishes of their constituents, extraparliamentary associations to bring public opinion to bear upon Parliament, and petitions and remonstrances on a national basis were highly innovative procedures that portended both the enlargement of the articulate political nation and the development of "'the public' as an independent force in politics." Similarly, what Lucy S. Sutherland has called the "critical attitude to existing institutions"[34] would lead in the next century to campaigns for more sweeping constitutional reforms. For the moment, however, the Wilkites were just as thoroughly committed to "Revolution principles" and to the ideal of parliamentary supremacy as the leading figures in the political establishment.

The identification of their own sufferings with those of the Americans was easy enough as long as the problems of both seemed to be soluble simply by the removal of power-thirsty ministers and the restoration of the constitution to its proper strength. But when, in 1774, it began to become clear that the logic of American arguments had led them to a total denial of parliamentary authority over the colonies and that that denial implied a fundamental reconception of the nature of sovereignty and of constitutional arrangements within the empire, few of the Wilkites, however sympathetic they may have remained toward the "oppressed" Americans, were willing to go along.

The alliance had always been potentially incompatible, for, although the Wilkites hoped to make Parliament more susceptible to the wishes of a broader segment of the political nation and to make it impossible for Parliament to abridge certain basic individual rights of citizens, their main concern was not to diminish the authority of Parliament but to restore its ancient vigor and to immunize it against future enfeebling attacks from corrupt combinations surrounding the crown, objectives that required far less sweeping constitutional changes than those ultimately sought by the Americans. The radical movement may have drawn its support from a different segment of society and, as James T. Boulton has recently shown in his analysis of the political discourse of the period,[35] may also have appealed to a somewhat different audience in a distinctive idiom, but the content of their appeals, especially their ideas about the constitution, did not differ substantially from the more

---

[34] Lucy S. Sutherland, *The City of London and the Opposition to Government, 1768–1774: A Study in the Rise of Metropolitan Radicalism* (London, 1959), 6.

[35] James T. Boulton, *The Language of Politics in the Age of Wilkes and Burke* (Toronto, 1963), xiii, 282. This volume, which examines political rhetoric from the time of the Wilkite agitation through the debate over the French Revolution, makes clear the value of literary critical analyses of political materials, though the nature of the findings suggests that it would be even more useful in studying periods in which political disagreements were more fundamental.

restrained and polite rhetoric of Burke and the portions of the political establishment he represented.

Despite its limited objectives, the Wilkite agitation appeared dangerously radical to the establishment. Not only the administration and its supporters at whom the attacks of the Wilkites were aimed but, as Sutherland has pointed out,[36] the opposition groups in Parliament with whom the Wilkites were allied regarded them with profound suspicion and apprehension. The effect of the movement was, therefore, not simply, as Black indicated, "to seat Lord North's conservative government" firmly in power but also, and more importantly, to reinforce the commitment of all segments of the establishment to the existing system and thereby to make them and the system even more resistant to change. Because of the association of American protests with the Wilkite movement, they were inevitably, to borrow a phrase from Christie, "tarred with the same brush" and thought to represent the same frightening brand of political and social radicalism. The result was, ironically, that Wilkite support, far from helping the Americans, ultimately made Parliament and the establishment even less receptive to their proposals.

The picture that emerges both from these recent studies and from earlier post-Namier works is that of a political culture in which there was a remarkable agreement upon fundamentals, at least among politically relevant segments of society. On the surface the factional struggles within the establishment along with the popular clamor associated with Wilkes gave the impression of a chaotic political system marked by sharply divergent views on the nature, organization, and function of the polity. But when one looks behind the churn of factional politics and the bravado of the Wilkite agitation to "the system of empirical beliefs, expressive symbols, and values" which defined the ground rules and the limits of political action, one discovers an extraordinarily deep and pervasive consensus extending over almost the entire spectrum of active political groups, from the king and his immediate associates down through the Wilkites, and made possible both by a relatively stable and prosperous society and, as Mansfield pointed out, by the settlement of the great religious and political questions of the seventeenth century.

At the heart of this consensus was the almost universal belief in the sanctity and essential appropriateness of the Settlement of 1688–1714

---

[36] Sutherland, *City of London*, 25–26.

and in the assumptions about the nature of the constitution, the proper distribution of power among political institutions, and the correct relationship of these institutions to the nation at large upon which that settlement was commonly understood to have been based. So powerful and so "generally taken for granted" was this belief that it was virtually "unchallengeable."[37] That is, no basic change in any major component of this belief or the constitutional arrangements associated with it could be entertained because any such changes, it was widely believed, would be inimical to the best interests of the nation. This internal consensus, this "self-satisfaction," was bolstered, as Caroline Robbins has remarked, "by two generations of continental visitors heaping praise upon the system which allowed enjoyment of so many liberties."[38] It was reinforced and vindicated by the amazing success of British arms in the Seven Years' War and the resulting enlargement of the British Empire in territory, population, and wealth to an extent unknown since antiquity.

With such widespread agreement at home, so much adulation from abroad, and so resounding a victory in war, it is not surprising that the British political system was so successfully repressive in the 1760s and 1770s and that during the American crisis the only Britons who could appreciate and support American constitutional arguments were those few who were sufficiently alienated from the system that they could take a detached and critical view of it. The only group so alienated was that small but articulate knot of radical dissenting and republican thinkers comprehensively described by Caroline Robbins in *The Eighteenth Century Commonwealthman.* To such members of this group as Richard Price and, to a lesser extent, James Burgh, the American position was both comprehensible and meritorious.[39] But these men were able to take such a position not because of their superior vision but because they were, by the standards of the day, political deviants whose position on the outermost fringes of politics exempted them to a large extent from many of the central imperatives of British political life and by giving

---

[37] The quotations are from Sidney Verba, "Comparative Political Culture," in Lucian W. Pye and Sidney Verba, eds., *Political Culture and Political Development* (Princeton, N.J., 1965), 513, 518–19.

[38] Caroline Robbins, *The Eighteenth-Century Commonwealth: Studies in the Transmission, Development and Circumstance of English Liberal Thought from the Restoration of Charles II until the War with the Thirteen Colonies* (Cambridge, Mass., 1961), 379.

[39] Ibid., 320–77. A fuller discussion of Burgh is Oscar and Mary Handlin, "James Burgh and American Revolutionary Theory," Massachusetts Historical Society, *Proceedings* 73 (1961): 38–57.

them a wider and more critical perspective enabled them to entertain a much larger range of alternatives than any of the groups at the center of politics. Significantly, however, they had, despite their prolific writings and their connections with establishment politicians such as Shelburne, no effective voice in politics, and their support of any measure was an almost certain indication that it did not have the approval of the vast majority within the political nation.

The stability and cohesiveness that derived from the widespread agreement on fundamentals within the British political nation helped give it enormous strength against both domestic upheaval and foreign attack. As Machiavelli remarked, however, even the "best instituted governments . . . carry in them the seeds of their destruction,"[40] and during the American crisis this source of internal strength, and the self-satisfaction associated with it, was one of the major ingredients of metro-politan weakness. Not only did it prevent British political leaders from making the constitutional adjustments necessary to bring the crisis to an end and retain the North American colonies in the empire but also, as several new books on the British military effort suggest, it caused them drastically to underestimate both the depth and extent of the colonial opposition and the capacity of Americans to resist. In addition to Brown's study of Germain which has already been discussed, the most important and ambitious of these studies are Piers Mackesy, *The War for America, 1775–1783*,[41] a comprehensive attempt to assess the British war effort "in the context of eighteenth-century warfare," and William B. Willcox, *Portrait of a General*,[42] a masterful and elegantly constructed examination of British strategy from the perspective of Sir Henry Clinton, the commander-in-chief of British forces during the final years of the war.

Both Mackesy and Willcox are concerned with explaining why the British lost the war. At least partly because they approach the question from such totally different perspectives—Mackesy from the macro-cosmos of Whitehall, Willcox from the microcosmos of Clinton—they come up with quite divergent answers. For Mackesy the British lost—despite the energetic, forceful, and competent leadership of George III and the two ministers most directly responsible for the war, Germain and Sandwich—because of the peculiar and almost insurmountable problems

---

[40] As quoted by Mansfield, *Statesmanship and Party Government*, 77.

[41] Piers Mackesy, *The War for America, 1775–1783* (Cambridge, Mass., 1964), xx, 565.

[42] William B. Willcox, *Portrait of a General: Sir Henry Clinton in the War of Independence* (New York, 1964), xxiv, 534, xiv.

presented by the war: the maintenance of a large army three thousand miles away in a hostile country; the vastness of the territory to be conquered and the popular character of the revolt; the coalition after 1778 of "maritime enemies undistracted by war in Europe"; and inadequate administrative machinery. Adding to these many handicaps the strong opposition to the war within the British political nation and the series of inept field commanders, who because of the nature of the war had the primary "responsibility for bringing strategy to the battlefield," it is, Mackesy seems to imply, remarkable that the British did as well as they did. By contrast, Willcox presents a highly unflattering picture of the directing of the war in Britain, and, although he too emphasizes the importance of "the internecine struggle that went on within the British command in America" and his subject's "singular inability to get his plans carried out," he leaves no doubt that he thinks that "the almost unbelievable ineptitude of the Cabinet" was the major ingredient in Britain's defeat.

However much they may disagree about the proper classification of reasons why the British lost the war, both Mackesy and Willcox, as well as Brown, concur in their judgments that the loss was at least partly attributable to the ministry's failure, as Mackesy puts it, "to assess the enemy correctly." For Mackesy, the failure was largely the result of the unprecedented character of the war and the difficulties of obtaining accurate intelligence. "A revolutionary struggle which involved an armed insurgent population," he points out, "was unique in the memory of the age," and with no precedents to guide them, the ministers persisted in the notion that the patriots were a small "mob led by demagogues," that the American army was a ragged, inexperienced, and poorly officered organization incapable of serious resistance, and that the loyalists were sufficiently strong and numerous to be an effective adjunct to the British army.[43]

For Willcox, these notions persisted not because of any lack of intelligence—Clinton, at any rate, had a clear understanding of the magnitude of the task and did not hesitate to place his opinions before his superiors—but of the illusions of the cabinet and especially of Germain. "Germain," Willcox writes, "was living in a dream world, in which the American problem was always just on the verge of solution: Washington's army was withering away, hordes of loyalists were waiting for the word to rise and declare themselves, and nothing prevented victory but lethargic

---

[43] A thorough analysis of the place of the Tories in British strategy is Paul H. Smith, *Loyalists and Redcoats: A Study in British Revolutionary Policy* (Chapel Hill, N.C., 1964).

generals." Fed by his "incredible optimism," "these illusions," Willcox declares, simply made Germain "deaf to home truths," and time and time again he "went on pressing ideas that by the time they arrived [in America] were utterly unrelated to American realities." But Germain was not the only one suffering from these illusions, a situation which suggests that their persistence had less to do with the difficulties of obtaining proper intelligence or Germain's "incredible optimism" than with the inability of the political establishment to accept the possibility that there could be any widespread, persistent, and successful opposition to a political system of such obvious merit.

Neither the series of military and naval reverses in America and on the seas in the period 1777–81 nor the eventual loss of the thirteen colonies could destroy this wholesale confidence in the political system. Opposition to the war in Parliament grew steadily between 1775 and 1781, with the Rockinghams eventually coming to advocate independence for the colonies as the only way out of a costly and humiliating war and the Chathamites, now under the leadership of Shelburne, continuing to hope for peace without independence. But there was no group in Parliament that was willing to go so far as to advocate changes in the constitutional structure of the kind and magnitude demanded by the Americans back in 1774 as a way of luring the Americans to the peace table.[44]

Similarly, the "dismay, condemnation, bitterness and frustration" that may have been in part the result of the war with the colonies[45] and were manifest beginning in 1779 in the Yorkshire movements and the associated demands for economic and parliamentary reform, the Gordon riots, and the demands of the Irish under Grattan for a significant measure of home rule signified an amount of internal political unrest unparalleled since the Glorious Revolution and perhaps even, as Herbert Butterfield has argued, the existence of a "quasi-revolutionary" situation.[46] Again though, however much discontent there may have been with the existing government and however potentially revolutionary the situation, the most striking feature of the reform movement of 1779–85 was the limited

---

[44] For a discussion of the opposition to the war in Parliament, see Namier and Brooke, *History of Parliament* 1:80–87; I. R. Christie, *The End of North's Ministry, 1780–1782* (London, 1958); and Alison Gilbert Olson, *The Radical Duke: Career and Correspondence of Charles Lenox, Third Duke of Richmond* (Oxford, 1961), 51.

[45] Christie, *Wilkes, Wyvill, and Reform,* 222–23.

[46] For a discussion of these various internal difficulties, see ibid.; Black, *The Association;* Christie, *End of North's Ministry;* and Herbert Butterfield, *George III, Lord North, and the People, 1779–80* (London, 1949), quotation from vi.

character of its demands. Like the Wilkite agitation a decade earlier, it spawned no program for sweeping changes in the basic structure of the political system. That it did not strongly suggests that only a failure of truly massive proportions can bring about significant innovation in the values, conventions, customary modes of procedure, and institutional structure of any political culture with such thorough and unquestioning internal support and such built-in resistance to change.

As a result of all of these new studies as well as a spate of critical essays of varying lengths on Namier and his work,[47] it is clear that a number of modifications or elaborations are required in the picture Namier originally drew of British politics in the age of the American Revolution. Most importantly, it seems, his preoccupation with the "instrumental, loaves-and-fishes aspect of politics,"[48] with "the intricate maneuverings of parliamentary leaders and factions" and "electoral 'arrangements' in manageable constituencies,"[49] led him to neglect what Mansfield has called the "appearance of politics" and thereby to overemphasize the role and power of the crown and its ministers and to underestimate the importance of party labels, factional programs, parliamentary debates, polemical discourse, idealized imperatives (such as those recommended by Bolingbroke or imbedded in traditions and habits of thought), great national issues (like naturalization in 1753 or economical reform in 1779–

---

[47] The most unfavorable and ambitious criticism of Namier is by Herbert Butterfield in *George III and the Historians* (London, 1937), 193–299. Other shorter criticisms are W. R. Fryer, "The Study of British Politics between the Revolution and the Reform Act," *Renaissance and Modern Studies* 1 (1957): 91–114, and "Namier and the King's Position in English Politics, 1744–84," *Burke Newsletter* 5 (1965): 246–58; Harvey C. Mansfield, Jr., "Sir Lewis Namier Again Considered," ibid., 3 (1963): 109–19; J. Steven Watson, "Parliamentary Procedure as a Key to the Understanding of Eighteenth Century Politics," ibid., 3 (1962): 107–29; and Thomas W. Perry, *Public Opinion, Propaganda, and Politics in Eighteenth-Century England: A Study of the Jewish Naturalization Act of 1753* (Cambridge, Mass., 1962), 189–93. More appreciative commentaries not previously cited are Ved Mehta, "The Flight of the Crook-Taloned Birds," *New Yorker*, Dec. 8, 1962, 59–147, and Dec. 15, 1962, 47–129, and Isaiah Berlin, "L. B. Namier: A Personal Impression," *Encounter* 27 (Nov. 1966): 32–42. Quite sympathetic to Namier and critical of his critics are Jacob M. Price, "Party, Purpose, and Pattern: Sir Lewis Namier and His Critics," *Journal of British Studies* 1 (1961): 71–93, and Robert Walcott, "'Sir Lewis Namier Considered,' Considered," ibid., 3 (1963): 85–108.

[48] Mansfield, "Sir Lewis Namier Again Considered," 114.

[49] Perry, *Public Opinion, Propaganda, and Politics*, 190.

80), and extraparliamentary movements (such as the Wilkite or Wy-villite agitations).

But Namier's neglect of these aspects of British political life, his admitted engrossment with questions involving "the locus, structure and transmission of power,"[50] and his repeated emphasis of "material factors" over "ideal ones,"[51] of "interests over ideas and principles,"[52] does not necessarily mean that he is guilty of the charge that was made most emphatically by Butterfield and that has since become a favorite cliché about Namier: that he washed the ideas out of history and was a mere "behaviorist" who had little comprehension of the tremendous power of ideas in shaping human behavior.[53] As both Jacob M. Price and John Brooke have pointed out, Namier's skepticism of the importance of ideas in history applied largely to certain categories of ideas: to men's purposive declarations, their rational and often ex post facto explanations of what, in many cases, were highly irrational acts, and their attempts to endow with high idealism sordid deeds of ambition and self-interest.[54]

In another and, for Namier's work, crucially important sense, ideas were central to his whole interpretation of British politics. But the ideas upon which he put such great, if only in most instances implicit, stress were not the avowed purposes of men but the "modes of thinking," "cherished lore," "inherited, historically conditioned ideas and words," and "dominant terms" which in "every country and every age . . . seem to obsess men's thoughts" and shape their behavior into predictable and familiar patterns.[55] As both Christopher Hill and Henry Winkler have suggested,[56] it was perhaps precisely because ideas of this type were one of the *givens* of eighteenth-century British political culture and as givens were beyond dispute that Namier's "method" was so peculiarly appropriate to the study of that culture.

---

[50] Price, "Party, Purpose, and Pattern," 80.

[51] Berlin, "L. B. Namier," 41.

[52] Winkler, "Sir Lewis Namier," 19.

[53] See, for instance, Gordon S. Wood, "Rhetoric and Reality in the American Revolution," *William and Mary Quarterly*, 3d ser., 23 (1966): 21–24.

[54] Price, "Party, Purpose, and Pattern," 88–92; Brooke, "Namier and Namierism," 340–42.

[55] Namier, *England in the Age of the American Revolution*, 21, 32; "Human Nature in Politics," *Personalities and Powers*, 6; and "History," in Fritz Stern, ed., *The Varieties of History* (New York, 1956), 374.

[56] Christopher Hill, "Recent Interpretations of the Civil War," *History* 41 (1956): 78; Winkler, "Sir Lewis Namier," 19.

For all his absorption with the intricacies of interest and intrigue, however, Namier never lost sight of the important extent to which these underlying ideas established the boundaries of political activity, and his treatment of the imperial problem is a case in point. For what enabled Namier to achieve his fundamental insight into the character of the British response to that problem was his acute awareness of the inhibitive role of traditional ideas and customary modes of procedure, ideas and procedures that were built into "the very structure and life of the Empire" and were so thoroughly internalized that most members of the British political nation thought them to be essential to the successful operation of the empire. As Namier suggested in 1930, and as the findings of scholars in recent work touching on the subject abundantly confirm and amplify, it was not so much a failure of vision among British political leaders of the 1760s and 1770s as the repressive character of those ideas and modes of procedure—the powerful and nearly universal commitment to habitual ways of doing things, established institutional forms, and fixed notions about the indivisibility of sovereignty and the omnipotence of the king-in-Parliament over the whole British political community—that prevented those leaders from considering seriously the constitutional and institutional innovations suggested by the Americans and, once those ideas and modes of procedure had been called into question by the Americans, made the American Revolution and the demise of the First British Empire as certain as "the revolutions of planets, . . . the migrations of birds, and . . . the plunging of hordes of lemmings into the sea."[57]

After I had submitted "The Flight from Determinism" (chapter 17 above) to the *South Atlantic Quarterly* in 1961, William Baskerville Hamilton asked me to write a companion piece on interpretations of the British side of the Revolutionary controversy. Other writing obligations and four time-consuming moves prevented me from completing this assignment until June 1967 when my then colleague at The Johns Hopkins University, Alfred D. Chandler, Jr., loaned me and my family his beach house on Nantucket. Presented to The Seminar, Department of History, The Johns Hopkins University, October 25, 1967, this chapter was also offered as a Phi Alpha Theta Lecture at American University in Washington, D.C., on December 11, 1967. Previously reprinted in The Bobbs-Merrill Reprint Series in American History, no. H-397 (Indianapolis, 1972), it is here reprinted with permission and minor verbal changes from the *South Atlantic Quarterly* 57 (1968): 141–75, Copyright Duke University Press, 1968.

---

[57] Namier, *England in the Age of the Revolution,* 40–41.

NINETEEN

The Reappraisal of the American Revolution in Recent Historical Literature

BOTH BECAUSE of its crucial position in modern history as the first of the great revolutions and because it gave birth to the United States of America, the American Revolution has always exercised a powerful appeal for historians. Its causes and consequences, its nature and meaning have never ceased to fascinate—and to puzzle—them, and each generation of historians has approached it anew, seeking to understand it in terms that would be meaningful to them. The result has been a welter of interpretations of why the Revolution occurred and what exactly it was. Those interpretations can be explained partly by changing intellectual styles, social, economic, and political imperatives, and psychological currents in the public world and partly by shifting conceptions of human nature and historical change within the community of historians. But they also stand as dramatic testimony to the one indisputable truth about the event itself: the American Revolution, like every other historical phenomenon of comparable magnitude, was so complex and contained so many diverse and seemingly contradictory currents that it can support a wide variety of interpretations and may never be comprehended in full. Yet the extensive and intensive reappraisal of the Revolution that has occurred since World War II may have brought us closer than ever before to such a comprehension.

Through most of the nineteenth century it was customary to view the Revolution as a classic struggle for liberty. The most celebrated, detailed, influential, and authoritative exposition of this Whig view came from George Bancroft, a fervid nationalist and devoted democrat who had grown to manhood in the years of intense national self-consciousness and democratic pride in American institutions that followed the War of 1812. His monumental *History of the United States,*[1] which brought the story of American development through the formation of the Constitution, was above all a patriotic ode to the foundation of American freedom. Sharing the conventional nineteenth-century Whig and democratic belief that the desire for freedom was the strongest drive in man, he limned a vivid portrait of the colonists' relentless striving for freedom, from the first landing at Jamestown in 1607 to the final victory at Yorktown in 1781, against a background of more or less continuous oppression from mother England. Although the Revolution was occasioned by the tyrannical assaults of George III upon American liberties in the 1760s and 1770s, it was merely the logical culmination of a century and a half of struggle against arbitrary English interference in American affairs.

For Bancroft, however, the final victory for freedom, the real triumph of American democracy and the successful conclusion of the Revolution, came not with the Treaty of Paris in 1783 but with the adoption of the Constitution in 1788. Immediately after the war, during what John Fiske, one of Bancroft's younger contemporaries, movingly described as *The Critical Period,*[2] petty local jealousies, uncertainty, and political impotence almost deprived Americans of the fruits of victory. Only with the embodiment of the libertarian and democratic principles of the Revolution in the Constitution and the establishment of a strong federal union were the achievements of 1776 and 1783 firmly secured.

That Americans had been blessed with an environment peculiarly well suited to the growth of freedom and, above all, with the special favor of God, Bancroft had little doubt, and in his conception of the Revolution as part of the "grand design of Providence" he found its deepest meaning. Americans were God's chosen people marked out for a special purpose, and their Revolution was the necessary prelude to the "political regeneration" of mankind, an important milestone on man's inevitable march toward a freer and a more nearly perfect world.

Shared in large measure by such respected British contemporaries as

---

[1] George Bancroft, *History of the United States,* 10 vols. (Boston, 1834–74).

[2] John Fiske, *The Critical Period* (Boston and New York, 1888).

W. E. H. Lecky[3] and George Otto Trevelyan,[4] Bancroft's simple Whig-gish view of the Revolution as well as his intense patriotism did not set well with a new generation of American historians who, trained in the methods of scientific history during the closing decades of the nineteenth century, demanded a more objective reading of the American past. After 1890 two new tendencies in Revolutionary scholarship profoundly al-tered the traditional interpretation.

The first of these tendencies was manifest in the work of a large group of historians who have since come to be referred to as the imperial school. Deeply offended by Bancroft's narrow nationalism and thoroughly caught up in the general movement toward Anglo-American accord that gained increasing vigor in the decades immediately preceding World War I, these historians insisted that the Revolution could be understood only when considered in terms of the empire as a whole, that the impe-rial, as well as the colonial, point of view had to be taken into account.

One of the most prominent of the imperial historians was Herbert Levi Osgood. Though he himself never produced a major work on the Revolution, he anticipated both the direction and many of the conclu-sions of the imperial historians in a notable essay published in 1898.[5] Calling for a "more just and scientific view of the Revolution," Osgood boldly suggested that the British government not only was not "guilty of intentional tyranny toward the colonies" but also had ample provoca-tion for pursuing the measures that led to revolution after 1763. From the perspective of imperial officials in London, he argued, the "vexatious delays" that resulted from the "narrow, prejudiced and unstatesmanlike" behavior of colonial lower houses of assembly during the Seven Years' War clearly justified the attempted reform of colonial administration at the end of the war. Like Bancroft, Osgood thought that the roots of the American Revolution were deeply embedded in the colonial past, but unlike Bancroft he expected to find them not in British oppression but

---

[3] W. E. H. Lecky, *A History of England in the Eighteenth Century*, 8 vols. (London and New York, 1878–90).

[4] George Otto Trevelyan, *The American Revolution*, 4 vols. (London and New York, 1899–1913).

[5] Herbert L. Osgood, "The American Revolution," *Political Science Quarterly* 13 (1898): 41–59.

in the "social and political tendencies . . . toward independence" within the colonies.

George Louis Beer, a tobacco merchant turned scholar and a protégé of Osgood, was the first to amplify and work out the implications of Osgood's suggestions in a study of *British Colonial Policy, 1754—1765,* which appeared in 1907.[6] As Beer carefully pointed out, he wrote strictly within the framework of imperial history, and his study made it clear that from the point of view of British administrators at Whitehall, American conduct during the Seven Years' War was marked not only by extreme provincialism, as Osgood had suggested, but also by patent disloyalty. Unmindful that the struggle extended beyond the narrow confines of the North American continent, Americans continued to trade with the French and Spanish in the West Indies throughout the war. Such behavior understandably persuaded metropolitan officials to try to tighten imperial ties and increase the administrative efficiency of the empire when the war was over. But this movement for centralization unfortunately—unfortunately because Beer tended to regard the Revolution as a tragic mistake, a "temporary separation of two kindred peoples"— came into direct and violent conflict with a movement for independence that dated from the very foundation of the colonies. Previously restrained only by the presence of the French and Spanish at the rear of the colonies, this movement could proceed without restraint after the removal of the French and Spanish menace in 1763. For Beer, then, as for Osgood and Bancroft, the ultimate cause of the Revolution was the incipient and long-developing desire for independence among the colonists.

The origin and nature of those desires were not spelled out in any detail until the 1920s when Charles McLean Andrews, the most influential and productive of all the imperial historians, turned after years of working on earlier colonial developments to speculate about the origins of the Revolution in a brilliant series of essays[7] and in his presidential address to the American Historical Association in 1925.[8] Like both Osgood and Beer, Andrews was strongly influenced by a conception of historical change that stressed the overwhelming influence of the physical environment, the evolutionary character of historical development, and

---

[6] George Louis Beer, *British Colonial Policy, 1754—1765* (New York, 1907).

[7] Charles M. Andrews, *Colonial Background of the American Revolution: Four Essays in American Colonial History* (New Haven, 1924).

[8] Charles M. Andrews, "The American Revolution: An Interpretation," *American Historical Review* 31 (1926): 219–32.

a view of human nature that saw man as the agent of vast, impersonal forces largely beyond his control. The supreme challenge to historians, he indicated in his presidential address, was to discover those many "deep-lying and almost invisible factors and forces which influence and often determine human action." Revolutions, he argued, were never sudden and never made by men; rather, they were the products of complex long-range developments which were the "masters, not the servants, of statesmen and political agitators."

A sound explanation of the American Revolution had therefore to be sought not in the behavior of individuals or groups during the 1760s and 1770s but in the differing "states of mind" produced by profoundly divergent conditions in the colonies and Great Britain during the previous century and a half. The American environment had given birth to "new wants, new desires, and new points of view," to a completely "new order of society" characterized by growth and change and contrasting sharply with a way of life in Britain that seemed to Andrews to have been "intellectually, socially, and institutionally in a state of stable equilibrium." Andrews was convinced that a collision between two such disparate and incompatible "yokefellows," the one absolutely committed to keeping the colonies dependent and the other demanding, through its ever-maturing representative assemblies, an ever-increasing amount of self-government, was inevitable.

The most notable contribution of these historians was a deeper understanding of the metropolitan side of colonial development. No one could read either the more substantial works of Osgood, Beer, Andrews, and their contemporaries or important contributions from the second generation of imperial historians—such as Leonard Woods Labaree's *Royal Government in America*,[9] which surveyed in detail the political relations between the metropolitan government and the colonies, and Lawrence A. Harper's *The English Navigation Laws*,[10] which described at length the rationale and operation of the mercantile system—and still regard the British as tyrants. By the late 1920s, in fact, no serious student of early American history could doubt that the British had, or at least thought they had, good and substantial reasons for undertaking the measures they did, however the colonists might have interpreted them.

Perhaps because they were so thoroughly engrossed in exploring the nature of metropolitan administration during the seventeenth and early eighteenth centuries and in putting colonial developments into their

---

[9] Leonard Woods Labaree, *Royal Government in America* (New Haven, 1930).

[10] Lawrence A. Harper, *The English Navigation Laws* (New York, 1939).

proper imperial setting, none of the first generation of imperial historians ever produced a systematic or detailed treatment of the critical decades just before the Declaration of Independence. That task was not undertaken until the 1930s, when Lawrence Henry Gipson, Andrews's most prolific student, began to publish a massive study, *The British Empire before the American Revolution,* which in fifteen volumes carried the story from 1748 to 1776. From these volumes as well as from two shorter studies[11] has emerged what may be assumed to be the final version of the imperial interpretation of the origins of the American Revolution. In its broader outlines it does not differ substantially from the more tentative formulations of Beer and Andrews. Like Andrews, Gipson places heavy emphasis upon the role of the American environment in causing the colonists to develop ideals and interests that diverged sharply from those of metropolitan English people. With Beer, he views the removal of the French menace as the decisive event in the coming of the Revolution. Already "politically mature, prosperous, dynamic, and self-reliant" by the 1750s, Americans gained physical security as well with the conquest of Canada; and when the British government justifiably sought to exert stricter controls over them in the 1760s and 1770s, nothing was left to deter them from throwing off the burdensome responsibilities of membership in the empire. By providing a solid substructure of detailed evidence to support these notions, Gipson finally supplied what Osgood had called for in 1898: a comprehensive study, free from the patriotic distortions of the nineteenth-century nationalists, that seeks to account rationally and historically for the conduct of the British government on the eve of the American Revolution.

At the very time Osgood and Beer were calling for a more dispassionate analysis of the British side of the American Revolution, another group of historians was focusing its attention upon internal divisions within the colonies. Where Bancroft had found unanimity among the Patriots, they found disagreement and conflict. Where the imperial historians emphasized the political and constitutional aspects of the controversy, they stressed the social and economic. To a very large extent, their interpretations were shaped by the rhetoric and assumptions of Progressive politics

---

[11] Lawrence Henry Gipson, *The Coming of the Revolution, 1763–1775* (New York, 1954), and "The American Revolution as an Aftermath of the Great War for Empire, 1754–1763," *Political Science Quarterly* 61 (1950): 86–104.

and social thought and by a conception of revolution that derived largely from the experience of the great European revolutions. Their sympathies, like those of all good Progressives, lay with the little man—the yeoman farmer, agricultural tenant, artisan, and town laborer. Not only the Revolutionary era but all of American history seemed to have been dominated by a fundamental conflict between such groups, who stood for human rights and democracy, and the upper classes, who advocated property rights and the political predominance of special interest groups.

The American Revolution was thus thought to have exhibited patterns of class conflicts and internal political and social upheaval similar to those of the French Revolution; and it came to be seen largely and most importantly as part of a sweeping struggle for democracy on the part of disfranchised and unprivileged groups, who by their constant pressures were slowly bringing about that equality of condition that was characteristic of the age of Andrew Jackson but had subsequently been undermined and subverted by the machinations of selfish businessmen and manufacturers in the decades after the Civil War. Also, like all good Progressives, they automatically assumed that man was primarily an economic creature and that economic interest largely determined political behavior and developments. Believing that men could both see their interests clearly and perceive the best way to secure them, most of these historians were profoundly skeptical of ideas, which they regarded as either simple reflections of deeper social forces or mere abstractions designed to cloak "real" motives so sinister and selfish that they were best concealed. Their mission was, therefore, to break down the dominant political abstractions of the Revolution and, by "employing the ruthless methods of modern scholarship," to ferret out and expose the concrete interests and motives that lay behind them—to discover, as it were, the "real" American Revolution.

Two early works by Charles H. Lincoln on Pennsylvania[12] and Carl L. Becker on New York[13] provided the foundations for the Progressive interpretation of the Revolution. Lincoln and Becker found that the Revolutionary controversy in both colonies was strongly conditioned by preexisting conflicts within them. In Pennsylvania there were "two opposing forces, one radical," composed of Scotch-Irish Presbyterians and

---

[12]Charles H. Lincoln, *The Revolutionary Movement in Pennsylvania, 1760–1776* (Philadelphia, 1901).

[13]Carl L. Becker, *History of Political Parties in the Province of New York, 1760–1763* (Madison, Wis., 1909).

Germans in the west and non-Quaker lower- and middle-class Philadelphians in the east, and the other "conservative," consisting of the Quaker
mercantile oligarchy in the east. In New York the radical unprivileged
and unfranchised common freeholders, tenants, mechanics, and artisans
were aligned against a tightly knit landowning and commercial aristocracy.

In both colonies the conflicts between these groups and the struggle of
the radicals to push their way into the political arena and to achieve a
wider area of economic and social freedom—the fight over "who should
rule at home" and the radical demands for the "democratization of . . .
politics and society"—and not the debate with Great Britain were most
important in shaping political developments in the years between 1763
and 1776. The aristocratic elements in both colonies took the lead in
opposing the Grenville program in 1764 and 1765, but they began to draw
back as it became increasingly clear over the next decade, as Lincoln
wrote, that "the arguments . . . used against English misrule" could be
"turned against minority control and misgovernment" within the colonies. In the crucial years from 1773 to 1776 the extralegal·committees,
conventions, and congresses, not the conservative-dominated and legitimate colonial legislatures, were chiefly responsible for the achievement
of independence, and in the process they also effected—more thoroughly
in Pennsylvania than in New York—the "internal revolution" for which
they had primarily been striving over the previous decade. The contest
with Britain, then, was chiefly important not because it brought the colonies their independence but because it unleashed the "latent opposition
of motives and interests between the privileged and the unprivileged"
and provided the opportunity for the latter to score the first great victory for American democracy by driving some of the privileged to become loyalists and compelling others to give the forces of democracy a
larger share in the direction of public affairs.

The striking similarity between developments in Pennsylvania and
New York strongly suggested that what was true for those colonies was
also true for the others, that the debate with Britain had everywhere
been accompanied by an internal struggle for democracy between radicals and conservatives, unprivileged and privileged, democrats and aristocrats. Added weight was given to this suggestion in 1918 with the publication of Arthur Meier Schlesinger's *The Colonial Merchants and the
American Revolution.*[14] In this volume Schlesinger argued at length that

---

[14] Arthur Meier Schlesinger, *The Colonial Merchants and the American Revolution* (New
York, 1918).

the merchants in all of the colonies exhibited a similar pattern of behavior between 1763 and 1776. Strongly opposed to the new commercial restrictions introduced in 1763 and 1764, they spearheaded the protest against the Stamp and the Townshend Acts. When, however, they began to lose control of the situation to "political agitators" and the "proletarian element," first during the riots over the Stamp Act and then during the enforcement of nonimportation from 1768 to 1770, they realized that they "were unavoidably releasing disruptive forces which, like Frankenstein, they were finding it impossible to control." Thereafter, they discouraged or at least sought to moderate the intensity of further opposition to British policy. Only when the Tea Act of 1773 raised the specter of Parliament-granted monopolies did the merchants again encourage a firm stand, and the results thoroughly confirmed their earlier fears as the radicals seized the initiative, pushed the colonies down the road to independence and to a more democratic polity, and left the merchants with the unsatisfactory alternatives of either becoming loyalists or acquiescing in the political domination of their "natural" rivals.

In a brilliant article[15] which appeared just after the publication of his book, Schlesinger spelled out the implications, for an understanding of the coming of the Revolution, of his own and other recent works on the political, social, and economic divisions within the colonies. In the process he erected a general framework of interpretation which for the next three decades determined the limits of much of the discussion of the Revolutionary controversy. The Revolution, he argued, could no longer be looked upon simply as a "great forensic controversy over abstract governmental rights." At best, Schlesinger declared, the history of the constitutional defenses of the colonies was "an account of their retreat from one strategic position to another," and, in any case, the big merchants (and presumably the planters)—the men who "dominated colonial opinion"—were, like all "practical men of affairs,. . . contemptuous, if not fearful, of disputes upon questions of abstract right." Rather, the Revolution had to be seen in the context of the "clashing of economic interests and the interplay of mutual prejudices, opposing ideas and personal antagonisms."

In general, Schlesinger emphasized, those interests and prejudices, those ideals and antagonisms, were determined by conflicting economic interests within the empire and by sectional and class considerations within the colonies. Hard economic interests—the fear among the mer-

---

[15] Arthur Meier Schlesinger, "The American Revolution Reconsidered," *Political Science Quarterly* 34 (1919): 61–78.

chants in the middle and northern colonies of the new commercial regulations and later of Parliament-granted monopolies and the desire among
the southern plantation aristocracy to repudiate their enormous debts—
and not devotion to constitutional principles per se drove the colonial
upper classes to oppose the new colonial policy. Inside the colonies there
were not "thirteen units of population thinking alike on most public
questions" but instead, he argued, in applying the frontier hypothesis
of Frederick Jackson Turner, two "major groupings" of population—the
eastern seaboard, divided into the commercial North and the agricultural South, and the West—which were "differentiated by physiographi-
cal conditions, economic interests and political ideals." The union between the "interior democracies" and the "democratic mechanic class" in
the cities, a union promoted by a new breed of professional revolutionaries epitomized by Samuel Adams, shaped the course of internal politics
between 1763 and 1776. "Fundamentally," Schlesinger concluded, "the
American Revolution represented the refusal of a self-reliant people to
permit their natural and normal energies to be confined against their
will, whether by an irresponsible imperial government or by the ruling
minorities in their midst."

That the deep-seated economic forces and sectional and class divisions
in the pre-Revolutionary years emphasized by Lincoln, Becker, and
Schlesinger were, in fact, fundamental to early American political life
had been confirmed in 1913 by Charles A. Beard in *An Economic Interpretation of the Constitution*,[16] a study of the other end of the Revolutionary era and one of the half dozen most influential books ever written in
American history. Assuming that "real economic forces . . . condition
great movements in politics," Beard analyzed the economic interests of
all members of the Constitutional Convention of 1787. A close examination of a group of previously unused Treasury records revealed that most
members of the convention owned government securities. Along with
other evidence, this discovery led him to conclude that the Constitution
"was not the product of an abstraction known as 'the whole people [as
jurists were prone to argue],' but of a group of economic interests which
must have expected beneficial results from its adoption."

Specifically, Beard argued, the holders of personalty—personal property in money, manufactures, trade and shipping, and especially public
securities, which promised to rise in value with the establishment of a
stronger and more effective central government—as opposed to real

---

[16]Charles A. Beard, *An Economic Interpretation of the Constitution* (New York, 1913).

property in land and slaves provided the "dynamic element in the movement for the new Constitution." Welded together by economic concerns that cut across state lines, a "small and active group of men" with strong personalty interests and expectations of large profits inaugurated the movement for the new Constitution, which was written in secrecy by a convention which was with few exceptions composed of men who were "immediately, directly, and personally interested in, and derived economic advantages from, the establishment of the new system." Despite strong opposition from small farming and debtor interests, the personalty interests were able to push the Constitution through the ratifying conventions because a large majority of adult males did not vote either because they were disfranchised or because they did not realize what was happening.

The Constitution thus became "essentially an economic document" written by a group of self-interested men to forward their own personal economic interests and to secure the rights of property; it was, therefore, necessarily inimical to the interests of the vast bulk of Americans, who had either no property or only small holdings. Implicit in Beard's conclusions was the idea that the Constitution, instead of being the logical culmination of the Revolution, as Bancroft and Fiske had argued, was actually a repudiation of it, a counterrevolutionary instrument conceived by conservatives to curb the democratic excesses of the war and Confederation periods.

Around the theme of a deeply rooted and pervasive conflict over democracy between rival groups of radicals and conservatives representing fundamentally antagonistic sectional and class interests, Becker and Lincoln, Schlesinger and Beard had together built what appeared to be a coherent explanation of the entire Revolutionary era. The pressures of 1774–76 finally gave the radicals the opportunity they had been waiting for to wrest the lion's share of political power from the conservatives. Over the next decade they pushed through the Declaration of Independence and inaugurated a program of democratic reform that succeeded in the various states according to the strength of radical domination but was checked, if only temporarily, in 1787–88 by the Constitution and the conservative resurgence it represented.

In 1926 J. Franklin Jameson added significantly to this interpretation with *The American Revolution Considered as a Social Movement*,[17] a sur-

---

[17] J. Franklin Jameson, *The American Revolution Considered as a Social Movement* (Princeton, N.J., 1926).

vey of the democratic achievements of the radicals. Allan Nevins had described in detail some of these achievements two years earlier in *The American States during and after the Revolution*,[18] but it was Jameson who fitted them all together to support the thesis that the American Revolution, like the French Revolution, was truly revolutionary in character and profoundly altered many aspects of colonial society. "The stream of revolution," he wrote in a now famous sentence, "once started, could not be confined within narrow banks, but spread abroad upon the land." The extension of the suffrage, abolition of feudal holdovers such as quitrents, primogeniture, and entail, redistribution of loyalist estates to small holders, disestablishment of the Anglican church, abolition of slavery and the slave trade in many states, and changes in the relation of social classes to one another were all products of the democratic impulses set free by the Revolution. Taken together they represented a significant advance toward a "levelling democracy."

Still other studies published in the 1920s and 1930s amplified the Progressive interpretation of the coming of the Revolution in significant ways. Two analyses of the arguments of the colonial opposition between 1763 and 1776 by Randolph G. Adams[19] and Carl L. Becker[20] agreed, as Becker put it, that the colonists had "step by step, from 1764 to 1776, . . . modified their theory to suit their needs." Denying only Parliament's right to levy internal taxes at the time of the Stamp Act, they extended their argument to include all taxes for revenue after Parliament had humored them by levying external duties with the Townshend Acts; and, after Parliament had threatened the internal constitutions of the colonies by legislation as well as taxation with the Coercive Acts of 1774, they denied that Parliament had any authority over the colonies whatever. Neither Becker nor Adams said as much, but their conclusions could be taken to indicate that the colonies had no firm devotion to the constitutional arguments they employed, that, in fact, it was the economic motive, the desire to escape any form of taxation, that lay behind their behavior.

From this position it was a short step to the idea that the colonists had not taken seriously any of the ideas they spouted in the vast flood of literature that poured from colonial presses in the pre-Revolutionary debate. This was the clear inference of two other studies, by John C.

---

[18] Allan Nevins, *The American States during and after the Revolution* (New York, 1924).

[19] Randolph G. Adams, *The Political Ideas of the Revolution* (Durham, N.C., 1922).

[20] Carl L. Becker, *The Declaration of Independence* (New York, 1922).

Miller[21] and Philip Davidson,[22] both of which were written in the dark days of the Great Depression when the Progressive view of the American past had an especially powerful appeal and when in Fascist Italy and Nazi Germany the manipulation of large segments of the population by clever propaganda made it easy to see propaganda as a major element in American politics at virtually every stage in the nation's history. Both Miller and Davidson recognized that propaganda might be true or false, sincere or insincere, but they tended in general to treat it as a mask for deeper motives. The net results of their studies were to throw still greater doubt upon the depth of the Americans' commitment to the ideas they advanced and, along with the works of Randolph Adams and Becker, to contribute to the conception of the Revolution as a movement begun by a group of wealthy conservatives for essentially economic motives and subsequently arrogated by a small band of radical conspirators using the debate with Britain to accomplish other, more important political, economic, and social ends within the colonies.

By the early 1940s the only parts of the Revolutionary era that had not been thoroughly studied from the Progressive point of view were the war and Confederation periods, the years between the Declaration of Independence and the adoption of the Constitution. Two general surveys, Charles and Mary Beard's *The Rise of American Civilization,*[23] a popular text, and Vernon Louis Parrington's *Main Currents in American Thought: The Colonial Mind,*[24] the first of a vivid three-volume account of the struggle between aristocratic and democratic forces in the American past as expressed in intellectual life, had traced the conflicts of the 1760s and 1770s through the 1780s and the debate over the Constitution. Other studies had described the conflict in two critical states: New York and Pennsylvania.[25] But it remained for Merrill Jensen to present the first really comprehensive study in *The Articles of Confederation*[26] and

---

[21] John C. Miller, *Sam Adams: Pioneer in Propaganda* (Boston, 1936).

[22] Philip Davidson, *Propaganda and the American Revolution* (Chapel Hill, N.C., 1941).

[23] Charles and Mary Beard, *The Rise of American Civilization,* 2 vols. (New York, 1927).

[24] Vernon Louis Parrington, *Main Currents in American Thought: The Colonial Mind* (New York, 1927).

[25] Most notably, E. Wilder Spaulding, *New York in the Critical Period, 1783–1789* (New York, 1932); J. Paul Selsam, *The Pennsylvania Constitution of 1775: A Study in Revolutionary Democracy* (Philadelphia, 1936); and Robert L. Brunhouse, *The Counter-Revolution in Pennsylvania, 1776–1790* (Harrisburg, Pa., 1942), all of which, it should be reiterated, dealt with New York and Pennsylvania.

[26] Merrill Jensen, *The Articles of Confederation* (Madison, Wis., 1940).

The New Nation,[27] the most important books written in the Progressive tradition on the Revolutionary era, with the single exception of Beard's great work on the Constitution.

Jensen's primary achievement was to demonstrate that the Confederation period was not one of complete "stagnation, ineptitude, bankruptcy, corruption, and disintegration," as Fiske and others had suggested. The Confederation government, Jensen showed, made significant accomplishments in the disposition of western lands, and within its framework states and individuals were able both to survive a postwar depression in the mid-1780s and to make a strong beginning toward solving the problems of developing a foreign trade, paying off wartime debts, and paving the way for smoother commercial intercourse among the states. The Fiske view derived, Jensen argued, from the "uncritical acceptance of the arguments of the victorious party in a long political battle" over the nature of the central government, which had been carried on from the outset of the Revolution by the adherents of "two consistently opposed bodies of opinion" deriving to some extent from differing material interests and representing fundamental economic, social, and political divisions in American society. The nationalists, composed largely of those members of the colonial aristocracy who became Patriots and new men who gained economic power during the war, demanded a stronger central government that could preserve them from the "horrors of unchecked democracy" by suppressing internal rebellions, regulating trade, collecting taxes, and checking the "power of the states and the democracy that found expression within their bounds." On the other side were the true federalists, consisting primarily of the prewar radicals described by earlier writers and inaccurately labeled antifederalists. This group was generally satisfied with the Articles, which by providing for decentralization and states' rights were the embodiment of the "agrarian democracy" for which they stood, the constitutional expression of the philosophy of the Declaration of Independence, and the "natural outcome of the revolutionary movement." Having won their real goal, local self-government, with the war, the radicals displayed little interest in maintaining the organization they had created to bring about the Revolution; as a result, they were caught off guard by the dedicated, well-disciplined efforts of the nationalists to overturn the Articles and with them some of the major achievements of the Revolution, and the nationalists were able in 1787 to engineer a "conservative counter-revolution" and erect a "nationalistic

---

[27] Merrill Jensen, *The New Nation* (New York, 1950).

government whose purpose in part was to thwart the will of 'the people' in whose name they acted."

With the works of Jensen, the Progressive conception of the Revolutionary era achieved its fullest expression. It was a story of internal revolution and counterrevolution, the rise and fall of democratic radicalism. Everywhere in the years between 1765 and 1776 radical leaders "seized on British acts as heaven-sent opportunities to attack the local aristocracy . . . under the guise of a patriotic defense of American liberties" and to unite the masses "in what became as much a war against the colonial aristocracy as a war for independence." It was the course of social revolution within the colonies—which Jensen argued was often far more important in determining political behavior than the more remote dangers of British policy—and not the debate with Britain which thus came to receive primary emphasis. The Revolution was to be viewed as "essentially, though relatively, a democratic movement within the thirteen American colonies," and its significance lay in its "tendency to elevate the political and economic status of the majority of the people." With the Constitution the movement was temporarily reversed, but all was not lost, because the nationalists—the aristocratic enemies of democracy—had failed to reckon with the possibility "that the government they created might be captured by the radicals united on a national scale."

By calling attention to the importance of internal divisions, the Progressive historians added a new dimension to the study of the Revolution; more importantly, for over four decades they supplied most of the leading ideas and intellectual energy in Revolutionary scholarship. They had never won the complete endorsement of all of the specialists who wrote about the Revolution, and most of the standard narrative accounts continued to treat it as a struggle for liberty, albeit in much more moderate tones than Bancroft and with a heavy imperial and Progressive veneer.[28] Among the vast body of American historians, however, and

---

[28] This statement refers especially to Claude H. Van Tyne, *The Causes of the War of Independence* (Boston and New York, 1922), and *The War for Independence* (Boston and New York, 1929); H. E. Egerton, *The Causes and Character of the American Revolution* (Oxford, 1923); and John C. Miller, *Origins of the American Revolution* (Boston, 1943), and *The Triumph of Freedom, 1775–1783* (Boston, 1948). The statement is even more applicable to the several important studies of constitutional and political thought published between 1920 and 1940: Charles Howard McIlwain, *The American Revolution: A Constitutional Interpretation* (New York, 1923); Robert Livingston Schuyler, *Parliament and the British Empire* (New York, 1929); Benjamin F. Wright, Jr., *American Interpretations*

especially among the writers of the most widely used American history texts, the Progressive interpretation by the late 1930s had become the standard version of the Revolutionary experience.

Since World War II a new group of scholars has subjected the writings of the imperial and Progressive historians to a massive, critical reassessment. Reexamining and rethinking the evidence at almost every major point, they have proceeded along two distinct yet complementary and overlapping lines of investigation. One line has been concerned mainly with exploring the substantive issues both in the debate with Britain and in the politics of the new nation between 1776 and 1789 and in examining the nature of internal political divisions and assessing their relationship to the dominant issues. A second line of investigation has been through the history of ideas, especially through the underlying assumptions and traditions of social and political behavior, and has sought to explain the relationship between those ideas and the central developments of the Revolutionary era.

Each line of investigation rests upon a conception of human nature that contrasts sharply with older interpretations. For the new group of scholars, man is no longer simply a pawn at the mercy of powerful, incomprehensible forces entirely beyond his control, as he was for both the nineteenth-century nationalists and the imperial historians. Nor is he a creature so strictly devoted to the pursuit of his own self-interest and so extraordinarily prescient as to be able to calculate ends and means as he so often appeared in the writings of the Progressives. Instead, he is an extraordinarily limited and insecure being, tenaciously attached to what he conceives to be his own interests and, often more importantly, to those principles, values, institutions, and aspirations around which he has built his life, and he responds intensely and emotionally to every contingency that seems to threaten any portion of his existence—his ideals as well as his interests. Man's limitations necessarily mean that his perceptions of the threat will rarely be accurate (indeed, he will probably see

of Natural Law (Cambridge, Mass., 1931); Andrew C. McLaughlin, Foundations of American Constitutionalism (New York, 1932), and A Constitutional History of the United States (New York, 1935); Charles F. Mullett, Fundamental Law and the American Revolution, 1760–1776 (New York, 1933); and Edmund Cody Burnett, The Continental Congress (New York, 1941).

threats that do not exist), that he will be perpetually subject to self-delusion so that even his understanding of his own behavior will be distorted, and that he will rarely be able to foresee the results of his actions, though he will often try to do so.

In short, he is a creature who, as A. O. Lovejoy has put it, "is forever 'rationalizing' but . . . is scarcely ever rational," a being who is at once at the mercy of history—of the larger developments within his lifetime—and, within the limits imposed by his nature and the physical and cultural environment in which he lives, free to make choices and take actions—perhaps even great creative and selfless actions—which impinge upon and perhaps even alter in significant ways the course of history. To understand the historical process, then, the new group of scholars assumes, one must understand the nature of broad historical forces, the behavior of individuals and groups, and the interaction between historical forces and human behavior. To understand human behavior, moreover, one must understand man's explanations of his own actions, because, no matter how grossly distorted those explanations may be, man does act upon them and they become, therefore, powerful causative forces.

The new investigations have focused upon seven major problems: (1) the nature of the relationship between Britain and the colonies before 1763; (2) the nature of social and political life within the colonies and its relationship to the coming of the Revolution; (3) the reasons for the estrangement of the colonies from Britain between 1763 and 1776; (4) the explanations for the behavior of the British government and its supporters in the colonies between 1763 and the loss of the colonies in 1783; (5) the revolutionary consequences of the Revolution; (6) the character of the movement for the Constitution of 1787 and its relationship to the Revolution; and (7) the nature and the meaning of the Revolution to the men who lived through it.

In the evaluation of the causes of the Revolution, one of the central problems has been the character of the relationship between Great Britain and the colonies before 1763. Most earlier interpretations viewed that relationship as essentially an unhappy one for the colonists, who, it was suggested, deeply resented the navigation system and chafed under the political restrictions imposed upon them by the home government. This view, which was widely held in Britain and among British officials in the colonies during the eighteenth century, has been sharply challenged by several of the newer investigations.

In *The Navigation Acts and the American Revolution*,[29] Oliver M. Dickerson examined the navigation system as it operated in the eighteenth century and concluded that it did not work serious hardships upon the colonies. He challenged the view of earlier imperial historians, especially George L. Beer, that widespread smuggling was symptomatic of American discontent with the Navigation Acts, denying that before 1763 the colonists either regarded the system as a grievance or seriously attempted to evade it except in the cases of tea and sugar after the passage of the Molasses Act in 1733. Only after 1764, when the British undertook to substitute a policy of trade taxation for the older system of trade protection and encouragement and then in 1767 tried to enforce that policy by establishing a separate Board of Customs for the continental colonies, Dickerson contended, did the colonists become discontented with metropolitan trade regulations. Between 1768 and 1772 the commissioners of the new board employed legal technicalities and unscrupulous methods to plunder large amounts from colonial merchants, including such future Revolutionary leaders as John Hancock and Henry Laurens. This wholesale attack on American liberty and property, not American opposition to the old navigation system or addiction to smuggling, Dickerson argued, provided the only real foundation for the subsequent charge by later historians that colonials were unhappy with the Navigation Acts.

Other historians have disagreed with Dickerson about the colonial attitude toward the navigation system and the effects of the system on the colonial economy. In his detailed study of the operation of the customs service,[30] Thomas C. Barrow agreed with Dickerson that American discontent with the navigation system in the years immediately before the Revolution stemmed largely from the reforms adopted after 1763. But he argued convincingly that the early opposition of the colonists to the system, between 1660 and 1720, indicated that they found it and the philosophy behind it fundamentally objectionable and that their acquiescence between 1720 and 1760 depended not upon their acceptance of the system, as Dickerson contended, but upon its lax enforcement.

---

[29] Oliver M. Dickerson, *The Navigation Acts and the American Revolution* (Philadelphia, 1951). A fuller discussion of this work can be found in chap. 17 above.

[30] Thomas C. Barrow, *Trade and Empire: The British Customs Service in Colonial America, 1600–1775* (Cambridge, Mass., 1967).

Two other students, Lawrence A. Harper[31] and Curtis P. Nettels,[32] argued that the burdens placed on the colonies by the Navigation Acts far exceeded the benefits. Although both admitted that there was little overt dissatisfaction with the acts among the colonists before 1763, they argued, like Barrow, that the colonists' failure to protest the acts was not because they were the cement of empire but because they were not strictly enforced. And while Harper and Nettels also admitted that colonial objections after 1763 were limited primarily to the new regulatory and revenue measures, they suggested that those objections implied, even if few colonists were conscious of the implication, a fundamental discontent with the intent and thrust of the navigation system.

On the basis of more sophisticated and systematic analytical techniques, however, Robert Paul Thomas has recently indicated that Dickerson was closer to the truth than either Harper or Nettels. Finding that between 1763 and 1772 the annual per capita loss to the colonists averaged only about twenty-six cents per person, or about one-half of 1 percent of estimated per capita income, Thomas concluded that neither the Navigation Acts nor the new trade regulations adopted after 1763 imposed significant economic hardships upon the colonial economy.[33]

Of course, Thomas's discoveries do not mean that powerful and articulate segments of the colonial population such as the New England merchants or the large Virginia planters might not have borne an unduly high proportion of the total loss or that for some such groups the Navigation Acts as they were enforced after 1763 might not have constituted a serious grievance, as Harper and Nettels suggested. Obviously, additional research will be required before these arguments can be evaluated more fully, but one point seems to have been rather firmly established: the colonists were not unhappy with the navigation system as it operated in the decades just before 1763, that is, when it was loosely administered.

That political relations were equally satisfactory to the colonists be-

---

[31] Lawrence A. Harper, "The Effects of the Navigation Acts on the Thirteen Colonies," in Richard B. Morris, ed., *The Era of the American Revolution: Studies Inscribed to Evarts Boutell Greene* (New York, 1939), 1–39, and "Mercantilism and the American Revolution," *Canadian Historical Review* 23 (1942): 24–34.

[32] Curtis P. Nettels, "British Mercantilism and the Economic Development of the Thirteen Colonies," *Journal of Economic History* 12 (1952): 105–14.

[33] Robert Paul Thomas, "A Quantitative Approach to the Study of the Effects of British Imperial Policy upon Colonial Welfare: Some Preliminary Findings," ibid., 25 (1965): 615–38.

fore 1763, for much the same reason, was my argument in *The Quest for Power*.[34] From the last decades of the seventeenth century, colonial offi- cials in London had envisioned a highly centralized empire with a uni- form political system in each of the colonies and with the metropolitan government exercising strict supervision over the subordinate govern- ments. But during the first half of the eighteenth century, they had made no sustained or systematic attempt to achieve these goals. The result, if the experience of the four southern royal colonies is typical, was the development of a working arrangement that permitted colonial lower houses considerable latitude in shaping the constitutions of the colonies without requiring crown officials explicitly to relinquish any of their goals. Sporadic and largely ineffective opposition from London officials and royal governors did not prevent the lower houses from acquiring an impressive array of de facto powers and privileges and, in the process, from transforming themselves from the dependent lawmaking bodies they originally were intended to be into miniature Houses of Commons and, in almost every colony, shifting the constitutional center of power from the executive to themselves. The growing divergence between im- perial ideals and colonial reality mattered little so long as each side refrained from openly challenging the other.

Severe friction in this area did not develop until after 1763, when Par- liament and the crown in its executive capacity challenged at several important points the authority of the lower houses and the constitu- tional structures they had been forging over the previous century and a half. Then, the sanctity of the rights and privileges of the lower houses became a major issue between the home government and the colonists when metropolitan officials insisted upon an adherence to the old goals and colonial legislators, in the course of trying first to draw a line be- tween the authority of Parliament and the lower houses and then to de- limit the boundaries of royal power in the colonies, demanded rigid guar- antees of colonial rights and, eventually, metropolitan recognition of the autonomy of the lower houses in local affairs and the equality of the lower houses with Parliament. Like the navigation system, then, which the colonists tolerated largely because it was laxly enforced, political and constitutional relations were not a source of serious tension before 1763 largely because metropolitan authorities had never made any sustained attempt to make colonial practice correspond to metropolitan ideals.

Carl Bridenbaugh reached a somewhat different conclusion about the

---

[34] Jack P. Greene, *The Quest for Power: The Lower Houses of Assembly in the Southern Royal Colonies, 1689–1776* (Chapel Hill, N.C., 1963).

impact of the Anglican attempt to secure a complete episcopal establishment in the colonies. His detailed exploration of that subject, *Mitre and Sceptre*,[35] not only pointed out the importance of this concrete religious issue in the coming of the Revolution in the Middle Colonies and New England but also argued that the "aggressive" tactics of the Anglicans in those colonies and the long, and at times bitter, debate over the episcopacy question between 1689 and 1760 already had helped to alienate many American dissenters from the mother country long before 1763. Because the advocates of episcopacy were never able to persuade the custodians of the empire to take any concrete steps toward implementing their program, however, the threat of an American bishopric remained no more than a threat and, however alarming to the dissenting clergy and others actively engaged in opposing it, it does not seem to have created sufficient discontent among the colonists at large to have made them unhappy with their connection with Britain. Significantly, as Bridenbaugh indicated, the climax of the episcopacy dispute came during the crucial years between 1760 and 1765 when the vigorous efforts of Archbishop Thomas Secker to secure an American episcopate convinced many American dissenters that an Anglican plot was in the making, caused them to fear lest the Grenville legislation and an American bishopric might be part of the same general scheme to curtail American liberties, and contributed substantially to the explosive reaction to the Stamp Act in the northern colonies. If, however, the furor over the episcopacy question helped to increase the intensity of the northern reaction to other measures in 1764–65, the issue also appears to have loomed much more seriously because of its association with those measures and to have been distinctly secondary to them.

With the profusion of British patriotism that poured from the colonies throughout the Seven Years' War and their notable propensity for quarreling among themselves, the absence of serious friction between the mother country and her North American possessions in 1763, whether in the economic, the political, or the religious realm, made the possibility of a united revolt by the colonies against Britain seem remote indeed. But the patriotism and the bickering, like the absence of friction, were, several writers have recently indicated, extremely deceptive. As Clinton Rossiter has argued in his lengthy discussion of the formal concepts of colonial political thought, *Seedtime of the Republic*,[36] by the middle of

---

[35] Carl Bridenbaugh, *Mitre and Sceptre: Transatlantic Faiths, Ideas, Personalities, and Politics, 1689–1775* (New York, 1962).

[36] Clinton Rossiter, *Seedtime of the Republic* (New York, 1953).

the eighteenth century colonial Americans had developed, out of their English intellectual heritage and a century and a half of practical experience, a common political faith. At the heart of that faith was a philosophy of "ethical, ordered liberty" that found expression in and served as the foundation for the arguments advanced by Americans during the Revolutionary crisis.

That the development of these common political ideas was accompanied by the emergence of common attitudes, values, and traditions in all other areas of colonial thought was the thesis of Max Savelle in *Seeds of Liberty*,[37] a general survey of eighteenth-century colonial culture. By 1750, Savelle contended, the colonists were one people culturally, with a latent American loyalty and American nationalism. Savelle was careful to emphasize that during the closing years of the Seven Years' War this American loyalty was submerged under an orgy of British patriotic sentiment as Americans celebrated the great British victories in Canada, the West Indies, and Europe; the accession of a vigorous young king, George III, in 1760; and the great Peace of Paris in 1763, which made the British Empire, contemporary panegyrists claimed, the most extensive and powerful empire in the world since Rome. Never, Savelle admitted, had British nationalism been stronger in the colonies. Yet, he argued, the effusions of British patriotism, however sincere, served to conceal a powerful, if still largely dormant, spirit of American nationalism that was waiting to be nourished by the British challenge between 1763 and 1766.[38]

Richard L. Merritt has recently confirmed these conclusions.[39] Seeking some way to measure more precisely the American sense of community, he turned to colonial newspapers, the importance of which in stimulating opposition to Britain after 1763 had been emphasized earlier by Arthur M. Schlesinger.[40] By using content analysis and counting the explicit verbal symbols of identification—e.g., "American," "Europe," "Great Britain," "Virginia," "Massachusetts"—in a carefully selected sample of the newspapers, he discovered that the colonists had already "developed a fairly high degree of community awareness" well before

[37] Max Savelle, *Seeds of Liberty: The Genesis of the American Mind* (New York, 1948). Savelle expanded on this theme later in "Nationalism and Other Loyalties in the American Revolution," *American Historical Review* 67 (1961): 901–23.

[38] For another discussion of this point, see Paul A. Varg, "The Advent of Nationalism, 1758–1776," *American Quarterly* 16 (1964): 160–81.

[39] Richard L. Merritt, *Symbols of American Community, 1735–1775* (New Haven, 1966).

[40] Arthur Meier Schlesinger, *Prelude to Independence: The Newspaper War on Britain, 1764–1776* (New York, 1958).

1763. By stimulating the colonists' pride in being Britons and by demanding an unusual amount of American attention to the home country and its military exploits, the Seven Years' War had, in fact, actually operated as a temporary brake upon the growth of that awareness. As soon as the war was over, however, the American sense of community increased perceptibly. The "takeoff" point, Merritt found, came during the early summer of 1763, well before any of the British measures that Americans found objectionable had gone into effect. The nature of his data did not enable him to explain *why* the colonists were becoming increasingly interested in one another. To answer that question he fell back upon some of the integrative forces—the emergence during the middle decades of the eighteenth century of intercolonial trading patterns and communications networks, an interlocking elite, and closer interurban ties—previously emphasized by Michael Kraus[41] and Carl Bridenbaugh.[42] Whatever "caused" this development, however, it was, Merritt suggested, an important element in enabling the colonists to offer united resistance during the Stamp Act crisis, "which, in its turn, made a further contribution to the developing sense of American community."

The debate with Britain, then, was, as Savelle had suggested, not the origin of American national sentiment but a powerful "impetus to a moving political force already underway." Each successive crisis reinforced "the colonists' growing sense of American separatism" until by 1775 they had crossed what Merritt called the "threshhold" of functional and psychological political amalgamation which enabled them to form national political institutions and to fight a war against Britain. This growing sense of American community, then, helps to explain how thirteen diverse and often quarreling colonies could in just twelve short years sufficiently overcome their differences to unite against the mother country.

That the colonists' strong feelings of British patriotism in 1763 depended to a large extent upon a conception of the role of the colonies in the British Empire that itself reflected the expanding sense of community among the colonies was suggested by Richard Koebner in *Empire*,[43] a study in political semantics. This investigation of the history of the terms *empire, imperial,* and *imperialism* in the language of western Eu-

---

[41] Michael Kraus, *Intercolonial Aspects of American Culture on the Eve of the Revolution, with Special Reference to the Northern Towns* (New York, 1928).

[42] Carl Bridenbaugh, *Cities in Revolt: Urban Life in America, 1743–1776* (New York, 1955).

[43] Richard Koebner, *Empire* (Cambridge, 1961).

rope from Rome to the Congress of Vienna contained a large section on British and colonial uses of the terms in the seventeenth and eighteenth centuries. It showed that the notion of the British Empire did not acquire a prominent place in British historical consciousness until after the Glorious Revolution and that even then it was an extremely restricted concept that referred only to Great Britain and Ireland and not to British possessions overseas. Only after 1740 did the colonies acquire a place in the empire, and then, the impetus for that development came from the colonies, not the home islands. Aware of their increasing importance to Britain and exhilarated by their vision of future greatness, Americans began to conceive of the colonies as the "British Empire in America," and out of this concept emerged the idea of the empire as a worldwide political system held together by mutual allegiance and the harmony of interests among the constituent parts.

This vision was, however, strictly an American creation, and in the decade preceding the Revolution it became clear that British officials had not yet come to regard the colonies as part of the empire, much less as the equal partners some Americans thought them to be. That, with the notable exception of Massachusetts governor Francis Bernard, British officials did not understand that the American view of the empire included the colonies and could not, therefore, appreciate the implications of equality inherent in that concept helps to explain why they were constantly surprised at the extent of American demands, were unable to grasp the fundamental assumptions behind American constitutional arguments, and so thoroughly misconstrued the nature of American intentions. When they did begin in the 1760s to employ a broader concept of empire that took in the colonies, they used it as a device to bring about a more unified constitutional arrangement that would guarantee the subordination, not the equality, of the colonies. This profound divergence of thought between Great Britain and the colonies about the current and future role of the colonies in the British political community—a divergence that contributed substantially to the breakdown in communications that occurred between 1763 and 1776—explains why American leaders felt such an extraordinary sense of betrayal at the new measures adopted after 1763 and also how the extreme British national feeling they expressed in the early 1760s could dissipate so quickly over the next decade as it became increasingly clear that the metropolitan government did not share their conception of the colonies' place in the empire.

What all of these newer studies seem to indicate, then, is that imperial-colonial relations were largely satisfactory to the colonies before 1763 only because potentially objectionable aspects of British economic

and political policy were loosely enforced and that British national sentiment in the colonies remained high to an important extent because of
the colonists' exaggerated view of their own economic importance within
the imperial community. In retrospect, it is clear that the shattering of
that view by the strict enforcement of metropolitan policy was bound to
stir resentment and opposition in the colonies. Had relations continued
to follow the same pattern after 1763 as before, however, it is entirely
possible that the colonists would have been as pleased with their British
connection in 1776 and 1787 as they were in 1763. Whig and imperial
historians to the contrary notwithstanding, recent studies strongly suggest that the Revolution cannot be attributed either primarily or directly
to colonial discontent with conditions as they operated before the 1760s.

Other scholars have directed their attention to the detailed study of political life within the individual colonies during the era of the Revolution,
and their findings indicate that major modifications are required in the
Progressive conception of both early American politics and the Revolution. Investigators of Maryland, New Jersey, Connecticut, Pennsylvania, Rhode Island, Georgia, and Virginia have analyzed the impact of
the debate with Britain upon local politics and assessed the importance
of the peculiar configuration of the economic, social, and political life of
each colony in shaping its response to that debate.[44]

Although these works reveal that the relative importance of the major
substantive issues and the pattern of the Revolutionary movement varied considerably from colony to colony and that there were special, and
occasionally extremely significant, local grievances against the metropolitan government in almost every colony, they also call attention to some

---

[44]Charles A. Barker, *The Background of the Revolution in Maryland* (New Haven, 1940);
Donald L. Kemmerer, *Path to Freedom: The Struggle for Self-Government in Colonial New
Jersey, 1703–1776* (Princeton, N.J., 1940); Oscar Zeichner, *Connecticut's Years of Controversy, 1750–1776* (Chapel Hill, N.C., 1949); Theodore Thayer, *Pennsylvania Politics and
the Growth of Democracy, 1740–1776* (Harrisburg, Pa., 1953); David Hawke, *In the Midst
of a Revolution* (Philadelphia, 1961); Arthur L. Jensen, *The Maritime Commerce of Colonial Philadelphia* (Madison, Wis., 1963); David S. Lovejoy, *Rhode Island Politics and the
American Revolution, 1760–1776* (Providence, 1958); Kenneth Coleman, *The American
Revolution in Georgia, 1763–1789* (Athens, Ga., 1958); W. W. Abbot, *The Royal Governors
of Georgia, 1754–1776* (Chapel Hill, N.C., 1959); and Thad W. Tate, "The Coming of
the Revolution in Virginia: Britain's Challenge to Virginia's Ruling Class, 1763–1776,"
William and Mary Quarterly, 3d ser., 19 (1962): 323–43.

important common features. Everywhere, relations with Britain were relatively harmonious before 1763, and politics within the colonies were primarily elitist in nature. Public office—both appointive and elective— and political leadership were securely in the hands of the upper-class groups, and, although there were occasional manifestations of social and economic discontent among the lower classes, that discontent never resulted in widespread demands for basic changes in the customary patterns of upper-class leadership. Political divisions, despite the earlier contentions of Lincoln and Becker, were not along class lines and not between rival ideological groups of radicals and conservatives. Rather, they revolved around the ambitions of rival factions among the elite. The debate with Britain was in many instances the occasion for one faction to gain political predominance at the expense of its rivals, but, significantly, the faction that stood for the strongest line of resistance to British policy usually emerged victorious.

Within the colonies, then, the direction of local politics and the balance of political forces were influenced, and in some cases altered profoundly, by the debate after 1763 over Parliament's authority and the extent of the crown's prerogative in the colonies. The constitutional debate was thus not only the primary political concern within most colonies from 1763 to 1776, these studies seem to indicate, but also the most powerful agency of political change.

An even more direct challenge to the Progressive conception of the Revolution came from Robert E. and B. Katherine Brown in two studies of the relationship between politics and social structure in Massachusetts and Virginia.[45] The Browns' discoveries that in both colonies the economic structure was highly fluid, property widely distributed, and lower-class economic and social discontent minimal indicated that neither colony was so rigidly stratified as to produce the kind of social conflicts which Progressive historians thought were the stuff of colonial politics. By showing as well that the franchise was considerably wider than had previously been supposed, the Browns also demonstrated that the predominance of the upper classes in politics did not depend upon a restricted franchise, that they had to have the support of men from all classes to gain elective office.

That both of these conclusions are probably also applicable to most other colonies is indicated by the findings of several other recent indepen-

---

[45] Robert E. Brown, *Middle-Class Democracy and the Revolution in Massachusetts, 1691– 1780* (Ithaca, N.Y., 1955), and Robert E. and B. Katherine Brown, *Virginia, 1705–1786: Democracy or Aristocracy?* (East Lansing, Mich., 1964), respectively.

dent investigations of Connecticut, New York, New Jersey, Pennsylvania, and Rhode Island.[46] All of these studies argue that the franchise in these colonies was very wide and that the vast majority of free adult males could expect to acquire enough property during their lifetimes to meet suffrage requirements. Similarly, Jackson Turner Main in *The Social Structure of Revolutionary America*[47] demonstrated that, although there were great extremes in wealth and in standards and styles of living in American society during the late eighteenth century, it was everywhere relatively free from poverty, and among the free population it had, especially by European standards, a high rate of vertical mobility, great social and economic opportunity, and a remarkably supple class structure. This combination of economic abundance and social fluidity, Main concluded, tended "to minimize those conflicts which might have grown out of the class structure and the concentration of wealth" that was occurring in older settled areas on the eve of the Revolution.

Other studies of the underlying assumptions and modes of behavior of early American politics by J. R. Pole[48] and Richard Buel, Jr.,[49] have helped to resolve what, within the modern democratic conceptions employed by the Progressive historians and such recent writers as Robert E. Brown, was such a massive and incomprehensible paradox: why, in the words of Pole, "the great mass of the common people might actually have given their consent to concepts of government" that by "systematically" excluding them "from the more responsible positions of political power" restricted "their own participation in ways completely at variance with the principles of modern democracy."

Revolutionary society, these studies have found, was essentially what Walter Bagehot called "a deferential society" that operated within an integrated structure of ideas fundamentally elitist in nature. That structure of ideas assumed, among other things, that government should be

---

[46] Charles S. Grant, *Democracy in the Connecticut Frontier Town of Kent* (New York, 1961); Milton M. Klein, "Democracy and Politics in Colonial New York," *New York History* 40 (1959): 221–46; Richard P. McCormick, *The History of Voting in New Jersey: A Study of the Development of Election Machinery, 1664–1911* (New Brunswick, N.J., 1953); Thayer, *Pennsylvania Politics;* and Lovejoy, *Rhode Island Politics.*

[47] Jackson Turner Main, *The Social Structure of Revolutionary America* (Princeton, N.J., 1965).

[48] J. R. Pole, "Historians and the Problem of Early American Democracy," *American Historical Review* 67 (1962): 626–46.

[49] Richard Buel, Jr., "Democracy and the American Revolution: A Frame of Reference," *William and Mary Quarterly*, 3d ser., 21 (1964): 165–90.

entrusted to men of merit; that merit was very often, though by no means always, associated with wealth and social position; that men of merit were obliged to use their talents for the benefit of the public; and that deference to them was the implicit duty of the rest of society. All society was therefore divided between the rulers and the ruled, and the rulers, including the representatives of the people, were not the tools of the people but their political superiors. "The mass of the people," Buel argued, thus "elected representatives not to order them around like lackeys to do the people's bidding, but to reap benefit from the distinguished abilities of the few upon which the safety of society might in large measure depend" and to utilize the "political *expertise* of the realm in the people's behalf." To be sure, representative institutions provided the people with the means to check any unwarranted abuses of power by their rulers, but the power the people possessed was "not designed to facilitate the expression of their will in politics but to defend them from oppression." Both Pole and Buel concluded that, although these assumptions were undermined by the Revolution and eventually gave way after 1790 to an expanded conception of the people's role in the polity, they continued to be the predominant elements underlying American political thought over the whole period from 1763 to 1789.

Obviously, many more specialized studies of developments within individual colonies will be required before the nature of internal political divisions and their relationship to the coming of the Revolution are fully understood. The investigations already published do, however, suggest four tentative conclusions that flatly contradict earlier arguments of the Progressive historians: the configuration of politics and the nature of social and economic divisions varied enormously from state to state; social and political opportunity was remarkably wide; class struggle and the demand for democracy on the part of unprivileged groups were not widespread and not a primary causative factor in the coming of the Revolution; and colonial political life operated within a structure of commonly accepted values that assigned positions of leadership in the polity to members of the social and economic elite.

One of the results of the discoveries that tensions between Britain and the colonies before 1763 were relatively mild and that political rivalries within the colonies were, in most cases, distinctly secondary in importance to the constitutional debate with Britain between 1763 and 1776 has been that historians have increasingly come to focus more directly upon that debate in their search for an explanation for the coming of the Revolution. The guiding question in this search has been why, in the years after 1763, the colonists became unhappy enough to revolt. To answer this question a number of historians have sought to identify and assess the importance of the several substantive issues between the colonies and Great Britain.

Thus Bernhard Knollenberg explored the nature and areas of American discontent during the early 1760s in *Origin of the American Revolution, 1759—1766.*[50] Although he agreed with other recent writers that Americans were generally happy with existing political and economic relationships with Britain through the middle decades of the eighteenth century, he contended that trouble began not in 1763 but in 1759, when British military successes made it unnecessary to placate the colonies further and permitted metropolitan authorities to inaugurate a stricter policy. Over the next four years a wider and more intensive use of such traditional checks as the royal instructions and legislative review produced a significant amount of discontent throughout the colonies.

That discontent increased measurably beginning in the spring of 1762, when first the Bute and then the Grenville ministries undertook a variety of general reform measures designed to tighten the colonial system. In 1763 came a series of steps that were particularly unpopular in New England, including the decision to use the Royal Navy to curb smuggling and to enforce the previously laxly administered Molasses Act of 1733 and various white pines acts. Also in 1763, metropolitan officials decided to station a large standing army in the colonies and to limit western expansion into the region beyond the Allegheny Mountains. Security was the primary consideration behind both measures, but it was easy for Americans to interpret the former as an attempt to overawe them with force and the latter as a stratagem to confine them to the seacoast—motives, Knollenberg found, which actually did play some small part in the decisions. The necessity of paying for the army led to the decision to tax the colonies and to Parliament's passage in 1764 of the Sugar Act, which provided for extensive reforms in colonial administration, and in 1765 of the Stamp Act, which touched off the colonial uprising in 1765–66. According to Knollenberg, then, the cumulative effect of British policy over the previous six years, and not the Stamp Act alone, brought the colonies to the brink of rebellion during the Stamp Act crisis.

That the Stamp Act and the threat of parliamentary taxation which

---

[50] Bernhard Knollenberg, *Origins of the American Revolution, 1759—1766* (New York, 1960). A fuller discussion of this work can be found in chap. 17 above.

it contained were easily the most important sources of American dissatisfaction in the uprising of 1765–66 has, however, been persuasively argued by Edmund S. Morgan and Helen M. Morgan in *The Stamp Act Crisis: Prologue to Revolution*,[51] one of the two or three most important books published on the era of the Revolution since World War II. On the basis of a new and thorough reexamination of what was probably already the most studied of the events preceding the Revolution, the Morgans reached several important new conclusions that fundamentally challenged old interpretations.[52] Most importantly, they found that Americans objected to all forms of parliamentary taxation for revenue in 1764–65 and not simply to internal taxes, as both imperial and Progressive historians had implied. By showing that American legislators and pamphlet writers categorically denied Parliament's authority to levy any taxes for revenue purposes, a principle to which they consistently adhered for the next decade,[53] they effectively refuted the traditional charge that Americans were inconsistent and continually enlarged their claims as the situation changed.

As the subtitle suggested, the Morgans' study argued for the decisiveness of the Stamp Act crisis in the unfolding Revolutionary drama. Not only did it raise the issue of the extent of Parliament's jurisdiction in the colonies by forcing American leaders and Parliament into a precise formulation of directly opposing views; it also created an atmosphere of mutual suspicion that pervaded all subsequent developments and quite possibly precluded any peaceful settlement of the issue. Thereafter, Americans scrutinized every parliamentary action for possible threats to their constitutional rights, while British authorities became increasingly convinced that American opposition was simply a prelude to an eventual attempt to shake off the restraint of the Navigation Acts and perhaps even political dependence.

Other scholars analyzed in detail the American reaction to still other issues during the period from 1760 to 1776. The works of Dickerson, Barrow, Bridenbaugh, and myself, treating respectively the colonial reaction to the new trade restrictions, customs regulations, proposals for an

---

[51] Edmund S. Morgan and Helen M. Morgan, *The Stamp Act Crisis: Prologue to Revolution* (Chapel Hill, N.C., 1953). A fuller discussion of this work can be found in chap. 17 above.

[52] See also the more detailed analysis in Edmund S. Morgan, "The Postponement of the Stamp Act," *William and Mary Quarterly*, 3d ser., 7 (1950): 353–92.

[53] For a more thorough elaboration of this point, see Edmund S. Morgan, "Colonial Ideas of Parliamentary Power," ibid., 5 (1948): 311–41.

American episcopate, and attacks on assembly rights, have already been discussed. Carl Ubbelohde[54] and John Shy[55] have explored the response to the vice-admiralty courts and the army.

Although the vice-admiralty courts had been in existence since 1696, they never, Ubbelohde found, became the object of deep colonial hostility before 1763, largely because colonial merchants and others involved with them had been able to avoid them. When, however, metropolitan authorities sought after 1763 to make the courts a "cornerstone in the new imperial rule" through a series of new and stricter regulations, colonial opposition hardened noticeably. Still, the courts did not come under major attack until after Parliament had given them jurisdiction over the enforcement of first the Sugar and Stamp Acts and then the Townshend Revenue Act. Americans, drawing a fundamental distinction between the old trade regulations and the new revenue laws, argued that to try cases arising under the revenue laws in juryless vice-admiralty courts deprived them of their ancient right of trial by jury. In Britain such cases were tried before juries in the common-law Court of Exchequer, and to alter that procedure in the colonies seemed to create an invidious distinction, as well as a basic inequality of rights, between Englishmen and Americans.[56] Yet, Ubbelohde concluded, however intrinsically objectionable Americans found the courts, their hostility to them ebbed and flowed with their dissatisfaction over questions of greater moment, and it was really the association of the courts with the new revenue laws and other broad objectives of British policy after 1763 that made them seem so onerous to the colonists.

Shy reached a similar conclusion about the army. Kept in the colonies after the Seven Years' War largely to occupy and defend the non-English rim of the expanded North American empire and to help in the management of Indian affairs, the army was viewed with suspicion by some colonials, who suspected that it might be intended as a coercive force. These suspicions, Shy found, were in part true: the possibility that an American garrison could help to put "some teeth in the imperial system" actually was a secondary consideration with British administrators, although

---

[54] Carl Ubbelohde, *The Vice-Admiralty Courts and the American Revolution* (Chapel Hill, N.C., 1960).

[55] John Shy, *Toward Lexington: The Role of the British Army and the Coming of the American Revolution* (Princeton, N.J., 1965).

[56] This aspect of the issue is treated more fully in David S. Lovejoy, "Rights Imply Equality: The Case against Admiralty Jurisdiction in America, 1764–1776," *William and Mary Quarterly*, 3d ser., 16 (1959): 459–84.

not until the Stamp Act crisis did they come to conceive of the army as "a police force" primarily. Yet because metropolitan authorities did not use the army in that way during the crisis, there was relatively little overt colonial opposition to it.

Only after September 1768, when troops had been sent to Boston specifically to quell the disturbances over the Townshend Acts, Shy found, did colonial leaders begin to suggest widely that the ostensible motive—the security of the colonies from external attack—for originally stationing the army in America was simply a pretext for forcing the colonists to obey the authority of Parliament and the directions of the ministry. Thereafter, polemicists repeatedly warned of the dangers of a standing army to the liberties and morals of the public, and the Boston Massacre, though it led to the removal of most of the troops from Boston and the eventual diminution of hostility to the army, only seemed to justify the warnings. Like the vice-admiralty courts, however, the army did not in the years before Lexington and Concord become "a major grievance in itself." Rather, Shy concluded, its primary importance lay in the fact that it "reinforced American attitudes on other issues."

Benjamin Woods Labaree analyzed the final crisis of the pre-Revolutionary years in detail in *The Boston Tea Party*.[57] The tea party, he argued, was the decisive event in the chain of events that led to the outbreak of war and the Declaration of Independence. The tea party, he pointed out, produced a new spirit of unity among the colonies, after more than two years of disharmony following the abandonment of the nonimportation agreements against the Townshend duties in 1770, and finally determined British officials to take a firm stand against colonial opposition to parliamentary taxation by making an example of Boston. The punitive measures they adopted posed the new and disturbing question of whether the colonists had any rights at all with which to protect themselves from the naked power of Parliament. These acts caused the rest of the colonies to unite behind Boston, drove Patriot leaders to deny that Parliament had any authority whatever over the internal affairs of the colonies, and put both sides into an inflamed state that made war a virtual certainty.

In an important modification of a long-accepted interpretation, Labaree also discovered that among American smugglers of Dutch tea the fear that the Tea Act of 1773 would enable the East India Company to undersell them and so gain a monopoly of the American market was less important in stirring resistance to East India Company tea than Pro-

---

[57] Benjamin Woods Labaree, *The Boston Tea Party* (New York, 1964).

gressive historians had suggested. Although he did not deny that the tea smugglers, who were largely confined to New York and Philadelphia, were concerned over the threat of monopoly, he found it a distinctly secondary issue among Patriot leaders and the public at large. What concerned them far more was the possibility that the Tea Act was simply a clever ruse to inveigle them into paying the tea duty and admitting the long-contested right of Parliament to tax the colonies for revenue. By this discovery Labaree strongly seconded the conclusions of other recent writers that constitutional rights, especially Parliament's attempts to tax the colonies for revenue, were the primary issues between Britain and the colonies in the fateful years from 1763 to 1776.

Although other important issues, such as metropolitan prohibition of legal tender paper currency[58] and western expansion,[59] still await study, these investigations have together made it possible to achieve a rather clear understanding of the importance and relative weight of the several substantive issues in the American case against the British government. Important segments of the colonists had occasionally been offended or alarmed by such things as the Anglican effort to secure an American episcopate or the sporadic attempts by metropolitan officials to curtail the power of the lower houses of assembly, but the colonists were generally satisfied with their connection with Britain before metropolitan officials adopted stricter measures after 1760 that fundamentally challenged American rights and property.

Parliament's attempts to tax the colonies for revenue were far and away the most serious of these measures. Though the colonists found them profoundly disturbing in themselves and though their concentration over so short a period unquestionably contributed to the intensity of the colonial response to the challenge from Parliament, none of the other measures—the effort to tighten the navigation system, the attempt to undermine the authority of the lower houses, the employment of the army as a coercive force, the increased use of the vice-admiralty courts, or the threat to establish an American episcopate—loomed so

---

[58] A brief treatment of this issue is Jack P. Greene and Richard M. Jellison, "The Currency Act of 1764 in Imperial-Colonial Relations, 1764–1776," *William and Mary Quarterly*, 3d ser., 18 (1961): 485–518.

[59] The conclusions of the classic study of British western policy—Clarence W. Alvord, *The Mississippi Valley in British Politics*, 2 vols. (Cleveland, 1917)—have been modified by the findings of several scholars, most notably Jack M. Sosin, *Whitehall and the Wilderness: The Middle West in British Colonial Policy, 1760–1775* (Lincoln, Nebr., 1961), although neither Alvord nor Sosin explored in detail the extent and nature of colonial discontent with that policy.

importantly or stirred such widespread, determined, and pointed opposition. The remarkable consistency of their constitutional demands down to 1774 revealed both the intense commitment of the colonists to the constitutional principles on which they stood and their genuine concern about the constitutional question. Only after 1774, as I emphasized in *The Quest for Power*, did the American protest cease to be largely a series of defensive responses to immediate provocations by the metropolitan government and become an aggressive movement intent not just on securing exemption for the colonies from all parliamentary measures but also, in a striking escalation of their earlier demands, strict limitations upon the crown's use of many of its traditional devices of royal control over the colonies.

Throughout the entire debate the primary issues in the minds of the colonists were, then, essentially of a political and constitutional nature, involving matters of corporate rights, political power, individual liberty, security of property, and rule of law. Although, as Edmund S. Morgan has taken pains to emphasize,[60] all of these objects of concern were intimately coupled with "self-interest" and were conceived of as the necessary safeguards of the colonists' fundamental well-being—social and economic, as well as political—the opposition to Great Britain, these new studies would seem to indicate, was much less directly social and economic in character than earlier historians had suggested.

These conclusions have been considerably enriched and somewhat altered by several recent explorations of the assumptions, traditions, conventions, and habits of thought that underlay and conditioned the American response to the substantive issues in the quarrel with Britain. These studies of what is essentially the psychology of colonial resistance have been especially concerned with the role of the Americans' conception of human nature. At least since the early nineteenth century it has been conventional to attribute to the eighteenth century an optimistic conception of man and a belief in his ability, to paraphrase one of the most famous expositions of this view, to perfect the "good life on earth."[61] But this view, A. O. Lovejoy has insisted,[62] is a "radical historical error." Some eighteenth-century writers did indeed subscribe to such a view of human nature, but, Lovejoy convincingly argued, the "most widely prevalent opinion about human nature" was that men were imperfect

---

[60] Edmund S. Morgan, *The Birth of the Republic, 1763–89* (Chicago, 1956).

[61] Carl L. Becker, *The Heavenly City of the Eighteenth-Century Philosophers* (New Haven, 1932).

[62] A. O. Lovejoy, *Reflections on Human Nature* (Baltimore, 1961).

creatures who were usually actuated "by non-rational motives—by 'passions,' or arbitrary and unexamined prejudices, or vanity, or the quest for private economic advantage." Only because of their "craving for reputation, praise, and applause," which, eighteenth-century thinkers believed, was the "dominant and universal passion" in man, were men ever driven to behave in a manner "necessary for the good order of society and the progress of mankind."

This unflattering view of human nature provided the foundation for an elaborate theory of politics which, in its essential elements, was traceable as far back as antiquity and which—as Z. S. Fink,[63] J. G. A. Pocock,[64] and, especially, Caroline Robbins,[65] among others, have shown—manifested itself in several forms in seventeenth- and eighteenth-century English thought and was especially congenial to those political groups on the fringes or completely out of political power. At the heart of this theory were the convictions that man in general could not withstand the temptations of power, that power was by its very nature a corrupting and aggressive force, and that liberty was its natural victim. The protection of liberty against the malignancy of power required that each of the various elements in the polity had to be balanced against one another in such a way as to prevent any one of them from gaining ascendancy over the rest. A mixed constitution was the means by which this delicate balance was to be achieved, but power was so pervasive and so ruthless that nothing was safe from it.

That this theory of politics with its underlying view of human nature was widely diffused throughout the colonies had been indicated earlier by Gerald Stourzh in *Benjamin Franklin and American Foreign Policy*[66] and by Caroline Robbins and Richard Buel, Jr., in the works referred to previously, but it remained for Bernard Bailyn in *The Ideological Origins of the American Revolution,*[67] perhaps the most penetrating and original

---

[63] Z. S. Fink, *The Classical Republicans: An Essay in the Recovery of a Pattern of Thought in Seventeenth-Century England* (Evanston, Ill., 1945).

[64] J. G. A. Pocock, "Machiavelli, Harrington, and English Political Ideologies in the Eighteenth Century," *William and Mary Quarterly*, 3d ser., 22 (1965): 547–83.

[65] Caroline Robbins, *The Eighteenth-Century Commonwealthman: Studies in the Transmission, Development, and Circumstances of English Liberal Thought from the Restoration of Charles II until the War with the Thirteen Colonies* (Cambridge, Mass., 1959).

[66] Gerald Stourzh, *Benjamin Franklin and American Foreign Policy* (Chicago, 1954).

[67] Bernard Bailyn, *The Ideological Origins of the American Revolution* (Cambridge, Mass., 1967). This volume originally appeared as the Introduction to vol. 1 of *Pamphlets of the American Revolution* (Cambridge, Mass., 1965).

new study of any segment of the era of the Revolution, to show precisely how the theory shaped the American response to British measures after 1763. Within the context of the ideas associated with this theory of politics, Bailyn found, after an intensive examination of American polemical literature in the pre-Revolutionary years, that the succession of restrictive and regulatory measures taken by the British government and royal officials in the colonies after 1763 appeared to be unmistakable "evidence of nothing less than a deliberate conspiracy launched surreptitiously by plotters against liberty both in England and in America." Far from being "mere rhetoric and propaganda," as Progressive writers had charged, such words as *slavery, corruption,* and *conspiracy* "meant something very real to both writers and their readers" and expressed "real fears, real anxieties, a sense of real danger." "In the end," Bailyn argued, this reading of British behavior and "not simply an accumulation of grievances" was what primarily "propelled" the colonists into rebellion. The gross distortions in their interpretation of the actions of the British government, Bailyn implied, mattered much less than that Americans believed that interpretation.

The inner reality behind the ostensible issues and concrete grievances, the "real" Revolution that had so successfully eluded the Progressive historians, Bailyn thus suggested, was not economic or even social in character but intellectual and psychological. Not only hard economic interests or considerations of political power or constitutional principles, then, but also and, Bailyn strongly implied, more importantly, ideas "lay behind the manifest events of the time" and provided the key to understanding the "contemporary meaning" of the Revolution. They revealed, Bailyn insisted, "not merely positions taken but the reasons why positions were taken" and the inner logic of American behavior.[68] Ideas thus played a dual role in the coming of the Revolution. They both provided a framework within which Americans could explain British and their own behavior and determined in significant and fundamental ways their responses to the developing situation.

The place of American conceptions of the past in this framework was the subject of H. Trevor Colbourn's monograph, *The Lamp of Experience: Whig History and the Intellectual Origins of the American Revolution.*[69]

---

[68] Richard J. Hooker makes a similar point about Revolutionary toasts in "The American Revolution Seen through a Wine Glass," *William and Mary Quarterly,* 3d ser., 11 (1954): 52–77.

[69] H. Trevor Colbourn, *The Lamp of Experience: Whig History and the Intellectual Origins of the American Revolution* (Chapel Hill, N.C., 1965).

As Colbourn's subtitle suggested, it was the conception of history as set forth by seventeenth- and eighteenth-century Whig writers to which colonials were largely devoted. That conception saw the past as a continual struggle between liberty and virtue on the one hand and arbitrary power and corruption on the other. Rome fell only after its citizens sacrificed their temperance and virtue to luxury and vice. And, although the Glorious Revolution in England had restored the ancient Saxon virtues and the free constitution in abeyance ever since the Norman invasion, it had not been accompanied by a reformation in English character. As a result, the early eighteenth century presented a dreary scene of continuing moral decline and political irresponsibility—the harbingers, English Whig writers warned, of the total collapse of constitutional government and the eventual fall of Britain. This interpretation of Roman and British history, Colbourn argued, led American leaders to the inevitable conclusion that the behavior of the British government toward the colonies after 1763 was proof of its degeneration. By suggesting that resistance would preserve not merely their liberty and property but their virtue as well, this view of the past helped to turn a political and constitutional debate into a moral conflict.

Two separate articles by Edmund S. Morgan[70] and Perry Miller[71] further explored the moral and emotional dimension of the American response to British policy. Both writers called attention to an important aspect of the Revolutionary experience that had largely eluded earlier historians: the extent to which the reactions of Americans to British measures had been accompanied and conditioned by an uneasy sense that it was not just British degeneracy but their own corruption that was responsible for their difficulties. Arguing that the American response to the Revolution "in all its phases" was "affected" by a group of inherited beliefs in industry, frugality, and simplicity which, for convenience, he called the Puritan ethic, Morgan showed how the widespread fear that British measures were a threat to those values both increased the intensity of the resistance movement and, ultimately, helped to persuade Americans that British persistence in such measures was a sure indication that "the British government had fallen into the hands of a luxurious and corrupt ruling class" and that the only way to preserve American virtue was to sever all connection with Britain.

---

[70] Edmund S. Morgan, "The Puritan Ethic and the American Revolution," *William and Mary Quarterly*, 3d ser., 24 (1967): 3–43.

[71] Perry Miller, "From the Covenant to the Revival," in James Ward Smith and A. Leland Jamison, eds., *The Shaping of American Religion* (Princeton, N.J., 1961), 322–68.

Equally important, however, Morgan suggested both that the colonists, "always uncomfortable in the presence of prosperity," were afraid that the rapid increase in colonial wealth during the eighteenth century had, by encouraging idleness, extravagance, and luxury, led to a precipitous decline in the old values and that these fears gave added impetus and meaning to the nonimportation and nonconsumption agreements employed by the colonists as weapons against British policy at various times between 1765 and 1766. Those agreements, Morgan pointed out, were seen as a means not simply of forcing the British government to repeal the measures in dispute but also of restoring American virtue. By removing the temptations to luxurious living represented by British imports and requiring "self-denial and industry" on the part of all colonials, those agreements, colonial spokesmen expected, would force the colonists to return to the old values and arrest the moral decay that was threatening the colonies with internal ruin. Americans thus conceived of "Parliamentary taxation" as "both a danger to be resisted and an act of providence to recall Americans from declension."

Miller explained how these same fears of moral and spiritual decline affected and were revealed by the American reaction to the outbreak of fighting in 1775. Analyzing the religious ritual that became so manifest a part of the Revolutionary process immediately after Lexington and Concord, Miller discovered a deep concern over the spiritual health of the colonists and a marked tendency to interpret the British government and the British army as the agencies of God's punishment for colonial sin. Receiving wide expression in public sermons in 1775–76, as well as later in the war, this concern was behind the days of humiliation and prayer set aside by Congress and the local governments and was revealed through the traditional Protestant philosophy of the jeremiad. That philosophy assumed both that "the sins of individuals brought calamity upon the commonwealth" and that humiliation before God, an acknowledgment of sin, and a sincere resolution, "not only separately but in unison, to mend their ways, restore primitive piety, suppress vice, [and] curtail luxury" were absolutely necessary before God would intervene to help them in their afflictions. The vindication of American rights and privileges and the success of American arms were thus, the clergy argued, "inextricably dependent upon a moral renovation." What was even more important, they realized in applying the philosophy of the social compact that was so integral to Protestant thought, moral renovation was equally dependent upon immediate and vigorous action against the agencies of their affliction. Resistance to British corruption, the clergy implied, was the means of reviving American virtue.

Although Miller did not explore either the sources or the nature of the social, religious, or psychological tensions that may have been behind the sense of guilt and moral and spiritual decline that gave this conventional, almost instinctual, procedure such compelling force in 1775–76,[72] he suggested that the crisis in imperial relations over the previous decade had caused Americans to go through a process of intensive self-examination, to become acutely aware of the vicious tendencies within themselves and their societies, and to come to the conclusion that it was not just the degeneracy of the British government and British society that they had to fear but also their own imperfect natures and evil inclinations. Like Morgan, Miller thus inferred that the Revolution was an internal fight against American corruption as well as an external war against British tyranny. "The really effective work" of the clergy, he wrote, was therefore "not an optimistic appeal to the rising glory of America, but their imparting a sense of crisis by revivifying Old Testament condemnations of a degenerate people." What gave their message such power with the populace at large was its vivid portrayal of the "vengeance God denounced against the wicked [and of] . . . what dreary fortunes would overwhelm those who persisted in sloth." Yet, Miller pointed out, the words of the clergy carried an implicit promise as well as an explicit threat. Social regeneration and the removal of British corruption, the successful assertion of "native piety against foreign impiety," would, many of the clergy came to infer, usher in a bright new day of "prosperity and temporal happiness beyond anything the world" had thitherto experienced.

Alan Heimert explored the religious aspects of the Revolution in far greater detail and over a much longer period in *Religion and the American Mind from the Great Awakening to the Revolution.*[73] An analysis of the intellectual divergence between "Liberal" (Arminian / Old Light) and Calvinist relgious leaders that grew out of the Great Awakening and of their contrasting responses to the debate with Britain after 1763 convinced Heimert that the evangelical Calvinist followers of Jonathan Edwards were far more deserving of the title "spokesmen of rebellion" than the Liberals for whom it had usually been reserved. The elitist social ideology and the fear of mass popular uprisings manifested by the Liber-

---

[72] Some of the possible sources of these tensions are discussed briefly in Gordon S. Wood, "Rhetoric and Reality in the American Revolution," *William and Mary Quarterly,* 3d ser., 23 (1966): 3–32.

[73] Alan Heimert, *Religion and the American Mind from the Great Awakening to the Revolution* (Cambridge, Mass., 1966).

als made them, Heimert argued, at best only timid revolutionaries, while the millenarian aspects of Calvinist thought—the hope for the establishment of a more affectionate union of Christians and the gradual restoration of the influence of the holy spirit in America—gave it a radical posture that made it far more congenial to the underlying thrust of the Revolution.

Already in the habit of contrasting the corruption of the Old World with the promise of the New in the years before 1763, Calvinist clergymen were among the earliest and most persistent exponents of the theme that the degeneracy of Britain was responsible for and gave coherence to the various measures Americans found objectionable in the 1760s and 1770s. For them, resistance to Britain became the means not only to escape the seductive influences of British depravity and to secure the blessings of liberty for America but also to revitalize "what for thirty and more years had been the social [and religious] goals of the evangelical scheme." By calling forth a vigorous exertion of will on behalf of liberty, by inspiring "sinners to oppose sin," the Revolution, the Calvinists hoped, would serve as the instrument for forging a spiritual union among Americans, "exorcising from America, not merely sinners, but the sinful spirit of selfishness itself," and thus initiating that moral revolution "within men" that would lead irresistibly to the creation of the "earthly Kingdom of the Calvinist Messiah" in America.

Like Miller, Heimert thus stressed that the spirit of 1775–76 was "not universally one of moderation and calculated assessment of political privileges and rights." For the Calvinists, at least, the Revolution was "not so much the result of reasoned thought as an emotional outburst similar to a religious revival." Like both Miller and Morgan, Heimert pointed out the intensely introspective side to the Calvinist's response to the Revolution. Beneath his "zealous opposition to tyranny," Heimert declared, "lay an anxious awareness that, were something not done to change the course of history, the American character, his own included, might well not prove to be completely different from that of the British tyrant whom he opposed."

These studies of the psychology of American resistance have added several new dimensions to our understanding of the colonial reaction to British policy after 1763. First, they have shifted the focus from the ostensible to the underlying issues in the dispute by making fully explicit what, in the several investigations of substantive grievances, had been largely only implicit: that it was not only the *desire* to preserve their traditional rights and privileges against attacks by the metropolitan government but also the *fear* of what might happen to them once those bulwarks against arbitrary power had been removed that drove the colonists to revolt. Second, they have traced the origins of this fear directly to the colonists' conception of human nature, with its strong sense of man's imperfections and especially of his inability to resist the corrupt influences of power. Third, they have shown that that conception derived both, as Bailyn has argued, from a long philosophical tradition which came to the colonists largely through the writings of British dissenters and, as Morgan, Miller, and Heimert have suggested, from experiential roots. From their individual and collective experience the colonists understood how frail and potentially evil man was, and their deep-seated anxieties about the state of individual and social morality within the colonies helped to sharpen and shape their response to and was in turn heightened by the several manifestations of what they took to be corruption and the corrosive effects of power on the part of the metropolitan government. Finally, on the basis of these conclusions it becomes much clearer why the colonists had such an exaggerated reaction to what, in retrospect, appear to have been no more than a series of justifiable and not very sinister actions by the parent state and why they so grossly misunderstood the motives and behavior of the ministry and Parliament and insisted upon interpreting every measure they found objectionable as part of a malign conspiracy of power against colonial, and ultimately all British, liberty.

From the perspective of these studies, then, the Revolution has become on the part of the Americans not merely a struggle to preserve the formal safeguards of liberty against flagrant violations by the British but, in a deeper sense, a moral crusade against British corruption, a crusade made all the more compelling by the American belief that only by a manly opposition to and, after 1776, a complete separation from that corruption could they hope to restore American virtue and save themselves from becoming similarly corrupt.

In their preoccupation with discovering and explaining the nature of American discontent between 1763 and 1776, most recent writers have neglected to give much attention to the Tory and British side of the Revolutionary controversy.[74] This is not to say that they have written

---

[74] This neglect can be explained in large part as a reaction to the writings of the imperial historians, who, as Edmund S. Morgan suggested ("The American Revolution: Revisions in Need of Revising," *William and Mary Quarterly*, 3d ser., 14 [1957]: 3–15), had

"as partisans of the Revolutionaries" or that, like the men of the Revolution and the nineteenth-century patriotic historians, they have assumed either implicitly or explicitly that the Patriots were right and their antagonists wrong. They have not, contrary to recent charges by Gordon S. Wood, attempted "to justify the Revolution."[75] Their findings and emphases do, however, raise two important questions. If, as they infer, the Patriots stood for the maintenance of the status quo and represented the dominant drift of colonial opinion, what can be said of the Tories, the classic conservatives in the Revolutionary drama? If the British government was not trying to establish a tyranny in the colonies, as everyone now would agree, why did it continue to pursue policies that Americans found so objectionable? Both of these questions have been the subject of recent study.

That the Tories represented a small minority of the total colonial population and were clearly out of step with their compatriots has been confirmed by the findings of two new works on loyalism. In *The King's Friends*[76] Wallace Brown concluded on the basis of a systematic analysis of the social, economic, and geographical backgrounds of those loyalists who submitted claims for compensation to the British government that the total number of loyalists constituted no more than 7.6 to 18 percent of the total white adult population. Earlier writers[77] had emphasized the upper-class character of loyalism, but Brown found that, although loyalism was "a distinctly urban and seaboard phenomenon"—except in New York and North Carolina where there were "major rural, inland pockets" of loyalists—with a clear "commercial, officeholding, and professional bias," its adherents came from all segments of society and represented a rough cross section of the colonial population. Only in Massachusetts, New York, and to a lesser degree Georgia were substantial numbers of the upper class represented, and even in those colonies the vast majority of the upper classes were clearly not loyalists. If, in terms of general social and economic background, the Tories were virtually in-

---

gone so far in presenting a sympathetic case for British officials that they had made it difficult to understand why the colonists revolted.

[75] Wood, "Rhetoric and Reality." These charges are valid in the case of the works of Dickerson and Knollenberg.

[76] Wallace Brown, *The King's Friends: The Composition and Motives of the American Loyalist Claimants* (Providence, 1966).

[77] Most notably, Claude H. Van Tyne, *The Loyalists in the American Revolution* (New York and London, 1902).

distinguishable from the Whigs, as Brown's investigation suggested, the question remains exactly how they were different.

William H. Nelson has taken up this question in *The American Tory*,[78] a penetrating study that focuses on the psychological character of the loyalists. The key to loyalism, Nelson argued, was weakness, weakness arising from the loyalists' inherent disparateness, lack of organization, unpopular political views, and marginal position in colonial society. Unlike their opponents, Tory leaders did not consult among themselves, never developed a community of feeling or a common sense of purpose, had no clear alternative to the Whig drift, and did not even know each other. Unable to cultivate public opinion, they held social and political ideas and values that could prevail in the colonies only with British assistance. Many, like Thomas Hutchinson, were passive and narrowly defensive with a sense of fatality, of inevitable misfortune and failure, that prevented them from taking the offensive. Others, like Joseph Galloway, found British measures as unacceptable as the Patriots but waited until the opposition was too far advanced for them to seize the initiative. Similarly, rank-and-file Tories were concentrated among non-English and religious minorities and among people in peripheral areas, "regions already in decline, or not yet risen to importance" such as the western frontier and the maritime region of the Middle Colonies, and represented a series of conscious minorities who looked to Britain for support against an external enemy like the Indians or the dominant majority.

Weakness, then, Nelson argued, along with alienation from or suspicion of the prevailing Whig majority, and not simple loyalty, tied the Tories to Britain and, he implied, was responsible for their choice after the Declaration of Independence. Nelson's conclusions were seconded both by Brown, who suggested that most loyalists "had, or thought they had, something material and spiritual to lose from the break with Britain," and by Douglass Adair and John Schutz in their introduction to *Peter Oliver's* Origin and Progress of the American Rebellion: *A Tory View*,[79] where they explained that Oliver's loyalism was in part attributable to his inability "to adapt himself to the fast-changing events of American life after 1760."

If the work on American grievances did not imply that British politicians were in the wrong, it did suggest that they seriously misjudged the

---

[78] William H. Nelson, *The American Tory* (Oxford, 1961).

[79] Douglass Adair and John A. Schutz, eds., *Peter Oliver's* Origin and Progress of the American Revolution: *A Tory View* (San Marino, Calif., 1961).

situation in the colonies at almost every point between 1763 and 1783 and that, if the preservation of the empire was one of their primary objectives, they blundered badly. If, as imperial historians have argued, the measures of the metropolitan government were wise, just, and well calculated to serve the interests of the empire as a whole, metropolitan authorities failed utterly to persuade the colonists of that fact. How this breakdown in understanding could have occurred in a political community so celebrated for its political genius has been partially explained by Sir Lewis Namier in his exhaustive analyses of British politics during the opening years of the reign of George III[80] and by other scholars in a number of studies working out the implications of his work.[81] A long line of earlier historians from Horace Walpole to Sir George Trevelyan had charged George III with attempting to destroy the influence of the Whig oligarchy and reestablish the supremacy of the crown over Parliament. The king's American program, they suggested, was part of the same pattern, and the English Whigs and the Americans were aligned against a common enemy in a common struggle against tyranny. Had the Whig party been in power, the argument ran, it would have pursued a more conciliatory course and prevented the Revolution.

Namier and his followers sharply challenged this interpretation at every point. They argued that there were no parties in the modern sense, only loosely organized factions and family groups; that what mattered most in politics was neither ideology nor principle but the struggle for office, power, and advantage; that political issues revolved about local rather than national or imperial considerations; that the "political nation"—the people who took an active role in politics—was largely restricted to a narrow elite in the middle and upper echelons of British social structure; that all groups, as well as the king, accepted the traditional Whig principles that had evolved out of the Revolutionary Settle-

---

[80] Lewis Namier, *The Structure of Politics at the Accession of George III*, 2 vols. (London, 1929); *England in the Age of the American Revolution* (London, 1930); and *Crossroads of Power: Essays on Eighteenth-Century England* (London, 1962).

[81] The most important among these studies are Richard Pares, *King George III and the Politicians* (Oxford, 1953), a general discussion of the politics of the reign in the light of Namier's conclusions; John Brooke, *The Chatham Administration, 1766–1768* (London, 1956), and Ian R. Christie, *The End of North's Ministry, 1780–1782* (London, 1958), two detailed studies of the structure and course of British politics during important segments of the Revolutionary years; Charles R. Ritcheson, *British Politics and the American Revolution* (Norman, Okla., 1954), a narrative of the impact of the American troubles upon British politics; and Eric Robson, *The American Revolution in Its Political and Military Aspects, 1763–1783* (London, 1955), a collection of interpretive essays.

ment; and that George III did not have to subvert the constitution to gain control over Parliament because, as in the case of his predecessor and grandfather, George II, his power to choose his own ministers and his control over patronage assured him of considerable influence in determining Parliament's decisions.[82]

What these conclusions mean in terms of the misunderstanding with the colonies, though no one has worked them out in detail, is fairly clear. They reinforce the suggestions of the students of American grievances that British policy was shortsighted and inept. If British political leaders were so preoccupied by the struggle for office and so deeply involved in local matters, it is not difficult to see why they were unable to take a broader view in dealing with the colonies. The engrossment of the ministers and the leaders of Parliament in internal British politics and, before 1770, the frequent changes in administration meant, as several recent books have shown,[83] that much of the responsibility for shaping the details of colonial policy devolved upon the bureaucracy—second-line officials in the Treasury, Board of Trade, American Department, and Law Offices who remained in office despite shifts in administration.

Two books, Michael Kammen, *A Rope of Sand*,[84] and Jack M. Sosin, *Agents and Merchants*,[85] have demonstrated that colonial agents and merchants concerned in the colonial trade operated as a kind of rudimentary lobby to present the views of the colonists and actually managed to secure several important concessions from the government. But neither the agents nor the merchants always had accurate and up-to-date information about the situation in the colonies, and, in any case, most colonial information came to the bureaucracy either from British officials in the colonies, most of whom were unsympathetic to the American cause, or from self-styled experts in both Britain and the colonies who, as John

---

[82] Namier's conclusions have been challenged by Herbert Butterfield, *George III and the Historians* (London, 1957), and others on the grounds that they do not give sufficient weight to the role of ideas and present too atomistic a view of British politics. One of the best replies to Namier's critics is Jacob M. Price, "Party, Purpose, and Pattern: Sir Lewis Namier and His Critics," *Journal of British Studies* 1 (1961): 71–93.

[83] Especially Dora Mae Clark, *The Rise of the British Treasury: Colonial Administration in the Eighteenth Century* (New Haven, 1960); Franklin B. Wickwire, *British Subministers and Colonial America, 1763–1783* (Princeton, N.J., 1966); Sosin, *Whitehall in the Wilderness*; and Shy, *Toward Lexington.*

[84] Michael Kammen, *A Rope of Sand: The Colonial Agents, British Politics, and the American Revolution* (Ithaca, N.Y., 1968).

[85] Jack M. Sosin, *Agents and Merchants: British Colonial Policy and the Origins of the American Revolution, 1763–1775* (Lincoln, Nebr., 1965).

Shy has remarked, often "had some ax to grind or private interest to serve." There was, in short, no sure way for colonial officials to obtain a clear and undistorted version of American views, and this absence of effective channels of communication could lead only to a massive breakdown in understanding during a crisis such as the one that developed after 1773.

Even more important in inhibiting effective action by metropolitan officials, still other studies have indicated, were their preconceptions about what colonies were and ought to be. Reinforced by the association in the official mind of the opposition in the colonies with the radical and, to many members of the British political nation, profoundly disturbing Wilkite agitation in Britain,[86] those preconceptions, according to recent investigations of four of the key figures in British politics—Townshend, Shelburne, Dartmouth, and Germain[87]—were of the utmost importance in shaping the responses of individuals of every political stripe to the imperial crisis. Similarly, Bernard Donoughue[88] has demonstrated how severely those preconceptions limited the range of choices open to the government in the critical period between the Boston Tea Party in December 1773 and the outbreak of war in April 1775. No one either in or out of office, Donoughue found, was able to escape from the oppressive weight of dominant ideas and habits of thinking to grapple with the possibility that, as Americans were insisting, the empire might be preserved without totally subordinating the colonies to Parliament.

The traditional explanation for this failure has been that the men in power lacked vision, magnanimity, and statesmanship. But Donoughue's work pointed to more than a mere series of individual weaknesses. If men could not go beyond the prescribed boundaries of thought and language within which the system required them to work, then perhaps the system itself was incapable of adjustment at that time and the old British Empire may have been less the victim of the men who presided over its dissolution than they were the victims of the system of which

---

[86] The nature and impact of this agitation has recently been analyzed in Ian R. Christie, *Wilkes, Wyvill, and Reform: The Parliamentary Reform Movement in British Politics, 1760 to 1774* (Oxford, 1962), and Eugene Charlton Black, *The Association: British Extraparliamentary Political Organization, 1769–1793* (Cambridge, 1963).

[87] Sir Lewis Namier and John Brooke, *Charles Townshend* (London, 1964); John Norris, *Shelburne and Reform* (London, 1963); B. D. Bargar, *Lord Dartmouth and the American Revolution* (Columbia, S. C., 1965); and Gerald Saxon Brown, *The American Secretary: The Colonial Policy of Lord George Germain, 1775–1778* (Ann Arbor, Mich., 1963).

[88] Bernard Donoughue, *British Politics and the American Revolution: The Path to War, 1773–75* (London, 1964).

the empire was a part. Given his commitment to the Revolutionary Settlement and to the supremacy of Parliament, George III could not possibly have stood apart from Parliament as a royal symbol of imperial union as the colonists desired.[89]

The net effect of the new studies of the coming of the Revolution has been to reestablish the image of the Revolution as a conservative protest movement against what appeared to the men of the Revolution to have been an unconstitutional and vicious assault upon American liberty and property by a tyrannical and corrupt British government. The Revolution, Daniel J. Boorstin argued in *The Genius of American Politics*,[90] had now to be understood as "a victory of constitutionalism." The major issue was "the true constitution of the British Empire," and because the leaders of the Revolution regarded it as an "affirmation of faith in ancient British institutions," the "greater part of the institutional life of the community . . . required no basic change." To Boorstin, the Revolution thus appeared a conservative and "prudential decision taken by men of principle," remarkable chiefly because "in the modern European sense of the word, it was hardly a revolution at all."

Recent investigations of the concrete political and social changes that accompanied the Revolution have tended to reinforce this image. Detailed studies of the political development of three states after 1776 have indicated that there was virtually no change in the traditional patterns of political leadership and little identifiable interest among any segment of society in achieving a more democratic polity. In a careful examination of Maryland,[91] Philip A. Crowl found that after 1776 "a relatively small class of planters, lawyers, and merchants" dominated the politics of that state without serious challenge from below, just as it had throughout the late colonial period. There was plenty of political conflict in Maryland, much of it over hard economic issues, and a bitter struggle

---

[89] A more detailed and comprehensive analysis of the implications of recent writings on British politics in the eighteenth century for the understanding of the Revolution will be found in Jack P. Greene, "The Plunge of Lemmings: A Consideration of Recent Writings on British Politics and the American Revolution," *South Atlantic Quarterly* 67 (1968): 141–75 [chap. 18 above].

[90] Daniel J. Boorstin, *The Genius of American Politics* (Chicago, 1953).

[91] Philip A. Crowl, *Maryland during and after the Revolution: A Political and Economic Study* (Baltimore, 1943).

over the emission of cheap paper money in 1785–87 saw debtors aligned against creditors. But the conflict was not along class lines—the debtors were mostly from the upper classes—and had few democratic overtones. Rather, it consisted of a series of battles over opposing interests, ideas, and personalities between ad hoc coalitions of opposing groups of leading men.

Richard P. McCormick[92] and John A. Munroe[93] reached similar conclusions about New Jersey and Delaware. "Men of interest" loosely organized into two broad factions deriving from long-standing sectional divisions peculiar to each state played the preponderant role in politics without interference from or unrest within the lower classes. These factions took opposing sides on a variety of issues, including the issuance of more paper money, but democracy per se was not an overt issue.[94]

By contrast, as Robert J. Taylor has shown,[95] the Revolution seems to have served as a much more profound educative and democratizing force among the people of western Massachusetts. Traditionally conservative and deeply suspicious of the commercial east, westerners were slow to join easterners in opposing the British, but once they had thrown in their lot with the Patriot cause they took the Revolutionary doctrine of popular sovereignty very seriously. In normal situations they were content to leave political leadership where it had always been—in the hands of local gentry. There were unmistakable signs, however, that the people at large now expected to play an expanded role in the polity. Between 1776 and 1780 they were among the most militant supporters of the demand for a state constitution written by a specially elected convention representing the sovereign authority of the people and then ratified by the people, and the unrest which began in 1781 and culminated in 1786 in Shays' Rebellion dramatically revealed similar tendencies.

The unrest was primarily the result of deteriorating economic conditions and was oriented largely toward economic ends, but the fact that western demands for a more equitable tax system and debtor relief were

---

[92] Richard P. McCormick, *Experiment in Independence: New Jersey in the Critical Period, 1781–1789* (New Brunswick, N.J., 1954).

[93] John A. Munroe, *Federalist Delaware, 1775–1815* (New Brunswick, N.J., 1954).

[94] Similarly, Oscar and Mary Handlin found in a survey of Massachusetts politics ("Radicals and Conservatives in Massachusetts after Independence," *New England Quarterly* 17 [1944]: 343–55) that there were not two stable parties, one radical and the other conservative, but a series of shifting alliances that showed little ideological continuity.

[95] Robert J. Taylor, *Western Massachusetts in the Revolution* (Providence, 1954).

couched in the language of popular sovereignty and made through conventions called by the people on the basis of their "natural right to . . . revise the fundamental law when it became oppressive" served notice that at least in that corner of the new United States the contest with Britain had been accompanied by a potentially powerful revolution in the political expectations of ordinary citizens, a revolution that, to the profound disturbance of political leaders up and down the Atlantic seaboard, might ultimately spread to other regions and other states.

This revolution in expectations did not, however, proceed very far during the period of the Revolution. As Elisha Douglass showed in *Rebels and Democrats*,[96] a study of the process of constitution making in the states, the internal political revolution that, according to the Progressive historians, had occurred in 1776 was a very modest revolution indeed. There was, Douglass found, an articulate, if not very large, group of "democrats" who viewed the Revolution not as an end in itself but as a means to rebuild society on the principles of the Declaration of Independence, and to that end they demanded "equal rights for all adult males and a government in which the will of the majority of citizens would be the ultimate authority for political decision." Ardently opposed by the dominant Whig leaders, who were suspicious of democracy and wanted governments that would check majority rule and retain the traditional system of political leadership, the democrats scored only limited gains in just three states—North Carolina, Pennsylvania, and Massachusetts—and even in those states they were unable to secure permanent control.

A more subtle and, ultimately, more important democratizing force was the increase in popular participation in politics described by Jackson Turner Main.[97] By opening up a large number of new political opportunities, the Revolution drew an increasingly greater number of ordinary citizens into politics, with the result, Main found, that the social base of both the upper and lower houses of the legislature was much broader after 1776 than it had been in the late colonial period. This development did not, however, lead to either a wholesale turnover in political leadership or immediate repudiation of the ideals of upper-class leadership.

---

[96] Elisha Douglass, *Rebels and Democrats* (Chapel Hill, N.C., 1955).

[97] Jackson Turner Main, "Government by the People: The American Revolution and the Democratization of the Legislatures," *William and Mary Quarterly*, 3d ser., 23 (1966): 391–407, and "Social Origins of a Political Elite: The Upper House in the Revolutionary Era," *Huntington Library Quarterly* 27 (1964): 147–58.

Along with the new ideology of popular government fashioned by some of the democrats and described by Douglass and Merrill Jensen,[98] it nevertheless did help to pave the way for the eventual breakdown of the old habits of deference, the ascendancy of the belief in a more popular government, and the veneration of majority rule in the early part of the nineteenth century.[99]

Although the Revolution contained some implicitly or potentially powerful democratic tendencies, all of these studies seemed to indicate that, at least insofar as it affected internal politics, it was fundamentally an elitist movement with only a modest amount of explicit striving among either the people at large or any of the dominant political factions for a wider diffusion of political power.

Although more work remains to be done before firm conclusions can be drawn, it also seems clear, as Frederick B. Tolles noted in a 1954 survey of recent studies,[100] that the concrete social changes Jameson emphasized were less sweeping and less significant than he had thought. Louis Hartz presented the most elaborate statement of this theme in *The Liberal Tradition in America*.[101] Taking for his text Tocqueville's observation that the great advantage of Americans lay in the fact that they did not have to "endure a democratic revolution," Hartz argued that "the outstanding thing about the American effort of 1776 was . . . not the freedom to which it led, but the established feudal structure it did not have to destroy." Living in "the freest society in the world" in 1776 and taking for granted the continued "reality of atomistic social freedom," the Americans, unlike revolutionaries elsewhere, did not have to destroy an ancien régime. The relics of feudalism abolished during the Revolution were just that, *relics* with no necessary social function, and the success and nature of the Revolution—its "outright conservatism"—were, Hartz insisted, directly attributable to "the social goals *it did not need to achieve*."

The view thus came to be that the Revolution was predominantly a conservative Whiggish movement undertaken in defense of American liberty and property, preoccupied throughout with constitutional and

---

[98] Merrill Jensen, "Democracy and the American Revolution," *Huntington Library Quarterly* 20 (1957): 321–41.

[99] In this connection, see, especially, David Hackett Fischer, *The Revolution of American Conservatism: The Federalist Party in the Era of Jeffersonian Democracy* (New York, 1965).

[100] Frederick B. Tolles, "The American Revolution Considered as a Social Movement: A Re-Evaluation," *American Historical Review* 60 (1954): 1–12.

[101] Louis Hartz, *The Liberal Tradition in America* (New York, 1955).

political problems, carried on with a minimum of violence—at least when seen in the perspective of other revolutions—and with little change either in the distribution of political power or in the structure and operation of basic social institutions, and reaching its logical culmination with the Federal Constitution. Whatever democratic stirrings may have accompanied it were incidental, subordinated to the main thrust of events and to the central concerns of its leaders.[102]

As Benjamin Fletcher Wright insisted,[103] the Spirit of '76 seemed to be represented less accurately by the writings of Thomas Paine—whose ideas, as Cecelia M. Kenyon has shown,[104] were decidedly atypical of the dominant patterns of thought among American Revolutionary leaders— or even the Declaration of Independence than by the state constitutions of 1776, 1777, and 1780, constitutions which were shaped out of traditional materials and revealed the commitment of the men of the Revolution to "order and stability as well as liberty," to the ancient British concept that "liberty required constitutional order." This continuity between the new and the old as well as the amazing "consensus on political and constitutional principles" represented both in the state constitutions and the Federal Constitution of 1787, Wright argued, cast far more light upon the nature of the American Revolution than the rather narrow range of conflict and disagreement or the relatively minor elements of discontinuity in the Revolutionary experience.

The Revolution, in short, came to be viewed largely from the perspective of the dominant Whig elite which, with very few exceptions, had managed to retain control of political life as well as the confidence of the public throughout the period from 1763 to 1789. According to the new interpretation, the urban mobs and rural populists who so thoroughly fired the imaginations of the Progressive historians for the most part played only supporting parts in the drama of the Revolution, however

---

[102] This view appears with some variations in most general treatments of the Revolution published in the 1950s and early 1960s. See, for example, John R. Alden, *The American Revolution, 1775–1783* (New York, 1954); Robert E. Brown, "Reinterpretation of the Revolution and Constitution," *Social Education* 21 (1957): 102–5, 114, and *Reinterpretation of the Formation of the American Constitution* (Boston, 1963); Richard B. Morris, *The American Revolution: A Short History* (New York, 1955), "Class Struggle and the American Revolution," *William and Mary Quarterly*, 3d ser., 19 (1962): 3–39, and *The American Revolution Reconsidered* (New York, 1967); and Esmond Wright, *Fabric of Freedom, 1763–1800* (New York, 1961).

[103] Benjamin Fletcher Wright, *Consensus and Continuity, 1776–1787* (Boston, 1958).

[104] Cecelia M. Kenyon, "Where Paine Went Wrong," *American Political Science Review* 45 (1951): 1086–99.

important the roles they were in the process of creating came to be on the American political stage after 1789. Political conflict thus no longer seemed to have been among classes or discrete and "naturally" antagonistic social and economic groups but among rival elements within the elite which competed against one another within a broad ideological consensus not so much over issues as for power and advantage. To be sure, the Revolution was accompanied, as Edmund S. Morgan has indicated in his masterful survey of the whole period,[105] by a creative search for principles first to defend American constitutional rights and then to build a new nation, but that search, at least during the years of the Revolution, was distinctly less radical in its results than earlier historians had assumed.

This overwhelming stress upon the defensive and preservative character of the Revolution tended to divert attention from any revolutionary or radical implications that may have accompanied it, and not until the early 1960s did a few scholars set out to discover and explain just what was actually revolutionary about the Revolution. The most systematic and thorough exploration of this theme was by Bernard Bailyn in a 1962 article[106] and in *The Ideological Origins of the American Revolution.* What "endowed the Revolution with its peculiar force and made of it a transforming event," Bailyn declared, was not the "overthrow of the existing order"—which nowhere occurred—but the "radical idealization and rationalization of the previous century and a half of American experience." Many of the social and political goals of the European Enlightenment, Bailyn pointed out, had already "developed naturally, spontaneously, early in the history of the American colonies, and they existed as simple matters of social and political fact on the eve of the Revolution." Because habits of mind and traditional ways of thinking lagged far behind these fundamental changes in the nature of colonial social and political life, however, there was on the eve of the Revolutionary debate a sharp "divergence between habits of mind and belief on the one hand and experience and behavior on the other."

By requiring a critical probing of traditional concepts and forcing the colonists to rationalize and explain their experience—"to complete, formalize, systematize, and symbolize what previously had been only partially realized, confused, and disputed matters of fact"—the Revolution helped to end this divergency. Most of the political ideas that emerged

---

[105] Morgan, *Birth of the Republic.*

[106] Bernard Bailyn, "Political Experience and Enlightenment Ideas in Eighteenth-Century America," *American Historical Review* 67 (1962): 339–51.

from this process—the conceptions of representative bodies as mirrors of their constituents, of human rights as existing above and limiting the law, of constitutions as ideal designs of government, and of sovereignty as divisible—were at once expressive of conditions that had long existed in the colonies and basic reconceptions of traditional notions about the "fundamentals of government and of society's relation to government." By "lifting into consciousness and endowing with high moral purpose" these "inchoate, confused elements of social and political change," the Revolutionary debate thus both released social and political forces that had long existed in the colonies and "vastly increased their power."

The movement of thought, Bailyn observed, quickly spilled over into other areas and produced a critical discussion of the institution of chattel slavery, the principle of the establishment of religion, and even conventional assumptions about the social basis of politics and the constitutional arrangements that followed from those assumptions. Ultimately, in the decades after the Revolution, these "changes in the realm of belief and attitude" and, more especially, the defiance of traditional order and distrust of authority contained within them affected the very "essentials" of American social organization and, Bailyn pointed out, helped permanently to transform the nature of American life.

Although Cecelia M. Kenyon[107] insisted that independence and the creation and adoption of the Constitution of 1787 were genuinely radical results of the Revolution, the two other consequences that she singled out as radical—the establishment of republicanism and the "crystallization of the individualism and egalitarianism of the Declaration of Independence into an operative as well as a formal political philosophy"—also fell largely within the realm of ideas. What was so remarkable and so innovative about the former, she observed, was not the formal institution of republican government, which was accomplished with ease and brought no pervasive or "fundamental changes, either in private or public life," but the sudden development among Americans, who only a short time before had been committed monarchists, of a deep "ideological attachment to republicanism" and the association in the public mind of "all the characteristics of good government with republicanism, and with republicanism only."

Far more innovative, Kenyon argued, was the radical individualism, the "political and ethical egoism," which was central to the developing philosophy of the Revolution and was symbolized by the substitution in

---

[107] Cecelia M. Kenyon, "Republicanism and Radicalism in the American Revolution: An Old-Fashioned Interpretation," *William and Mary Quarterly*, 3d ser., 19 (1962): 153–82.

the Declaration of Independence of "the *pursuit of happiness* for *property*" in the traditional trilogy of inviolable rights. Because happiness was "a subjective goal dependent on individual interpretation," it was, as an end of government, "far more individualistic" than the protection of property and necessarily strongly egalitarian in its implications. Clearly, no individual could decide for another what would promote his happiness, and, as Kenyon pointed out, if all men had by nature an equal right to the pursuit of happiness, it followed "logically that every man should have a voice in the determination of public policy." Although this philosophy of radical individualism was a clear invitation to political relativism and to the acceptance, even idealization, of the pursuit of self-interest as a legitimate form of behavior to be protected, even encouraged, by government, its full effect, Kenyon emphasized, was not realized until well after the Revolutionary era because the men of the Revolution, despite the individualistic trend of their thought, continued to think in terms of an objective common good and "to deplore man's tendency toward self-interest and bias."

Alan Heimert similarly emphasized the radical thrust of the thought of the Revolution in *Religion and the American Mind.* The double focus of the Calvinist Revolutionary crusade, he noted, the emphasis upon both securing the benefits of liberty and achieving an affectionate Christian union free of invidious social and political distinctions, had a millennarian character that made it a potentially "highly radical political movement." The Revolution was expected to inaugurate the moral renovation of man, and once that renovation was under way, Calvinists implied, government—that badge of lost innocence and symbol of man's corruption—could be placed more directly in the hands of the people, who in turn would "persevere in the Christian warfare until all despots, great and petty, had been overthrown." Perhaps because the Calvinists did not, in general, speak for "the more respectable and presumably . . . most powerful elements of colonial society," who, as other writers have shown, retained control of American political life, this movement did not, however, make much headway during the Revolution.

Gordon S. Wood has built upon these foundations a comprehensive analysis of the development of American political thought from the Declaration of Independence to the adoption of the Federal Constitution.[108] Like Bailyn, Wood stressed the radicalism of the Spirit of '76, locating

---

[108]Gordon S. Wood, *The Creation of the American Republic, 1776–1787* (Chapel Hill, N.C., 1969).

it not in the relatively minor (outside Pennsylvania) transfer of political leadership from old to new men emphasized by older historians, and not in the radical reconception of politics described by Bailyn, but in the Americans' expectation that the Revolution would usher in a "new era of freedom and bliss" not only for themselves but for the whole of mankind. In Wood's view millennial aspirations of the sort Heimert associated only with the evangelical clergy constituted the very core of American political and social thought during the first stages of the Revolution.

What lay behind these utopian impulses and what gave the "revolution its socially radical character," according to Wood, was the confident expectation that separation from a degenerate Britain and the institution of a republican government would purge America of its moral and social impurities. These developments, American spokesmen hoped, would alter the very character of the American people by transforming them into virtuous citizens who would eschew the vices and luxuries of the Old World in favor of the simple virtues, put aside all individual concerns for the common good, and reconstruct their societies so that the only meaningful social distinctions would be those arising from natural differences among men. Precisely because they put such extraordinarily high hopes upon the regenerative effects of republican government, the construction of new state governments became a work of enormous importance.

That these hopes were misplaced became abundantly clear to a significant number of Americans over the following decade. A spirit of extreme localism came to pervade politics, and representatives were elected not because of their virtue or talent but because of their popularity and willingness to abide by the wishes of their electors. Instead of governments devoted to the selfless pursuit of the common good, Americans seemed to have produced a series of petty, excessively mutable legislative tyrannies which provided neither stable government nor protection for the liberty and property of their citizens. Even worse, it became obvious that republican government had not brought about the change in the character of the American people that had been hoped for in 1776. "The self-sacrifice and patriotism of 1774-75 soon seemed to give way to greed and profiteering at the expense of the public good."

As these tendencies were accelerated by prosperous economic conditions in the 1780s, many leaders and intellectuals came to the conclusion that Americans simply did not have the virtue "necessary to sustain republican governments." Even more than the political malfunctioning of the states, this disillusionment, the fear that the great republican hopes of 1776 would be sacrificed to the self-interest and parochialism of Americans themselves, Wood suggested in a significant new conclusion, was what made the 1780s "truly critical for American intellectuals."

If the Revolution failed to achieve the millennial visions of 1776, however, it nonetheless succeeded, Wood showed, in generating an emerging *American* conception of politics. That sovereignty resided in the people rather than in any institution of government, that constitutions were compacts established by the sovereign power of the people and were unalterable by government, that government should be divided into separate parts not because each part represented a different social constituency but simply because it would act as a check upon the others, that every part was equally representative of the people, that because all sovereignty derived from the people power could be distributed among various levels of government, that republican government might be founded on self-interest because the clashing of interests would always prevent any one from gaining the ascendancy, and that liberty involved not merely the right of the subject to participate in government but "the protection of individual rights against *all* government encroachments"— all of these ideas which we now recognize as fundamental to the "American science of politics" had been hammered out gradually and fitfully by many different individuals in response to the pressure of democratic politics between the Declaration of Independence and the Constitution. The achievement of Revolutionary political thinkers, Wood showed far more clearly than any previous writer, was "to bring together into a comprehensive whole [these] diffuse and often rudimentary" ideas and "to make intelligible and consistent the tangles and confusions" among them.

If, then, as most recent writers have indicated, the Revolution was at its center a fundamentally conservative movement concerned primarily with the preservation of American liberty and property, it also had some distinctly radical features, as the works of Bailyn, Kenyon, Heimert, and Wood make clear. Its radicalism was to be found, however, less in the relatively modest social and political changes that accompanied it than in the power of its ideas. Bailyn and Kenyon discussed some of the immediate and tangible results of the workings of those ideas during the Revolutionary era. R. R. Palmer[109] has emphasized another. From the broad perspective of general western European political development, Palmer argued, the "most distinctive work of the Revolution," and its most novel institutional achievement, was in devising an institu-

---

[109] R. R. Palmer, *The Age of the Democratic Revolution: A Political History of Europe and America, 1760–1800*, vol. 1, *The Challenge* (Princeton, N.J., 1959).

tion—the constitutional convention—through which the people could in practice, and not just in theory, exercise their sovereign power to constitute their own governments. Used for the first time in preparing the Massachusetts Constitution of 1780, the device of a convention chosen solely for the purpose of writing a constitution, then to be popularly ratified, was institutionalized with the Federal Constitution of 1787 and has since served as a model for constitution writing throughout the world.

But the full impact of the radical ideas of the Revolution, their complete expression in the institutions and values of American life, Heimert, Bailyn, Kenyon, and Wood all seemed to agree, came not during the Revolution but over the next half century in the political movements associated with Thomas Jefferson and Andrew Jackson. Thus, as William H. Nelson remarked in an essay on "The Revolutionary Character of the American Revolution,"[110] even "if the American revolutionists did not fight for democracy, they contributed to its coming[,] . . . because their individualistic concepts of government by consent and republican equality led irresistibly in a democratic direction."

The forces for and against the movement for a stronger central government in the 1780s, the nature of the divisions over the Constitution of 1787, and the relationship of the Constitution to the Revolution have also received considerable attention over the past quarter century. Much of this attention has been focused upon Charles A. Beard's economic interpretation of the Constitution, and the clear consensus has been that that interpretation is seriously deficient in almost every respect. In separate articles published in the early 1950s, Richard Hofstadter[111] and Douglass Adair[112] argued that the Beard book was a Progressive tract and showed to what a large extent his interpretation had been warped by his inability to resist viewing eighteenth-century phenomena through Progressive lenses. One of the most serious of the resulting errors was

---

[110] William H. Nelson, "The Revolutionary Character of the American Revolution," *American Historical Review* 70 (1965): 998–1014.

[111] Richard Hofstadter, "Beard and the Constitution: The History of an Idea," *American Quarterly* 2 (1950): 195–212.

[112] Douglass Adair, "The Tenth Federalist Revisited," *William and Mary Quarterly*, 3d ser., 8 (1951): 48–67.

pointed out by Edmund S. Morgan in 1957.[113] By reading back into the Revolution the conflict between property rights and human rights that seemed to him so fundamental to early twentieth-century American politics, Beard and other Progressives had completely distorted and misread the eighteenth-century conception of liberty, which was always coupled with, not set in opposition to, property, and thereby built their whole account upon an anachronism. In the most devastating critique, Robert E. Brown, on the basis of a meticulous paragraph-by-paragraph analysis of the Beard volume,[114] convicted Beard of rank mishandling of his evidence.

The most ambitious analysis of the Beard thesis was presented in 1958 by Forrest McDonald in *We the People*.[115] After doing much of the research that Beard had said would be necessary to validate his interpretation, McDonald was able to state categorically that Beard's "economic interpretation of the Constitution does not work." Far from being as unrepresentative of the American electorate as Beard had inferred, the Philadelphia Convention, McDonald argued, "constituted an almost complete cross-section of the geographical areas" and organized political interest groups "existing in the United States in 1787." Thirty-nine of fifty-five major geographical areas and thirty-one of thirty-four major political factions from twelve of the thirteen states were represented. Neither did the delegates compose a "consolidated economic group," nor did "substantial personalty interests" provide the dynamic element in the movement for the Constitution, as Beard had argued. Furthermore, in both federal and state conventions the amount of real property in land and slaves held by the proponents of the Constitution far exceeded the value of their holdings in public securities and other forms of personal property, wealth in both personal and real property was substantially represented among both Federalists and Antifederalists, and in "no state was the Constitution ratified without the consent of the farmers and a majority of the friends of paper money."

Indeed, McDonald implied, such broad categories as those employed by Beard—real property versus personal property, commerce versus agriculture, creditors versus debtors, lower classes versus upper classes—

---

[113] Morgan, "American Revolution: Revisions in Need of Revising" and *Birth of the Republic*.

[114] Robert E. Brown, *Charles Beard and the Constitution* (Princeton, N.J., 1956).

[115] Forrest McDonald, *We the People: The Economic Origins of the Constitution* (Chicago, 1958).

were virtually meaningless when applied to the struggle over the Constitution. With at least six basic forms of capital and "twenty basic occupational groups having distinctly different economic characteristics and needs," there were, obviously, so many diverse and conflicting interests that it was impossible, McDonald concluded, to devise a single set of polar classifications that would adequately explain the alignment over the Constitution.

Although in *We the People* McDonald was primarily concerned with clearing the decks so that he could subsequently write "something meaningful about the making of the Constitution" without constantly stopping to do battle with Beard, the thrust of the book was by no means entirely negative. Scattered throughout the text and in three concluding chapters were conclusions and hypotheses that indicated what McDonald considered the central elements in a more plausible economic interpretation of the Constitution.

The whole story, he implied, could be told entirely without reference to class conflict and the struggle for democracy—the two themes that had received most emphasis from Progressive historians. Not class but state, sectional, group, and individual interests and the complex interplay among them comprised the economic forces behind the Constitution. Any economic interpretation of the Constitution would therefore necessarily be pluralistic, but, McDonald indicated, the primary organizing unit would be the individual states. Not only were the activities of most interest groups circumscribed by state boundaries, but those interests that reached across state boundaries, such as the interest in the public debt, "operated under different conditions in the several states, and their attitudes toward the Constitution varied with the internal conditions in their states."

The contest over the Constitution was thus "at once *a contest* and *thirteen contests*," and, McDonald suggested in his most important new general conclusion, the outcome in each state seemed to depend upon how satisfied its citizens were—how well their economic interests were being served—under the Articles of Confederation. "Those states that had done well on their own were inclined to desire to continue on their own," he noted, "and those that found it difficult to survive independently were inclined to desire to cast their several lots with a general government."

That McDonald had overstated his case against Beard and that his focus upon narrow and specific interests tended to obscure the larger, and presumably more significant, divisions over the Constitution was the argument of two formidable critics: Jackson Turner Main and Lee

Benson. Main, who had been over much of the same material as McDonald, published a long critical analysis of *We the People*[116] in which he convicted McDonald of a number of factual errors, argued that because "there was not a single delegate who spoke for the small farmers" the Philadelphia Convention was not as representative as McDonald had contended and the delegates were therefore a "consolidated economic group" representing the commercial east coast, and maintained that the Constitution was indeed "written by large property owners and that the division over its acceptance followed, to some extent, class lines," as Beard had affirmed.

A year later Main presented the evidence for these propositions and his own explanation of the fight over the Constitution in his book *The Antifederalists.*[117] In some respects Main's conclusions, as McDonald remarked in his rebuttal, appeared to be the same old Progressive story of the rich guys against the poor guys, but there were significant new qualifications and shifts of emphasis. Insisting that there were important ideological and economic differences between Federalists and Antifederalists, Main subscribed to the traditional Progressive view that the ideological split was between advocates of aristocracy and advocates of democracy. He carefully pointed out, however, that not all Antifederalists were democrats. Most Antifederalist leaders were, in fact, well-to-do and were interested less in democracy than in local self-rule and a weak central government. These leaders, who were the chief spokesmen for antifederalism, tended to mute the democratic voices of rank-and-file Antifederalists, the small property holders who were "fundamentally anti-aristocratic" and "wanted a government dominated by the many rather than the few." Similarly, Main argued that the economic division over the Constitution was in general along class lines, with small property holders opposing large property holders, debtors against creditors, and paper money advocates opposed to hard money supporters. As he carefully pointed out, however, there were so many exceptions to his general conclusion that the contest could not possibly be explained "exclusively in terms of class conflict."

A far more important division, he suggested, which cut across class lines, was that between the commercial and noncommercial regions, be-

[116] Jackson Turner Main, "Charles A. Beard and the Constitution: A Critical Review of Forrest McDonald's *We the People* with a Rebuttal by Forrest McDonald," *William and Mary Quarterly,* 3d ser., 17 (1960): 86–110.

[117] Jackson Turner Main, *The Antifederalists: Critics of the Constitution, 1781–1788* (Chapel Hill, N.C., 1961).

tween "the areas, or people, who depended on commerce, and those who were largely self-sufficient." Again there were important exceptions, but, he maintained, this "socio-economic division based on a geographical location" was "the most significant fact" about the ratification struggle, "to which all else is elaboration, amplification, or exception." For Main, then, class conflict and the struggle for democracy were still significant elements in the fight over the Constitution, though neither was nearly so important nor so clear-cut as early Progressive historians had thought.

In *Turner and Beard*[118] Lee Benson subjected McDonald's work to a different kind of criticism and offered his own hypotheses about the contest over the Constitution. The primary difficulty with McDonald's book, Benson argued, was the assumptions on which it rested. Based upon a "crude version of economic determinism that assumes men behave primarily as members of interest groups that keep a profit-and-loss account of their feelings and calculate the cash value of their political actions," McDonald's interpretive system, Benson charged, was even more grossly distorting than Beard's. That system might conceivably be applicable to the activities of pressure groups in the normal legislative process, but it was clearly inappropriate to the study of a national "Constitutional revolution" like the one that occurred in 1787–88. Such a revolution inevitably involved a conflict of ideology, and ideology, Benson argued, was never the "direct product of self-interest" and "always cuts across the lines of interest groups."

On the assumption that "social environment and position in the American social structure mainly determined men's ideologies, and, in turn, their ideologies mainly determined their opinions on the Constitution," Benson proposed to devise a system of interpretation based not on narrow economic interest groups but upon broad symbolic social groups. The principal division in this "social interpretation of the Constitution" was between *"agrarian-minded"* men and *"commercial-minded"* men. Ostensibly, the division was over what kind of central government the United States would have, with the agrarian-minded favoring a government of strictly limited powers that was close to the people and the commercial-minded a government that could "function as a creative, powerful instrument" for realizing broad social ends. Agrarians thus tended to be satisfied with the Articles of Confederation while commercialists tended to be supporters of the Constitution. But, Benson insisted in reading back into the ratification struggle the conflict of the 1790s

---

[118] Lee Benson, *Turner and Beard: American Historical Writing Reconsidered* (Glencoe, Ill., 1960).

over Hamiltonian finance, the real question at issue was what kind of society—agrarian or commercial—the United States would have, and the struggle over the Constitution, over whether the central government would be weak or strong, was merely a reflection of this larger ideological conflict which had been waged with "great intensity" by the opposing groups and presumably had been behind most political issues ever since 1776.

What these hypotheses amounted to, as Benson freely admitted, was a reformulation of Beard's thesis in broader social terms, but they also contained two new, if also highly tentative, propositions: that broad social environment rather than narrow economic interests was the primary determinative force in the struggle over the Constitution and that political behavior in the 1780s was "influenced more strongly by ideas of the Good Society than by ideas of the Good State."

The controversy over Beard's interpretation of the Constitution had thus generated three alternative and partially contradictory sets of hypotheses about the hard social and economic forces behind the Constitution. All three scholars were in general agreement on a number of key points: there were discernible socioeconomic divisions over the Constitution; those divisions exerted a profound, and probably primary, influence in the struggle; their nature and operation were enormously more complicated than Beard had ever imagined; and, whether class divisions were important or not, the contest was not a match between the haves and the have-nots.

The dispute was mainly over which divisions were most important and what was the precise nature of the divisions. The possibility of achieving some synthesis between Main's "commercial" and "noncommercial" categories on the one hand and Benson's "commercial-minded" and "agrarian-minded" on the other was clear enough, but McDonald's insistence that the struggle was between strong (satisfied) states and weak (dissatisfied) states and was shaped by the conflicting ambitions of a multitude of special-interest groups seemed completely irreconcilable with the arguments of either Main or Benson. Clearly, as Main pointed out, an enormous amount of work would be required before these competing propositions could be evaluated.

E. James Ferguson and McDonald have subsequently performed some of that work. In *The Power of the Purse*,[119] Ferguson explored the relationship between public finance and the movement for constitutional re-

---

[119] E. James Ferguson, *The Power of the Purse: A History of American Public Finance, 1776–1790* (Chapel Hill, N.C., 1961).

form. Ferguson's thesis was that the question of how the public debts incurred during the War for Independence were to be paid, whether by the states or by Congress, was the "pivotal issue in the relations between the states and the nascent central government" during the Confederation period. On this question the alignment was broadly the same as that Main and Benson had seen in the struggle over the Constitution: mercantile capitalists versus agrarians. The former were "nationalists" who favored some money backed by specie, strong central financial institutions, and the absolute sanctity of contracts and property, while the latter were localists who wanted cheap paper money, state-oriented finance, and easy ways of discharging debts.

Seeing in the debt a lever by which they could secure the taxing power for the Congress, the nationalists, led by Robert Morris,[120] endeavored between 1780 and 1786 to vest the debt in Congress and give Congress the taxing power to support it. But these endeavors ran into opposition from the advocates of state-oriented finance, some states began to take care of the interest on the debt, and the nationalist movement, for all practical purposes, collapsed between 1784 and 1786. Except for the foreign debt, on which Congress partially defaulted, the period was not critical in terms of finance, and what produced the nationalist resurgence that led to the Constitution of 1787 was not public bankruptcy and currency depreciation but the nationalists' "fear of social radicalism" following the flood of paper money emissions in 1785–86 and Shays' Rebellion.

Though it was not entirely clear from Ferguson's account whether the merchants advocated a strong central government so that they could handle the debt or, as he seemed to suggest, the debt was simply a means of achieving the anterior goal of a strong central government, Ferguson had demonstrated, as he later remarked,[121] that the political goals of the nationalists were "interwoven with economic ends, particularly the establishment of a nationwide regime of sound money and contractual obligation."

---

[120] Morris's role as superintendent of finance is dealt with at greater length by Clarence L. Ver Steeg, *Robert Morris: Revolutionary Financier* (Philadelphia, 1954).

[121] Stuart Bruchey, "The Forces behind the Constitution: A Critical Review of the Framework of E. James Ferguson's *The Power of the Purse* with a Rebuttal by E. James Ferguson," *William and Mary Quarterly*, 3d ser., 19 (1962): 429–38. For consideration of other economic developments during the Revolution, see Clarence L. Ver Steeg, "The American Revolution Considered as an Economic Movement," *Huntington Library Quarterly* 20 (1957): 361–72; Robert A. East, *Business Enterprise in the American Revolutionary Era* (New York, 1938); and Curtis P. Nettels, *The Emergence of a National Economy, 1775–1815* (New York, 1962).

McDonald, who presented the results of his work in a paper[122] and a book-length essay,[123] agreed with Ferguson that the public debt and the public lands were the "material sinews of union" and served as the basis for a national economic interest which formed around Robert Morris and provided the impetus for the movement to give Congress the taxing power in the early 1780s. He also agreed that the virtual collapse of that movement in 1783–84 did not bring economic disaster. "It was a critical moment only for the United States as United States," for "those who thought the American Republic was worth creating and saving," he wrote, but "not for the several states or their inhabitants," who in general "had it better than they had ever had it before." Where he differed from Ferguson was on the nature of the major political alignments and the central issue that divided them. The debate over whether to augment the powers of Congress, as McDonald saw it, only masked a deeper and much more fundamental issue—whether the United States would be politically one nation or not. Where individuals stood on that question depended on a number of variables, including where they lived, whether their states were thriving, their economic interests, and their ideological commitments.

By suggesting that "accessibility to transportation—and through it to communication—predisposed Americans to be narrow or broad in their loyalties, to oppose or favor the establishment of a national government," McDonald seemed to be adopting categories similar to those earlier used by Main and Benson, albeit with a significant twist in emphasis: for McDonald it was the broad-minded versus the narrow-minded, not the commercial-minded versus the agrarian-minded. But McDonald left no doubt that in his mind this division was distinctly secondary to the interplay of competing economic interests. Then, as now, McDonald implied, the primary determinative force in American politics was the pocketbook, the "irresistible and illimitable compulsion to get More." Although the number of separate interests was vast, the most important division, McDonald contended in an important elaboration of his central conclusion in *We the People*, was between those who thought their interests would best be served by a strong national government and those who had a vested interest in the continued primacy of the state governments. The behavior of some men, however, could not, McDonald ad-

---

[122] Forrest McDonald, "The Anti-Federalists, 1781–1789," *Wisconsin Magazine of History* 46 (1963): 206–14.

[123] Forrest McDonald, *E Pluribus Unum: The Formation of the American Republic, 1776–1790* (Boston, 1965).

mitted, be explained purely in terms of self-interest. Some of the Anti-federalists were republican ideologues who would have opposed the Constitution no matter what their interests were. More important, the constitution was so impressive an achievement—"the miracle of the age . . . and of all ages to come"—that the men who wrote it—McDonald called them "giants"—obviously had to have been inspired by something more than the sordid materialism that normally characterized American politics.

McDonald's admission that the behavior of the men who wrote and pushed through the Constitution, as well as that of *some* of their opponents, could not be explained entirely or even largely in terms of their economic and social interests underlined the fundamental weakness in most of the post–World War II literature on the Confederation and Constitution. McDonald and Ferguson, Benson and Main, have together brought an enlarged and more precise understanding of the tangible economic and social forces at work in the United States during the 1780s and of their relationship to the critical political developments of the decade. They have, in short, succeeded remarkably well in refining Beard's conclusions and categories in such a way as to make them accord much more closely with existing evidence. The very nature of their success, however, only revealed how giant a shadow Beard had cast, how severely constricting his influence had been, even for scholars, like McDonald, who have specifically sought to free themselves from his intellectual domination.

In sharp contrast to recent writers on the pre-Revolutionary period, historians of the Confederation and Constitution have not, in other words, advanced very far beyond the Progressive historians in explaining what the ostensible and immediate *political* issues and underlying assumptions were, how men of all political hues saw and reacted to the problems of the Confederation and the issues raised by the Constitution, and how they explained their behavior to themselves, their contemporaries, and posterity, whatever social and economic considerations may have consciously or unconsciously helped to shape their behavior. There seems to be a general agreement that the Constitution was a bold political stroke, but the exact nature of that stroke, what it represented to the people who supported and opposed it, has not been made completely clear.

Though an enormous amount of work still needs to be done on developments within several key states and on the relationship between the states and Congress before the political contours of the 1780s can be fully reconstructed, several recent writers have indicated what the main outlines of that reconstruction may be. Thus, in a suggestive article,[124] John P. Roche emphasized the extent to which the Constitution was at once the product of democratic political procedures and a reflection of the founders' aspirations for the new country. The founders, he argued, had to be understood "first and foremost" as "superb democratic politicians" who were spokesmen for "*American* nationalism," a "new and compelling credo" that emerged out of the American Revolution. As they saw it, the Philadelphia Convention was "an all-or-nothing proposition." Either "national salvation or national impotence" would be the result, and to achieve the former they persistently demonstrated a willingness to submerge "their parochial interests in behalf of an ideal which took shape before their eyes and under their ministrations," an ideal that was at best a "patchwork" of compromises over structural details necessary to overcome a variety of differences among the delegates and to make the final document acceptable to the public at large.

Far from being an antidemocratic document, as Progressive historians had claimed, the Constitution, Roche concluded, was a "vivid demonstration of effective democratic political action" and a clear indication that the founding fathers had to operate, and were aware they had to operate, "with great delicacy and skill in a political cosmos full of enemies to achieve the one definitive goal—popular approbation."[125] Implicit in Roche's analysis was the assumption that the Constitution, however much it may have been tailored to fit the fancies of the public, was a striking victory for the "*American* nationalism" represented by the men who wrote it and secured its ratification.[126]

As both Jackson Turner Main and, more recently, Robert Allen Rutland[127] have suggested, the extreme continental nationalism of the Federalists and the possibility that they might have sacrificed the libertarian inheritance of the Revolution to it, was precisely what worried their Antifederalist opponents. To the Antifederalists the Constitution seemed not just a threat to local control and state-centered vested interests but, at least to many diehards, an ominous betrayal of the ideals

---

[124] John P. Roche, "The Founding Fathers: A Reform Caucus in Action," *American Political Science Review* 55 (1961): 799–816.

[125] Clinton Rossiter expands on this theme in *1787: The Grand Convention* (New York, 1966).

[126] This point was made more explicitly by Richard B. Morris, "The Confederation Period and the American Historian," *William and Mary Quarterly*, 3d ser., 13 (1956): 139–56.

[127] Robert Allen Rutland, *The Ordeal of the Constitution: The Antifederalists and the Ratification Struggle of 1787–1788* (Norman, Okla., 1966).

and achievements of the Revolution, the diabolical instrument of a counterrevolutionary conspiracy against American liberty.

That the Antifederalists were correct in thinking that they smelled
a conspiracy but that they seriously misunderstood its character and
intent was the conclusion of Stanley Elkins and Eric McKitrick in a
perceptive article analyzing the nature of both the divisions over the
Constitution and the nationalistic aspirations of the Federalists.[128] The
Federalist conspiracy, Elkins and McKitrick contended, was against not
liberty but "particularism and inertia," which in the mid-1780s seemed
to the Federalists on the verge of robbing the young nation of its future
promise. Significantly younger than their opponents, many leading Federalists, Elkins and McKitrick pointed out, had "quite literally seen their
careers launched in the Revolution."

In contrast to most Antifederalist leaders, whose careers were already
well under way before 1776 and who remained largely state-oriented
thereafter, the younger Federalists necessarily had been preoccupied
with putting together a continental war effort and in the process came
to "view the states collectively as a 'country' and to think in continental
terms." What made them nationalists, then, what gave them the "dedication, the force and éclat" to attempt to overcome the "urge to rest, to
drift, to turn back the clock" that was represented by the Antifederalists
and seemed to have a stranglehold on the country from 1783 to 1787, was
not "any 'distaste' for the Revolution . . . but rather their profound and
growing involvement in it." Behind "the revolutionary verve and ardor
of the Federalists, their resources of will and energy, their willingness to
scheme tirelessly, campaign everywhere, and sweat and agonize over every vote" was this inspired vision of what the nation could and should
be. Fundamentally, then, Elkins and McKitrick concluded, the struggle
was not between rival economic groups, not between competing ideologies, not even between nationalism and localism, but between energy
and inertia, and the Constitution was "sufficiently congenial to the underlying commitments of the whole culture—republicanism and capitalism—that," once inertia had been overcome and the basic object of discontent, the absence of a Bill of Rights, removed, opposition to the new
government melted away. After a dozen years of anxiety, the men of the
Revolution could be reasonably confident in 1788–89 that "*their* Revolution had been a success." Far from trying to overturn the Revolution,
the Federalists were thus trying to bring it to a favorable conclusion.

---

[128] Stanley Elkins and Eric McKitrick, "The Founding Fathers: Young Men of the Revolution," *Political Science Quarterly* 76 (1961): 181–216.

Beneath the political maneuvering described by Roche and behind the desire for a more energetic government emphasized by Elkins and Mc-Kitrick, other writers have recently demonstrated, were certain basic ideas that were central to the state constitutions and indeed to the whole Revolutionary experience. As A. O. Lovejoy has shown,[129] the framers of the Constitution had not changed their minds about human nature as a result of their experience during the Revolution: they still "had few illusions about the rationality of the generality of mankind." Indeed, with the paper money mania of 1785–86 and Shays' Rebellion in Massachusetts fresh in their minds, they were more fearful than ever of the "giddiness of the multitude." To prevent social anarchy and to guarantee the success of—even to save—the republican experiment in America from the unhappy fate it had suffered everywhere else,[130] they were persuaded, clearly required a stable and vigorous political system that would check such popular excesses.[131] Yet, as Martin Diamond has indicated,[132] they were also deeply devoted to popular government, to the idea that political authority should be "'derived from the great body of the society, not from . . . [any] favoured class of it.'"

However considerable were the roles of economic interests, broad social forces, the personal and social aspirations of the founders, or the pressures for political compromise, the interaction between these two ideas, between the pessimistic conception of human nature and the commitment to popular government, these writers have argued, exercised a profound shaping influence upon the proceedings of the Philadelphia Convention in 1787. Inspired, as Douglass Adair has shown,[133] by the possibilities that politics might be reduced to a science, they believed, in Lovejoy's words, that it was entirely possible by employing the method of counterpoise, the balancing of harmful elements against one another, "to construct an ideal political society out of bad human materials—to

---

[129] Lovejoy, *Reflections on Human Nature.*

[130] On this point, see Douglass G. Adair, "'Experience Must Be Our Only Guide': History, Democratic Theory, and the United States Constitution," in Ray E. Billington, ed., *The Reinterpretation of Early American History* (San Marino, Calif., 1966), 129–48.

[131] Among several excellent analyses of the relation of Shays' Rebellion to the movement for stronger central government, see the discussion in J. R. Pole, *Political Representation in England and the Origins of the American Republic* (London, 1966).

[132] Martin Diamond, "Democracy and *The Federalist:* A Reconsideration of the Framers' Intent," *American Political Science Review* 53 (1959): 52–68.

[133] Douglass Adair, "'That Politics May Be Reduced to a Science': David Hume, James Madison, and the Tenth *Federalist,*" *Huntington Library Quarterly* 20 (1957): 343–60.

frame a rational scheme of government, in which the general good will be realized, without presupposing that the individuals who exercise ultimate political power will be severally actuated in their use by rational motives, or primarily solicitous about the general good." The framers were thus trying not just to put together a structure of government that would be acceptable not only to all of the interests at the convention but to a majority of the public at large, as Roche argued, but also, as Adair remarked, to discover through a "genuinely 'scientific' attempt . . . the 'constant and universal principles' of any republican government in regard to liberty, justice, and stability."[134]

The central problem facing the framers, then, was, to quote Lovejoy again, "not chiefly one of political ethics but of practical psychology, a need not so much to preach to Americans about what they *ought* to do, as to predict successfully what they *would* do." That the people would behave irrationally and constantly fall under the sway of factions devoted to their own selfish ends rather than to the good of the public was clear enough from the fate of all previous experiments in republican government. To moderate the flightiness of the people and to prevent the formation of a majority faction that would stop at nothing, even tyranny, to secure its own interest, the framers agreed, were their primary tasks. The first task they sought to accomplish by the creation of the Senate which, as Diamond has pointed out, was designed to protect property against popular excesses and to provide a check on the popular House of Representatives without in any respect going "beyond the limits" permitted by the "'genuine principles of republican government.'" The framers thus rejected the conventional "*mixed* republic," in which the polity was divided into separate and distinct elements and the aristocracy balanced against the democracy, in favor of a "*democratic* republic," in which the body representing stability and moderation was not hereditary but popularly elected, if not directly by the people, by representatives who were elected directly by the people.

To prevent the formation of a majority faction, the framers came up with an equally "republican remedy," a major intellectual breakthrough and the peculiar insight, as Adair has demonstrated, of James Madison. What would save the United States from the tyranny of a majority fac-

---

[134]The founders' quest for fame—distinction—and the importance of that quest in both shaping their behavior in 1787 and determining the character of the Philadelphia Convention and the Constitution are discussed by Adair in "Fame and the Founding Fathers," in Edmund P. Willis, ed., *Fame and the Founding Fathers* (Bethlehem, Pa., 1967), 27–52.

tion and the fate of earlier republics, Madison argued in applying to the American situation an idea suggested to him by his reading of Scottish philosopher David Hume, was its enormous size and the multiplicity of factions and interests that would necessarily result from that size. With so many separate and diverse interests, Madison contended, there would be no possibility of enough of them submerging their differences and getting together to form a majority faction. In a large republic, then, Madison suggested, the struggle of manifold interests would operate, to quote Diamond, as a "safe, even energizing" force that in itself would guarantee "the safety and stability of society."

Their inability to accept Madison's contentions, Cecelia M. Kenyon has argued,[135] constituted the chief ideological difference between Antifederalists and Federalists. An intensive analysis of Antifederalist writings, she argued, revealed that they held the same pessimistic conception of human nature, with the distrust of the masses and fear of factions implied in that conception, as the Federalists. Far from being devoted to simple majoritarianism, as earlier writers had assumed, they were afraid of oppression from all quarters—from the people at large as well as from corrupt factions among the upper classes. So fearful were they of the malignant effects of power from whatever source it emanated, that the proposed federal government would have required "a more rigid system of separation of powers, more numerous and more effective checks and balances" to have met their full approval. But, in fact, they were fundamentally suspicious of any form of a truly "national" government because they were convinced both that no government with such extensive authority could be prevented from yielding to the temptations of power and because, unlike Madison, who thought republican government would work only in a large state, they thought that it would never work except in small polities where the government could be "an exact miniature of the people."

From the perspective of the ideas of those who favored and opposed the Constitution, recent writers have thus indicated, the Federalists were those who were committed to the notion that politics might be reduced to a science, that Americans, despite their imperfections, might be able to devise a workable political mechanism for the entire United States, while the Antifederalists so feared the incapacities of man that they had "little faith" in his ability to construct a national political sys-

---

[135] Cecelia M. Kenyon, "Men of Little Faith: The Anti-Federalists on the Nature of Representative Government," *William and Mary Quarterly*, 3d ser., 12 (1955): 3–43.

tem which would function efficiently and energetically and still preserve the essences of republican government.

The Constitution has thus come to be seen not as the repudiation of the Revolution but as the fulfillment of the aspirations and ideas of its dominant group of leaders. To the extent it was intended to check the popular excesses that had been one of the incidental, if also entirely logical, results of the Revolution, it was also mildly counterrevolutionary, an attempt to neutralize the radical tendencies of thought and behavior before they threw the young republic into a state of political and social chaos that, the founders believed, would perforce lead to a tyranny as objectionable as that they had just fought a long and bloody war to escape. Through the Constitution and the powerful central government it created they hoped to reassert and provide the necessary institutional and constitutional framework for achieving the original goals of the opposition to and subsequent break with Britain: a stable and orderly government in which men, despite their imperfections, would be free to enjoy the blessings of liberty and the security of property that was so essential a part of those blessings.

Gordon S. Wood has challenged this view in part in *The Creation of the American Republic.* The disagreement over the proper remedy for the ills of the country during the 1780s, Wood argued, revealed a long-standing, though previously largely concealed, rift in American political ideology. One side—Calvinists and future Antifederalists—clung to "moral reform and the regeneration of men's hearts" as the only effective cures, while the other—Liberal Christians and future Federalists—looked "to mechanical devices and institutional contrivances as the only lasting solution." Seeking to salvage the Revolution and to restrain its many unintended excesses by constructing a national *republican* government that would neutralize the "vices" of the state governments and not be dependent, like them, on the virtue of the people for its success, men of the latter persuasion spearheaded the movement for a stronger central government culminating in the adoption of the Federal Constitution in 1788.

In treating the bitter struggle over the Constitution, Wood seemed to align himself with older historians in declaring that the conflict was fundamentally social, "between aristocracy and democracy," and that the Constitution was "intrinsically" an aristocratic document designed to check the democratic tendencies of the period. But his analysis seems to suggest that, no matter how contemporaries conceived of it, the debate was really over what kind of *democratic* government Americans should have. The Federalists, who believed that only virtuous and talented men—the "natural aristocracy"—were capable of providing effective republican government, stood for an elitist, nationally oriented democracy, while the Antifederalists, who thought that such men were not sufficiently close to the people in general to be responsive to the true interests of the entire society, favored a popular, locally based democracy.

Wood's argument that the Constitution was a repudiation of the Revolution was based upon the questionable assumption that the utopian impulses of 1776 were the central components of the Spirit of '76. But it is by no means clear that the optimism of most Revolutionary leaders in 1776 did not derive more from their confidence that they could contrive constitutions that would neutralize the viciousness of men rather than from the hope that republican government would effect a wholesale renovation in human nature.

Because of its very newness and because it did so much to reshape not simply the political ideas but the political aspirations of men both in America and elsewhere in the world, the original system of politics encapsulated by the Federalists in the Constitution, far more than the genuine but transitory and perhaps not very broadly diffused millennialism of 1776, may have been not only the most lasting but also the most radical—socially as well as politically—contribution of the Revolution.

What lay behind the manifest events, concrete issues, and manifold interests of the era of the American Revolution, what gave them shape and coherence for the men of the Revolution, scholarship over the past quarter century seems to indicate, were their preconceptions about the nature of man and the function of government. Given the intense preoccupation of American leaders, from the Stamp Act crisis to the adoption of the Constitution of 1787, with human nature and its relationship to the political process, it is now clear that they were grappling with and were fully conscious that they were grappling with the knottiest and most challenging of human problems. The central concern of the men of the American Revolution was not merely the reaffirmation and preservation of their Anglo-colonial heritage and not simply the protection of liberty and property but, as Edmund S. Morgan has put it,[136] the discov-

---

[136] Edmund S. Morgan, "The American Revolution Considered as an Intellectual Movement," in Arthur M. Schlesinger, Jr., and Morton White, eds., *Paths of American Thought* (Boston, 1963), 11–33.

ery of means "to check the inevitable operation of depravity in men who wielded power."

This "great intellectual challenge," Morgan argued, engaged the "best minds of the period" as politics replaced theology as "the most challenging area of human thought and endeavor" and the intellectual leaders in America "addressed themselves to the rescue, not of souls, but of governments, from the perils of corruption." This fear of human nature, Morgan emphasized, lay behind the resistance of the colonists to Britain between 1763 and 1783 and their insistence that "the people of one region ought not to exercise dominion over those of another" unless those subject to that dominion had some control over it. This same fear, Morgan noted, drove them to adopt written constitutions that would, by establishing "the superiority of the people to their government," give the people some protection against "man's tyranny over man."

The meaning of the American Revolution has thus come to be seen primarily in the constitutions it produced and the ideas that lay behind them. Hannah Arendt presented the fullest and most systematic exposition of this view in *On Revolution*,[137] a trenchant analysis of the great revolutions of the late eighteenth century and the revolutionary tradition they spawned. The most significant fact about the American Revolution, Arendt argued, was that armed uprising and the Declaration of Independence were accompanied not by chaos but by a "spontaneous outbreak of constitution-making." And, she contended, the "true culmination" of the Revolutionary process was not the struggle for liberation from Britain but the effort to establish the freedom represented by those constitutions. Fear of human nature, of the "chartless darkness of the human heart," and the conviction that, in John Adams's phrase, there would be nothing "without a constitution," were initially behind this fever of constitution making.

But the possibility of creating a "community, which, even though it was composed of 'sinners,' need not necessarily reflect this 'sinful' side of human nature," the exhilarating hope, as Hamilton expressed it, that men might establish "good government from reflection and choice" and not be forever dependent "for their political constitutions on accident and force," was what eventually made them conceive of constitution making as the "foremost and the noblest of all revolutionary deeds" and emboldened them to try the great experiment in federalism in 1787. To devise a national system which would, as Madison put it, "guard . . . society against the oppression of its rulers" by checking the various pow-

---

[137] Hannah Arendt, *On Revolution* (New York, 1963).

ers of government against one another and still have sufficient power to
protect "one part of society against the injustice of the other part" was
not, and the founders never understood it to be, an easy task that could
be accomplished to perfection.

But they had the confidence of the public and a degree of confidence
in one another present elsewhere only among conspirators, Arendt contended, and their accomplishment was notable. With the Constitution
of 1787 they managed both to consolidate the power of the American
Revolution and to provide a foundation for the freedom that was the
ultimate concern of the Revolution.

When in the early 1960s the Service Center for Teachers of History asked Edmund S.
Morgan to revise his *The American Revolution: A Review of Changing Interpretations*
(Washington, D.C., 1958), he suggested that I be engaged to write an entirely new pamphlet, which eventually appeared as *The Reappraisal of the American Revolution in Recent Historical Literature,* Publication no. 68 (Washington, D.C.: Service Center for
Teachers, 1967). The following year I published with the same title a modest expansion
of this booklet as the introduction to my anthology, *The Reinterpretation of the American
Revolution, 1763–1789* (New York: Harper & Row, 1968), 2–74, which with minor verbal
changes is reprinted here. This chapter was also published in a slightly different form
and with additions that are incorporated into the present version as "Revolution, Confederation, and Constitution, 1763–1787," in William H. Cartwright and Richard L.
Watson, Jr., eds., *The Reinterpretation of American History and Culture* (Washington,
D.C.: National Council for the Social Studies, 1973), 259–96. Portions of the original
essay were derived from "The Flight from Determinism: A Review of Recent Literature
on the Coming of the American Revolution," *South Atlantic Quarterly,* 61 (1962): 235–59
(chap. 17 above), and "Changing Interpretations of Early American Politics," in Ray A.
Billington, ed., *The Reinterpretation of Early American History: Essays in Honor of John
Edwin Pomfret* (San Marino, Calif., 1966) (chap. 5 above). The chapter formed the basis
for a talk at Wayland Baptist College, Plainview, Texas, on April 15, 1967.

Twenty

Beyond the Neo-Whig Paradigm:

Trends in the Historiography of the American Revolution, 1968–76

T HE TWO DECADES following World War II witnessed the emergence of a powerful new interpretation of the American Revolution. Over the previous thirty years, the socioeconomic or "Progressive" view of the Revolution as primarily an internal struggle between conservatives and radicals, aristocrats and democrats, over who should govern within the colonies and only secondarily as a quarrel between Britain and the colonies over home rule for the colonies exercised an extremely strong appeal among American historians. During the 1950s and early 1960s, several developments combined to weaken that appeal. As the general affluence throughout much of the Western world and especially in the United States seemed to produce a lessening of social conflict, economic problems came to appear less paramount and class antagonisms less central at all points in the American past. Moreover, the almost global routinization of revolutions over the same period, revolutions that were in many instances characterized by violent internal conflict and wholesale efforts at social reformation, often at enormous human cost, made the late eighteenth-century American Revolution seem by comparison like an extraordinarily orderly, mild, almost unrevolutionary event. Finally, from a burgeoning community of early American historians there issued a spate of detailed studies of many aspects of the era of the Revolution that effectively challenged at almost every major point the principal studies on which not only the Progressive but most previous interpretations of the Revolution had been based.

The new "neo-Whig" paradigm[1] that gradually took shape as a result of these studies almost totally reversed the central focus of Revolution scholarship. Detailed investigations of the configurations of sociopolitical life in most of the major colonies revealed that politics was primarily elitist in character and that political divisions, the precise character of which varied enormously from one colony to another, were rarely along class lines and in no colony sufficiently intense to produce a genuinely revolutionary situation. Political conflict there was aplenty, but it took place within a deferential political system in which most white male members of the lower and middle orders of society either were or could expect to be enfranchised and, far from demanding a greater role in politics, routinely deferred to the superior political expertise of their economic and social betters and returned them to office.[2] Although, assuredly, political conflicts influenced the character of—and were in turn influenced by—the Revolution, the work of the neo-Whig historians seemed to show, they did not cause it. With the discovery that there was no generalized demand for democracy among a large excluded group in any colony, the search for an explanation for the Revolution shifted back to the pre-Progressive subject of focus: the conflict between Britain and the colonies.

A careful reexamination of most aspects of the relationship between Britain and the colonies before 1763 and of the central issues in dispute between 1763 and 1776 led neo-Whig scholars to several important new conclusions. First, they found that lax enforcement of potentially objectionable metropolitan economic and political restraints had prevented the development of any deep or serious colonial discontent with the British connection before 1763 and that, furthermore, a combination of growing cultural and economic ties between Britain and the colonies through the middle decades of the eighteenth century and of colonial pride in Britain's stunning victory over the French and Spanish in the Seven Years' War made British patriotism in the colonies in 1763

---

[1] See, for a much fuller analysis of this literature, Jack P. Greene, "The Flight from Determinism: A Review of Recent Literature on the Coming of the American Revolution," *South Atlantic Quarterly* 61 (1962): 235–59 [chap. 17 above]; *The Reinterpretation of the American Revolution* (New York, 1968), 2–74 [chap. 19 above]; and "Revolution, Confederation, and Constitution, 1763–1787," in William H. Cartwright and Richard L. Watson, Jr., eds., *The Reinterpretation of American History and Culture* (Washington, D.C., 1973), 259–96.

[2] This literature is analyzed in detail in Jack P. Greene, "Changing Interpretations of Early American Politics," in Ray Allen Billington, ed., *The Reinterpretation of Early American History* (San Marino, Calif., 1966), 151–84 [chap. 5 above].

stronger than it had ever been before. Second, they discovered that what did create colonial discontent and what eventually in 1775–1776 drove the colonists to rebellion were the efforts of metropolitan authorities after 1763 to tighten their control over colonial economic and political life through parliamentary taxation and a variety of other economic and political restrictions. The colonists saw such restrictions as fundamental violations of the traditional relationship between them and the parent state and as ominous challenges to the security of American rights and property.

Why the metropolitan government should initially undertake such measures was nowhere systematically explained. But a whole series of investigations of the major figures, groups, and episodes in British politics during the 1760s and 1770s underlined still a third new conclusion: that metropolitan authorities persisted in such measures because colonial claims for exemption from parliamentary taxation and, after 1774, from any parliamentary legislation seemed, by challenging the supremacy of Parliament over the whole of the British diaspora, to strike at the most cherished component of the Revolutionary Settlement of 1688–89, the belief in the absolute sovereignty of Parliament.[3] A fourth discovery was that a large number of the Tory or loyalist opponents of American resistance agreed with resistance leaders upon the necessity for strict constitutional guarantees of colonial rights and property and went into opposition only after the outbreak of armed conflict in April 1775. Perhaps as many as a fifth of the total population of the colonies, they came not predominantly from the upper classes as had previously been supposed but from a rough cross section of the population with a heavy representation from social groups and regions which were unusually dependent upon the parent state.

Still other studies reshaped understanding of the period between the Declaration of Independence and the Constitution of 1787. Investigations of the concrete political and social changes that accompanied the Revolution found them much less sweeping than had previously been supposed. Although there was a significant increase in the political expectations of ordinary citizens in a number of states, a noticeable lowering of the socioeconomic base of officeholding, and the elimination of many of the remaining social relics of traditional European society, there was no wholesale turnover in political leadership, immediate repudiation

---

[3] See Jack P. Greene, "The Plunge of Lemmings: A Consideration of Recent Writings on British Politics and the American Revolution," *South Atlantic Quarterly* 67 (1968): 141–75 [chap. 18 above], for a close analysis of this literature.

of the ideals of upper-class leadership, or fundamental redistribution of socioeconomic power during the era of the Revolution. After, as well as before, 1776, political divisions continued to be incredibly complicated within the states, albeit on the great question of whether or not to strengthen the Union, there was a rough division, the product of both interest and ideology, between cosmopolitans and locals, with the former in favor and the latter wary of a strong national government. For the cosmopolitans the Federal Constitution was not only, as earlier scholars had emphasized, a means to check some of the popular excesses that had grown naturally out of the Revolution but also, and much more importantly, an instrument to achieve the original goal of the initial opposition to and eventual break with Britain: a stable and orderly government in which men, despite their imperfections, would be free to enjoy the blessings of liberty and the security of property that was so essential a part of those blessings.

Between 1945 and 1965, then, the prevailing view of the Revolution came to be that it was predominantly a conservative Whiggish movement undertaken in defense of American liberty and property, preoccupied throughout with essentially political and constitutional questions, carried on with a minimum of violence—at least when seen in the perspective of other revolutions—and with little change in the distribution of political power or in the structure and operation of society, and reaching its logical culmination with the Federal Constitution. Whatever democratic stirrings may have accompanied it were subordinate and incidental to the main thrust of events and to the central concerns of its leaders. The Revolution, in short, came to be seen primarily from the vantage point of the dominant Patriot elite which, with very few exceptions, had managed to retain control of political life as well as the confidence of the public throughout the whole period from 1763 to 1789. The urban mobs and rural populists who had so thoroughly fired the imagination of the Progressive historians were now seen for the most part to have played only supporting parts in the drama of the Revolution, however important the roles they were creating would come to be on the American political stage after 1789. Political conflict no longer seemed to have been between classes or discrete and naturally antagonistic social groups but among rival elements within the elite, competing with one another within a broad ideological consensus not so much over issues as for political power and advantage.

Bernard Bailyn and Gordon S. Wood supplied the mortar for this new and, it has turned out, extraordinarily sturdy intellectual edifice during the late 1960s in their important studies of the ideological dimensions of the Revolution. In *The Ideological Origins of the American Revolution,* published in 1967, Bailyn examined the intellectual framework of colonial political life in the middle of the eighteenth century and showed to what a remarkable extent that framework conditioned the American reaction to the controversy with Britain between 1763 and 1776. The most important ingredients in that framework, according to Bailyn, were drawn from opposition political writers in Walpolean Britain. Distrustful of human nature, they thought that liberty was always in imminent danger of being corrupted by conspiracies of men who were unable to withstand the temptations of power. Within the context of the ideas associated with this theory of politics, Bailyn found, the succession of regulatory measures taken by the British government after 1763 appeared to be "evidence of a deliberate conspiracy launched by plotters against liberty both in England and in America." Far from being "mere rhetoric and propaganda," such words as slavery, corruption, and conspiracy "meant something very real to both writers and their readers" and expressed "real fears, real anxieties, a sense of real danger." Above all else, Bailyn argued, it was this reading of British behavior and "not simply an accumulation of grievances" that "in the end propelled" the colonists into rebellion.[4]

In *The Creation of the American Republic, 1776—1787,* published in 1969, Wood analyzed the role of ideas in the period between the Declaration of Independence and the Federal Constitution. Bailyn had emphasized the radical drift of American political and social thought in the years before 1776. Building upon this foundation, Wood argued that the American expectation in 1776 that the Revolution would usher in a "new era of freedom and bliss" not only for themselves but for the whole of mankind gave the Revolution a "socially radical character." That these expectations had been misplaced, however, became abundantly clear to a significant number of Americans over the following decade as the "self-sacrifice and patriotism of 1774–1775 . . . seemed to give way to greed and profiteering at the expense of the public good" and the governments of many of the states seemed to degenerate into a series of myopic, petty, and excessively mutable legislative tyrannies that provided neither stable government nor protection for the liberty and property of their citizens. Declining virtue and political malfunction during the 1780s fed a growing fear that the great republican hopes of 1776 would be sacrificed to the self-interest and parochialism of Americans themselves.

---

[4] Bernard Bailyn, *The Ideological Origins of the American Revolution* (Cambridge, Mass., 1967).

The debate over how to respond to this ominous situation, Wood argued, revealed a fundamental rift in American political ideology, with
one side clinging to "moral reform and the regeneration of men's hearts"
as the only effective cures, while the other side looked "to mechanical
devices and institutional contrivances as the only lasting solution." Men
of the latter persuasion, who sought to salvage the Revolution and to
restrain its unforeseen excesses by constructing a national republican
government that would neutralize the "vices" of the state governments
without, like them, depending on the virtue of the people for its success,
spearheaded the movement for a stronger central government; while
men of the former persuasion opposed such efforts because they feared
that so complicated a system of political contrivances could not possibly
be responsive to the true interests of the entire society.[5]

The stream of scholarship on the American Revolution has actually increased in volume since the mid-1960s, but most of it has been firmly
set within the neo-Whig paradigm elaborated over the previous quarter
century. Thus, several scholars have investigated the relationship between Britain and the colonies before 1763 and found it far less stable
than earlier neo-Whig writers had suggested. The systematic appropria-
tion of American patronage to reward administration followers in Britain after 1725 undermined the already declining influence of many colonial executives; the growing power of metropolitan commercial interests
in British politics after 1750 made it increasingly difficult for colonial
interests to make themselves heard whenever the two came into conflict;
and residual anxieties among colonial political leaders over the ineffectiveness of existing constitutional safeguards of colonial liberty and
property were always close to the surface and easily activated.[6]

---

[5] Gordon S. Wood, *The Creation of the American Republic, 1776–1787* (Chapel Hill, N.C., 1969).

[6] See Bernard Bailyn, *The Origins of American Politics* (New York, 1968); Jack P. Greene, ed., *Great Britain and the American Colonies, 1606–1763* (New York, 1970), xi–xlvii, and "Political Mimesis: A Consideration of the Historical and Cultural Roots of Legislative Behavior in the British Colonies in the Eighteenth Century," *American Historical Review* 75 (1969): 337–67; James A. Henretta, *"Salutary Neglect": Colonial Administration under the Duke of Newcastle* (Princeton, N.J., 1972); Michael Kammen, *Empire and Interest: The American Colonies and the Politics of Mercantilism* (Philadelphia, 1970); Alison Gil-bert Olson, *Anglo-American Politics, 1660–1775: The Relationship between Parties in England and Colonial America* (New York, 1973); and Alison Gilbert Olson and Richard

Moreover, a growing awareness of the economic importance of the colonies to Britain and the apparent decline of British authority in the colonies called forth a systematic, largely unsuccessful, and highly frustrating effort by metropolitan authorities beginning in 1748 to bring the colonies under stricter control through the use of executive authority; and the failure of this effort evoked a rising chorus of demands during the 1750s for parliamentary action to shore up British authority in the colonies.[7] Finally, manifestations of this "assertive imperialism" during the Seven Years' War, in particular the high-handed activities of British military commanders in America, stimulated, Alan Rogers has argued, strong anti-imperialist feelings among the colonists and caused them to question whether colonial liberty was compatible with empire.[8]

Yet, the consensus seems to be, none of these potentially destabilizing developments was sufficiently powerful to weaken significantly the strong ties of interest, affection, and habit that throughout the eighteenth century had been the primary elements binding the colonies to Britain. Economically profitable for the colonists as well as for Britain,[9] the Anglo-American connection before 1763 was, still other studies have suggested, cemented by growing economic and cultural ties and, despite the emergence of an increasingly self-conscious "American patriotism" after 1740, by the continuing dependence of provincial America upon the metropolis for models of social, cultural, and moral behavior.[10]

Maxwell Brown, eds., *Anglo-American Political Relations, 1675–1775* (New Brunswick, N.J., 1970).

[7] Jack P. Greene, "An Uneasy Connection: An Analysis of the Preconditions of the American Revolution," in Stephen G. Kurtz and James H. Hutson, eds., *Essays on the American Revolution* (Chapel Hill, N.C., 1973), 32–80.

[8] Alan Rogers, *Empire and Liberty: American Resistance to British Authority, 1775–1763* (Berkeley and Los Angeles, 1974).

[9] See Robert Paul Thomas, "A Quantitative Approach to the Study of the Effects of British Imperial Policy upon Colonial Welfare: Some Preliminary Findings," *Journal of Economic History* 25 (1965): 615–38; Roger L. Ransom, "British Policy and Colonial Growth: Some Implications of the Burden from the Navigation Acts," ibid., 28 (1968): 427–35, with a comment by Thomas, 436–40; Peter D. McClelland, "The Cost to America of British Imperial Policy," *American Economic Review* 59 (1969): 370–81, with discussions by Jonathan R. T. Hughes and Herman E. Kroos, 382–85; Joseph D. Reid, Jr., "On Navigating and Navigation Acts with Peter D. McClelland: Comment," ibid., 60 (1970): 949–55, with a reply by McClelland, 956–58; and Gary M. Walton, "The New Economic History and the Burdens of the Navigation Acts," *Economic History Review*, 2d ser., 24 (1971): 533–42.

[10] See, especially, Lawrence A. Cremin, *American Education: The Colonial Experience* (New York, 1970); Jack P. Greene, "Search for Identity: An Interpretation of the Mean-

Still other scholars have broadened and deepened without fundamentally altering the neo-Whig view of the process of estrangement between Britain and the colonies after 1763. Thus, Neil R. Stout demonstrated how British use of the Royal Navy to enforce the trade laws after 1760 contributed to widespread resentment against metropolitan authority within the maritime regions of the colonies.[11] Joseph Albert Ernst analyzed the adverse American reaction to the tangled conflict over metropolitan attempts to restrict colonial use of paper money and the mounting crisis of liquidity in the colonies afer 1764.[12] James Kirby Martin suggested how the monopolization of major offices by British placemen and a few colonial favorites created significant "political immobility" and "pent-up frustrations" among excluded members of the colonial elite that may have helped to give "motion to the developing American Revolution."[13]

Other scholars took a more general approach. Arguing that their deep affection for Britain had to be largely dissipated before the colonists could move from resistance to Revolution, Pauline Maier traced in greater detail than any previous scholar the progressive disillusionment of colonial leaders with the metropolitan government and showed how colonial resistance was punctuated throughout by a compulsive concern for restraint, even on the part of its most militant leaders.[14] In his reexamination of the American response to the Coercive Acts, David Ammerman made a strong case for the proposition that the "enormous unpopularity" of those measures made the period from their passage in

ing of Selected Patterns of Social Response in Eighteenth-Century America," *Journal of Social History* 3 (1970): 189–220; and Carl Bridenbaugh, *The Spirit of '76: The Growth of American Patriotism before Independence* (New York, 1976).

[11] Neil R. Stout, *The Royal Navy in America, 1760–1775: A Study of Enforcement of British Colonial Policy in the Era of the American Revolution* (Annapolis, 1973).

[12] Joseph Albert Ernst, *Money and Politics in America, 1755–1775: A Study in the Currency Act of 1764 and the Political Economy of Revolution* (Chapel Hill, N.C., 1973).

[13] James Kirby Martin, *Men in Rebellion: Higher Governmental Leaders and the Coming of the American Revolution* (New Brunswick, N.J., 1973), and "A Model for the Coming of the American Revolution: The Birth and Death of the Wentworth Oligarchy in New Hampshire, 1741–1776," *Journal of Social History* 4 (1970): 41–60.

[14] Pauline Maier, *From Resistance to Revolution: Colonial Radicals and the Development of American Opposition to Britain, 1765–1776* (New York, 1972). The strong American aversion to republicanism as a form of government, a factor which was reinforcive of American affection for Britain, is discussed by W. Paul Adams, "Republicanism in Political Rhetoric before 1776," *Political Science Quarterly* 85 (1970): 397–421. Hiller B. Zobel presents a somewhat less benign view of Boston mobs in his detailed study of *The Boston Massacre* (New York, 1970).

early 1774 to the outbreak of war a year later "the high-water mark of American consensus," "notable for the temporary muting of discord," the achievement of a remarkable degree of unanimity, and the enlistment of at least seven thousand persons into the active leadership of the resistance movement by the spring of 1775.[15] Finally, John M. Head speculated that powerful social factors shaped the subsequent division over independence, with those colonies that were politically united but economically ailing favoring independence and those that were both disunited and prosperous tending to be more cautious.[16]

Also reinforcive of earlier conclusions have been a series of recent works on British politics during the era of the Revolution. In a detailed study of the impact of the American question upon British parliamentary politics from 1763 to 1767, P. D. G. Thomas demonstrated beyond all doubt what had already been strongly suggested by many earlier studies: that there was an "almost universal belief" among the British political nation "in Britain's right to exercise full sovereignty over" the colonies "through Parliament."[17] Already "without any fund of good will toward the colonies" during the early 1760s, the British political community reacted to American resistance to the Stamp Act with "a virtual unanimity of mind" in favor of Parliament's sovereignty over the colonies. As studies by Paul Langford, Frank O'Gorman, and Ross J. F. Hoffman have confirmed, the Rockingham Whigs shared this sentiment and backed into the repeal of the Stamp Act only after they had been persuaded by British mercantile and manufacturing interests that direct taxation was inexpedient.[18] Despite his vaunted friendship for the colonies, both Chatham and his administration, Thomas also shows, not only accepted the same orthodoxy but made a "sustained attempt to assert the supremacy of the Crown and Parliament over the colonies" in

---

[15] David Ammerman, *In the Common Cause: American Response to the Coercive Acts of 1774* (Charlottesville, Va., 1974).

[16] John M. Head, *A Time to Rend: An Essay on the Decision for American Independence* (Madison, Wis., 1968).

[17] P. D. G. Thomas, *British Politics and the Stamp Act Crisis: The First Phase of the American Revolution, 1763—1767* (Oxford, 1975).

[18] Paul Langford, "The Rockingham Whigs and America, 1767–1773," in Anne Whiteman, J. S. Bromley, and P. G. M. Dickson, eds., *Statesmen, Scholars, and Merchants: Essays in Eighteenth-Century History Presented to Dame Lucy Sutherland* (Oxford, 1973), 135–52, and *The First Rockingham Administration, 1765—1766* (Oxford, 1973); Frank O'Gorman, *The Rise of Party in England: The Rockingham Whigs, 1760—82* (London, 1975); and Ross J. S. Hoffman, *The Marquis: A Study of Lord Rockingham, 1730—1782* (New York, 1973).

1766–67.[19] Continuation of American resistance through the repeal of the Townshend duties in 1770 and its renewal in 1773 following passage of the Tea Act fed the emerging suspicion within Britain that there was a malign conspiracy in the colonies bent upon achieving colonial independence,[20] activated deep-seated anti-American feelings within a broad spectrum of British opinion in 1774 and 1775,[21] and stiffened the determination of men in power never to admit the American claim for exemption from parliamentary authority. With very little sentiment in favor of pursuing a conciliatory line, Lord North and George III, as recent biographies have shown, moved irresistibly toward the position that force was necessary to put down the rebellion and retain the colonies within the empire.[22]

Recent work on most of the other central problems of the Revolution has exhibited a similar tendency to amplify the details of neo-Whig views without altering the basic terms of understanding. Thus, several scholars, notably J. G. A. Pocock,[23] have enormously enriched our knowledge of the genealogy and character of those radical British opposition political ideas that Americans found so congenial during the Revolution,

---

[19] See also Derek Watson, "The Rockingham Whigs and the Townshend Duties," *English Historical Review* 84 (1969): 561–65; Robert J. Chaffin, "The Townshend Acts of 1767," *William and Mary Quarterly*, 3d ser., 27 (1970): 90–121; Peter Brown, *The Chathamites: A Study in the Relationship between Personalities and Ideas in the Second Half of the Eighteenth Century* (New York, 1968); and Stanley Ayling, *The Elder Pitt, Earl of Chatham* (London, 1976).

[20] Ira D. Gruber, "The American Revolution as a Conspiracy: The British View," *William and Mary Quarterly*, 3d ser., 26 (1969): 360–72.

[21] Benjamin W. Labaree, "The Idea of American Independence: The British View, 1774–1776," Massachusetts Historical Society, *Proceedings* 82 (1970): 3–20.

[22] P. D. G. Thomas, *Lord North* (London, 1976); John Brooke, *King George III* (London, 1972); and Allan J. McCurry, "The North Government and the Outbreak of the American Revolution," *Huntington Library Quarterly* 39 (1971): 141–57.

[23] J. G. A. Pocock, *The Machiavellian Moment: Florentine Political Thought and the Atlantic Republican Tradition* (Princeton, N.J., 1975). See also Isaac Kramnick, *Bolingbroke and His Circle: The Politics of Nostalgia in the Age of Walpole* (Cambridge, Mass., 1968); John Dunn, "The Politics of Locke in England and America in the Eighteenth Century," in John W. Yolton, ed., *John Locke: Problems and Perspectives* (Cambridge, 1969), 45–80; Nathan O. Hatch, "The Origins of Civil Millennialism in America: New England Clergymen, War with France, and the Revolution," *William and Mary Quarterly*, 3d ser., 31 (1974): 407–30. For a detailed summary of the main discoveries of students of American political ideology through the early 1970s, see Robert E. Shalhope, "Toward a Republican Synthesis: The Emergence of an Understanding of Republicanism in American Historiography," ibid., 29 (1972): 49–80.

while other scholars, like Staughton Lynd and Gerald Stourzh,[24] have insisted upon the importance of other ideological strains without challenging the centrality of the opposition tradition. Similarly, a large volume of work on the loyalists, the most comprehensive of which is Robert M. Calhoon, *The Loyalists in Revolutionary America, 1760—1781,* have considerably enlarged our understanding of the sources, motives, number, and fate of individuals and groups who opposed American independence and opted to remain loyal to Britain.[25] In particular, William Allen Benton and Mary Beth Norton have emphasized the quintessential Whiggery of most loyalists and the consequent inapplicability of the denotation *Tory.*[26] Norton, in a skillful and important analysis of loyalist exiles in Britain, has also shown, among many other things, how their tragedy was intensified by the sharpening of their sense of American identity as a result of their experiences in Britain.[27] Likewise, although several scholars have produced evidence that there was a powerful fear among upper-class lenders of lower-class involvement in politics, especially during the crucial years of transition from colonial to independent

[24] Staughton Lynd, *Intellectual Origins of American Radicalism* (New York, 1968); Gerald Stourzh, "William Blackstone: Teacher of Revolution," *Jahrbuch für Amerikastudien* 15 (1970): 184–200, and *Alexander Hamilton and the Idea of Republican Government* (Stanford, Calif., 1970); J. G. A. Pocock, "Virtue and Commerce in the Eighteenth Century," *Journal of Interdisciplinary History* 3 (1972): 119–34; Greene, "Political Mimesis"; Richard Bushman, "Corruption and Power in Provincial America," in *The Development of a Revolutionary Mentality* (Washington, D.C., 1972); and Paul K. Conkin, *Self-Evident Truths: Being a Discourse on the Origins and Development of the First Principles of American Government* (Bloomington, Ind., 1974).

[25] Robert M. Calhoon, *The Loyalists in Revolutionary America, 1760—1781* (New York, 1973). Wallace Brown, *The Good Americans: The Loyalists in the American Revolution* (New York, 1969), though less penetrating and ambitious, is another general study. Bernard Bailyn, *The Ordeal of Thomas Hutchinson* (Cambridge, Mass., 1974), L. S. F. Upton, *The Loyal Whigs: William Smith of New York and Quebec* (Toronto, 1969), and Carol Berkin, *Jonathan Sewall* (New York, 1972), are perhaps the best of several recent biographies. Paul H. Smith, "The American Loyalists: Notes on Their Organization and Numerical Strength," *William and Mary Quarterly,* 3d ser., 25 (1968): 259–77, is a well-informed consideration of the problems posed in the title. John A. Neuenschwander, *The Middle Colonies and the Coming of the American Revolution* (Port Washington, N.Y., 1974), analyzes some of the social conditions that tended to make leaders in the middle colonies of New York, New Jersey, and Pennsylvania fear independence.

[26] William Allen Benton, *Whig-Loyalism: An Aspect of Political Ideology in the American Revolution* (Rutherford, N.J., 1969); Mary Beth Norton, "The Loyalist Critique of the Revolution," in *Development of a Revolutionary Mentality,* 137–48.

[27] Mary Beth Norton, *The British-Americans: The Loyalist Exiles in England, 1774—1789* (Boston, 1972).

government after 1774,[28] Merrill Jensen's sweeping and authoritative discussion of the relationship between local political divisions and resistance
to Britain in all of the colonies during the 1760s, along with several other
new studies of the same subject in individual colonies, tends to reinforce
the earlier neo-Whig emphases upon the elite character of colonial political divisions, the rarity of class conflict in colonial political life, the deferential character of colonial politics, and the relative weakness of lower-
class political aspirations.[29]

Studies of the period after Independence also tend to be broadly confirmatory of positions worked out between 1945 and 1965. The libertarian ideology unleashed by the Revolution had sufficient power to stimulate most states to disestablish formerly legally established churches and
to enunciate principles of religious toleration and equality of all denominations.[30] It was not, however, strong enough to produce any basic
change in traditional conceptions of which groups should be accorded
full civic rights in political society;[31] it did not force the abolition of chattel slavery anywhere that the institution was economically significant,
nor did it extend citizenship to those people who successfully escaped from
slavery during the Revolution.[32] Nevertheless, as several works have

---

[28] See, especially, Merrill Jensen, "The American People and the American Revolution,"
Journal of American History 57 (1970): 5–35; Ronald Hoffman, *A Spirit of Dissension:
Economics, Politics, and the Revolution in Maryland* (Baltimore, 1974); David Curtis
Skaggs, *Roots of Maryland Democracy, 1753–1776* (Westport, Conn., 1973).

[29] Merrill Jensen, *The Founding of a Nation: A History of the American Revolution, 1763–
1776* (New York, 1968); Jere R. Daniell, *Experiment in Republicanism: New Hampshire
Politics and the American Revolution, 1741–1794* (Cambridge, Mass., 1970); Stephen E.
Patterson, *Political Parties in Revolutionary Massachusetts* (Madison, Wis., 1973); Bernard Mason, *The Road to Independence: The Revolutionary Movement in New York,
1773–1777* (Lexington, Ky., 1966); Larry Gerlach, *Revolution or Independence: New Jersey, 1760–1776* (New Brunswick, N.J., 1976); James H. Hutson, *Pennsylvania Politics,
1746–1770: The Movement for Royal Government and Its Consequences* (Princeton, N.J.,
1972); Hoffman, *A Spirit of Dissension.*

[30] See William G. McLoughlin, "The Role of Religion in the Revolution: Liberty of Conscience and Cultural Cohesion in the New Nation," in Kurtz and Hutson, *Essays on the
American Revolution,* 197–255.

[31] Jack P. Greene, *"All Men Are Created Equal": Some Reflections on the Character of the
American Revolution* (Oxford, 1976).

[32] Winthrop D. Jordan, *White over Black: American Attitudes toward the Negro, 1550–
1812* (Chapel Hill, N.C., 1968); Duncan J. McLeod, *Slavery, Race, and the American
Revolution* (Cambridge, 1974); Arthur Zilversmit, *The First Emancipation: The Abolition
of Slavery in the North* (Chicago, 1967); David S. Lovejoy, "Samuel Hopkins: Religion,

emphasized, slavery was at the root of fundamental sectional divergencies that began to manifest themselves strongly in national politics during the 1780s and required major political compromise at the Philadelphia Convention in 1787.[33]

Perhaps the most extensive work has been done on the character of political divisions in the independent states between 1776 and 1787. New investigations of politics in several states[34] and Jackson Turner Main's ambitious investigation of *Political Parties before the Constitution*[35] underscored a point emphasized by previous writers: each state had unique political configurations. But, as a result of Main's painstaking analysis of roll-call votes in all the states, he discovered, and many of the state studies tended to confirm, the existence of two distinct legislative blocs of a character that Main and other scholars had earlier suggested lay at the heart of political divisions between the time of the Declaration of Independence and the Constitution. One bloc was "Localist" and consisted largely of men who lived in noncommercial farming areas (usually remote from urban centers and the seaboard), were of relatively moderate means, were most often farmers but occasionally small businessmen,

---

Slavery, and the Revolution," *New England Quarterly* 40 (1967): 227–43; and David B. Davis, *The Problem of Slavery in the Age of Revolution, 1770–1823* (Ithaca, N.Y., 1975).

[33] See H. James Henderson, *Party Politics in the Continental Congress* (New York, 1974), and "The Structure of Politics in the Continental Congress," in Kurtz and Hutson, *Essays on the American Revolution*, 157–96; Staughton Lynd, *Class Conflict, Slavery, and the United States Constitution* (Indianapolis, 1968); Howard A. Ohline, "Republicanism and Slavery: Origins of the Three-Fifths Clause in the United States Constitution," *William and Mary Quarterly*, 3d ser., 28 (1971): 563–84; and Donald L. Robinson, *Slavery in the Structure of American Politics, 1765–1820* (New York, 1971). Except for these studies of the importance of the slavery issue, there has been relatively little work on the Constitution over the past decade. But see Robert A. Feer, "Shays's Rebellion and the Constitution: A Study in Causation," *New England Quarterly* 42 (1969): 388–410, for an interesting questioning of the conventional wisdom that Shays' Rebellion was an important "cause" of the Constitution.

[34] Daniell, *Experiment in Republicanism*; Patterson, *Political Parties in Revolutionary Massachusetts*; Van Beck Hall, *Politics without Parties: Massachusetts, 1780–1791* (Pittsburgh, 1972); Irwin H. Polishook, *Rhode Island and the Union, 1774–1795* (Evanston, Ill., 1969); Alfred F. Young, *The Democratic Republicans in New York: The Origins, 1763–1795* (Chapel Hill, N.C., 1967); Linda Grant DePauw, *The Eleventh Pillar: New York State and the Federal Constitution* (Ithaca, N.Y., 1966); Owen S. Ireland, "The Ethnic-Religious Dimension of Pennsylvania Politics, 1778–1779," *William and Mary Quarterly*, 3d ser., 30 (1973): 423–48; and James R. Morrill, *The Practice and Politics of Fiat Finance: North Carolina in the Confederation, 1783–1789* (Chapel Hill, N.C., 1969).

[35] Jackson Turner Main, *Political Parties before the Constitution* (Chapel Hill, N.C., 1973).

and were extremely parochial in their point of view. The second bloc was "Cosmopolitan" and was composed mostly of men who resided in urban or commercial farming areas, had considerable wealth, were usually large planters, merchants, or professional men, had had extensive political experience, and represented a broader, more "continental, cosmopolitan, urbane" worldview. The first group stood for low government costs, light taxes, debtors, and agrarian interests, and the latter for more government spending, sound credit, and commercial interests. Reflecting two distinctive social environments undefined by state boundaries, this alignment quickly became manifest after 1776 and, Main contends, prefigured divisions over the Constitution.

Most of an impressive volume of scholarship over the past decade has thus sharpened the nuances but done little to change the broad outlines of the picture of the Revolution that took shape during the previous twenty years. Thus, just as Thomas C. Barrow could assert confidently in 1968 that the American Revolution, unlike the French Revolution, was not "the product of unbearable tensions within . . . society" but "a colonial . . . war of liberation," the purposes of which were "the achievement of self-determination" and the "fulfillment of an existing society, rather than its destruction,"[36] so Edmund S. Morgan could declare five years later that while Revolutionary America was indeed riven with social conflict, the Revolution tended "to suppress or to encompass" much of that conflict, which, in any case, was mostly sectional rather than class in character.

If such conflicts inevitably found expression in the Revolution, they neither caused the Revolution nor were they sufficiently pervasive to exercise a determinative influence upon its basic character. What did chiefly determine that character and what constituted the central themes of the Revolution, Bernard Bailyn affirmed in 1973, were the widespread fear of power that he and other scholars had previously identified as an animating force in Revolutionary America and the deep antagonism to the "artificial, man-made and man-secured privilege" that, Americans thought, had been such a crushing weight upon man's aspirations in the Old World.[37]

---

[36] Thomas C. Barrow, "The American Revolution as a Colonial War for Independence," *William and Mary Quarterly,* 3d ser., 25 (1968): 452–64.

[37] Edmund S. Morgan, "Conflict and Consensus in the American Revolution," in Kurtz and Hutson, *Essays on the American Revolution,* 289–309; Bernard Bailyn, "The Central Themes of the American Revolution: An Interpretation," ibid., 3–31.

If the work of most students of the Revolution over the past decade can be marshaled to support this general view, a growing number of scholars have been self-consciously, if cautiously, groping for alternative ways of looking at the Revolutionary experience. They have pursued several separate lines of inquiry.

One line has explored more fully and imaginatively than ever before the psychological dimensions of British behavior toward the colonies and the American response to it. This promising effort to penetrate below the ideological, political, and socioeconomic considerations emphasized by most writers to the emotional roots of the Revolutionary process has focused upon the family metaphor—the parent-child analogy—that was almost invariably used to characterize the relationship between Britain and the colonies. Several scholars have pointed out the extent to which the logic of that metaphor helped to give concrete shape to those metropolitan fears of colonial independence that underlay the shift toward a less permissive colonial policy after 1748 and conditioned the anxious assertions of parental authority by the metropolis after the colonists had challenged it during the 1760s.

They have also stressed the degree to which the "intense affection" felt for Britain by the colonists well into the 1770s was rooted in a "deep . . . sense of comparative weakness and inferiority" that derived from several sources: "the objective disparity between British power and colonial power," colonial need for protection against the imperial ambitions of France and Spain in North America, and colonial dependence upon Britain for moral and cultural authority. By arousing widespread resentment against such illegitimate exertions of maternal authority, metropolitan imposition of new forms of control and punishment gradually weakened these bonds of affection during the 1760s and 1770s and in 1774–76 finally drove many colonists, whose actual dependence upon Britain had been slowly eroded by the growing strength and competence of the colonies after 1740, to revolt. Paine's *Common Sense* had such an electrifying impact because it satisfied the need to justify—and thereby to absolve the guilt that arose from—this rejection of parental authority, this radical break from "the mother-country and from the father-king."[38]

---

[38] The most important of these works are Greene, "An Uneasy Connection," ibid., 32–80, and, most especially, Edwin G. Burrows and Michael Wallace, "The American Revolution: The Ideology and Psychology of National Liberation," *Perspectives in American*

An even more tentative approach has been the attempt to revive an economic interpretation of the Revolution by Marc Egnal and Joseph A. Ernst in a suggestive article published in 1972.[39] On the assumption that the "time has come to reassert the essential reasonableness and necessity of the American Revolution in terms of the overall economic situation of the colonies and of the specific interests of the actors," Egnal and Ernst put forward the proposition that "two developments—the long-term growth of the whig elite's self-conscious strength and . . . the increasing awareness of a need for economic sovereignty in the face of [a] . . . post-1745 spurt in British exports and of new British policies after 1763—called into existence the Revolutionary movement." With regard to the second development, the argument is that the heavy intrusion of British merchants and capital into the colonial economies after 1745 increased the volatility of colonial economic life, restricted the autonomy and undermined the economic well-being of commercial elites in both city and country, and thereby contributed to the gradual rise of a powerful demand "for economic sovereignty" among those elites. Although the evidence is too skimpy and the argument too preliminary to establish that colonial discontent with the economic aspects of the Anglo-American connection was sufficiently great to bear the degree of causal weight the authors assign to it, they have offered some interesting evidence to show specifically how short-term changes in the business cycle affected merchant participation in the controversy with Britain.

Similar observations can be made about a much more extensive literature that has been used to construct several tentative social interpretations of the Revolution. The growing interest in social history has identified a variety of changes taking place in colonial society during the half century before the Revolution, and several scholars have suggested that these changes might be linked causally to the Revolution. Two main hypotheses have emerged: first, that colonial society was becoming increasingly constrictive and polarized, as population became more dense, land less plentiful, poverty more widespread, society more differenti-

History 6 (1972): 167–306. See also Winthrop D. Jordan, "Familial Politics: Thomas Paine and the Killing of the King, 1776," *Journal of American History* 60 (1973): 294–308; J. M. Bumstead, "'Things in the Womb of Time': Ideas of American Independence, 1633–1763," *William and Mary Quarterly*, 3d ser., 31 (1974): 533–64; Greene, "Search for Identity"; and Philip J. Greven, Jr., *Four Generations: Population, Land, and Family in Colonial Andover, Massachusetts* (Ithaca, N.Y., 1970), 280–83.

[39] Marc Egnal and Joseph A. Ernst, "An Economic Interpretation of the American Revolution," *William and Mary Quarterly*, 3d ser., 29 (1972): 3–32. See also Ernst, *Money and Politics in America.*

ated, and power-dependency relationships more manifest; and, second, that colonial society was coming apart as a result of a dramatic erosion of internal social cohesion by rapid territorial, demographic, and economic growth.[40]

Either way, it has been suggested, the result by the 1760s was an exceptionally brittle society that was ripe for internal upheaval: a society, in short, that was highly prone to upheaval and revolution. So far, however, no one has been able to show that the social changes generated by the Revolution were strong or sweeping enough to support the view that the break with Britain was in any major way a response to massive social dysfunction within the colonies or that the Revolution constituted or was accompanied by a large-scale social transformation. Yet these writers have made an important contribution by underlining and amplifying the earlier neo-Whig observation that the peculiar socioeconomic character of each colony affected both its responses to the controversy with Britain and its behavior following Independence and that, in fact, the many variations in the "face" of the Revolution from one state to the next can only be explained in terms of the widely differing circumstances of political society in each.

Yet other writers have been concerned with the process of political mobilization that occurred in the colonies in response to the pre-Revolutionary crises.[41] They have concentrated upon the crowds, mobs, and informal committees and associations that participated in the protests against British policy, and more especially upon the beliefs, objectives, organization, and activities of such groups. Most of the literature has thus far emphasized the degree to which members of these groups shared the general objectives and remained under the tutelage of tradi-

---

[40] The voluminous literature that has been invoked in support of a social interpretation of the Revolution is analyzed in more detail by Jack P. Greene, "The Social Origins of the American Revolution," *Political Science Quarterly* 88 (1973): 1–22, and Kenneth A. Lockridge, "Social Change and the Meaning of the American Revolution," *Journal of Social History* 6 (1973): 403–39. See also the recent special issue of the *Journal of Interdisciplinary History* 6 (Spring 1976), on the American Revolution.

[41] Gary B. Nash, "The Transformation of Urban Politics, 1700–1765," *Journal of American History* 60 (1973): 605–32, argues that the process of political mobilization was already well advanced before the 1760s, but the consensus seems to be that it was the result of the debate with Britain. See Merrill Jensen, "The American Revolution and the American People," ibid., 57 (1970): 5–35, and Jack P. Greene, "The Growth of Political Stability: An Interpretation of Political Development in the Anglo-American Colonies, 1660–1770," in John Parker and Carol Urness, eds., *The American Revolution: A Heritage of Change* (Minneapolis, 1975), 26–52.

tional political leaders, even when they came from the lower social orders.[42] But some scholars have shown that some participants, notably merchant sailors, had additional motives for their action and a penchant for independent behavior that both set them off from traditional leaders and created, at the very least, latent antagonism within the resistance movement.[43]

Even more promising, if much more difficult, a few scholars have begun to look in detail at the socioeconomic composition of the various informal resistance organizations and groups. Thus, Richard A. Ryerson's case study of Philadelphia shows how the Revolutionary committees of that city represented an ever-broadening and massive mobilization of people who had formerly been on the periphery of public life and makes clear that the broadening of the socioeconomic base of politics already observed by Jackson Turner Main in his studies of the composition of the legislatures of the new state governments was well under way in some places before Independence.[44]

Finally, several other scholars, particularly John Shy and Don Higginbotham, have sought to integrate the history of the War for Independence with the history of the political revolution. Following World War II, relatively few people showed much interest in the Revolutionary War

---

[42] See Maier, *Resistance to Revolution,* "The Charleston Mob and the Evolution of Popular Politics in Revolutionary South Carolina, 1765–1784," *Perspectives in American History* 4 (1970): 173–96, and "The Beginnings of American Republicanism," in *Development of a Revolutionary Mentality,* 99–117; Richard D. Brown, *Revolutionary Politics in Massachusetts: The Boston Committee of Correspondence and the Towns, 1772–1774* (Cambridge, Mass., 1970); Richard Maxwell Brown, "Violence and the American Revolution," in Kurtz and Hutson, *Essays on the American Revolution,* 81–120; Alan and Katherine Day, "Another Look at the Boston 'Caucus,'" *Journal of American Studies* 5 (1972): 19–42. For an analysis of this literature, see Edward Countryman, "The Problem of the Early American Crowd," ibid., 7 (1974): 77–90.

[43] Jesse Lemisch, "Jack Tar in the Streets: Merchant Seamen in the Politics of Revolutionary America," *William and Mary Quarterly,* 3d ser., 25 (1968): 371–407; James H. Hutson, "An Investigation of the Inarticulate: Philadelphia's White Oaks," ibid., 28 (1971): 3–25; Jesse Lemisch and John K. Alexander, "The White Oaks, Jack Tar, and the Concept of the 'Inarticulate,'" ibid., 29 (1972): 109–34; Bernard Friedman, "The Shaping of the Radical Consciousness in Provincial New York," *Journal of American History* 66 (1970): 781–801; and Charles S. Olton, "Philadelphia's Mechanics in the First Decade of Revolution, 1765–1775," ibid., 59 (1972): 311–26.

[44] R. A. Ryerson, "Political Mobilization and the American Revolution: The Resistance Movement in Philadelphia, 1765–1776," *William and Mary Quarterly,* 3d ser., 31 (1974): 565–88. See also Jackson Turner Main, *The Upper House in Revolutionary America, 1763–1788* (Madison, Wis., 1967).

itself, and those who did tended to focus rather narrowly upon things exclusively military.[45] The importance of the newer work has been the effort to sort out the relationship between the war and the political society in which it occurred. Thus, Higginbotham has emphasized the ways in which social conditions in America shaped the character of the American military effort throughout the war, and Shy has stressed how the war involved large numbers from among the broad mass of Americans and thereby contributed both to further the process of political mobilization begun before the war and to act as an integrative force in the new nation by nourishing a kind of "hot-house nationalism."[46]

It is not yet clear that any of these new approaches to the Revolution, each of which represents a deliberate effort to try to break out of the neo-Whig paradigm, has altered that paradigm in any fundamental way. Like other recent writers who have been content to work within the framework supplied by that paradigm, they have extended and amplified it in important and interesting ways and have thereby considerably deepened our understanding of the Revolution. We now know far more about the emotional, economic, and social dimensions of the Revolution as well as about the ways—and the extent to which—the debate with Britain and the war contributed to the mobilization of the population. But most of this knowledge can be easily incorporated into the neo-Whig paradigm. The facade of that apparently durable edifice may require some alterations and its internal supports some reinforcement from some new sorts of materials. But the overall appearance and the basic structure of the building have been remarkably little changed.

This chapter was written in the spring of 1976 for the Bicentennial Seminar on "The American Revolution and Its Meaning to Asians and Americans," held at the East-West Center, University of Hawaii, Honolulu, June 29, 1976. It is reprinted with permission and with minor corrections from Cedric B. Cowing, ed., *The American Revolution: Its Meaning to Asians and Americans* (Honolulu: East-West Center, 1977), 35–62.

[45] Earlier literature is analyzed in Don Higginbotham, "American Historians and the Military History of the American Revolution," *American Historical Review* 70 (1964): 18–34.

[46] Don Higginbotham, *The American War for Independence: Military Attitudes, Politics, and Practice, 1763–1789* (New York, 1971), and John Shy, "The American Revolution: The Military Conflict Considered as a Revolutionary War," in Kurtz and Hutson, *Essays on the American Revolution*, 121–56.

Twenty-One

Jeffersonian Republicans and the "Modernization" of American Political Consciousness

For WELL OVER a decade now in a penetrating series of articles and in her important monograph, *Economic Thought and Ideology in Seventeenth-Century England*,[1] Joyce Oldham Appleby has been exploring the question of how during the early modern era economic change influenced Anglo-American social and political perceptions and the behavior associated with those perceptions. In *Capitalism and a New Social Order*, an admirably succinct volume that is an outgrowth of her 1982 Anson G. Phelps Lectures in Early American History at New York University, she builds on this earlier work and on other recent scholarship to produce a bold new reading of the meaning of the political conflicts of the 1790s. Quite as much as the debates over independence and the Federal constitution, she contends, those conflicts involved a debate over fundamental political and social values. Indeed, in her view, the Jeffersonian victory in 1800 was the single most important change in the history of American political culture. At once, she argues, it signaled both a rejection of the deeply rooted sociopolitical perceptual system that Americans had inherited from the Old World and a triumph of those values that have ever since been regarded as "quintessentially American."[2]

Far from being "born free, rich, and modern," Americans throughout the colonial era, Appleby argues in her first chapter, operated within an

---

[1] Joyce O. Appleby, *Economic Thought and Ideology in Seventeenth-Century England* (Princeton, N.J., 1978).

[2] Joyce O. Appleby, *Capitalism and a New Social Order: The Republican Vision of the 1790s* (New York, 1984), 14.

"English Frame of Reference." No less than Britons in the home islands, they were devoted to liberty. More often than not, however, the liberty they celebrated was quite limited in scope. When they used the term, it usually referred to one or the other of three quite distinct, potentially contradictory, but usually complementary, concepts: liberty as "a corporate body's right of self-determination"; liberty, in the classical republican sense, as the right of free men to participate in civic affairs; or liberty, "in the historic rights tradition," as the "secure possession" of property or certain specified rights. In each of these conceptions, liberty was both rooted in historical circumstances and confined to particular segments of the population, and the classical republican notion was highly elitist in its presumption that the liberty of civic participation should be limited to those few individuals who were capable of attaining virtue in the public realm.[3]

Americans were also familiar with a fourth concept of "liberty as personal freedom bounded only by such limits as are necessary if others are to enjoy the same extensive personal freedom." Deriving out of the writings of Thomas Hobbes and John Locke and fundamentally "instrumental, utilitarian, individualistic, egalitarian, abstract, and rational" in its intellectual thrust, this essentially modern and liberal conception of liberty was both highly subversive in its implications and fundamentally in conflict with the classical republican idea of liberty. As Appleby explains, however, Americans were prevented from coming to a full appreciation of these implications and contradictions by their continuing devotion to the inherited tradition that a legitimate civil order should be based on "hierarchical values" and characterized by "deferential political practices" and reverence for history and constitutional authority.[4]

The process by which this inherited frame of reference was weakened, brought under vigorous assault, and finally wholly supplanted in the wake of the election of 1800 is the subject of the final three chapters. For well over a century before the American Revolution, the growth of commercial capitalism in Britain had been slowly undermining the "structural underpinnings for this traditional world view." As "population growth, inflation, agricultural innovations, new forms of business association, and the intensification of European and world trade . . . worked cumulatively and interactively to transform the economy," traditional restraints were relaxed and "the ambit of economic freedom" grad-

---

[3] Ibid., 7, 16–18.

[4] Ibid., 3, 16, 21.

ually widened. The fact that "quite ordinary men" often played a central role in this process both stimulated the development of a "productive ideal" of activity and enterprise and carried it from the great merchants and commercial centers "down the social ladder and out into the country- side" to "cattle drovers and cheesemongers, peddlars and teamsters." The American colonies were not excluded from these developments. As metropolitan capital and labor flowed into America to take advantage of an abundant land supply and new market opportunities, rising popu- lation and agricultural production enabled colonists to become signifi- cant partners in the burgeoning capitalism that characterized much of the Atlantic world.[5]

By "unsettling old understandings," raising individual expectations, and giving the pursuit of self-interest an enhanced legitimacy, these eco- nomic developments helped both to challenge the "fixed hierarchy of so- cial statuses that formed so visible a part of early modern life" and to produce a fundamental "reconceptualization of economic life." Fully elaborated in 1776 by Adam Smith in *The Wealth of Nations,* the new conception viewed economic relations as both voluntary and self- regulating, in Appleby's words, "undirected but patterned, uncoerced but orderly, free but predictable." "Conspicuous social distinctions" in- hibited full acceptance of this new conception in Britain, where it served primarily "as a device for understanding how nations grow wealthy through trade" and never managed wholly to supplant traditional notions of the social order.[6]

In America, by contrast, "more equal social conditions" and the "structural looseness of . . . society," Appleby believes, "made it possible to think of the economists' description of the market as a template for society." Yet even in America this model and the liberal idea of liberty that informed it continued throughout the Revolutionary era to coexist with the ancient view that a legitimate social order was necessarily hier- archical in nature. Indeed, Americans did not clarify "the full implica- tions of the liberal concept of liberty" or recognize "its fundamental in- compatibility with the venerable classical tradition" until the French Revolution had presented the world with two contrasting models of civil society: "England, as the model of sober, ordered constitutional govern- ment committed to securing the maximum personal freedom consonant with the flawed nature of man, and France, presenting a vision of what

---

[5] Ibid., 27–29.

[6] Ibid., 33–35, 38, 50.

a society of free men might be if the chains of customs and outworn creeds were cast off."[7]

Inspired not just by the French example but also by the widespread prosperity associated with the commercial age and the "American record in political inventiveness—first in establishing governments in 1776 and then in refashioning the federal concept eleven years later—" Jeffersonian Republicans in the 1790s developed an optimistic vision of America as a "society of economically progressive, socially equal, and politically competent citizens." Rejecting the old "belief in inherent, ineradicable differences among men" that lay at the heart of the British social order, they looked forward to the achievement in the United States of a "classless" society of free and independent men in which ordinary men, unrestrained by the dead hand of tradition or the operation of "Privilege," would, through the pursuit of self-interest, rise "to the level of competence and autonomy."[8]

This reading of the political developments of the 1790s directly challenges several earlier interpretations. Far from being a "class of men . . . tied together by common economic interests," as Charles Beard and his followers have argued, Jeffersonians, Appleby insists, were a "kind" of men who coalesced around a common demand for the reform of political life and "the liberation of the human spirit." Even more important, she persuasively argues against the currently fashionable interpretation that Republicans represented an American variant of British country party ideology and that the party struggles of the 1790s can best be understood as "a replay of the British political wrangles between court and country." In contrast to British country theorists, Jeffersonians were in no sense anticommercial, and they rejected conventional notions of social hierarchy. They extolled the pursuit of happiness and the "enjoyments of comforts" rather than the "pristine values of thrift and frugality." They regarded virtue not as an appurtenance of the public realm but as a matter of public rectitude. They put far less stress upon virtue than upon "the independence of individuals and the voluntary cooperation of private persons." They eschewed "the past as a repository of wisdom." Most significant of all, they had a far more benign view of human nature and "a faith in the future that was altogether novel."[9]

One of many strengths of this volume is its systematic explication

---

[7] Ibid., 22, 50, 57, 104.

[8] Ibid., 50, 74, 85, 97.

[9] Ibid., 4, 79–80, 90, 94.

of the differences between Federalists and Republicans. Both parties, Appleby contends, were "dominated by modernists" who were committed to commercial capitalism and looked forward to economic change. Both also "warmly affirmed the freedom of self-governing, autonomous men," accepted "the extended suffrage of the American states," and "embraced the mobility of the meritorious." Primarily, they differed "over the social and political context in which . . . change would take place," with the "natural harmony of autonomous individuals freely exerting themselves to take care of their own interest while expanding the range of free exchange and free inquiry" being "the liberating alternative [which] Republicans juxtaposed to the Federalists' expectations of orderly growth within venerable social limits." Federalists, who, Appleby argues, remained far closer to the classical republicanism of British country ideologists than did Republicans, believed that the future would not "be fundamentally different" from the past and clung to "traditional expectations about the role of authority in public life," the "permanence of social classes," and the necessity for "elite leadership and [a] passive citizenry." The widespread appeal of the Republican vision, according to Appleby, lay precisely in its proposal to liberate Americans and "human nature from the implicit slurs" of such doctrines, which, as she emphasizes, were so thoroughly discredited after the election of 1800 that "no politician would again think of defending" them.[10]

This otherwise powerful and generally convincing interpretation is open to question on two major points. The first concerns its portrait of colonial British-American society. Although most American leaders continued to think of their societies in traditional terms well into the 1790s, it is highly misleading to insist so strongly on their societies' traditional character. Granted, most elite Americans wanted a traditional society. But only the orthodox Puritan colonies of Massachusetts and Connecticut, the two colonies which deviated most sharply from the norms of early modern British overseas colonization, came close to achieving that aim at any time during the colonial period and then only for two, or at most three, generations during their earliest decades. While, over time, the other colonies came to look and to behave more like Old World societies, in each of them authority, habits of deference, and feelings of community were far too weak and social relations far too disorderly and individualistic to make possible the creation of anything more than a pale reflection of a traditional western European society.

Appleby recognizes that the Federalists in the 1790s lacked the power

---

[10] Ibid., 4–5, 59, 79, 94.

to impose their vision of social order upon American society. But, except for the early Puritans, other early American elites were equally powerless. A strong case can be made that the broad passivity of the citizenry throughout much of the eighteenth century was the product of disinterest rather than deference, that personal independence was always accorded more emphasis than civic virtue in the classical republican sense, and that colonials never held authority, sovereign or otherwise, in "awe and reverence."

If, as seems probable, colonial societies were, in all these ways, far more modern in their operation than Appleby suggests, then she may have both considerably underestimated the radical character of the Federalists' effort to establish—not, as she would have it, to "restore"—"the august majesty of government" and have given far too little emphasis to the internal social roots of the Republican vision of the 1790s. By providing Americans with a conceptual framework to explain and legitimate their societies, that vision may have functioned not only as "a blueprint" for the future but also, and even more significantly, as a device for enabling Americans finally to come to terms with their unruly presents—and pasts.

A second and perhaps equally important objection involves Appleby's failure to give sufficient emphasis to the exclusive character of the Republican vision and, as a consequence, to have misread its relationship to chattel slavery, a basic early American institution to which she pays far too little attention. Although she briefly acknowledges that the Republican vision did not extend to women, Indians, and black slaves, she appears not to appreciate the extent to which those wholesale exclusions drastically limited the scope of the Republican creed. For Jeffersonian Republicans, as for other residents of the early modern world, *independents* constituted an exclusive social category that was in major part defined by its symbiotic opposite, that of *dependents.* No known societies, least of all the slave societies of the New World (and before the Revolution every British-American colony was a slave society), were without masses of dependents. So far from representing a "glaring contradiction," slavery, as one of many forms of contemporary social dependency, was perfectly compatible with a social ideology that put a high premium upon personal independence. Along with the marginalization of the Indians, the extensive use of chattel slaves and the deep racism that accompanied it made clear that commercial agriculture in early modern British America was, simultaneously, both a regressive and a progressive force.

Nor does Appleby's suggestion that the American Revolution seriously weakened the slave-powered staple economies appear to be correct.

In the 1790s those still profitable and dynamic areas were just as essential to the Republican triumph as was the fast-growing and less slave-commercial wheat belt she sees as the core of Republican strength. These reservations notwithstanding, *Capitalism and a New Social Order* is the most persuasive analysis yet published of the underlying thrust and meaning of the Jeffersonian Republican movement of the 1790s.

Written in the late summer of 1984, this chapter is reprinted with permission and with the addition of citations to quotations from *Reviews in American History* 13 (1985): 37–42.

—TWENTY-TWO—

From the Perspective of Law:
Context and Legitimacy in the Origins of the American Revolution

THE DRAMATIC expansion of early American history over the past two decades has not produced an explosion of interest in the American Revolution, traditionally the most important subject of study in the field. Instead, a burgeoning group of scholars has concentrated more and more upon reconstructing and analyzing aspects of the new societies that developed in colonial British America during the *pre*-Revolutionary years.

While historians have been paying less attention to the Revolution, however, legal scholars have, for the first time, taken it up as a subject of serious study. Since the publication in 1970 of Hiller B. Zobel's detailed analysis of the climate of law and opinion surrounding the Boston Massacre,[1] there have appeared no fewer than four monographs, one anthology,[2] one edited work, and fourteen articles written by lawyers on aspects of the origins of the Revolution. These include M. G. Smith's exhaustive study of the writs of assistance case in Massachusetts[3] and important articles by William E. Nelson,[4] Barbara A. Black,[5] and Thomas C.

---

[1] Hiller B. Zobel, *The Boston Massacre* (New York, 1970).

[2] Hendrik B. Hartog, ed., *Law in the American Revolution and the Revolution in the Law* (New York, 1981), a collection of eight essays in American legal history. Five of the essays deal with the Revolution.

[3] M. G. Smith, *The Writs of Assistance Case* (Berkeley and Los Angeles, 1978).

[4] William E. Nelson, "The Legal Restraint of Power in Pre-Revolutionary America: Massachusetts as a Case Study, 1760–1775," *American Journal of Legal History* 18 (1974): 1–32.

[5] Barbara A. Black, "The Constitution of Empire: The Case for the Colonists," *University of Pennsylvania Law Review* 124 (1976): 1157–1211.

Grey.[6] But by far the most prolific contributor to this growing body of work has been John Phillip Reid, professor of law at New York University. Since 1967, when he produced his first review article on the Revolution,[7] his publications on the Revolution include three monographs,[8] a book-length edition of the debates between Governor Thomas Hutchinson and the Massachusetts council and House of Representatives in 1773,[9] nine articles,[10] one chapter in a book,[11] and another review article.[12]

Perhaps because it appeared at precisely the point at which they were

---

[6] Thomas C. Grey, "Origin of the Unwritten Constitution: Fundamental Law in American Revolutionary Thought," *Stanford Law Review* 30 (1978): 843–93.

[7] John Phillip Reid, "The Apparatus of Constitutional Advocacy and the American Revolution: A Review of Five Books," *New York University Law Review* 42 (1967): 185–211.

[8] Reid, *In a Defiant Stance: The Conditions of Law in Massachusetts Bay, the Irish Comparison, and the Coming of the American Revolution* (University Park, Pa., 1977); *In a Rebellious Spirit: The Argument of Facts, the Liberty Riot, and the Coming of the American Revolution* (University Park, Pa., 1979); and *In Defiance of the Law: The Standing-Army Controversy, the Two Constitutions, and the Coming of the American Revolution* (Chapel Hill, N.C., 1981).

[9] Reid, ed., *The Briefs of the American Revolution: Constitutional Arguments between Thomas Hutchinson, Governor of Massachusetts Bay, and James Bowdoin for the Council and John Adams for the House of Representatives* (New York, 1981).

[10] Reid, "A Lawyer Acquitted: John Adams and the Boston Massacre Trials," *American Journal of Legal History* 18 (1974): 189–207; "In a Defensive Rage: The Uses of the Mob, the Justification in Law, and the Coming of the American Revolution," *New York University Law Review* 49 (1974): 1043–91; "In a Constitutional Void: The Enforcement of Imperial Law, the Role of the British Army, and the Coming of the American Revolution," *Wayne Law Review* 22 (1975): 1–37; "'In Our Contracted Sphere': The Constitutional Contract, the Stamp Act Crisis, and the Coming of the American Revolution," *Columbia Law Review* 76 (1976): 21–47; "In the First Line of Defense: The Colonial Charters, the Stamp Act Debate and the Coming of the American Revolution," *New York University Law Review* 51 (1976): 177–215; "In an Inherited Way: English Constitutional Rights, the Stamp Act Debates, and the Coming of the American Revolution," *Southern California Law Review* 49 (1976): 1109–29; "In Accordance with Usage: The Authority of Custom, the Stamp Act Debate, and the Coming of the American Revolution," *Fordham Law Review* 45 (1976): 335–68; "In Legitimate Stirps: The Concept of 'Arbitrary,' the Supremacy of Parliament, and the Coming of the American Revolution," *Hofstra Law Review* 5 (1977): 459–99; and "The Irrelevance of the Declaration," in Hartog, *Law in the American Revolution*, 46–89.

[11] Reid, "Civil Law as a Criminal Sanction: The Use of the Jury in the Coming of the American Revolution," in Edward M. Wise and Gerhard O. W. Mueller, eds., *Studies in Comparative Criminal Law* (Springfield, Ill., 1975), 211–47.

[12] Reid, "The Ordeal by Law of Thomas Hutchinson," *New York University Law Review* 49 (1974): 593–613.

losing interest in the Revolution, the implications of this substantial body of literature for our understanding of the origins of the Revolution seem not to have been fully appreciated by historians. This essay explores some of those implications and considers how they modify existing interpretations of the Revolution.

Of all the legal historians who have contributed to this literature, Reid is the most explicit in articulating the assumptions that both underlie and animate it. Because most historians who have analyzed the Revolution have lacked expertise in the law, Reid suggests, they have both failed to appreciate the relevance of law and "misunderstood the legal and constitutional history of the American Revolution." As a result, Reid charges, they have too often "confuse[d] the political with the legal," failed to appreciate "the role played by law both in setting the stage for rebellion and formulating the conditions under which it would be fought," and told the story of the Revolution "incorrectly." Digging "more deeply than historians and asking questions historians are not trained to ask," legal historians, Reid claims, have been able to show both that legal and constitutional concerns "played an all-pervasive and highly central role in the politics of pre-Revolutionary America" and that "law and the constitution" will have to "be returned to center stage if we are [ever going] to gain a true understanding of the prerevolutionary struggle."[13]

According to Reid and other writers considered here, the most significant errors committed by nonlegal historians of the Revolution have derived from a single source: their anachronistic conception of law. Specifically, they have usually employed a modern definition of "law as nothing but the command of a sovereign." As Hendrik Hartog points out, however, this definition derives from a "positivist jurisprudence" that was only just coming into vogue during the last half of the eighteenth century and would not gain full ascendancy until the nineteenth and twentieth centuries. For Britons on either side of the Atlantic during the pre-Revolutionary crisis, by contrast, law "did not always mean 'command' or 'will,'" and theorists did not "necessarily associate 'law' with sovereignty." On the contrary, in the context of British and British-

---

[13] Reid, "In an Inherited Way," 1109; "A Lawyer Acquitted," 189, 191; *Defiance of the Law,* 222; "Irrelevance of the Declaration," 46; and "Apparatus of Constitutional Advocacy," 190.

American legal traditions, law in the 1760s and 1770s was still thought of as being "as much custom and community consensus as sovereign command." Failure to appreciate this fact, according to Reid and other scholars, has led historians both to endow "eighteenth-century law with [far] greater coercive power than it possessed" and to underestimate the legitimacy of American consitutional arguments in the pre-Revolutionary debates.[14]

The basis for the argument that eighteenth-century law was considerably less coercive than earlier writers have suggested derives from William E. Nelson's important investigation of the legal restraints upon governmental power in pre-Revolutionary Massachusetts.[15] Arguing that "one of the most intense concerns of Americans in the pre-Revolutionary period was to restrain governmental power and to render individuals secure in their lives, liberties and properties from abuses of that power," Nelson shows that, at least in Massachusetts, they managed to realize those concerns "to an extraordinary degree."[16]

Because Massachusetts had no permanent police force and only a tiny bureaucracy, the provincial courts were the only governmental institutions with much coercive power. No other "agency . . . possessed jurisdiction to fine or otherwise punish and hence ultimately coerce a man." Because they "wanted to be ruled by law, not by judges possessing vast discretionary powers that could be put to the use of potentially arbitrary rulers," however, colonial legislators were careful "to deprive judges of all discretion in administering their vast powers and of effective ability to bring those powers to bear upon individuals." In part, legislators were aided in this task by long-standing custom, according to which courts never went against precedent. As in England itself, precedent, usage, or custom both had the force of law and was invariably used "to fill in [the] interstices in statute or common law." But legislators also gave juries

[14] Hartog, "Losing the World of the Massachusetts Whig," in Hartog, *Law in the American Revolution*, 147; Reid, "Irrelevance of the Declaration," 60.

[15] First published in his 1974 article cited in note 4 above, the results of this investigation were republished as the second chapter in Nelson's important book *Americanization of the Common Law: The Impact of Legal Change on Massachusetts Society, 1760—1830* (Cambridge, Mass., 1975), 13–35.

[16] Nelson, "Legal Restraint of Power," 1.

wide jurisdiction in both civil and criminal cases and, even more important, "vast power to find both the law and the facts in those cases."[17]

The "virtually unlimited" power of juries to find law in effect meant both that judges had very "little law-making power" and that "representatives of local communities assembled as jurors"—not judges or other provincial officials—"generally possessed effective power to control the content of the province's substantive law." Indeed, the broad "law-finding power of juries" functioned to ensure that judges would "adhere to precedent and so not alter the [customary] rules of law." Moreover, although juries seem usually to have given priority to provincial statutes and rules of English common law over local custom, they nonetheless "possessed the power to reject the common law" and, at least occasionally actually "permit[ted] local custom to prevail over clear common law." "The communities of pre-Revolutionary Massachusetts," Nelson notes, thus "freely received the common law of England as the basis of their jurisprudence, but simultaneously reserved [to juries] the unfettered right to reject whatever parts of that law were inconsistent with their own views of justice and morality or with their own needs and circumstances."[18]

Other provincial officials—both provincial and metropolitan—had even less power than judges. Almost entirely without coercive resources of their own, they were, in fact, "subject to judicial supervision" and liable to both "common law actions for damages whenever in the exercise of their duties they committed a wrong" and "monetary penalities imposed" by statute. "In substance," officials were thus "incapable of exercising their coercive powers without the consent of local communities," and the "crucial fact about government in pre-Revolutionary Massachusetts was that subordinate officials like sheriffs, deputy sheriffs and constables—the men with legal responsibility for enforcing judgments—could do so only when local communities were willing to permit judgments to be enforced."[19]

Colonial Massachusetts was thus a standing example of the truth of one of the most frequently reiterated maxims of early modern British political theorists: the idea that, as Edmund Burke put it, no government could function "without regard to the general opinion of those who were to be governed." No less than Britain itself, Massachusetts, and,

---

[17] Ibid., 7, 10, 14, 26.

[18] Ibid., 23–24, 26, 28.

[19] Ibid., 7–9, 26, 30.

presumably, all the other British-American colonies, thus functioned within that venerable "Anglo-American tradition," according to which "government did not possess vast bureaucratic armies of officials to enforce its laws, but instead relied upon its subjects to aid the few [existing] officials . . . in their task of law enforcement." "In sum," Nelson observes, "the only way for officials to ensure enforcement of the law was to obtain community support for the law, and the best way to obtain that support was to permit local communities to determine the substance of the law, through legal institutions such as the jury."[20]

Nelson's findings that the Massachusetts legal system was consensual, lacking in coercive power, and subject to local control constituted an implicit challenge to the view of the Boston Massacre set forth by Hiller B. Zobel four years earlier in his 1970 study. Zobel had depicted pre-Revolutionary Boston as a place of increasing disorder and lawlessness in which radical conspirators, probably led by Samuel Adams, presided over a situation in which rule of law had been steadily replaced by rule of the mob. During the five years preceding the massacre, according to Zobel, "resistance to authority" had come to pervade "the spirit of the times," "order had gradually disappeared from the streets, untrammeled law had slowly been barred from the courts," and "violence had become . . . common."[21]

Reviewers immediately challenged Zobel's interpretation as essentially "a law-and-order" and "Tory account of the Boston Massacre" and emphasized the extent to which a "concern for law was central not only to the radicals' ideology, but to their tactics as well."[22] But Reid was the one who fully revealed the anachronistic character of Zobel's point of view. In two monographs on what he called "the conditions of law" in Massachusetts, he explored the implications of Nelson's findings for understanding the origins of the Revolution in that colony. By the phrase

---

[20] Edmund Burke, *A Letter from Mr. Burke, to John Farr and John Harris, Esqrs., Sheriffs of the City of Bristol; on the Affairs of America* (1777), in *The Works of Edmund Burke*, 16 vols. (London, 1826), 3:187; Nelson, "Legal Restraint of Power," 31–32.

[21] Zobel, *Boston Massacre*, 48, 303. For a more explicit statement of Zobel's point of view, see his earlier "Law under Pressure: Boston, 1769–1770," in George A. Billias, ed., *Law and Authority in Colonial America* (Barre, Mass., 1965), 187–208.

[22] See, especially, the penetrating critiques by Jesse Lemisch and Pauline Maier. In his "Radical Plot in Boston (1770): A Study in the Use of Evidence," *Harvard Law Review*, 84 (1970): 485–504 (quotations from 501, 503), Lemisch focuses on Zobel's law and order bias, while Maier, in her "Revolutionary Violence and the Relevance of History," *Journal of Interdisciplinary History* 2 (1971): 119–35 (quotation from 129), examines other aspects of the ahistorical character of his account.

conditions of law, Reid "meant not merely substantive rules of law, but the certainty, the power, and the effectiveness of that law, and whether it was directed by a unicentric or multicentric authority."[23]

Published in 1977, *In a Defiant Stance* compared the conditions of law in two late-eighteenth-century British colonies, Massachusetts and Ireland, during two ostensibly comparable situations, the American resistance movement of the 1760s and the Irish rising of the 1790s. Published in 1979, *In a Rebellious Spirit* recounted how Massachusetts resistance leaders employed law in three different incidents during the 1760s: the Malcolm affair in 1766, the celebration of the repeal of the Stamp Act in 1768, and the *Liberty* riot, also in 1768.

In Reid's view the crucial fact about the conditions of law in pre-Revolutionary Massachusetts was that it was bicentric and not unicentric. That is, there was not a single law but two laws. Generated by Parliament and royal officials in London, *imperial law* was indeed "anemic." With no effective legal institutions at their command, Massachusetts officials charged with its enforcement "were helpless without the support and acquiescence" of the local community. Already weak before the Revolutionary crisis, imperial law became even more so over time, as local opinion increasingly came to perceive it as in large part a series of arbitrary measures intended to undermine their traditional constitutional rights and autonomy of economic and political behavior.[24]

But the decline of respect for imperial law, Reid insists, emphatically did *not* lead to "a breakdown of respect for law in general." On the contrary, at the same time that imperial law was becoming steadily weaker, *local law*—those provincial statutes, judicial precedents, and customs that were upheld by the courts, grand jury, traverse juries, magistrates, and other institutions that comprised the colony's effective legal system—retained its full vigor. As Nelson had explained earlier, the two essential features of that law were that it was "a reflection of community consensus" and that it was under local, not metropolitan, control.[25]

No less than imperial law, local law lacked strong formal instruments of coercion and depended upon public support for its enforcement. In an original article published in 1970, Pauline Maier showed how, through-

---

[23] Reid, *In a Defiant Stance,* 2.

[24] Ibid., 118; Hartog, "Losing the World of the Massachusetts Whig," 147.

[25] Reid, *In a Defiant Stance,* 63, 65. Reid tendentiously refers to local law as "whig law" and thereby overemphasizes its partisan character and draws attention away from the more important point that for the vast majority of people in Massachusetts it was the legitimate instrument of local opinion.

out Britain's American colonies during the eighteenth century, popular uprisings had repeatedly acted to defend "the urgent interests" of communities both to enforce the "will of local magistrates" and to compensate for the failure or inability of "lawful authorities . . . to act." Although she emphasized that such uprisings were at least as common in Britain as they were in America, Maier seemed uncertain about whether they were or were not "outside the bounds of law."[26]

Making essentially the same point at much greater length and building on Willard Hurst's insight "that violence in the form of extra-judicial self-help constitutes a legitimate strain in the history of American law," Reid displays no such ambivalence. As he points out, it was a well-established *British* tradition for the people to take matters into their own hands in two different types of situations: first, when "ordinary legal processes failed or did not exist," and, second, when they had no other means to nullify "arbitrary," unconstitutional measures. So long as popular uprisings "served a public, not [a] private function" and confined their actions to harassing those charged with enforcing "unconstitutional statutes of parliament," they were thus perfectly in accord with British legal traditions as expressed in "the eighteenth-century constitutional doctrine" that it was legal "to resist unlawful government power." So far from being outside the bounds of law, then, according to Reid, the popular uprisings described by Zobel and others as expressions of lawless violence actually functioned as the "police unit," in the words of the Massachusetts House of Representatives, the *"posse comitatus,"* of local law. No wonder, then, as Reid illustrates at length, that in Massachusetts between 1765 and 1775 such uprisings were almost invariably "supported by most of the institutions of local government."[27]

Although he admits that customs and other metropolitan officials and supporters who were the victims of these uprisings saw them in much the same way as they had been depicted by Zobel, Reid insists that "the legal perspective of the tory was not that of the [majority] whig" population of the colony and that the "prerevolutionary American political

---

[26] Pauline Maier, "Popular Uprisings and Civil Authority in Eighteenth-Century America," *William and Mary Quarterly,* 3d ser., 27 (1970): 3–35. This article in a somewhat abbreviated form also constituted the first chapter of Maier's *From Resistance to Revolution: Colonial Radicals and the Development of American Opposition to Britain, 1765–1776* (New York, 1972), 3–26, quotations from 4–5, 10.

[27] Reid, "Violence in American Law: A Review of Five Books," *New York University Law Review* 40 (1965): 1208; "In a Defensive Rage," 1051, 1055, 1061, 1068, 1086; "Apparatus of Constitutional Advocacy," 210; "In Legitimate Stirps," 461–62; *In a Rebellious Spirit,* 52; "Irrelevance of the Declaration," 53–54; and "In a Constitutional Void," 7, 17.

crowd" was at least "as lawful as it was lawless." Far from being illegal, Reid explains, resistance to imperial law was actually undertaken in defense of local law. "When the prerevolutionary era is [thus] viewed from the perspective of law and of legal institutions," he concludes, it becomes clear that American mobs served largely "as an auxiliary enforcement" agency for locally dominated "legal institutions such as the jury and the justices of the peace" and thereby operated "primarily to supplement" local law.[28]

Acting in concert and with overwhelming public support, the formal instruments of law—juries, magistrates, etc.—and the informal instrument—the crowd—managed in one incident after another after 1765 to nullify those many parliamentary statutes and metropolitan regulations that were deemed both arbitrary and contrary to the vital interests of the colony. In the process they effectively underlined the impotence of metropolitan agents to enforce any measures opposed by locals. Nor was the force of imperial law in any way strengthened by the stationing of British troops in Boston after 1768: that event did not lead to arrests and executions of resistance leaders. Never empowered to act as a police force, the army remained subject to civilian control. The result was that it could not be used as an instrument of coercion and was easily neutralized by the same agencies of "local law" that had already—by *legal* means—rendered imperial law a dead letter in the colony. According to Reid, the neutralization of metropolitan power after 1765 thus occurred not, as so many earlier historians have suggested, because metropolitan representatives were restrained or timid in their use of power but because they were so rapidly and fully "immobilized by [local] law."[29]

Reid uses the comparison with Ireland in the 1790s to buttress this line of argument. The substance of law in Ireland and in Massachusetts did not differ in any fundamental respect, being equally British in origin. What differed profoundly, according to Reid, were the conditions of law, specifically "the tradition[s] of law and the degree of local control over the institutions of law." In contrast to Revolutionaries in Massachusetts, the rebelling Irish, who constituted at least three-fourths of the colony's population, not only did not have effective control over the Irish legal

---

[28] Reid, "In a Defensive Rage," 1044; "In a Constitutional Void," 35–37; and *In a Defiant Stance,* 170–71.

[29] Reid, *In a Defiant Stance,* 71, 170–72; "Civil Law as a Criminal Sanction," 211, 213, 216, 246–47; "In a Constitutional Void," 3, 7–10, 26, 35–37; and *In Defiance of the Law,* 226–27. Smith, *Writs of Assistance,* 519, is a recent example of the suggestion that metropolitan officials could have been more assertive.

system but were actually excluded from any formal role in the political process and had few civil rights. As a result, local institutions were both weaker and far less responsive to their needs, while imperial law, supported by a large military establishment and uninhibited by local law from acting in the most draconian ways to suppress local dissent, was infinitely stronger, and genuinely lawless violence was the rule. Whereas Massachusetts Revolutionaries "had a law for which to fight," Reid writes, Irish rebels "had a law to fight against."[30]

Strictly speaking, of course, Reid's Irish-Massachusetts comparison is not a rigorous one. According to his analysis, the key variables in the comparison were the conditions of law and the degree of local control. But the most important difference between the two situations would seem to lie in the character of the revolting segments of society. In Massachusetts the governing class was in revolt. In Ireland it was the excluded class. The one characteristic these two groups had in common was their discontent with the existing regime. In every other sense the Irish rebels were more similar to slaves and other excluded groups in the American colonies, that is, they were subject to the law but had no role in making it.

Nor does the fact that the Catholic Irish were excluded from an active role in civic life mean, as Reid seems to imply, that traditions of local self-government in Ireland were weak. Indeed, in Ireland as well as in the American colonies the seventy years following the Glorious Revolution had witnessed the growth of parliamentary institutions and local autonomy. In response to repeated claims by Irish leaders for exemption from its authority, the British Parliament passed a declaratory act in 1720 asserting its jurisdiction over Ireland in "all cases whatsoever." As J. C. Beckett has shown, however, Parliament continued thereafter, as it had done from the Tudor period onward, to exert its right to legislate for Ireland "with great caution." After 1720, as before, British legislation for Ireland "was, in fact, very largely economic or administrative," and the crown, as had long been its custom, usually sought the concurrence of the Irish Parliament to any British statutes that applied specifically to Ireland. According to Beckett, "there was never any question of taxing Ireland by British legislation; and even in less vital matters ministers were very unwilling to stir up trouble by using the authority of a British statute to over-ride the will of the Irish Parliament." Nor did the British Parliament customarily legislate on Irish internal affairs. With a "nervous regard for Irish opinion" and a grave "apprehensive[ness] of the con-

---

[30] Reid, *In a Defiant Stance,* 26, 135, 172–73.

sequences that might follow rash punitive measures," the metropolitan government occasionally threatened to take unpopular measures but repeatedly backed down in the face of Irish resistance. In Ireland, as in the American colonies, government thus seems to have been consensual, and metropolitan officials could not enforce measures that were actively opposed by the local ruling class.[31]

The vital difference between the ruling segment of the population in Ireland and that of Massachusetts was that the former ultimately had to depend upon the metropolitan government to keep the large excluded population of Catholic Irish in line. In this sense the Anglo-Irish ruling class was similar to the small governing class of white planters in Britain's Caribbean colonies. Thus, it can be argued that in the eighteenth-century British colonial world the relative internal strength of the governing class rather than its control over local institutions was the main variable in determining the strength of imperial law and the forces behind it in any given colonial polity.

Notwithstanding these problems with Reid's comparison, it does help to underline the extent to which local revolutionaries did have effective control of legal processes in Massachusetts.

The discovery that effective law in the American colonies was both local and consensual inevitably helped to reopen the classic question debated by Charles H. McIlwain and Robert L. Schuyler more than fifty years ago, the question of the legitimacy of American constitutional pretensions during the pre-Revolutionary debate.[32] Once again, Reid has produced the largest volume of work on this subject. An important theme in both *In a Defiant Stance* and *In a Rebellious Spirit*, it is the central focus of many of his articles and his 1981 monograph, *In Defiance of the Law*, a work devoted to an assessment of the validity of American arguments against stationing troops in the colonies. But Reid's analysis

---

[31] See J. C. Beckett, "The Irish Parliament in the Eighteenth Century," Belfast National History and Philosophical Society, *Proceedings*, 2d ser., 4 (1955): 18–23, and "Anglo-Irish Constitutional Relations in the Later Eighteenth Century," *Irish Historical Studies* 14 (1964): 20–23; J. L. McCracken, "The Conflict between the Irish Administration and Parliament, 1753–6," ibid., 3 (1942): 169, 179; and F. G. James, "Irish Smuggling in the Eighteenth Century," ibid., 12 (1961): 299–317.

[32] Charles Howard McIlwain, *The American Revolution: A Constitutional Interpretation* (New York, 1923); Robert Livingston Schuyler, *Parliament and the British Empire: Some Constitutional Controversies concerning Imperial Legislative Jurisdiction* (New York, 1929).

of this subject has been supplemented by two important articles, by Barbara A. Black and Thomas C. Grey. In terms both of its imaginative insights and its rigor and depth of analysis, Black's article is, in fact, the most impressive and important single piece of historical analysis considered in this essay.[33]

Historians will not be surprised to be told that two competing views of the constitutional organization of the British Empire emerged out of and animated the pre-Revolutionary debate. The metropolitan "government premised its claims on the eighteenth-century British constitution of parliamentary supremacy." Developing gradually in the wake of the Glorious Revolution, this view represented a "new constitutionalism" in which law was conceived of as "the 'power' of coercive force" and the "constitution came to be seen . . . as a set of institutions headed by Parliament that possessed ultimate authority to change customary constitutional arrangements by legislation." The herald of "an emerging positivist theory of an active and unified state," this view conflated power with right and saw the constitution as a flexible one, "whose only fixed doctrine was that Parliament was legally free to do as it liked."[34]

In opposition to this position, American resistance leaders appealed to "the seventeenth-century English constitution of customary restraints on arbitrary power." Grounded in "the old constitutionalism" of Sir Edward Coke, John Hampden, and John Pym, the American view saw law as the product of "the 'right' of consent, custom, or consensus" and conceived of the constitution as a bundle of customary rights—"primarily common law property rights, and rights to traditional institutional arrangements and legal procedures"—that "were the products of social evolution." Because it was the source of legislative authority, the constitution was both superior to and a limit on that authority. Relatively inflexible, it could be modified only by precedent "based upon consent"— and not by legislative enactments. Whereas the metropolitan argument implied that the British Empire was a unified state under the direction of an omnipotent Parliament, the colonial view suggested that it was a "decentralized" entity that, through custom and consent, had slowly developed a "legally binding unwritten constitution" that severely limited Parliament's authority over the colonies.[35]

---

[33] Black, "Constitution of the Empire"; Grey, "Origins of the Unwritten Constitution."

[34] Reid, *In Defiance of the Law*, dust jacket, 3, 41–42, 48, 121; Grey, "Origins of the Unwritten Constitution," 857, 867.

[35] Reid, *In Defiance of the Law*, dust jacket, 3, 48, 121; Grey, "Origins of the Unwritten Constitution," 863–67, 892.

As Black notes, "twentieth-century scholarship" has been "virtually unanimous in holding that," in this debate, "Americans . . . were 'wrong on the law,'" in Reid's words, that "American constitutional pretensions" should not be "take[n] seriously because the constitution was what Parliament declared it to be." This is, in fact, the view of most earlier legal historians. But Reid, Black, and Grey together offer a powerful case against this conventional view. They argue that, so far from being right, that interpretation is "really an incorrect conclusion of law."[36]

These scholars do not deny that London authorities thought "of the governance of their empire in terms of [a] . . . unicentric power applying one law laid down by parliament." What they contend is that the "imperial constitution of eighteenth-century British North America was not [nearly] as precise as today's historians insist it must have been" and that it by no means "furnish[ed] definitive answers" about the scope of Parliament's authority within the empire. "A development of the mid-eighteenth century" that was "not reasonably foreseeable in 1689," the doctrine of parliamentary supremacy was still sufficiently new as not yet to be fully understood or accepted even within England itself. By no means yet having lost its "historical respectability and constitutional legitimacy," the "old idea of a . . . fixed constitution standing above and limiting the working institutions of government . . . [still] remained a respectable idea in England in the 1760s." In fact, as Reid remarks, the very concept of the constitution was still so imprecise that "definition [was] more a matter of personal usage than of judicial certainty," and it was still possible, even, "to accept the new constitution of parliamentary supremacy while clinging to the old constitution of fixed restraints."[37]

If the precise nature of the British constitution remained unclear in Britain, its status was even more ambiguous in America. In regard to "both Ireland and North America," Reid notes, the exact nature of the constitution continued to be "one of . . . many points of controversy on

---

[36] Black, "Constitution of the Empire," 1157; Reid, *In Defiance of the Law,* 168–69, and "Irrelevance of the Declaration," 60. Julius Goebel is chief among the legal historians who have taken the conventional view. See his volume in *The Oliver Wendell Holmes Devise History of the Supreme Court of the United States: Antecedents and Beginnings to 1801* (New York, 1973). See also the more recent article by another legal historian, William F. Swindler, "'Rights of Englishmen' since 1776: Some Anglo-American Notes," *University of Pennsylvania Law Review* 124 (1976): 1083–1103, that the American case was "substantially inaccurate" (1089).

[37] Reid, *In a Defiant Stance,* 70, *In Defiance of the Law,* 25, 33, 36, 205, and "Ordeal by Law of Thomas Hutchinson," 602; Black, "Constitution of the Empire," 1210–11; Grey, "Origins of the Unwritten Constitution," 858.

which even crown lawyers did not agree." "Unwritten and without a judiciary to settle conflicts, the imperial constitution was," in fact, "whatever could be plausibly argued and forcibly maintained," and "competent lawyers could write convincing briefs for both sides of the question." Under these conditions, Reid contends, the issue was "seen as debatable on both sides of the Atlantic." Presumably, that is why George Grenville went to such pains to try to refute American arguments against taxation without representation before he pushed through the Stamp Act. "The test of whether an argument was then legally sound," Reid writes, was "whether that argument was not only one that enjoyed substantial public support but also one that a lawyer could seriously defend." In his view the question "therefore is not whether . . . American constitutional arguments were 'right' or even 'sound'" but "whether they were at least tenable."[38]

That they certainly were "at least tenable" is the verdict of both Black and Reid. Historians have tended to treat the American view as "an archaism." As Reid explains, however, the fact that "the seventeenth-century constitution of customary rights would never be reestablished as the constitution of Great Britain does not prove that the eighteenth-century British constitution of parliamentary supremacy had been established in the North American colonies." On the contrary, Reid and Black both argue that the colonies operated under the aegis not of the British constitution but of an emerging "imperial constitution," the "Constitution of the Empire" referred to in the title of Black's article. Almost a century and a half old by the 1760s, this constitution was not, contrary to the opinions of many historians, to any significant degree based upon the charters. As documents that, like Magna Charta, were merely confirmatory of existing rights and not grants of new ones, charters served as little more than a "first line of defense"—for those few colonies that still had them. They were "part of the American constitutional case," Reid writes, but "not the case itself." Rather, the American case rested primarily on three other, legally much more solid foundations.[39]

---

[38] Reid, *In a Defiant Stance,* 12; "Ordeal by Law of Thomas Hutchinson," 610; "In a Defensive Rage," 1087; *In Defiance of the Law,* dust jacket; "In Accordance with Usage," 341; and "Apparatus of Constitutional Advocacy," 194.

[39] Reid, "Apparatus of Constitutional Advocacy," 194, *In Defiance of the Law,* 32, 159, 162–63; and "In the First Line of Defense," 177, 208, 209, 211; Black, "Constitution of the Empire," 1203. While the distinction between the British constitution and the imperial constitution is a necessary and useful one, it is also important to emphasize that within the empire there was also a third kind of constitution, namely the constitution of each separate colony, no one of which was precisely the same as another. The implications

Intensively explored by Black, the first of these was the *doctrine of irrevocable surrender.* Much of the scholarly discussion of the merits of the American case has revolved around the opinions of Edward Coke in two early seventeenth-century cases that were also "central to the contemporary debate over parliamentary power in the dominions": *Bonham's Case* (1607), in which Coke held that the common law was superior to parliamentary statutes, and *Calvin's Case* (1608), a contrived case in which he ruled, favorably, on the question of whether James I's Scottish subjects born after his accession to the English throne in 1603 had "the rights of Englishmen, despite the fact that they lived under separate law in Scotland, and the English Parliament had no authority there."[40]

In *Calvin's Case* Coke made a sharp distinction between Scotland, "a *kingdom by descent* . . . by whose laws the king came into his title," and Ireland, "a *dominion by conquest.*" In the former, people could "live under allegiance to the King of England without subjection to the English Parliament." But, Coke argued, in conquered territories like Ireland the situation was quite otherwise. As conqueror, the king could "at his pleasure alter and change the laws." Once he had introduced the laws of England into the conquered territory, however, as Henry II had done in Ireland, neither he nor his successors could thenceforth "alter the same without Parliament." The standard interpretation of this clause has been that Coke intended by it "to maximize the power of the English Parliament" over the dominions; and, as Black remarks, this view seems to gain support from the fact that, elsewhere in the case, "Coke went out of his way . . . to underline the power of the English Parliament over Ireland" by including "the so-called 'naming doctrine.'" According to that doctrine, Parliament could bind the dominions by any statute merely by naming those dominions in the statute.[41]

In an ingenious reconsideration of *Calvin's Case*, however, Black casts considerable doubt upon this interpretation. Indeed, she argues that, "far from displaying an anxiety that the power of the English Parliament over the dominions be secured," Coke instead exhibited both "a distinct

---

of this fact are explored in Jack P. Greene, *Peripheries and Center: Constitutional Development in the Extended Polities of the British Empire and the United States, 1607–1788* (Athens, Ga., 1986). Reid implicitly acknowledges the existence and importance of these local constitutions, though to speak of them collectively as an "American constitution" (e.g., *In Defiance of the Law,* 160) is anachronistic, albeit they all were founded upon and expressed a common set of underlying principles.

[40] Black, "Constitution of the Empire," 1175–76.

[41] Ibid., 1176–79.

recognition that the power of the English Parliament over Ireland (and, presumably, over any dominion ruled by English law)" was "anomalous" and "a reluctance to admit that power." "Current opinion notwithstanding," Black asserts, "there is no reason to think that when Coke" declared "that the king must, after the institution of English law [in a conquered territory], work through parliament, it" was "the *English* Parliament that he" had "in mind!" "To the contrary," she believes, "Coke's assumption" seemed to be "that the parliament [in question] would be one granted the conquered territory."[42]

Persuasively insisting that Coke, both in *Calvin's Case* and in his *Institutes*, "evidently believed that the grant of English laws to Ireland put the English king in Ireland in the position of the English king in England—that is, without legislative power on his own, but only through a parliament," Black characterizes Coke's position as "that of a parliament-man, not a Parliament-man," and emphasizes his reluctance to allow the English Parliament any power "over a conquered country *to which had been given the laws of England.*" Thus, "far from assuming that the grant of English law" was "equivalent to the imposition of English rule through the English Parliament and courts," as the standard interpretation has assumed, Coke, argues Black, "obviously . . . saw it merely as a requirement that the conqueror act in Ireland as he did in England"—through the local parliament.[43]

By this line of interpretation, Black shifts the emphasis in *Calvin's Case* away from Coke's conquest doctrine, on which most earlier writers have focused, to what she calls his "new-hatched doctrine of limitation on the conqueror's prerogative," the idea that the crown's grant of English rights to a conquered territory represented an "irrevocable surrender" of those rights. Stressing Coke's attachment to the concept of "principled limitation," she contends that, notwithstanding his inclusion of the naming clause in *Calvin's Case*, his "major concern," in the dominions, as well as in England, "was for what we should call government by consent," for both doing "away with absolute royal rule" and giving "to all who lived under English law the benefits of representative government." Denying that it is possible to find any "sign" in either his writings or his behavior "that Coke saw the English Parliament as appropriately representing any but the King's subjects in England, except . . . in the absence of a representative body in the dominion—and then only until such a body appeared," she concludes that the "standard . . . reading of

[42] Ibid., 1179–80.
[43] Ibid., 1181, 1186–87.

Calvin's Case," by which "all signs of Coke's wish to stamp principled limitation upon imperial rule" have been converted "into an avidity for the establishment of the supremacy of the English Parliament throughout the Empire," is wholly "inaccurate."[44]

If the doctrine of irrevocable surrender as elaborated by Black provides one foundation for the American case,[45] the *doctrine of settlement* furnishes a second. In *Calvin's Case,* as Black explains, "Coke recognized only descent and conquest as possible modes" of acquiring new dominions. This formulation was dictated by English property law, according to which "all land" was "in tenure," "all titles" were "derivative," and there was "no recognition of *res nullius.*" There was, therefore, "no room for the mode of acquisition which later came to be called colonization, plantation, or settlement."[46]

To resolve this situation, later jurists, Black points out, abandoned "the restrictions of English real property law" and "recognized colonization as well as descent and conquest" as a way of acquiring new areas. A product of this new distinction, the doctrine of settlement held that, as "subjects of the British crown," colonists automatically carried with them to their new homes "all rights traditionally associated with the ancient English constitution." Because all but two of the American colonies settled before 1760 had been acquired by settlement rather than by conquest, the effect of this doctrine was dramatically to "decrease . . . the number of territories subject at all, for any length of time, for any period, to the conqueror's absolute power." As metropolitan law officers held in *Campbell v. Hall* in 1774, moreover, "grants of legislative assemblies" to conquered colonies such as Jamaica and New York "constituted an irrevocable surrender of the king's rights as conqueror."[47]

Although such a noted authority as Sir William Blackstone thought the opposite, "the cumulative force of these doctrines," Black cogently argues, was "considerable." By the era of the American Revolution, it had been clearly established in law that "colonies were not conquests" and "that conquests which had been granted legislative assemblies were not conquests." Like the idea of principled limitation that she sees as the

---

[44] Ibid., 1184, 1191, 1196, 1198, 1203.

[45] Its use by both crown lawyers and colonial commentators from North America, the Caribbean, and Ireland during the first six decades of the eighteenth century would seem to justify the importance Black attributes to the doctrine of irrevocable surrender. See Greene, *Peripheries and Center,* chaps. 2–4.

[46] Black, "Constitution of the Empire," 1177.

[47] Ibid., 1199; Reid, *In Defiance of the Law,* 79–80.

ultimate goal of Coke's concept of irrevocable surrender, the doctrine of settlement, in Black's view, was obviously "a legal development . . . in the direction of self-determination."[48]

But the most solid of the three *legal* foundations on which the Americans rested their case, Reid, Black, and Grey all seem to agree, was the third: the *doctrine of usage*, or custom. The primary "source of authority underlying both the seventeenth-century English constitution, and the contemporary American constitution[s] that colonial whigs were defending against the eighteenth-century British constitution," writes Reid, "was custom." The eighteenth-century Cambridge natural law theorist Thomas Rutherforth agreed. "The content of a nation's constitution," he noted in 1750, was largely "a question of fact, to be determined by considering the history and customs of a people." To a very important extent, the American case ultimately rested on the contention, first asserted during the Stamp Act crisis, that both "interference in local affairs by Parliament through legislation" and "direct parliamentary taxation" were "contrary to the principles of the contemporary" colonial constitutions, as those "constitution[s] had been established by long custom and as" that custom "was currently sanctioned by accepted usage."[49]

As historians have long recognized, evidence for these claims is by no means insubstantial. During the eighteenth century, as Black notes, Britain's various overseas dominions had been "much, if not equally, blessed by the extension of the benefits of government by consent." As is well known, while the king's prerogative in Britain was reduced considerably as a result of various statutory restrictions following the Glorious Revolution, it remained, at least in theory, extensive in the colonies. While it is certainly an exaggeration to say, as Reid does, that by the 1760s the "case had been won against the royal prerogative" in America, over the previous seven decades the assemblies in most colonies had certainly managed, through a combination of statutes and custom, largely to neutralize the prerogative. These achievements, moreover, had been sanctioned not only by custom, as "'constantly' reaffirmed both by usage and British reacknowledgement," but also, in many cases, by rulings of crown law officers, who repeatedly upheld and thereby reiterated the continuing legitimacy of "the doctrine of usage" in colonial cases. As Black observes, it is impossible to read "the pertinent cases and opinions of crown officers over the years from Coke to Mansfield" without being

---

[48] Black, "Constitution of the Empire," 1199–1200.

[49] Reid, *In Defiance of the Law*, 79–80, 160, "In an Inherited Way," 1127, and "In Accordance with Usage," 341; Grey, "Origins of the Unwritten Constitution," 863.

"struck not by the support which emerges for royal power over the king's dominions but by the progressive diminishment of" that power—in law. To an extraordinary degree royal government in the colonies had come "more and more" to mean "government by the elected representatives of the people."[50]

The corollary to this diminution of royal power through a combination of custom and recognition of its legally binding character by metropolitan law officers was the failure of Parliament to take an expansive role in colonial affairs. "Except in the areas of trade, imperial defense, and some minor matters," Reid notes, "the authority of Parliament to bind the North American colonies had not been established by custom or precedent." Precisely because Parliament thus played only a limited, "essentially conciliar" role in colonial affairs, the fact "that the prerogative was at its height in the colonies reinforced the sense of" the colonies "as the king's dominions." As a result, Black observes, the "reduction of the king's power by English law, as well as by the ingenuity and effort of the colonial assemblies[,] . . . irresistibly [suggested] the reduction in law of all external power"—that of Parliament as well as that of the king— and thereby gave legitimacy to the American claim that rights established through custom "were beyond modification by [either] Parliament" or king. By the 1760s most of the customary colonial constitutions had existed for at least eighty to a hundred years, and the colonial assemblies, under the aegis of those constitutions, "had long performed [all of the] functions Parliament and the British ministry were [then] attempting to assume." As far as Americans were concerned, however, "the supremacy of Parliament," as Reid puts it, "had not yet been established as part of their customary constitution[s] and, now that the Stamp Act [had] exposed the danger of parliamentary supremacy, it would never be [so] established."[51]

Most historians, including some earlier legal historians, have treated the disparity between the actualities of colonial self-government and metropolitan theory as a distinction between "fact and law" or, in the

---

[50] Black, "Constitution of the Empire," 1193, 1198, 1200, 1203; Reid, "Ordeal by Law of Thomas Hutchinson," 599, and "In Accordance with Usage," 366. Earlier historical works that do emphasize the importance of custom and the customary constitutional changes that occurred as a result of the gains of the assemblies and the character of metropolitan supervision include Bernhard Knollenberg, *Origin of the American Revolution, 1759–1766* (New York, 1960), and Jack P. Greene, *The Quest for Power: The Lower Houses of Assembly in the Southern Royal Colonies, 1689–1763* (Chapel Hill, N.C., 1963).

[51] Reid, *In Defiance of the Law,* 162, 169, and "In Accordance with Usage," 357, 364; Black, "Constitution of the Empire," 1202.

case of the present writer, between fact and theory. But, and herein lies one of the principal contributions of the legal historians considered in this article, such distinctions seriously underestimate the legal force of custom in English law. The supposed "tension between fact and law," Black states, was actually a "tension within law." In English jurisprudence, as Reid explains, custom obtained "the force of law by a combination of time and precedent. Whatever had been done from time immemorial in a community was legal; whatever had been abstained from was illegal." "Historical fact was the source of constitutional custom," and, according to contemporary English practice well into the late eighteenth century, "rights established by custom and proven by time were legal rights" that, as Grey notes, were "*judicially* enforceable, even against the highest legislative and executive organs of government."[52]

The colonists, Grey observes, did not condemn British policies as "merely . . . unjust or untraditional or even 'unconstitutional' in the extra-legal sense of that term." They denounced them "as *illegal*—and the law" they invoked "was the unwritten fundamental law of reasonable custom and customary reason that [had traditionally] made [and still continued to make] up [so much of] the British constitution."[53] Historians who have treated "custom as a source of or authority for 'law' that in fact" was "not law, or" was "something less than law" have thus been wrong. As Black insists, colonial "gains made over the years in the direction of self-determination by means of the doctrines of settlement, irrevocable surrender, and usage" were "gains made *in and by law*," and the "reduction of the king's power and the increase of the representative dimension of the imperial constitution" were developments "in law [as well] as in fact."[54]

---

[52] Black, "Constitution of the Empire," 1202; Reid, *In Defiance of the Law*, 81, 160, 165, "In Accordance with Usage," 356–57, and "Irrelevance of the Declaration," 61; Grey, "Origins of the Unwritten Constitution," 850.

[53] Grey, "Origins of the Unwritten Constitution," 890. As Grey points out, notwithstanding the growing authority of the doctrine of parliamentary supremacy in Britain, English lawyers continued, even into the third quarter of the eighteenth century, to invoke a legal tradition that regarded fundamental law as "*legally* supreme" and saw custom as "the most reliable evidence of the content of natural [or fundamental] law." Unlike modern historians, fundamental law theorists thus did not see reason and custom as being in conflict. Instead, as Grey explains, they blended them "into a single system," according to which "the old was the reasonable and the reasonable was the old." Ibid., 850, 853–54.

[54] Reid, "In Accordance with Usage," 344; Black, "Constitution of the Empire," 1203, 1210.

Just as there was more than one law in each colony, a local law and an imperial law, so, the writers considered here show, there was more than one constitution in the British Empire. If by the 1760s the British constitution had become the constitution of parliamentary supremacy, the emerging imperial constitution, like the separate constitutions of Britain's many overseas dominions, remained a customary constitution. An important aspect of custom was that it depended upon consent. As Rutherforth noted in 1750, usage that had "obtained in any civil society [from] . . . time immemorial . . . may be presumed to have obtained with its consent." And just as, in Rutherforth's words, "whatever is consented to by a civil society, becomes a law of such society," so it was a hallowed English constitutional principle that nothing could become law without such consent.[55]

This principle lay at the heart of the familiar idea of a constitutional contract between the rulers and the ruled. According to this idea, neither party could change the contract without the consent of the other. No political or constitutional changes, in short, could take effect without the consent of *both* concerned parties as indicated either by long-standing acceptance through usage or by a formal legislative enactment by a representative body empowered to give such consent. Because historians have tended to trace the colonists' use of this argument to the writings of John Locke and various natural law theorists, they have failed to appreciate, as Reid writes, that it had also been "a central dogma in English and British constitutional law since time immemorial." Contract theory did not therefore rest only on philosophical grounds but, like the doctrine of custom, was also deeply rooted in "customary [English] jurisprudence" and had firm legal standing.[56]

Recognition of the legal status of the doctrines of consent and contract tends to give still further legal weight to the Americans' argument that "parliament and the ministry in London, not they, [had] defied the ancient law" and had attempted to violate their "old rights" by altering their "customary constitution[s]." The Americans admitted that it was legal for Parliament to regulate colonial trade because, as a quid pro quo for protection, they had, through usage, "'chearfully' consented" to such regulations. But they vehemently argued that it was *il*legal for Parliament to tax the colonies or otherwise interfere in unaccustomed ways

---

[55] Grey, "Origins of the Unwritten Constitution," 863–64; Reid, "Irrelevance of the Declaration," 65.

[56] Reid, "Irrelevance of the Declaration," 72, and "In Our Contracted Sphere," 22.

with their internal affairs because they had never given their consent to such exertions of parliamentary power. Through both formal parliamentary enactments in the wake of the Glorious Revolution and usage during succeeding decades, British people in Britain had obviously consented to the doctrine of parliamentary supremacy. In the colonies, however, neither the people at large through custom nor their representatives in the several colonial assemblies had given such consent. For Parliament to attempt to bind the colonies without that consent was nothing less than "a unilateral breach of an agreement that could properly be changed only by bilateral negotiation."[57]

However strong its case in law, the American claim that the imperial constitution was one of "principled limitation" by which colonists were guaranteed "government by consent" of course found little support in Britain. There, constitutional theory was running in an entirely different direction, one, in Black's words, that "in theory involved the obliteration of every trace of principled limitation from law and its relegation to the precarious plane of practice." Once metropolitan officials had subjected the American claim to the test of this new theory, any hope of winning a favorable hearing for their case in London was "pretty much lost."[58]

But the fact that they would not take these claims seriously does not mean that metropolitan officials were "right about the law." As these legal historians have so cogently stressed, constitutional arrangements within the British Empire were far from precise, and each side could marshal effective legal arguments in behalf of its position. Nor, as Reid emphasizes, was there within the empire any "tribunal to which [such] a constitutional dispute could be taken for resolution except parliament itself—the very institution against which the colonists were contending." In this fluid situation questions "of sovereignty and legitimacy" were by no means so clear as they were said to be in London and as so many later historians have assumed. The *legal* question of "whether usage was . . . the authority for the [imperial] constitution," the primary issue "dividing American Whigs from their fellow subjects in Great Britain" during the 1760s and 1770s, was thus still very much an open question.[59]

---

[57] Reid, "Irrelevance of the Declaration," 83, "In Our Contracted Sphere," 31, 40, and "In a Defensive Rage," 1087; Black, "Constitution of the Empire," 1202–3.

[58] Reid, "In Accordance with Usage," 344; Black, "Constitution of the Empire," 1203, 1210.

[59] Reid, "In a Defensive Rage," 1063; *In a Defiant Stance,* 162; "A Lawyer Acquitted," 191; and "In Accordance with Usage," 344.

The picture of the American Revolution that emerges from the new legal history literature is one in which the quarrel was not over a right and a wrong interpretation of the constitution but a "struggle . . . between different levels of government," each of which had a legitimate constitutional case. By no means yet a modern unitary state, the British Empire was directed by a "multicentric" rather than a "unicentric . . . authority." Imperial institutions in the colonies had little coercive power and depended for their effectiveness upon the consent of local populations. Authority within the empire was dispersed into the hands of authoritative, powerful, and "largely autonomous local institutions." Not dependent for their effectiveness "on the support or the acquiescence of a central authority" and highly "resistant to centralized control," these institutions were regarded, both by those who composed them and those whom they served, as largely "independent recipients of constitutional power and authority." As Hartog notes, in this "diffuse and decentralized" political entity, local institutions invariably "defined the meaning of 'law' as much as did imperial institutions." The same can be said in reference to constitutional arrangements. In view of this new understanding of its legal context, the colonial argument in behalf of constitutional limits on metropolitan authority over the colonies, which scholars have so long and so widely regarded as ad hoc, contrived, and insubstantial, now has to be regarded as having strong legal as well as experiential foundations.[60]

This body of work also provides a caution for students of extended polities in the era before the French Revolution and the development of the modern consolidated state in its wake. In regard to such polities, it can no longer be automatically assumed that the perspective of the center is the correct or even the dominant one. What these new legal history studies powerfully suggest, in fact, is that in any polity in whose localities the authority and ideology of the center are weak while local power and traditions are strong, local institutions and customs will be at least as important as those of the center in determining existing legal and constitutional situations. In such an entity a *center* perspective will almost automatically be a *partisan* perspective. In the particular case of the American Revolution, the antiquity of the notion of a customary

---

[60] Reid, *In a Defiant Stance*, 2, 161, and "In a Defensive Rage," 1091; Hartog, "Losing the World of the Massachusetts Whig," 146, 147, 152–53, 160.

imperial constitution of principled limitation and the strength of local institutions, on the one hand, combined with the comparative recentness of the doctrine of parliamentary supremacy and the weakness of metropolitan authority in the colonies, on the other hand, to make the perspective of the center a "tory perspective." Perhaps even more important, the failure of the center to establish the legitimacy of its perspective in the colonies rendered that perspective anachronistic when applied to legal and constitutional arrangements within the empire as a whole.[61]

The line of interpretation elaborated here would be still further strengthened by a systematic analysis of the development of colonial constitutional thinking before the 1760s, not just in North America but in Ireland and the West Indies as well. The cursory nature of existing studies of this subject[62] contributes to the misperception, voiced explicitly by Grey, that "during the colonial period Americans had not been much given to debate over issues of constitutional theory." To be sure, they had not given much thought to the specific problem of the relationship between the colonies and Parliament. That was a question that would not be raised explicitly until the early 1760s. By then, however, they had been involved for over a century in a long series of controversies over the nature of the relationship between the colonies and Britain, controversies that involved elaborate considerations of questions concerning the access of colonists to the benefits of English laws and constitutional rights and the status of their elected assemblies. Even a casual analysis of the considerable literature generated by these controversies reveals that they had fostered the development of coherent constitutional traditions that, on the eve of the pre-Revolutionary debate, were both explicit and vital.[63]

In view of this development, it is certainly misleading to say, as Reid does, that the colonists were merely "the heirs, not the progenitors, of

---

[61] Reid, *In a Defiant Stance*, 162.

[62] Lawrence H. Leder, *Liberty and Authority: Early American Political Ideology, 1689–1763* (Chicago, 1968), 79–139, and Bernard Bailyn, *The Origins of American Politics* (New York, 1968), 124–61, contain brief considerations of colonial constitutional thought. The former is at best a superficial analysis, though the research behind that analysis is extensive. The second is only tangentially concerned with constitutional issues per se.

[63] For a more extensive discussion of this development, see Greene, *Peripheries and Center*, chaps. 1–4. The quotation is from Grey, "Origins of the Unwritten Constitution," 865.

their constitutional world" and that their "guiding principles" were backward-looking and "English, not American." More accurately, it might be said that their principles were both American *and* English, that those principles were grounded in their own as well as in the English past, and that they had been the active progenitors as well as the heirs of the constitutional world in which they lived. The same literature also shows that the American view "of how authority was distributed throughout the empire" was by no means "peculiar," as Reid suggests, but was shared by the dominant populations of Ireland and the West Indian and other island colonies. The fact that this *colonial* view extended to all of the well-developed peripheral areas of the empire adds considerable weight to the conception, so powerfully and persuasively developed in the works treated in this essay, of the early modern British Empire as an entity in which the dispersion, not the concentration, of authority was a central fact of its legal and constitutional character.[64]

Twenty years ago in the pages of the *South Atlantic Quarterly* I described a new interpretation of the American Revolution that was then emerging from literature produced after World War II. For want of a better term, I called that interpretation *neo-Whig*. The product of the newer writings of older scholars like Oliver M. Dickerson and Bernard Knollenberg and a large group of younger scholars, including especially Edmund S. Morgan, the early contributions to that interpretation were primarily concerned with explaining why the colonists opposed British policies in the 1760s and 1770s.[65] Taking the ideas of American resistance leaders seriously, they explored the context and character of the colonial position on most of the important substantive issues involved in the pre-Revolutionary disputes and stressed the importance of constitutional considerations. A few of them even suggested that the colonial case against parliamentary taxation was stronger than most scholars had supposed.[66] By showing just how strong—in law—it was, the legal historians discussed in this article have both placed themselves

---

[64] Reid, *In Defiance of the Law,* 31, 34, 54, 229.

[65] Jack P. Greene, "The Flight from Determinism: A Review of Recent Literature on the Coming of the American Revolution," *South Atlantic Quarterly* 61 (1962): 235–59 [chap. 17 above].

[66] Knollenberg, *Origin of the American Revolution,* 157–75; Jack P. Greene, ed., *The Nature of Colony Constitutions: Two Pamphlets on the Wilkes Fund Controversy in South Carolina by Sir Egerton Leigh and Arthur Lee* (Columbia, S.C., 1970), 49–55.

squarely within the neo-Whig tradition and made a major contribution
to it.

In the early 1980s Richard L. Watson, Jr., editor of the *South Atlantic Quarterly,* asked
me to write a general piece on the historiography of the American Revolution to be
published on the twentieth anniversary of "The Flight from Determinism" (chap. 17
above). Because the literature published on this subject since the early 1960s was far too
vast and complex to be considered in a single article, I offered instead to do a piece on the
contribution of legal history scholars to the literature on the origins of the Revolution, a
subject I then was considering in connection with my book *Peripheries and Center.* The
chapter was published and is here reprinted with permission and a few verbal changes
from the *South Atlantic Quarterly* 75 (1986): 56–77, Copyright Duke University Press,
1986.

—Twenty-Three—

The American Revolution Revisited

CONTEMPORARY SPOKESMEN for the resistance movement that led to the American Revolution in 1776–83 invariably depicted that movement as a defense of the Americans' constitutional rights as British people against a metropolitan government intent upon depriving them of those rights. Few among the articulate minority of colonists who either supported the metropolis or counseled only limited opposition to its measures found this interpretation credible, however. Eventually denominated by the "whig" leaders of resistance as "tories" or "loyalists," these opponents of resistance rarely defended the wisdom or politesse of the specific measures being resisted. With resistance leaders, in fact, many of them questioned the constitutionality of those measures. But they emphatically did not agree that either the offending measures or the metropolitan use of force to compel colonial obedience to them constituted sufficient grounds for armed resistance in 1775 or the decision to separate from the British Empire in 1776.

For both contemporary opponents of armed resistance and independence in America and defenders of government actions toward America in Britain, the behavior of participants in the colonial resistance movement seemed to require a deeper explanation. In their view the "*pretence* for such outrageous proceedings, conducted with such indecent and unjust precipitation," as one analyst remarked in 1774, was "much too slight to account for them. The *true* cause of such violent animosity, must have existed much earlier and deeper."[1] Variously, they explained colonial resistance as a result of one or more of several unacknowledged motives or forces. These included the alleged republicanism and religious

[1] Joseph Priestley, *An Address to Protestant Dissenters of All Denominations* (London, 1774), 5, as quoted by J. C. D. Clark, *The Language of Liberty, 1660–1832: Political Discourse and Social Dynamics in the Anglo-American World* (Cambridge, 1994), 45.

[493]

independence of New Englanders, an intellectual and religious inheritance that, ever since the Restoration, had seemed to put them out of step with political and ecclesiastical trends in the parent state; the desire of Virginia tobacco planters to repudiate their large debts to British merchants; the overweening ambitions of colonial leaders to enhance their political status by making the colonies independent; or the aspirations of colonial producers and merchants to escape the trading restrictions imposed by the Navigation Acts.

Inescapably the intellectual heirs of nineteenth-century social and psychological theory, modern historians have continued to search for the unstated or unconscious, "deeper" sources of the American Revolution. Indeed, during the early stages of the Anglo-American cultural rapprochement that, contemporary with the development of professional historical studies, has continued now for more than a century, the search became compelling. In the United States during the early decades of this century, the imperial school of historians led by Charles M. Andrews showed that, so far from having tyrannical intent, as nineteenth-century patriotic American historians like George Bancroft had claimed, the measures American resistance leaders found objectionable were little more than early, somewhat tentative, and wholly unsystematic efforts to grapple with specific problems arising out of a burgeoning empire. In Britain beginning around 1930, Sir Lewis Namier and his intellectual associates and descendants demonstrated that, so far from being the products of a conservative Tory reaction against the Whig ascendancy, as earlier British Whig historians like George Otto Trevelyan had argued, those measures often were rooted in and always deeply affected by the conflicts and mutability of factions within the British political establishment.

By seemingly absolving successive metropolitan ministries of any malicious intent toward the colonies, the findings of these historians suggested that the contemporary colonial contention that new metropolitan initiatives beginning in 1764 put their constitutional rights at serious risk was a palpable exaggeration that represented either a conscious contrivance to cover up some deeper motive or an unconscious self-deception that enabled them to disguise their true motives from themselves. Together, the imperial historians and the Namierites effectively reopened the question of why the colonies rebelled.

Throughout the first half of the twentieth century, one of the most popular answers to this question derived from the work of the Progressive historians, so called because they built their historical explanations upon the prevailing social assumptions of the era of "progressive" politics in the America in which they lived. Searching for the early roots of the contemporary conflicts they saw all around them, these historians put primary emphasis on the conflict not between Britain and the colonies but between rival sociopolitical groups within the colonies, between an entrenched ruling class, on the one hand, and a group of challengers representing the excluded and less powerful classes, on the other. For these historians colonial demands for home rule, to paraphrase Carl Becker, one of the most prominent of the Progressive historians, had far less salience than internal rivalries over who should rule at home, and metropolitan challenges to colonial liberties had considerably less significance than deep and long-standing fissures within the colonial bodies politic. Indeed, from this new perspective contemporary Whig explanations for the Revolution came to be depicted as propaganda designed by the ruling classes to elicit the popular support necessary to preserve their hold upon colonial political life against a formidable challenge from below.

Beginning in the 1940s, many detailed investigations revealed that class struggle was by no means the defining or even a very prominent component of late colonial political divisions and thereby wholly undermined the Progressive explanation for the Revolution; and in the 1950s a new generation of historians, led by Edmund S. Morgan, reexamined in detail relations between Britain and the colonies in the 1760s and 1770s. Taking the declarations and writings of contemporary resistance leaders seriously, they concluded, in contrast to so many of their modern predecessors, that those leaders not only believed what they said in their protests but that those beliefs provided the most accurate guide to their actions. As they said in the Declaration of Independence and many other state papers, Americans separated from the British Empire because the behavior of the metropolitan government after 1764 had persuaded them that it had no respect for their constitutional rights and that separation was the only way they could secure those rights.[2]

But by no means all historians of the post–World War II generation found this "neo-Whig" explanation for the Revolution fully compelling. Notwithstanding the fact that African Americans were at precisely that moment exhibiting a powerful emotional investment in the struggle to secure their civil rights, historians of the Revolution in the 1960s and 1970s, almost all of whom were whites who had long since come to take

---

[2] See Jack P. Greene, "The Flight from Determinism: A Review of Recent Literature on the Coming of the American Revolution," *South Atlantic Quarterly* 61 (1962): 235–59 [chap. 17 above].

their constitutional rights for granted, challenged the contention that so large a proportion of the free colonial population could have been mobilized in revolt around an objective with no more emotional charge than constitutional rights. The facts that colonial economic, demographic, and social success within the empire had been so spectaculer since 1740, that colonists' expressions of pride in their connection with Britain were so widespread and so fulsome, that colonial material grievances against the metropolis were minor, and that overt British oppression, at least before 1775, was minimal—all seemed to add credence to this challenge and stimulated a renewal of the search for the deeper causes of the Revolution.

This search has proven to be a rich field for speculation and for the display of intellectual virtuosity. Based on his brilliant investigation into the ideological origins of the Revolution, Bernard Bailyn in the mid-1960s denied that the Revolution could be understood in terms of the Revolutionaries' often expressed resentment against alleged violations of their rights and focused instead on their widely reiterated fears of a conspiracy among metropolitan ministers and their minions to overturn the British constitution on both sides of the Atlantic and destroy British liberties.

According to Bailyn, the Revolutionaries derived these fears from opposition political writers in Britain, writers who had long warned hyperbolically about the endangerment of British liberty in the face of the rampant corruption and unchecked power of the metropolitan government. The Revolutionaries' extensive familiarity with opposition writings, Bailyn argued, culturally programmed them to put a sinister construction on the behavior of the metropolitan government and produced the exaggerated and "seemingly paranoic" reaction that, far more than their devotion to what seemed to Bailyn "abstract" constitutional rights, provided the emotional fuel behind the colonial decision to revolt.[3]

During the quarter century since Bailyn wrote, other scholars have tried to push the search for the deeper or "true" causes of the American Revolution in other directions. In an influential gloss on Bailyn's argument, his former student Gordon S. Wood agreed that the frenzied and "paranoiac" rhetoric stressed by Bailyn could not possibly be explained as a result of the Revolutionaries' determination to defend their constitutional rights. In a serious departure from Bailyn that was obviously inspired by the then popular explanatory models of structural-functional

---

[3] Bernard Bailyn, *The Ideological Origins of the American Revolution* (Cambridge, Mass., 1967), quotation from 158.

sociology, Wood suggested that such language must have been the product of "severe . . . social strain" within the colonies.[4] In *The Fall of the First British Empire*, published in the early 1980s, Robert W. Tucker and David C. Hendrickson suggested that the Revolution should be understood as an aggressive colonial challenge to British authority that was driven by a powerful, if at the time unacknowledged, nascent American nationalism.[5]

J. C. D. Clark's *The Language of Liberty* is the latest entry in this ongoing search for "a deeper understanding of the causes of" the Revolution. Operating on the assumption that British and loyalist observers "were best able to discern" the "novel and sensational features" of the Revolution, Clark joins them and the scholars referred to above in judging contemporary Whig explanations of the Revolution "strangely inadequate." In contrast to earlier scholars, however, he seeks to explain the Revolution in terms not of class conflict, underlying social strain, or frustrated American nationalism but of transatlantic sectarian divisions, especially as they took shape and functioned within the colonies.[6]

With this ambitious volume Clark continues his effort to rescue the history of the early modern English-speaking world from the clutches of secular historians. A decade ago in several important works, he articulated a powerful case that the traditional institutions of monarchy, court, church, and aristocracy and the hierarchical conceptions of the social order for which they stood were far more central to the identity and operation of English society and politics than modern historians had allowed.[7] Before 1832, he suggested, the "old order" in England could be described, as he reiterates in this volume, as an "ancien regime" or a "confessional state" in which the political "discourse of the Anglican, monarchical, hereditary order" was nothing less than "hegemonic."[8]

This volume explores the implications of these contentions for our understanding of the development of the wider early modern English Atlantic world. Throughout that world, Clark suggests, law and religion "dominated men's understanding of the public realm," functioned as the

---

[4] Gordon S. Wood, "Rhetoric and Reality in the American Revolution," *William and Mary Quarterly*, 3d ser., 23 (1966): 3–32, quotation from 25.

[5] Robert W. Tucker and David C. Hendrickson, *The Fall of the First British Empire: Origins of the War of American Independence* (Baltimore, 1981).

[6] Clark, *Language of Liberty*, 45, 93, 279.

[7] Clark, *Revolution and Rebellion: State and Society in England in the Seventeenth and Eighteenth Centuries* (Cambridge, 1986), and *English Society, 1688–1832* (Cambridge, 1985).

[8] Clark, *Language of Liberty*, 23, 141.

"dominant idioms" of public discourse, and formed the "conceptual structure" around which collective identity took shape. The proud boast that English people enjoyed liberty and security under a representative government and a prescriptive system of common law that bound even the monarch combined with a conception of England as an elect nation with a providential destiny to form the basis for a "hegemonic English myth." Exerting a powerful attraction not just for Englishmen in the home islands but for Scots, Irish, and American colonists, this myth, Clark emphasizes, helped both to give cultural and intellectual unity to an expanding empire and to provide powerful continuities in the midst of dynamic social changes.[9]

Like most earlier historians Clark acknowledges the significance of English legal traditions in shaping colonial public discourse, but he goes well beyond any earlier scholar in his efforts to suggest the many ways in which religious concerns also contributed to that discourse. Indeed, his contention that law and religion were "profoundly related" in the construction of the language of liberty throughout the English-speaking world is one of three large propositions that he asks his readers to consider. Insisting that religion was "a central component both of daily, grassroots communal practice and of the various discourses of political theory in which transatlantic relations were discussed," he argues that religion had a powerful effect upon "the way in which British and colonial legal thinking developed."[10]

On both sides of the Atlantic, Clark writes, societies were "denominationally-defined" and "essentially sectarian in their dynamics: traditions of political thought and action were carried within and articulated by the mosaic of religious denominations which made up the British Isles and, still more, the North American colonies," where by the 1770s extraordinary religious diversity was, in his view, the "most salient" social characteristic. Challenging Bailyn's contention that British opposition thought served as a harmonizing element in American political thought, he asserts that each denomination "at all times . . . necessarily brought to the public arena long-rehearsed and still keenly-debated doctrines about their origins, purposes, and destinies, and about what these entailed for the kingdom or empire in which they found themselves."[11]

[9] Ibid., 1, 11, 47.

[10] Ibid., 4, 5, 16.

[11] Ibid., 22, 41, 286.

In the shaping of colonial political discourse, Clark claims a special role for the religious doctrines of the "various denominations of Protestant Dissenters, whose perspective on the Anglican ascendancy, its theology, its liturgy and its social forms, crucially shaped the theoretical foundations of liberty which triumphed or failed in the years between 1776 and 1787." A new Dissenting conception of liberty, according to him, was the principal source of the ideas of popular sovereignty that some colonists employed against Sir William Blackstone's "quintessentially Anglican" version of the traditional English "unitary, absolutist doctrine of sovereignty." To an important degree, he concludes, the "heightened [American] language of 1776" had been "already fully formed as a language of spiritual liberty" well "before the question of political independence [ever] arose."[12]

By his own admission Clark has not done the detailed research and analysis necessary to provide an authoritative foundation for this argument, and colonial challenges to Blackstonian notions of sovereignty, efforts that were common to Anglicans and Dissenters, almost certainly derived more from their long-standing experience with the practical division of authority within the empire than from either Dissenting religious or better-known political idioms. Nevertheless, he makes a strong enough case for the significance of religious thought in colonial political discourse to suggest that this subject is worth pursuing at greater length and in more depth.

Clark's second major proposition is that "1776 may be understood as a revolution of natural law against common law." Carefully eschewed by "non-Congregationalist propagandists in the middle and southern colonies," the use of natural law to defend colonial rights, according to this argument, was largely limited in the 1760s to Dissenting thinkers such as the Massachusetts lawyer James Otis. Over the following decade, however, the weakness of their legal case increasingly drove Whig opponents of metropolitan measures to ground it very largely upon natural law. Whereas the English legal tradition conceived of common law and natural law as "closely related," the colonists' increasing emphasis on natural law, Clark suggests, shattered this long-standing "shared legal tradition" by creating an evident "antithesis" between them.[13]

Again, Clark has not done the necessary empirical work in colonial polemical literature to demonstrate the plausibility of this contention.

---

[12] Ibid., xii, 5, 66, 114, 148.

[13] Ibid., 2–3, 4, 96.

But the detailed analyses of other scholars do not suggest that it would be a promising line of investigation. Doubtless, the Tory critics from whom Clark takes his cue were fully persuaded that the Whig legal case was weak, but the Whigs themselves regarded it as strong. As John Philip Reid and several other legal historians have shown with great force in a large body of recent writings, the findings of which Clark seems not to have absorbed, Whig theorists not only were persuaded that they had a solid legal case but also, in what they regarded as the best English tradition, continued throughout the years of controversy between 1764 and 1776 to rest their case primarily upon customary law and the British constitution. As Reid's work makes clear, moreover, when they employed natural law, they thought of it not as antithetical to but as virtually isomorphic with common law, custom, and what they took to be the fundamental principles of the English constitution.[14]

Even more problematic is Clark's third—and boldest—general proposition: that the American Revolution was in essence "a rebellion by groups within Protestant Dissent against an Anglican hegemony." The author grounds the complicated argument he constructs to support this proposition in the numerical predominance of Dissenters in the colonial population. Whereas "less than a tenth of Englishmen in 1776 were Dissenters," he notes, "more than three quarters of Americans were enlisted in" non-Anglican denominations: Baptists, Congregationalists, Presbyterians, Quakers, and a variety of smaller sects. These groups formed competing social constituencies that, he asserts, contributed both to produce levels of political conflict that were "significantly higher than in the British Isles" and to make civil insurrection a phenomenon that was "increasingly experienced."[15]

These insurrections often took the form of a challenge "to the authority of a newly-emergent east-coast oligarchy of gentry landowners." But, Clark asserts, they "generally drew on a relatively clearly-defined social constituency which was often denominational in nature," and, he contends, "it was their religious implications which raised practical grievances to a higher plane of collective action." Thus, even though conflict was "usually negotiated, or disguised, within the constitutional struc-

---

[14] For a discussion of Reid's work, see Jack P. Greene, "From the Perspective of Law: Context and Legitimacy in the Origins of the American Revolution," *South Atlantic Quarterly* 85 (1986): 56–77 [chap. 22 above]. The most recent of Reid's nine substantial books is *The Authority of Law*, vol. 4 of *Constitutional History of the American Revolution* (Madison, Wis., 1993).

[15] Clark, *Language of Liberty*, 5, 7, 41, 42.

tures of representation and law," once rebellion had "lifted the lid," denominational dynamics provided the "essential explanatory key."[16]

An antagonism to the Anglican establishment and to the British imperial rule that sought to foster it had, Clark points out, been "long latent" in the several denominations' "inherited ideas on polity." Most Dissenting denominations "carried a right of resistance as part of their definitions of their ecclesiastical polities." For much of the colonial era, however, conflict with French Canada functioned to keep such latent antagonism from rising to the surface. Before the expulsion of the French at the end of the Seven Years' War in 1763, Canada had obviously posed a far greater "threat to liberty, property and Protestantism." No sooner had the French gone, however, than Dissenting colonists, appalled by the "confident expansionary drive" by the Church of England in the colonies after 1760, projected their ancient association of popery and tyranny upon the Anglican social order, which, Clark avers, they "increasingly pictured . . . in terms of sinister feudal, monarchical and clerical anachronisms."[17]

But, Clark contends, the principal stimulus for the transformation of their antagonism to Anglicanism into more general opposition to British rule came from Blackstone's *Commentaries*. By endeavoring to restructure English law "in the interest of the monarchy and the established Church," Blackstone, according to Clark, made Dissent the enemy and thereby offered "a sensational affront to colonial and English Dissenters." From the perspective of Blackstone's formulation, Dissenters more and more tended to perceive the traditional English idea of sovereignty as nothing less than "an affront to God's sovereignty as expressed in fundamental law," and they spearheaded a building opposition to it in the colonies.[18]

In his preface Clark explicitly denies that he offers this hypothesis as a "mono- or even duo-causal explanation" and declares his intention not to supplant but merely to "supplement . . . and so profoundly to modify" earlier interpretations. But his language suggests considerably grander objectives. Directly challenging the traditional view that an external threat emanating from Britain activated colonial resistance, he argues that the American decision to rebel "is chiefly to be explained by new developments in the colonies" arising out of "the inner dynamics of

---

[16] Ibid., 42, 244, 246.

[17] Ibid., 16, 224, 264, 310, 339.

[18] Ibid., 83, 84, 112.

colonial life," specifically by the widespread colonial adoption in the mid-1770s of the Dissenting view of sovereignty. As had been the case in England in the 1680s when wholesale Stuart political reforms became grounds for rebellion only after James's indulgence of "'popery' identified a reformed monarchy as an agency of 'arbitrary power,'" in the American case, Clark argues, "Religious predispositions among anti-Catholic colonists," now displaced upon the Anglicans, "acted to translate practical problems into triggers of armed resistance." "At their core," he concludes, the reasons the "American revolutionaries chose to fight to escape" the empire were thus "largely . . . sectarian ones."[19]

In Clark's opinion the "world of discourse populated by such idioms as the ancient constitution, chartered rights and common-law freedoms" was far too "cautious" ever to produce the "extravagant mind set" required to propel Americans into armed rebellion. Only religious enthusiasm, he writes, could possibly have turned dry and, he implies, unemotive "constitutional issues raised by questions of taxation, executive prerogative and parliamentary jurisdiction . . . from negotiable ones into non-negotiable grievances which evoked the passionate, uncalculating commitment of great numbers of ordinary men by their engagement with a much wider nexus of ideas and feelings." Only "ancient [religious] divisions and hatreds," in his view, could ever have produced the "frenzied" rhetoric, the "paranoia, mass hysteria, [and] virulent hostility" that resulted in the violent overthrow "of the Anglican order" in 1776, an overthrow that, he suggests, made the rebellion less a revolution than a civil war between what he comes close to characterizing as a Whig Dissenting majority and a largely Anglican Tory minority, "a holy war" that, he announces in warming to his theme, was "the last great war of religion in the western world."[20]

In an effort to generalize this line of argument, Clark employs it to construct an explanatory model of political rebellion in the early modern English-speaking world. This model involves "a hierarchy of causation in which denominational polities often established the boundaries of and potential for political mobilisation; theological developments, acting on those polities, acted as accelerators; [and] practical grievances over land and defence, justice and taxation, religious discrimination and the perceived threat of 'Popery and arbitary power' acted as catalysts." Ac-

[19] Ibid., xii–xiii, 7, 62, 239, 273, 307.

[20] Ibid., 45, 180, 222, 273, 301, 302, 305.

cording to this model, "practical grievances" are "seldom sufficient to activate those preconditions without specific [religious] triggers."[21]

No reader can fail to admire the ingenuity of this explanation, the impressive learning on which it is based, or the sustained rendering given to it. It is a significant reinterpretation that demands careful evaluation. Unfortunately, it is also subject to many obvious objections. For one thing, it turns on the highly problematic assumption that throughout the early modern Anglophone world, religious concerns dictated conduct, more specifically, that at the time of the American Revolution the "political commitments of most men were still an aspect of their religion." This may be true, but Clark asserts it without demonstrating it.[22]

A second objection to Clark's explanation is that it rests upon several unsubstantiated contentions about the extent and nature of colonial political divisions and the sources of colonial opposition. Thus, he uncritically accepts the suggestions of earlier scholars that political conflict was "significantly higher" in America than in Britain and that rebellion was becoming more common as time went on. Yet, by almost any conceivable standard for the measurement of such phenomena, these suggestions are both wrong. Neither, without considerably more evidence, will many accept his argument that religious commitments were more important than the colonists' long and sustained experience in the civil realm in shaping their political perceptions and determining their political actions. Similar objections can be made to his suggestion that Dissenters qua Dissenters exerted a prominent role in spearheading the revolt. Both leaders and politically involved constituents of all religious denominations, Congregationalists in New England and Anglicans in Virginia, broadly shared the fear of an omnipotent imperial Parliament and an aggressive ministry, and among Dissenting enclaves in the western backcountry, opinion was sharply divided.[23]

Precisely because Dissenters elsewhere were so divided, Clark's explanation requires him to exaggerate the role of New England in precipitating the Revolution. Indeed, his explanation works best for New England. There, Dissenters were most prominent and least divided. There, the fear of Anglican aggression was most pronounced. There, in the only colonies other than Pennsylvania in which religious motives were central

---

[21] Ibid., 224.

[22] Ibid., 274.

[23] Ibid., 41.

at their founding, people continued, at least to some extent, to subscribe to "a doctrine of identity, origins, purpose and destiny as a New Israel, a chosen people defined by religious allegiance and practice" that found scant expression in other colonies.[24]

As much recent work has shown, however, the New England experience was atypical. An earlier generation of scholars often wrote as if New England, with its rich and easily accessible print heritage, could serve as a convenient proxy for the rest of the colonies or even that it provided the dominant cultural pattern for colonial British America. But such assumptions have been thoroughly discredited.[25] We now know that, contrary to Clark's claim, New England religious and political writings were not "massively exported" to other colonies—indeed, few of them penetrated much beyond the boundaries of New England—and that New England providential discourse was not widely diffused in American cultural centers before the last quarter of the eighteenth century.[26]

Another objection to Clark's explanation is that it is highly partisan— in two senses. First, it is partisan in the sense that it endorses the contentions of contemporary loyalist and metropolitan observers that the colonists had no legal case. Again and again, he follows the lead of those early observers, dismissing the Whig distinction between trade regulations and taxation, based on long-standing custom, as "unconvincing," the Whig argument that the colonies were immediately dependent on the crown as "suspiciously anachronistic," and the catalog of grievances in the Declaration of Independence as "implausible." Moreover, by labeling the Whig response as excessive and hysterical, he suggests that it had no substance. By joining Bailyn and Wood in applying the clinical term *paranoia* to that response, he suggests, as did the loyalists, that it was also pathological.[27]

Clark's explanation is also partisan in the sense that it uncritically endorses London definitions of how the extended polity of the British Empire worked. He takes for granted the existence of an authoritarian center. Thus, he believes that the Declaratory Act of 1720 "was sufficient to establish the Westminster Parliament's supremacy over Dublin." But this judgment ignores the fact that that statute was a unilateral decision

---

[24] Ibid., 154.

[25] See Jack P. Greene, *Pursuits of Happiness: The Social Development of Early Modern British Colonies and the Formation of American Culture* (Chapel Hill, N.C., 1988).

[26] Clark, *Language of Liberty,* 44.

[27] Ibid., 101, 103, 284.

that in the face of Irish resistance in the early 1780s proved unenforceable and had to be repealed. As he seems not to understand, in an extended political entity in which fiscal and coercive resources were limited, fiats from the center carried little weight and effective authority derived out of a delicate process of negotiation in which the peripheries had a significant voice in determining which metropolitan measures would be obeyed. During the early modern era, then, colonial empires were not, like the new composite states that sought to preside over them, "unified by doctrines of sovereignty" but by a consensual political process that rested on a shared attachment to the common traditions that defined residents of both centers and peripheries as English.[28]

Such an arrangement could work well only so long as neither party decided to pursue some action opposed by the other. In a situation involving such a profound disagreement as that which obtained in the mid-1770s, however, the absence of an impartial and authoritative agency for adjudication made the "pragmatic adjustment" of "legal disagreements" almost impossible. To suggest, as does Clark, that "grievances legally expressed" should have been legally redressed without resort to war and revolution is to ignore this serious structural weakness in the early modern British Empire, a weakness that needs to be taken into account in any successful explanation of the American Revolution.[29]

Clark is certainly correct to stress the importance of law and religion in the construction of an English-speaking identity.[30] In doing so, however, he has singled out only two of the threads in a complex fabric. The traditional discourses of law and religion coexisted with the more forward-looking language of civility, politeness, and improvement. As a result of a growing volume of contacts between Europeans and the many seemingly savage, impolite, and backward peoples in the new worlds that Europeans encountered overseas, beginning in the fifteenth century, this language became an integral part of the public discourse of all western European societies. During the eighteenth century these contacts provided much of the stimulus for the articulation, principally by Scottish conjectural historians, of an elaborate theory of social development that depicted societies as proceeding through four distinct stages, from

[28] Ibid., 74, 111.

[29] Ibid., 4, 110.

[30] Linda Colley, *Britons: Forging the Nation, 1707–1837* (London, 1992), and Richard Helgerson, *Forms of Nationhood: The Elizabethan Writing of England* (London, 1992), explore similar themes more fully.

simplicity, represented by the aboriginal inhabitants of the eastern wood-lands of North America, to refinement, epitomized by Europeans.[31]

In their collective self-conceptions of colonists in America, this lan-guage of improvement occupied a place fully as important as the lan-guages of law and religion with which it was intimately associated. In the process of implanting European-style social landscapes upon the American environment, successive generations of settlers had undergone just such a social passage from rudeness to civility, and they measured their success as collectivities in part by their achievements in this regard. Perhaps even more for colonists in New World outposts than for Britons at home, to be English was thus not merely to be Protestant and legally free but also civil, polite, and cultivated. Of these three sets of attri-butes, only their Protestantism, the one to which Clark accords special emphasis, was not at issue in the 1760s and 1770s.

In stressing the comparative religious and ethnic diversity of the colo-nies, Clark chooses to single out only one of several features that contem-poraries thought distinguished the societies of colonial British America from those of the Old World. They attached equal, if not greater, impor-tance to the extraordinary demographic and economic growth after 1715 and to the presence of racial slavery. But the social feature they regarded as most distinctive and most significant, one that Clark wholly ignores, was the remarkably wide distribution of property among free people. A much higher proportion of the free colonial population owned real prop-erty than was the case in England or in any other Old World society.

One does not have to subscribe to an "image of America as a wholly new, unindebted and morally free-standing culture from the outset of colonisation" to appreciate, as did virtually every contemporary ob-server, the radical social effects of this phenomenon. In early modern English societies, civic competence was a function not alone of adulthood or gender but of the personal independence, that is, exemption from con-trol by any other person, that possession of property was thought to bestow. If all English people lived under a constitutional government of laws, only those who were independent had an active voice in choosing the representatives through whom they gave their consent to those laws. Only such independent men fully enjoyed the freedoms associated in the emerging identity of Englishness.[32]

Much higher levels of property holding in the colonies thus meant

[31] Jack P. Greene, *The Intellectual Construction of America: Exceptionalism and Identity from 1492 to 1800* (Chapel Hill, N.C., 1993), 117–22.

[32] Clark, *Language of Liberty,* 303.

much higher levels of civic competence, and the colonial assemblies, which, with the notable exceptions of Pennsylvania and New York, everywhere took the lead in mobilizing resistance to Britain, represented and spoke not just for the local magnates who usually dominated them but for a vast empowered group that reached far down into the colonial population. For this extensive population their status as civic, that is, empowered, people formed a principal component of both their individual identities and the corporate identities of the political societies in which they lived and was almost certainly the most potent symbol of their Englishness. In ordinary times, as they went about their private domestic pursuits, most members of this extensive group might indeed have been "politically quietist." Taking great pride in their civic status, however, they could, as was revealed during each of the several crises that preceded the Revolution, be quickly mobilized in the face of any challenge to that status.[33]

One may accept Clark's judgment that British colonial policy in the 1760s and 1770s is most "convincingly explicable in functional terms as a series of pragmatic responses to administrative problems." As they reiterated in pamphlets, newspaper essays, sermons, petitions, addresses, resolutions, and speeches, however, Americans interpreted the new spirit of "confident interventionism" represented by that policy as a major threat to their inherited and long-standing rights—and identities—as propertied and civically competent Englishmen. To colonial resistance leaders, the part of their identities that was most at risk was their claim to that essential badge of Englishness: the right to live freely under an English system of constitutional governance.[34]

When Americans pondered the effects of parliamentary claims, they of course considered their spiritual dimensions, which now appear much more clearly as a result of Clark's analysis, and their argument that "the legitimacy of government" was grounded "on the consent of the governed" may well have drawn some force "from the idea of the covenant in religion," as he contends. To say, however, as he does, that "representation was not centrally at issue in 1776" is to miss both the intimate connection among representation, civic competence, and identity in the colonial world and the extraordinary emotive force behind that connection.[35] Unlike many modern historians, including Clark, Americans at

---

[33] Ibid., 194.

[34] Ibid., 264, 306.

[35] Ibid., 80, 99.

the time of the Revolution, as John Phillip Reid has shown at length, "took rights seriously."[36] Charles Inglis, the Tory rector of Trinity Church in New York, underlined this point in a passage quoted by Clark when he noted in 1776 that "civil liberty," and not religion, "was the bait that was flung out to catch the populace at large and engage them in rebellion."[37]

Reinforcing this deep and passionate concern for civil liberty and the fear of civil emasculation that underlay it was resentment arising out of what seemed to many colonists an implicit denial of their civility as a people. Clark writes that Englishmen did not "define Americans as 'the other,'" but this was by no means evident to Americans. Both in the condescending language that metropolitans used to describe the colonists and in the subordinate and unequal status for colonists implicit in the policies that the metropolitan government sought to implement in the colonies, colonial protesters found abundant evidence that metropolitans regarded them as uncivil residents of a still wild and savage country who were by no means entitled to the English identity to which they aspired.[38]

If Clark's explanation gives far less weight to such fears and resentment than the evidence seems to demand, he is on firmer ground when he characterizes the events of 1776–83 as a civil war. He is certainly right to question those who have argued that the Revolution was the product of a homogenizing ideological consensus. At the same time, however, his stress on internal division obscures the extent to which there was a solid consensus on many general issues. Virtually everyone in the colonies agreed that, as Britons, colonists should enjoy a government of laws, not men, a government that rested on the consent of the governed and allowed no person to be deprived of life, liberty, or property without due process of law and trial by peers. A very large majority, moreover, also seems to have agreed that metropolitan efforts to tax and regulate the colonies in ways that were contrary to long-standing customary arrangements were impolitic. Considerably more disagreement was evident on the question of whether the metropolis had a constitutional right to undertake such measures. Most divisive was the question of how far the colonists should go in resisting the metropolis. Clark's speculations about

---

[36] Reid, *The Authority of Rights*, vol. 1 of *Constitutional History of the American Revolution* (Madison, Wis., 1986), 3.

[37] Charles Inglis to Society for the Propagation of the Gospel, Oct. 31, 1776, as quoted by Clark, *Language of Liberty*, 358.

[38] Clark, *Language of Liberty*, 61.

the role of religious predispositions in the divisions over this question and in the internecine strife that accompanied the American War for Independence are worth further study.

No doubt historians will persist in the search for the deeper causes of the American Revolution. Before they do so, however, they would do well to ponder the words of the Philadelphia physician Hugh Williamson. "If the Americans had gone out of the way to seek for some grievance, if they had gone back to revive some ancient claim, or discuss some doubtful theorem," he declared in 1777, "then indeed we might have said that the ostensible cause was not the true one, and that they sought for something which they did not avow." But, insisted Williamson, in the colonists' case the ostensible causes had been the true ones, their "complaints [had] immediately followed the injuries they had received," those injuries had not been "trifling or imaginary" but "gross and palpable," and the failure of the metropolitan government to remove those injuries had brought "the miserable colonists" to the very edge of the "pit of despotism."[39]

The obvious emotion behind this statement powerfully suggests that, at least in the early modern American world, the constitutional issues central to both corporate and individual identity were thoroughly capable of mobilizing the population in opposition and revolt. So far, historians have failed to find a better explanation.

Written in February 1994, this essay was published under the title "Why Did They Rebel?: Looking for the Deeper Causes of the American Revolution," in the *Times Literary Supplement*, no. 4758 (June 7, 1994), 3–5. It is here reprinted with permission and with the addition of notes.

---

[39] [Hugh Williamson], *The Plea of the Colonies on the Charges Brought against Them by Lord Mansfield* (Philadelphia, 1777), 9, as quoted by Reid, *Authority of Rights*, 212–13.

Index

Abbot, W. W., 325
Absenteeism, 168–69
Acadia, 11
Act for Establishing Freedom of
    Religion, 210
Adair, Douglass, 409, 423, 434–35
Adams, John, 69, 439
Adams, Randolph G., 378–79
Adams, Samuel, 376, 472
Admiralty (British department
    of), 355
Africa: in study of history, 17–18,
    21, 26–28, 30–31, 33–35, 37; as
    origin of slaves, 161, 164; trade
    with, 47, 234, 263, 291, 299;
    heritage from, 21, 36, 118
Africanization, 32–33
Africans (also African Americans):
    as immigrants, 234; effects
    of, on American culture, 295,
    301; in study of American his-
    tory, 6–10, 21, 27, 29–41, 495;
    in New York, 184, 192; in
    West Indies, 157–78; see also
    Slavery
Agents, British, role in colonial
    politics of, 411–12
Agriculture, in New England,
    261–64

Albany, N.Y., 187, 192
Albany Congress, 73
Alden, John R., 222, 323–24,
    330–31
Allegheny Mountains, 318, 395
Allen, David Grayson, 244
American, as identification, 72–
    73, 148, 388
American Department (of British
    government), 411
American Historical Association,
    role in American historiogra-
    phy, 42, 121, 221
Americanization, 124, 224
American studies approach, 223,
    232
Amerindians: effects of, on Ameri-
    can culture, 295, 298, 301;
    European conception of, 48,
    506; exclusion of, from repub-
    lican vision, 465; in Anglo-
    American relations, 397, 409;
    in New England, 250, 269; in
    southern literature, 215–18; in
    study of American history,
    6–8, 12, 23, 27, 29, 35, 37–39,
    41, 231; relations of, with
    whites, 98, 100, 236, 298–
    300

Ammerman, David, 202–3, 207, 448–49
Anderson, Terry, 256
Andes, the, 8
Andover, Mass., 139–52, 241, 244–45
Andrews, Charles M., 12–13, 76–77, 222, 293, 311, 370–71, 494
Andros, Sir Edmund, 96–97, 182
Anglicans: comparison of, with Puritans, 52–53, 122, 217; disestablishment of church, as Revolutionary goal, 378; efforts of, to establish American episcopate, 318, 387, 399, 501; in Connecticut, 92, 325; in New England, 256; in Pennsylvania, 100, 325; in Virginia, 86, 209, 211–12; resistance of dissenters to, 499–503
Anglicization, of American society, 63, 124, 238, 384
Angola, 344
Annales school of history, 3, 24–26, 227, 230–32
Anthropology: in study of Amerindians, 20–21; in study of Virginia politics, 208, 213
Antifederalists, 380–81, 424, 426, 429, 431–38, 453
Antigua, 9, 36, 158, 167, 235
Appleby, Joyce, 230–33, 460–66
Araucanian Indians, 20
Archdeacon, Thomas, Jr., 183–86, 195, 197
Arendt, Hannah, 439–40
Armenians, 92
Army (British), in colonies, 319–20, 323, 354, 397–98, 477
Articles of Confederation, 379–81, 425, 427
Asia, 17–18, 26
Assembly: colonial, 60–63; lower houses of, 109, 331, 349, 369, 386, 399, 485, 507
Association movement, 357
Atlantic approach, 15–16, 27–29, 31, 35, 40

Atlantic History and Culture Program, 15, 35–36, 41
Auchmuty, Robert, Jr., 322
Australia, 17–18, 74

Bacon's Rebellion, 98–99
Bagehot, Walter, 106, 393–94
Bahamas, the, 9, 235, 304
Bailyn, Bernard, 42, 64, 70, 77, 96, 98, 104, 109–10, 120, 225–26, 259, 290–91, 295–307, 401–2, 407, 418–23, 444–46, 454, 496, 498, 504
Baltic, 47
Baltimore, Lord, 51
Bancroft, George, 80, 311–12, 333, 368–72, 377, 381, 494
Baptists, 212, 500; Separate, 92, 209
Barbados: culture in, 219; in study of American history, 9, 11, 128, 235; slavery in, 66; society in, 157–58, 160–61, 165–69, 173, 178
Bargar, B. D., 350–52
Barker, Charles Albro, 90–91, 325
Barrow, Thomas C., 384–85, 396, 454
Bastide, Roger, 30, 33
Beard, Charles, 82, 223, 376–77, 379–80, 423–31, 463
Beard, Mary, 82, 379–80
Becker, Carl, 81–82, 89, 103, 311–12, 324–25, 373–74, 376–79, 392, 495
Beckett, J. C., 476
Beckford, Peter, 170
Bedford, John Russell, 4th duke of, 339, 341
Beer, George Louis, 311, 315, 319, 370–72, 384
Behavior, revolution in, in New England, 154–55, 275–76
Belcher, Jonathan, 97
Belize, 9
Bennett, J. Harry, 157
Benson, Lee, 425–31
Benton, William Allen, 451
Berkeley, Sir William, 98–99

Bermuda, 9, 13, 75, 231, 235, 304
Bernard, Francis, 390
Billias, George Athan, 97
Bill of Rights, 433
Birmingham, David, 31
Black, Barbara A., 467, 478–88
Black, Eugene Charlton, 356–57, 359
Blackstone, Sir William, 483, 499, 501
Blue Mountains, 180
Bolingbroke, Henry St. John, 1st viscount, 344–45, 364
Bonham's Case, 481
Bonomi, Patricia U., 183, 189, 291
Boorstin, Daniel J., 77, 332–33, 413
Boston, 59, 139, 154, 172, 190, 249, 325; as mercantile center, 54, 256, 259, 262; British troops in, 316, 324, 398, 475; court in, 322; punitive measures against, 353; resistance in, 324, 472; society in, 151; wealth in, 55, 246
Boston Massacre, 316, 324, 398, 467, 472
Boston Tea Party, 342, 350, 352, 398, 412
Boulton, James T., 358
Bradford, William, 145
Braintree, Mass., 137
Brathwaite, Edward, 39–40, 173–78
Brazil, 11, 15, 23, 35, 37, 164, 177
Brebner, John Bartlett, 89–90
Breen, Timothy H., 230, 232, 236, 247, 302–4
Bridenbaugh, Carl, 77, 156–62, 165–66, 169–70, 172, 174, 176–78, 214, 221–22, 225, 386–87, 389, 396
Bridenbaugh, Roberta, 158–62, 165–66, 169–70, 172, 174, 176–78
Bristol (in New England), 144
Bristol, Eng., 203
Britain, 97, 165, 236–39, 303, 371, 374; colonial attitudes to-

ward, 73–76, *see also* Patriotism; colonies of, 9–16; conflict with, 209–10, 493–509, *see also* Revolution; institutions from, 60–63; politics in, 327–28, 335–43, 409–13, 449–51, 474; relationship of, with colonies, 350–54, 382–95; study of history in, 24, 30; trade with, 263
British Empire, 22; colonial view of role in, 73–74, 291, 389–91; failure of First, 338, 366
Brooke, John, 327, 335–36, 339, 346, 365
Brown, B. Katherine, 85–88, 106, 392
Brown, Gerald Saxon, 349–50
Brown, Richard D., 289
Brown, Robert E., 85–88, 106, 326–27, 361–62, 392–93, 424
Brown, Wallace, 408–9
Buel, Richard, Jr., 106, 393, 401
Burgh, James, 360
Burk, John Daly, 200–201
Burke, Edmund, 74, 342–46, 359, 471–72
Bushman, Richard L., 136–37, 152, 230–32, 275, 277
Bushnell, Amy Turner, 8
Bute, Lord (and his ministry), 318, 339, 357, 395
Butterfield, Herbert, 80, 363, 365

Cabot, John, 46
Calder, Angus, 291
Calhoon, Robert M., 451
Caliban, 48
California, 7, 11, 14–15
Calusus Indians, 20
Calvinists, 405–6, 420, 437
Calvin's Case, 481–83
Cambridge Group for the History of Population and Social Structure, 25, 227
Campbell v. Hall, 483
Canada, 9, 192; British victories in, 73–74, 372, 388; French, 11–12, 15, 300, 501

Capitalism, 461–64
Caribbean, 65, 128, 180, 477; as region, 235; comparison of, with New England, 149, 151, 154; in study of American history, 11, 15, 37, 231; society in, 156–79
Carolinas, the, 12, 46, 61, 63, 128, 150, 205, 297; as region, 301; comparison of, with West Indies, 171, 178; slavery in, 65–66
Carr, Lois Green, 205
Carter, Landon, 66–67
Carteret, John, Lord Granville, 344
Cary, John, 86
Central America, 37, 46
Center perspective, 489–90
Central-place theory, 232
Champagne, Roger, 103
Charles II, 60–62, 181
Charleston, S.C., 55, 94, 322
Charlestown (in New England), 192
Charter of 1691, 97
Chatham, William Pitt, earl of, 327, 318, 339, 342–44, 348–49, 352–53, 449
Chathamites, 363, 340
Chesapeake, 54, 180, 229; as region, 10–11, 235–36, 287, 304; comparison of, with New England, 154, 241–42, 247, 249; comparison of, with the West Indies, 159, 178; society in, 116, 200–213
Chevalier, François, 25
Chichimeca Indians, 20
Chile, 20
China, 27
Christie, Ian R., 356, 359
Church of England, see Anglican
Clark, Dora Mae, 329, 331, 354
Clark, J. C. D., 497–509
Class conflict, American politics as, 81–83
Clergy, in New England, 69, 253, 404–6

Clinton, Lord, 361
Cobb, Richard, 76
Coercive Acts, 342, 352, 378, 448
Coke, Sir Edward, 478, 481–88
Colbourn, H. Trevor, 402–3
Collingwood, R. G., 239
Colonies of exploitation, as explanatory concept, 233–34
Colonies of settlement, as explanatory concept, 233–35
Colonization, as explanatory concept, 19–22, 33, 46–49
Common law, 470–71, 481, 498–500
Commons House of Assembly, Georgia, 94
Community: in Massachusetts, 133–38; in New England, 51, 149–52; in Plymouth, 145–47
Comparative approach, 15, 28–30
Concord, Mass., 324, 343, 352, 398, 404
Confederation government, 377, 379–81, 431
Congo, 34
Congregationalists, 500, 503
Congress, Federal, 429–31
Connecticut, 111, 194, 218–19, 235, 464; politics in, 91–93, 391, 393; resistance to Britain in, 320, 325–26; society in, 137, 140, 167, 170–71, 240–41, 245, 247–50, 258–62
Connecticut River valley, 257, 264
Consensus, importance of: in Massachusetts, 134–38; in American politics, 224, 449
Consensus school, 232
Consent, as basis of law, 478, 482, 484, 487
Constitution, British: American view of, 356–60, 394–400, 478–80, 490–93, 496; dedication to, in Britain, 336, 344–56, 360
Constitution, colonial, 386, 484–85
Constitution, Federal, 84, 201,

Constitution, Federal (*cont.*)
226, 383, 444; as conservative
document, 381, 417, 437–38;
as radical document, 368,
419, 432–33; debate over, 379,
436–37, 426–28, 454, 460; economic interpretation of, 376–
77, 423–27; political issues of
431–38; social interpretation
of, 427–28
Constitution, imperial, 479–80,
488
Constitution, Massachusetts, 423
Constitutional Convention, 376
Constitutional conventions, as radical innovation of Revolution,
423
Constitutions, state, 414–15, 417,
434
Continental Congress, 343
Cook, Edward M., Jr., 132, 136
Cook, Edward Marks, 261, 268
Core-periphery framework,
297–301
Cortlandt Manor, 187, 190
Country ideology, 107–9, 463–64
Courten, Myndert, 193
Court of Exchequer, in Britain,
322, 397
Courts, colonial, 321–23; in Massa-
chusetts, 470–71; vice-
admiralty, 321–23, 397
Craton, Michael, 170–73, 178
Craven, Wesley Frank, 77, 181,
201, 222–23, 225
Credit, importance of, in colonies,
55, 67
Creoles: among slaves, 33, 161,
163; in colonial society, 174,
203, 206–7, 237
Creole societies, as interpretive
framework, 302–3
Creolization, 40, 284–85, 306, 163,
177
Cremin, Lawrence A., 120–25
Crime: in New England, 272–73;
in New York, 191–95
Crowl, Philip A., 91, 413–14
Cuba, 15

Cultural diffusion model, 232, 293,
298, 307
Culture: African influence on, 21,
30, 34; American, 124–25,
285–88, 329; Amerindian influence on, 295, 298, 301;
British influence on, 120–25,
295–99, 304, 442, *see also* Inheritance; regional, 293–95,
301; slave, in West Indies,
162–67, 175–76
Curaçao, 12
Curtin, Philip D., 31–33, 35
Customs, Board of, 316, 322, 355,
384

Dartmouth, Lord, 342–43, 350–
52, 354, 412
Davidson, Philip, 379
Davis, Richard Beale, 215–20
Debt: desire of planters to repudi-
ate, 376; public, 425, 429–30
Declaration of Independence, 84,
377, 380, 398, 415, 417, 419–
20, 439, 495, 504
Declaratory Act, 351, 353, 504
Declension model, 129, 248–61,
277–80, 282, 285–86, *see also*
Gemeinschaft-gesellschaft
model
Dedham, Mass., 129–33, 135, 139,
141, 143, 147–48, 150–52
Defoe, Daniel, 123
DeLancey family (of New York),
102
Delaware, 94, 111, 235, 414
Delaware River valley, 7, 293, 297
Democracy: American, 85–86;
Revolution as struggle for,
373–74, 377–78, 380–81
Demography, in New England,
140–41, 241–42, 248–51; *see
also* Population
Demos, John, 136, 138, 143–48,
150–51
DePeyster, Abraham, 185
Developmental model, 237–39,
282–88, 305–6
Diamond, Martin, 434–36

Diamond, Sigmund, 50
Diaspora, 33, 38, 40–41
Dickerson, Oliver M., 315–20, 330, 333, 384–85, 396, 491
Dike, K. O., 31
Diversity, 131, 146–47, 506
Doctrine of consent, 487–88
Doctrine of implicit importance, 4
Doctrine of irrevocable surrender, 481
Doctrine of settlement, 483–84
Doctrine of usage, 484
Dominica, 9
Dongan, Thomas, 182
Donoughue, Bernard, 342–43, 412
Douglass, Elisha, 415–16
Dublin, Ire., 504
Du Bois, W. E. B., 21
Dunn, Richard S., 13–14, 16, 96, 158, 160–62, 165–67, 169–70, 172–74, 176–78, 230
Dutch, 11–12, 16, 236; in New York, 180–99; in West Indies, 158; trade with, 57, 59

Earle, Carville, 204
East India Company, British, 398
Economy: colonial, 54–56, 63–65, 116–17; in New England, 61–66, 246–47, 256–59; role in Revolution, 372–79; ties with Britain involving the, 442
Education, 120–25; in New England, 245; in South, 217
Edwards, Jonathan, 405
Eggleston, Edward, 293
Egnal, Marc, 426
Elites, colonial, 118–19, 160, 257–59, 266–70
Elizabeth I, 46
Elkins, Stanley, 29, 164, 433–34
Encounter, as explanatory concept, 37–40
England, 9, 63, 75, 160–61, 172, 227, 244, 291, 403; economy of, 46–49; inheritance from, 72–73, 121–22, 279, 293; migration from, 140, 241; relationship of, with colonies,

56–59, 64, 368; trade with, 54–55, 256–57
English Civil War, 57, 241
Enlightenment, Scottish, 123
Enlightenment, 418
Erikson, Erik, 143
Ernst, Joseph Albert, 448, 456
Essex County, Eng., 272
Essex County, Mass., 260
Ethnohistory, 20–21, 37–38
Europe, 17, 25, 35, 148–49, 388; trade with, 54, 257, 263
Europeanization, 32, 131–32, 142–43; see also Anglicization
Europeans, in colonies, 6–7, 39, 234
Exceptionalism, American, 224, 232
Exchange, as explanatory concept, 40, 175–76
Expansion, European, as explanatory concept, 22, 33, 63
Experience, as explanatory concept, 239, 304

Factionalism: chaotic, as explanatory concept, 110–11; stable, as explanatory concept, 111
Family: as metaphor, 455; in New England, 138–48, 151–52; in Virginia, 204–5; role of, in education, 122
Federalists, 380–81, 424, 426, 429, 433–38, 464–65
Ferguson, E. James, 428–31
Fink, Z. S., 107, 401
Fischer, David Hackett, 292–307
Fiske, John, 368, 377, 380
Flaherty, David H., 136, 146, 272
Florida, 7, 9, 11–12, 14–15, 20, 301, 321
Folkways, 294–96, 304
Foord, Archibald S., 343–44
Foster, George M., 294–95, 301
Foster, Stephen, 243, 245, 247, 254, 260
France, 9, 24, 25, 30, 455, 462–63
Franklin, Benjamin, 73, 401
French: in America, 11, 14–16, 25,

French: in America (*cont.*)
89, 165, 184–85; trade with,
59, 370; war with, 75, 236,
372, 442
French and Indian War, 68, 73,
75; *see also* Seven Years' War
French Revolution, 27, 76, 378,
454, 462
Freyre, Gilberto, 23, 29

Gadsden, Christopher, 75
Gadsden election controversy, 318
Gage, General Thomas, 324, 343
Galloway, Joseph, 409
Games, Alison, 6, 13, 15–16
Garraty, John A., 45–78
Gaspar, David Barry, 36
Gaspee affair, 316, 351
Gemeinschaft-gesellschaft model,
232–33, 282, 289; *see also*
Declension model
George II, 328, 411
George III, 311, 327–28, 335–38,
342, 348, 350, 356, 361, 368,
388, 410–11, 413, 450
Georgia, 12, 66, 73, 94, 128, 150,
178, 200, 215, 235, 325, 391,
408
Germain, Lord George, 349–51,
354, 361–63, 412
Germans: in America, 65, 68; in
Pennsylvania, 81, 100, 374
Ghana, 163
Gibson, Charles, 15, 28–29, 37
Gilbert, Sir Humphrey, 48
Gilman, John, 267
Gilman, Nicholas, 267
Gipson, Lawrence Henry, 222,
311, 320, 372
Glorious Revolution, 25, 61–62,
123, 183, 187, 227, 403; Eng-
land after, 336, 363, 390, 476,
478, 484, 488
Gloucester, Mass., 262, 276
Goen, C. C., 136
Gold Coast, 34, 163
Gordon, Governor Patrick (of
Pennsylvania), 100
Gordon riots, 363

Goveia, Elsa, 174–75
Government: English constitutional, 462, 506; local institutions of, 476, 489–90; popular, 434; republican, 421–22,
435–38; royal, in America,
371; representative, lack of,
in New York, 181–83; self,
485
Grant, Charles S., 136, 270
Grattan, 363
Great Awakening, 69, 72, 91–92,
113, 115–16, 118, 196, 277–78,
405–6
Great Lakes, the, 9
Great Rebellion of 1766, 103, 187,
189–90
Greenberg, Douglas, 191–95, 197
Greene, Evarts B., 13
Greene, Jack P. (works by, specifically cited), 13, 281–92,
303–9, 386, 396, 400
Green Spring faction, 98
Grenada, 9
Grenville, George, 313–14, 317–18,
329–30, 339–40, 350, 374,
387, 395, 480
Greven, Philip, 138–43, 148, 150–
52, 241, 245
Grey, Thomas C., 467–68, 487,
484, 490
Guadeloupe, 11
Gura, Philip, 242

Hakluyt, Richard, 48
Half-way covenant, 252
Halifax, George Montague Dunk,
earl of, 75, 317
Halifax, 89–90; court in, 321–22
Hall, David D., 230–32, 253
Hall, Michael Garibaldi, 96
Hamilton, Alexander, 428, 439
Hampden, John, 478
Hancock, John, 316, 384
Handlin, Oscar, 189, 225
Hardy, Governor (of New York),
193
Harper, Lawrence A., 371, 385
Harris, R. Cole, 301

Hartford, Conn., 262, 266
Hartog, Hendrick, 469–70, 489
Hartz, Louis, 294, 332–33, 416
Harvard College, 122
Haskins, George Lee, 106
Hawaii, 6
Hawke, David, 101–2
Head, John M., 449
Heimert, Alan, 77, 405–7, 420–23
Hendrickson, David C., 497
Henretta, James A., 230–31, 289
Henry VII, 46
Henry VIII, 46, 48
Henry, Patrick, 99, 207
Herskovits, Melville J., 30, 33
Heyrman, Christine, 276
Higginbotham, Don, 458–59
Hill, Christopher, 365
Hillsborough, Wills Hill, 2d viscount, 341, 351
Hispanic America, 25, 31, 37
Histoire totale, 24, 227, 231
Hobbes, Thomas, 160, 461
Hoffman, Ross J. F., 449
Hofstadter, Richard, 113–19, 150, 423
Hopkins, Stephen, 93, 325
Horn, James, 203
House of Burgesses, Virginia, 98
House of Commons, British, 335, 346
House of Delegates, Maryland, 90
House of Representatives, Massachusetts, 97, 134, 468, 474
House of Representatives, United States, 435
Hudson River, 192, 297
Hudson River valley, 7, 116, 182–83, 301
Hudson's Bay, 9, 301
Human nature, views of, 53–54, 79, 370–71, 382–83, 400–401, 403–7, 434, 436, 438–39
Hume, David, 436
Hunter, Governor Robert (of New York), 102
Hurst, Willard, 474
Hutchinson, Anne, 247

Hutchinson, Governor Thomas (of Massachusetts), 409, 468
Hutchinson letters, 342

Iberian peninsula, New England trade with, 256
Ideology: role of, in Revolution, 400–407, 418–23; in creation of Constitution, 426–38, 452
Illinois, 11, 14–15
Immigration: to Chesapeake, 202–3; to New England, 241; role of, in affecting culture, 295–99
Imperial school: interpretation of colonial history, 22–23, 28, 222–23, 232, 494; interpretation of Revolution, 222, 311–12, 332, 338, 369–72
Implantation, as explanatory concept, 300, 302
Improvement, in public discourse, 238, 305, 505–6
Indentured servitude, 55, 63, 65–66, 203
India, 9, 27–28, 73, 234, 291
Indians, *see* Amerindians
Indigenismo, 23
Indigo planting, 70
Industrial Revolution, 166, 296
Industry, regulation of, 64
Ingersoll, Jared, 322
Inglis, Charles, 508
Inheritance, as analytic concept, 121, 239, 298, 302, 304, 461–62
Innes, Stephen, 258
Isaac, Rhys, 207–13
Islands: Atlantic, as region, 9–10, 235, 241; tropical, as region, 301
Institute of Early American History and Culture, 202, 221, 225
Intellectual life, 379–81; in South, 214–20
Interactionist model, 232
Ireland (also Irish), 9, 263, 291,

Ireland (also Irish) (*cont.*)
303, 363, 390, 473–77, 479–
82, 490–91, 498, 505
Iron Act, 64
Iron manufacturing, 63–64
Iroquois Indians, 20

Jackson, Andrew, 83, 373, 423
Jamaica, 9, 11–12, 61, 180, 235,
483; slavery in, 36, 66, 157–
58, 160, 162–65, 168–70;
society in, 39–40, 157–58,
160, 162–65, 168–74,
178
James I, 481, 502
James II, 60, 62
Jameson, J. Franklin, 312, 377–78,
416
Jamestown, 80, 204, 368
Jedrey, Christopher, 276
Jefferson, Thomas, 67, 207, 423,
460
Jenkinson, Charles, 330
Jensen, Merrill, 222, 225, 312,
379–81, 416, 452
John Reeves's Association for the
Preservation of Liberty and
Property, 357
Johnson, Augustus, 322
Jordan, David W., 205
Jordan, Winthrop D., 29, 56, 66,
78
Juries, 397, 470–71, 475

Kammen, Michael, 180, 195–98,
411
Katz, Stanley N., 230–31
Kea, Ray, 35
Kelly, Kevin P., 205
Kemmerer, Donald L., 325
Kenyon, Cecelia M., 417, 419–20,
422–23, 436
Ketcham, Ralph, 101
Kim, Sung Bok, 186–91
King Philip's War, 250, 257
King's County, N.Y., 193
Klein, Milton M., 103
Knight, Franklin, 35

Knollenberg, Bernard, 317–21,
330, 333, 395, 491
Koebner, Richard, 389–91
Konig, David T., 260
Kraus, Michael, 389

Labaree, Leonard Woods, 12–13,
371
Labaree, Benjamin Woods, 398–99
Labor, 10–11, 55, 65–66; *see also* Indentured servitude; slavery
Langford, Paul, 449
La Raza, 23
La Rochfoucauld-Liancourt, 200
Latin America, 15, 23, 26, 41
Laurens, Henry, 67, 316, 384
Laurens-Leigh controversy, 322
Law, 483, 487, 508; common, 470–
71, 481, 498–500; conditions
of, 473, 475–76; consensus as
basis of, 470, 473; enforcement, 193–94; force of cus-
tom in, 470–71, 473, 478,
484–86, 508; imperial v. lo-
cal, 473–75, 487; importance
of, in forming identity, 497–
98, 505; natural, 499–500;
precedent, 470–71; pre-
Revolutionary concept of,
469–70; regarding conquest,
481–84
Law Offices, British, 411
Lecky, W. E. H., 369
Leder, Lawrence H., 102
Lee, Richard Henry, 207
Leeward Islands, 234–35; society
in, 157–58, 160, 165, 167–69,
173, 175, 178
Legislatures: colonial, 74, 415–16;
state, 458; *see also* Assembly
Leisler, Jacob, 183
Leisler's Rebellion, 102, 111, 183,
185–86
Lemisch, Jesse, 76
Lemon, James T., 230–32
Lexington, Mass., 324, 343, 352,
354, 398, 404
Levant, the, 47

Liberty: as motive of Revolution, 331, 508; colonial philosophy of, 329, 388, 422, 444–46, 461–63, 496, 499
Liberty, the, 322
Liberty riot, 473
Lincoln, Charles H., 81–82, 89, 101, 373–74, 376–77, 392
Littlefield, Daniel C., 36
Liverpool, Eng., 203
Livingston, Robert, 102
Livingston family (of New York), 102–3
Livingston Manor, 187, 189
Lloyd, David, 100
Localists, *see* Antifederalists
Locke, John, 123, 461, 487
Lockhart, James, 28
Lockridge, Kenneth A., 129–33, 135–38, 141–43, 148, 150–53, 241, 270, 291
Logan, James, 100
London, 54, 73–74, 89, 93, 95, 134, 203, 259, 272; government in, 369, 386
Long Island, 182–83, 192, 196
Louisiana, 11, 14–15, 20, 301
Lovejoy, A. O., 383, 400–401, 434–35
Lovejoy, David S., 93, 181, 325
Lower South, 10–11, 231, 235–36, 287, 304
Loyalists, 451, 493; *see also* Tories
Lucas, Paul, 253
Lynd, Staughton, 76, 451

McCormick, Richard P., 92–93, 414
McCurry, Allan J., 450
McCusker, John J., 13, 279, 290, 307
MacDonald, Forrest, 104, 424–31
Machiavelli, 361
McIlwain, Charles H., 320, 477
Mackesy, Piers, 361–64
McKitrick, Eric, 433–34
McMahon, Sarah F., 271
McNeill, William H., 27–28
Madison, James, 207, 435–36, 439

Magna Charta, 480
Maier, Pauline, 448, 473–74
Main, Jackson Turner, 88, 258, 261, 269–71, 393, 415–16, 425–26, 428–32, 453–54, 458
Maine, 250, 264
Malcolm affair, 473
Manhattan, 192
Manorial system, in New York, 187–91, 197
Mansfield (crown officer), 484
Mansfield, Harvey C., Jr., 344–46, 348, 359, 364
Marblehead, Mass., 262, 268, 276
Maroons, 168
Marshall, John, 207
Martin, James Kirby, 448
Martinique, 11, 165
Maryland, 51, 54–55, 57, 64–65, 77, 215, 235; causes of Revolution in, 320, 325; politics in, 90–92, 100, 110–11, 391, 413–14; society in, 201, 204–5
Mason, George, 207
Massachusetts, 54, 73, 161, 194, 235, 286, 313–14, 318, 322, 388, 408, 434, 464, 467–68; community in, 51, 131–35; conflict with New York, 189–90; culture in, 218–19, 293; middle class in, 85–88, 326–27; law in, 470–77; politics in, 96–98, 107, 110–11, 392, 414–15; resistance to British in, 320, 324, 342; society in, 241, 244–45, 247–50, 259–62, 264, 267, 272; towns in, 133–38
Master class, rise of, in West Indies, 160
Masur, Louis, 269
Mather, Cotton, 254, 277
Mauger, Joshua, 89
Mediterranean, 25
Meinig, D. W., 292, 299–307
Menard, Russell R., 205, 279, 290, 307
Mercantile system, 315–21, 331, 371

Mercantilism, 58, 65, 320
Merchants: role of, in colonial politics, 411–12; role of, in Revolution, 374–76
Merivale, Herman, 234
Merritt, Richard L., 388–89
Metropolitanization, 284–85, 306; *see also* Anglicization
Mexico, 8, 20, 23, 25, 29, 37, 46, 299
Middle Colonies, 10, 81, 235–36, 283–87, 304, 387, 409
Middle East, 26
Middlesex County, Mass., 264, 272
Middlesex County, Va., 204–5
Middlesex election controversy, 352, 357
Middletown, Conn., 262
Migration: in New England, 131, 141, 250–51; to West Indies, 158, 167; *see also* Immigration
Miller, John C., 222, 378–79
Miller, Perry, 52, 76–77, 106, 126, 216, 222–26, 232, 242, 254–55, 279, 403–5, 406–7
Mintz, Sidney, 35
Mississippi River valley, 7, 9
Modernization model, 282, 289
Molasses Act, 65, 315, 318, 384, 395
Money, paper, 55, 67–68, 95, 399, 414, 424, 429, 434, 448
Monopoly, 58, 375–76
Monroe, James, 207
Montserrat, 9, 158, 167, 235
Morgan, Edmund S., 53, 77, 106, 222, 225, 313–15, 317, 320, 328, 330, 332–33, 339, 396, 400, 403–7, 418, 424, 438–39, 454, 491, 495
Morgan, Helen S., 313–15, 317, 320, 330, 396
Morris, Richard B., 225, 331
Morris, Robert, 429–30
Mortality: in Chesapeake, 204–5; in New England, 241–42
Mullin, Gerald W., 36
Multicultural approach, 39–41

Munroe, John A., 414
Murrin, John M., 136, 223, 230

Namier, Lady, 346
Namier, Sir Lewis, 89, 327–31, 334–39, 346, 364–66, 410–11, 494
Naming doctrine, 481
Narragansett Bay, 177
Narragansett region, Rhode Island, 264, 269
Nash, Gary B., 230, 236
Nationalism, American, 329, 388–91, 432, 497; *see also* Patriotism
Nationalists, *see* Federalists
Nation-state perspective, 7–19, 40–42
Navigation Acts, 57, 60–63, 74, 80, 166, 315–21, 325, 371, 384–85, 396, 494
Navigation system, British, 65, 74–76, 383–85
Navy, Royal, 318, 395, 448
Nelson, William E., 467, 470–72
Nelson, William H., 409, 423
Neo-Whig school: interpretation of colonial history, 442–54, 457, 459; interpretation of Revolution, 313–33, 442, 446, 448, 491–92, 495
Netherlands, the, 9, 25
Nettels, Curtis P., 13, 385
Nevis, 9, 158, 167, 235
Nevis, Allan, 378
New Castle, 94
New England, 10, 12, 21, 49–51, 59, 61, 67–68, 70, 73, 117–18, 183, 194, 214–15, 229, 286, 494; as cultural region, 235–36, 287, 297, 301, 304; comparison of, with other colonies, 159, 178, 180–81, 186, 195, 202–4; decline of parental authority in, 140–41, 273–74; economy in, 54–55; education in, 121–23; family in, 138–48, 151–52; merchants in, 77, 96, 385; mind, 76, 216, 222–23;

New England (*cont.*)
  political discontent in, 318,
  395; political society in,
  245–46; religion in, 54, 69,
  217, 252–53, 387, 503, *see also*
  Puritans; rise of autonomy
  in, 152–54; role of, in Revolution, 126, 503–4; slavery in,
  269–70; society in, 76–77,
  116, 126–55, 232–33, 237,
  240–80; social stratification
  in, 261–70; trade in, 64, 67,
  256–57, 263
Newfoundland, 9, 46, 231, 321
New France, 20
New Granada, 12
New Hampshire, 46, 75, 93–94,
  110–11, 140, 200, 235, 249–
  50, 259, 262, 264, 267–68,
  330
New Haven, Conn., 245, 247–48,
  262, 266
New history, 3–5, 382–400
New Jersey, 61, 75, 205, 235, 325;
  politics in, 88, 92–93, 111,
  318, 391, 393, 414
New Left, interpretation of Revolutionary history, 76
New Lights, 92, 325
New London, Conn., 262
New Mexico, 7, 11, 14–15, 20
New Netherlands, *see* New York
Newport, R.I., 55, 93, 262,
  266–71
New Spain, 11, 15, 20; *see also*
  Mexico
Newton, Sir Isaac, 123
New West, as possible regional
  classification, 235
New York, 12, 20, 55, 61, 70, 75,
  123, 128, 178, 235, 250, 323,
  325, 330, 373–74, 379, 408,
  483, 507; antiauthoritarian-
  ism in, 193–94; materialism
  in, 195–98; politics in, 81, 88,
  100, 102–3, 110–11, 318, 393;
  slavery in, 184; society in,
  180–99; unrest in, 192–
  96

New York City, 59, 67, 181–87,
  192, 194, 197
New Zealand, 74
Norris, John, 352–54
North, Frederick, 7th baron, 341–
  42, 350, 352, 359, 450
Northampton, 252
North Carolina, 68, 75, 215, 235,
  330, 408, 415; politics, 95,
  110–11
Norton, Mary Beth, 451
Norwich, Conn., 262
Nova Scotia, 9, 13, 46, 89–90, 94,
  111, 231, 235, 240, 250

O'Gorman, Frank, 449
Ohio River valley, 9
Old Lights, 92, 405–6
Oliver, Peter, 409
Oliver, Roland, 31
Onuf, Peter S., 285–86
Opposition, in British politics,
  344, 445, 450, 496, 498
Osborne, Francis, 121
Osgood, Herbert Levi, 369–72
Otis, James, 499

Paine, Thomas, 417, 455
Palmer, R. R., 27, 422–23
Pares, Richard, 157, 327, 339–40
Parliament, British, 68, 386; authority of, in colonies, 392,
  412, 449, 476, 485, 502; internal struggles in, 107, 363, *see
  also* Opposition; role of, in colonies, 61–63; struggle with
  crown, 327–28; supremacy of,
  335–43, 348–58, 413, 443,
  478, 480–82, 487–88; *see also*
  Taxes
Parliament, Irish, 61, 476
Parrington, Vernon Lewis, 51–52,
  82, 223, 379
Parties, political, 108; in America,
  453; in Britain, 344–46; *see
  also* Tories; Whigs
Patriotism, 347; American, 447;
  British, in colonies, 73–74,
  347, 387–91, 442

Patriots, 380, 408
Patterson, Orlando, 36, 162–65, 170, 172, 174–78
Paxton affair, 101
Peace at Utrecht, 116
Peace of Paris, 388
Pearce, Roy Harvey, 29
Pelhams, the, 330
Penn, William (the elder), 61
Penn, William, 198
Pennsylvania, 51, 61, 64–65, 70, 123, 150, 178, 205, 235, 286, 301, 325, 503, 507; politics in, 81, 88, 100–102, 107, 110–11, 391, 393, 415, 421; society in, 373–74, 379
Peopling, as explanatory concept, 295–99
Peru, 11, 20, 23, 28, 37, 46, 299
Philadelphia, 55, 59, 67, 73, 77, 100–101, 172, 322, 374, 399, 458
Philadelphia Convention, 424, 426, 432, 434, 453
Philipsburgh, 187–88, 190–91
Pierson, William D., 36
Pitman, Frank Wesley, 157–58, 176
Plantation colonies, as analytic concept, 234–35
Platt, Gerald M., 150
Pluralism, 115; in Middle Colonies, 283–86; in New York, 180–99
Plymouth colony, 88, 143–47, 150, 241, 249
Pocock, J. G. A., 107, 293, 401, 450–51
Pole, J. R., 13, 106, 289–91, 393–94
Policy, British colonial, 347–56, 370, 375, 397, 406, 507–8
Political culture, as explanatory concept, 105–14, 460
Political nation, British, as analytic concept, 334–35, 339–43, 348, 355–56, 361–62, 412, 449
Politics, British, 327–28, 335–38, 409–13, 449–51

Politics, colonial, 59–60, 70, 205, 386–93, 422, 442–43; elitist nature of, 103–4, 392; factionalism in, 104–5; local, 391–93; process of mobilization in, 457–59; popular participation in, 415–16
Pontiac's rebellion, 319
Poor Richard's Almanack, 115
Pope, Robert, 277
Population: in New England, 130, 140–42; slave, in West Indies, 167–68; *see also* Demography
Porter, John A., 303
Portsmouth, N.H., 262, 266, 268
Portugal, 8
Portuguese, in America, 11, 16, 25
Potter, David, 27
Potter, Jim, 230–31
Power, paradigm of, 18–42
Poyning's Law, 61
Presbyterians, 81, 100, 209, 393, 500
Price, Charles, Sr., 171, 173
Price, Charles, Jr. (the Patriot), 171, 173
Price, Charles III, 172
Price, Francis, 170
Price, Jacob M., 229, 232, 365
Price, Richard, 35, 360
Price, Rose, 172
Price family (of Jamaica), 170–73, 178
Progressive school: critique of, 87, 89–90, 96, 100, 103, 105–6, 382–440; interpretation of colonial history, 223–24, 232, 494–95; interpretation of Revolution, 80–85, 311–12, 332, 372–82, 441, 444
Prospero, 48
Protestant Association, 357
Protestant Dissenters, 499–506
Providence, R.I., 93, 262, 266, 271
Pruitt, Bettye Hobbs, 261–63
Pueblo Indians, 20
Puritans, 48, 51–53, 76, 106, 117, 122, 226, 403, 464–65; cul-

Puritans (*cont.*)
　　ture of, 126–55, 214–19; in
　　Massachusetts politics,
　　96–97; in New England soci-
　　ety, 240–80
Pym, John, 478
Pynchon family, 257–58

Quakers, 77, 93, 107, 247, 326,
　　500; in Pennsylvania, 51, 81,
　　100–102, 374
Quartering Act, 349
Quashee personality syndrome,
　　164
Queen Anne's War, 63
Quitt, Martin H., 205

Ragatz, Lowell J., 157–58, 176
Raleigh, Sir Walter, 48
Randolph, Edward, 61, 96
Regional model, 233–37, 282–83,
　　295, 302
Regulator movement, 95
Reid, John Phillip, 468–70, 472–
　　91, 500, 508
Religion, 69, 77, 242; changes in,
　　in New England, 252–56; in
　　constructing identity, 505; in
　　Revolution, 387, 404, 419–20,
　　497–99; in Virginia, 209–12
Rensselaerwyck, 187, 189
Reorganization, as analytic con-
　　cept, 300, 302
Republicanism, as concept in
　　America, 419, 433
Revolution, American, 27, 85–86,
　　90–93, 123, 126, 132, 174,
　　195, 200–201, 212, 226, 230,
　　306, 311–509; as civil war,
　　508; as conservative move-
　　ment, 313–14, 413–18, 422; as
　　political conflict, 331–32; as
　　social conflict, 373–79; Brit-
　　ish policy during, 364; eco-
　　nomic interpretation of, 456;
　　effects of, on local develop-
　　ments, 324–26; ideology of,
　　78, 400–407, 444–46; imperial

school interpretation of, 222,
　　311–12, 332, 338, 369–72; in-
　　ternal struggles as cause of,
　　372–79, 509; legal history of,
　　469–92; moral dimensions of,
　　403–7, 420–22; neo-Whig in-
　　terpretation of, 313–33, 442,
　　446, 448, 491–92, 495; origins
　　of, 113–19, 311–33, 469–509;
　　Progressive interpretation of,
　　80–85, 311–12, 332, 372–82,
　　441, 444; radicalism of,
　　418–23; role of British politics
　　in, 334–49; social interpreta-
　　tion of, 456–57; Whig inter-
　　pretation of, 80, 311–12, 367–
　　69, 494–95, 497, 504
Revolutionary Settlement, 328,
　　335, 344, 346, 359, 410–11,
　　413, 443
Rhode Island, 219, 230, 249, 260,
　　325; politics in, 88, 93, 111,
　　391, 393; society in, 250, 259,
　　262, 264–65, 269
Rice planting, 36, 63, 70, 156
Rio Grande River valley, 301
Ritcheson, Charles, 339
Ritchie, Robert C., 181, 195
Robbins, Caroline, 107, 360–61,
　　401
Robinson, John, 330
Robson, Eric, 327–28
Roche, John P., 432, 434–35
Rockingham, Charles Watson-
　　Wentworth, Lord, 339, 340,
　　344–45, 350, 363, 449
Rockingham, Lord (second), 340,
　　352, 363
Rogers, Alan, 447
Rome, Whig view of fall of, 403
Rose, Francis, 170
Rose, Willie Lee, 35
Rossiter, Clinton, 329, 331, 333,
　　387–88
Rude, George, 76, 356
Russell-Wood, A. J. R., 35
Russians, 7, 47
Rutherford, Thomas, 484, 487

Rutland, Robert Allen, 432
Rutman, Anita H., 204–5
Rutman, Darrett B., 151, 204–5
Ryerson, Richard A., 458

St. Christopher, 9, 235
St. Domingue, 11, 27, 165
St. John (Prince Edward Island), 9
St. John's Parish, Jamaica, 170
St. Kitts, 158, 167, 169
St. Lawrence River valley, 7, 301
St. Vincent, 9
Salem, Mass., 246, 249, 255–56,
    258–59, 262, 266
Salutary neglect, 74
Sandwich, earl of, 361
Savelle, Max, 13, 222, 329, 331,
    388
Schlesinger, Arthur Meier, Sr.,
    311–12, 374–77
Schlesinger, Arthur Meier, Jr.,
    388–89
Schutz, John A., 97, 409
Schuyler, Robert L., 477
Scotch-Irish, 68, 94
Scotland, 9, 121, 291, 293, 481, 498
Scots, in colonies, 68, 169
Secker, Archbishop Thomas, 318,
    387
Secularism, 69, 117–19, 196–97
Senate, United States, 435
Senegambia, 36
Seven Years' War, 195, 317, 501;
    British patriotism during,
    387–91, 442; effect of, on Brit-
    ish colonial policy, 327–29,
    337–38, 360, 369–70, 397,
    446–47; *see also* French and
    Indian War
Sewell, Jonathan, 322
Shakespeare, William, 48
Shammas, Carole, 206–7
Shay's Rebellion, 98, 414–15, 429,
    434
Shelburne, William Petty, 2d earl,
    352–54, 361, 363, 412
Sheridan, Richard B., 13–14, 165–
    70, 177–78, 229, 232

Shirley, William, 97
Shy, John, 354, 397–98, 411–12,
    458–59
Slavery: in colonies, 55–56, 65–67,
    233, 506; effect of, on whites,
    66–67, 118; failure to abolish,
    378, 452–53; in Revolution-
    ary ideology, 402, 465; in
    southern culture, 217, 219; in
    study of American history,
    10, 21, 23, 29, 33; opposition
    to, 65, 419; trade based on,
    31–32, 70, 265
Smith, Adam, 462
Smith, Ebenezer, 267
Smith, M. G., 467
Smuggling, 59, 316, 318, 321, 384,
    395, 398–99
Sobel, Mechal, 39–40
Social development, as analytic
    concept, 132, 304, 505–6
Social elaboration, as analytic con-
    cept, 238, 305
Social replication, as analytic con-
    cept, 238, 305
Social sciences, use of, in study of
    history, 4, 24–27, 198, 225–27,
    230, 233
Social simplification, as analytic
    concept, 112, 237, 305
Society: British, effect of changes
    in, for colonies, 285; colonial,
    113–19, 235–37, 285, 392–93,
    442, 465; colonial, changing
    nature of, 45–46, 68–69, 443;
    efforts to re-create British, in
    America, 49, 62, 72, 114–15,
    119, 206, 211–12, 237–39,
    266–67, 284, 506; elitist na-
    ture of colonial, 106, 393–94,
    461–63
Sons of Liberty, 103, 314
Sosin, Jack M., 354, 355–56, 411
South: as region, 195, 376; culture
    in, 214–20; distinctiveness of,
    214, 218–20
South Carolina, 63, 67, 70, 70–71,
    73, 75, 77, 116, 128, 178, 235,

South Carolina (*cont.*)
330; culture in, 215; politics
in, 94–95, 110–11, 318, 322;
slavery in, 36, 67
Southern Department, in British
government, 355
Spain: colonies of, 9, 11, 14–16,
22, 28, 37, 56, 180, 455; Brit-
ish imperial wars with, 236,
370, 442; example of, in colo-
nization, 46–47
Spanish Town, Jamaica, 171, 173
Speck, William, 230
Spirit of '76, radicalism of, 417,
420
Spotswood, Lieutenant Governor
Alexander, 99
Springfield, Mass., 262
Spry, Dr. William, 321–22
Stamp Act, 62–63, 75, 77, 92, 100,
190, 313–15, 317, 330, 338–41,
349–51, 355, 375, 378, 387,
389, 395–98, 438, 449, 473,
480, 484–85
Stamp Act Congress, 75
Stampp, Kenneth M., 29
Staple and population model, 232
Steele, Ian K., 290
Steele, Richard, 123
Stoddard, Solomon, 252
Stourzh, Gerald, 401, 451
Stout, Neil R., 448
Structural-functional model, 283,
496–97
Sudbury, Mass., 244
Suffolk County, N.Y., 192, 194
Sugar Act, 313–15, 318, 321–22,
395, 397
Sugar planting, 64–65, 156–70
Surinam, 12
Surrey County, Eng., 194–95
Surry County, Va., 205
Susquehannah Company, 92
Sutherland, Lucy S., 358–59
Sydnor, Charles S., 99

Tannenbaum, Frank, 29
Tate, Thad W., 201–3, 207
Taxes: in United States, 380, 414,

429–30; parliamentary, colo-
nial resistance to, 331, 378,
395–400, 404, 443, 480, 484,
491, 502, 504; right of parlia-
ment to levy, 62, 314–21, 339–
40, 348, 353–54, 395–98,
478–88
Taylor, Robert J., 414
Tea Act, 375, 398–99, 450
Tempest, the, 48
Tenantry, in New York, 186–91
Texas, 7, 15, 301
Thayer, Theodore, 326
Thomas, P. D. G., 449–50
Thomas, Robert Paul, 385
Thompson, Roger, 272
Thornton, John, 37
Tobacco planting, 54, 64, 156,
205–6
Tobago, 9
Tocqueville, 416
Toleration, religious, 54, 69, 116–
17, 452; in New England, 52,
254
Toleration Act, 54
Tolles, Frederick B., 77, 107, 222,
416
Tories: in America, 407–9, 443,
451, 493, 503, *see also* Loyal-
ists; in Britain, 344
Townshend, Charles, 341, 346–49,
351, 353, 412
Townshend Acts, 62, 316, 322,
324, 338, 341, 349–50, 355,
375, 397–98, 450
Trade, Board of, 75, 318, 330, 348,
351, 355, 411
Trade, Lords of, 60–61
Trade regulation, British, 57–59,
64, 321, 384–85, 487, 504
Traditional-modern framework,
233
Transatlantic perspective, 27, 296
Treasury, British, 329–30, 355, 411
Treaty of Paris, 368
Trevelyan, Sir George Otto, 327–
28, 369, 410, 494
Troops, *see* Army
Tucker, Robert W., 497

Tudor monarchy, 46
Turner, Frederick Jackson, 232, 297, 376
Two-Penny Act, 318

Ubbelohde, Carl, 321–23, 330, 333, 397
Ulster, Eng., 293
United States, 415, 435; creation of, 367, 436; government in, 427–28, 430; history of, 6–7, 12, 15, 23, 27, 80, 224, 367–68; politics in, 112, 415, 424, 431; regions in, 300; study of social sciences in, 24, 226–27; study of history in, 31, 39
Urbanization, of New England, 262–63

Value-and-society approach, 232
Van Cortlandt, Jacobus, 185
Van Cortlandt, Stephen, 190
Van Dam, Rip, 185
Van Deventer, David E., 267
Van Rensselaers family (of New York), 189
Vansina, Jan, 31, 34
Virginia, 13, 50, 54–55, 57, 61, 70, 73, 222, 235, 320, 330, 385, 388, 494; comparison of, with West Indies, 161, 171; culture in, 219, 293, 301; education in, 121, 123; politics in, 70, 86–88, 98–100, 110–11, 318, 391–92; religion in, 54, 503; slavery in, 36, 39–40, 65–66, 201, 206, 208–9; society in, 45–46, 180, 200–213
Virginia Company, the, 50
Virgin Islands, 9

Wales, 9, 291
Wales, Princess Dowager of, 357
Walpole, Horace, 327–28, 330, 410
Walsh, Lorena S., 204–5
Walvin, James, 170–73, 178
Wantons (of Newport), 93
Ward, Samuel, 93, 325

War for Independence, *see* Revolution
Washburn, Wilcomb E., 98
Washington, George, 207, 362
Washington, Margaret Creel, 36
Watson, J. Steven, 339
Weinstein, Fred, 150
Wentworth, Governor Benning, 93
West Africa, 9, 159
Westchester County, 187
West Indies, 6, 9, 12–16, 35, 50, 65, 70, 180, 490–91; as region, 10–11, 301, 304; British victories in, 73, 388; creole society in, 173–74; culture in, 291, 299, 304; failure to establish white society in, 159–63, 173–79; slavery in, 56, 66, 157–70, 172, 175–76; trade with New England, 54–55, 64, 257, 263; trade with Spanish and French in, 370; white society in, 170, 173–79
Whateley, Thomas, 330
Whig interpretation of American history: colonial period, 224; ideology of colonists, 402–3; politics, 79–80, 83–84; Revolution, 80, 311–12, 367–69, 494–95, 497, 504
Whigs: in Britain, 327–28, 335–36, 339, 344, 410; in America, 409, 484, 488, 493, 499–500, 502
Whitehall, 75, 361, 370
Wickwire, Franklin B., 354–55
Wilkes, John, 318, 356
Wilkites, 356–59, 364–65, 412
Willcox, William B., 361–64
William III, 62
William and Mary Quarterly, in American historiography, 16, 25, 222, 225
Williams, Eric, 29, 157
Williams, Roger, 247
Williamson, Hugh, 509
Wine Islands, New England trade with, 256
Winkler, Henry, 365

Winthrop, John, 52
Wolf, Eric, 20
Wood, Gordon S., 109, 226,
    408–9, 420–23, 437–38, 444–
    46, 496–97, 504
Wood, Joseph, 244
Wood, Peter H., 36, 41
Woolen Act, 64
Worcester County, Mass., 137,
    262, 264
Worthy Park, Jamaica, 170–72
Wright, Benjamin Fletcher,
    417
Wright, Governor James, 94
Wright, Louis B., 77, 201, 214,
    222, 293

Wyoming Valley (Pennsylvania),
    92
Wyvillites, 356–57, 365

York, duke of, 181
Yorkshire movements, 363
Yorktown, 368
Young, Arthur, 156

Zavala, Silvio, 23
Zeichner, Oscar, 91–92, 325–26
Zemsky, Robert, 134
Zobel, Hiller B., 467, 472–74
Zuckerman, Michael, 128–29, 133,
    146–48, 150–52, 154, 276,
    281–88

Sr. DISTINCTIVENESS 214-220. — the "Good life" 220

**171 that transcultural acculturation between white and black